Inside Network Perimeter Security

Second Edition

Inside Network Perimeter Security

Second Edition

Stephen Northcutt, Lenny Zeltser, Scott Winters,
Karen Kent, and Ronald W. Ritchey

Sams Publishing, 800 East 96th Street, Indianapolis, Indiana 46240 USA

Inside Network Perimeter Security

International Standard Book Number: 0-672-32737-6

Library of Congress Catalog Card Number: 2004096804

Printed in the United States of America

First Printing: March 2005

08 07 06   4   3   2

Trademarks

All terms mentioned in this book that are known to be trademarks or service marks have been appropriately capitalized. Sams Publishing cannot attest to the accuracy of this information. Use of a term in this book should not be regarded as affecting the validity of any trademark or service mark.

Warning and Disclaimer

Every effort has been made to make this book as complete and as accurate as possible, but no warranty or fitness is implied. The information provided is on an "as is" basis.

Bulk Sales

Pearson offers excellent discounts on this book when ordered in quantity for bulk purchases or special sales. For more information, please contact

> **U.S. Corporate and Government Sales**
> 1-800-382-3419
> corpsales@pearsontechgroup.com

For sales outside of the U.S., please contact

> **International Sales**
> international@pearsoned.com

Acquisitions Editor
Linda Bump Harrison

Development Editor
Songlin Qiu

Managing Editor
Charlotte Clapp

Project Editor
George E. Nedeff

Copy Editor
Bart Reed

Indexer
Ken Johnson

Proofreader
Kathy Bidwell

Technical Editors
Todd Chapman
Anton Chuvakin
Dan Goldberg
John Spangler

Publishing Coordinator
Vanessa Evans

Book Designer
Gary Adair

Page Layout
Kelly Maish

Contents at a Glance

Table of Contents

About the Authors

Stephen Northcutt is a graduate of Mary Washington College. Before entering the field of computer security, he worked as a Navy helicopter search and rescue crewman, whitewater raft guide, chef, martial arts instructor, cartographer, and network designer. Stephen is author/coauthor of *Incident Handling Step-by-Step, Intrusion Signatures and Analysis, Inside Network Perimeter Security, 2nd Edition, IT Ethics Handbook, SANS Security Essentials, SANS Security Leadership Essentials,* and *Network Intrusion Detection, 3rd Edition.* He was the original author of the Shadow Intrusion Detection System before accepting the position of Chief for Information Warfare at the Ballistic Missile Defense Organization. Stephen currently serves as Director of the SANS Institute.

Lenny Zeltser's work in information security draws upon experience in system administration, software architecture, and business administration. Lenny has directed security efforts for several organizations, co-founded a software company, and consulted for a major financial institution. He is a senior instructor at the SANS Institute, having written and taught a course on reverse-engineering malware. Lenny is also a coauthor of books such as *SANS Security Essentials* and *Malware: Fighting Malicious Code.* He holds a number of professional certifications, including CISSP and GSE, and is an incident handler at SANS Internet Storm Center. Lenny has earned a bachelor of science in engineering degree from the University of Pennsylvania and a master in business administration degree from MIT. More information about Lenny's projects and interests is available at www.zeltser.com.

Scott Winters has been working in all aspects of networking and computer security for over 14 years. He has been an Instructor, Network Engineer, and Systems Administrator and is currently employed as a Senior Consultant for Unisys at the Commonwealth of Pennsylvania Enterprise Server Farm. He has SANS GIAC Firewalls and Incident Handling certifications, as well as MCSE, CNE, Cisco CCNP, CCDP, and other industry certifications. Other accomplishments include authoring and editing of SANS GIAC Training and Certification course content, as well as exam content. He was a primary author of the first edition of *Inside Network Perimeter Security* and a contributing author for *SANS Security Essentials with CISSP CBK.* He has also been involved in the SANS GIAC Mentoring program and has served on the SANS GCFW Advisory Board.

Karen Kent is an Associate with Booz Allen Hamilton, where she provides guidance to Federal agencies on a broad range of information assurance concerns, including incident handling, intrusion detection, VPNs, log monitoring, and host security. Karen has earned a bachelor's degree in computer science from the University of Wisconsin-Parkside and a master's degree in computer science from the University of Idaho. She holds the CISSP certification and four SANS GIAC certifications. Karen has contributed to several books, including *Intrusion Signatures and Analysis*, published numerous articles on security, and coauthored several publications for the National Institute of Standards and Technology (NIST), including NIST Special Publication 800-61: Computer Security Incident Handling Guide.

Ronald W. Ritchey has an active interest in secure network design and network intrusion techniques. He gets to exercise this interest regularly by conducting penetration testing efforts for Booz Allen Hamilton, where he has had the opportunity to learn first-hand the real-world impact of network vulnerabilities. He is also an active researcher in the field with peer-reviewed publications in the area of automated network security analysis. Ronald has authored courses on computer security that have been taught across the country, and he periodically teaches graduate-level courses on computer security. Ronald holds a masters degree in computer science from George Mason University and is currently pursuing his Ph.D. in information technology at their School of Information Technology and Engineering. His doctoral research involves automating network security analysis.

About the Technical Editors

Todd Chapman has 10+ years of experience delivering IT services as varied as systems management, security, networking, clustering, Perl programming, and corporate development and training. Currently, Todd is a consultant for gedas USA, Inc., in Auburn Hills, Michigan, where he provides security consulting services for Volkswagen/Audi of America. For the last three years Todd has been an active member of the SANS GCFW advisory board and has written SANS certification exam questions in a number of disciplines. Todd's certifications include Red Hat Certified Engineer (RHCE), Microsoft Certified Systems Engineer (MCSE), GIAC Certified Firewall Analyst (GCFW), GIAC Certified Intrusion Analyst (GCIA), and GIAC Systems and Network Auditor (GSNA).

Anton Chuvakin, Ph.D., GCIA, GCIH, is a Security Strategist with netForensics, a security information management company, where he is involved with designing the product, researching potential new security features, and advancing the security roadmap. His areas of infosec expertise include intrusion detection, UNIX security, forensics, honeypots, and more. He is the author of the book *Security Warrior* (O'Reilly, January 2004) and a contributor to "Know Your Enemy II" by the Honeynet Project (AWL, June 2004) and "Information Security Management Handbook" (CRC, April 2004). In his spare time he maintains his security portal www.info-secure.org website.

Dan Goldberg recently created MADJiC Consulting, Inc., to provide network design and architecture reviews, intrusion detection and response, and vulnerability assessments in Central Virginia. He also works on research and writing projects for the SANS Institute and as technical director for Global Information Assurance Certification (GIAC). When not occupied by these activities, you may find him riding a mountain bike in the Blue Ridge Mountains.

John Spangler is a freelance Network Systems Engineer. Having over 10 years of experience, he has worked on everything from small office systems to large enterprise and ISP networks. John has worked as a technical editor for Cisco certification manuals.

Acknowledgments

Creating a book of this breadth and depth would not have been possible without the support of our colleagues, families, and friends. We would like to express our humble thanks to the individuals who helped make this book a reality.

Our acquisitions editor, Linda Harrison, and our development editor, Songlin Qiu, have meticulously guided us through the process of creating and revising this book. They, and the staff at Sams Publishing, have been wonderful partners in this venture.

This edition's technical editors, Todd Chapman, Anton Chuvakin, Dan Goldberg, and John Spangler, have carefully examined each chapter's draft to ensure the accuracy of the book's content. We thank them for the time they've devoted to the project, and for the expertise they've loaned to this book.

We also thank our coauthors and technical editors who played a major role in creating the previous edition of this book. Their expertise, thoughtfulness, and attention to detail have already assisted thousands of readers in protecting their network's perimeter.

First edition contributing authors:

Brent Deterding

Mark Edmead

Dr. Neil F. Johnson

Brian O'Berry

Daniel Martin

First edition technical editors:

Bill Bauer

Sam Campbell

Clement Dupuis

Jeff Stevenson

Sergei Ledovskjj

Lastly, we thank our families and friends for their incredible patience while we worked on this project. Their support, love, and understanding helped make this book possible.

We Want to Hear from You!

As the reader of this book, *you* are our most important critic and commentator. We value your opinion and want to know what we're doing right, what we could do better, what areas you'd like to see us publish in, and any other words of wisdom you're willing to pass our way.

You can email or write me directly to let me know what you did or didn't like about this book—as well as what we can do to make our books stronger.

Please note that I cannot help you with technical problems related to the topic of this book, and that due to the high volume of mail I receive, I might not be able to reply to every message.

When you write, please be sure to include this book's title and author as well as your name and phone or email address. I will carefully review your comments and share them with the author and editors who worked on the book.

E-mail: networking@samspublishing.com

Mail: Mark Taber
          Associate Publisher
          Sams Publishing
          800 East 96th Street
          Indianapolis, IN 46240 USA

Reader Services

For more information about this book or another Sams Publishing title, visit our website at www.samspublishing.com. Type the ISBN (excluding hyphens) or the title of a book in the Search field to find the page you're looking for.

Preface

The flight from Lihue to San Francisco is about five and a half hours and allows me some of my most productive work time. The phone doesn't ring, the dog doesn't ask to go outside, and my personal firewall doesn't start blinking because someone is trying to scan my computer. The flight attendant crews are starting to know me; I don't want any airplane food, I brought my own recycled water bottle filled with water from my own reverse osmosis filter, just let me write. I am very thankful for a bit of understanding from the crew of United FLT 30 for the time to write this preface. If any of my words give you insight into the current state of affairs with perimeter and internal network management, don't attribute that to me. I rely more each day of my life on the words in James 1:5; I am just the messenger.

I was enjoying working on the second edition of this book when a scene on the airplane entertainment televisions caught my eye. It was a video history of United Airlines, which started by delivering airmail in rickety old airplanes with exposed cockpits. Today, modern, fast, sophisticated aircraft have an incredible safety record. The airline industry has gone from an oddity—a great tool to entertain the crowds at county fairs—to an industry that is crucial to our way of life and economy. The airlines in the United States were essentially grounded for about three days following the terrorist attacks of September 11, 2001. The U.S. Congress debated whether to give the airlines money; they decided against it and United is now in chapter 11.

By exploring what has changed in the airline world, you will see both the past and the future of our industry, information technology (IT). Like the airline industry, IT has historically been accomplished on rickety platforms. We have benefited from rapid advances in technology. We have seen a decline in personal service. We are headed for continuous inspections, a defense-in-depth approach, and we are every bit as vulnerable and at the same time crucial to the economy.

Rickety Planes

What if we flew in computers? That gives "crash" a whole new meaning, doesn't it? Well, if we did, I am sure you would agree that we would all be dead. I would love to say operating systems are really improving, but it isn't so. I installed XP SP2 beta, one of the least-rickety operating systems I have worked with in a long time, on a clone of my primary laptop a couple months ago, and it has been interesting. As soon as I submit the remainder of my chapters for this book, I will upgrade my production box. As I write this, the Windows update version has still not been released, and it will be very interesting to see what breaks when the home users get upgraded. A lot of people died in the early days of the airline industry, and as I say, if we flew in those early planes today, most of us would be dead.

Now here is the kicker: IPS systems and intelligent switches are nothing but software applications or ASICs that are built on these rickety operating systems. One of the primary themes of this book is never to trust the operating system, to expect perimeter components to fail. This book will show you techniques for failover, layering defense components, segmenting internal networks, using instrumentation to detect anomalies, and troubleshooting. In the early days of perimeter defense, the only choice that information security practitioners had was to layer their perimeter software on these rickety operating systems.

Fires in the West

For years, I was a network builder for the Department of Defense, which uses large, high-end, fast networks. The most effective security mechanism for separation of sensitive information was implemented with a physical solution—an airgap. If you want to protect one network from another, just don't connect them together. Worms such as Blaster taught us that many networks that supposedly were not connected to the Internet actually were in one way or another, but if you audit carefully and never allow an exception, airgaps work.

The problem with an airgap is the two networks cannot interoperate, a concept directly in contradiction with the Internet philosophy and electronic business. The past few years have been a bad time for the U.S. West, as rain has been minimal, with fires starting earlier and earlier each year it seems. One of the most effective tools for managing fires is a firebreak; it isn't as powerful as an airgap (sometimes the fire will bridge it), but segmenting the forest into zones is a powerful technique. The information technology analog for a firebreak is to segment the internal network. This can be done with internal intelligent Network Intrusion Prevention Switches (NIPS), with some elbow grease using current generation switches and applying access control to VLANs, or with low-cost appliance-type firewalls used on the internal network. It can even be done manually using anomaly IDS to detect switch ports heating up, which is usually a signature of a worm, and shutting down the switch. Segmenting internal networks with "firebreaks" allows us to have the interoperability and reduce the risk of losing all our internal systems to a destructive worm "wildfire."

This book discusses a number of perimeter and internal network designs. Some are more focused on security, whereas others are focused on performance. Some focus on uptime and help you to understand how to choose these designs based on your organization's requirements.

> **Note**
> One of the reasons that early airplanes were so dangerous is that a large number of them were hand built. Even if the planes were built in a factory, after a couple of years, they might as well be hand built because of the number of times they were repaired and modified.

Can you see how similar the early airplanes are to our server and desktop operating systems? We all agree that patching to reduce the vulnerability footprint is critical, but if no two servers are alike, exactly how do you test the patch? Repeatable builds give an IT shop a major increase in security just like factory-built aircraft.

So do appliance firewalls. They are factory built, plug and go. It's not guaranteed that their OS is hardened, but you do know that the OS on the appliance is factory built, consistent, and probably stripped of unneeded programs. These low-cost appliances are very useful for segmenting an internal network.

Rapid Advances in Technology

Modern aircrafts have wings, fly through the air, and land on the ground—and that is about all they have in common with the first airplanes. The advances in airframe design, materials, avionics, navigation and route selection, and airport operations make it difficult to believe that people ever considered getting into the early airplanes.

I would love to say that modern perimeter systems are so advanced that it is inconceivable that we ever tried to protect our systems with those early firewalls, but we haven't made that much progress yet. However, hope prevails, and we certainly see evidence of improvement. Perimeter defense systems have come way down in price for any given bandwidth point; many can be upgraded by just downloading a new image.

Deep packet inspection at gigabit speed is possible right now for the well-funded organization. Subscription models that update daily or weekly are the norm and support an architecture of perimeter components to create hybrid systems that combine classic perimeter defense, reporting sensors, and possibly even vulnerability assessments that allow performing internal correlation.

This book discusses the importance of using the information collected by perimeter devices to help defend the network. The data collected and reported by these devices fuels the most advanced analysis capability in the world—the Internet Storm Center (ISC). Organizations such as ISC and Internet Security Systems's X-Force are often the first groups to detect a new worm beginning to cause trouble on the Internet. One of the upcoming models for security is continuous reporting, or operational readiness, and this requires sensors all over the network to constantly report in. The technology of network security is dynamic. It's important to have constant updates to maintain security in the face of the ever-changing threat.

It is worth mentioning that ease of use and good security might be orthogonal. If it were as easy to get into an airplane and fly as it is to get into a car and drive, the skies would be a dangerous place. Appliance wireless access points often aggregate all wireless and built-in wired ports into the same broadcast domains. Possibilities for attacks exist based on MAC address spoofing, sniffing the internal traffic from outside the plant in the parking lot, the use of rogue, unapproved access points bought at Best Buy and plugged into the Net, access points with a bit more power than the FTC allows being broadcast into the internal network from the parking lot, and failures of the authentication system. The most common reason for aircraft crashes today is poor maintenance, and we are going to see the same thing with wireless implementations as better security technology becomes available.

Decline in Personal Service

More has changed on the human side of the airline equation than just the name change from *stewardesses* to *flight attendants*. First class isn't first class, and it goes downhill from there. The airlines seem to be testing the limits to see just how much abuse people will take—and they wonder why they occasionally deal with passenger rage. Sadly, the IT industry has never been big on personal service. There were exceptions, back in the glory days of big blue. We had a bit of trouble with an IBM mainframe, and they tossed a squad of technicians into an airplane and dropped them by parachute into our parking lot. Until the technicians dropped on target, vice presidents would call every 15 minutes to apprise us of the location of the plane. Okay, I am kidding, but not by much. Those of us in IT security should take heed. I hope you understand what your CEO is thinking right now. He gave you money for security after 9/11 because it seemed to be the right thing to do. You still got hit by worms. He increased ITSEC to 5% of the IT budget. You still got hit by worms. Now you are in a meeting thinking about asking the CEO for unplanned money to implement a NIPS or HIPS solution. I strongly suggest you invest time in looking at your requirements, making sure that you choose the best technology for your needs and that customer service is part of the budget request so the people impacted by the active defense layer you are thinking about implementing will have someone intelligent and caring to call.

Nowadays, the IT industry has two primary features: bad software and worse service. One of the advantages of this book is that the entire author team has pragmatic experience with most of the commercial and freeware perimeter products on the market, including the rapidly changing personal firewall market. We can't do much to help you with the bad software, and we never intend to bash any vendor—each has its foibles. However, we can help you in finding ways to meet your mission goals despite the flaws in the technology we each use. We devote an entire chapter of the book to implementing defense components, such as personal firewalls at a host level, to help you avoid some of the common pitfalls and know what technology is available. The latest generation of Host Intrusion Protection Systems (HIPS), which are essentially personal firewalls with operating system shims to trap dangerous operating system interrupts, have already proved themselves in production and are an important and valuable layer of defense.

Continuous Inspections

One of the primary reasons the aircraft industry has been able to make gigantic leaps in improving safety is the rigorous, complete, and continuous inspections for every component and process related to flying. This is also the most important change that we need to make. When I teach at the SANS Institute, a security research and education organization, I often say, "Who reads the event logs every day?" Some hands go up. I try to memorize their faces and catch them alone at the break. Then I ask them, "What is in the logs? What recurring problems are there?" They usually cannot answer. This book can help you deploy sensors and scanners. An entire chapter is devoted to intrusion detection. Even your organization's software architecture is a security perimeter component, as you will learn in the software architecture chapter.

If you were to ask me what the growth industry in IT was, I would answer that consoles, sensors, and agents to collect and display information would be a strong candidate. Computer systems change rapidly. They are analogous to the barnstormer bi-planes that flew around county fairs. When something broke, a blacksmith, automobile mechanic, or seamstress fabricated a new part. We can add and uninstall software in a heartbeat, but when we do, we cannot get back to the place where we were before the change. We need to monitor for change continuously, and until we learn how to do this and rigorously enforce change control, flying in computers will be nearly certain death.

Defense in Depth

It is a tragedy when a single passenger plane crashes, worse when a plane full of people goes down, and an unspeakable horror when a plane is used as a weapon of terrorism. Today, airports are transforming into examples of *defense in depth*. Defense in depth is a primary focus of this book, and the concept is quite simple: Make it harder to attack at chokepoint after chokepoint. How many security systems or defensive layers would you have to defeat to rush through an airport race to a waiting, fueled, long-range jet, commandeer the plane, drive it out on the tarmac to take off, and use it as a missile? Many are obvious, such as security checkpoints, armed National Guard troops, locked doors, and tarmac controls. If you did manage to get the plane in the air, you would also have to defeat fighter aircraft. It isn't impossible, but it is unlikely that you could defeat the defense in depth that is now employed at airports.

Defense in depth is present in every chapter of this book, and it's becoming easier to implement in information technology. High-speed programmable hardware boxes, such as UnityOne from TippingPoint, can help protect our network borders from worm outbreaks. Technologies we have already discussed in this preface, such as next-generation intelligent switches and HIPS, allow us to implement multiple layers for our perimeter and internal networks, albeit at a significant cost. No matter what role you play in your organization, it is important to read the intrusion prevention chapter and make sure the folks in charge of the budget know what is on the horizon. As you read this book, you will learn how to architect your network so that it is resistant to attack. As we evolve as an information-based society, the importance of protecting intellectual property assets continues to rise.

Core Business Sector

In less than a century, airplanes have gone from being an oddity to being vitally important to the economy. Information technology has done the same in less time and continues to grow in importance. We have been more than a bit lazy. I often wonder what the effect of a worm with the infection rate of Blaster that overwrote (not deleted, overwrote) every location on the hard drive of an infected computer four hours after infection would be. If the Congress of the United States did not vote on a bailout package for the airline industry, IT should not expect one. One of the primary keys to survival in business over the next few years will be managing the flow of information so that resources are available when they are needed with full integrity, while the confidentiality of proprietary and sensitive information is maintained. It is a big task, so we had better get started.

—Stephen Northcutt and the authoring team

Introduction

WELCOME, AND THANK YOU FOR CONSIDERING the second edition of *Inside Network Perimeter Security*. This book is a unique volume because it has a consistent phrasing and style, yet it consolidates the experience of more than a dozen information security professionals working together as a team of writers and reviewers. Our goal was to create a practical guide for designing, deploying, and maintaining a real-world network security perimeter. This is a crucial topic because robust network defenses form the foundation of a reliable and trustworthy computing infrastructure.

As Richard Clarke, the former U.S. cyber-security czar, pointed out during a keynote address at a SANS Institute conference: "The perimeter is crumbling. Wireless technologies, worms, and our gadget mentality are the reason." Given the porous nature of the modern perimeter, protecting the network is not an easy task; it requires that you get to know different types of technologies and understand how they relate to each other. This is why we discuss key perimeter security components, such as firewalls, VPNs, routers, as well as intrusion detection and prevention systems. We also explain how to integrate these devices with each other to form a unified whole. There is no single gadget that can protect our networks against all threats, which is why we focus on layered security architectures. This concept of defense in depth is present throughout the book, and we believe it holds a key to the practical use of the perimeter security techniques discussed here.

Who Should Read This Book

This is an intermediate- to advanced-level book for security professionals and system and network administrators who have a good understanding of TCP/IP and related technologies. This book is a valuable reference for individuals who are interested in examining best practices of perimeter defense and in expanding their knowledge of network security tools and techniques. Because the book was developed in close coordination with the SANS Institute, it is also an excellent supplementary resource for those pursuing the GIAC Certified Firewall Analyst (GCFW) certification.

Why We Created This Book's Second Edition

The world of information security is evolving, as attackers develop new tools and techniques, and as defenders create new protective mechanisms. In turn, we have updated this book to ensure that it continues to be a useful resource for those responsible for protecting their organizations' network resources. We have expanded the coverage of perimeter security by adding two brand new chapters: one focusing on intrusion prevention systems, and the other on security of wireless networks. We also carefully went through the book's other chapters, revising them where appropriate to address current threats, to describe advancements in defensive technologies, and to improve the way we explain core concepts. No book is perfect; revising this book has given us the opportunity to come a bit closer to this unattainable goal.

Overview of the Book's Contents

We would like to introduce this book from a 50,000-foot view. Part I, "The Essentials of Network Perimeter Security," covers the first five chapters and serves as a foundation for later chapters. The first chapter presents an overview of everything we will talk about throughout the book. Other chapters in Part I discuss core perimeter security concepts, such as packet filtering, stateful firewalls, proxies, and security policy.

Part II, "Fortifying the Security Perimeter," comprises Chapters 6 through 11 and concentrates on additional components that make up a network security perimeter. Here, we examine the role of routers, virtual private networks (VPNs), network intrusion detection systems (IDSs), intrusion prevention systems (IPSs), and host-centric defense mechanisms.

Good design is covered in Part III, "Designing a Secure Network Perimeter," where we focus on integrating perimeter components into a unified defense architecture. Chapters 12 through 18 describe ways of achieving defense in depth that are appropriate for your needs and budgets, letting you apply what you have learned about security devices and approaches. In addition to discussing design fundamentals, we focus on topics such as resource separation, wireless network security, software architecture, and VPN integration. We also explain how to tune a security design to achieve optimal performance, and we look at several sample architectures.

Part IV, "Maintaining and Monitoring Perimeter Security," which comprises Chapters 19 through 24, concludes the book by answering the famous question, "How do you know?" It presents a discussion of understanding what the perimeter systems are telling us and of ensuring that the perimeter operates according to its design. We examine perimeter maintenance procedures, log analysis, and troubleshooting approaches. We also describe techniques for assessing the strength of your defenses and explain how to conduct an adversarial review of the network architecture. The last chapter summarizes defense-in-depth concepts that have been described throughout the book. It is a mirror in some sense of the first chapter, but it is used to wrap up prime concepts of the book.

We have also outfitted the book with two appendixes, where we provide sample Cisco access list configurations and discuss fundamentals of cryptography that are relevant to network defense. Designing, deploying, and maintaining a network security perimeter is a challenging journey, and we hope that our approach to network defense makes your path more comfortable.

Conventions

This book follows a few typographical and stylistic conventions:

- New terms are set in *italic* the first time they are introduced.

- Whenever possible, we reference the Common Vulnerabilities and Exposures (CVE) database to allow you to obtain additional information about the vulnerabilities—for example, http://cve.mitre.org/cgibin/cvename.cgi?name= CAN-2004-0965.

- Commands, file locations, variables, and other "computer language" instructions are set in a monospace font—for example, `GET`, `AllowHosts`, and `access-list`.

- We also use italic to indicate the use of a placeholder in the text. For example, in the following IOS command, you should substitute "gateway IP" with an actual IP address: `ip route 0.0.0.0 0.0.0.0 `*`gateway IP`*.

- When a line from command, code, or log listing is too long to fit on the page, we use the code-continuation character to indicate that we wrapped the line that did not originally have a line break. Here's an example:

```
Jan 28 03:15:26 [10.20.30.40] 265114: %SEC-6-IPACCESSLOGP: list 105 denied
➡tcp 172.30.128.12(1947) -> 10.20.1.6(80), 1 packet
```

- We often use sidebars to describe our own experiences and to present illustrative examples. Therefore, the text in most sidebars is worded in a first person voice. Here's an example:

At Least Lock the (Screen) Door

I once encountered a network without a screened subnet or a DMZ. The DNS server resided on the internal network, which was a hub-based environment. When an attacker compromised the DNS server, he installed a sniffer and was able to glean internal passwords. If the DNS server had been on a switched screened subnet, the attacker's ability to sniff passwords would have been greatly inhibited.

- Finally, within each chapter, you will encounter several Notes and Tips:

Tip

Tips are used to highlight shortcuts, convenient techniques, or tools that can make a task easier. Tips also sometimes provide recommendations on best practices you should follow.

Note

Notes provide additional background information about a topic being described, beyond what is given in the chapter text. Often, notes are used to provide references to places you can find more information about a particular topic.

I

The Essentials of Network Perimeter Security

1

Perimeter Security Fundamentals

THE SECURITY OF YOUR NETWORK IS EVALUATED daily. A rich question to ask is, "Are you the one doing it?" The answer, hopefully, is that someone on your side is involved in assessing the effectiveness of your defenses; however, overwhelming evidence reports that you are not the only party probing your network's perimeter. Internet-facing systems—computers with IP addresses that can be reached from the Internet—receive between several and hundreds or even thousands of attack attempts every day. Many of these are simple scans that we know how to defend against, but others catch us by surprise, unexpectedly shifting us into incident investigation and cleanup mode.

Does your organization have access to expertise in all aspects of perimeter security, including networking, firewalls, intrusion detection systems (IDSs), intrusion prevention systems (IPSs), Virtual Private Networks (VPNs), UNIX security, and Windows security? In the pages ahead, we will show you how all these protective measures work together. Can you definitively say how secure or insecure your network is? Does everyone in your organization understand the policies related to information security and their implications? One hint that they do not is the famous expression, "But we have a firewall!" If you work in information security, you probably hear this phrase more often than you would like to, because it seems to express the opinion of many people, both technical and nontechnical.

One of the most challenging aspects of securing modern networks, even those that already have firewalls, is that they exhibit porous properties. Wireless connections, portable storage devices, mobile systems, and links to partner sites offer a multitude of ways in which data can get in and out of our networks, bypassing our border defenses. This is one of the reasons why a single security component cannot properly defend a network. However, many components working together can. *Defense in depth*, a major theme of this chapter and this book, is the process of layering these components to capitalize on their respective strengths. It is flexible, in that it allows us to select components based on technical, budgetary, and organizational constraints and combine them in a way that doesn't compromise the overall security or usability of the network.

We will begin this chapter by defining some common terms of the trade to ensure that we're all on the same page. Then we'll discuss core components of defense in depth, to illustrate how various aspects of the security perimeter can complement each other to form a balanced whole. We will close with a discussion of the Nimda worm and show how defense in depth can help protect your network against such an attack.

Terms of the Trade

We need a common frame of reference when it comes to terms used throughout the book, because one person's definitions might not be the same as someone else's. To that end, we'll define the perimeter, the border router, a firewall, an IDS, an IPS, a VPN, software architecture, as well as De-Militarized Zones (DMZs) and screened subnets.

The Perimeter

What exactly is the perimeter? Some people, when they hear the term *perimeter*, may conjure up an image of a small squad of soldiers spread out on the ground in a circular formation. Others may come up with the circling-the-wagons image. Before we move on, ask yourself, "What is a perimeter?"

In the context of this book, a perimeter is the fortified boundary of the network that might include the following aspects:

- Border routers
- Firewalls
- IDSs
- IPSs
- VPN devices
- Software architecture
- DMZs and screened subnets

Let's take a look at these perimeter components in closer detail.

Border Routers

Routers are the traffic cops of networks. They direct traffic into, out of, and within our networks. The *border router* is the last router you control before an untrusted network such as the Internet. Because all of an organization's Internet traffic goes through this router, it often functions as a network's first and last line of defense through initial and final filtering.

Firewalls

A *firewall* is a chokepoint device that has a set of rules specifying what traffic it will allow or deny to pass through it. A firewall typically picks up where the border router leaves off and makes a much more thorough pass at filtering traffic. Firewalls come in several different types, including static packet filters, stateful firewalls, and proxies. You might use a static packet filter such as a Cisco router to block easily identifiable "noise" on the Internet, a stateful firewall such as a Check Point FireWall-1 to control allowed services, or a proxy firewall such as Secure Computing's Sidewinder to control content. Although firewalls aren't perfect, they do block what we tell them to block and allow what we tell them to allow.

Intrusion Detection Systems

An *IDS* is like a burglar alarm system for your network that is used to detect and alert on malicious events. The system might comprise many different IDS sensors placed at strategic points in your network. Two basic types of IDS exist: network-based (NIDS), such as Snort or Cisco Secure IDS, and host-based (HIDS), such as Tripwire or ISS BlackICE. NIDS sensors monitor network traffic for suspicious activity. NIDS sensors often reside on subnets that are directly connected to the firewall, as well as at critical points on the internal network. HIDS sensors reside on and monitor individual hosts.

In general, IDS sensors watch for predefined signatures of malicious events, and they might perform statistical and anomaly analysis. When IDS sensors detect suspicious events, they can alert in several different ways, including email, paging, or simply logging the occurrence. IDS sensors can usually report to a central database that correlates their information to view the network from multiple points.

Intrusion Prevention Systems

An *IPS* is a system that automatically detects and thwarts computer attacks against protected resources. In contrast to a traditional IDS, which focuses on notifying the administrator of anomalies, an IPS strives to automatically defend the target without the administrator's direct involvement. Such protection may involve using signature-based or behavioral techniques to identify an attack and then blocking the malicious traffic or system call before it causes harm. In this respect, an IPS combines the functionality of a firewall and IDS to offer a solution that automatically blocks offending actions as soon as it detects an attack.

As you will learn in Chapter 11, "Intrusion Prevention Systems," some IPS products exist as standalone systems, such as TippingPoint's UnityOne device. Additionally, leading firewall and IDS vendors are incorporating IPS functionality into their existing products.

Virtual Private Networks

A *VPN* is a protected network session formed across an unprotected channel such as the Internet. Frequently, we reference a VPN in terms of the device on the perimeter that enables the encrypted session, such as Cisco VPN Concentrator. The intended use might be for business partners, road warriors, or telecommuters. A VPN allows an outside user to participate on the internal network as if connected directly to it. Many organizations have a false sense of security regarding their remote access just because they have a VPN. However, if an attacker compromises the machine of a legitimate user, a VPN can give that attacker an encrypted channel into your network. You might trust the security of your perimeter, but you have little control over your telecommuters' systems connecting from home, a hotel room, or an Internet café. Similar issues of trust and control arise with the security of nodes connected over a VPN from your business partner's network.

Software Architecture

Software architecture refers to applications that are hosted on the organization's network, and it defines how they are structured. For example, we might structure an e-commerce application by splitting it into three distinct tiers:

- The web front end that is responsible for how the application is presented to the user
- The application code that implements the business logic of the application
- The back-end databases that store underlying data for the application

Software architecture plays a significant role in the discussion of a security infrastructure because the primary purpose of the network's perimeter is to protect the application's data and services. When securing the application, you should ensure that the architecture of the software and the network is harmonious.

De-Militarized Zones and Screened Subnets

We typically use the terms *DMZ* and *screened subnet* in reference to a small network containing public services connected directly to and offered protection by the firewall or other filtering device. A DMZ and a screened subnet are slightly different, even though many people use the terms interchangeably. The term DMZ originated during the Korean War when a strip of land at the 38th parallel was off-limits militarily. A DMZ is an insecure area between secure areas. Just as the DMZ in Korea was in front of any defenses, the DMZ, when applied to networks, is located outside the firewall. A firewall or a comparable traffic-screening device protects a screened subnet that is directly connected to it. Remember this: A DMZ is in front of a firewall, whereas a screened subnet is behind a firewall. In the context of this book, we will adhere to these definitions. Note the difference in Figure 1.1.

A screened subnet is an isolated network that is connected to a dedicated interface of a firewall or another filtering device. The screened subnet is frequently used to segregate servers that need to be accessible from the Internet from systems that are used solely by the organization's internal users. The screened subnet typically hosts "public" services, including DNS, mail, and web. We would like to think these servers are *bastion hosts*. A bastion is a well-fortified position. When applied to hosts on a network, fortifying involves hardening the operating system and applications according to best practices. As attacks over time have shown, these servers are not always well fortified; in fact, they are sometimes vulnerable despite being protected by a firewall. We must take extra care fortifying these hosts because they are the target of the majority of attacks and can bring the attacker closer to accessing even more critical internal resources.

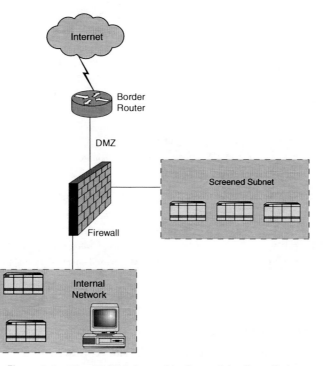

Figure 1.1   The DMZ is located in front of the firewall; the
screened subnet is isolated from the internal network, but it
still enjoys the protections that the firewall offers.

Now that we have defined core components of the network perimeter, let's look at how
they can be applied in an architecture according to the principle of defense in depth.

Defense in Depth

A well-structured defense architecture treats security of the network like an onion.
When you peel away the outermost layer, many remain underneath it. No concept carries more importance when discussing network security than *defense in depth*. Defense in
depth helps you protect network resources even if one of the security layers is compromised. After all, no single security component can be guaranteed to withstand every
attack it might need to face.

We operate in a real world of system misconfigurations, software bugs, disgruntled
employees, and overloaded system administrators. Moreover, any practical security design
needs to accommodate business needs that might require us to open certain firewall
ports, leave additional services running on the server, or prevent us from applying the
latest security patch because it breaks a business-critical application. Treating perimeter
security components as parts of a coherent infrastructure allows us to deploy them in a
way that accounts for the weaknesses and strengths of each individual component. Of

course, given the requirements of your organization, you might choose not to implement every component discussed in this chapter. The extent to which you need to apply network security layers depends on the needs and capabilities of your business.

After introducing defense in depth in this section, we will use it as the guiding principle behind designs and implementations throughout this book. In fact, this topic is so important, we will conclude the book with a chapter devoted specifically to this topic.

Crown Jewels

Think of any information that would have significant adverse affects if compromised as your organization's crown jewels. What are your company's crown jewels? How well protected are they?

Take the case of CD-Universe. Maxim, a Russian cracker, compromised 300,000 credit card numbers late in 1999. CD-Universe refused to pay his $100,000 ransom demand. In response, Maxim posted 25,000 numbers on a website on Christmas Day 1999.

CD-Universe had their crown jewels compromised and undoubtedly felt the effects in lost sales and consumer confidence. When mitigating such risks, we must consider what our organization's crown jewels are and what protecting them is worth when we implement defense in depth if we want to avoid similar problems for our organizations.

Components of Defense in Depth

What exactly does defense in depth entail? The simple answer is the perimeter, the internal network, and a human factor. Each of these comprises many components, which are independently not enough to secure a network. The key lies in each component complementing the others to form a complete security picture.

The Perimeter

When we think of network security, we most often think of the perimeter. As we mentioned earlier in this chapter, the perimeter includes any or all of the following:

- Static packet filter
- Stateful firewall
- Proxy firewall
- IDS and IPS
- VPN device

We have already introduced these security components to you. Now, let's take a look at how they might work together to form a defense-in-depth infrastructure.

Static packet filters inspect basic information within every packet and are typically implemented as routers. The border device is the first incoming and the last outgoing layer of your network security. It contributes to defense in depth by filtering traffic before it enters or exits your network. All too often, we only consider filtering incoming traffic, but then we don't get the full usability of our border router.

Improperly destined traffic might be internal addresses that hit your external interface, or vice versa, and they can be addressed with ingress and egress filtering. Border routers can also block traffic that is considered high risk from entering your network, such as traffic on the SANS Top 20 Vulnerabilities list (http://www.sans.org/top20). ICMP is a favorite of attackers both for DoS attacks and reconnaissance, so blocking this protocol in whole or in part is a common function of a border router. You may also consider blocking source-routed packets at the border router because they can circumvent defenses. The border router can also block out-of-band packets, such as SYN-FIN packets.

On February 9, 2000, websites such as Yahoo! and CNN were temporarily taken off the Internet, mostly by distributed denial of service (DDoS) Smurf attacks. A Smurf attack involves sending spoofed ICMP echo requests (ping) to the broadcast address, resulting in a response from every host. In this case, spoofing allowed attackers to direct the large number of responses to a victim network. Ingress and egress filtering would have blocked the spoofed traffic and allowed them to weather the DDoS storm. Every network should have ingress and egress filtering at the border router to permit only traffic that is destined for the internal network to enter and traffic that is destined for the external network to exit. We will cover filtering—including ingress and egress filters—in Chapter 2, "Packet Filtering."

Static packet filters, such as routers, are faster at screening traffic than stateful or proxy firewalls. This speed comes in handy when you are under attack or when the firewall is already under a heavy load. What if you don't have a border router under your exclusive control? If your Internet connection is relatively small (T1 or less), then performing filtering solely on a firewall might be sufficient.

Unlike static packet filtering devices, stateful firewalls keep track of connections in a state table and are the most common type of firewall. A stateful firewall blocks traffic that is not in its table of established connections. The firewall rulebase determines the source and destination IP and port numbers permitted to establish connections. By rejecting nonestablished, nonpermitted connections, a stateful firewall helps to block reconnaissance packets, as well as those that may gain more extensive unauthorized access to protected resources.

Recon Is the Name of the Game

My cable modem at home receives several scans per day. Previously with the IPChains firewall I had in place, Nmap ACK scans would pass through and successfully scan me. They were successful because non-stateful, static packet filters, such as IPChains, evaluated each packet independently and did not track state. The presence of the ACK bit made it appear that I had initiated the connection and the ACK was the response. Without a stateful firewall in place, reconnaissance of my machine was relatively easy.

Stateful firewalls are able to recognize and block traffic that is part of a nonestablished, nonpermitted connection, such as attempts at reconnaissance. The ability to block reconnaissance attempts that hit your firewall, such as the Nmap ACK scan, make stateful firewalls a valuable part of defense in depth by adding another layer of security to your network. An alternative, and sometimes a complement to a stateful firewall, is a proxy firewall.

Proxy firewalls are the most advanced and least common type of firewall. Proxy firewalls are also stateful, in that they block any nonestablished, nonpermitted connections. As with stateful firewalls, the firewall rulebase determines the source and destination IP and port numbers that are permitted to establish connections. Proxy firewalls offer a high level of security because internal and external hosts never communicate directly. Rather, the firewall acts as an intermediary between hosts. Proxy firewalls examine the entire packet to ensure compliance with the protocol that is indicated by the destination port number. Ensuring that only protocol-compliant traffic passes through the firewall helps defense in depth by diminishing the possibility of malicious traffic entering or exiting your network.

Using proxy firewalls diminishes the possibility of malicious traffic entering or exiting your network by ensuring that only protocol-compliant traffic passes through. However, what happens if malicious traffic appears to be appropriate material and adheres to the protocol?

An IDS represents the eyes and ears of a network by monitoring the network and hosts from critical points for malicious activity. Typical network IDS sensor placement includes each network segment directly connected to the firewall, as well as critical points within the network. If malicious traffic bypasses your other defense mechanisms, an IDS should be able to detect it, as well as communicate what it sees. This is precisely how an IDS helps with defense in depth.

For example, a network IDS could identify and alert on the following:

- DNS zone transfer requests from unauthorized hosts
- Unicode attacks directed at a web server
- Buffer overflow attacks
- Worm propagation

There are numerous incidents where successive fast-spreading worms have brought down large international networks. If these companies had been able to identify and isolate the infected machines quickly each time a new worm hit, they could have kept their networks functioning. An IDS with the correct signature would facilitate that identification. An IDS can help identify malicious traffic that might otherwise appear normal to an untrained eye. For example, a DNS zone transfer is a legitimate and common operation for peered DNS servers to engage in. However, we should consider zone transfers outside of those hosts dangerous.

An IDS contributes toward a defense-in-depth architecture by detecting and reporting suspicious activity. This functionality can be augmented by deploying an IPS, which, in addition to detecting attacks, attempts to automatically thwart them. *Intrusion prevention* is becoming a popular term in literature describing firewall and IDS products—such "active response" technology gives us an opportunity to block malicious activity in situations where the likelihood of falsely identifying an attack is low.

An IDS allows us to tune our defenses to match the current threats. Furthermore, correlation of router, firewall, VPN, and system logs can yield some information about suspicious activity on the network. These logs are not meant to replace the granularity and extensiveness of IDS logs, but to augment them. Logs from non-IDS perimeter components can help significantly when the network IDS logs are of no use, such as when the traffic is encrypted in route to a VPN device.

VPNs protect communications over unprotected networks, such as the Internet. They improve security by offering confidentiality, integrity, and nonrepudiation. For example, a VPN can allow your employees working from home to connect to your servers in a trustworthy manner even while traversing the Internet. In this scenario, the VPN will make sure that no one can monitor the protected traffic, that no one can modify it without being detected, and that the data really came from the expected user. VPNs are appropriate for a wide range of applications and are often useful when dedicated private lines are too expensive or impractical for connecting network nodes. Protecting communications over unprotected networks helps us defend our networks with depth.

VPNs are wonderful tools or wonderful weapons, depending on who is using them. By providing protected communications over unprotected channels, a VPN is a tool to legitimate users. If, however, the endpoints of a VPN connection are not secure, an attacker might be able to gain a protected channel into your internal network, giving him an awesome weapon. In our experience, many large networks that have been severely crippled by worms were affected by the same type culprit during every infection: a VPN user who was working from home. Users would surf the Web using their personal broadband connections at night before logging onto the internal network the following day via the VPN. A worm infected their machines when they were connected to the Internet at night. When they connected to the internal network the following day, the worm propagated to the internal network and ran rampant.

VPNs offer significant cost savings over the previous alternative of frame relay or a private line. We can use a VPN to protect all traffic from one network to another (network to network), between two hosts (host to host), or from a single host to a network (host to network). Knowing this, the way in which we configure our networks becomes increasingly important.

All too often, security is not a primary concern to a business when putting a network in place. A thought-out network architecture is vital to defense in depth because it segregates resources and provides for performance and redundancy. A well-designed infrastructure can act as a business enabler, rather a stumbling block to the organization.

We need to do the following when evaluating a network security architecture:

- Determine what resources need to be protected.
- Determine the risk.
- Determine business requirements.

With this information, we can make educated decisions regarding our network defenses.

A solid network architecture created with security in mind will segregate resources and provide for performance and redundancy. Segregating resources is vital to defense in depth, and we will look at it closely in Chapter 13, "Separating Resources." We must keep in mind that no matter how segregated a host is from a network viewpoint, its configuration must also be hardened.

At Least Lock the (Screen) Door

I once encountered a network without a screened subnet or a DMZ. The DNS server resided on the internal network, which was a hub-based environment. When an attacker compromised the DNS server, he installed a sniffer and was able to glean internal passwords. If the DNS server had been on a switched screened subnet, the attacker's ability to sniff passwords would have been greatly inhibited.

The Perfect Onion?

Recently I was on site with a client who was telling me all about his company's layered security. The company had proxy firewalls, a big border router, IDSs, VPNs, a good design—you name it. When I asked about the security of the public DNS server, he told me that "it was fine" and that with so much security in front, the company wasn't too worried about it. Talk about locking the door but leaving the window open!

The organization had segregated and protected this DNS server quite well. However, in neglecting to harden the host, the company had wasted a lot of work on securing the rest of the perimeter. Further investigation revealed that an attacker could have easily compromised the server, obtained a shell, and exploited a trust relationship with the internal DNS server, leaving him inside the network with a critical server.

We've discussed how various components of the perimeter contribute to the overall security of our network through defense in depth. Although vital, the external perimeter is only one piece of defense in depth. Next, we examine a piece that many organizations neglect to properly address: the internal network.

The Internal Network

The internal network is the network that is protected by the perimeter and that contains all the servers, workstations, and infrastructure with which a company conducts business.

So often, administrators of various types say, "We can trust our own people." Organizations often neglect the security of the internal network because they don't consider an internal attack a risk. An internal attack doesn't have to be a malicious employee; it can be a careless employee as well. As organizations are learning each time a new worm comes out, they cannot afford to overlook the security of the internal network!

Let's shift gears for a minute. Conjure up an image of what you consider a highly skilled attacker. Imagine him breaking into your most sensitive systems...while sitting at your desk. What would stop him?

On the internal network, we could have the following "perimeter" devices:

- Ingress and egress filtering on every router
- Internal firewalls to segregate resources
- IDS sensors to function as "canaries in a coal mine" and monitor the internal network

On protected systems, we can use the following:

- Host-centric (personal) firewalls
- Antivirus software
- Operating system hardening
- Configuration management
- Audits

Host-centric (personal) firewalls are generally implemented as software modules that run on individual machines, screening network traffic as it enters and leaves the system. Many are configurable on a per-application basis, meaning that the user determines which applications have rights to access the Internet or function as servers (accept incoming connections). Personal firewalls help defense in depth by augmenting the perimeter on every host.

You might ask, "Why do I need a personal firewall if I'm already behind a network firewall at work?" A personal firewall at work can protect you from malicious programs, such as Trojans, and other internal hosts, as is the case with malicious internal users. If you do not have a personal firewall and connect to the Internet outside of work (such as the hotel room while traveling or the home office when working from home), you cannot assume that you are being protected.

Personal Firewall to the Rescue

Recently, a nontechnical co-worker asked me why a personal firewall on her office desktop kept popping up alerts. My curiosity immediately piqued, as I seriously doubted there was a hole in the company firewall. I discovered that she used a dial-up connection to check her personal email, and it had created a tunnel to her machine. She was being probed through the dial-up network for a vulnerability her machine had. If she had not had a personal firewall in place, an attacker could have run rampant on the internal company network.

Host-centric firewalls are wonderful pieces of software that augment the perimeter. If a traditional firewall cannot be deployed at the network's entry point, host-centric firewalls are cost-effective alternatives, especially if the network hosts a small number of systems. Host-centric firewalls are also useful for mobile users who connect to a network outside of work. Almost every network needs firewall technology of some sort, be it with static packet filters, stateful firewalls, or proxy firewalls on the perimeter or the individual machines. Most networks with user-level workstations also need an antivirus capability.

In many respects, antivirus software and network IDSs are similar in that they frequently operate by examining data for signatures of known malicious intent. Antivirus software typically looks at the data on the file system and in RAM, whereas a network IDS examines data on the network. As vendors package antivirus, personal firewall, and IDS technology into a single product, the line distinguishing the three becomes increasingly vague. The role of antivirus in defense in depth is clear—it protects against malicious code.

We can augment our antivirus capability on the desktop through products that couple with perimeter components, such as firewalls and email servers. The effectiveness of antivirus software drastically decreases if it is not regularly updated, or if it does not yet provide a signature to identify the latest virus or worm. This is often the case with worms, which propagate very quickly. Locking down the host's configuration becomes critically important in the case of ineffective antivirus software.

Host hardening is the process of tightening the configuration of the host's OS and applications with the purpose of securing any unnecessary openings on the system. This typically involves applying relevant OS and application patches, setting file system permissions, disabling unnecessary services, and enforcing password restrictions. If everything else fails, host hardening is the last layer protecting an individual system. That makes it vital to defense in depth.

Consider the nontechnical co-worker who was checking her personal email through a hotel's dial-up connection. What if she had not installed a personal firewall or antivirus software? If basic hardening had been performed, she would have likely presented the attacker with a variety of vulnerabilities to exploit. It is all too easy to forget about host hardening when multiple layers of defense are surrounding the system. The fact remains that those defenses are not perfect, and we need that last layer. The question of how to keep on top of host hardening naturally arises.

Configuration management is the process of establishing and maintaining a known configuration for systems and devices that are on the network. Large companies might have an automated means of manipulating the configuration of all hosts, whereas small companies might perform the process manually. Defense in depth benefits from the ability to enforce a standard configuration.

Configuration management can enforce the following:

- That all Windows machines have a particular service pack installed
- That all Linux machines have a specific kernel running
- That all users with remote-access accounts have a personal firewall
- That every machine has antivirus signatures updated daily
- That all users agree to the acceptable-use policy when they log on

Some of these tasks naturally lend themselves to large-scale automation, whereas others we can accomplish manually.

Who Is Responsible for Configuration Management?

A client recently called me in to handle a worm outbreak. My first question of the systems administrator was whether the OS on all hosts was up to the latest patch level. It turned out that he had not kept up with the latest patches because every host had antivirus software that each user was to update weekly. As you can imagine, many hosts had out-of-date antivirus signatures, which resulted in the worm freely exploiting unpatched OS vulnerabilities. We ended up spending at least a week eradicating worm infections and updating system configurations to make them more resilient to such attacks.

Configuration management is the best way to establish a standard, secure configuration so that damage from incidents is limited. It can also enable your organization to control unauthorized software installation. Configuration management is an important piece of defense in depth because it enforces a standard configuration. How can we verify that a configuration is a secure one that remains unchanged?

Auditing is the process of resolving perception to reality and improving upon that. Internal staff or external consultants can perform audits. The information that we present next was written from a perspective of an external consultant, but it applies to either situation. Verifying the current state of security and improving upon it is vital to defense in depth.

An audit typically progresses like this:

1. An informational meeting is held to plan the audit. At the first informational meeting, the auditor finds out what the client wants and expects and establishes risks, costs, cooperation, deliverables, timeframes, and authorization.

2. Fieldwork begins (implementing the audit). When the client is ready, the auditor performs the audit in line with what we established in the planning session.

3. The initial audit report (technical report) takes place. The auditor might prefer to give an initial audit report to the technical representatives of a client before their management sees the final report. This provides the technical staff with an opportunity to address some concerns before the final report goes to management. This also ensures that the technical representatives know what their management will see and can offer clarification on any issues.

4. The final audit report (a nontechnical report with the final technical report) takes place. The final audit report typically contains an executive summary, the general approach used, the specific methodology used, and the final technical report.

5. Follow-up occurs (verified recommendations are performed).

When the client is ready, the auditor may return to verify that the issues have been resolved.

Just like you go to your doctor on a regular basis for a physical to make sure you're as healthy as you think you are, you should check your network on a regular basis to ensure that your perception and the reality of your defenses coincide. Consider an audit preventative maintenance. An audit is the only tool in defense in depth to verify that everything is as it should be.

Securing the internal network with host-centric firewalls, antivirus software, and host hardening is not a trivial task. Configuration management and audits can help you accomplish this. Addressing security on the external perimeter and the internal network is not enough. Next, we will complete the defense-in-depth picture by discussing the human factor.

The Human Factor

Frequently, we get caught up in the technical aspect of network security without considering its nontechnical element. Tasks such as optimizing the firewall rulebase, examining network traffic for suspicious patterns, and locking down the configuration of systems are certainly important to network security. What we often forget is the human end of things, such as the policies and awareness that go along with the technical solution.

Policy determines what security measures your organization should implement. As a result, the security policy guides your decisions when implementing security of the network. An effective defense-in-depth infrastructure requires a comprehensive and realistic security policy.

Hallmarks of good policy include the following:

- **Authority**—Who is responsible.
- **Scope**—Who it affects.
- **Expiration**—When it ends.
- **Specificity**—What is required.
- **Clarity**—Can everyone understand it?

The Importance of Having a Documented Security Policy

In the initial planning meeting with clients, the first thing I always ask for is the security policy. Many times, the client gives me a quizzical look and asks why I would need it. I try to explain that policy and security are not separate entities, but determine one another.

If only a lawyer could read your security policy, it needs to be reevaluated. We'll take a good, long look at this issue in Chapter 5, "Security Policy." A caveat about policy: It only works if someone reads it.

User awareness is like driver's education. Users can reduce risk and help defense in depth if they know and follow the security policy. Here are some of the actions you can take to increase user awareness of your organization's security policy:

- Have every user sign an acceptable-use policy annually.
- Set up a security web page with policies, best practices, and news.
- Send a "Security Tip of the Week" to every user.

A direct benefit of aware users comes when considering social-engineering attacks. For example, if users know not to give their password to other people, a potential attack might be thwarted. When users are aware of policy, there tends to be fewer incidents and misunderstandings, and users feel more involved in security. Additionally, in the case of policy violations, if the users are educated, it's harder for people to claim that they didn't know they were doing something wrong.

> **Get It in Writing**
>
> I'm reminded of a time in my intemperate youth when I used the phrase, "I didn't know that; it was never communicated to me," regarding an acceptable-use policy. I've heard this same phrase repeated in a number of different circumstances. There is not much to be said when you have a signature affirming that a user agrees to and understands a policy. I have found a signed policy statement to be more valuable than gold in terms of time and effort saved.

Remember: Defense in depth hinges on the human factor of policy and user awareness. Policy determines what security measures your organization should implement. Those security measures should reflect policy. Defense in depth is the means to policy implementation; it depends on it.

We've examined the components of defense in depth and how they contribute to security of the network. Defense in depth is a flexible concept that allows you to create an effective security infrastructure that reflects the requirements of your organization. For example, smaller organizations might not be able to afford some of the components we discussed, but alternatives usually exist. Regardless of the size of your organization, policy and user awareness are necessary.

We'll wrap up this chapter by looking at a real-world case where defense in depth could have saved an organization a lot of time, effort, and money.

Case Study: Defense in Depth in Action

The Nimda worm hit the Internet on September 18, 2001, causing a costly denial of service (DoS) condition for many organizations. Nimda was unique in that it spread via several distinct methods:

- IIS exploits
- Email
- HTTP browsing
- Windows file shares

The use of several distinct propagation methods made Nimda particularly vicious, because it could infect server-server, server-client, and client-client. As a result, Nimda was able to infect the entire range of Windows operating systems.

A large international network of 10,000 servers was brought to its knees in a matter of hours because of Nimda. This organization discovered first-hand the cost of not heeding the defense-in-depth concept. Defense in depth could have mitigated Nimda.

How could this company have used the perimeter to mitigate Nimda? Using routers to preemptively block or restrict web access (HTTP) and file access (SMB) traffic in the inbound direction could have prevented infection via the first and fourth methods. A rate-limiting switch would have been able to dampen the effects of a DoS in the case of mass infections. Static filters or stateful firewalls, set up to block or restrict HTTP and SMB packets, also would have helped. Proxy firewalls, configured to block known strings within Nimda, would be effective as well. If the company had properly segregated public services on a screened subnet, few machines would have been facing the Internet. Given that Nimda achieved saturation in approximately 2.5 hours, it is safe to say that most organizations did not know of Nimda until it had penetrated their internal network. What could have mitigated Nimda on the internal network?

The internal network could have used many of the same components that the external perimeter had available, such as routers, firewalls, IDSs, and IPSs. Additionally, the internal network could have contained host-centric (personal) firewalls capable of blocking some IIS and windows file share access. The company could have attempted to use antivirus software to mitigate Nimda, although reliable antivirus signatures for Nimda were not available until the end of the day when this worm hit. Host hardening had the highest potential of success in blocking Nimda by preventing infection entirely. Nimda used an old exploit that administrators should have patched well before the worm began spreading. Had the company applied the patch, it would have stopped all four propagation methods. Additionally, this vulnerability was widely known, and regular audits would have found that the organization was open to such an attack.

A robust security policy could have also helped mitigate the spread of Nimda. Given a thought-out incident-handling procedure, sections of the network could have been isolated to patch the vulnerabilities or contain the spread of the worm. If the company had established a user-awareness program before the attacks, user behavior might have prevented infection (especially via email).

Why did Nimda run rampant when so many methods were available to mitigate its spread? Perhaps organizations had one or more important components of defense in depth missing. Perhaps organizations had the wrong pieces of defense in depth in place by focusing entirely on the perimeter while neglecting the internal network. Perhaps organizations didn't follow policy. Perhaps this particular organization and countless others like it will learn to address security before an incident rather than during or after.

Summary

This first chapter has set the stage for the book; as you can see, you must understand defense in depth to improve the security of a networked organization. No silver bullets exist, and no single component can properly defend a network. You can deploy many components working together in such a way as to make attack difficult. Defense in depth describes the process of layering these components to capitalize on their respective strengths. It is flexible, but no single roadmap can select and deploy the various perimeter components. Our role is to design, build, and maintain the perimeter so that the overall security of the network is at an acceptable level, while providing an environment that supports business operations of the organization. A defense-in-depth approach can be used to secure an individual machine or the largest network in the world. It is a powerful tool for defenders.

2

Packet Filtering

PACKET FILTERING IS ONE OF THE OLDEST and most widely available means to control access to networks. The concept is simple: Determine whether a packet is allowed to enter or exit the network by comparing some basic identifying pieces of information located in the packet's header. Packet-filtering technology can be found in operating systems, software and hardware firewalls, and as a security feature of most routers.

The goal of this chapter is to explore the highlights and weaknesses of packet-filtering technology and how to implement this technology successfully. We discuss the basics of TCP/IP and how it applies to packet filtering, along with the rules of how to implement packet filters using Cisco router access lists. We explore uses for rules that filter on source address, such as the allowance and prohibition of traffic from given hosts and ingress and egress filters. We also cover filters that examine destination addresses and make decisions based on port numbers and their uses for improved control of traffic flow. We examine the problems of the packet filter, including its weaknesses to spoofing, fragmentation, control of return traffic, and the problems with poking an always-open hole in your defense. Finally, we explore the power of dynamic packet filters and the ways they can help correct many of the downfalls of static packet filtering.

TCP/IP Primer: How Packet Filtering Works

Before we go into the details of packet filtering, it is necessary to understand the construct and technologies behind the TCP/IP protocol and its associated packets.

> **Note**
> The next several sections provide a basic overview of the TCP/IP protocol. Advanced readers might find this review unnecessary and might prefer to skip ahead to the section "The Cisco Router as a Packet Filter."

When systems on a network communicate, they need to speak the same language, or *protocol*. One such protocol suite is TCP/IP, the primary communications language of the Internet. To facilitate such communications, the information you send needs to be broken down into manageable pieces called *packets*. Packet headers are small segments of information that are stuck at the beginning of a packet to identify it.

The IP portion of TCP/IP stands for *Internet Protocol*. It is responsible for identifying the packets (by their IP address) and for guiding them to their destination. IP packets are directed, or *routed*, by the values located in their packet headers. These identifiers hold information about where the packets came from (source address), where they are going (destination address), as well as other information describing the type of service the packet might support, among other things.

IP Version 6

The version of IP protocol that is most commonly used on the Internet today and that we are referring to in this chapter is IP version 4 (IPv4). It was created in the 1980s and has many limitations that have required expansions to keep it valid into the twenty-first century. Those limitations include a restricted address space, no integrated security, no integrated means to automatically assign addresses, and the list goes on. Although technologies were created as "band-aids" to help overcome these issues (NAT, IPSec, and DHCP), it wasn't long before development began on a replacement version. In the 90s, IP version 6 (IPv6) was born. It has a much larger potential address space made up of eight 16-bit values, instead of IPv4's four 8-bit values. IPv4 addresses are most commonly notated as decimals in the format 192.168.1.1, where the decimal numbers are some value between 0 and 255 (2^8). IPv6 addresses are notated as hexadecimal in the format 1234:ABCD:1A2B:4321:CDEF:C5D6:789D:F12A, where the hexadecimal numbers are some value between 0 and FFFF (or 0 and 65535 decimal, 2^16). Hexadecimal is used to keep the already long IPv6 addresses notation more concise and readable. One shorthand method of IPv6 notating involves abbreviating lists of zeroes with double colons (::). For example, the IPv6 address 1234:5678:0000:0000:0000:0000:0000:1AF4 can instead be listed as 1234:5678::1AF4. The double colons indicate that all digits between those listed are zeroes. Other improvements that IPv6 offers are integrated authentication and encryption methods, automatic address assignment capabilities, improved Quality of Service (QoS) methods, and an improved header format that moves anything but essential routing information to extension headers, allowing for quicker processing. Despite all its advantages, IPv6 is still not heavily implemented. As a network administrator it is important that you are aware of IPv6 and its possible advantages for your environment, even though you may not be required to use it for years to come. For more information on the IPv6 standard, refer to RFC 2460.

When an IP packet arrives at a router, the router checks its destination to see whether it knows how to get to the place where the packet wants to go. If it does, it passes the packet to the appropriate network segment. The fact that a router passes any packet whose destination it is aware of is called *implicit permit*. Unless further security measures are added, all traffic is allowed in as well as out. For this reason, a method is required to control the information entering and exiting the interfaces of the router.

TCP and UDP Ports

The TCP part of TCP/IP stands for *Transmission Control Protocol*, and it is a reliable transport-oriented way for information to be communicated. User Datagram Protocol

(UDP) is an unreliable transport protocol that works well with programs that don't rely on the protocol to make sure their payload gets where it's going. Both TCP and UDP use ports to keep track of communication sessions. Certain ports are set aside as the particular ones through which to contact a server running a given service such as HTTP (port 80), FTP (port 21), Telnet (port 23), DNS (port 53), or SMTP (port 25). (These services and how to secure them are discussed in more detail later.) The original RFC that documents well-known ports is RFC 1700. However, for a more up-to-date informative list of all of TCP's and UDP's server-side ports and the services to which they are assigned, check out this link to the IANA website: http://www.iana.org/assignments/port-numbers. IANA is the Internet Assigned Numbers Authority—the good people who track the number standards for the Internet as we know it.

When a client contacts a server, it randomly picks a source port numbered above 1023 to go out through. Then the client contacts the server on a set port, such as port 23 for Telnet. When the server replies, the information leaves on port 23 and returns to the client on the random greater-than 1023 port from which it left. This port information is the only way that a packet filter can determine the service it is filtering.

For example, you might want to filter out all Telnet traffic; you do so by blocking all traffic directed at TCP port 23. You might also want to allow all HTTP traffic coming to port 80. However, if someone is running a Telnet server on port 80 somewhere on your network, and all you have for protection is the aforementioned packet filter, the traffic passes. Packet-filtering systems don't have the intelligence to look beyond the port number to determine what service is running at the application layer. You need to keep this in mind when constructing filtering rules to block access to a service that you are running on an alternative port. Sometimes, web servers run on alternative ports, such as 8000, 8080, and the like; if you wanted to allow access to said web servers, then creating a packet-filtering rule that allows in standard HTTP traffic on port 80 wouldn't be effective.

TCP's Three-way Handshake

To begin communicating, connection-oriented TCP uses what's known as the *three-way handshake*. When Host A wants to connect to Host B to transfer data, it has to let Host B know that it wants to connect. Host A does this by sending a packet to Host B with the SYN (or synchronization) flag set, meaning, "I want to start a new conversation." If Host B can and wants to converse back to Host A, it returns a packet with the SYN and ACK (or acknowledgment) flags set, meaning, "I want to start a conversation with you, too, and I am acknowledging that I will be a part of your conversation." Finally, Host A returns the third part of the handshake, a packet with just the ACK flag set, meaning, "I will also take part in your conversation, so let's start talking!" With that, data begins transferring. In a simplified view, the two hosts are simply exchanging SYN flagged packets to say they want to start a conversation and ACK flagged packets to say they acknowledge the receipt of the SYN. The second host simply "piggybacks" its acknowledgment onto the same packet that contains its initiating SYN.

Packet-filtering systems can use these flags to determine the stage of the current three-way handshake. For example, if you didn't want to allow new connections from the outside, you could choose to only permit traffic flagged with ACK; the packets starting a new connection contain the SYN flag only.

The Cisco Router as a Packet Filter

The Cisco ACL is one of the most available packet filters found today. The means by which a Cisco router filters packets is known as an *access control list (ACL)*. An ACL serves as a laundry list of things for the router to look at in the packet header, to decide whether the packet should be permitted or denied access to a network segment. This is the basis of the traffic-control features of a Cisco router.

Routers are a convenient choice for network filtering because they are already a part of your network's infrastructure. One is located at your network's furthermost edge as well as at the intersections of all your network segments. If you want to keep something out of a network segment, the furthermost point is the best place to screen it. This section covers the basic syntax and usage of the Cisco ACL and its environment, the Cisco IOS. All examples in this chapter are illustrated through the use of Cisco ACLs (IOS version 12.1 or greater), although the theories demonstrated can be applied to any packet-filtering system.

An Alternative Packet Filter: IPChains

Although examples in this chapter are given as Cisco access lists, other software programs and devices use similar technology. Following is an example of IPChains, one such program. IPChains is a packet-filtering system that comes bundled with many versions of Linux. Though IPChains is not as popular as it once was, being superseded by IPTables, you may still run into it or choose to deploy it as an effective packet filtering mechanism for your server or network.

If you wanted to block HTTP traffic from anywhere to your host 200.200.200.2 and log the matches, you would use the Cisco ACL:

```
access-list 111 deny tcp any host 200.200.200.2 eq 80 log
```

With IPChains, you would use

```
ipchains -A input -i eth1 -p tcp -s 0.0.0.0/0 -d 200.200.200.2/32 80 -l -j DENY
```

where -A input means to place this rule on the end of the existing input chain.

-i eth1 tells IPChains to apply this rule to the interface eth1, -p tells the protocol to watch for TCP, the -s parameter sets the source address, and 0.0.0.0/0 indicates to watch for any source address.

The /0 is the wildcard, and it means to match the specified bits exactly. Because the wildcard is 0 in this case, it means "don't match anything exactly or allow anything." This is equivalent to the Cisco any keyword.

The `-d` parameter is the destination address. In this example, it is equal to the host address 200.200.200.2 because the `/32` wildcard mask is used. It tells IPChains to match the first 32 bits (or everything) exactly. This is equivalent to using the 0.0.0.0 wildcard or the `host` keyword in Cisco ACLs.

The destination address in this case is followed by the port number of the blocked protocol (80, for HTTP traffic). If the source port were filtered as well, it would have followed the source address.

Finally, the `-l` parameter means "log this information," and `-j DENY` stipulates that any matching packets should be dropped and not to send any information of this back to the sender. It is the counterpart to the Cisco `deny` keyword.

As you can see, although similar in function, static packet filters come in different forms. Despite the differences in appearance and syntax, after you have a grasp of packet-filtering concepts, your knowledge can be applied to any of these filtration systems.

The Cisco ACL

The Cisco ACL is simply a means to filter traffic that crosses your router. It has two major syntax types—numbered and named lists—and it comes in several filtering types, including standard, extended, and reflexive, all of which will be discussed in this chapter. Numbered access lists are entered in the format

```
access-list number criteria
```

where `number` is a given range that represents the type of access list it is. The range 1–99 represents standard IP lists, and the range 100–199 represents extended IP lists. Over time, these basic ranges have been expanded to include 1300–1999 for standard and 2000–2699 for extended. Other access list number ranges are reserved for alternative protocols, and so on.

The named access list uses the format

```
ip access-list type name
```

where the `type` code stands for standard, extended, and so on, and the `name` code represents a unique name for the list. This can help make the list more identifiable. For example, "dnsinbound" might mean more to someone than the number "113" does.

Upon entering the preceding command to start list creation, you are dropped into a configuration mode just for that access list. Here, you can enter filtering commands in the following format:

```
permit|deny  criteria
```

Either type of ACL works well and can be used separately or together. Although standard and extended lists can be written in either format, reflexive access lists can use only the named format. To remove either type of ACL, reenter it preceded by the word `no`.

Rule Order

Many of the access lists demonstrated throughout this text are "deny" access lists that show how to block a particular address or port. However, because of a concept called *implicit deny*, dropping such a list into an otherwise empty router configuration could cause the blocking of all traffic! Implicit deny takes place when as little as one access list is added to an interface on a Cisco router. The router stops its standard behavior of forwarding all routable traffic and instead begins comparing all packets received to the newly added access list. If the traffic doesn't match the applied access list(s), it is dropped. Adding one simple access list changes the behavior of the router entirely. Only packets that match the added access list as permitted traffic are allowed.

When multiple rules are added, even more concerns arise. Because rules are processed from the top down and a packet only has to pass or fail one rule to be dropped or allowed into the network, it is imperative to put specific filters before general filters. Otherwise, a more general rule might allow a packet access that may have been denied by another more specific rule later in the access list. When a packet "matches" a rule, the packet is immediately dropped (if it is a deny rule) or forwarded (if it is a permit rule) without being tested by the rest of the access list entries.

Be careful when planning the order of access list rules. That is why a complete access list rulebase needs to be laid out in advance and built from the ground up. Adding rules carelessly is a sure recipe for disaster.

> **Note**
>
> Whenever possible, assemble your access lists following the precept "allow what you need" rather than "deny what you don't."

Cisco IOS Basics

Before we go into detail on the syntax of Cisco access lists, it is necessary to discuss the interface by which Cisco routers are configured. Cisco routers can be configured in one of several ways. They can be accessed through a serial connection to the console port on the back of the router, through a Telnet session, or via a web browser with newer models. After you have access to the router, actually getting it into configuration mode is a relatively easy process, as outlined here:

1. You receive the standard prompt (designated by the > symbol) `routername>`.

2. You must go into enable mode before configuration mode. Typing `enable` and pressing the Enter key accomplishes this. You are prompted for a secret password. After entering it, you are in enable mode, which is identified by the `routername#` prompt (designated by the number sign [#]).

3. To configure the router, enter terminal configuration mode by typing `config t` (which is short for *configure terminal*) and pressing Enter. You then see the global configuration prompt: `routername(config)#`. This is where you enter global configuration commands, including access lists.

4. You can enter interface configuration mode from the global configuration mode by typing `int s1`, where `int` stands for interface and `s1` is the interface name (in this case, serial 1). This format is also carried into Ethernet interfaces (`e0`, `e1`, and so on) as well as other interface types. Typing the interface command changes the prompt to the interface configuration prompt: `routername(config-if)#`. From here, you can type interface-specific commands, and this is where you can apply access lists to individual interfaces with the `access-group` command.

5. Exit any configuration level by typing the `exit` command. Completely exit out of configuration mode from any sublevel by pressing Ctrl+Z. Leave enable mode by typing `disable`.

Effective Uses of Packet-Filtering Devices

Because packet filtering is older technology and lacks the capability to differentiate between types of network traffic, you might be wondering why we are discussing it. What could be the possible use for this technology in a world that is filled with hi-tech firewalls that can track protocols using knowledge of the way they work to intelligently differentiate between incoming and outgoing traffic streams? Good question! Why use a PC when we have supercomputers? Sometimes a lighter-weight, less expensive means to get things done is a major advantage. Because packet filters don't go to great depth in their analysis of traffic streams, they are faster than other firewall technologies. This is partially due to the speed at which the header information can be checked and partially due to the fact that packets don't have to be "decoded" to the application level for a decision to be made on them. Complex decisions are not necessary, simply a comparison of bits in a packet to bits in an ACL.

Filtering Based on Source Address: The Cisco Standard ACL

One of the things that packet-filtering technology is great for is the blocking or allowing of traffic based on the IP address of the source system. Some ways that this technology can be usefully applied are filters blocking specific hosts (blacklisting), filters allowing specific hosts (such as business partners), and in the implementation of ingress and egress filters. Any of these examples can be implemented on a Cisco router by using a "standard" access list.

The standard access list is used to specifically allow or disallow traffic from a given source IP address only. It cannot filter based on destination or port number. Because of these limitations, the standard access list is fast and should be preferred when the source address is the only criteria on which you need to filter.

The syntax for a standard access list is as follows:

```
access-list list number 1-99 or 1300-1999 permit |deny source address mask log
```

Notice that when ACLs were first created, the list number had to be 1–99. This range was expanded in IOS version 12.0(1) to include the numbers 1300–1999. The only way that the Cisco IOS can identify the list as a standard ACL is if a list number in one of these two ranges is used. The *mask* option is a required wildcard mask, which tells the router whether this is a single host we are filtering or an entire network range. (For more information on wildcard masks, check out the sidebar "The Cisco Wildcard Mask Explained" later in this chapter). The `log` option can be appended to tell the router to specifically log any matches of this filter. These log entries can be saved in local memory or more appropriately sent to a remote Syslog server. For more information on router logging, see Chapter 6, "The Role of a Router," and Chapter 20, "Network Log Analysis."

The previously listed access list notation is entered in global configuration mode and can be applied to the interface in the interface configuration mode with the `access-group` statement, as shown here:

```
ip access-group list number in|out
```

The `access-group` command is used to specifically apply an ACL to an interface (by its list number) either inbound or outbound. Only one access list can be applied in one direction (in or out) per interface. This means a maximum of two applied ACLs per interface: one inbound and one outbound.

One of the confusing concepts of router ACLs is the way that applying filters "in" or "out" works. This is confusing because people normally visualize "in" as traffic moving toward their internal network and "out" as traffic moving away from their network toward outside entities. However, this premise does not necessarily hold true when talking about the `in` and `out` keywords in Cisco router access lists. Specifically, the keywords tell the router to check the traffic moving toward (in) or away from (out) the interface listed.

In a simple dual-interface router, this concept is more easily illustrated. Let's assume you have an interface called `e1` (hooked to your internal network) and an external interface called `s1` (hooked up to the Internet, for example). Traffic that comes into the `s1` interface moves toward your internal network, whereas traffic that goes out of the `s1` interface moves toward the Internet.

So far this seems to be pretty logical, but now let's consider the internal `e1` interface. Traffic that comes into `e1` moves away from your internal network (toward the Internet), and traffic that goes out of `e1` goes toward your internal network.

VLAN Interfaces and Direction

When determining direction, VLAN interfaces are a little more confusing than physical router interfaces. Applying an access group "in" on a VLAN interface means that traffic moving away from the network will be filtered, whereas "out" means that traffic coming into the VLAN will be filtered.

Keep in mind when you apply `access-group` commands to your interfaces that you apply the access list in the direction that the traffic is traveling, in regards to the router's interface. You might be thinking, "What is the difference, then, between inbound on the `s1` interface and outbound on the `e1` interface? Both refer to traffic that is moving in the same direction. Which is more appropriate to use?"

Tip

To maximize performance, filter traffic as it enters the router.

The less work the router has to do, the better. Always try to filter traffic at the first interface it enters, or apply your filters "inbound" as much as possible.

Returning to our example, if something should be blocked (or permitted, for that matter) coming in from the Internet, it would make the most sense to block it coming in to the s1 (outside) interface. In addition, if something should be filtered leaving your network, it would be best to filter it inbound on the e1 (inside) interface. Basically, you should show preference to the in keyword in your access lists. Some specific exceptions to this rule exist, which involve certain access list types (such as reflexive ACLs) that require being placed outbound.

These examples often list the actual prompt for a router named "router" to remind you of the command modes that the router will be in when entering the various commands.

The following is an example of an actual filter that uses the previous syntax and 190.190.190.x as the source network's IP address that you want to deny:

```
router(config)#access-list 11 deny 190.190.190.0 0.0.0.255
```

This filter's list number is 11. It denies any packet with a source network address of 190.190.190 with any source host address. It is applied to the interface inbound, so it filters the traffic on the way into the router's interface.

The command to apply the access list to your serial 1 interface would be

```
router(config-if)#ip access-group 11 in
```

where we are in interface configuration mode for the interface to which we are applying the access list, inbound.

The Cisco Wildcard Mask Explained

The wildcard mask is one of the least understood portions of the Cisco ACL syntax. Take a look at the following example:

```
access-list 12 permit 192.168.1.0 0.0.0.255
```

In this case, 0.0.0.255 represents the wildcard mask. It looks like a reverse subnet mask and represents the portion of the listed IP address range to filter against the traffic in question. Zeros mean, "Test this portion of the address," and ones mean, "Ignore this portion of the address when testing."

In our example, let's say a packet comes in with a source address of 192.168.2.27. Because the first octet of the wildcard mask is a zero, the router compares the first octet of the incoming packet to the value 192, listed in the access list. In this case, they are the same, so the router continues to the second octet of the wildcard mask, which is also a zero. Again, the second octet of the value of the source address of the incoming packet is compared to the value 168. Because they are also the same, the router continues to the third octet. Because the wildcard mask specifies a zero in the third octet as well, it continues to test the address, but the value of the third octet does not match, so the packet is dropped.

For the sake of example, let's continue to look at the fourth octet, even though in actuality the packet would have been dropped at this point. The wildcard's fourth octet is valued at 255. In binary, this equates to 11111111. In this example, the value 0 in the access list does not match the value 27 of the compared packet; however, because the wildcard wants us to ignore this octet, the access list allows the packet to pass (assuming it hadn't failed on the previous octet). The concept might seem pretty easy with a wildcard value that deals with entire octets, but it gets tricky when you need to deal with an address range that is smaller than 255. The reality is that the router doesn't test octet by octet, but bit by bit through each of the octets.

What if you want to allow traffic from systems in the address range 192.168.1.16–192.168.1.31 only? The first three octets of the wildcard are easy: 0.0.0. It's the last octet that is difficult. It's time to grab your handy-dandy binary calculator. Consider what 16 looks like in binary: 0001 0000. Now look at 31: 0001 1111. The difference between these two binary values occurs in the last four bits. Therefore, the values between 16 and 31 are covered in the range 10000–11111. To allow those values, you need to place zeros in your wildcard mask for the portions that need to match exactly, and ones for the binary values that change. Because the last four bits are the only bits that change in the desired range, the wildcard mask reflects those four bits with ones. In binary, our wildcard mask is as follows:

```
00000000.00000000.00000000.00001111
```

Translated with our binary calculator, that is 0.0.0.15.

This wildcard mask works for any range of 15 addresses you are comparing, so to make it work for 16–31, you must properly reflect the range in the IP address portion of the access list. Your final access list looks like this:

```
access-list 10 permit 192.168.1.16 0.0.0.15
```

A wildcard mask is always contiguous zeros and ones, without interruption, as in the example listed previously. In some cases, you need more than one ACL statement and wildcard mask to cover a range of network addresses. For example, if you want to block addresses in the range 232–255, you need the command

```
access-list 110 deny ip 192.168.1.232 0.0.0.7 any
```

to block the range 232–239, and you also need to specify

```
access-list 110 deny ip 192.168.1.240 0.0.0.15 any
```

to block the range 240–255.

Blacklisting: The Blocking of Specific Addresses

One popular use of the standard access list is the "blacklisting" of particular host networks. This means that you can block a single host or an entire network from accessing your network. The most popular reason for blocking a given address is mischief. If your intrusion detection system (IDS) shows that you are being scanned constantly by a given address, or you have found that a certain IP address seems to be constantly trying to log in to your systems, you might simply want to block it as a preventative measure.

For example, if your intranet web server should only be offering its information to your business locations in the continental United States, and you are getting a lot of hits from a range of IPs in China, you might want to consider blocking those addresses.

Warning

The blocking of "spoofed" addresses can lead to a denial of service condition. Always research IP addresses before uniformly blocking them.

The blocking of address ranges is also a popular way to "band-aid" your system against an immediate threat. For example, if one of your servers was being attacked from a certain IP address, you could simply block all traffic from that host or network number. As another example, if you just found out that you had a widespread infection of a Trojan that contacted a remote IRC server, you could block all traffic coming from that IRC server. It would be more appropriate to block the traffic leaving your network to that destination, however, but that would require an extended access list because standard ACLs only filter on source address.

A sample access list to block access from an outside address range would be

```
router(config)#access-list 11 deny 192.168.1.0 0.0.0.255
router(config-if)# ip access-group 11 in
```

where the network number of the outside parties to be blocked would be 192.168.1.0–255. (Of course, this address range is part of the ranges reserved for private addressing, and it's simply used as an example in this instance.) This access list would be applied to the external router interface, inbound.

Spyware

Once I was perusing my logs to check for Internet connections from my network during off-hours to see if anything peculiar was going on. I noticed some connections that were initiated in the middle of the night from various stations, repeatedly contacting a similar network address. I did some research on the address and determined that the maker of a popular freeware program owned it.

After a brief inspection of one of the "beaconing" stations, I found that the freeware program in question was loaded on the system. Being completely paranoid (as all good security professionals are), I immediately set up a rule on my perimeter router to block all access to the network address in question. Many software packages search for updates regularly and do not use these automatic "phoning home" sessions for malicious activity. However, as a firewall administrator, I have to be in control of my network's traffic flow. Besides, I do question why these packages need to "call out" several times a night.

Of course, my block was just a quick fix until I could unload the software at all the "infected" stations, but if it somehow appeared again, I had no fear of the software gaining outside access. The moral of the story: It can be a lot more efficient to block a single network address at your perimeter router than to run from station to station to audit software.

"Friendly Net": Allowing Specific Addresses

Another way you can use a standard access list is to permit traffic from a given IP address. However, this is not recommended. Allowing access to an address in this manner, without any kind of authentication, can make you a candidate for attacks and scans that use spoofed addresses. Because we can only filter on source address with a standard ACL, any inside device with an IP address can be accessed. Also, it's impossible to protect individual services on those devices. If you need to set up access like this and can't do it through a solution that requires authentication or some type of VPN, it is probably best to at least use an access list that considers more than the source address. We'll discuss this more in the section on extended access lists. However, this type of access may be suitable in situations requiring less security, such as access between internal network segments. For example, if Bob in accounting needs access to your intranet server segment, a standard ACL would be a simple way to allow his station access.

Ingress Filtering

RFC 1918 pertains to reserved addresses. Private/reserved addresses are ranges of IP addresses that will never be distributed for public use. This way, you can use these addresses in internal networks without worry of accidentally picking network addresses that might correspond with a public address you might want to access some day.

For example, imagine that you are in a world in which reserved private addresses don't exist. You are installing a new private network for your business that will have access to the Internet and will be running TCP/IP, so you will have to come up with a range of IP addresses for your stations. You don't want these stations to have public addressing because they won't be serving information to the Internet, and you will be accessing the Internet through a proxy server. You pick a range of IP addresses at random (say, 190.190.190.0–255). You configure your stations and set up Internet access.

Everything is working great until the first time you attempt to access your bank's website and receive an error. You call the bank, and the bank says that everything is fine on its end. You eventually come to discover that the bank is right. The bank's system you were trying to contact has a public IP address of 190.190.190.10, the same address you have configured for one of your own stations. Every time your web browser goes to send information to the bank, it never even leaves your internal network. You've been asking your CAD station for a web page, and because your CAD station doesn't run web server software, you've just been getting an error. This example paints a clearer picture of why reserved addresses are so important for the interrelationship of public and private TCP/IP networks.

The reserved ranges are as follows:

- Class A: 10.0.0.0–10.255.255.255
- Class B: 172.16.0.0–172.31.255.255
- Class C: 192.168.0.0–192.168.255.255

Because these ranges are often used as internal network numbers, they are good candidates for someone who is crafting packets or doing other malicious packet-transmitting behavior, including denial of service. Therefore, these ranges should be blocked at the outside of your network. In addition, the loopback address 127.0.0.1 (the default address that all IP stations use to "address" themselves) is another candidate for being blocked, for the same reason. While you are blocking invalid addresses, you should also block the multicast address range 224.0.0.0–239.255.255.255 and the invalid address 0.0.0.0. Following is a sample access list to accomplish this:

```
router(config)#access-list 11 deny 10.0.0.0 0.255.255.255
router(config)#access-list 11 deny 127.0.0.0 0.255.255.255
router(config)#access-list 11 deny 172.16.0.0 0.15.255.255
router(config)#access-list 11 deny 192.168.0.0 0.0.255.255
router(config)#access-list 11 deny 224.0.0.0 15.255.255.255
router(config)#access-list 11 deny host 0.0.0.0
router(config-if)# ip access-group 11 in
```

These access lists are similar to the last one, denying access to the IP address ranges listed in an inbound direction on the applied interface. Notice the host keyword when blocking 0.0.0.0 in the previous example. When blocking a single host, instead of following the IP address with the wildcard 0.0.0.0, you can precede the address with the keyword host. These lists have the same "implicit deny" that any access list does. This means that somewhere in access list number 11, a permit statement would have to exist; otherwise, all inbound traffic would be denied! An example of an appropriate permit statement might be one that allows the return of established traffic, like the following:

```
router(config)# access-list 111 permit tcp any any established
```

This is, however, an extended access list, which we'll talk more about later in the section "Filtering by Port and Destination Address: The Cisco Extended ACL."

It is also advisable that you create a rule to block traffic coming into your network that claims to have a source address matching that of your internal network, to complete your ingress access list. Valid traffic from the outside world doesn't have to have the same addressing as your stations. However, if this traffic is allowed to pass, it could bypass security mechanisms that think the traffic is local. If you are using one of the standard private address ranges, this is already done. If you're not, it would look like this:

```
router(config)#access-list 11 deny 201.201.201.0 0.0.0.255
```

Here, your network address range is 201.201.201.0–255. This rule would be added to the previous list before the line that allows return traffic.

Ingress filters are an excellent example of a means to use packet-filtering technology to its fullest, on any network. Even if you have a stateful or proxy firewall, why not let your perimeter router use packet filtering to strip off this unwanted traffic? Let perimeter routers be the "bouncers" of your network, stripping off the undesirables before they even reach other internal protection devices.

Egress Filtering

Another use of standard access lists is for egress filters. The concept behind an egress filter is that only packets with your network's source address should be leaving your network. This seems like a forgone conclusion, but as stated in the section on ingress filters, Trojans and other nefarious programs might use a station on your network to send spoofed traffic to the rest of the world. By creating an ACL that only allows your subnet's address in from your network, you prevent this type of traffic from touching the outside world. Of course, this won't help if the program doesn't spoof the source address, but many such programs do to help slow the rate at which they can be traced. Such an access list would look like this, assuming an internal network address of 192.168.100.0:

```
router(config)#access-list 11 permit 192.168.1.0 0.0.0.255
```

Implicit deny takes care of denying all other source addresses. You could use an extended access list to tighten this down even more and limit things such as the types of traffic and destinations your stations are allowed to access. This ACL would be applied to the inside interface inbound, effectively on the outside edge of your router's network interface.

You might be wondering what the advantage is in implementing a rule such as this. "What will this do for me?" you might be asking yourself. Well, it is no different from dumping your tray at the local fast food restaurant; it's the good neighbor policy. It doesn't do anything for you directly (other than possibly prevent you from facing outside litigation), but if everyone did it, oh what a world we would live in. Imagine the effect on distributed denial of service attacks that use zombies stationed on innocent people's networks. These filters (assuming that the denial of service [DoS] zombies take advantage of some type of packet spoofing) could help cripple such zombies.

It is also possible to set up filters that prevent traffic from leaving your network from specified systems. For example, imagine that you have a top-secret file server that has no Internet access. This system should only be contacted from inside stations, and it should never contact the outside world or be contacted from the outside world. You can place an ACL on the inside router interface, inbound. It could be a part of the same access list that you used for your egress filter, but it would have to be placed above the egress filter because of the importance of rule order. If the top-secret file server's IP address was 192.168.100.7, here is how the entire egress list would look:

```
router(config)#access-list 11 deny 192.168.100.7 0.0.0.0
router(config)#access-list 11 permit 192.168.100.0 0.0.0.255
```

The given host's packets would be filtered before the rule that allows all other systems on the 192.168.100 network to enter the router. It should be noted that this will deny all outbound traffic, so no Internet security updates or downloading of the latest virus-definition file directly to this server.

Tracking Rejected Traffic

When creating Cisco router access lists, one of the greatest downfalls of the `log` keyword is that it only records matches to the rule in question. Therefore, if the rule is a permit rule, you lose the profoundly important information about which packets are being denied. To track the traffic that is being filtered by an implicit deny, add a "deny any" ACL with the `log` keyword (as seen in the following example) to the bottom of the list in question. Functionally, the `deny any log` command does the same thing as the assumed implicit deny, but it facilitates the logging of denied traffic. One good application of this concept is to track abnormal traffic that is being filtered by the implicit deny at the end of an egress filter access list. Using this method allows a means to track all outbound traffic that has a source address other than that of your network. This is a great way to keep a handle on any strange things that might be trying to sneak out of your network! Here is a simple example of how you would tell the router to log blocked traffic:

```
access-list 11 deny any log
```

Filtering by Port and Destination Address: The Cisco Extended ACL

Another powerful use of packet-filtering technology involves filtering on packet header information and port numbers. These examples can be applied in the form of specific "conduits" that allow one system to access another (extranets), allow access to a specific public access system (web or DNS server), or allow a specific type of traffic into the network (ICMP `packet-too-big` unreachables). This functionality is enabled on a Cisco router using the extended access list.

The Cisco Extended ACL

The Cisco extended ACL offers additional features that allow more control of network traffic flow. Instead of only being able to filter on source address, we have the additional flexibility of destination address filtering, filtering based on protocol type, filtering on specific layer 4 port number information, flags, and more. With this additional granularity, the effectiveness of the Cisco router as a packet filter is greatly increased, making it viable for many security concerns.

The extended access list syntax is as follows:

```
access-list number 100-199 or 2000-2699 permit|deny protocol  source
➥source-mask source-port destination  destination-mask
➥destination port log|log-input options
```

You should recognize the first entries in the syntax from the standard access list, up to the `protocol` keyword. This is where you would specify the protocol you are interested in filtering. Possible selections are IP, TCP, UDP, and ICMP. Because TCP, UDP, and

ICMP are all forms of IP-based traffic, when you use IP as the protocol on an access list, it permits or denies any of the other three traffic types. If we had used an extended access list to substitute for one of the standard access lists from the previous section, IP would have been the appropriate choice because it would have blocked all IP traffic types (UDP, TCP, and ICMP).

Remember the importance of rule order. Each incoming packet is checked by each access list in order from top to bottom. When a packet matches the criteria in any one of the access lists, an action is performed. If it is a permit filter, the packet is forwarded; if it is a deny filter, the packet is dropped. No rules test the packet beyond the rule that the packet matched. Use the following code to allow a particular packet in (let's say that its IP address is 205.205.205.1) if it is TCP but to deny it entry if it uses any other IP protocol:

```
access-list 111 deny ip host 205.205.205.1 any
access-list 111 permit tcp host 205.205.205.1 any
```

The first rule would test true for a TCP packet of address 205.205.205.1. Because it is a "deny" rule, the packet would be dropped. The packet would never get to be tested by the second rule. If the two rules were reversed in order, with the TCP rule first, the filter would work correctly.

In the extended access list's syntax, the source address and mask should look familiar; the destination address and mask follow the same format, and simply mean "where it is going" instead of "where it is from." The keyword any can be used to represent the numerical range 0.0.0.0–255.255.255.255, or all addresses.

This is the first time you see ports listed as part of an access list. As mentioned previously, ports are an important part of TCP/IP and the access lists. The *source port* or *destination port* entry can specify the type of traffic you want to allow or disallow. When specifying a port number or name, you must also include an operator, such as eq (meaning equal to this port number), gt (for any port above this number), lt (for any port less than this number), or my favorite range (to list an entire contiguous range of port numbers; use the syntax range *port1 port2*, where *port1* is the first port in the range and *port2* is the last).

Extended access lists are configured and applied just like standard access lists, including the association of an access group to an interface. Many options can be added to the end of the access list, such as log (as mentioned in the standard access list) or log-input (which also displays the input interface and source MAC address), flags to check for, and the established keyword.

"Friendly Net" Revisited

As mentioned previously, allowing access to a given IP address is not a favored practice. The main reason for this is lack of control and the dangers of spoofing. Using a standard ACL to allow access is a problem because the only thing we have control over is which IP address (or range) can access the entire inside network. This means that not only can the host or range of hosts specified access any station on the inside, but it also can do so on any port number. This is not good. Extended access lists can at least help tighten up that control. We can specify the destination host (or range) to which the host can connect, as well as the port on which they can communicate. This way, we can allow an outside trusted host to access our web server (only) on port 80 (only). Take a look at this example:

```
access-list 111 permit tcp host 100.100.100.1 gt 1023 host
➥200.200.200.2 eq 80 log
```

This example assumes that the trusted host is at address 100.100.100.1 and our target web server is at address 200.200.200.2. We only allow traffic from the trusted host on ephemeral ports, and only to port 80 on our web server. We add the `log` keyword to track traffic that is passing this rule.

This is not secure. All this guarantees is that we have control over those specified items, helping to lessen the ability of outsiders to exploit our defense. This ACL can be subverted in other ways.

Only allowing port 80 traffic doesn't ensure that only web traffic will transpire from the outside host to our web server. As a matter of fact, if a flaw exists to be exploited in our web server, and an attacker can get a Telnet program or other backdoor running on our web server on port 80, the server might as well be wide open. If this system is on a private network and not on a separate screened subnet, we are just a few leaps away from being fully compromised, especially if the web server has a trust relationship with any other mission-critical servers on our network.

Be sure to tightly harden the system if you elect to control access to its resources solely through the use of packet filters, without further authentication. If possible, run a multiple interface router (or packet-filtering device) or multiple levels of packet-filtering devices where you can structure a separate subnet for public access systems.

Filtering TCP and UDP Ports and ICMP Types

Another handy function of the extended access list is the filtering of certain types of traffic. You can control the types of traffic that leave your network, in effect enforcing your security policy. You can allow or disallow certain types of traffic that enter your network. Denying traffic to a list of popular Trojan program ports or to ports that programs use that conflict with your Internet usage or security policies (IRC, Kazaa, instant messaging programs, and so on) can also be an extra layer of defense. As stated previously, it makes more sense to only allow what you need. A more common use of port filtering is allowing traffic types that can enter or leave your network, like the example in the previous section. For a list of mission-critical ports that any environment should consider defending, see Appendix A of the SANS Top 20 Vulnerabilities, available at http://www.sans.org/top20.

Another use for this type of filtering is to allow or disallow certain informative ICMP messages entrance to your network. ICMP is one of the most exploited of the protocols. It is being used for reconnaissance, denial of service attacks (such as `smurf`), and more. It is recommended that you block incoming echo requests (ping and Windows traceroute), block any outgoing echo replies, and block time exceeded, for maximum security. All the ICMP traffic types can be blocked with extended ACLs. The use of any ICMP blocking filters could affect network traffic control.

ICMP doesn't work like the other protocols. Instead of having port numbers, it uses type and code identifiers. It is basically set up to send error messages for protocols that can't (such as UDP and IP) and to send informational messages (such as router error messages telling that a host is unreachable). ICMP is used by popular end-to-end troubleshooting utilities such as ping and traceroute. ICMP can be controlled by using Cisco access lists with special ICMP keywords or ICMP type numbers, instead of port numbers such as TCP and UDP access lists.

To block ICMP echo requests (ICMP type 8), we could use a line in an extended access list such as this:

```
router(config)#access-list 111 deny icmp any any echo-request
```

The main difference between this access list and others we have looked at is the keyword at the end of the line. This keyword represents the ICMP type and code for echo requests. It means, "deny any ICMP traffic from anywhere to anywhere with the type and code set to `echo-request`." This filter would be applied on the external router interface to the Internet. Other ICMP traffic types can be filtered in the same way using their type-of-service keywords.

A better way to handle the ICMP blocking would be to allow only the types of traffic that you want and then deny the rest. For example, one important ICMP packet type to allow in is the `packet-too-big` ICMP unreachable messages (type 3, code 4). This is because without this message, you could have major communications issues. What if a host can't receive a packet because it is too large for the router to handle and the router isn't allowed to return information to the host telling it that the packet is too large? How will the sender ever find out what is wrong and successfully communicate with the host? Luckily, in this example, Cisco has an ICMP keyword for the `packet-too-big` message. This keyword could be applied as follows, permitting the `packet-too-big` messages, but denying all other ICMP messages:

```
router(config)#access-list 111 permit icmp any any packet-too-big
router(config)#access-list 111 deny icmp any any
```

The filter would be applied as usual with an `ip access-group 111 in` command.

Problems with Packet Filters

Despite the many positive uses of packet filters, problems exist due to inherent limitations in the way packet filters work. Spoofed and fragmented traffic can bypass the packet filter if protections aren't properly implemented. In addition, because of the always-open nature of a "permit" static packet filter, issues exist with opening such a "hole." Finally, allowing return traffic can be difficult using a technology that lacks the ability to track the state of the current traffic flow. To successfully defend a network with packet filtering, these weaknesses must be understood.

Spoofing and Source Routing

Spoofing means sending a packet that is addressed with false information, so it appears to come from somewhere other than where it did. A packet can be addressed as if it came from an internal host on the target network, one of the private address ranges, or even another network entirely. Of course, a packet doesn't do this on its own; the packet has to be crafted or created with special packet-crafting software.

If your defense isn't set up correctly and the packet gets through, it's possible that an internal host could believe the packet came from a "trusted" host that has rights to private information, and could in turn reply to the spoofed address! You might be asking yourself, "If the packet appeared to come from a station other than the one that sent it, where will the response go?" Well, the answer in typical TCP/IP communication is to the real host, which wouldn't know what to do with the packet, and would drop it and send a reset to the originator. However, if source routing is enabled, the imposter packet could carry source-routing information that would allow it to tell the station where it needs to be sent to go home.

Source routing allows a packet to carry information that tells a router the "correct" or a better way for it to get back to where it came from, allowing it to override the router's prescribed routing rules for the packet. This could allow a devious user to guide return traffic wherever he wants. For this reason, it is imperative to have source routing disabled. It is easily disabled in a Cisco router with the following command typed at the global configuration prompt:

```
router(config)#no ip source-route
```

However, by blocking any packet that claims to have an unusable address before it can enter, we can help remove the problem. This is where ingress filters come into play. The best place to cut off packets like these is where they enter: on the perimeter router's interface that connects your network to the Internet.

Fragments

Many of the great fragmenting attacks were originally designed to defeat packet-filtering technology. Originally, some packet-filtering technologies allowed all fragments to pass, which wasn't good. After this was recognized as a security concern, many systems began checking the first fragment to verify that the header information passed the tests set forth by the ACLs. If this initial fragment failed the test and didn't pass through the router, the rest of the fragments could never be reformed at the other side, in theory solving the problem.[1]

Because of the way packet filtering examines the header information, it could be defeated by splitting up the packet into such small pieces that the header containing TCP or UDP port information was divided. Because the first fragment was often the only fragment that many popular packet-filtering systems checked and that the IP address information would pass, the entire reassembled packet would be passed. In addition, packet filtering was discovered to be vulnerable to other fragmenting attacks, including attacks that allowed a second fragment to overlap a seemingly harmless TCP or UDP port in the initial fragment with deviously chosen port information.[2] Many clever ways were determined that could bypass the packet filter's inspection capabilities.

As time went by, packet-filtering product manufacturers advanced their technology, and solutions were proposed to many of the common fragment attack methods. RFC 1858 defined methods to deter fragment flow, including dropping initial fragments that were smaller than a defined size or dropping a second fragment based on information found in it.[3]

The most important point on using a packet-filtering defense to protect your network from fragment attacks is to verify that you have the latest firmware and security patches (or in the case of Cisco routers, the latest IOS software). These updates reflect the changes made to defend against fragment attacks such as those mentioned. For more complete fragment protection, some firewall technologies include methods such as fragment reassembly before packets are ruled on, the forming of tables that track decisions regarding initial fragments, and the basing of outcome of noninitial fragments on their predecessors. These technologies are not inherent in packet-filtering systems, and they must be checked for when purchasing an individual product.

Cisco access lists can disallow fragmented traffic using the following access list as the first in an ACL series:

```
router(config)# access-list 111 deny ip any any fragments
```

This access list disallows any noninitial fragments that have matching IP address information, but it allows non-fragments or initial fragments to continue to the next access list entry because of the `fragments` keyword at the end of the ACL. The initial fragments or non-fragments are denied or allowed based on the access lists that follow the preceding example. However, fragmented traffic is a normal part of some environments, and a statement like the previous example would deny this normal traffic, as well as maliciously fragmented traffic. This example would only be used in an environment that warrants the highest security to fragmentation attacks, without fear of the loss of potential usability.

Opening a "Hole" in a Static Packet Filter

One of the great flaws of static packet filtering is that to allow a protocol into a network, you need to open a "hole." It is referred to as a hole because no additional checking takes place of the type of traffic allowed in or out based on more intelligent methods of detection. All you can do is open an individual port on your protective wall; as with a bullet hole through a three-foot wall, you can't shoot anywhere else on the other side, but you can fire straight through the existing hole repeatedly. The importance of this analogy is that something must be on the other side at the port in question; otherwise, you won't be able to hit it.

It is recommended when opening a port using an access list of this type that you limit the target hosts as much as possible with the access list. Then, if you have a secured server with all patches and no vulnerabilities (found as often as elves and four leaf clovers) that you are allowing to service this port, this isn't such a bad thing. However, if your host system is exploitable through whatever port number you have open, it is possible that any traffic can be sent through that "hole," not just the protocol that was running on the host inside.

Two-way Traffic and the `established` Keyword

When we communicate with another host, it's not just us connecting to the host, but also the host connecting to us—a two-way connection. This presents a problem when it comes to preventing unwanted access with a packet filter. If we try to block all incoming traffic, we prevent the return connection from hosts we are trying to contact.

How can we allow only return traffic? The original answer that Cisco came up with was the `established` keyword for extended access lists. With the word `established` added to an access list, any traffic, other than return traffic, is blocked, theoretically. The `established` keyword checks to see which flags are set on incoming packets. Packets with the ACK flag set (or RST flag) would pass, and only response traffic of the type specified could ever get through, right? Wrong! The combination of certain pieces of software and sneaky, nefarious users results in what's known as a *crafted packet*, which is a packet that the communicating host does not create in the normal way, but builds Frankenstein-style from software residing on a host. Users can set any flag they want.

What happens if a packet that was crafted with malicious intent appears with the ACK flag set in an attempt to sneak by the router's filters? The `established` keyword access list lets it go through, which isn't good. The good news is that an internal system that is listening for a new connection (initiated by a SYN packet) would not accept the ACK packet that is passed. It would be so offended by the packet that it would send a reset back to the originator, telling it to try again.

This sounds like a good thing, but it has two flaws. First, it proves that a station exists at the address to which the packet was sent. If a station didn't exist there, a reset packet wouldn't be returned. This scanning technique works and is pretty stealthy as well. Second, because it is eliciting a response from a private system, this technique might be used successfully for a denial of service attack. Internal systems could be repeatedly hit with scores of ACK packets, causing those systems to attempt reply after reply with RST packets. This is further accentuated by spoofing the source address on the ACK packets, so the targeted network would be feverishly firing resets back to another innocent network. Fortunately, the innocent network does not respond to the resets, preventing a second volley from being thrown at the target network.

Despite the drawbacks of the `established` keyword, it is one of the only static means by which a Cisco router can allow only return traffic back in to your network. The following is an example of an established access list:

```
router(config)#access-list 101 permit tcp any any est log
```

This basic extended access list allows any TCP traffic that has the ACK bit set, meaning that it allows only return traffic to pass. It is applied inbound on the outside router interface, and it can log matches with the appended `log` keyword. It also allows RST packets to enter (by definition) to help facilitate proper TCP communication. A more secure version of this same list would be this:

```
router(config)#access-list 101 permit tcp any eq 80
➡192.168.1.0 0.0.0.255 gt 1023 est log
router(config)#access-list 101 permit tcp any eq 23
➡192.168.1.0 0.0.0.255 gt 1023 est log
router(config)#access-list 101 permit tcp any eq 25
➡192.168.1.0 0.0.0.255 gt 1023 est log
router(config)#access-list 101 permit tcp any eq 110
➡192.168.1.0 0.0.0.255 gt 1023 est log
```

In this case, the inside network address is 192.168.1.0–255. These access lists are applied inbound on the external router interface. By writing your access list this way, you allow traffic only from approved protocol port numbers (web traffic, Telnet, email, and so on) to your internal network addresses, and only to ephemeral ports on your systems. However, an access list of this type still has problems. It would not support FTP for reasons we will go over in an upcoming section, and it only handles TCP traffic.

The `established` **Keyword and the Problem of DNS**

Remember that the previous ACL did not allow UDP traffic or ICMP traffic. The `established` (or `est`) keyword is only valid for TCP access lists. Access lists allow needed ICMP and UDP traffic, which would have to be included along side of this `established` access list, to form a comprehensive filter set. Without UDP, outside DNS is a real problem, disabling Internet functionality. This shows one of the biggest flaws of the `est` keyword as an effective defense mechanism. To facilitate Internet access with the `est` keyword, a UDP access list must be included, allowing any DNS return traffic. Remember that return traffic is coming to a randomly chosen port above 1023, which means that to effectively allow any DNS responses, you need an access list like this:

```
access-list 101 permit udp host 192.168.1.1 eq 53
➡172.16.100.0 0.0.0.255 gt 1023 log
```

This ACL assumes that the external DNS server's address is 192.168.1.1 and that your internal network is 172.16.100.0–255. By adding this line to your existing access list 101, you allow DNS responses to your network. However, you also leave yourself open to outside access on ports greater than 1023 from that external DNS server. Your security red alert should be going off about now! This would be a great argument for bringing DNS inside your perimeter; however, that DNS server would then need to be able to access outside DNS servers for queries and zone transfers. To allow the DNS server to make outbound DNS queries, a similar access list would need to be added to the router:

```
access-list 101 permit tcp any host 172.16.100.3 eq 53
access-list 101 permit udp any host 172.16.100.3 eq 53
```

This allows all traffic through port 53 to your inside (and hopefully well-hardened) DNS server. Ideally, such a public access server would be on a separate screened subnet for maximum security.

Remember that neither solution provides for additional UDP or ICMP support. If access to either is needed in your specific environment, more "holes" have to be opened.

Protocol Problems: Extended Access Lists and FTP

File Transfer Protocol (FTP) is a popular means to move files back and forth between remote systems. You need to be careful of outside FTP access because it could allow a malicious user to pull company information or server information (including password files) from inside servers. A user could upload files in an attempt to fill a hard drive and crash a server, upload a Trojan, or overwrite important server configuration files with ones that allow compromise of the server.

FTP is also one of the more complicated services to secure because of the way it works. Securing (or blocking) an incoming connection is relatively easy, but securing outgoing FTP connections is considerably more difficult. Let's take a look at a trace that shows standard FTP communication between a client and a server.

First is the outgoing connection with TCP/IP's three-way handshake:

```
client.com.4567 > server.com.21: S 1234567890:1234567890(0)
server.com.21 > client.com.4567: S 3242456789:3242456789(0) ack 1234567890
client.com.4567 > server.com.21: . ack 1
```

Next is the incoming connection when establishing data channel:

```
server.com.20 > client.com.4568: S 3612244896:3612244896(0)
client.com.4568 > server.com.20: S 1810169911:1810169911(0) ack 3612244896
server.com.20 > client.com.4568: . ack 1
```

The first part of the communication is a normal three-way handshake, but when the data channel is established, things become complicated. The server starts a connection session from a different port (TCP 20) than the one the client originally contacted (TCP 21), to a port greater than 1023 port on the client that differs from the one the client originally used. Because the server starts the connection, it is not considered return traffic and won't pass through extended access lists with the established keyword or dynamic reflexive access lists. In turn, to open the router for standard FTP, you must allow any traffic with a destination TCP port greater than 1023 and a source port of 20, which is a significant security hole.

One way to get around this problem is to use passive (PASV) FTP. PASV FTP works like standard FTP until the data connection. Instead of connecting to the client from port 20 to a random port greater than 1023, the FTP server tells the client (through the port that the client last used to connect to it) what greater-than 1023 port it wants to use to transfer data. With this port number, the client establishes a connection back to the FTP server. Now let's look at a trace of our previous example's data connection, this time using PASV FTP:

```
client.com.4568 > server.com.3456: S 1810169911: 1810169911(0)
server.com.3456 > client.com.4568: S 3612244896:3612244896(0) ack 1810169911
client.com.4568 > server.com.3456: . ack 1
```

All traffic that comes from the server is established traffic, permitting extended lists with the `established` keyword to function correctly. Using PASV mode FTP requires both the FTP server and client to support PASV mode transfers. Changing to passive FTP clients isn't a problem for most sites because most popular FTP clients support PASV mode. Most of the major web browsers support PASV mode FTP as well; however, this might require some minor setup, such as going to a preferences section and selecting PASV or passive FTP mode support. Using an ACL like the following example would be one way to handle inbound return PASV FTP traffic:

```
router(config)#access-list 101 permit tcp any gt 1023 192.168.1.0
➥0.0.0.255 gt 1023 est log
```

The Case of the Covert Channel

As a young security practitioner, I had the scare of my life. I randomly grabbed some log files and started looking through them, just giving a random spot check for anything that seemed out of the ordinary. About halfway through, I ran into a conversation between one of my network stations with an outside, unrecognized IP address.

The ports in question were disconcerting. The inside station was using TCP port 1741, and the outside port was much higher, in the 3000s. The higher number was an undefined port, but with a quick check of some port listings, I found that port 1741 happened to be defined as "Cisco net management." I wasn't familiar with this, but we were in a Cisco environment. The terror! The 3000 range port must have been a generated port, and the outside entity was contacting me on port 1741.

This log file caught the middle of the conversation, so I couldn't look at the beginning to verify that my theory was sound. I needed more information, so I went to my proxy log to check specifics on the connection. The outside entity appeared to be uploading some kind of FTP program to the station in question. This was getting worse instead of better.

I did more research to find out whose station had the DHCP assigned address in question during the transfer. The "malicious" IP address belonged to an FTP server. A tiny light bulb went off in my head. I went to the user and asked if he had been doing any FTP downloads at the time in question. He concurred. He had been downloading a new version of an FTP client. Because we used PASV FTP, the data channel port number was not the default port 20, but a high-numbered port determined as previously stated.

If you choose PASV FTP, be aware of false alarms regarding covert channels!

This ACL assumes that our internal network addresses are 192.168.1.0–255 and that they are part of a more complete access list allowing other, more standard traffic types. The problem with this access list is that despite the fact that only return traffic is allowed (in theory), you must leave open all greater-than 1023 TCP ports for return access because you don't know what data channel port the FTP server you are contacting will choose.

Although this ACL is more secure than some of the previous options, it still isn't a strong security stance. Wouldn't it be nice if it were possible to find out what port number you were using to contact the PASV FTP server every time, and use that information to allow the traffic back in?

Dynamic Packet Filtering and the Reflexive Access List

Many of the problems that face static packet filtering, the Cisco standard, and extended access lists can be alleviated by dynamic packet-filtering technology. The concept is that filters are built on-the-fly as needed and torn down after connections are broken.

Reflexive access lists are examples of dynamic packet-filtering technology. A criterion is set up on the outbound interface that watches defined connection types to the outside world. When the traffic returns, it is compared to an access list that was dynamically created as the outgoing traffic left the network.

For example, perhaps you have a client that has an IP address of 192.168.100.2 and have set up a reflexive access list to check for TCP traffic using the Telnet port. The reflexive access list would see the client sending the Telnet packet out the greater than 1023 port (let's say 1072 was randomly picked) to port 23 on some IP address (let's say 100.100.100.1) of a Telnet server. The reflexive access list would then generate an incoming access list based on this outgoing connection. It would take the outgoing connection

```
Client 192.168.100.2.1072 > telnet server 100.100.100.1.23
```

and reverse it into an incoming access list that permits traffic from 100.100.100.1 on port 23, to client 192.168.100.2 on port 1072, like this:

```
permit tcp host 100.100.100.1 eq 23 192.168.100.2 eq 1072
```

This dynamically generated list would be deleted after the connection was ended (a graceful FIN exchange or RST packet was sent). Because this access list type doesn't rely on the TCP flag bits set, it works with UDP and ICMP traffic as well. For non-TCP traffic, the connection is torn down after a timeout value expires. The timeout can be set per access list, or it can default to the global timeout of 300 seconds. This feature allows maximum security for return traffic because lists are created and removed for individual communication sessions. This capability to keep track of connections makes the reflexive access list the safest of the three access list types, but also the slowest.

Syntactically, reflexive access lists are basically a subset of extended access lists—specifically, "named" extended access lists. Named lists were created in Cisco IOS version 11.2 for two main reasons. First, large enterprises could run out of numbers for access lists using the old method. Second, its name could explain for what purpose the list was being used.

Sequence and the Named Access List

One of the best features of the named access list is that individual entries can be added or deleted without the list having to be completely re-created. You simply enter the access list configuration mode by typing

```
ip access-list extended name
```

where *name* is the name of the access list you want to edit. The prompt will change to look like this:

```
router(config-ext-nacl)#
```

At this point, you can delete entries by typing an existing entry preceded by `no`, or you can enter additional entries that will automatically be added to the end of the list. The fact that entries are added to the end of the list can be an issue, due to the problems with rule order. In previous versions of IOS, the only way this could be corrected was by re-creating the entire list or by deleting all the commands at the end of the list that you want the new entry to be placed before and then re-adding them back in after adding the new entry. Anyone who has done this knows it is a major hassle.

Now in versions 12.2(15)T and 12.3(2)T and later, the sequence feature has been introduced. Before entering the `permit` or `deny` keyword, you can add a sequence number, enabling the placement of a new access list entry anywhere in an access list. To demonstrate this feature, let's look at the following access list:

```
ip access-list extended test
    10 permit tcp any any
    20 permit ip any any log
```

In the past, a new entry would be placed after the last listed entry. However, with the sequence feature, we can choose a value below 10 to place the entry at the beginning of this list, between 10 and 20 to put the entry between the two listed entries, or greater than 20 to add it to the end of the list. If an initial sequence number is not specified when you create an entry, numbers will automatically be assigned (starting with the number 10). The auto-numbering then increments by 10 for each additional entry added.

We start by defining the list with `ip access-list extended` *name*, where *name* is the descriptive name used to define the access list. We follow this line with `permit` and `deny` lines, as shown next. They follow similar logic to numbered extended access lists. To move to a reflexive access list, all we have to do is add the `reflect` keyword to the end, followed by a name for the reflexive access list:

```
router(config)#ip access-list extended outfilter
router(config-ext-nacl)#permit tcp any any eq 80 reflect mypackets
router(config-if)#ip access-group outfilter out
```

Notice the way that the prompt changes after entering the initial command, which shows that we are now entering specific information into the named access list. In the permit line, we have the `reflect` keyword and the name of the reflexive access list with which we will be keeping track of our packet's connection information. Of course, the last line applies the list to the network interface, just like all previous examples, but now we do it by name. You might remember from the explanation of reflexive access lists that every connection has a dynamically created access list. These dynamic lists are created based on an access list like the one in the previous example. However, we need a component in the reverse direction to examine the packets when they come back in. Take a look at a sample inbound filter:

```
router(config)#ip access-list extended infilter
router(config-ext-nacl)#evaluate mypackets
router(config-if)#ip access-group infilter in
```

This access list should look familiar, except for the second line. The `evaluate` line checks the incoming packet flow versus the reflexive access list information (in this case, `mypackets`) to see if it will pass the test of one of its dynamically created lists. We now have a complete reflexive access list with all its components!

FTP Problems Revisited with the Reflexive Access List

Following is an example of a reflexive mode FTP filter that blocks incoming FTP traffic but allows outgoing passive FTP, along with any valid TCP traffic. This is a popular use of the reflexive access list—to allow anything outbound and to allow return (or response) traffic inbound.

```
router(config)#ip access-list extended filterout
router(config-ext-nacl)#permit tcp any any reflect packets
router(config-ext-nacl)#permit udp any any reflect packets
router(config-ext-nacl)#permit icmp any any reflect packets

router(config)#ip access-list extended filterin
router(config-ext-nacl)#evaluate packets

router(config-if)#ip access-group filterin in
router(config-if)#ip access-group filterout out
```

The `filterout` on this list permits all types of traffic out. Only TCP is necessary for FTP, but the others are added to demonstrate a popular configuration selection used with reflexive access lists, as mentioned previously. The `filterin` evaluates the return traffic of the previous outbound filter, and by the implied "deny all," it drops non-return FTP traffic (and any other non-return traffic). The last group shows the application of the `filterin` inbound and `filterout` outbound on the appropriate internal and external ports. Filter order isn't an issue, as the example appears here. It is possible to add other permit and deny access lists into this filter, being careful to ensure that nothing permitting TCP port 21 traffic comes before the rule in `filterin` and that the `evaluate` line terminates the list. The `evaluate` line must always terminate the list.

You can test the effectiveness of this filter using a properly implemented PASV FTP client. This filter, though the most secure of the FTP options you have seen so far, still only works with PASV FTP. The only way to securely allow standard FTP outbound through a Cisco router is by using a part of the Cisco Secure Integrated Software (formerly the Firewall Feature Set) called *context-based access control (CBAC)*, which inspects traffic and watches for inbound connections based on common behaviors of known protocols. Therefore, if you have to do secured outbound standard FTP on a Cisco router, consider the Cisco Secure Integrated Software.

Reflexive ACLs with UDP and ICMP Traffic: Clearing Up DNS Issues

One of the greatest advantages of reflexive ACLs over extended ACLs with the `established` keyword is that reflexive access lists can handle UDP and ICMP traffic. One place that this is helpful is with DNS traffic.

As previously mentioned, incoming UDP DNS return traffic is an issue because it can't be tracked by the `established` command; therefore, a specific access list must be made to allow DNS return traffic. With the reflexive access list, this is no longer necessary. Using the same access list used in the "FTP Problems Revisited with the Reflexive Access List" section, DNS return traffic is handled dynamically. Because the outgoing connection is aware of the ephemeral port that the DNS request is using, the dynamically created ACL can reflect (pardon the pun) that information, making a much more secure access control list.

Trouble in Paradise: Problems with Reflexive Access Lists

Yes, just when you thought you had found the panacea of packet filtering, the disclaimer comes about. Even reflexive access lists aren't perfect. However, due to the dynamic nature by which they are created and deleted, they are much more difficult to pass than other packet filters. One reset packet is all that is required to entirely remove a reflexively generated ACL.

Another issue with reflexive access lists is that they keep no record of TCP flags, so initial traffic could flow in without an alarm being sounded. How feasible is this? Look at the following example:

```
permit tcp host 100.100.100.1 eq 23 192.168.100.2 eq 1072
```

This is a dynamically generated reflexive access list example from a previous section. For someone to be able to use this access list as a conduit through to your internal network, the following would have to transpire:

1. Someone would have to know that this access list exists.
2. This access list would have to be created by an internal host contacting an outside entity.
3. Only a host at 100.100.100.1 using port 23 could start a viable communications channel through this access list.
4. The only host that could be contacted would be at address 192.168.100.2.
5. The contacted host would have to be listening on the ephemeral port 1072.

6. The sending host would have to know exactly what stage of communication the contacted host would be expecting to keep it from tearing down the dynamic access list.

7. This would all have to transpire before the generated access list was torn down.

If someone is this in-tune with your network and security structure and you don't have the reconnaissance capabilities to recognize that this person is watching you, you might be vulnerable on more levels than this one.

One thing can walk right through reflexive access lists: outbound traffic. If a virus or Trojan is on the internal network and wants to contact a malicious outside entity, the reflexive access list would let the traffic out and the return traffic from the conversation back in. The only way to defend against this with packet filtering is by limiting outbound access with an access list like the following (for an even stronger security stance, replace the second any with your internal network number):

```
router(config)#ip access-list extended filterout
router(config-ext-nacl)#permit tcp any any eq 21 reflect packets
router(config-ext-nacl)#permit tcp any any eq 22 reflect packets
router(config-ext-nacl)#permit tcp any any eq 23 reflect packets
router(config-ext-nacl)#permit tcp any any eq 25 reflect packets
router(config-ext-nacl)#permit tcp any any eq 53 reflect packets
router(config-ext-nacl)#permit tcp any any eq 80 reflect packets
router(config-ext-nacl)#permit tcp any any eq 110 reflect packets
router(config-ext-nacl)#permit tcp any any eq 119 reflect packets
router(config-ext-nacl)#permit tcp any any eq 143 reflect packets
router(config-ext-nacl)#permit tcp any any eq 443 reflect packets
router(config-ext-nacl)#permit udp any any eq 53 reflect packets
router(config-ext-nacl)#permit icmp any any packet-too-big
router(config-ext-nacl)#deny ip any any log-input


router(config)#ip access-list extended filterin
router(config-ext-nacl)#evaluate packets

router(config-if)#ip access-group filterin in
router(config-if)#ip access-group filterout out
```

This way, controls exist for the types of traffic leaving the network. However, if the virus or Trojan happens to use one of these popular traffic types, you are just as vulnerable. This is why it is important to deploy extra layers of defense, such as virus checkers and host firewall defenses. Despite the fact that reflexive ACLs can be a more effective means to defend your network using dynamically generated host and port access lists, they still have the inherent limitations of packet-filtering technology that need to be considered before choosing them as your protection method of choice. They also put more of a burden on your router than static ACLs, so implement them with caution.

For two complete examples of reflexive access lists, refer to Appendix A, "Cisco Access List Sample Configurations."

Cisco IPv6 Access Lists

With the advent of IP version 6, Cisco access lists have changed. IPv6 extended access list support started to be accommodated for in IOS versions 12.0(23)S and 12.2(13)T or later. Previously there were limited IOS versions that supported features similar to standard access list functionality for IPv6, only allowing filtering based on source addressing. The IPv6 extended access lists, though similar to their IPv4 predecessors, require slightly different commands. Because IPv6 is not backward compatible with IPv4, new commands needed to be created for IPv6-related functions.

Access lists are still created in config mode, but the process of creating an IPv6 access list is instead started with the following command:

```
Router(config)#ipv6 access-list name
```

Here, name is some descriptive name for the IPv6 access list. This will place you into IPv6 access-list configuration mode. The prompt will change to look like this:

```
Router(config-ipv6-acl)#
```

Now permit or deny access list statements can be added. Here is an example of a permit statement for this access list:

```
Router(config-ipv6-acl)#permit ipv6 any A2b2:A:132::1234/64 log
```

It follows the same format as IPv4 extended access lists—permit or deny, followed by protocol identifier. Supported keywords include ipv6 for layer 3 access lists using IPv6 addressing, along with protocol identifiers ahp, esp, tcp, udp, pcp, stcp, and icmp. This is followed by the source and destination address in IPv6 format, and the any and host keywords can still also be used. This version of access list can accommodate the double-colon abbreviation, as shown in the example. One minor difference in the source and destination address notation is the new way the subnet mask is entered. Instead of listing out the value of the subnet mask, as was commonly done with IPv4, it is now shown as /xxx where xxx is some number between 0 and 128. This number represents the number of bits in the subnet mask. The entry can be ended with a trailing keyword. It can be any of the trailing keywords used in IPv4, with the exception of keywords that only refer to IPv4 features (tos and precedence). Also, there are several new keywords to accommodate IPv6 features. IPv6 extension header information can be filtered with the flow-label and routing keywords. Also, the sequence keyword allows similar functionality to the IPv4 named access list feature of the same name. However, in IPv6 lists, the sequence keyword is added after the list instead of at the beginning:

```
permit tcp any any sequence 5
```

IPv6 extended access lists also have support for reflexive access list capability with the use of the `reflect` keyword. This functionality is identical to IPv4 reflexive access lists.

IPv6 access lists are displayed using the following command:

```
Router# sh ipv6 access-list name
```

The `name` option can be left off to display all IPv6 access lists.

As IPv6 continues to be more and more supported throughout the Internet, understanding IPv6 access list features will become a crucial part of securing your network environment.

Summary

Throughout this chapter, we've discussed the many ways that packet filtering can be used as a means to secure the perimeter. We discussed the positive and negative points of using a packet filter as the means to control traffic flow based on address and port, and the weaknesses of the packet-filtering technology. We also discussed the improvement of packet-filtering technology through the use of dynamic packet filters.

Despite weaknesses in the packet filter's capability to track information and understand what it is tracking, it still has many uses that can make it a valuable part of your perimeter defense. Filters can be utilized to screen out unwanted traffic at the perimeter, to prevent possibly dangerous traffic from leaving your network, and even to tailor incoming traffic that is allowed.

Packet filters can be used in conjunction with other firewalls as a layer of an intricate defense-in-depth posture or as a standalone solution in lower-risk areas or where budgets are tight. After all, protection of information is a balancing act between the value of the data and the cost to protect it.

Packet-filtering technology can be a useful means to protect your network as long as you implement it with due consideration to its strengths and weaknesses.

References

1 "Access Control Lists and IP Fragments." Cisco Systems, Inc. http://www.cisco.com/_warp/public/105/acl_wp.html. December 2001.
2 "Access Control Lists and IP Fragments." Cisco Systems, Inc. http://www.cisco.com/_warp/public/105/acl_wp.html. December 2001.
3 RFC 1858 "Security Considerations for IP Fragment Filtering." http://www.ietf.org/rfc/_rfc1858.txt. October 1995.

3

Stateful Firewalls

THE FOCUS OF THIS CHAPTER IS ON STATEFUL firewalls, a type of firewall that attempts to track the state of network connections when filtering packets. The stateful firewall's capabilities are somewhat of a cross between the functions of a packet filter and the additional application-level protocol intelligence of a proxy. Because of this additional protocol knowledge, many of the problems encountered when trying to configure a packet-filtering firewall for protocols that behave in nonstandard ways (as mentioned in Chapter 2, "Packet Filtering") are bypassed.

This chapter discusses stateful filtering, stateful inspection, and deep packet inspection, as well as state when dealing with various transport and application-level protocols. We also demonstrate some practical examples of how several vendors implement state tracking as well as go over examples of such firewalls.

How a Stateful Firewall Works

The stateful firewall spends most of its cycles examining packet information in Layer 4 (transport) and lower. However, it also offers more advanced inspection capabilities by targeting vital packets for Layer 7 (application) examination, such as the packet that initializes a connection. If the inspected packet matches an existing firewall rule that permits it, the packet is passed and an entry is added to the state table. From that point forward, because the packets in that particular communication session match an existing state table entry, they are allowed access without call for further application layer inspection. Those packets only need to have their Layer 3 and 4 information (IP address and TCP/UDP port number) verified against the information stored in the state table to confirm that they are indeed part of the current exchange. This method increases overall firewall performance (versus proxy-type systems, which examine all packets) because only initiating packets need to be unencapsulated the whole way to the application layer.

Conversely, because these firewalls use such filtering techniques, they don't consider the application layer commands for the entire communications session, as a proxy firewall would. This equates to an inability to really control sessions based on application-level traffic, making it a less secure alternative to a proxy. However, because of the stateful firewall's speed advantage and its ability to handle just about any traffic flow (as opposed to the limited number of protocols supported by an application-level proxy), it can be an excellent choice as the only perimeter protection device for a site or as a role player in a more complex network environment.

> **Note**
>
> Using a single perimeter protection device is often a financial necessity for smaller sites. However, despite the fact that only a single firewall is being implemented, other defense-in-depth options such as intrusion detection systems (IDSs), logging and monitoring servers, and host-level protection should also be used for a more secure network implementation.

Now that we have discussed the stateful firewall, for a better understanding of its function, let's discuss the meaning of *state* and how it is tracked in network communications.

> **Using a Firewall as a Means of Control**
>
> An important point that should be considered when discussing perimeter security is the concept of a firewall as a network chokepoint. A *chokepoint* is a controllable, single entry point where something is funneled for greater security. However, as the name implies, this area of limited entry also can be a place where bandwidth is restricted. A good example of a chokepoint in the real world is a metal detector at an airport. Imagine if the metal detector was the size of an entire hallway in the airport, and 20 or more people could walk through a single gate at one time. If the detector goes off, it would be difficult for the inspectors to determine which party had triggered it and to be able to stop that person to examine him or her further. More fine-grained traffic control is needed in such a situation. That is why the concept of a chokepoint is necessary in such a case; it allows one inspector to watch one party go through one metal detector at a time. The chokepoint offers additional control of the parties entering the airport. Like other chokepoints, this channeling of people for additional control can also lead to slowdowns in the process; therefore, lines often form at airport metal detectors.
>
> Similar to an airport metal detector, a firewall offers a chokepoint for your network segment. All traffic that enters or leaves your network needs to pass through it for inspection. This additional control not only helps protect inbound and outbound traffic flows but also allows a single point for examining and logging such traffic, verifying that if a breach exists, it is recorded.

The Concept of State

One confusing concept to understand when discussing firewall and TCP/IP communications is the meaning of *state*. The main reason this term is so elusive is that it can mean different things in different situations. Basically, state is the condition of being of a given communication session. The definition of this condition of being for a given host or session can differ greatly, depending on the application with which the parties are communicating and the protocols the parties are using for the exchange.

Devices that track state most often store the information as a table. This state table holds entries that represent all the communication sessions of which the device is aware. Every entry holds a laundry list of information that uniquely identifies the communication session it represents. Such information might include source and destination IP address information, flags, sequence and acknowledgment numbers, and more. A state table entry is created when a connection is started out through the stateful device. Then, when traffic returns, the device compares the packet's information to the state table information to determine whether it is part of a currently logged communication session. If the packet is related to a current table entry, it is allowed to pass. This is why the information held in the state table must be as specific and detailed as possible to guarantee that attackers will not be able to construct traffic that will be able to pass the state table test.

Firewall Clustering and Tracking State

It is possible to cluster firewalls together for redundancy, or to allow more bandwidth than a single firewall can handle on its own. In this clustered state, any of the firewall partners could possibly receive any part of a traffic flow. Therefore, although the initial SYN packet for a connection might be received on firewall 1, the final ACK response might come back to firewall 2. To be able to handle traffic statefully when firewalls are clustered, a single shared state table must be available to all the cluster members. This facilitates the complete knowledge of all traffic that other cluster members have seen. It is often accomplished using a dedicated communications cable between the members as a sort of direct link, solely for the sharing of vital state information. Such a mechanism affords an efficient means for the propagation of said state table information, allowing even the fastest communication links to operate without the problem of an incompletely updated state table.

The only other means to implement clustered firewalls without having to share state is by placing the firewalls in a "sandwich" between load-balancers. This way, a given traffic stream will always hit the same firewall it was initiated through. For more information on design choices for firewall clustering, take a look at Chapter 17, "Tuning the Design for Performance."

Transport and Network Protocols and State

Transport protocols can have their connection's state tracked in various ways. Many of the attributes that make up a communication session, including IP address and port pairings, sequence numbers, and flags, can all be used to fingerprint an individual connection. The combination of these pieces of information is often held as a hash in a state table for easy comparison. The particulars depend on the vendor's individual implementation. However, because these protocols are different, so are the ways the state of their communications can be effectively tracked.

TCP and State

Because TCP is a connection-oriented protocol, the state of its communication sessions can be solidly defined. Because the beginning and end of a communication session is well defined in TCP and because it tracks the state of its connections with flags, TCP is considered a stateful protocol. TCP's connection is tracked as being in one of 11 states, as defined in RFC 793. To truly understand the stateful tracking of TCP, it is important to realize the many stages a TCP connection goes through, as detailed in the following list:

- **CLOSED**—A "non-state" that exists before a connection actually begins.
- **LISTEN**—The state a host is in when waiting for a request to start a connection. This is the true starting state of a TCP connection.
- **SYN-SENT**—The time after a host has sent out a SYN packet and is waiting for the proper SYN-ACK reply.
- **SYN-RCVD**—The state a host is in after receiving a SYN packet and replying with its SYN-ACK reply.
- **ESTABLISHED**—The state a connection is in after its necessary ACK packet has been received. The initiating host goes into this state after receiving a SYN-ACK, as the responding host does after receiving the lone ACK.

During the process of establishing a TCP connection, a host goes through these states. This is all part of the three-way handshake, as shown in Figure 3.1.

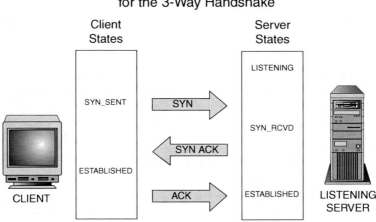

Figure 3.1   The TCP three-way handshake connection establishment consists of five well-defined states.

The remaining 6 of the 11 TCP connection states describe the tearing down of a TCP connection. The first state is used during an active close by the initiator and a passive close by the receiver, as shown in Figure 3.2.

TCP STATES
for a standard connection close

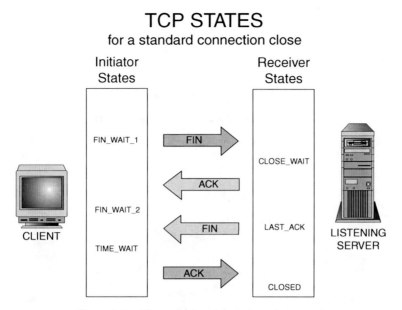

Figure 3.2   The active/passive closing of a normal
TCP connection consists of six states.

- **FIN-WAIT-1**—The state a connection is in after it has sent an initial FIN packet asking for a graceful close of the TCP connection.
- **CLOSE-WAIT**—The state a host's connection is in after it receives an initial FIN and sends back an ACK to acknowledge the FIN.
- **FIN-WAIT-2**—The connection state of the host that has received the ACK response to its initial FIN, as it waits for a final FIN from its connection partner.
- **LAST-ACK**—The state of the host that just sent the second FIN needed to gracefully close the TCP connection back to the initiating host while it waits for an acknowledgment.
- **TIME-WAIT**—The state of the initiating host that received the final FIN and has sent an ACK to close the connection. Because it will not receive an acknowledgment of its sent ACK from the connection partner, it has to wait a given time period before closing (hence, the name TIME-WAIT); the other party has sufficient time to receive the ACK packet before it leaves this state.

Note

The amount of time the TIME-WAIT state is defined to pause is equal to the Maximum Segment Lifetime (MSL), as defined for the TCP implementation, multiplied by two. This is why this state is also called 2MSL.

- **CLOSING**—A state that is employed when a connection uses the nonstandard simultaneous close. The connection is in this state after receiving an initial FIN and sending an ACK. After receiving an ACK back for its FIN, the connection will go into the TIME-WAIT state (see Figure 3.3).

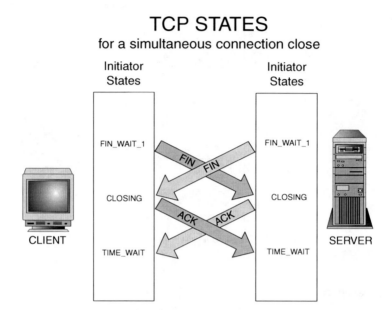

Figure 3.3   The simultaneous close of a TCP connection, where both parties close actively, consists of six states.

You can determine the state of the TCP connection by checking the flags being carried by the packets, as alluded to by the various descriptions of the TCP states. The tracking of this flag information, in combination with the IP address/port address information for each of the communicating parties, can paint a pretty good picture of what is going on with the given connection. The only other pieces of the puzzle that might be needed for clarity are the sequence and acknowledgment numbers of the packets. This way, if packets arrive out of order, the dialog flow of the communication can be more easily discerned, and the use of replay attacks against a device tracking state will be less likely to succeed.

Entries for TCP communication sessions in a state table are removed when the connection is closed. To prevent connections that are improperly closed from remaining in the state table indefinitely, timers are also used. While the three-way handshake is transpiring, the initial timeout value used is typically short (under a minute), so network scans and the like are more quickly cleared from the state table. The value is lengthened considerably (to as long as an hour or more) after the connection is established, because a properly initiated session is more likely to be gracefully closed.

It would seem from what we have just covered that the state of any TCP connection is easily definable, concrete, and objective. However, when you're tracking the overall communication session, these rules might not always apply. What if an application that employs nonstandard communication techniques was being used? For example, as discussed in Chapter 2, standard FTP uses an atypical communication exchange when initializing its data channel. The states of the two individual TCP connections that make up an FTP session can be tracked in the normal fashion. However, the state of the FTP connection obeys different rules. For a stateful device to be able to correctly pass the traffic of an FTP session, it must be able to take into account the way that standard FTP uses one outbound connection for the control channel and one inbound connection for the data channel. We will cover this issue in greater detail in the "Application-Level Traffic and State" section, later in this chapter.

UDP and State

Unlike TCP, UDP is a connectionless transport protocol. This makes the tracking of its state a much more complicated process. In actuality, a connectionless protocol has no state; therefore, a stateful device must track a UDP connection in a pseudo-stateful manner, keeping track of items specific to its connection only. Because UDP has no sequence numbers or flags, the only items on which we can base a session's state are the IP addressing and port numbers used by the source and destination hosts. Because the ephemeral ports are at least somewhat random, and they differ for any connection coming from a given IP address, this adds a little bit of credence to this pseudo-stateful method of session tracking. However, because the UDP session is connectionless, it has no set method of connection teardown that announces the session's end. Because of this lack of a defined ending, a state-tracking device will typically be set up to clear a UDP session's state table entries after a preconfigured timeout value (usually a minute or less) is reached. This prevents entries from filling the table.

Another point of concern with UDP traffic is that because it cannot correct communication issues on its own, it relies entirely on ICMP as its error handler, making ICMP an important part of a UDP session to be considered when tracking its overall state.

For example, what if during a UDP communication session a host can no longer keep up with the speed at which it is receiving packets? UDP offers no method of letting the other party know to slow down transmission. However, the receiving host can send an ICMP source quench message to let the sending host know to slow down transmission of packets. However, if the firewall blocks this message because it is not part of the normal UDP session, the host that is sending packets too quickly does not know that an issue has come up, and it continues to send at the same speed, resulting in lost packets at the receiving host. Stateful firewalls must consider such "related" traffic when deciding what traffic should be returned to protected hosts.

ICMP and State

ICMP, like UDP, really isn't a stateful protocol. However, like UDP, it also has attributes that allow its connections to be pseudo-statefully tracked. The more complicated part of tracking ICMP involves its one-way communications. The ICMP protocol is often used to return error messages when a host or protocol can't do so on its own, in what can be described as a "response" message. ICMP response-type messages are precipitated by requests by other protocols (TCP, UDP). Because of this multiprotocol issue, figuring ICMP messages into the state of an existing UDP or TCP session can be confusing to say the least. The other, easier-to-track way in which ICMP is used is in a request/ reply-type usage. The most popular example of an application that uses this request/reply form is ping. It sends echo requests and receives echo reply messages. Obviously, because the given stimulus in these cases produces an expected response, the session's state becomes less complicated to track. However, instead of being tracked based on source and destination addresses, the ICMP message can be tracked on request message type and reply message type. This tracking method is about the only way ICMP can enter into a state table.

Another issue with ICMP is that, like UDP, it is connectionless; therefore, it must base the retention of a state table entry on a predetermined timeout because ICMP also does not have a specific mechanism to end its communication sessions.

Application-Level Traffic and State

We have covered in some detail the ways that state can be tracked at the transport and network protocol levels; however, things change when you are concerned about the state of the entire session. When a stateful device is deciding which traffic to allow into the network, application behaviors must be taken into account to verify that all session-related traffic is properly handled. Because the application might follow different rules for communication exchanges, it might change the way that state has to be considered for that particular communication session. Let's look at an application that uses a standard communication style (HTTP) and one that handles things in a nonstandard way (FTP).

HTTP and State

HTTP is the one of the main protocols used for web access, and it's the most commonly used protocol on the Internet today. It uses TCP as its transport protocol, and its session initialization follows the standard way that TCP connections are formed. Look at the following tcpdump trace:

```
21:55:46.1 Host.1096 > maverick.giac.org.80: S 489703169:489703169(0)
win 16384 <mss1460,nop,nop,sackOK> (DF)
21:55:46.2 maverick.giac.org.80 > Host.1096: S 3148360676:3148360676(0)
 ack 489703170win 5840 <mss 1460,nop,nop,sackOK> (DF)
21:55:46.5 Host.1096 > maverick.giac.org.80: . ack 1 win 17520 (DF)
```

This tcpdump trace shows the three-way handshake between a contacting client named Host and the SANS GIAC web server, Maverick. It is a standard TCP connection establishment in all aspects.

The following packet lists the first transaction after the TCP connection was established. Notice that in the payload of the packet, the GET / HTTP/1.1 statement can be clearly made out (we truncated the output for display purposes):

```
21:55:46.6 Host.1096 > maverick.giac.org.80: P 1:326(325) ack 1 win 17520 (DF)
E..m."@....6.....!...H.P.OG...+.P.Dpe$..GET./.HTTP/1.1..Accept:.image/gif,.image
```

This is the first HTTP command that a station issues to receive a web page from a remote source.

Let's look at the next packet, which is truncated for display purposes:

```
21:55:46.8 maverick.giac.org.80 > Host.1096: P 1:587(586) ack 326 win 6432 (DF)
➡E..r..@.2..6.!.......P.H..+..OHGP.......HTTP/1.1.301.Moved.Permanently..
➡Date:.Wed,.06.Feb.2002.02:56:03.GMT..Server:.Apache..Location:
➡.http://www.sans.org/newlook/home.php..Kee
```

Notice that this reply packet begins to return the home page for the SANS GIAC website at http://www.sans.org. As shown in the preceding example, protocols such as HTTP that follow a standard TCP flow allow an easier definition of the overall session's state. Because it uses a single established connection from the client to the server and because all requests are outbound and responses inbound, the state of the connection doesn't differ much from what would be commonly tracked with TCP. If tracking only the state of the TCP connection in this example, a firewall would allow the HTTP traffic to transpire as expected. However, there is merit in also tracking the application-level commands being communicated. We cover this topic more in the section "Problems with Application-Level Inspection," later in this chapter. Next, we look at how this scenario changes when dealing with applications that use a nonstandard communication flow, such as standard FTP traffic.

File Transfer Protocol and State

File Transfer Protocol (FTP) is a popular means to move files between systems, especially across the Internet. FTP in its standard form, however, behaves quite differently from most other TCP protocols. This strange two-way connection establishment also brings up some issues with the tracking of state of the entire connection. Would a firewall that only tracks the state of the TCP connections on a system be able to pass standard FTP traffic? As seen in Chapter 2, the answer is no. A firewall cannot know to allow in the SYN packet that establishes an FTP data channel if it doesn't take into account the behavior of FTP. For a stateful firewall to be able to truly facilitate all types of TCP connections, it must have some knowledge of the application protocols being run, especially those that behave in nonstandard ways.

When the application-level examination capabilities of a stateful inspection system are being used, a complicated transaction like that used by a standard FTP connection can be dissected and handled in an effective and secure manner.

The stateful firewall begins by examining all outbound traffic and paying special attention to certain types of sessions. As we know from Chapter 2, an FTP control session can be established without difficulty; it is the inbound data-channel initialization that is problematic. Therefore, when a stateful firewall sees that a client is initializing an outbound FTP control session (using TCP port 21), it knows to expect the server being contacted to initiate an inbound data channel on TCP port 20 back to the client. The firewall can dynamically allow an inbound connection from the IP address of the server on port 20 to the address of the client. However, for utmost security, the firewall should also specify the port on which the client will be contacted for this exchange.

The firewall discovers on which port the client is contacted through the use of application inspection. Despite the fact that every other piece of information we have needed thus far in this exchange has been Layer 4 or lower, the port number used by the server initializing the data channel is actually sent to it in an FTP `port` command from the client. Therefore, by inspecting the traffic flow between client and server, the firewall also picks up the port information needed for inbound data channel connection. This process is illustrated in Figure 3.4.

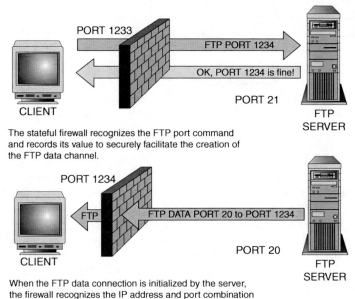

Figure 3.4   The stateful firewall examines the FTP `port` command to determine the destination port for the establishment of the FTP data channel.

Multimedia Protocols and the Stateful Firewall

Multimedia protocols work similarly to FTP through a stateful firewall—just with more connections and complexity. The widespread use of multimedia communication types, such as H.323, Real Time Streaming Protocol (RTSP), CUSeeME, Microsoft's NetShow, and more, have demanded a secure means to allow such traffic to pass into the networks of the world.

All these protocols rely on at least one TCP control channel to communicate commands and one or more channels for multimedia data streams running on TCP or UDP. The control channels are monitored by the stateful firewall to receive the IP addresses and port numbers used for the multimedia streams. This address information is then used to open secure conduits to facilitate the media streams' entrance into the network, as shown in Figure 3.5.

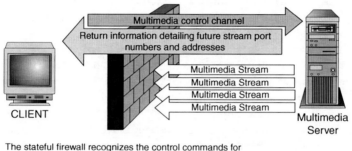

The stateful firewall recognizes the control commands for the multimedia session to securely facilitate inbound access for incoming multimedia streams to follow.

Figure 3.5   The stateful firewall tracks the multimedia protocol's communication channel to facilitate the passing of incoming media streams.

Note

Stateful firewalls now allow the use of multistream multimedia applications, such as H.323, in conjunction with Port Address Translation (PAT). In the not-so-distant past, this was a long-time problem with multistream protocols because the multiple ports used per connection could easily conflict with the PAT translation's port dispersal.

Problems with Application-Level Inspection

Despite the fact that many stateful firewalls by definition can examine application layer traffic, holes in their implementation prevent stateful firewalls from being a replacement for proxy firewalls in environments that need the utmost in application-level control. The main problems with the stateful examination of application-level traffic involve the abbreviated examination of application-level traffic and the lack of thoroughness of this examination, including the firewall's inability to track the content of said application flow.

To provide better performance, many stateful firewalls abbreviate examinations by performing only an application-level examination of the packet that initiates a communication session, which means that all subsequent packets are tracked through the state table using Layer 4 information and lower. This is an efficient way to track communications, but it lacks the ability to consider the full application dialog of a session. In turn, any deviant application-level behavior after the initial packet might be missed, and there are no checks to verify that proper application commands are being used throughout the communication session.

However, because the state table entry will record at least the source and destination IP address and port information, whatever exploit was applied would have to involve those two communicating parties and transpire over the same port numbers. Also, the connection that established the state table entry would not be properly terminated, or the entry would be instantly cleared. Finally, whatever activity transpired would have to take place in the time left on the timeout of the state table entry in question. Making such an exploit work would take a determined attacker or involve an accomplice on the inside.

Another issue with the way stateful inspection firewalls handle application-level traffic is that they typically watch traffic more so for triggers than for a full understanding of the communication dialog; therefore, they lack full application support. As an example, a stateful device might be monitoring an FTP session for the `port` command, but it might let other non-FTP traffic pass through the FTP port as normal. Such is the nature of a stateful firewall; it is most often reactive and not proactive. A stateful firewall simply filters on one particular command type on which it must act rather than considering each command that might pass in a communication flow. Such behavior, although efficient, can leave openings for unwanted communications types, such as those used by covert channels or those used by outbound devious application traffic.

In the previous example, we considered that the stateful firewall watches diligently for the FTP `port` command, while letting non-FTP traffic traverse without issue. For this reason, it would be possible in most standard stateful firewall implementations to pass traffic of one protocol through a port that was being monitored at the application level for a different protocol. For example, if you are only allowing HTTP traffic on TCP port 80 out of your stateful firewall, an inside user could run a communication channel of some sort (that uses a protocol other than the HTTP protocol) to an outside server listening for such communications on port 80.

Another potential issue with a stateful firewall is its inability to monitor the content of allowed traffic. For example, because you allow HTTP and HTTPS out through your firewall, it would be possible for an inside user to contact an outside website service such as http://www.gotomypc.com. This website offers users the ability to access their PC from anywhere via the web. The firewall will not prevent this access, because their desktop will initiate a connection to the outside Gotomypc.com server via TCP port 443 using HTTPS, which is allowed by your firewall policy. Then the user can contact the Gotomypc.com server from the outside and it will "proxy" the user's access back to his desktop via the same TCP port 443 data flow. The whole communication will transpire over HTTPS. The firewall won't be able to prevent this obvious security breach because the application inspection portion of most stateful firewalls really isn't meant to consider content. It is looking for certain trigger-application behaviors, but most often (with some exceptions) not the lack thereof. In the case of http://www.gotomypc.com, application-level inspection has no means to decipher that this content is inappropriate.

> **Note**
>
> Despite the fact that standard stateful examination capabilities of most such firewalls could not catch deviant traffic flows such as the covert channels based on commonly open ports, many vendors also offer content filtering or Deep Packet Inspection features on their stateful firewall products to prevent such issues. FireWall-1 and the PIX both offer varying levels of content filtering, for example. However, such features are often not enabled by default or need to be purchased separately and must be configured properly to be effective.

Another popular example of traffic that sneaks out of many otherwise secure networks involves programs such as AOL Instant Messenger, Kazaa, and other messaging and peer-to-peer file-sharing programs. These programs have the potential to transmit through any port, and because most stateful firewalls have at least one outbound port open, they will find their way out. Like the aforementioned "covert channel" example, the standard stateful firewall does not differentiate this type of traffic; it allows the traffic to pass as long as it is using one of the available ports. Content-level filtering or a true proxy firewall that considers all application-level commands could be used to prevent such traffic.

Deep Packet Inspection

Some of the biggest problems security professionals face today are allowed through their firewalls by design. As mentioned in the previous section, covert channels, nefarious content traversing known ports, and even malicious code carried on known protocols are some of the most damaging security threats your business will be exposed to. It is true that even a defense mechanism as simple as a packet filter could block most of these threats if you blocked the port they were carried on, but the real issue is that they travel over protocols you want to allow into your network and are required for your business! For example, many of the most widespread worms travel over NetBIOS, HTTP, or SQL-related protocols—all of which can be an important part of your Internet or network business. Obviously, it is not good form to allow NetBIOS or SQL into your network from the Internet, but if an attack is launched from an email attachment received at a user's PC, it is very likely that you might allow these protocols to traverse security zones on your network. How can we prevent issues carried by protocols that our businesses require to function? The answer is Deep Packet Inspection.

Deep Packet Inspection devices are concerned with the content of the packets. The term Deep Packet Inspection is actually a marketing buzzword that was recently coined for technology that has been around for some time; content examination is not something new. Antivirus software has been doing it at the host and mail server level, and network IDSs have been doing it on the wire for years. However, these products have limited visibility and capability to deal with the malicious payloads they find. A major disadvantage of content filtering at these levels is that the worm, Trojan horse, or malicious packet has already entered your network perimeter. Firewalls offering Deep Packet Inspection technology have the ability to detect and drop packets at the ingress point of the network. What more appropriate place to stop malicious traffic than at the firewall?

In the past, you have been able to use router or firewall content-filtering technologies to enter the signature of a worm or other malicious event and block it at the exterior of your network. However, what newer Deep Packet Inspection devices bring to the table are preloaded signatures, similar to those used by an antivirus solution. This way, your firewall is aware of and able to detect and remove malicious content as it arrives at your network. Also, because the packet's content is being considered at the application layer, traffic anomalies representative of an attack or worm can also be considered and filtered even if a specific signature isn't available for it. For example, if some attack uses a command that is considered nonstandard for a particular protocol, the device doing Deep Packet Inspection would be able to recognize it and drop the malicious content.

Note

The Deep Packet Inspection technology used in many popular firewall solutions is very similar to the content examination capabilities inherent in Intrusion Prevention Systems (IPSs). However, despite the fact that the technology is similar, the firewall-based solutions lack the volume of signatures and the thoroughness of analysis that a true IPS offers. Firewall-based Deep Packet Inspection could be considered "IPS-Lite." For more information on IPS, take a look at Chapter 11, "Intrusion Prevention Systems."

A Deep Packet Inspection firewall is responsible for performing many simultaneous functions. The entire content of a packet's application layer information needs to be reviewed against a list of attack signatures as well as for anomalous traffic behaviors. These firewalls also have to perform all the standard functions a stateful firewall typically handles. Therefore, advanced hardware is required to perform all these processes in a timely manner. This advanced hardware integration (typically dedicated "processors" just for this task) is what has set Deep Packet Inspection firewalls apart from their predecessors. It enables the swift processing and removal of anomalous traffic, with the added advantage of the stateful firewall's perspective on the overall communication flow of the network. This offers a major edge when determining which traffic is malicious and which is not.

Note

It is important to remember that for Deep Packet Inspection to work on SSL encrypted traffic flows, some means to decrypt the traffic must be employed. SSL certificates must also be loaded on the Deep Packet Inspection device and SSL flows must be decrypted, reviewed, and reencrypted before they are sent on to their destination. This process will cause some network latency and requires additional processing power to achieve efficient communications.

Most vendors are either already offering or are considering to offer solutions that incorporate this type of Deep Packet Inspection technology. Major vendors, including Check

Point, Cisco, and Juniper, are using some form of Deep Packet Inspection in their products and are constantly advancing it to help handle the new attacks that arrive at our networks on a daily basis.

As heavy-hitting worms such as SQL-Slammer, Blaster, Code-Red, and Welchia pound on our networks, transported via protocols that we use on a regular basis, the need for devices that consider the content of packets as well as its application become more and more urgent. Deep Packet Inspection is an excellent method to shut down some of the most used attack vectors exploited by malicious content today.

Stateful Filtering and Stateful Inspection

The definition of stateful filtering seems to vary greatly among various product vendors and has developed somewhat, as time has gone on. Stateful filtering can mean anything, from the ability to track and filter traffic based on the most minute of connection details to the ability to track and inspect session information at the application level. With this loose interpretation in mind, let's define these terms for the purpose of this chapter.

Stateful filtering has been used to define the stateful tracking of protocol information at Layer 4 and lower. Under this definition, stateful filtering products exhibit no knowledge of application layer protocols. At the most basic level, such products use the tracking of the IP addresses and port numbers of the connecting parties to track state. As mentioned previously, this is the only way that connectionless protocols can be tracked, but at best, this is only "pseudo-stateful." What about using this same method of stateful filtering for the tracking of the connection-oriented TCP? As mentioned previously, this method does not in any way track the TCP flags. TCP's flags define its connection states; therefore, although this method might be tracking some information from the various communication sessions, it is not truly tracking the TCP connection state.

More advanced forms of stateful filtering can also track sequence and acknowledgment numbers and the TCP packet flags. With the addition of these criteria, we can get truly stateful connection tracking for TCP, although we still lack the ability to differentiate traffic flows at the application level.

Stateful inspection, in contrast, has come to be used as a description of the devices that track state using all the Layer 4–type information listed previously, as well as the tracking of application-level commands. All this information can be combined to offer a relatively strong definition of the individual connection's state. Also, because Layer 7 information is being examined, extra insight into nonstandard protocol behaviors is available. This allows normally troublesome protocols such as FTP and H.323 to be securely passed by the device without complication.

> **Note**
>
> *Stateful inspection* is a term originally coined by the security product manufacturer Check Point, the maker of FireWall-1, for the way FireWall-1 handles the tracking of state information. It comprises both the tracking of state using Layer 4 protocol information and the tracking of application-level traffic commands.[1]

In both stateful filtering and stateful inspection, the tracked state information is most often recorded into a state table that tracks the information until a connection is torn down (as with TCP) or until a preconfigured timeout is reached (TCP, UDP, and ICMP). Every vendor has its own implementation of these methods, and in the next several sections, we will look at some vendors' definitions of stateful filtering/stateful inspection as used in their products.

Stateful Firewall Product Examples

As stated previously, various firewall products handle the tracking of state in many different ways. This section lists some popular firewall products and provides explanations of how they handle state. We also show examples of each product's state table and examine a sample configuration of a stateful firewall.

Netfilter/IPTables

Netfilter and IPTables are the two main pieces of the most recent incarnation of a firewall product that is freely available for Linux distributions. IPTables is the construct that is used to build the firewall rule sets. Netfilter is the bridge between the Linux kernel and the IPTables rule structure. Netfilter/IPTables is the successor of the ipfwadm and IPChains products, with an ever-increasing list of features and functionality. Now thanks to its connection-tracking feature, IPTables offers stateful filtering capability.[2]

Connection tracking records the state of a connection based mostly on protocol-specific information. Administrators create rules specifying what protocols or specific traffic types should be tracked. When a connection is begun using a tracked protocol, IPTables adds a state table entry for the connection in question. This state table entry includes such information as the following:

- The protocol being used for the connection
- The source and destination IP addresses
- The source and destination ports
- A listing with source and destination IP addresses and ports reversed (to represent response traffic)
- The time remaining before the rule is removed
- The TCP state of the connection (for TCP only)
- The connection-tracking state of the connection

Following is an example of a state table entry for IPTables:

```
tcp 6 93 SYN_SENT src=192.168.1.34 dst=172.16.2.23 sport=1054 dport=21 [UNREPLIED]
➥src=172.16.2.23 dst=192.168.1.34 sport=21 dport=1054 use=1
```

The first line starts out listing the protocol in question, followed by the protocol's numerical designation (6 for TCP). The next value, 93, represents the time remaining before the entry is automatically cleared from the state table. Then is shown the state that the TCP connection is in. The source and destination IP addresses follow, and then the source and destination ports are listed. Because this is an initial connection (as demonstrated by the connection's TCP state), this line lists that IPTables sees this connection as [UNREPLIED] and hasn't increased its timeout value yet. Next in the listing, we see a reversal of the original source and destination address and port information to allow return traffic. After the connection is established, the state table entry is altered, as you can see in the next example:

```
tcp 6 41294 ESTABLISHED src=192.168.1.34 dst=172.16.2.23 sport=1054 dport=21
➥src=172.16.2.23 dst=192.168.1.34 sport=21 dport=1054 [ASSURED] use=1
```

The [UNREPLIED] marker is removed after the first return packet. Upon establishment of the connection, the [ASSURED] marker is placed on the entry, and the timeout value (41294) is greatly increased.

Now let's consider the rules of IPTables.

Note

The following rule examples are basic and for demonstration purposes only. They do not take into account egress filtering or the lockdown or allowance of specific services. For optimum security, rules that specifically designate only those individual applications allowed would be more appropriate.

To begin, we'll look at the syntax and how it works. This first sample rule is considered an *output* rule because it defines which traffic can leave through the firewall (-A specifies that this rule will be appended to already existing rules):

```
iptables -A OUTPUT -p tcp -m state --state NEW,ESTABLISHED -j ACCEPT
```

This output rule determines which outbound communication will be accepted (as specified by the -j option). This particular rule deals only with the TCP protocol, as specified by the -p tcp option.

Note

IPTables and Netfilter now support IPv6. All you need is kernel version 2.4.x or above and all necessary modules and kernel patches loaded. Then you can use the ip6tables command for creating rules for IPv6, which supports the new 128-bit addresses. The -p protocol switch supports both ICMPv6 and IPv6. For more information on whether your system supports IPv6 or how to set up IP6Tables, check out the Linux Documentation Project site at http://www.tldp.org/HOWTO/Linux+IPv6-HOWTO/.

It specifies in the --state section that NEW and ESTABLISHED traffic is allowed out of our network. This rule, as listed, allows no egress protection. All new outbound TCP traffic will be allowed because the NEW option is specified. NEW tells the firewall to watch for packets with a lone SYN flag that are initiating a connection and to create entries in the state table for every such occurrence. The ESTABLISHED option allows traffic that is part of an existing session that has previously been recorded in the state table to pass as well, which means that any standard TCP communications will be able to leave the network.

Another part of the command worth mentioning is `-m state`. The `-m` denotes what module should be used for the rule in question—in this case, the standard `state` module that comes with IPTables. Now let's examine the rule that will allow the return traffic for our connection back into our network:

```
iptables -A INPUT -p tcp -m state --state ESTABLISHED -j ACCEPT
```

This command appears identical to the preceding one, except that it is an *input* rule, and only ESTABLISHED is listed under the `-state` section of the command. This means that only return traffic will be allowed inbound to our network, as defined by the state table. IPTables determines whether incoming traffic is return traffic for the connection entered into the state table by checking it against the reversed connection information located in the state table entry. No new connections will be able to enter our network from the outside.

Even though most of the requirements of TCP stateful tracking are available in IPTables, one exception to this is the tracking of sequence and acknowledgment numbers, which can be added with the tcp-window-tracking patch.[3]

From our previous definition of the items held in the state table, you can see that the items needed to do a pseudo-stateful job of tracking ICMP and UDP are present. Examples of basic UDP output and input rules would be as follows:

```
iptables -A OUTPUT -p udp -m state --state NEW,ESTABLISHED -j ACCEPT
iptables -A INPUT -p udp -m state --state ESTABLISHED -j ACCEPT
```

These rules appear identical to those specified for TCP, except for the `-p udp` option listing.

ICMP rules look about the same:

```
iptables -A OUTPUT -p icmp -m state --state NEW,ESTABLISHED,RELATED -j ACCEPT
iptables -A INPUT -p icmp -m state --state ESTABLISHED,RELATED -j ACCEPT
```

The main differences are the `-p icmp` specification for protocol and a new entry in the `--state` section: RELATED.

The RELATED option is the means by which IPTables allows traffic that is already in some way associated with an established traffic flow to initiate a new connection in the state table and be passed through the firewall. This related traffic might be an ICMP error message that is returned for a UDP or TCP connection already held in the state table. It could also be the initialization of an inbound FTP data channel on TCP port 20, after state table information had already been logged for an inside station starting a control channel connection on TCP port 21.

As listed, our rule allows ICMP traffic inbound and outbound that is related to existing ESTABLISHED traffic flows. Therefore, errors returned in response to existing TCP and UDP connections will pass. Because the NEW option is listed for outbound traffic, requests from ICMP programs such as `ping` will be able to leave our network, and the ESTABLISHED option specified for inbound traffic will allow the replies to said traffic to return back through. However, inbound ping requests will not be allowed in because the NEW option is not specified inbound.

The rules of conduct for defining related traffic are included in connection-tracking modules. They facilitate the examination of application-specific commands, such as the way the `ip_conntrack_ftp` module facilitates the inspection of FTP's `port` command to allow the secure handling of standard FTP traffic. (For more information on how stateful firewalls handle FTP traffic, see the "File Transfer Protocol and State" section, earlier in this chapter.) These modules can be added on as new protocols are used in your environment.

To implement a module such as `ip_conntrack_ftp` to allow standard outbound FTP communications to be properly initialized through our IPTables firewall, it first has to be loaded with a command such as the following:

```
modprobe ip_conntrack_ftp
```

Next, a specific rule has to be created to inspect the related traffic. This can be accomplished in the case of FTP by making an INPUT rule that allows inbound TCP port 20 traffic with the state option of RELATED. This will allow the inbound port 20 traffic to connect if the inspection process deems it related to an existing connection in the state table. Here is a listing of such a rule:

```
iptables -A INPUT -p tcp --sport 20 -m state --state ESTABLISHED,RELATED -j ACCEPT
```

An OUTPUT rule will be needed as well to allow response traffic to return:

```
iptables -A OUTPUT -p tcp --dport 20 -m state --state ESTABLISHED -j ACCEPT
```

Notice that the `-sport 20` option representing the source port in the INPUT rule has changed to the `-dport 20` (or destination port) option in the OUTPUT rule. This change is due to the reversal of communication roles for outbound versus inbound traffic.

Check Point FireWall-1

The Check Point FireWall-1 (FW-1) is one of the most popular stateful firewalls in use today. It is software based and can be loaded onto hardware server solutions of various platform types, including Windows, Solaris, and Red Hat Linux. It is also offered as a hardware appliance solution by Nokia. FireWall-1 uses a state table for the basic tracking of connections at the protocol level and an INSPECT engine for more complicated rules involving application layer traffic and nonstandard protocol behavior.

When deciding whether to allow a packet to pass, FireWall-1 tests it against the following data structures, in the order specified:

- First, FireWall-1 checks to see whether a connection is already logged in the state table for this particular incoming packet. If so, it is forwarded without further scrutiny.

- Next, if the state table did not contain an entry for the packet, the packet is compared against the security policy. If a rule allows the packet to pass, it will be forwarded on, and an entry for its communication session will be added to the state table.

TCP traffic is handled at a protocol level, much like previously shown examples. When a communication ensues, because the first packet of a connection will not be reflected in the state table, it is tested against the security policy. If it is accepted based on one of the rules, it is added into the state table.

> ### Tip
> For the most complete stateful protection of TCP communication flows, be sure to use the latest vendor-recommended version and feature pack of FireWall-1. In this text, all commands and examples use FW-1 NG. Also, for the highest level of security protection, be sure that all suggested hot fixes are applied.

The rules that might allow traffic to pass are either one of the implied rules set up in the FireWall-1 section of the Global Properties of SmartDashboard or are part of the rulebase created and maintained in FireWall-1's SmartDashboard GUI interface. For an example of a rule's listing and what the SmartDashboard interface looks like, refer to Figure 3.6.

> ### Implied Rules
> Be aware that even though FW-1's implied rules are not seen by default when you are viewing a firewall policy, they will allow certain types of traffic through your firewall. To ease your troubleshooting efforts, you may want to check the Log Implied Rules box in the FireWall-1 section of Global Properties. Also, to keep yourself cognizant of the implied rules when building your rulebase, you can check the Implied Rules option under the View menu of SmartDashboard so these rules appear when you view your firewall policy.

As shown in Figure 3.6, designing a rule set for firewall products such as FireWall-1 can be less demanding than some of the less user-friendly choices, such as IPTables. FireWall-1 allows you to use a GUI interface to represent your networks and systems as objects. You can elect to allow or disallow traffic for specific services by selecting appropriate options and referencing relevant objects. Rule order is one of the most critical things to keep in mind when designing such a rule set. It is vital to list specific rules at the top of the rule list before more general rules that might inadvertently apply to unwanted traffic types.

> ### Note
> For more information on building a FireWall-1 rulebase, see Lance Spitzner's paper titled "Building Your Firewall Rulebase" at http://www.spitzner.net/rules.html.

FireWall-1 enforces timeouts for TCP connections to ensure that improperly terminated sessions that lack the common FIN packet exchange do not remain in the state table indefinitely. The initial timeout on a half-open connection (before the three-way handshake has been completed) is logged at 60 seconds by default. Upon completion of the three-way handshake, this timeout is increased to 60 minutes to allow for latency in communications. After the closing of the connection is initiated with a FIN packet, the timeout is dropped to 50 seconds to ensure that the state table entry is more quickly cleared if the graceful FIN exchange is not completed successfully.

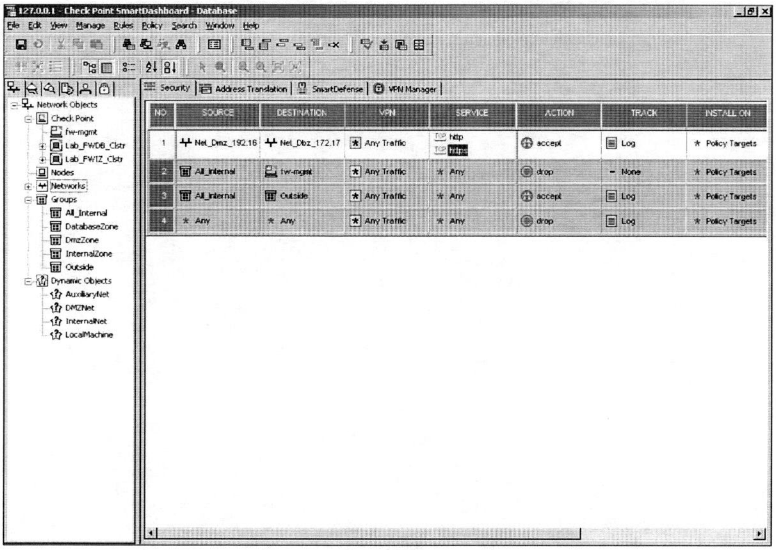

Figure 3.6   Check Point FireWall-1 NG offers a user-friendly
GUI interface called SmartDashboard (formerly Policy
Editor in previous versions) for editing its rule set.

Note

The 60-minute timeout setting for TCP connections, as well as the default UDP timeout, can be adjusted in the Stateful Inspection section of the Check Point NG Global Properties dialog box, as shown in Figure 3.7. In Check Point NG, all TCP and UDP services will use the shown timeout values by default, or you can manually configure a specific service with its own timeout value by clicking the Advanced button in the properties box for that particular service.

FireWall-1 handles UDP traffic in much the same way that other stateful firewalls do. It uses a pseudo-stateful method of tracking outbound UDP connections, and it allows inbound UDP packets that match one of the currently recorded communication flows. This process is accomplished through the recording of the IP addressing and port numbers that the communication partners use. A timer is used to remove the session from the state table after a predetermined amount of inactivity (see Figure 3.7).

For a better understanding of FireWall-1's tracking of state, look at its state table. Listing 3.1 is the Check Point FireWall-1 state table as decoded (it normally appears as rows of difficult-to-decipher numbers) by a Perl script (fwtable.pl) available from Lance Spitzner's website at http://www.spitzner.net/fwtable.txt.[4]

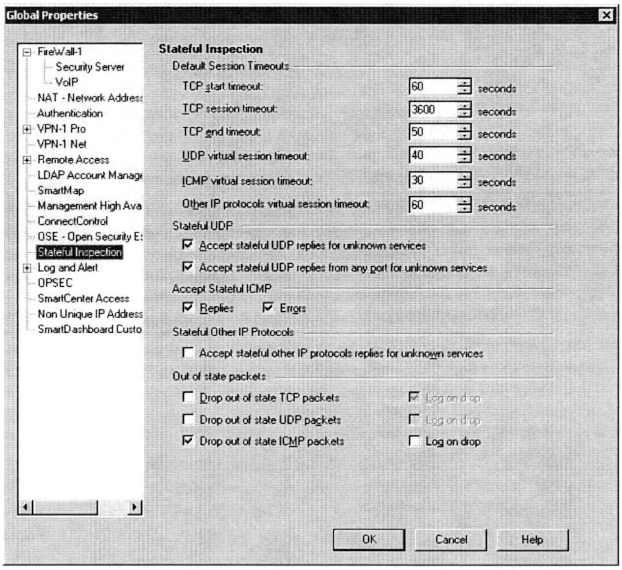

Figure 3.7   The Stateful Inspection section of the Global Properties dialog box for FireWall-1 NG contains many settings that define how FireWall-1 handles state.

Listing 3.1   **A Check Point FireWall-1's State Table as Translated by fwtable.pl**

Src_IP		Src_Prt	Dst_IP		Dst_Prt	IP_prot	Kbuf	Type	Flags	Timeout
192.168.1.202	1783	192.168.1.207	137		17	0		16386	ffffff00	18/40
192.168.1.202	1885	192.168.1.207	80		6	0		28673	ffffff00	43/50
192.168.1.202	1884	192.168.1.207	80		6	0		28673	ffffff00	43/50
192.168.1.202	1797	192.168.1.207	23		6	0		16385	ffffff00	35/50
192.168.1.202	1796	192.168.1.207	22		6	0		16385	ffffff00	35/50
192.168.1.202	1795	192.168.1.207	21		6	0		16385	ffffff10	35/50
192.168.1.202	1798	192.168.1.207	25		6	0		16385	ffffff00	35/50
192.168.1.202	1907	192.168.1.207	80		6	0		28673	ffffff00	43/50

IP addresses, port numbers, and even timeout values can be clearly seen in the FireWall-1 state table represented by fwtable.pl.

Tip

Dr. Peter Bieringer has updated Lance Spitzner's fwtable script to support versions of FW-1 through NG. For a copy, check out http://www.fw-1.de/aerasec/download/fw1-tool/fw1-tool.pl.

FW-1 supports the stateful inspection of many popular protocols. These include the following TCP protocols: H.323, FTP-BIDIR, RTSP, IIOP, SQLNET2, ENC-HTTP, Netshow, DNS_TCP, SSH2, FW1_CVP, HTTP, FTP-Port, PNA, SMTP, FTP-PASV,

FTP_BASIC, SSL_V3, Winframe, CIFS, FTP, INSPECT, CitrixICA, and RSHELL. It also pseudo-statefully inspects the following UDP protocols: CP-DHCP-reply, SNMP Reads, SIP, H.323 RAS, NBDatagram, DNS, CP-DHCP-request, NBName, and Freetel. FW-1 has additional capabilities to track RPC traffic of many varieties. It has the capability to allow many nonstandard protocols, including not only RPC, but also H.323, FTP (standard), and SQLNET2. For example, FireWall-1 statefully handles traffic based on remote procedure calls (RPCs), such as Network File System (NFS), whose ports are randomly generated by the portmapper service. The portmapper service runs on TCP and UDP ports 111 and handles the automatic generation of RPC programs' access ports. Because these ports are generated randomly, it would be nearly impossible to write a secure rule that could effectively permit such traffic. FireWall-1 solves this problem by tracking all specified portmapper traffic and actually caching the port numbers that portmapper maps to the RPC programs in use. This way, such traffic can be effectively tracked.

Configuring an FW-1 Service for Stateful Inspection

It should be mentioned that FW-1 does not automatically realize that it should track a service statefully by its port. The object representing the service must be configured for the protocol type in question. If you chose one of the predefined service objects from Check Point, this should already be done for you. However, if you created your own service object for some reason (different naming convention, alternate port setting, and so on), you need to manually configure the protocol that the object represents. For example, if your company runs standard FTP over port TCP/1021 (instead of TCP/21), it would seem that creating a TCP object and assigning it a name and port 1021 would be enough. However, FW-1 would handle this as a standard single-session TCP service and would not allow the return data channel to ensue. To configure the service object for FTP protocol, edit the object, click the Advanced button, and change the protocol type drop-down box to FTP-PORT. To make this change take place, you will need to reinstall the policy containing the object.

A new feature of FW-1 NG is the Smart Defense component. It is available in Feature Pack 3 and higher or can be loaded as a hotfix with Feature Pack 2. It allows advanced application layer examination (akin to Deep Packet Inspection) for a list of known attacks, worms, and types of malicious behavior. Applying this additional level of support to your existing FW-1 policy is as easy as switching to the SmartDefense tab in SmartDashboard and checking the protection options you want to employ. For additional information on the many elements of SmartDefense, check out the SmartDefense Technical White Paper on Check Point's website (http://www.checkpoint.com/products/downloads/smartdefense_whitepaper.pdf).

The Cisco PIX Firewall

The PIX firewall statefully inspects traffic using Cisco's Adaptive Security Algorithm (ASA). The ASA is used to make a representative hash of each outgoing TCP and UDP packet and then store it in a state table. When the TCP and UDP traffic return, because a representative entry is recorded in the state table, the traffic will be allowed to pass. ICMP traffic is a different matter. Inbound ICMP traffic is denied through the outside interface of the PIX, and a specific access list must be created to allow any such traffic.

Outbound ICMP is allowed, but it will not work by default, because the inbound responses will be blocked, like the `echo-reply` response to a `ping` command. Here's an example of an access list that will let ICMP traffic from a given test address cross through the PIX (as commonly used for troubleshooting new PIX installations):

```
access-list ICMP-ACL permit icmp test address inside address range
access-group ICMP-ACL in interface outside
```

The first command creates an access list called ICMP-ACL that permits ICMP traffic from a specified test address to our inside address range. The second line applies that ACL inbound on the outside interface.

The command that the PIX firewall uses to configure the stateful examination of traffic flows for a given protocol is the `fixup` command. The `fixup` command starts an advanced application-specific examination of outbound traffic of the protocol type listed to the designated port. The Cisco PIX firewall supports this application-level examination of traffic for the following protocols through the standard `fixup` command: CTIQBE, ESP-IKE, FTP, HTTP, H.323 (now supporting version 3 and 4), ICMP ERROR, ILS, MGCP, PPTP, RSH, RTSP, SIP, SIP UDP, SKINNY (now supporting PAT), SMTP, SNMP, SQLNET, and TFTP. The fixups for these protocols can be added or removed from a PIX configuration and reconfigured for various port specifications. They are considered extraneous to the operations of the PIX.

The PIX also offers built-in fixup support for these protocols: RTSP, CUSEEME, DNS, SUNRPC, XDMCP, H.323 RAS, TCP, and UDP. These integrated fixups are not seen in the PIX's configuration. They work in the background in conjunction with the normal fixups for the advanced inspection of these particular types of traffic. Even if a fixup is not installed for a particular TCP or UDP traffic type, the PIX will still track the session in its state table and allow its return traffic re-admittance to the network.

Not all fixups are created equal. Each fixup tracks application layer information at different levels. This level of inspection might vary from making sure the traffic passes through NAT successfully to the monitoring for specific application-level commands. For example, the SMTP fixup is the most stringent of them all. Since PIX software version 4.2, the SMTP fixup has supplied a protection feature called "mailguard." This fixup allows only SMTP commands to pass through it successfully. Non-SMTP traffic commands are dropped, but the PIX still returns an OK to the sender as if the information were passed. This helps protect poorly defended mail servers from outside attacks. Other fixups, such as FTP and H.323, allow the return of nonstandard communication traffic by monitoring the application-level commands that control the formation of their data channels.

Because the standard `fixup` command allows the specifying of the port number to be examined for the protocol, alternative configurations are supported. (This is not true for the built-in fixups.) For example, if you need to access a web server that is running on port 8080, use the following command:

```
Pixprompt(config)#fixup protocol http 8080
```

Such a `fixup` command will allow the creation of state table information for the listed outbound traffic type. Multiple fixups can be listed if more than one port number is used per protocol. The PIX's state tables contain ASA hashes based on the source and destination addresses, port numbers, sequence numbers, and TCP flags. Because PIX firewalls use truly random TCP sequence number generation, the connection is kept more secure.[5]

When the reply returns, the PIX checks the response against the state table and information that it knows about the behavior of the protocol in question. If the information checks out, it is allowed to pass. All other information is dropped unless it is specifically allowed using an access list.

The table listing connection state for a Cisco PIX can be viewed using the `show conn` command. Such a table can be seen in Listing 3.2.

Listing 3.2   **The Output from a Cisco PIX Firewall's** `show conn` **Command**

```
TCP out xx.yy.zz.129:5190 in 172.16.1.33:1960 idle 629:25:50 Bytes 6737 flags UIO
TCP out xx.yy.zz.254:23 in 172.16.1.88:1053 idle 0:11:33 Bytes 226696 flags UIO
TCP out xx.yy.zz.254:23 in 172.16.1.76:1146 idle 256:09:15 Bytes 78482 flags UIO
TCP out xx.yy.zz.254:23 in 172.16.1.100:1660 idle 145:21:19 Bytes 9657 flags UIO
TCP out xx.yy.zz.254:23 in 172.16.1.100:1564 idle 641:51:05 Bytes 132891 flags UIO
UDP out xx.yy.zz.12:137 in 172.16.1.12:137 idle 0:00:03 flags
```

Notice that standard IP address and port information is tracked, along with the time that entries will remain in the table. Also notice on the last entry for a UDP connection that no flags are listed. Despite the fact that this output shows current connections and can give you a good idea of what information is in your PIX's state table, this is not a true dump of the state table because it lacks the information provided by the stored ASA hash. You will notice, for example, that sequence numbers are not listed in this output.

To learn more about the way the PIX firewall operates and to better understand the configuration of a stateful firewall, we will look at a PIX firewall configuration using software version 6.3(4). The configuration will only include those items that have to do with passing standard protocol information.

First, in the PIX configuration listing are commands that define the interfaces:

```
nameif ethernet0 outside security0
nameif ethernet1 inside security100
```

This is a simple configuration with only two interfaces: an inside interface and an outside interface. Notice the security levels (shown as `security0` and `security100`). By default, all traffic can flow from a higher security numbered interface to a lower one on a PIX, but none can flow from a lower interface to a higher one. By default, this PIX cannot receive inbound traffic connections, but it can send anything out. These default behaviors can be adjusted by using NAT and access lists.

To allow an inbound connection, two criteria must be met:

- A static NAT mapping must be configured to allow the inbound traffic flow to bypass NAT translation, assuming that NAT is used in your environment. If it is not, this criterion can be ignored.
- An access list must be made to allow the type of traffic in question. For highest security, inbound traffic should only be allowed when using a firewall with a DMZ port; public servers can be placed on their own screened subnet.

Because NAT will not be an issue, you only need to add an access list to disallow outbound connections. This prevents the traffic types that you want to disallow. You can also create an egress filter to verify that only authentic local traffic is leaving your network.

Note

This configuration as listed does not include support for egress protection. For optimum security, egress protection of some sort is suggested. For more information on egress filters, see Chapter 2.

The `nameif` interface commands are followed by the backbone of the PIX configuration: the `fixup` commands (as mentioned earlier in the section). These commands list the protocols and their associated port numbers that the PIX will inspect. Listed next are some popular choices:

```
fixup protocol ftp 21
fixup protocol http 80
fixup protocol h323 1720
fixup protocol rsh 514
fixup protocol smtp 25
fixup protocol sqlnet 1521
fixup protocol sip 5060
```

The next lines of this listing show the IP addresses and subnet masks assigned to both the inside and outside ports. These are displayed here as a point of reference for the NAT-related commands to follow:

```
ip address outside 192.168.2.178 255.255.255.240
ip address inside 172.16.1.10 255.255.0.0
```

In the next portion of the listing, we create two address pools of outside addresses for our NAT pool, reflected by the first line, `(outside) 2`, and for PAT, `(outside) 1`. If we were only using PAT, the first line would not be necessary.

```
global (outside) 2 192.168.2.180-192.168.2.190 netmask 255.255.255.240
global (outside) 1 192.168.2.179
```

Next, we define the inside addresses for pool 2 and pool 1. The first statement lists the pool of inside addresses that will be NAT address translated. All other IP addresses will be forced to use PAT.

```
nat (inside) 2 172.16.1.96 255.255.255.248 0 0
nat (inside) 1 0.0.0.0 0.0.0.0 0 0
```

The second line demonstrates a wildcard so that any IP address (other than those listed on the previous line) will be PAT translated. We know that this is a PAT translation command because it maps to the previous `global (outside) 1` command, which only has one public address.

PIX firewalls allow return traffic in conjunction with the NAT statement. The NAT and state tables combine to let the firewall know which traffic is returning as part of an already started conversation.

The next statements are the defaults of a PIX configuration and were not added in this example. However, they are displayed to show the default timeouts for the NAT translation table (`xlate`), the connection listings (state table, `conn`), and user authentication traffic listings (`uauth`):

```
timeout xlate 3:00:00
timeout conn 1:00:00 half-closed 0:10:00 udp 0:02:00 rpc 0:10:00 h323 0:05:00 sip
➥0:30:00 sip_media 0:02:00
timeout uauth 0:05:00 absolute
```

> **Note**
>
> When you're troubleshooting broken connections through a PIX firewall, one good step is to raise the `xlate` timeout. If out-of-state traffic is seen getting dropped in the firewall logs, the `conn` timeout values may need adjusted.

These timeouts can be adjusted at any time by simply retyping the preceding commands with new timeout values.

The PIX Device Manager (PDM) has simplified PIX firewall management. The PDM is a GUI interface that's used to edit most of the PIX firewall's settings. It allows the editing of firewall access rules, NAT translation settings, host and network objects, and general firewall configuration changes. It also has a Monitoring section (see Figure 3.8) that allows the viewing of statistical information about the PIX and its performance as well as provides the ability to generate attractive exportable graphs.

To use the PDM, you simply have to add the appropriate PDM image to your PIX. This is done by copying the PDM file to the PIX's flash memory with the following command:

```
copy tftp://ipaddress/pdmfilename flash:pdm.
```

Here, *ipaddress* is the IP of the TFTP server holding the PDM image you are copying, and *pdmfilename* is the name of the PDM file. If there is already a PDM file on your PIX, it will be erased. Your PIX will need to be configured to allow HTTP access from any clients needing to do PDM administration. This is done as follows:

```
Pix(config)#http 10.0.0.1 255.255.255.255 inside
```

Here, 10.0.0.1 is the station you want to manage the PIX with. This is followed by a 24-bit mask so that it is the only station allowed to make contact. This could be any legal IP address mask allowing access from one to an entire network segment of addresses. Finally, the statement is ended with the name of the interface you want to manage the PIX through—preferably the inside interface!

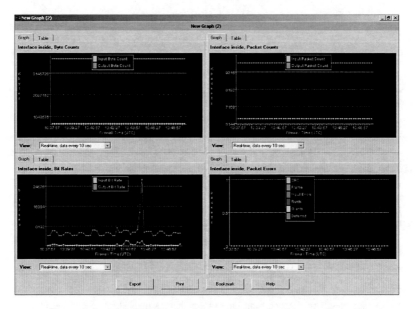

Figure 3.8   The PIX Device Manager's Monitoring tab allows the generation of aesthetically pleasing graphs that can be exported.

Now all you have to do is type `HTTPS://10.0.0.100` into the URL line of any web browser (where 10.0.0.100 is the IP address of the interface you specified in the HTTP access line). Be sure to specify HTTPS in your web browser! Trying to access the PIX via HTTP is disallowed and will return a "Page cannot be displayed" message. If your configuration was successful, you should be prompted to accept a certificate and then receive a pop-up window asking for authentication information. You can use any username and password you already have configured in your PIX for management, or if none are configured you can leave the Username box blank and type the PIX's enable password in the password box. You should be greeted with the PDM's home startup screen, as shown in Figure 3.9.

If you click the Configuration button, you will be taken to the area in the PDM where most of the important firewall rule and NAT management takes place. The Access Rules tab (see Figure 3.10) is where the firewall rules configured in your PIX can be viewed and edited.

> **Note**
>
> The first time you access the PDM, the configuration screen information may not be populated. If so, go to the File menu and choose Refresh PDM with the Running Configuration on the Firewall. You will be prompted that the PDM needs to query the PIX for the first time to get the information it needs to populate the PDM tabs. Thereafter, all information should appear as expected.

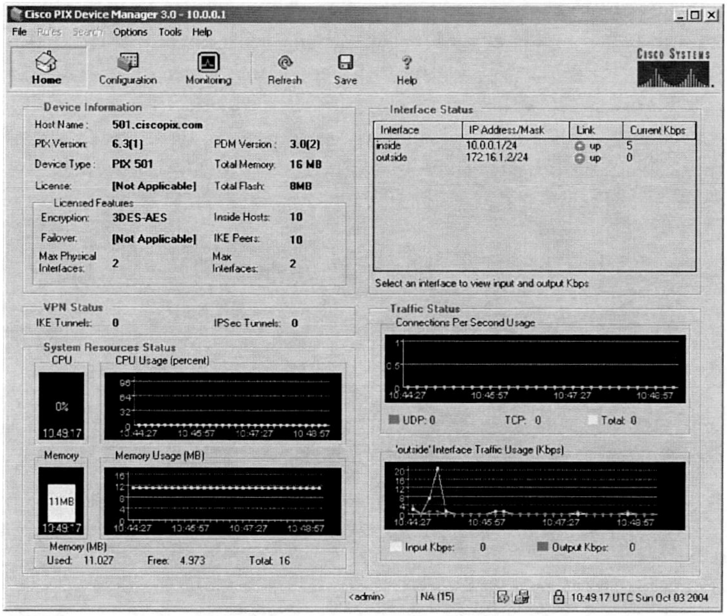

Figure 3.9 The PDM home page shows many useful pieces of information about your PIX, including version, license, and status information.

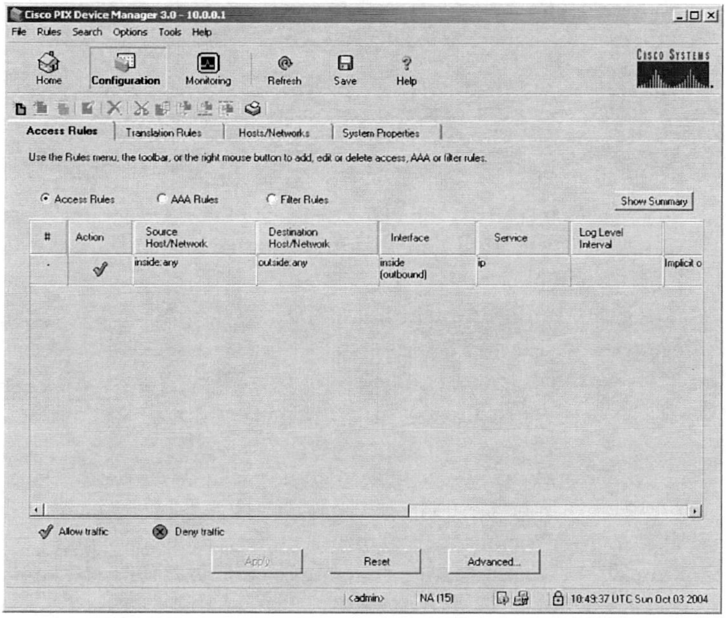

Figure 3.10 The Configuration section of the PDM allows viewing and editing of the access rules that make up the firewall policy.

If no specific rules have been added to the PIX, the Access Rules tab will appear, as shown in Figure 3.10, with the implicit permit rule for outbound traffic.

The Translation Rules tab shows the NAT configuration for the PIX firewall, per interface (see Figure 3.11). When the radio button Translation Rules is enabled, all NAT commands specified in the PIX and their associated global commands are displayed. Clicking the Manage Pools button allows you to edit the NAT pools for the given interface.

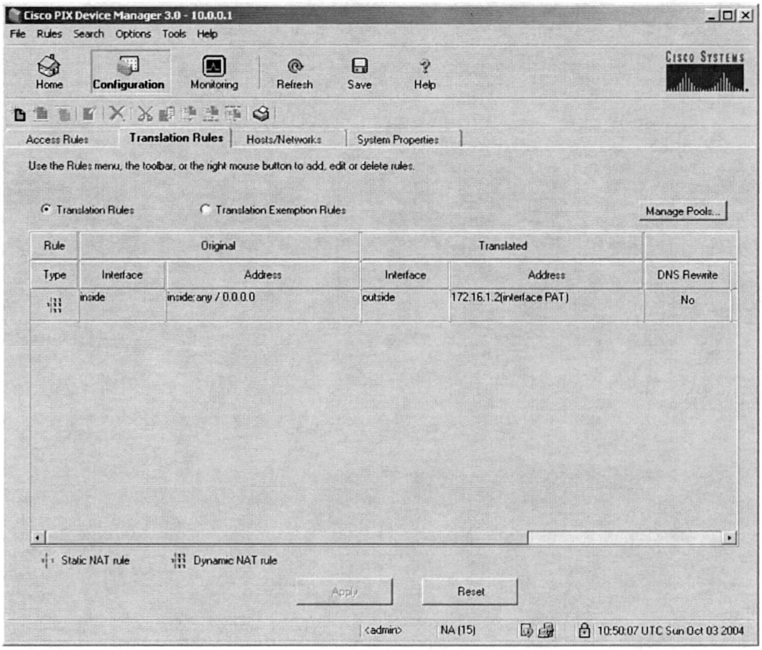

Figure 3.11   The PDM Translation Rules screen shows all NAT information for the PIX.

If the radio button Translation Exemption Rules is selected, the configuration of any NAT 0 commands in the PIX are displayed.

The Hosts/Networks tab is where objects can be viewed and edited for use in the PDM. These objects will be used to populate the access rules when creating a firewall policy.

Finally, you can perform many basic PIX administration tasks on the System Properties tab, including interface configuration, DHCP server and client configuration, logging and AAA settings, various management settings, and more. The PDM is an excellent tool to ease the administrative burden of the firewall for a PIX novice—or even a seasoned professional.

Now that 10Gb networking is being incorporated into the enterprise and Internet connection speeds are getting faster, the speed with which a firewall can statefully process information is becoming increasingly important. An exciting addition to the PIX line is the FireWall Services Module (FWSM). This is a full PIX firewall on a card that fits into an available slot in the 6500 series Cisco enterprise switches. It supports most of the features of the standard PIX but takes advantage of the port density and speed of the 6500. The bandwidth for connectivity is supplied by the backplane of the 6500 (which by default supports 32Gbps), letting the FWSM support an astounding throughput of up to 5.5Gbps! If that's not enough throughput for you, up to three more FWSMs can be added to the 6500 series chassis for a combined throughput of 20Gbps. The FWSM uses the VLAN interfaces of the 6500 for ingress and egress of traffic. In turn, the FWSM can support as many as 250 virtual interfaces!

Note

Be sure to use an up-to-date version of the FWSM code. Major vulnerabilities that could cause a DoS condition were announced in late 2003 (documented as CSCeb16356 and CSCeb88419). Both problems have been corrected in software version 1.1.3.

Virtual firewalls can be configured, allowing management of separate policies by different groups of administrators. The FWSM supports active-passive and active-active configurations as well as management via the PDM. When considering a means to protect intra-VLAN communication on a 6500 series switch or considering a solution in an enterprise environment that requires the maximum in throughput, you would be remiss not to take into account the power and flexibility of the FWSM.

High-Speed NetScreen Firewall Appliance

As network bandwidth requirements grow higher and content gets richer, the need for faster firewalls becomes greater. That is the focus of the Juniper Networks NetScreen firewall, which is an appliance-based stateful firewall that is particularly well-regarded due to its fast performance. Using specialized microchips called Application-Specific Integrated Circuits (ASICs), rather than relying solely on a central microprocessor, NetScreen is able to achieve very high throughput, especially on its carrier-class model. ASICs that are designed to perform a particular task are much more efficient and much faster then a processor running code to do the same task.

The core functions that NetScreen offers are typical for what you would expect of a stateful firewall aimed at the enterprise market. Along with the standard access control features, NetScreen also includes basic QoS capabilities, and integrated high speed VPN support (6 Gb/s throughput with 3DES as of this writing). NetScreen is also able to screen for and block some of the more popular network attacks such as the Ping of Death, Land and Teardrop attacks, as well as port scans and various types of network floods. Despite all of these features, the filtering and logging capabilities of the NetScreen still leave some room for improvement. Never-the-less, the NetScreen firewall's performance is demonstrative of ASIC-based firewall appliances becoming an integral part of network access control.

Summary

The firewall provides a secured method of controlling what information moves in to or out of a defined ingress/egress point of your network. This concept of a network "chokepoint" allows increased control and a single target for the monitoring and logging of network traffic. This extra control does come at a price: an overall cost in performance.

The stateful firewall adds intelligence to the packet-filtering method of network communication control. Stateful filtering has been popularly used to define the filtering of the state of packet flows based on information from Layers 4 and below. This definition is ambiguous because the amount of protocol information that is considered in the filtering can deviate among vendor implementations. Items such as source and destination IP addresses and port numbers, sequence and acknowledgment numbers, as well as flags and other Layer 4 information can all be considered.

Stateful inspection also monitors Layer 4 information (just like stateful filtering) and adds application-level examination to provide insight into the communication session. This offers a secure means to handle nonstandard TCP/IP traffic flows. Stateful inspection offers a much more secure environment than a "dumb" packet filter as well as performance advantages over a proxy firewall, making it an excellent compromise between the two technologies. However, the same features that give stateful application inspection a performance advantage over a proxy firewall also make it less secure in environments where all aspects of application-level communication must be considered.

In any case, the stateful firewall is an excellent fit as a single perimeter security solution for smaller environments. It performs well as a role player in larger or more complex environments where multiple firewall technologies are implemented. Clearly, the stateful firewall is a solid choice and a strong performer in the current network landscape. In the next chapter, we examine a way to filter network traffic by taking advantage of application-level restraints that can be implemented using proxy firewalls.

References

1 Check Point. "Stateful Inspection Technology Tech Note." http://www.checkpoint.com/ products/security/whitepapers/firewall-1_statefulinspection.pdf. March 2002.

2 Netfilter/IPTables Documentation. "What Is Netfilter?" http://www.iptables.org/ documentation. March 2002.

3 Fabrice Marie. "Netfilter Extensions HOWTO." http://netfilter.samba.org/ documentation/HOWTO//netfilter-extensions-HOWTO.html. March 2002.

4 Lance Spitzner. "Understanding the FW-1 State Table." November 29, 2000. http://www.spitzner.net//fwtable.html. March 2002.

5 Cisco Systems, Inc. "Cisco's PIX Firewall Series and Stateful Firewall Security." http://www.cisco.com/warp/public/cc/pd/fw/sqfw500/tech/nat_wp.pdf. March 2002.

4

Proxy Firewalls

In this chapter, we introduce you to proxy techniques and how they have been used to create proxy firewalls. Proxy firewalls serve a role similar to stateful firewalls. Both are designed to allow or deny access between networks based on a policy. The method they use to accomplish this is very different, though. As described in the last chapter, with a stateful firewall, network connections flow through the firewall if they are accepted by the policy. This type of firewall acts like a router, passing packets through that are deemed acceptable. In contrast, a proxy firewall acts as a go-between for every network conversation. Connections do not flow through a proxy. Instead, computers communicating through a proxy establish a connection to the proxy instead of their ultimate destination. The proxy then initiates a new network connection on behalf of the request. This provides significant security benefits because it prevents any direct connections between systems on either side of the firewall.

Proxy firewalls are often implemented as a set of small, trusted programs that each support a particular application protocol. Each proxy agent has in-depth knowledge of the protocol it is proxying, allowing it to perform very complete security analysis for the supported protocol. This provides better security control than is possible with a standard stateful firewall. However, you only receive this benefit for the protocols included with the proxy firewall. If you must allow the use of a protocol that your proxy firewall does not specifically support, you are reduced to using a generic proxy. Generic proxies do not have any in-depth knowledge of the protocols they proxy, so they can only provide basic security checks based on the information contained within the headers of the packets (IP address, port, and so on).

This chapter describes the basics of proxy firewalls and how they may fit into your security architecture. Although proxies are not as popular as they once were, they can still offer value when deployed appropriately. This chapter will help you to understand how proxies work, what their strengths and weaknesses are, and when you may want to use them.

Fundamentals of Proxying

A proxy acts on behalf of the client or user to provide access to a network service, and it shields each side from a direct peer-to-peer connection. Clients needing to communicate with a destination server first establish a connection to the proxy server. The proxy then establishes a connection to the destination server on the client's behalf. The proxy server sends data it receives from the client to the destination server and forwards data it receives from the destination server to the client. In the process of performing this role, the proxy server can examine the requests to ensure they are valid and allowed by the policy.

The proxy server is both a server and a client. It is a server to the client and a client to the destination server. One way to keep this straight is to call the listening end of the proxy the *listener* and the initiating side of the proxy the *initiator*. This leaves the terms *client* and *server* for the endpoints.

Another important issue is whether the proxy is transparent to the client. Originally, all proxy servers required clients to be aware of them. This meant that a client's software would need to include specific code to properly use a proxy, and the client would need to be configured to send its requests to the proxy. Client software that was not proxy aware could not communicate through the proxy.

Two approaches were used to overcome this software burden. First, an industry standard proxy protocol was developed. Called SOCKS, it allows client software developers to easily add proxy support to their products. We'll be covering SOCKS in more detail later in this chapter. The second approach was the development of transparent proxies. These products intercept connection requests by masquerading on the fly as the destination server being requested by the client. The transparent proxy then goes on to make the request to the destination server for the client. Using this method, the client is fooled into thinking that it is communicating directly with the server, while the proxy is actually handling the communications.

The following is an example of how a typical request from an internal client to an external server would be handled by a transparent proxy firewall:

1. The client requests an Internet service, such as HTTP, FTP, or Telnet.

2. The client computer starts by attempting to set up a session between the client and the server. Assuming the Internet service being requested is TCP based, this begins with the client sending out a SYN packet sourced from the client's IP address and destined to the server's IP address.

3. The proxy firewall intercepts the connection request and, if allowed by policy, replies with a SYN-ACK packet sourced from the destination server's IP address. It is important to mention that this does require the proxy to be on the network path between the client and the server.

4. Upon receipt of the proxy's SYN-ACK packet, the client finishes the three-way handshake by sending out the final ACK packet, again destined to the server's IP address. At this point, the client thinks it has a valid TCP connection to the external server. In reality, it only has a connection to the proxy.

5. The proxy is now responsible for establishing a connection to the external server. It accomplishes this by sending out a SYN packet sourced from its own IP address and destined to the external server. Upon receipt of the server's SYN-ACK packet, it replies with an ACK packet to establish the connection to the external server. At this point, the proxy has two valid TCP connections for the session: one between itself and the client, and the other between itself and the server.

6. Requests received over the client-proxy connection will be analyzed for correctness and policy compliance. If they are acceptable, the proxy will make a corresponding request using its proxy-server connection. Replies received over the proxy-server connection will also be analyzed for correctness and policy compliance and then, if acceptable, forwarded to the client over the proxy-client connection. This will continue until either side of the conversation terminates the connection.

A traditional, nontransparent proxy would similarly handle the request. However, there would be no need for the IP address manipulations required by the transparent proxy. Instead, the client would know about the proxy and would be able to send the request directly to the proxy server's IP address. In addition, because the client is proxy aware, if there are any special proxy functions for the client to choose from, the client can include this information in the request.

Proxy firewalls are often implemented as dual-homed bastion hosts running a set of proxy agents. Each agent supports one or more Internet protocols. The degree to which each agent understands the protocols it proxies determines how effective the agent can be in managing the connection. A generic agent that supports standard TCP protocols will likely only be able to restrict connections based on the TCP and IP headers (for example, IP address, port, TCP state). This functionality is similar to packet filter firewalls. However, if the protocol to be proxied is not standard, or if additional security functionality is desired, more sophisticated agents are required.

Note

Bastion hosts are systems that are expected to come under direct network attack, especially from the Internet. They are used to offer public services such as web, FTP, DNS, and email. Their exposed roles require them to be carefully hardened against attack. Chapter 9, "Host Hardening," provides a detailed description on how you can properly protect these exposed systems.

A good protocol to use as an example is the File Transfer Protocol (FTP). Remember from Chapter 2, "Packet Filtering," that FTP does not act like a standard TCP protocol. Instead, FTP uses two different TCP connections to enable file transfer. One (the command channel) is used to send instructions to the FTP server, the other (the data channel) is used to transfer files (see Figure 4.1). This makes it impossible to support FTP with a generic proxy. Unless the proxy agent was aware that this second TCP connection was needed, it would not be able to accept the second connection, blocking the FTP protocol from transferring files.

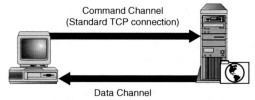

Command Channel
(Standard TCP connection)

Data Channel
(Initiated by Server on receipt of
RETR over Command Channel)

Figure 4.1   FTP requires two TCP connections
to transfer files across a network.

An agent specifically programmed to support FTP would be able to monitor the individual FTP commands being issued over the command channel. It would be able to watch for the command used to transfer a file and then begin listening for the TCP connection used to transfer the file. In addition, by being protocol aware, the agent has the ability to watch the FTP commands to detect suspicious activity.

FTP was created during the early days of the Internet, when security was not something the designers emphasized. The FTP protocol contains several, well-known security flaws that have been repeatedly exploited. Even today, it is not uncommon to locate FTP servers that are not properly protected. One classic flaw is related to how the data channel is set up between a client and a server.

When the client wants to request a file from the server, one option it has is to send a PORT command. PORT is used to configure the server to establish a TCP connection initiated from the server to the client. The format for the PORT command is as follows:

```
PORT h1, h2, h3, h4, p1, p2
```

The values h1 through h4 form an IP address (h1.h2.h3.h4). p1 and p2 are used to specify the destination port using the following formula:

$$256 \star p1 + p2$$

For example, if the client is at IP address 192.168.5.12, it might issue the command

```
PORT 192, 168, 5, 12, 4, 1
```

which would tell the server to transfer requested files to IP address 192.168.5.12 using TCP port 1025. To actually cause the connection to be established, the client uses the RETR command to request a file. At this point, the server will initiate the TCP session to the client on TCP port 1025 and transfer the file across the resulting connection.

The vulnerability is introduced because the client can provide any IP address and port to the PORT command. In some circumstances, this can allow an attacker to bypass firewall restrictions. We will use the network shown in Figure 4.2 to illustrate this attack. This network is composed of a screened subnet that contains a web server and an FTP server. To allow customers to upload files to the company, the FTP server is set up to allow anonymous connections. The web server is running a Telnet service to allow administrators to access the system from the internal network. Unfortunately, the Telnet service is susceptible to an invalid input attack that would allow anyone who connects to the service access to the computer without authentication. The good news is that the stateful inspection firewall is blocking all inbound network connections from the Internet except packets destined to TCP port 80 on the web server and TCP port 21 on the FTP server. This would prevent attackers from establishing a connection to the Telnet service running at TCP port 23 on the web server. On the surface it seems that even with the vulnerable Telnet service, the firewall has effectively kept the network secure. This is just an illusion, though, as the FTP server can be leveraged to reach the web server.

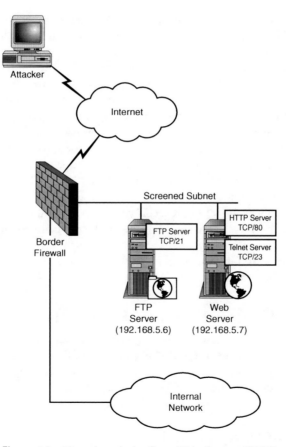

Figure 4.2   Even though the firewall blocks non-HTTP access to the web server, the FTP PORT command may allow attackers to access the web server's Telnet service.

The following steps would allow the attacker to bypass the firewall and attack the vulnerable web server:

1. Use a normal FTP connection to upload a file to the anonymous FTP server. This file needs to contain the exploit commands necessary to attack the web server.

2. Using the established FTP command channel, send the command PORT 192,168,5,7,0,23. This will tell the FTP server that the next file request should be sent to the web server using port 23 (for example, Telnet).

3. Again using the FTP command channel, send the RETR command specifying the name of the file transferred during step 1. This will cause the FTP server to initiate a TCP connection to the web server on port 23, then transfer the contents of the file over the connection.

Assuming the file contains the commands or data necessary to exploit the web server's Telnet service, the attacker will have successfully bypassed the firewall, gaining control of the web server.

A sufficiently sophisticated FTP proxy agent would have had little difficulty blocking this attack at step 2. When the agent receives the PORT command from the client, it could compare the parameters of the command to see if the IP address matches the IP address of the client. If it does not, the connection could be terminated and an alert generated. This is one example of how protocol-aware proxy agents can prevent vulnerabilities that would be difficult or impossible to eliminate using packet-filtering techniques.

Modern proxy firewalls provide proxy agents for a large set of Internet protocols. You can expect the core Internet protocols, such as HTTP, FTP, SMTP, DNS, and ICMP, to be supported by just about all the products. When selecting a proxy firewall, though, you should look carefully at the set of protocols your network will need to pass through the proxy. If a critical protocol is missing from the product you are considering, you may be able fall back to a generic proxy and live with the reduction in security enforcement. If the protocol you are trying to support is nonstandard (such as FTP), you may need to choose between the protocol and the firewall.

Pros and Cons of Proxy Firewalls

Proxy firewalls represent a balance between security and functionality. On the one side, well-written proxies offer security benefits that are significantly better than many other types of firewall technologies. However, they are often slower than other products, and they can limit what applications your network can support. In this section, we will itemize the advantages and disadvantages you should consider when choosing to use a proxy.

Advantages of Proxy Firewalls

Proxy firewalls have several advantages over other types of firewalls:

- Proxy firewalls provide comprehensive, protocol-aware security analysis for the protocols they support. By working at the application layer, they are able to make better security decisions than products that focus purely on packet header information.

- The topology of the internal protected network is hidden by proxy firewalls. Internal IP addresses are shielded from the external world because proxy services do not allow direct communications between external servers and internal computers. Although this can also be accomplished using Network Address Translation techniques, it occurs by default with proxy firewalls.

- Network discovery is made substantially more difficult because attackers do not receive packets created directly by their target systems. Attackers can often develop detailed information about the types of hosts and services located on a network by observing packet header information from the hosts. How different systems set fields such as the Time to Live (TTL) field, window size, and TCP options can help an attacker determine which operating system is running on a server. This technique, known as *fingerprinting*, is used by an attacker to determine what kinds of exploits to use against the client system. Proxies can prevent much of this activity because the attacking system does not receive any packets directly created by the server.

- Robust, protocol-aware logging is possible in proxy firewalls. This can make it significantly easier to identify the methods of an attack. It also provides a valuable backup of the logs that exist on the servers being protected by the proxy.

Proxy Firewall Log Discovers RingZero Trojan

The protocol-aware logging possible on proxy firewalls often leads to the early discovery of new exploits. Back in the fall of 1999, the defensive community noticed a large number of probes on ports TCP 80, 8080, and 3128. Analysts poured over router logs, but they could not figure out what was going on. However, Bill Royds in Canada detected similar activity on his proxy firewall. Here is one of the log entries he captured:

```
Oct 1 06:47:02 gate gwcontrol:
 201 http[3785494487]:
 access denied for smak.mplik.ru to www.rusftpsearch.net [default rule] [no
➥rules found]

Oct 1 06:47:02 gate httpd[7188]:
 121 Statistics: duration=0.15 id=w7Ii3 sent=357 rcvd=402
   srcif=hme1 src=195.58.0.243/61332 srcname=smak.mplik.ru
   dstif=hme1 dst=206.253.222.89/80 dstname=www.rusftpsearch.net
   op=GET
   arg=http://www.rusftpsearch.net/cgibin/pst.pl?
     pstmode=writeip&psthost=167.33.61.23&pstport=80
   result="403 Forbidden" proto=http (request denied by gwcontrol)
```

What this log entry shows is a client (smak.mplik.ru) trying to communicate through Bill's firewall to a web server (www.rusftpsearch.net). In addition, the web request reveals that the client was attempting to hand an IP address and port to the pst.pl program running on the web server. The contents of this log entry turned out to be critical in identifying a new Trojan horse program called RingZero (http://www.cnn.com/TECH/computing/9910/22/russian.trojan.horse.idg/).

What Bill's firewall caught was a message from a host infected by RingZero trying to report home. RingZero attempted to locate web servers and web proxies by scanning for hosts that have port 80, 8080, or 3128 open. When it found a live server, it reported this by connecting to the pst.pl program on www. rusftpsearch.net. By capturing this important application detail, Bill's proxy firewall led to the discovery of RingZero and the development of an effective response.

Disadvantages of Proxy Firewalls

Although proxy firewalls can provide increased security over packet-filtering firewalls, they do have their disadvantages. Here are some of the issues you should consider prior to fielding a proxy firewall:

- Proxy firewalls are not compatible with all network protocols. A new proxy agent must be developed for each new application or protocol to pass through the firewall. If the proxy product you choose does not provide support for a needed protocol, you may have to settle for a generic proxy. In some cases, even generic proxies may not work if the protocol is nonstandard.

- A reduction of performance occurs due to the additional processing requests required for application services. There is no such thing as a free lunch. The extra overhead implied by setting up two connections for every conversation, combined with the time needed to validate requests at the application layer, adds up to slower performance. In some cases, this can be balanced by choosing higher-end servers to run your proxy. However, for some extremely high-bandwidth networks, a proxy firewall may become a performance bottleneck.

- Virtual Private Networks (VPNs) may not function through a proxy firewall. As will be discussed further in Chapter 7, "Virtual Private Networks," VPN packet authentication will fail if the IP address of the sender is modified during the transmission. Although this is normally thought of as an issue with Network Address Translation, the same issue occurs with proxy firewalls. Of course, if the VPN endpoint is the firewall, this will not be a problem.

- The configuration of proxy firewalls can be more difficult than other firewall technologies. Especially when using older proxies, it can be difficult to properly install and configure the set of proxies necessary for your network.

It is also worth noting that the number of proxy firewall products on the market is decreasing. The commercial firewall industry is moving away from proxy firewalls, due mainly to performance and compatibility concerns. Many of these vendors are dropping their proxy product lines in exchange for stateful products that make use of Deep Packet Inspection techniques. These techniques, which we described in Chapter 3, "Stateful Firewalls," provide some, but not all of the benefits of proxy firewalls. Like proxy firewalls, Deep Packet Inspection allows security tests at the application layer. However, unlike proxies, it allows direct connections to occur between computer systems. As mentioned earlier, this makes it easier for attackers to perform operating system and application discovery. Deep Packet Inspection firewalls tend to be more flexible than proxies and they can be designed to handle very high-speed networks.

So far, we've looked into the basics of proxy servers and their role in developing a firewall solution. We've talked about how they operate and discussed some of their advantages and disadvantages. In this next section, we will talk about some of various ways proxy technologies are being used to secure networks.

Types of Proxies

Proxies can be used for several purposes. The classic use is as a proxy firewall located on the perimeter between the Internet and your private network. Proxies are not limited to this role though. Proxies can be used to accelerate web performance, provide remote access to internal servers, and provide anonymity for network conversations. In this section, we will highlight these other uses that can be made of proxy technology.

Web Proxies

Proxies are not just used to implement firewalls. One of their most popular uses inside a network is increasing web performance. Web conversations make up a large percentage of the traffic on many networks, so making the Web more efficient can have a dramatic impact on network operations. Proxies can help by monitoring web conversations and eliminating redundant requests. Web traffic is often characterized by frequent transmissions of nearly identical information. Some studies have shown that as much as half the requests for information across the Web are duplicates of other recent requests. Caching frequently requested web pages can dramatically speed up web browsing.

Proxy servers that provide web caching are often referred to as *proxy caches* or *web caches*. When a proxy cache is used, browsers are directed to make their HTTP requests to the proxy cache instead of directly to the destination web server (see Figure 4.3). The proxy then has the opportunity to determine whether it already has a copy of the requested information or if it needs to request a copy from the destination server. If the HTTP request is new, the proxy will make a TCP connection and HTTP request to the destination server, returning the resulting information to the browser and also storing a copy of the returned result for future use. Whenever any client of the proxy requests the same information, the proxy can reply using its local copy, eliminating the need to make a request from the destination server. This reduces network traffic as well as the load on the web server. However, it can introduce problems.

Caching works best when the information being retrieved does not change rapidly. However, some information is very time sensitive, such as stock quotes. This can cause problems if the client receives old information from the cache, when newer, more relevant data is available on the web server. The term for this is *freshness*. A file is "fresh" if the version on the cache is the same as the version on the web server. Web servers can specify when a file should no longer be considered fresh by placing an "Expires:" header in the returned request. This tells any caches being used (whether proxy or browser based) when to discard the file and request a new one. Many web servers do not provide good expiration guidance though. Because of this, it is important during the configuration of a proxy cache to establish good freshness policies.

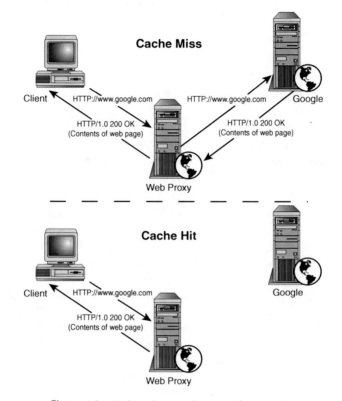

Figure 4.3 Web caches accelerate performance by eliminating unnecessary server requests.

Freshness policies are normally developed using several values associated with the file. The most important, if supplied by the web server, is the "Expires:" field. This field is part of the HTTP protocol and, if configured by the web administrator, is provided in the server's response to a browser request. It allows the website to provide specific guidance concerning when a file should be disregarded. When this information is not available, though, the web proxy server will need to look at other data to make a freshness decision. One simple method would be to set a fixed time to cache all files that lack "Expires:" headers. The problem with this approach is that many sites with dynamic content that do not support "Expires:" will not work correctly when cached. A better approach is to use the age of the file to determine how long to cache. If a file is received that is seconds old, you might not want to cache it because it is much more likely that it was dynamically generated. A file that is weeks old, though, is much less likely to change while its copy is held in the cache. Even with files that have not been modified for a long time, it is still a good idea to periodically refresh the cached files, so most web proxy servers set a maximum time a file can be considered fresh.

Another benefit that can be gained through web proxies is control over where users can browse. Security and productivity can be increased by limiting access to non-organization-related web browsing. It is not uncommon for viruses, worms, and other types of malicious code to be introduced into a protected network based on files downloaded by users from inappropriate websites. By limiting what sites users can reach, you can decrease the chance that this will happen to your network. Placing restrictions on browsing has also been shown to increase productivity by taking away the temptation to spend excessive time surfing the Web. However, not all organizations will want to or be able to place restrictions on user web behavior. Before considering web filtering, you must examine your site's policies and procedures regarding user web access. Often your Human Resources and Legal departments will need to be involved.

One last item to discuss with web proxies is the logging they can provide. As we showed earlier with RingZero, proxy logging can be very useful in detecting malicious activity on your network. With a web proxy, all the URLs that browsers request can be used for intrusion analysis. Looking for requests that do not appear normal can be a powerful method to discover attacks against your network. Often your proxy logs will contain the first indications that your network is under attack. Things to look for include excessive requests for files that do not exist on your web servers (such as those that return 404 errors). This can indicate that someone is scanning your websites looking for vulnerable software. Also looking for excessively long URL requests, or requests that contain special characters, can indicate that someone is attacking your site. If you do discover that someone has successfully attacked your site, these logs can also be invaluable at discovering what weakness led to the compromise, how extensive the damage is, and (rarely) who is responsible.

Reverse Proxies

Firewalls are frequently thought of as devices that restrict access, not enable it. However, proxy techniques can be used for both. If you have a need to support remote Internet users, reverse proxies can be the answer.

Reverse proxies are used to provide controlled access for external (normally Internet-based) users to internal servers. They act as a trusted intermediary that external users must use to gain access to internal servers that would not normally be Internet accessible. An external user attempting to gain access to an internal server first connects and authenticates to the reverse proxy. Normally this is done over a Secure Sockets Layer (SSL) connection to provide confidentiality and integrity for the session. If authentication is successful, the proxy will check its policy to see whether the user is allowed to access the requested server. If so, it will begin proxying the connection for the user.

The type of internal servers that can be accessed using a reverse proxy vary depending on the sophistication of the proxy. Simple reverse proxies can only support web-based services. These products are basically normal web proxies that have been enhanced to support user authentication. In many cases, they are sufficient because many sites provide a significant amount of their network content using web systems. If you are trying to grant access to other applications that do not have a web interface, you may need to work harder.

One approach is placing a web interface on top of the application you are trying to proxy. Once the application is web enabled, normal reverse proxy techniques can be used to grant remote access. An example of this is Microsoft's Outlook Web Access (OWA). OWA is part of Microsoft Exchange and provides a web version of the Outlook mail and calendaring application. Any clients who can make a web connection to the OWA application will be able to use most Outlook functions. In fact, it can be difficult to recognize that you're accessing Outlook through a browser because the interface you are interacting with inside the browser so closely resembles the desktop version of Outlook. OWA combined with a reverse proxy provides a secure mail and calendaring solution for remote users.

Alternatively, you can roll the web-enabling technology together with a reverse proxy. This is the approach taken by Citrix MetaFrame. Citrix allows common desktop and server applications to be accessed by web browsers, including applications such as Microsoft Word and Adobe Acrobat. In fact, Citrix can proxy an entire user desktop through a browser, giving a user experience that is highly similar to sitting in front of the actual computer. Citrix also provides extensive management controls, including role-based access to internal applications. Although a capable product, it is not necessarily cheap and simple to implement. If you're considering technologies such as Citrix, make sure to include acquisition and operational costs in your analysis. In some cases, though, Citrix-like products can actually save you money by allowing shared access to products too expensive to place on every user's desktop.

Anonymizing Proxies

Privacy can be an important security service but can be a hard commodity to come by on the Internet. Almost all actions taken on a computer leave a digital trail. If you don't want someone else following that digital trail back to you, an anonymizing proxy may be the answer.

Anonymizing proxies work exactly like normal proxies, but are used for the purpose of protecting your identity while you use services across the Internet. Your requests are forwarded to the anonymizing proxy (usually over an SSL connection), which hides your identifying details (such as IP address) by making the request on your behalf. The destination server you are using only learns about the proxy's information and does not learn who actually made the request. This assumes that you do not pass anything identifying in the actual request.

Also assumed is that no one is monitoring the anonymizing proxy. If they were, they might be able to match incoming requests to outgoing requests, breaching an important aspect of the connection's privacy. This is especially easy to do if the proxy is not busy. If yours is the only IP address connected to the proxy, it's not terribly hard to guess who it is making requests through the proxy!

Various approaches have been used to solve this problem. One of the most popular is *proxy chaining*. Tools such as SocksChain (http://www.ufasoft.com/socks) can be used to build connections through multiple anonymizing proxies. An observer at the first proxy in the chain will only see that you are sending a request to the anonymizer, but will not learn the destination because the next hop will only be another anonymizer. In this way, the ultimate destination of your request is hidden from any outside observers (see Figure 4.4). Another approach along the same lines is Onion routing (http://www.onion-router.net), which combines proxy chaining with multiple layers of encryption to ensure that a conversation cannot be followed through the proxy nodes.

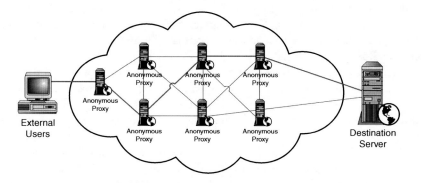

Figure 4.4   Proxy chains allow private communications by hiding the true source and destination of a packet from network eavesdroppers.

If you are in need of an anonymizer service, but do not want to set your own up, preexisting services are available on the Internet. Searching on Google for "anonymizers" will return many sites offering this privacy service. However, caveat emptor: You should trust that they maintain your privacy slightly less than you trust them.

A perfect case in point is the Java Anonymous Proxy (JAP). JAP is a anonymizer service run as a joint effort of the Dresden University of Berlin, the Free University of Berlin, and the Independent Centre for Privacy Protection, Schleswig-Holstein, Germain. It is available at http://anon.inf.tu-dresden.de/index_en.html. Back in July of 2003, it was discovered that they had, as a result of a court order, added code to JAP that was designed to monitor access to certain IP addresses. Whenever a user of the service accessed one of these forbidden sites, a message was generated recording the who, what, and when and sent to the police. This hidden behavior was uncovered several days later by an observant user of the service, but until this discovery was made, users of the JAP service were getting less privacy than they thought. For the record, the current version of JAP is supposed to be free of any tattle-tail code.

Tools for Proxying

Many available applications provide proxy capabilities. We've already mentioned some of them while describing proxy capabilities. However, it's becoming harder to find pure proxy products on the market. The major commercial vendors have embraced hybrid technologies that combine proxy and stateful technologies, making it harder to identify when proxy techniques are used in their products. Mergers and acquisitions in the field have also added confusion to this subject. A classic example of this is the Gauntlet firewall. Gauntlet was one of the first, and most popular, proxy firewalls. Originally created by TIS, its technology was first acquired in 1998 by Network Associates, Inc (NAI). NAI continued to sell the products under the Gauntlet name. In 2002 though, NAI sold Gauntlet to Secure Computing, which already owned a competing firewall called Sidewinder. Secure Computing then integrated both products together to create a hybrid product. If you were to read the marketing literature for this product (which retains the Sidewinder name), you would not see any reference to proxies. How do we know there is any proxy technology left in it? Well, certain keywords keep popping up that can clue you in. These include terms such as *secure gateway services* and *application layer protocol analysis*. The bottom-line impact of all this market activity is you are going to need to ask and to experiment to determine how commercial products protect your network.

In the rest of this section, we'll talk about some important proxy technologies. We'll start with one of the proxies that started it all: the Firewall Toolkit. In addition, we'll cover an important proxy-enabling technology called SOCKS. Finally, we'll cover Squid, the most popular open source web proxy.

Firewall Toolkit (FWTK)

Firewall Toolkit was one of the first proxy firewalls. It was developed by Trusted Information Systems (TIS) under an Advanced Research Projects Agency (ARPA) grant, and it was first released in October of 1993. The key technology of FWTK was used to create the first version of the Gauntlet firewall. FWTK is still available at http://www.fwtk.org, but has not been updated for many years. In fact, version 2.1, the last update, was released in early 1998, and there are no current plans to extend it further. Still, it can be used to implement a useful proxy firewall, especially if you do not need to support many protocols.

FWTK is available in source code, which is an important part of its appeal. Anyone from a security analyst to a potential attacker can review its design to look for defects. TIS referred to this as a *crystal box design*, a term coined by one of its first customers. In a crystal box design, nothing about the design is hidden. Therefore, the security of the system is totally dependent on the quality of the design, not any secrets buried inside the design. Put another way, FWTK does not depend on security through obscurity.

This same approach has been followed in the cryptographic community for decades. The belief is that if a design has not been peer-reviewed by the cryptographic community, no one should have any confidence in its security. This might seem an arrogant point of view, until you look at the history of proprietary cryptographic systems. To save you some research, they have not faired very well. This is something to consider when you select the products you will use to secure your network. It is important to remember that FWTK is currently unsupported. This, and the fact that it does not support many modern protocols (such as H.323), would make it a poor choice for an enterprise firewall. However, if your network does not require protocols unsupported by FWTK, and you are interested in learning the nuts and bolts of proxy implementation, FWTK can be an effective product.

SOCKS

As we discussed at the beginning of this chapter, SOCKS is a proxy toolkit that enables applications to be proxied without requiring specific proxy code to be re-created for each client application. Many proxy products support the SOCKS protocol, allowing any SOCKS-enabled client to make use of the proxy's services. This includes providing access to hosts on the other side of the SOCKS server without requiring direct IP connectivity. The SOCKS server performs authentication and authorization functions on requests, establishes proxy connections, and relays data between hosts. A SOCKS proxy server licensed for noncommercial use is available for free from http://www.socks.permeo.com/.

For applications to work with the SOCKS proxy server, they must be "SOCKS-ified." Most of the work involved in doing this has been packaged into the SOCKS software development kit (SDK). A reasonably skilled network application developer would have little difficulty adding SOCKS functionality to an application using the SDK.

SOCKS has evolved over time and gone through several revisions. SOCKS version 4 was the first popular version of SOCKS and is still in use. However version 5 adds important features, including the support of UDP proxying as well as a variety of authentication methods. The Internet Engineering Task Force (IETF) approved SOCKSv5 as the standard (RFC 1928) generic, proxy protocol for TCP/IP-based networking applications.

SOCKS is more of an enabling technology than a product in its own right. Many client software packages already support SOCKS. If they do, you can securely manage connectivity, authentication, and access control to them using any SOCKS-compliant proxy. Examples of common proxy servers that support SOCKS are Squid (described in the following section, "Squid"), Apache's mod_proxy module, and Permeo's proxy products. If you have an application that does not support SOCKS that you would like to add proxy support to, using the SOCKS API is a relatively quick and effective way of adding a robust proxy implementation to your product.

SOCKS Version 4

The SOCKSv4 protocol defines the message format and conventions to allow TCP-based application users transparent access across a firewall. During proxy connection setup, the SOCKS server grants access based on TCP header information, including IP addresses and source and destination host port numbers. The SOCKS server also authorizes users using Ident (RFC 1413) information.

SOCKS Version 5

The SOCKS version 5 protocol, also known as *authenticated firewall traversal (AFT)*, is an open Internet standard (RFC 1928) for performing network proxies at the transport layer. It resolves a few issues that SOCKS version 4 protocol did not fully address or omitted:

- **Strong authentication**—The SOCKSv5 authentication method negotiation is handled by the SOCKSv5 client/server communication. The application client identifies the authentication methods it can support to the SOCKSv5 server. The SOCKSv5 server, in turn, sends a message to the client identifying the authentication method the client should use. The authentication method is also determined based on the security policy defined in the SOCKSv5 server configuration. If the client's supported authentication methods fail to meet the security requirements of the proxy's policy, the SOCKSv5 server denies communication.

- **Address resolution proxy**—SOCKSv5's built-in address resolution proxy simplifies DNS administration and facilitates IP address hiding and translation. SOCKSv5 clients can pass the name, instead of the resolved address, to the SOCKSv5 server, and the server resolves the address for the client.

- **Proxy for UDP-based applications**—SOCKSv5 supports UDP association by creating a virtual proxy circuit for UDP-based application data.

There are two additional SOCKSv5-related standards to support authentication methods:

- Username/password authentication for SOCKSv5 (RFC 1929)
- GSS-API (Generic Security Service Application Programming Interface) authentication for SOCKSv5 (RFC 1961)

Squid

Squid is a highly regarded open source web proxy project. It provides high-performance proxy caching for HTTP, HTTPS, and FTP. Squid can be used in several web proxy scenarios. Its most frequent use is to cache browser requests for a site to accelerate and control web conversations. However, it is equally useful as a web server accelerator and as a reverse proxy server.

Squid was designed to run under UNIX and has been successfully compiled on a broad set, including Linux, FreeBSD, OpenBSD, Mac OS/X, Sun Solaris, IBM AIX, and HP-UX. (Note that this is only a partial list.) It can also be compiled to run under Windows if used in conjunction with the Cygwin (http://www.cygwin.com) and Mingw (http://www.mingw.org) packages. Squid is available at http://www.squid-cache.org.

Summary

In this chapter, we have examined the various ways that proxy technology can be used to secure your perimeter. We described how proxies work as well as some of their advantages and disadvantages. We also discussed proxy caching, how it can be used to accelerate network performance, provide secure remote access, and offer anonymity services.

Proxies can provide unparalleled network protection. They are considered by many to be the most secure type of firewall, providing better application layer protection than other techniques, including excellent protection against attacker network-discovery methods. The commercial firewall market, though, seems to be moving away from pure proxy solutions. Their perceived inflexibility and performance limitations have relegated them to smaller roles within many networks. That being said, keep in mind that many security techniques and services can be employed together to complement and enhance each other's capabilities. When used where they make the most sense, proxies can still provide tremendous value.

5

Security Policy

WHEN YOU TALK TO VENDORS OR ATTEND a security course, they tell you to do this or that according to your site's security policy, but they rarely attempt to explain what a security policy is or how to write or evaluate one. This is why we have included this chapter in the book. Firewalls and other perimeter devices are active security policy–enforcement engines. As we examine the material, we discuss the fact that organizations often have unwritten policies. In the first half of this chapter, we explore the task of mapping policy to perimeter architectures and translating policy to enforceable firewall rules. In the second half of this chapter, we consider an approach to developing policy that requires understanding authority, scope, expiration, specificity, and clarity. Developing and implementing policy is not easy, which is why we explicitly cover the hallmarks of good policy and bad policy.

> **Note**
>
> "A security policy establishes what you must do to protect information stored on computers. A well-written policy contains sufficient definition of 'what' to do so you can identify and measure or evaluate 'how.'"[1]

Firewalls Are Policy

The yin and yang of perimeter security policy can be referred to as access and control. When you come to fully understand these, it is hard to think of an access control list (ACL) in the same way. The point of a network is to provide access. *Access* pertains to accessibility—providing service, performance, and ease of use. *Control* focuses on denial of unauthorized service or access—separation, integrity, and safety. At one point as a community, we thought that two basic perimeter policy models existed:

- Everything is denied except that which is specifically permitted.
- Everything is permitted except that which is specially denied.

That sounds good, but it is bogus. In truth, one policy exists:

- Everything is denied except that which is specifically permitted or that which gets in anyway.

Let's illustrate this with the simple case of making the access control decision on the destination port. For example, if the destination is TCP port 27374 (the default port for SubSeven 2.2), and 27374 isn't on the allow list, control is applied, and the packet is dropped. Internally, what is happening? The firewall scoots to the second 16-bit field in the TCP header and grabs the destination port to compare it to its access control policy. What if the packet is a fragment? Only the first fragment has protocol information. Let's say this is the runt, the last fragment of the original datagram, but it arrives first. We aren't going to make an access control decision on 27374; it isn't there. To be sure, we can make many decisions when dealing with a fragment:

- Consult our state table to see if this is part of an existing connection.
- Buffer the fragment, reassemble the datagram, and then make the access control decision.
- Let the fragment through, but engage rate limiting to minimize harm.
- If outbound ICMP unreachables are disabled, let the fragment through.
- Drop the fragment and make the sender retransmit.

Firewall rules look simple when we are looking at a Check Point FireWall-1 GUI, but underneath there might be many complex decisions and assumptions. Complexity is the enemy of enforceable, consistent policy. Sometimes the result is that we are actually granting access when we think we are applying control. This is a case of unenforceable policy.

Access and Security Illustrated

Several years ago, I was talking with a perimeter analyst who was responsible for the site security policy for the Naval Space Command. He was overseeing the installation of a new application gateway firewall, a Sidewinder from Secure Computing. He wasn't sure what his organization should set for a security policy, so he decided to block everything and sit by the phone to see who called. This succeeded handily in providing security, but it fell a bit short in providing access. To this day, when I am reviewing an architecture, I cannot help but remember this approach.

Active Policy Enforcement

You can argue with your security officer or your boss, but you can't argue with the firewall. The firewall is a genuine policy-enforcement engine, and like most policy enforcers, it is none too bright. Much of this chapter is devoted to unenforceable policy. We are going to show that sometimes the problem is the firewall's limitations, but sometimes the firewall doesn't stand a chance. If you believe that a firewall can protect you, by the end of this section you should have some serious doubt. Often, the firewall is unable to enforce the site's policy; if you do not have defense in depth, you are running at a high risk.

Unenforceable Policy

One thing you should try to be sensitive to is unenforceable policy. We will first paint the picture clearly with nontechnical organizational examples, but then show how it is possible to create situations in which policy is unenforceable with perimeter systems. At one time, the U.S. Government had a policy that mandated "no personal use of Government computers." During the time of mainframes (ancient computers that were the size of a house with less processing power than an Intel 386), that was probably enforceable.

Times changed. By 1985, almost all technical workers had at least one personal computer or workstation on their desktops. The world had changed, but the policy hadn't. When people have their own operating and file systems, the rule of no personal use is unenforceable. Have you ever known you needed to finish that documentation, but on your way to bring up the word processor, clicked your email icon to check your mail for a second and neglected to get back to the document for an hour? Or brought up Google to look up one thing, saw something else that looked interesting, and never found the original fact? With tools like this, is "no personal use" possible? No way! That becomes an unenforceable policy—policy that is written but cannot be enforced. Unenforceable policy, whether unrealistic administrative policy or failed perimeter policy enforcement, is not a good thing.

Unofficial Official Policy

I still remember working for the Defense Mapping Agency, now the National Imagery and Mapping Agency (NIMA). Just before the Christmas holidays, we used to load a game of *Star Trek* on the Digital PDP 1170s for about two days. The game was primitive by today's standards, but these were huge graphics terminals used to edit maps. Playing *Star Trek* on these computers was the coolest thing I had ever seen. After the Christmas party, we would remove the game and search the file system for any file that was the same size as the game in case it had been copied and renamed.

I asked the system administrator, "Why can't we leave it on there for slow nights when we get our work done early?" He informed me that the head of the topography department was a powerful and authoritarian man and I really didn't want to cross him. He created an unofficial policy that we could play *Star Trek* for two days, but it had to be completely removed after the Christmas party. This is known as an *administrative control*.

Administrative controls don't work. During the years I was at the Mapping Agency, the game would pop up now and again. We would find the game and remove it, but there was no way to actively and consistently enforce the *Star Trek* policy.

The Effect of Unenforceable Policy

If you have an unenforceable administrative policy, then people are encouraged to either ignore it or push the rules. In fact, one of the reasons that attacks are so widespread is that many laws against them are virtually unenforceable, especially because some courts have ruled that the reconnaissance phase, scanning, is legal. Another classic unenforceable policy is a requirement to report all malicious code infections. After the problem is cleaned up, the tendency is to move on with life. The security office has no way of knowing how many infections the organization has. One Navy group went to a central antivirus console so that infections were automatically reported by the workstations. It went from seven reports the year before to more than 1,000 with the console. As a general rule, any policy that does not have a method to collect information and controls, the tools we use for enforcement, is probably unenforceable.

If You Were Told to Enforce "No Personal Use," Could You Do It?

I was once asked this question. It would be hard to get to a 100% solution, but I could block all incoming or outgoing traffic that wasn't to or from a .mil, .gov, or .int (NATO) address, and that would take care of a lot. This is some serious control!

In the case of no personal use, just like our simple example of making the access control decision on the destination port, we have those complicated cases such as fragmentation to deal with. Users might have the following types of questions:

- What if my wife sends me an email? Is it okay to read it?
- Can I check on my stocks at lunch?

The answer is, "Yes, these things are okay." The U.S. Government has retreated to a position called "limited personal use." Limited personal use is enforceable through a number of firewalls and other perimeter tools. One of the better examples of a limited personal use policy can be found at http://www.opm.gov/extra/itusepolicy.htm. In essence, this says that you can use your Government computer for personal use. Don't ask, don't tell, and don't overdo the personal use. Don't send chain letters, fundraise, or pass sexual, racist, or illegal files.

If you were assigned to enforce limited personal use, could you do it? Subscription-based services that have sets of banned URLs are available. You can load a set for sites that are banned because they have sexual content, and another set for hate speech, and so on. These go by names such as CYBERsitter and Net Nanny and are available for desktops and firewalls. They are known to be inflexible; they tend to apply control when they should be allowing access. For a while, it was a common sport on the Internet to make these tools look bad because they stopped web queries for "breast feeding" and so forth. Also, sometimes they allow access when they should apply control, such as a URL they don't know when the site is a bit cagey. That is why you have to pay the money for the subscription; if you want the tool to work, you have to keep it up to date. Most K–12 school systems employ these tools on their perimeters, and there we see one of the most extreme examples of the harmful effect of unenforceable policy. Kids become heroes by going through an open proxy to download porn directly to the library workstations. The good news is that progress is on the horizon, with content-aware tools such as MIMEsweeper for Web from Clearswift, but these tools are expensive and come with their own headaches. Are you starting to believe that complexity is the enemy of enforceable, consistent policy?

We have gone from administrative controls, such as manually searching for banned software, to perimeter tools that have protection-oriented security controls, such as blocking banned URLs. In our next section, we explore the ways we can create or find unenforceable policy in the perimeter. These problem vectors include coding errors, lack of understanding what the policy should be, web tunneling, email attachments, disks in briefcases, and every kind of backdoor you can imagine.

Vectors for Unenforceable Policy

If unenforceable policy is a problem because it enables people to access things that we would prefer to control, then we want to minimize it. On the organizational, administrative level, we can review our policies to see if they meet the criteria of good policy that we discuss later in this chapter. On the technical side, we can use tools such as PacketX and hping2 to throw crazy packets at the perimeter and see what gets through. What kind of packets? Try short fragments, or TCP packets with odd code combinations or every possible option set. This can alert us to how the assumptions and design decisions underneath the rules we are able to write are working. In addition to a fire-walking-type assessment, it is a good idea to ask yourself what vectors might allow unenforceable policy to manifest itself. We are the most likely culprits. Sometimes we forget how firewall rules are processed, or we add them willy-nilly.

Unwittingly Coding Unenforceable Policy

Have you ever heard the saying, "I know it is what I asked for, but it isn't what I wanted!"? This happens to firewall administrators, the folks who write firewall rules, all too often. Many times we get what we asked for, but not what we wanted, when our firewall has complex firewall rules. After all, a seemingly simple set of rules has underlying assumptions and rules, so a complex set of rules makes it pretty likely that a firewall administrator might accidentally arrange the rules in such a way that the firewall cannot enforce the policy that the administrator thinks he has defined. This is the reason you hear recommendations such as "never have more than 20 rules." That sounds good, but what if you live in the real world? You might need a bit more than 20 rules.

Firewall administrators become aware of unwittingly coding unenforceable firewall policy when they run into their first case of self-inflicted denial of service. Such denial of service often happens simply because we fail to create a match before the default deny all–style rule. The following are some examples of common errors you might make, with the first example showing the incorrect way to allow HTTP and FTP traffic:

```
allow tcp from any to any 80
allow tcp from any to any 21
deny tcp from any to any
```

The classic mistake here is forgetting FTP's data channel on port 20. That is easy, and in a three-rule set, we pick it up in seconds. In a 40-rule set, however, it might not be so easy.

Another simple mistake you might make is to write a broad match before a deny. The administrator intends to stop HTTP and FTP, but he writes an allow rule first and the intended deny rules are never processed. This is easy to see in a three-rule set, but it is much harder in a large rule set.

```
allow tcp from any to any
deny tcp from any to any 80
deny tcp from any to any 21
```

If you have a fairly large rule set, pour a cup of coffee, sit down, pay close attention to the keyword any, and ensure that you know exactly what kind of matching your firewall has (best fit, or the first or last rule to match wins). You are off to the races!

No Up-front Policy

The simple mistakes we just examined are why firewall books and instructors always stress that the first thing to do is to examine your site's policy and then create the rule set. If you just turn the firewall on and start adding rules, it is pretty easy to stuff an allow after a deny, or vice versa. It really pays off to write a rule set from the ground up. If you are not comfortable with the policy-first methodology we show in this book, create your own rule set, test it, test it some more, and stick with it. However, even with good rules that are properly organized, a policy can be subverted or made unenforceable through those two Mack truck–sized holes living at TCP ports 80 and 25.

TCP Port 80

Most of us configure our firewalls to allow outbound port 80 (HTTP, or the World Wide Web). If you go to your favorite search engine and do a search on "tunnel port 80," you will find enough to curl your hair. From GNU httptunnel to custom web tunnels to emerging Internet standards, an abundance of tools and techniques is available to encapsulate any kind of network traffic imaginable in packets that appear to be HTTP. Applications such as instant messaging (IM) and peer-to-peer (P2P) file sharing clients can typically use a variety of ports, including port 80, so that they can find a way out through firewalls.

Many client applications and tunneling tools aren't just using port 80; they are actually encoding their traffic in HTTP with get, put, POST, and markup language tags. Can the fake or encapsulated traffic be detected? Sometimes it can, but it is pretty difficult, and keyword searches or content inspectors are the best shot. This is a case where your organizational policy really matters. Either you are going to allow HTTP tunneling or you are not. Tunneling is usually for the purpose of evading the firewall, so let's say you don't. If you do catch someone, then your organizational policy needs to state clearly that the individual's head will be mounted on a pole outside the main entrance of the building as a deterrent to others. Port 80 tunneling generally requires intent by someone on the inside; email, however, is the most amazing policy destruction technology of all time.

Email

The primary policy problems with email include users sending sensitive information or binary attachments, automated forwarding, and over-responsive email clients.

Sensitive Information

I did a project for the U.S. Military once in which I collected nothing but the source, destination, and subject lines of outbound email for a month. I ran that through a keyword search for sensitive technologies. I will never forget watching the color drain from the face of a battle-tested senior officer as I showed him the results. Fortunately, it was only a 4.4-billion-dollar-a-year weapons program; it would be a real shame if we were talking serious money. This organization had an unenforceable policy: "Never send sensitive information unencrypted over the Internet." However, these merry tricksters didn't give their users any way to encrypt; they were against Pretty Good Privacy (PGP), and they had been implementing Public Key Infrastructure (PKI) for about five years.

As email has become a primary means of communication, we have become more familiar with it and less aware of the risks. As a rule of thumb, before an employee has finished drinking his first cup of coffee, he will attach and send any file you ask for and never remember that he did it.

Don't you just love those cute greeting card programs that people send back and forth? Ever wonder if they might do more than whir or chirp? Malicious materials in email can be detected by content scanners at the perimeter, especially antivirus software. (Some organizations use two types of scanners, because one scanner may pick up a virus and the other may miss it.) The Royal Canadian Mounted Police has the handle on binary attachments. Whether documents or programs, the Royal Canadian Mounted Police refuses them all and sends polite notes from its perimeter saying it doesn't accept attachments. Most of us lean way too far in the direction of access over control when it comes to email.

Outlook is the quintessential unenforceable policy engine; if it receives an email from some unknown party, it happily accepts the email's programming instructions. If someone is running Outlook internally, it is probably impossible to secure the perimeter.

Let's say you are in some super-duper secure place, such as the CIA or NSA. In the above-ground world, some wacky macro virus like Melissa variant 2,000,012 is jumping from address book to address book, and suddenly the same behavior starts on your classified network that is airgapped from the Internet! What happened? It's a good bet that infected media is being passed among systems.

Lessons That Melissa Taught Us

Before Melissa and Lovebug, not everyone understood how dangerous Outlook's behavior was. I still remember the day I saw the future and shook my head in disbelief. A friend was testing a personal firewall. Someone had sent her an email message with a URL. Outlook kindly retrieved the URL as soon as she highlighted the message so she didn't have to wait for the picture of a flower to which the URL pointed. When Outlook tried to get the flower, her ZoneAlarm alerted. I asked myself, "If Outlook will do that, what else will it do?" Even today as I write this, years after many crazy security flaws and Microsoft Office macro exploits, the answer seems to be, "Anything the sender wants it to." In this form-over-function world, I suppose organizations will continue to choose HTML-aware, macro-extendable programs such as Outlook, but I could live with plain, printable ASCII text in email if I had to.

Very Large, Very High-Latency Packets

When we do site security assessments, one of the things we like to do is the hurricane backup test. The idea is simple: A class five hurricane is expected to hit the site in 3–5 hours. Senior management directs that they get a backup of all the data out to a safe location in advance of the hurricane. After some initial scurrying, they start to run backups and load backup tapes. A classic old trick is to wait till they are about loaded and then ask, "Did you get all the data?" They usually nod yes. "What about the data on the user's local drives?" "That's the user's responsibility," they reply. "We back up the servers." "Ummm, and where will you be without your top salesman's contact list, or your CIO's notes?" In general, there is hopping around and a discussion of running to Costco to buy all the zip drives and disks they have. After some flapping, the hurricane only an hour away, we have to leave with whatever backups we have.

The first time we did this and watched the van loaded with all the tapes head off to discover whether cold backup sites really work, the guy standing next to me commented, "Wow, when disks are in motion, you can think of them as very large, very high-latency packets!" As a security analyst, this is a significant vector to defeat our perimeter's active policy enforcement. VLVHLPs fit in shirt pockets, briefcases, any number of form factors. One thing is certain: Every variation of sneaker net—physically moving data around on foot or by vehicle—has the capability to evade perimeter defenses. In fact, several of us on the team have worked in a number of secure facilities where disks are supposed to be registered as they go in and out, and they supposedly have spot checks, but in 20 years, we have never been stopped.

When the terrorists attacked the World Trade Center on September 11, 2001, several cold site vans were circling the blocks as administrators raced to get the VLVHLPs out of the trade center and surrounding buildings. We live in a time of increasing threat. If we are responsible for business continuity, we should think in a far smaller time horizon than 3–5 hours.

Backdoors

Backdoors make our security policy unenforceable by evading our perimeter defenses. Everyone knows that modems can breach perimeter defenses, especially when they are connected to operating systems that support IP forwarding. Many countermeasures are available for this, ranging from proactively scanning your phone lines to using digital phone lines. Wireless adds a whole new dimension of challenge; cell phones can surf the web, forward faxes, and connect laptops to the Internet. With 802.11 in wide use, organizations would be wise to walk their physical perimeters looking for signals. Don't be fooled by the box that claims they are only good for about a hundred meters. People with amplifiers and modified antennas can get significant range. You can run these tests yourself with a free copy of NetStumbler (http://www.netstumbler.com) and an inexpensive wireless network card. We need to think about our perimeter as a physical bubble drawn around our physical assets and be ready to test for breaches in a number of ways, from physical access caused by disks moving across the perimeter to RF signal. Access and security do not just apply to the computer or network, but to the organization as a whole. This is why the one true firewall maxim is, "Everything is denied except that which is specifically permitted or that which gets in anyway."

At this point, you should have a lot to think about. If you think of other vectors for unenforceable policy, we would love to hear from you! It is important to be alert for the situations in which policy cannot be enforced. These situations have a tendency to lead to chaos; they encourage people to either ignore the rules or push the envelope on the rules.

How to Develop Policy

Earlier, we pointed out the risks of trying to develop firewall rules without policy. The tendency is to do this willy-nilly, adding a rule here, modifying a rule there, until the rule set becomes difficult to maintain. Because we are in the active policy-enforcement business, sooner or later there will be controversy about why a certain service is either granted access or controlled. If the firewall administrator has a signed, approved, up-to-date policy to refer to, it can stifle the controversy. We need to have a policy on which to base our access and control decisions. Policy development can be approached in several ways, but in information security, we are probably best off to use a risk-based approach. For this to work, we identify the risk, communicate what we have learned to an authority, update or create security policy, and figure out how to measure compliance.

Identify Risks

It is time for a walkabout. Try not to let this stress you, but you will need to get out of your cubicle and go talk to some people. We realize that computer security types are a fairly introverted bunch, but users are a significant source of risk. Determine how your organization uses computers and networks in the conduct of business, both routinely and under emergency circumstances. You need to ask two questions:

- What data do you have or do you use from a different source that would really hurt the organization if it were not available?

- Do you use the Internet for anything other than email? (Of course, if your organization doesn't have a presumption of privacy, you can pull the logs and know what answer to expect before you meet.) Keep in mind that if no policy exists, the users in your organization aren't doing anything wrong. Make sure they understand you are simply trying to establish a baseline, not cause anyone trouble.

These questions will provide insight into the risks that your organization faces. Odds are, this will not be pretty. Just because you are using a personal firewall and keeping your antivirus software up to date doesn't mean anyone else is. You might find that people download games and other untested software, and that they run chat programs capable of transferring files. You might even find a copy of a web server on a workstation if you look long enough. The next step will be to pass your findings on the areas of risk to management, the folks who are paid to approve or mitigate business risk.

> **Where Is It Written?**
>
> For many years, I believed that people were rational, and that any two reasonable persons could be expected to make the same decision in a given situation. That isn't so. Really intelligent people will ask questions like, "If we have a firewall, why should we have to patch our systems?" We all know the perimeter cannot guarantee that a system will be 100% protected 100% of the time. But when people get a notion like that in their heads, logic ceases to be the drug of choice. You can try to explain things to them and they just don't get it. What is phenomenal, though, is the power of the written word. Someone might ask, "What instruction requires that we do it that way (or at all)?" If you show a written and dated policy signed by upper management, a surprising number of times the person nods and accepts the policy.

Communicate Your Findings

When communicating what you have learned to management, keep it simple, balanced, and fairly concise. If you mention an individual's name with respect to a problem or risk you have discovered at any point, management is likely to think of this as a personal attack and dismiss everything you have done. Keep the general tone on the types of problems you found and the implications. When possible, give an example of where this type of behavior was financially damaging to the organization.

> **SirCam as an Awareness Tool**
>
> I worked with a group that was pretty lax about antivirus, and nothing I said seemed to get them to understand the risks of malicious code. After SirCam hit in July 2001, I was at a restaurant with the group's senior manager. We were discussing a business deal, and I told him about a law firm that was hit by SirCam over the weekend. When the firm came in that Monday, the phones were lit up because sensitive documents of all sorts had been blasted over the Internet. It was fun to watch his face as he suddenly got it. The group added email screening to its firewall, and began updating workstation antivirus signatures regularly. SirCam created awareness of how malicious code could expose sensitive information in unexpected ways.

Offer management a range of options for managing those risks. It's probably best to use two different antivirus tools on the mail gateway, but if management decides to make the investment in only one, that is their choice. Our job is to give management the data in such a way they can make a reasonable decision. Don't try to do this by discussion only. Make sure you leave a written summary of your findings as well.

Create or Update the Security Policy as Needed

If no written policy is in place, write it and get it signed by upper-level management. Later in this chapter, we will cover the elements of policy and give you a few more tips for creating policy. However, life is too short to write policy from the ground up if you can avoid it. You don't write a makefile from scratch every time you build a new software distribution, do you? You usually modify an existing makefile. Many policy references are on the SANS web server (http://www.sans.org/resources/policies/), and an Internet search should turn up plenty of additional resources. We went through a lot of trouble to build the case for avoidance of unenforceable policy. One way to prevent unenforceable policy is to build in methods that allow us to audit compliance.

Determine Policy Compliance

If you cannot measure compliance (conformance), the policy is unenforceable. If the policy is specific enough, it should be easy to determine whether any item you are testing is in compliance. For instance, if we are only allowed to play *Star Trek* two days a year, it is possible to audit the system for the presence of that software. If trading sound files is against policy, we can monitor logs for the default ports of tools such as Kazaa clients, but also use Snort or a similar tool to look for the .mp3 file extension. One warning: If your plan is to spot check, make sure someone spot checks to see whether the spot checks actually happen. The spot checks should be logged and should occur quarterly. Audit the spot check log. Again, if there are no metrics and no controls to ensure compliance, it is probably unenforceable policy. If security supposedly spot checks for disk media at secure installations and it really isn't happening, the security function will not detect violations of their policy. A word of warning, though: Most people will choose compromise over confrontation. Management might have the best of intentions. They might say all the right words, but make sure you do not run afoul of your corporate culture, or your policy experience might be a very unpleasant one.

Sound Out the Organization's Rules and Culture

Every organization has a particular style, an ethic or image. Many times, a senior manager maintains this style and the organization buys into it to some extent. Does the organization favor managers over technical people? Does it favor seniority over excellent performance? Do the rules apply to everyone or only to some people? Is the organization laid back or aggressive? If you are writing policy, make sure it reflects the culture; otherwise, it is certainly going to be unenforceable.

We like to ask a few questions to determine the security posture of the organization before looking at policy. Some of those questions include the following:

- What is the presumption of privacy, including phone and network monitoring? Do employees have a reasonable expectation that what they store on their computers, what they say on the phone, and what they send on the Internet are protected communications?
- Are random physical searches permitted, and is there an active search program?
- Is the perimeter configured to allow all connections that are initiated from inside the organization?
- Are employees able to add software or modify settings on their desktop systems?
- Are administrators able to make changes without going through a formal configuration management approval program?

The answers to these questions can really help you see the "tone" you would expect the policy to have. Then you can continue to do an assessment of the culture by reading existing written policy and writing down unwritten policy.

Comparing Policy and Culture

Written policy can be found in a number of ways. It includes official policy, of course, but also directives from senior management, contracts, and other legal agreements, and even existing Human Resources cases. It can be an interesting experience to compare the official policy that is listed in documents with the other sources of policy we have described. The wise analyst examines the alternate sources and the cases of enforced policy to be alert for indications that the corporate culture does not completely agree with its stated policy. In a sense, this is just like Windows Active Directory: You have the Group Policy and the Local Security Policy, and they might not totally agree. If you want your Windows system to be secure, you need to be aware of what the effective policy is at all times. This is the same principle at work when we consider official policy and corporate culture.

> **Note**
>
> Policy must be documented and consistently enforced. Humans have trouble with this, but perimeter devices do not. This is why it is imperative to consider the human side of the equation before engaging the perimeter.

Written Policy

The first place to start looking for your corporate culture is the Human Resources handbook that is given to every new employee. At some point, this document was almost certainly approved by senior management as the document they wanted new employees to see. Be sure to check that the same management team that approved the employee handbook is still in power. Also, directives and other standard policy information might be available. It can't hurt to check those, being sensitive to when they were created. Checking these sources gives you an idea of what some combination of policy writers and management thought they wanted the policy to be.

Directives

Senior management will have approved the primary policy documents of their organization, but they might have modified them afterward by issuing directives. Generally, an executive secretary or administrative officer serves as the organizational memory. Clearly, this person would not be comfortable sharing all email or directives with you, but you are only interested in directives that modify either access or control. Even informal emails from senior management can have a large effect on a corporate climate.

How do you ensure that the administrative officer takes this exercise seriously? We suggest a checklist that lists the proposed perimeter policy based to the extent possible on the written policy. This should be in English, not in a firewall rules language. This checklist can be done with bullets, as in the following example:

- All internal systems are maintained according to the organization's best-practice checklist.

- All connections that are implemented from the inside are considered trusted.

- Acme Corporation, a strategic partner, has implemented a direct connection to us and is not blocked or monitored for the following services: file transfer, access to our product's database, and email.

Then you provide a place on the checklist for the administrative officer: "I have reviewed senior management directives, and the following directives and instructions indicate the proposed policy might need to be modified. If none, so state." This way, if the CEO or president of the company is offended by the perimeter's active policy enforcement, you have a layer of protection, a firewall between the angry manager and yourself.

Contracts and Human Resources Rulings

Legal contracts can effectively modify corporate policy, as can the hiring and firing disciplinary rulings from Human Resources. Many policies have a references section, and if you are aware of documents that modify the policy, you can include these in references as you update.

Unwritten Policy

If you immediately jumped to the conclusion, "No, policy *has* to be written," then we would ask you to consider the following:

- We have always done it that way!
- We have tried that five times and it always just dies.
- I wouldn't go there if I were you.

Every organization has hidden rules. Crossing these rules usually doesn't cause employment termination, but you can waste a lot of time. Every organization has wise folks who have been around for a long time, and these are the folks with whom to chat. Don't ask them to sign your checklist, but ask where the minefields are. You can always raise points with the senior manager who approves the implementation of the perimeter policy. Senior managers are paid to make the hard calls.

A chapter that is devoted to implementation of policy for perimeter devices cannot possibly cover all the elements of policy—that would be a book all by itself. That said, we do want to make sure we discuss the most common elements.

Elements of Policy

You can think about the elements of policy as the outline or skeleton. When we learned to code, many of us were taught to build the main program and put in dummy function calls. The idea was to call the function and make sure we returned so that the flow of the program would work. This limits troubleshooting to one function at a time, so we would be able to build the program efficiently. The elements of policy serve the same purpose; you can think of them as function calls in a main program.

We are not going to provide an exhaustive list of the elements of policy. This policy is tailored to a perimeter situation, so it will not need everything that you find in more Human Resource–related policies. Keep in mind that we need to focus on access and control with the policy. We will discuss authority, scope, and expiration next. We will also cover the characteristics of good policy.

Authority

We need to consider levels of authority: the manager who is authorized to sign the paper, and the policy under which this policy might fall. Often, a higher-level ruling policy exists. For instance, a perimeter policy might reference the organization's information security policy, and that might reference the organization's security policy. If this is not policy at the highest level, then to whom does it apply? Everyone, or perhaps everyone in a particular department or group? This is why we need to explicitly define the scope of the policy.

Scope

The scope section of policy identifies the depth and breadth of coverage (to whom or what the policy applies). Is it for one element of the organization, or will it also apply to contractor agencies that work for your organization? It is worth paying careful attention to the scope. If the scope proves to be incorrect, you might end up having to support two firewall policies: one for group A and another for group B. Of course, things change, and the policy should be reevaluated periodically. This is the purpose of the expiration information.

Expiration

Some policy is only valid for a short period of time. If your organization merges with another, you might have a transitional policy for 30–90 days. Policy is fairly static, with the exception of perimeter policy, which needs to be reviewed at least yearly. Taking the time to craft good policy makes it easier to check periodically.

Hallmarks of Good Policy

Anything worth doing is worth doing well, and that certainly applies to policy. Let's take a few minutes to define what good policy is and is not. It does *not* have to be wordy, use obscure words, or use acronyms. It *does* need to state the issue, state what is expected, and be a tool that can be used to measure compliance. To best accomplish this task, the policy should be specific, concise, and realistic.

Specificity and Clarity

Specificity is one of the most important aspects of good policy. One of the best ways to avoid unenforceable policy is to reduce ambiguity. Many times, people who write policy attempt to write in a formal tone that makes the policy hard to read. Just state the issue in plain, readable language. It is imperative to be specific about the following:

- **What needs to be done**—Enough information should be available from the policy to create a checklist that is sufficient to ensure compliance.

- **Why the policy exists and what the problem is designed to solve**— Rational people need to understand what the problem is to fully buy into the solution.

- **Who is responsible for accomplishing the tasks listed on the policy**—This is particularly important if procedures are developed from the policy. It must be clear who is responsible for completing the procedures.

The policy should be reviewed for clarity to make sure the reader can understand it. One simple way to test for clarity is to have one of the individuals identified as being responsible determine whether he understands the responsibility. Ask this person to read the policy and describe in his own words what the policy requires to be done. One of the best ways to make a policy clear is to make it concise.

Conciseness

Rules of thumbs are dangerous, so this is meant to challenge you to say what you need to say in a reasonable length. A specific policy topic (such as antivirus signature updates) shouldn't exceed two pages. Many organizations limit them to one page.

Realism

Perhaps you have heard of the mnemonic SMART. It stands for Specific, Measurable, Achievable, Realistic, and Time-based, and it is a good basis for effective policy. SMART also illustrates the importance of a realistic policy. Security policy shouldn't require people to try to implement things that can't be implemented. The *R* for Realistic is such an important characteristic; if the policy is not realistic, it is unenforceable.

Perimeter Considerations

Next, we consider how policy can be implemented in our perimeter architecture. If good policy already exists, we simply need to assess our perimeter technology, asking the question, "Is it possible for us to implement our policy with the technology we have?" Now that we have a firm foundation in what policy is and we are sensitive to unenforceable policy, let's go back to the notion of active policy enforcement. We will discuss how to map our architecture to our policy, and how the limitations of technology sometimes force us to modify our policy.

Real-world Operations and Policy

All too often we have to bend policy to match our architecture. This doesn't have to be the guiding principle, however. As we close out this chapter, let's cover some of the technologies and consider their implications for our policy position. Because perimeters examine and log packets, running a perimeter involves privacy issues. In addition, as email bounces or gets sent back to us, we might see a user's private thoughts. Our policy needs to prepare us for these situations in which limitations in our technology throw us information we might not expect to see. Policy must provide guidance to administrators and to those who operate content-sensing devices about what is and is not appropriate when private information is exposed.

> **Note**
>
> Every time we buy a new product or upgrade a system, our goal must be to build an architecture that actively enforces our policy.

Presumption of Privacy

If you are a student at a university in the United States, you have a presumption of privacy. Certainly, some speech is not protected; for example, you can't threaten the President or threaten to take your own life and expect confidence. However, on the whole, custom, practice, and law protects your communications.

If you are a uniformed member of the United States Armed Forces, you tend to live on the other side of the spectrum. Every time you enter a military base, you are greeted by a sign letting you know that you and your possessions are subject to search. The telephones have stickers warning that they might be monitored. You know that you do not have a presumption of privacy.

In an earlier section, we gathered and evaluated both the written and unwritten policy, which gives us the groundwork to determine what the presumption of privacy policy is for our organization. This helps us make perimeter design decisions. If you are designing for a university, you probably shouldn't collect content of packets. One of the engineering requirements for the Shadow IDS was to be able to detect attacks without looking at content. Widely deployed antivirus tools might be the "canary in the coal mine" that alerts us to a user who is circumventing the perimeter. Usually, we can use the information about the presence of a virus, but what do we do when we start getting arbitrary files from someone's hard disk courtesy of a W32.SirCam-type infection? It depends on the presumption of privacy. Email handling is another sticky point.

Email Handling

Have you ever worked in an organization in which people were fairly certain that the postmaster read their email? Needless to say, it should be grounds for termination if someone intercepts and reads mail without cause or written permission, but bounced mail comes to the postmaster. Anyone who has been a postmaster for any length of time has a story to tell about bounced mail. A postmaster must try to handle this by giving a quick look at the mail headers and ignoring the content, but sometimes it is inevitable. If the mail to the postmaster is a complaint from an outsider who received mail from our organization, what then? We probably do need to respond and help in the investigation by collecting the logs that corroborate or disprove the complaint. This is just one of the ways that working with the perimeter defenses can vault us into the wonderful world of incident handling.

Incident Handling: Preparation to Containment

Consider the six stages of incident handling:

- Preparation
- Detection
- Containment
- Eradication
- Recovery
- Lessons learned

It quickly becomes apparent that the perimeter is a crucial player in the process. Building a perimeter that allows flexible, active policy enforcement is one of the best ways to *prepare* for an incident. The event might well be detected by firewall or intrusion detection logs. After detection, we can use the perimeter to assist in the containment phase, where we typically make a decision between two approaches: contain and clean, or watch and learn.

If you have a system that you suspect is infected, your policy might be to contain and clean. You might choose to lock it down tight and prevent traffic from coming from the Internet to this system, and also prevent outbound traffic from the system to the Internet. In this book, we cover egress filtering, but it is worth emphasizing that a compromised box might be sending packets with spoofed source addresses. If you have a switched environment, you can often accomplish lockout right at the wall socket. Alternatively, you might decide to increase your instrumentation and see what you can learn about the motives and techniques of the hackers.

The watch-and-learn approach to incident handling takes access and control to the level of an art form. The Honeynet Project (http://www.honeynet.org/) has done more than any other group to advance the state of observing attackers in the wild who have been granted access, while maintaining control over the state of the system. If you are considering this approach to incident handling, you would be wise to visit Honeynet's website, get on the mailing list, and get involved. Tools such as rate-limiting switches can be helpful with this approach. Instead of denying the attacker access to the suspected machine, you throttle the bandwidth to make the attacker's experience a longer wait. This gives you a little more time to analyze the situation. Watch and learn is a higher risk strategy than contain and clean, but the potential payoff is also much higher.

Incident Handling: Eradication to Lessons Learned

At some point, usually within 24 hours of a suspected compromise, the primary focus is to get the system back in business. The first step is to completely clean the system and then to restore operations. The perimeter systems can be used for additional monitoring and filtering. Often, the attacker comes back, and we must remain alert for this. In addition, the logs from the perimeter help tell the whole story and are useful during the lessons learned phase of the process. If you don't understand how you were attacked and make the appropriate changes, it is all too likely it will happen again tomorrow. In the final section of this chapter, we will briefly consider policy that provides the security controls that apply to firewall administrators.

Rules of the Road

The perimeter sets the rules of the road. If we use active policy enforcement to manage access and control for various information assets, when and how do we have the authority to make changes in the perimeter? Who has the authority to request these changes, and under what circumstances? Who makes the final approval? Whatever your process is to approve changes, make sure you document them. Often, an apparently small change in filtering policy can have unintended side effects. If a change log exists, it can be of great help to those who have to troubleshoot the system.

The Firewall Admin Who Shouldn't Have

When I was working for the U.S. Department of Defense, I noticed some suspicious traffic on the Shadow IDS the department had deployed. After considerable analysis, it was fairly clear that there was a complete TCP connection, stimulated from HTTP, but on a high port with a three-way handshake, a data exchange, and a graceful close. How could this be? A sandbox violation seemed impossible. The client system was behind an application gateway firewall, and things such as Java and ActiveX were not permitted. How had the client been directed to open the connection from the inside of the facility? When I went to see the firewall administrator with the logs, I learned that the firewall administrator had turned off the HTTP proxy. My jaw dropped as I asked why. The reply was, "I got a phone call and someone complained it was too slow." Make sure you understand and follow the process in your organization for making changes to the perimeter's policy.

Summary

Policy is not something to be left to a nontechnical administrative worker. Everyone who is involved in perimeter design and operations is involved in policy. The perimeter can be viewed as an engine or series of engines that actively enforces your organization's policy relating to access and control of traffic. For the perimeter to do a good job of enforcing the rules of the road, you need a comprehensive policy. Be sensitive to situations in which your stated policy cannot be enforced. Strive for a policy that is clear, specific, and concise so that any reasonable, technically educated person can look at the policy and perimeter rules and understand the relation between the two. Never forget your responsibilities in terms of maintaining the privacy and dignity of others. You are the keeper of the gate for your organization; don't let an organization down by misusing the information and authority that is available to you.

References

1 "Security Policy." SANS Security Essentials Course, Version 2.3. September 2004.

II

Fortifying the Security Perimeter

6

The Role of a Router

A *ROUTER* IS A DEVICE THAT INTERCONNECTS TWO or more networks. Because of its role as a gateway between networks, it becomes a focal point of your network's security. Just like any entranceway to a secured perimeter, efforts must be made to reinforce the router's defenses to ensure your environment's safety.

The role that the router plays in your infrastructure's security depends greatly on its placement and the networks it joins together. The router might be a simple border device that joins your network to the Internet and relies on a firewall behind it to take care of the majority of the security concerns. Or perhaps the router is used as the lone perimeter security device for a small or low-risk network or a network subsegment. In either case, the main function of a router is the forwarding of packets from one network segment to another. Depending on the implementation you choose, you might strive to have the router focus on routing and perform routine security tasks as part of a larger defense-in-depth posture. Conversely, you could implement the router as an all-in-one perimeter security solution in an environment that has no other protection and reinforce this environment with additional defense in depth.

In this chapter, we discuss the router, its functions as a component of defense in depth, ways to implement it as an all-in-one security solution, and ways to protect the router through various hardening techniques. All examples use Cisco routers (Internetwork Operating System, or IOS, version 12.1 or greater), although the principles demonstrated could be applied to almost any brand of equivalent router.

The Router as a Perimeter Device

Simply stated, the main function of a router is the forwarding of packets between two network segments. This is often forgotten when it is time to implement a security structure. Many additional duties are thrust onto the router and, ultimately, performance suffers. Routers, like computers, have processors, memory, and storage space.

How Can You Tell Whether Your Router Is Overburdened?

When your router is overtaxed, many strange things can happen. Packets can be dropped, things can pass that shouldn't, and so on. To check whether your router is overburdened, look at its processor utilization. With a Cisco router, you can do this with the following command:

```
router#show processes cpu
```

This command shows the amount of central processing unit (CPU, or another word for *processor*) usage for each process. A command with even more interesting output is

```
router#show proc cpu history
```

Notice that this time, we abbreviated the word `processes` as `proc`. This command shows your CPU usage in a graphical format for the past 60 seconds, the past 60 minutes, and the past 72 hours. This can give you a much better idea of what kind of workload your router has had over given periods of time and when performing specific functions. If you are wondering how your router's memory is being dispersed, try the following command:

```
router#sh proc memory
```

This shows how much memory each of the running router processes is using. This can give you some major insight as to why you might need more RAM. With tools like these, the mysteries of an overworked router can be solved in record time!

You must consider these points when you're choosing a router for your specific network environment. Many of the features of expensive, high-power routers are also available in the lower power, more reasonably priced models; however, it is important to check under the hood. Make sure the router you choose can handle enough bandwidth to fit your site's needs. Also be sure it has enough memory and storage available to handle the features you plan to employ. Information is available from your router vendor on the amount of memory required for the features you need.

Routers usually don't have much storage space available, and storage upgrades are at a premium. When considering your design environment, think about the ramifications of implementing an external storage area for log files, configuration file backups, and operating software. Most likely, the router in question will use Syslog for remote logging and Trivial File Transfer Protocol (TFTP) for the transfer of configuration files and operating software updates. Therefore, ensure that you have systems that provide these services to the router to supplement its internal storage space.

Routing

To begin routing in a simple environment, a router needs little configuration. If you have two separate subnets that need to communicate, drop the router in and configure each connecting interface with an address for its attached network, make sure that routing is enabled, and—voilà—instant communication! The router knows the IP address of its two interfaces and can apply this knowledge to forward traffic sent from one network to the other. Complexities begin to arise as network segments the router isn't directly connected to are added to the configuration. Because the router doesn't have direct knowledge of these segments, it must be told about them with statements in its routing table. Such statements can be added manually by an administrator (static routes) or dynamically by updates from other routers. Static routes are easy to configure in a small environment. On Cisco routers, configuration can be accomplished with a command such as the following:

```
router_(config)#ip route 10.10.10.0 255.255.255.0 10.1.1.1 1
```

In this command, 10.10.10.0 is the network address range you want to tell the router about, and 255.255.255.0 is its subnet mask. 10.1.1.1 is the address of the router or gateway device to which the router should forward information that is destined for the 10.10.10.0 network. The single number 1 at the end of the statement is a route metric. It can be any number between 1 and 255, and it tells the router how much precedence should be placed on that path. If multiple choices are available, the router can make an informed decision about which route is the preferred.

The `ip route` statement can also be used in circumstances in which hundreds of networks might be unknown to our router, such as for a connection to the Internet. To forward all unknown traffic on to the Internet, we use the form

```
ip route 0.0.0.0 0.0.0.0 gateway IP
```

where `gateway IP` is the address of the next-hop router on the way to the Internet. Each of the following devices in the path to the Internet would also require a similar default route to the next upstream device. This statement is typically called the *default route* or the *gateway of last resort*.

Static routes offer a secure routing method for configuring a small environment, but what happens when we have 100 routers in our corporation? Do we want to program all the necessary static routes manually? Of course not! This is when dynamic routing protocols come into play.

Dynamic routing protocols allow properly configured routers to learn from each other about available routing paths. Protocols, such as Routing Information Protocol version 1 (RIPv1), Open Shortest Path First (OSPF), RIPv2, Interior Gateway Routing Protocol (IGRP), Enhanced Interior Gateway Routing Protocol (EIGRP), and so on, allow routers in a large environment to learn on the fly about one another. This process can simplify the configurations of what would be hundreds of static routing tables. This dynamic environment has its own set of problems, however. From a performance standpoint, all those updates travel around the network so that the routers can learn about each other. From a security standpoint, how do we know that the update being sent to our router is not from a nefarious outside party? Such updates could be sent in an effort to gain access to information on our network or sabotage its infrastructure.

Cisco Shorthand

Some of the examples throughout this chapter take advantage of Cisco router shorthand. On Cisco routers, you can use just enough letters of a command to differentiate it from all other commands. As long as the abbreviated form of the command cannot also represent another valid command, it will work. Otherwise, you will get this message:

`% Ambiguous command:`

This message is then followed by the characters you typed in, framed in quotes. An example of this is the popular command `show configuration` being entered as `sh conf`. `show` is the only other command that begins with `sh`, and `configuration` is the only appropriate command-line option to follow `show` that begins with `conf`. If you tried to use the command `sh con`, you would receive the `ambiguous command` message because `con` could represent `configuration` or `connection`, which are both valid options.

The command `copy run star` actually represents `copy running-config startup-config`. You save a lot of time in typing, and if you are a bad typist, the less typing the better!

Secure Dynamic Routing

One important part of keeping an environment that uses routing safe is secure implementation of dynamically updated routing protocols, such as RIP (versions 1 and 2), OSPF, Border Gateway Protocol (BGP), IGRP, and EIGRP. Dynamic routing protocols are often a necessary part of a complex internetworking environment. However, if they are not configured correctly, dynamic routing protocols can be an easily exploited security hole. Some routing protocols use numbering schemes that require some knowledge of the specific details of your network's routing configuration to send acceptable routing updates. However, these numbers are transmitted in the clear (without encryption), so they can be sniffed. In addition, often the numbers chosen are guessed easily and might not provide adequate protection. Unless the configuration steps listed in the upcoming sections are taken, the use of these protocols might leave a gaping hole in what would be an otherwise secure network environment.

Route Authentication

Some dynamic routing protocols offer advanced protection known as *route authentication*. On a Cisco router, the process of route authentication involves the use of a secret keyword that is configured into all routers that are to share their dynamic routing information. This keyword, used in conjunction with the routing update information, generates a Message Digest 5 (MD5) hash signature to be sent with dynamic route updates. If this hash information is not included with the updates or is incorrect, contacted routers will ignore the provided route information. Protocols that support routing authentication include RIPv2, OSPF, EIGRP, and BGP. Two dynamic routing protocols of note that don't support this feature are RIPv1 and IGRP. Cisco routers have a feature that performs a simple check to help secure these two protocols. The `validate-update-source` command (which is configured by default) checks the source address of incoming RIP and IGRP updates to verify that they are from a neighboring device on the same network segment as the interface on which the update was received. This feature helps prevent false router updates from outside of the network.

You could install route authentication on an OSPF routed network by using the `ip ospf message-digest-key 10 md5` *secretkey* command.

You must enter this statement at the interface that will be propagating the routing updates. (For a refresher on the Cisco IOS interface, check out Chapter 2, "Packet Filtering.") `10` is the key ID, which is a number that represents the unique secret key that you define, and *secretkey* is the actual key used to create the MD5 hashes that protect your routing updates. The importance of the key ID value comes into play if you want to change keys in an active environment. You can simply add the new *secretkey* value in a similar statement with a different key ID number. The router identifies that it has a new key and starts sending two routing updates: one with the new key value, and one with the original key value. This behavior is designed to allow a window of opportunity for you, the administrator, to change the keys on all other routers that share common routing information. After all routers have been updated, remove the original statement so that only the new key is used. After all, using two authentication updates simultaneously requires twice the bandwidth, and you are only as secure as the lesser of your two statements.

To activate the MD5 authentication, use the statement

```
area 0 authentication message-digest
```

This command is entered in global configuration mode. The `0` represents the OSPF area in which you will be using MD5 route authentication. It might differ depending on how OSPF is configured in your particular environment.

Implementation of router authentication varies slightly depending on the routing protocol, so be sure to check proper documentation before implementing in non-OSPF environments.

Other Dynamic Routing Defenses

Another way you can be sure to prevent tampering with your route tables is by blocking updates from networks that are deemed unsafe. For example, if you had an extranet connection to a customer, you might not want the customer's routers to have the ability to change the configuration of your routers (accidentally or on purpose). You can configure the interface that connects your router to the customer's to deny routing updates. Cisco routers use the `distribute-list` command, which prevents the propagation, or the acceptance of specified route updates through configured interfaces. For example, if you want to prevent outside routers from being able to make changes in routing information for a mission-critical network segment in your internal infrastructure, you can use `distribute-list 112 in` *e1*.

Here, *e1* is the interface that connects you to the outside routers, and `112` is an access control list (ACL) that defines the network address range of the mission-critical segment.

The access list can define ranges of allowed or disallowed IP routing information (depending on whether it is a permit or deny ACL). In a similar manner, a `distribute-list out` command can be used to disallow the sending of route updates that include information on how to route traffic to your top-secret lab. The syntax is `distribute-list 113 out e1`.

Again, `e1` is the interface you want to prevent routing information from leaving, and `113` is the access list number that defines the address range of the top-secret lab. Remember that the access list always defines the address range of the segment for which you don't want to accept or propagate routing information. It does not represent the addresses of segments that you want to prevent from receiving or sending the information.

To keep important details of your network infrastructure private, it may be necessary to prevent dynamic routing protocols from sharing internal route information with outsiders. To accomplish this on a Cisco router, use the `passive interface` command to prevent the router from broadcasting route updates out of the specified interface. Its syntax is as follows:

```
passive interface e1
```

In this case, `e1` is the interface through which you want to disallow the sending of updates, while still accepting updates inbound. This command behaves in a slightly different manner with the EIGRP and OSPF routing protocols, by disallowing both the sending *and* receiving of routing information via the specified interface.

The Router as a Security Device

Because the router is traditionally the entranceway to a network, it plays an important part in network security. For this reason, routers have been designed with many built-in security features, such as packet filters, stateful firewall features, Network Address Translation (NAT), and Virtual Private Network (VPN) support. The question is whether a router is utilized as your only security device or as a piece of a larger defense-in-depth security structure. In a perfect (secure) world, the answer would always be as a part of a larger security structure, letting the router focus on its primary function, and allowing firewalls, intrusion detection systems (IDSs), and so on handle the burden of the security concerns. In this section, we look at scenarios that use a router as part of defense in depth and also as the primary security solution. We also explore the technologies that are often implemented when using a router as a lone security device, such as NAT, context-based access control (CBAC), ACLs, and so on. In addition, we look at the technologies that can be employed to make the router a complement to a greater security scheme.

The Router as a Part of Defense in Depth

In Chapter 12, "Fundamentals of Secure Perimeter Design," we go into detail on the logistics of placing a router as part of the defense-in-depth structure and the functions it should perform. In this section, we predominately focus on the technologies to make a router an effective part of defense in depth and ways to implement those technologies.

A router's role as part of defense in depth can vary depending on the related pieces of the overall security scheme. For example, it would be foolish to implement a router with stateful inspection capabilities in conjunction with a stateful firewall. Typically, the rule of thumb is to keep the router from doing any more than it has to, and let it focus on what it is good at.

Packet Filtering

As stated in Chapter 2, blocking access from ranges of addresses is something that routers do well. It makes sense to take advantage of this strong suit when using the router as a role player in conjunction with a stateful firewall, by utilizing the router for ingress and egress filtering.

It is logical to implement ingress filters at the furthermost point on your perimeter, which is most likely your border router. Having the router perform this function offloads some of the burden from the firewall, allowing it to focus on the things for which it is better suited, such as the stateful inspection of defined protocols. Egress filtering is also a good choice for a router that is working in conjunction with other perimeter firewalls; blocking or allowing entire network ranges is something that packet filters are well suited for. Due to the structuring of the TCP/IP packet and the means by which matches are made with the standard packet filter, blocking a range of network addresses is simple bit matching that is difficult to circumvent on a router and that can be accomplished efficiently. For this reason, any time whole ranges of network addresses need to be blocked or allowed, the router is an excellent candidate for a point of implementation.

For more information on the best ways to implement egress and ingress filters and to utilize the packet-filtering features of a router, refer to Chapter 2.

Network-Based Application Recognition (NBAR)

Recently, routers have begun to be utilized in another way as a part of defense in depth. Cisco's network-based application recognition (NBAR) is a feature that was originally designed to help with Quality of Service (QoS) issues, with full functionality available in IOS 12.1(2)e or later. With the onset of bandwidth-devouring streaming-multimedia applications and applications that require high QoS, such as Voice over IP (VoIP), a method had to be created to allocate bandwidth based on the applications being used. NBAR can be used to allocate at least a certain amount of bandwidth to an activity or traffic type or to limit bandwidth for a given traffic type.

You might be wondering why QoS commands are being mentioned in a book about security. In today's world, security is more than disallowing or allowing access to resources. It also includes the protection of service demands and available bandwidth. Because of the increased threat of denial of service (DoS) attacks, protecting the bandwidth we have to offer our business or clients has become a major point of concern. A business relying on e-commerce whose storefront is inaccessible due to inadequate bandwidth can face a serious financial hardship. A lack of bandwidth equates to a DoS whether it is due to an outside malicious DoS attack or mismanaged use of internal bandwidth. Using solutions such as NBAR can prevent this mismanagement, keeping a "governor" on high-bandwidth activities that don't serve as an important resource for your business. For example, if your site relies on e-commerce to exist and you share bandwidth between e-commerce applications and Internet access for employees, NBAR would prevent a DoS condition caused from all your employees simultaneously tuning in to the latest Victoria's Secret streaming fashion show.

NBAR can recognize traffic based on HTTP information—including MIME types, URLs, and hostnames. It can also search on static and dynamic port information. After the traffic is identified, it can be marked, and then a policy determining the amount of bandwidth allowed can be applied. This policy can be used in many creative ways to control QoS and protect application bandwidth.

For example, in a business environment, you might want to limit the bandwidth for multimedia applications to a fraction of your total Internet connection bandwidth so that they don't interfere with higher priority business applications. Using the following commands limits the bandwidth for all defined multimedia applications to 12 kilobits per second (Kbps) total:

> **Tip**
> Cisco Express Forwarding must be enabled for NBAR to function.

```
router(config)#class-map match-any av
router(config-cmap)#match protocol http mime "audio/*"
router(config-cmap)#match protocol http mime "video/*"
router(config)#class-map match-any images
router(config-cmap)#match protocol http url "*.gif"
router(config-cmap)#match protocol http url "*.jpg|*.jpeg"
```

Here, av and images are the unique names for the class maps, and audio/* and video/* are the MIME types for which we want to control QoS. With the images class map, we specifically limit the bandwidth for defined picture types as well.

Then, both of these class maps can be combined into one all-inclusive class map:

```
router(config)#class-map match-any mmedia
router(config-cmap)#match class-map av
router(config-cmap)#match class-map images
```

Notice the use of the match-any keyword. The keyword match-all (not shown) requires that all the listed criteria be met, whereas match-any allows a match if any of the listed criteria is the same. Because we want to affect traffic that matches either of the listed class maps, we must use match-any.

Now we will create a policy defining how much bandwidth our mmedia class map will be allowed:

```
router(config)#policy-map mybusiness
router(config-pmap)#class mmedia
router(config-pmap-c)#police 12000 conform transmit exceed drop
```

Here, *mybusiness* is a unique policy name that represents all class maps for which we want to control QoS on an interface. Other class maps could be applied in this same policy map. We apply the class map `mmedia`, which we created previously, and then allow no more than 12Kbps of our total bandwidth to it with the `police` command.

Note

As you may have guessed by the syntax of the `police` command, *any* multimedia traffic exceeding the 12K bandwidth limitation is *dropped*. It is not queued in any way and will break multimedia communications.

Finally, we apply the policy to an interface using the following command:

```
router(config-if)#service-policy output mybusiness
```

Here, *mybusiness* is the policy name previously defined, and `output` is the correct direction on the interface to which we choose to apply it.

NBAR has also become a method to prevent outside attacks from causing a DoS condition. With the advent of the Code Red and Nimda and SQL Slammer worms, many sites that properly patched their servers still fell victim to the "noise" generated by other infected locations. They had no means to protect their bandwidth from the repeated assaults from outside infectors. By placing NBAR as a screening mechanism on border routers, you can effectively prevent just such a DoS condition.

The setup is similar to our previous example. We simply create another class map. This class map can be used to screen incoming malicious traffic that has a known uniquely identifiable structure, or *footprint*.

Note

Don't allow yourself to be lulled into a false sense of security. NBAR screening for malicious traffic is a dynamic process. As variants are discovered, the footprints used to screen content must be updated.

Our class map will include Cisco's suggested match information for Code Red, Nimda, and some current variants:

```
router(config)#class-map match-any web-attacks
router(config-cmap)#match protocol http url "*.ida*"
router(config-cmap)#match protocol http url "*cmd.exe*"
router(config-cmap)#match protocol http url "*root.exe*"
router(config-cmap)#match protocol http url "*readme.eml*"
```

This new class map can be added to an existing policy that is applied in the same direction on the same interfaces. If you don't have a like policy, you can create a new one:

```
router(config)#Policy-map attacks
router(config-pmap)#class web-attacks
router(config-pmap-c)#police 10000 3000 3000 conform-action
➥drop exceed-action drop violate-action drop
```

Notice that the policy map looks similar to the last example, with the exception of the `police` command. Because of the addition of the `violate-action` keyword, we need to add burst speeds after the first bandwidth listing. However, the three numbers specified are meaningless because all defined actions will drop the identified traffic. Cisco has documented this as a solution for bandwidth issues in these situations (http://www.cisco.com/warp/public/63/nbar_acl_codered.shtml).

To handle a worm like SQL Slammer with an unusual protocol and no particular URL-match criteria to filter on, we need to use other information to generate a "signature." First, a custom protocol needs to be created with the following command:

```
ip nbar port-map custom udp 1434
```

Then, the class map can be created to include this custom defined protocol and another unique piece of criteria, the packet length:

```
Class-map match-all slammer
Match protocol custom
Match packet length min 404 max 404
```

The packet length as part of the matching criteria is crucial, because it is what separates the Slammer traffic from possibly normal SQL traffic on UDP port 1434. Notice in this class map we specify to "match all" because we only want to drop UDP 1434 packets with the listed packet length. In the Nimda/Code Red example, payloads matching any of the criteria would have been dropped. Finally, this class map would be assigned to a policy map like the one in the Nimda/Code Red example and the traffic would be dropped using a like police statement.

Note

Realize that your border router will experience additional load from this NBAR screening process, and a seriously overburdened router can also create a DoS condition.

Tip

For more information on mitigating the effects of worms using Cisco technologies, refer to http://www.cisco.com/en/US/netsol/ns340/ns394/ns171/ns128/networking_solutions_white_paper09186a00801e120c.shtml. Also, additional settings can be added to your router to limit the effect of DoS attacks. For an article on protecting against various other DoS attacks on Cisco routers, see http://www.cisco.com/warp/public/707/newsflash.html.

No matter what security technology you take advantage of on your router—whether it's simple access lists for filtering out undesired packets, or NBAR to drop malicious Internet worms—you will find the router to be an excellent role player in your network's defense in depth. However, in some cases a router may need to supply the majority of the security features for the defense of a network segment.

The Router as a Lone Perimeter Security Solution

In some environments, the router can be used as an effective perimeter security solution on its own. It can be used as a sole means of defense for a remote or home office, for an internal segment of your network, or as a security solution for a low-risk facility where it wouldn't be cost effective to add an additional firewall or other security device. No matter what the deployment, a properly configured router can provide a good base for a perimeter defense. However, it is still important to apply defense-in-depth principles beyond the router. Relying on any single perimeter device as your only source of security leaves you only one step from being compromised. An outsider needs to find only a single flaw to have access to your entire network.

Router Placement

The placement of your router will help determine the technologies you should implement when securing your environment.

A border router that has to serve as an all-in-one security solution might have many duties to perform. Not only does it handle all the routing between your network and the outside world, but it must also block incoming attacks to provide security. Depending on the environment, this might be accomplished with ACLs or stateful CBAC support. (For more information on CBAC, look at the "Technology Choices" section later in this chapter.) Because it is at the border of your network, it may support NAT or Port Address Translation (PAT) to allow the use of a private addressing scheme internally. It may also be where VPN connections are decoded and information passed on to internal hosts. One important thing to remember when a border router is your sole security solution is its visibility. Because it is your gateway to the world, anyone on the Internet must be able to contact it for you to be able to communicate. In turn, that means it is vulnerable. Many border routers are configured to securely protect internal hosts, and yet are open to attack themselves. In the section on router hardening later in this chapter, we discuss means to defend the lone router from being exploited.

Routers can also be placed at internal subnetting points in your network. IP networks are subnetted for various reasons, including performance and security. A router must be placed at the points where the subnetted segments join together to facilitate communication. Depending on environmental circumstances, a router might be a good device for enforcing resource separation on the network. For example, when subnetting off a research and development lab, you might want to consider preventing inbound access from other internal subnets, while allowing outbound access from the lab to the rest of the network and Internet. Again, this can be accomplished with ACLs or CBAC, depending on the segment's security level. If the internal network is based entirely on a private addressing scheme, it is unlikely that NAT would be implemented on a router joining such subnets.

No matter the placement, several security technologies can be used to secure the network. In the following section, we will discuss these technologies.

Technology Choices

With the advancement of technology, routers are becoming more feature rich. Many options are available when implementing a router as a security solution, whether it is as part of an entire defense scheme or as a standalone device. All the technologies in the following list are discussed in depth in this section and can be used in either case, but they are often implemented as a lone solution:

- NAT/PAT
- CBAC
- Packet filtering and ACLs

NAT has long been a means to help solve the public IP address range shortage and help secure a network and its privacy. NAT allows the assignment of a public IP address on the "outside" of a device to a corresponding private IP address on the "inside." This way, the internal network addressing remains hidden from outside parties. As communication ensues, the NAT device is responsible for translating the traffic between the public outside and private inside addressing. Only the NAT device knows the internal addresses to which the outside public addresses relate. These translations can be statically assigned (to allow bidirectional communication) or dynamically assigned. When dynamic assignment is used, a pool of available public addresses needs to be created. This outside pool does not necessarily have to match one-to-one with the number of inside addresses, allowing many privately addressed stations to share a smaller group of public addresses. However, no more stations can make external connections at one time than there are available public addresses in the pool. When all available public addresses from this outside pool are in use, the next internal station attempting an outside connection will be unable to do so, unless a variation of NAT, called *overloading* or *PAT*, is also implemented.

> **Note**
>
> In the context of this section, we use the term *NAT* to define standard NAT using address-only translation. We use the term *PAT* to define NAT translation using port overloading.

The greatest conservation of addresses can be accomplished by using overloading or PAT (also called *NAPT*, or *single address NAT*). PAT maps multiple internal addresses to one external public address by tracking the communication sessions by the port number in use. As an example, an internal station at IP address 192.168.1.5 contacts an outside web server. It generates an ephemeral port of 1035 and sends the request to its gateway router, which happens to be a PAT device. The router translates the requesting station's address into the defined public IP address and assigns a new port number (1111 in this instance). This is accomplished by actually rewriting the packet's header information with the new IP address and port number information. It then enters this information as well as the station's original IP address information and the information of the server it is contacting into a table, like this:

```
Source IP/port - Translated IP/port - Contacted IP/port
192.168.1.5.1035 - 200.200.200.2.1111 - 225.225.225.1.80
```

Depending on the implementation, the PAT device may attempt to assign the same source port number on the outside that is being used by the station on the inside. However, if another connection is already using the port number, the PAT device might reassign a new port number in approximately the same port range, as in our previous example. Also, many implementations of PAT use a range of high port numbers (often 50,000 or more) that is assigned for the source port. When you're monitoring traffic, seeing ephemeral ports in this range is often a sign that a PAT device has translated the traffic.

When the traffic returns, the PAT device can refer to the NAT table and translate the response for IP 200.200.200.2 port 1111 back to IP address 192.168.1.5 port 1035. Subsequent connections from inside stations would be translated to other ports on the same 200.200.200.2 address. This way, thousands of sessions can successfully take place with only one public IP address, and each will be able to be differentiated from the other. PAT does not have to be limited to a single IP address. Some implementations of PAT will allow multiple IP addresses to be translated.

On a Cisco router, a NAT configuration can be implemented as follows:

1. Apply the command `router(config-if)#ip nat outside` on the external interface. This command sets this interface as the outside NAT interface.

2. Apply the command `router(config-if)#ip nat inside` to the internal router interface. For translation reasons, this command tells NAT that this is the inside interface.

3. Configure a pool of addresses for NAT to use with the following statement:

   ```
   ip nat pool natpool 200.200.200.2 200.200.200.10 netmask
   ➥255.255.255.240
   ```

   This statement defines a public address pool named `natpool` with the IP addresses 200.200.200.2–200.200.200.10.

4. Follow this with an access list to specify all internal addresses to be assigned public IP addresses from the NAT pool, as follows:

   ```
   access-list 1 permit ip 10.0.0.0 0.255.255.255
   ```

   If you are using this device for a VPN as well, additional access lists will need to be created to allow the VPN traffic to bypass NAT. (For more information on VPN implementations on Cisco hardware, refer to Chapter 7, "Virtual Private Networks.")

5. Execute the following command in global configuration mode (this command is the bread and butter of the NAT implementation on a Cisco router):

   ```
   ip nat inside source list 1 pool natpool
   ```

It starts by assigning 1 to the access list as the addresses to be translated. Next, it defines the pool of public addresses to dynamically be assigned. This is a standard configuration for dynamic NAT, with a pool of addresses to be assigned.

For PAT, the command would be changed as follows:

```
ip nat inside source list 1 interface Ethernet0 overload
```

First, the definition of a pool of addresses is not needed because only one IP address will be used externally, although the definition of a pool would be allowable. The keyword `overload` is added to the end of the NAT statement, signifying that multiple outgoing connections can overload or share one external IP address. Notice that the following command doesn't use a pool name. Instead, the `interface` keyword assigns the external address followed by the listing of the external interface's name. This way, PAT and the router's external interface can share one public IP address. This statement would be entered in global configuration mode.

The entering of these commands can make almost any Cisco router into a NAT or PAT device. To view the NAT or PAT translation table at any point, use the command `router#sh ip nat trans`.

Although NAT can be considered a privacy method, it offers limited inherent security after a connection is established from the inside. After an inside IP address is added to the NAT table, the address it was contacting can be accessed from the outside until the mapping is dynamically cleared. Some NAT implementations have no reference to port information in their NAT table, which leaves the inside station open to activity from the contacted outside host (or from spoofed traffic) on protocols other than the one which it had contacted. For example, if your internal web server contacted an outside DNS server for DNS information, and the DNS server tried to initiate communication to your web server before the original NAT table entry expired, it would be allowed access to any services your web server offers. This makes a good case for the addition of ACLs or CBAC as a complement to properly secure NAT traffic. PAT offers more security because it also tracks the port numbers used for each connection and logs them in its translation table. As long as the source port that your internal station is using is a dynamically generated ephemeral port on which no services are hosted, your configuration should be rather safe. However, if an attacker has the ability to detect your IP address, most likely he also will be able to detect the source and destination ports you are using. This means that if the translation table still holds the address/port combination in question, properly crafted traffic could pass. This assumes that the inside station is still listening on the port it was contacting when the table entry was created.

Another security issue with NAT is the lack of inherent outbound filtering. Any inside hosts can get out, which leaves an opening for Trojan software. The lack of granularity in the translation tables allows a greater likelihood of the occurrence of session hijacking or the infiltration of the network through an existing address translation. However, when used in conjunction with other technologies, such as static packet filtering, dynamic packet filtering, and even stateful inspection methods, NAT and PAT can provide an excellent privacy and security combination.

CBAC is a full-featured method of stateful inspection for Cisco routers. CBAC is available in the Cisco Secure Firewall Feature Set. (Some functionality was introduced in IOS version 11.2p, but many useful features have been added up to version 12.05t.) CBAC supports most popular protocols and keeps full track of the state of connections, dynamically creating access lists to allow return traffic from outside sources. The implementation of CBAC involves creating `inspect` statements that monitor the defined protocols. Following is an example of an `inspect` statement:

```
ip inspect name firewall http timeout 3600
```

Here, `firewall` represents the name of the inspection set we will be applying to our interface. `http` is a keyword that defines the protocol we are inspecting with this command, and the `timeout` option (which is not required) tells how long the dynamically generated access lists should exist after creation. This same formatting is applied to additional `inspect` statements for other protocols that you want to allow to exit your internal network. The set named `firewall` must be applied outbound on the external router interface with a command such as `ip inspect firewall out`. This command must be applied in interface configuration mode.

Because CBAC uses stateful inspection, not only does it make sure that ACLs are dynamically generated to allow return traffic, but it also verifies that the traffic being inspected is indeed what it claims to be at the application level. This prevents the use of well-known ports to facilitate possibly malicious activities (for example, using port 80 for Telnetting to a host instead of HTTP) and helps prevent session hijacking. For more information on stateful inspection and stateful filtering, see Chapter 3, "Stateful Firewalls."

Despite the fact that CBAC adds an extra layer of intelligence to the inspection of inbound and outbound traffic, it is not a security panacea. It is still wise to use ingress and egress filters in conjunction with CBAC. Despite CBAC's ability to inspect traffic, it will not provide NBAR-type screening of malicious content. Although CBAC provides stateful inspection-level protection for communications channels, it is still only one segment of a total defense-in-depth deployment. In addition, CBAC uses more resources and is slower, comparatively, than the other technology choices. Despite the fact that CBAC might be the most secure method to protect traffic with a router, it might not be the best selection in all scenarios.

Another way to secure a router is through ACLs that use static and dynamic packet filtering. This is what the router does best, and it is a complement to any security configuration. An ACL can also be a facilitator. Often, when other default security solutions don't allow a type of access, a static packet filter is created as an easy means to allow traffic in or out. This is often the way that a secure configuration can suddenly jump to insecure. ACLs are a powerful tool that must be carefully configured to prevent security holes. For more information on packet filtering with a router, see Chapter 2. For full sample listings of ACLs, see Appendix A, "Cisco Access List Sample Configurations."

Regardless of which security technologies you choose for your router, it is important to remember that they all have their strengths and weaknesses, and no method is impenetrable. Also, each of these technologies can benefit from defense-in-depth methodology, even in the simplest of networks. Keep these points in mind when designing your network's security structure, and remember that even the most secure interior configuration can still leave the perimeter router at a point of vulnerability.

Router Hardening

Having the device that provides all your network's security on the edge of the perimeter is like having an army's general placed ahead of his troops. The piece that is vital to your success or failure is in the most vulnerable position. When it comes to perimeter protection, we can use defense in depth to help, but in some environments, we might not have much support for our "general." This is why router hardening is so important to your network's security. In effect, it's like placing your general in a tank. Its focus is on protecting the protection device. This protection involves disabling all unneeded services and servers, blocking all unnecessary traffic types, locking down any methods we use to configure our security device, posting warning banners, and closely monitoring the device and the traffic that passes through it.

Operating System

Protecting a router isn't that much different from protecting a computer. (Hardening procedures applicable to hosts are described in Chapter 9, "Host Hardening.") One major concern that is often overlooked involves patches for the operating system. The operating system for Cisco routers is called the IOS. Keeping tabs on IOS updates and security flaws is imperative in defending your router from attack. Cisco's website posts security issues as they are discovered, and it is a good practice to check such sites regularly. For a list of Cisco security advisories, go to http://www.cisco.com/en/US/products/products_security_advisories_listing.html.

It is also wise to subscribe to an email/list such as @RISK: The Consensus Security Alert, which automatically sends multiplatform security advisory information to you as it becomes available. To subscribe, go to http://www.sans.org/newsletters.

Cisco also has a security mailing list at cust-security-announce@cisco.com.

Registration information is available at http://www.cisco.com/en/US/products/products_security_vulnerability_policy.html.

Locking Down Administration Points

One of the most important parts of securing a perimeter security device is locking down the ways it can be configured. Otherwise, it is like locking a door and leaving the key in the lock. Over the next few sections, we will discuss popular administration methods and some ways to secure them from outside attack.

Telnet

Telnet is probably the most popular way to remotely configure a router. Following are the two greatest concerns of Telnet:

- Properly securing the Telnet server from outside access to prevent remote nefarious users from reconfiguring your router.

- Realizing that all information, including logins and passwords, are sent in clear text. This means that a sniffer could assist in gaining access to your router configuration.

The Telnet server on board every Cisco router can be protected through username and password authentication. However, protection by authentication might be insufficient for securing of something as vital as a perimeter security device. For this reason, it is advisable to apply access lists that limit where Telnet sessions can originate. Following is an example of an ACL that allows an administrative station at IP address 192.168.1.1 to have Telnet access:

```
access-list 11 permit 192.168.1.1
```

This access list is applied to the virtual terminal lines (VTY) using the `access-class` command, which works similarly to the `access-group` command that applies ACLs to router interfaces. (For more information on ACLs or the `access-group` command, see Chapter 2.) This access list would be applied as follows:

1. To get into line configuration mode, enter normal configuration mode and type `router(config)#line 1 3`, where 1 through 3 is the range of VTY lines to which you want to apply the access list in question.

2. Enter the `access-class` command `router(config-line)#access-class 11 in`. One administrator's trick is to apply an ACL to the first several VTY lines (for example, 1 through 3) that allow access for the IP addresses of all administrators. Then, apply an ACL to the last VTY line, including only the IP address of the senior administrator's station. This way, the administrator can always get Telnet access, regardless of whoever else is connected. Not only do these access lists verify that you'll always have a free VTY session, but they also protect you from malicious outside users (and inside users for that matter).

3. Make sure that Telnet is the only input type your router will accept by using `router(config-line)#transport input telnet`. This command disables all other protocols from being used to access the VTY lines. (This is important to prevent access from alternate protocols such as rlogin.)

4. If you want to ensure that Telnet access is completely disabled at the router level, you can add the `login` keyword to the VTY line configuration of your router and then add the `no password` command. This disables Telnet usage because a password is required for access.

5. Though this causes a great headache for many an administrator, it is wise to enable timeouts for sessions with the `exec-timeout` command. Simply add it followed by the time, in minutes, you want an inactive session to remain open before you are disconnected.

The fact that Telnet transfers information in clear text can only be corrected by using an alternative configuration method such as Secure Shell (SSH), which utilizes encryption, or by adding IPSec support to run your Telnet sessions through encrypted ESP tunnels.

Telnet Trick

Sometimes you might want to separate VTY sessions on a Cisco router, such as when using lock and key access lists or other instances when you need to set different criteria for various VTY Telnet sessions. You might want to have certain settings for VTY lines 1–3 and others for 4–5. How do you then log in to line 4 or 5? Using the default Telnet port (23) connects you to the first available VTY. If that doesn't happen to be line 4 or 5, the alternatively defined criteria will not apply. `access-class` statements will not correct this problem. If your connection fails to one VTY line, you are simply denied access, not rolled on to the next line to see if its ACL will allow you.

I searched for a way to change this behavior, but to no avail. Then as I was perusing a firewall mailing list archive one day, I found a workaround. A gentleman sent in the advice that you can use the rotary # command to allow VTY Telnet access via an alternate port. This port is the number listed after the rotary command, added onto 3,000, 5,000, and 7,000. The result is that if you configure the option `rotary 13` on your last VTY line with alternate criteria, you can initiate a Telnet connection to ports 3013, 5013, or 7013. You will also access the alternate criteria instead of what is configured for the other VTY lines. This can be great in situations where you have to execute an autocommand, such as with lock and key ACLs. Personally, I don't like having all those ports available, so I lock down the line with an ACL such as `access-list 117 permit tcp host my IP any eq 3013` and apply it with an `access-class 117` on the VTY line in question. Not only does this verify that no one else will gain access, but it ensures that I can only access port 3013. (Of course, this port is based on the rotary number used.) Use this tip at your own risk—it is not the way the command was intended to be used, but it works!

SSH

SSH is a secure alternative to Telnet. Instead of passing login information in clear text, SSH uses encryption to protect login names and passwords while authenticating. Since version 12.1 of IOS (only those versions that support encryption), SSH version 1 only is supported in most of the Cisco router platforms. If you remotely manage your routers, you are in a high-risk environment, and you have concerns about the security of your authentication information, consider using SSH as your Telnet replacement. To configure SSH server capabilities on your router, do the following:

1. Enter the commands `hostname host` and `ip domain name domain`, where `host` specifies the unique hostname of the device and `domain` is the domain that the device resides in.

The host and domain name information must be entered before attempting to configure SSH. This information is required to enable key generation.

2. Our next goal is to create our RSA key with the statement `crypto key generate rsa`. This statement actually generates an RSA key and activates SSH. You can view generated RSA keys using the command `show crypto key mypubkey rsa`. You can verify that SSH is active by entering `sh ip ssh`.

Tip

Enter the `crypto key generate rsa` command at the global configuration command prompt. It is not part of your configuration file; therefore, it cannot be entered by editing and reloading the current configuration file.

3. We can set SSH options with the following commands:

```
ip ssh time-out 50
ip ssh authentication-retries 4
```

If these options are not entered, the defaults for each are assumed.

4. Use the `login local` command to enable local authentication or use Authentication, Authorization, and Accounting (AAA) commands if authenticating through Remote Authentication Dial-In User Service (RADIUS) or Terminal Access Controller Access Control System (TACACS) servers.

5. Of course, we also have to include the command `username` *name* `password` *pass*, where *name* is the username for authentication and *pass* is the password of choice.

6. The `transport input ssh` command can be entered for the VTY lines in question. It disables Telnet remote configuration, allowing SSH to be the only connection method. (Multiple items can be listed for more than one input type.)

7. The `exec-timeout` x command can be applied to verify that inactive sessions will be disconnected after *x* minutes of no activity.

The Cisco router (IOS version 12.1[3]t and up) also includes an SSH client implementation so that other SSH-capable devices can be contacted from the router's console prompt. The command to start such a session is `ssh -1` *user* 10.0.0.1, where *user* is the user ID you will use to connect, and 10.0.0.1 represents the SSH server device to which you are connecting. Additionally, the `-p` option allows the use of an alternate port number, and the `-c` option allows the preferred encryption strength to be specified—either Data Encryption Standard (DES), 3DES, or AES with 128-, 192-, or 256-bit key strength (for SSHv2 only).

The Console Port

Don't let the fact that the console port of your router is local lull you into a false sense of security. Even in facilities with high physical security, individuals may still be able to gain local access to your router. For this reason, all the same authentication precautions mentioned for the VTY lines using Telnet or SSH should be applied to the console port. Either add a local password with the `password` command, set it for local user login using the `login local` command, or set it for remote authentication using the `login tacacs` command. Finally, because the console port has a local transport, the `exec-timeout` statement is more important than ever. If you are configuring your router via the console port and don't properly exit before disconnecting your console cable and walking away, your session will remain active if no `exec-timeout` is set! When the next person plugs in to the port weeks, months, or years later (assuming there haven't been any reboots), the router will still be in whatever mode it was left in, most likely enable mode if you were in the configuration process! With `exec-timeout` set, reauthentication will be forced after x minutes.

TFTP and FTP

TFTP is a dangerous protocol. It has the file transfer power of FTP, but with zero security. No login or authentication is needed—just point and transfer. You can imagine that if TFTP were running on any systems on your network, you wouldn't want anyone to have outside access to it. TFTP can be run as a server on some versions of Cisco routers, although it should be disabled by default. (For more information on disabling the TFTP server on Cisco devices, see the "Disabling Servers" section later in this chapter.) TFTP can also be run as a client on all Cisco routers, enabling transfer of configuration files, IOS upgrades, and so on.

Many experienced administrators use TFTP as their administration method of choice instead of Telnet or other command-line type utilities. This brings up the greatest TFTP security concern, which is not the router, but the TFTP server where configuration files are held. A place must exist for administrators to upload and download the configuration files they edit, and these locations are a major point of concern. Many administrators use their personal station or an administration station for this purpose and only run the TFTP server while in the process of updating configurations. This is the preferred method.

Having a TFTP server running all the time with former or current configuration files and IOS updates on it is an outside attacker's dream. Those configuration files can be used as a map of your entire security structure. For this reason alone, it is imperative to block TFTP traffic coming in from the Internet. An access list to block traffic destined for a TFTP server using standard UDP port 69 would look something like this:

```
router(config)#access-list 110 deny udp any any eq 69
```

Of course, this wouldn't be necessary in an environment that only allows necessary traffic.

Since IOS version 12, FTP has also become available to transfer IOS and configuration information. Thankfully, FTP servers have the authentication controls that a TFTP server lacks. However, if you have administrative FTP servers running on your network, it is still advisable that you verify whether inbound FTP traffic is being blocked. Also, keep in mind that all FTP information travels in the clear, so it has the same "eavesdropping" issues that Telnet suffers from. If your router's IOS version supports encryption, it would be possible to protect your FTP sessions from eavesdropping with IPSec.

Configuration Management Tricks with TFTP and Scripts

Anyone who has configured a Cisco router via Telnet or another command-line interface has wondered, "Isn't there a better way?" Because the ordering of rules is so important to their effectiveness, reconfiguration of a long ACL via the command line is a chore of Herculean proportions. In addition, the retyping of key information for VPNs or other features that require encryption demands the utmost in accuracy. This is why many long-time Cisco administrators transfer config files to their station and use an editor to make router changes. Use the command `copy run tftp` and supply the details about where the TFTP server can be located. This will copy the running configuration from the Cisco device in question to your TFTP server. Then you can edit the document with an editor that handles formatting, such as WordPad in a Windows environment. (Other text editors might not be able to process the formatting, and the file will appear jumbled.) With Find and Replace, a changed IP address can be propagated throughout a complicated configuration with ease. Cut and Paste can allow the swift addition of ACL lines wherever you want them. When the process is complete, copy the saved file back to the router with the `copy tftp run` or `copy tftp star` command. If the update needs to be done without a reboot, you will need to copy to `run`. However, when you copy to the running configuration, commands are appended rather than overwritten, which can be messy. A better way, in environments that can afford a few minutes down time, is to copy the config to star (or the startup configuration) and then do a reload to reboot. Upon reload, the changed configuration will be loaded as typed. Watch for typing errors; with this method, you lose the error checking of the IOS until it's too late!

In environments where a reboot cannot be afforded, administrators can make scripts from copied configurations that can be pasted into the command-line interface. This way, the same speed can be afforded with Find and Replace, but without any service interruption.

Simple Network Management Protocol

Simple Network Management Protocol (SNMP) is a popular way to manage network devices (including routers), especially in large, cumbersome, complex, or geographically dispersed networks. Many different management products and systems use it. However, allowing Internet access to SNMP, despite the fact that it provides an easy way for a distant administrator to help manage the network, still opens a potential security hole that outside malicious users can exploit. If an attacker can figure out your SNMP security scheme, or if the scheme isn't properly secured, the attacker could be the person managing your network. Because we strive to avoid this, it is highly advisable that you simply block all SNMP traffic at the entrance to the network. SNMP devices may use several ports, but most typically operate on UDP ports 161 and 162. An access list to explicitly block such traffic would look like this:

```
router(config)#access-list 113 deny udp any any eq 161
router(config)#access-list 113 deny udp any any eq 162
```

Other SNMP-related ports that may need to be blocked in some environments are TCP ports 161, 162, 199, 391, 705, and 1993, and UDP ports 199, 391, and 1993. Of course, you would only use this access list if it were part of an existing access list that permits traffic by default. In other configurations, SNMP traffic would be most likely be blocked by an implicit deny.

The most effective way to mitigate SNMP-related risks is to disable SNMP in environments where it is not required. You can accomplish this by applying the following command in the configuration mode:

```
router(config)#no snmp-server
```

> **Note**
>
> In February 2002, vulnerabilities were discovered that left many vendors' SNMP implementations open to exploit (http://www.cert.org/advisories/CA-2002-03.html). It is imperative that your product is patched to the level required to fix these vulnerabilities, or that a workaround is implemented to prevent external access to the SNMP ports of your hosts and devices.

In Chapter 19, "Maintaining a Security Perimeter," we describe the benefits of using SNMP for monitoring the network devices on the internal network. If you want to take advantage of SNMP capabilities built in to Cisco routers, here are some suggestions on best practices for securing SNMP. If your environment allows it, implement at least SNMP version 3, which supports encryption and cryptographic authentication and is significantly more secure than its predecessors. (SNMP versions 1 and 2c, which are also supported by Cisco IOS, are limited to using community strings for authentication, and they transmit data in clear text.) If you cannot use version 3, consider implementing IPSec encryption to protect the clear-text SNMP traffic if it absolutely must travel across the Internet. When you need to resort to using plain community strings, by all means, carefully pick community string names. Don't use the universal choices of "public" and "private." The Cisco command for setting up a complex community name for SNMP version 1 reads as follows for read-only (RO) access:

```
router(config)#snmp-server community complex name RO
```

Substituting RO with RW (read-write) allows read-write access to the said community. It is in your best security interest to disallow read-write access from the outside network if possible. An IP access list number can be included to restrict access to certain stations by adding the number of a standard ACL to the end of the `snmp-server community` command, as follows:

```
snmp-server community complex name RW ACL #
```

The standard ACL represented by the listed number includes the IP address range of stations that are allowed to access the agent.

> **Note**
>
> This is an SNMPv1 command. Do not use this command in an SNMPv3 environment; otherwise, the router will think you are using SNMPv1 and disable the advantages associated with SNMPv3. For information about configuring SNMPv3 on Cisco devices, take a look at http://www.cisco.com/univercd/cc/td/doc/product/software/ios120/120newft/120t/_120t3/snmp3.htm.

Authentication and Passwords

When discussing the security of a managed device, it's imperative to mention authentication and passwording. In the Cisco router, each service has its own configuration options for the authentication method of choice (as mentioned in their individual sections). However, these options basically boil down to two types: remote and local authentication. Remote authentication is the preferred method, and it relies on an external RADIUS or TACACS+ server. Both RADIUS and TACACS+ are remote server methods of verifying a user's name and password credentials. To set this up for TACACS+, use the following commands.

To enable AAA from config mode, use the command

```
aaa new-model
```

Until this is typed in, no other `aaa` commands will be available. Then follow with this command:

```
aaa authentication login default group tacacs+ local
```

Here, `default` is the name of the AAA list (you can substitute a unique name here). Also, `group tacacs+` tells the router to authenticate with any servers defined in the tacacs+ group, and `local` indicates to use the local login as a backup if the remote server should fail.

> **Tip**
>
> Always have a backup for your AAA authentication command, especially when you're first configuring remote authentication! It is a good practice to leave an open session to the router while configuring and testing AAA commands. Also, do not save the configuration until it has been tested. This way, you can always recover by rebooting. Otherwise, you may find yourself completely locked out of your router!

Then go to the line you want to configure remote authentication for (con, aux, vty, and so on) and type the following:

```
login authentication default
```

This will force the line in question to use the authentication methods defined in the AAA authentication list `default`.

Finally, to specify your TACACS+ server, use these commands:

```
tacacs-server host 10.0.0.1
```

```
tacacs-server key THISISMYKEY
```

Here, 10.0.0.1 is the IP address of your TACACS+ server and *THISISMYKEY* is the unique key name you are using for authentication with your TACACS+ servers. This will be the default key used for *any* TACACS+ server. For unique server keys, append the `key` keyword to the `tacacs-server host` command, followed by the unique key value.

The advantage of remote authentication is not having all of your "eggs in one basket." If you use local authentication, your login and password information is accessible directly in the router. Moving this information to a remote location adds to its security. Also, when you are administering a lot of devices and dozens of users, setting up all your users on new devices is as easy as configuring them for RADIUS or TACACS. Also, because all the user and password information is securely held on a remote server, the security complications of having to transport and type in local users is eliminated. One negative point of remote authentication is that if your remote authentication source is down and you have no other authentication options available, you could be kept from logging in. However, remote authentication options can allow for many types of backups for just such circumstances, including the ability to use local or no authentication.

When a business decision is made not to implement a remote authentication server, the next best option is local authentication. As mentioned previously, this is accomplished by adding the `login local` command to the line you want to control access to. To configure a username and password, use the `username` command mentioned previously in the section on SSH. It is important to use best practices to select a username and password for configuration purposes. If you do remote configuration by Telnet or SSH, a good username and password might be all that stands between your network and an attacker.

For extra protection, passwords can be set to appear as an encrypted string when listing configuration information on the router. This is accomplished with the command `service password encryption`. This command is simply a means to help sanitize configurations, preventing accidental exposure of passwords to "shoulder surfers." However, the encryption method employed is weak and will not protect the passwords from serious cryptographic analysis. Don't let this encryption give you a false sense of security and start leaving configuration files lying about!

Disabling Servers

Several servers can be run on most Cisco routers, and as with a PC, any running server is a point of vulnerability. Therefore, all unneeded servers should be disabled. Depending on the IOS version, these servers might be disabled by default; however, it never hurts to double-check. We already discussed the Telnet server and ways to defend it. Following are a few of the more common server programs and the commands to disable them:

- The Bootp server is a forerunner of DHCP that can be configured to hand out necessary IP information to configured clients. Bootp can be disabled with the command `no ip bootp server`.

- The TFTP server on supported routers is disabled with `no tftp-server` *device-name*. Here, *device-name* is the device that is configured to receive files.

- The HTTP server offers alternative means to manage the router via a web browser. This can be a major security concern because web traffic is much more likely to be allowed into an environment than Telnet traffic is. You can disable HTTP by using the command `no ip http server`.

- If the HTTP server must be used for management, authentication can be enabled (much like the login local feature of Telnet) with the command `ip http authentication local`.

- For additional security, ACLs can be applied to allow only specified addresses access to the HTTP server with the command `ip http access-class ACL #`, where `ACL #` refers to the standard access list that defines stations that can gain access.

- You can change the HTTP server's port address with the command `ip http port` *port#*, where *port#* is the port used for HTTP access, numbered 0–65535. Picking an unusual port number helps promote "security through obscurity," making your Cisco router's web server harder to find.

Disable Unneeded Services

One key to securing any type of device is removing any services that are not needed. These services might not serve as a direct threat, but when you're maximizing security, any window that isn't needed should be boarded up. In this section, we will take a look at some services that are not used in some environments and that can be known troublemakers.

Small Services

Small services (ports below 20 TCP and UDP) and the Time service (TCP and UDP port 37) are seldom used and are more of a liability than a value to you. The small services can be disabled with the following commands:

```
router(config)#no service tcp-small-servers
router(config)#no service udp-small-servers
```

By typing these commands at the `config` prompt and saving the configuration, you will disallow small services on the router. (These services are disabled by default on IOS version 12.0 and later.) Access to these services should be blocked at your perimeter. In an environment where inbound access is allowed until explicitly denied, access to these services running on internal systems can be blocked using an ACL as follows:

```
router(config)#access-list 101 deny tcp any any lt 20
router(config)#access-list 101 deny udp any any lt 20
```

The Time service should also be blocked. Any time-related services should be handled by NTP (see "Configure NTP and NTP Authentication," later in this chapter). The rule of thumb in security is to block any service ports you know you don't need. It doesn't matter whether this is regarding an unpopular service, such as Time, or one as popular as FTP. If your security policy states that a service isn't used on your network, block it. In an environment where you only block traffic that you don't want, the Time service can be filtered with two extended access lists:

```
router(config)#access-list 101 deny tcp any any eq 37
router(config)#access-list 101 deny udp any any eq 37
```

The following line is used to apply the access lists to the interface:

```
router (config-if)#ip access-group 101 in
```

This is applied with the rest of the deny statements on the external router interface to the Internet.

Cisco Discovery Protocol

Another popular protocol specific to Cisco routers is the Cisco Discovery Protocol (CDP), which enables Cisco routers to discover specific details about each other. CDP can be a major security concern because detailed configuration information is propagated throughout the network. If you don't have a specific need for CDP, disable it. The command to do so by interface is router(config-if)#no cdp enable. To completely disable CDP, use router(config)#no cdp run.

Finger

Finger is a service that allows users to query a network device to discover information about other users by their email address or about currently logged-on users. Depending on the variation of Finger server, you might find out only if the user is currently logged on, or you might find more personal information, including the last time the user retrieved his mail, his telephone number, full name, address, and so on. Cisco routers specifically can give information about users who are logged in currently to the router via services such as Telnet. Most ISPs now disable Finger services for privacy reasons; we want to give out as little information as possible to prevent possible attacks. It is in your users' best interest to block the Finger service at the furthest contact point from your private network, most likely your border router. To disable the Finger server built in to the Cisco router, use the following command:

```
router(config)#no service finger
```

An access list to specifically block the Finger service would look like this:

```
access-list 122 deny tcp any any eq 79
```

It is unlikely that this access list would be used, however, because most environments only allow traffic they want.

PAD Service

The PAD service is used for Packet Assembler/Disassembler commands, which are used for connections between servers accessing the services and devices using PAD. If your Cisco configuration does not require this service, use the command `no service pad`.

Proxy-ARP

Cisco routers have the ability to respond to ARP requests on behalf of hosts that are shielded behind them. This proxy-ARP feature can allow hosts on routed subnets to communicate as if they are on one large, flat network. However, in a properly configured routed environment, this feature is not needed. Also, spoofing and denial of service attacks can be facilitated with proxy-ARP enabled. Therefore, it is a commonly accepted best practice to disable proxy-ARP. This is accomplished on all router interfaces by typing `no ip proxy-arp`.

Configure NTP and NTP Authentication

Network Time Protocol (NTP) is used to synchronize time sources on a network. You should disable access to NTP services through any interface that does not require them. Cisco includes a simple command to disable NTP on any router interface:

```
router(config-if)# ntp disable
```

NTP is disabled on all interfaces of Cisco routers by default. However, NTP is important from a security perspective, because it can be useful for synchronizing time sources when comparing log files from various devices and for tracking time-sensitive update information. To prevent update information from unwanted sources, authentication can be enabled that requires all updates to be "signed" with an MD5 hash. If you are using a local NTP source, verify that it is properly "hardened" and that you have these authentication mechanisms enabled. Also, if you use a remote NTP time source, be sure it is a known public source and audit that it is answering NTP requests from your hosts on a regular basis.

Note

For an updated list of publicly available time servers, check out http://ntp.isc.org/bin/view/Servers/ WebHome.

Often, public time servers ask that you use a DNS name to reach them instead of an IP address, because they want the flexibility to change the IP address of the server they are using for this service. However, many routers and switches can only support an IP address. For this reason, it is a good practice to set up a local NTP server to query the public source by DNS name and then configure routers and switches to synchronize with it. Here's the command to configure a Cisco router to query an NTP time server:

```
ntp server 10.0.0.1 key key#
```

In this example, 10.0.0.1 would be the address of the time server. If authentication is used, the key option is specified, followed by the number of the key being used. Multiple commands can be listed for redundancy, in case one time server is down. To choose a preferred time server, add the prefer keyword to the end of the corresponding NTP server statement. You can also append the version keyword, followed by the version of NTP you are using (1–3) and the source keyword followed by the name of the interface you want to be the source of the NTP request.

If you want to use authentication for NTP on a Cisco router, use the following command:

```
ntp authenticate
```

This command enables the ability to use authentication with NTP. Then, type in this next command:

```
ntp authentication-key 1 md5 thisismytestkey
```

Here, 1 is the key number, md5 is the hash algorithm being used, and *thisismytestkey* is the value used to generate the MD5 hash.

Finally, use the following command to let the router know that the previously defined key (identified as 1) is a trusted key and should be used for future NTP transactions.

```
ntp trusted-key 1
```

As a final means to protect your Cisco router's NTP services, you can apply an access list to it of all its peers (servers it is allowed to communicate with):

```
ntp access-group serve-only 1
```

Here, 1 is the standard access list defining allowed NTP communications partners and serve-only specifically states that this ACL will only allow server access to the router's NTP service. You can also specify peer, query-only, and serve for other combinations of allowed NTP access.

Cisco TCP Keepalives Services

The Cisco TCP Keepalives services ensure that connections are properly cleared when they are idle and improperly terminated. These services guarantee that connections cannot be used by nefarious users for diabolical purposes. To enable these services, add the statements service tcp-keepalives-in and service tcp-keepalives-out to your global router configuration.

Unicast Reverse Path Forwarding

Unicast Reverse Path Forwarding (RFP) verifies that packets come from a logically sound source based on routing information stored in the Cisco router. In turn, this feature helps prevent spoofed packets from being accepted on the router. To enable Unicast RFP, use the command `ip verify unicast reverse-path`. This feature requires Cisco Express Forwarding (CEF) to be enabled, which uses additional resources on the router.

Internet Control Message Protocol Blocking

Internet Control Message Protocol (ICMP) is a workhorse protocol in an IP-based environment. It is responsible for generating many of the error messages and informative messages that keep the Internet working. However, many popular attacks and reconnaissance techniques are based on this protocol. In this section, we will look at some ways to protect your router from these types of attacks.

Unreachables

We will now look at the filtering of host unreachables (ICMP type 3). A router sends the "host unreachable" message when it can't find the listed host because it is down or doesn't exist. This doesn't seem like such a bad thing, but if a malicious mapper compares the unreachables and other responses from an IP address range, she can determine which of the IP addresses represent valid, running hosts. This is yet another method for the devious to map out your network before an attack. A trace of communication (using a product such as Tcpdump) between a sender and a nonexistent recipient would look like this:

```
sender.com.31054 > receiver.com.23: S 3435678932:3435678932(0) win 8760
➥<ms 1460> (DF)
router > sender.com: icmp: host receiver.com unreachable
```

The trace shows an initiating Telnet packet from sender.com to a nonexistent host, receiver.com. Because the nonexistent receiver can't respond for itself (obviously!), the router (called "router" in our example) replies to sender.com with the ICMP host unreachable message.

Because of these mapping concerns, host unreachables are another traffic type that is popular to block. Cisco has the following integrated command to disable them:

```
router(config-if)#no ip unreachables
```

After applying this in global configuration mode, all host unreachable messages will be disabled. To test this, Telnet to an IP address that doesn't exist on your inside network while running a network trace program to see what packets are returned to you. Be sure that Telnet traffic will pass through to your inside network by altering any access lists that would deny such traffic. After the command has been applied, you shouldn't receive host unreachables. You might wonder, "If it's not returning host unreachables, what would the traffic look like?"

The answer is simply that there would be no reply. The sender would give up on its own because it didn't receive a response in the allotted amount of retries.

Disabling such informative ICMP messages from your network or from being propagated by your router has consequences. The "packet-too-big" unreachable message (a subtype of the standard ICMP unreachable) is often necessary for proper network functionality. If you can't let outside parties know that they need to fragment their information or adjust their maximum transmission unit (MTU) size to communicate with you, you might not successfully communicate.

Note

For information on excluding the packet-too-big ICMP unreachable messages (type 3 code 4) from your ICMP filtering, as well as suggestions for filtering the various ICMP types from your network, look at the "Filtering TCP and UDP Ports and ICMP Types" section of Chapter 2.

Blocking IP unreachables and other ICMP traffic types that facilitate smooth communications assumes either that you don't have any publicly accessible servers or that you do and aren't being a good Internet neighbor. If you have public servers, you might want to be a good Internet neighbor and allow certain ICMP interactions with them on your screened subnet. Apply all the ICMP filters to the router interface of the private network, protecting it, and allow chosen ICMP traffic to the screened subnet. This allows enhanced communications with outside parties who aren't familiar with your environment. Some allowed ICMP types might include outbound echo replies, time-exceeded messages, packet-too-big, administratively prohibited, and unreachables. Inbound, you might want to allow echo requests (perhaps just to a few particular servers' IP addresses). Your security policy and your ISP will decide the types you allow.

Most of these traffic types are security concerns because of an outsider's ability to map your network. This isn't as great of a concern on a publicly accessible segment. Echo replies and requests are of the most concern (due to exploits and covert channel concerns), but with properly patched, configured, and hardened servers, they shouldn't be a problem either. The proper logging of said traffic types is advised to verify that the traffic in question is not of a malicious nature. For more information on the logging and examination of malicious traffic, check out Chapter 8, "Network Intrusion Detection," and Chapter 20, "Network Log Analysis."

Directed Broadcasts

One command that is useful when securing Cisco routers against popular ICMP-based attacks is `router(config-if)#no ip directed-broadcast`.

This command disallows traffic to broadcast addresses, preventing amplification of Smurf-like attacks, where one echo request can generate hundreds of responses. For this reason, it is best to execute this command on all router interfaces on your network. As of IOS version 12.0, directed broadcasts are disabled by default. Although this command is popularly mentioned as a means to deter Smurf attacks that use the ICMP protocol, it is also effective against broadcast attacks using UDP, TCP, and IP.

Smurf Attacks

Smurfing is a type of denial of service attack that makes use of the broadcast behavior of IP networks. It is called *smurfing* because one of the first programs to implement the attack was named Smurf. The attack works by sending a series of spoofed ICMP echo packets to the broadcast address of a network. The attacker hopes that all the hosts on the network will send ICMP echo replies to the spoofed address. If the network segment is large, the attacker might be able to evoke hundreds of echo reply packets generated for every echo packet he sends. This allows the attacker to magnify the bandwidth of the attack, making it possible for a dial-up attacker connected at 56Kbps to bring down sites connected using a T1 line (1.544Mbps).

Redirects

Another popularly implemented Cisco ICMP type command is `router(config-if)#no ip redirects`.

This command is often used in conjunction with antispoofing access lists and is applied to any router interface from which malicious traffic can enter your network. It is a means by which a nefarious user could manipulate the path of return traffic, and it should be disabled.

Spoofing and Source Routing

As introduced in Chapter 2, source routing and spoofing can be an effective and hazardous combination. This is why it is so important to apply ingress filters and disable source routing. As mentioned previously, the command to disable source routing on Cisco routers is `router(config)#no ip source-route`.

For a review of ingress filtering and source routing, refer to Chapter 2.

Router Logging

Logging is an important feature of any firewall, especially one with a secured subnet. A router doesn't have much space onboard for logs, however. In addition, logging takes up extra resources on a possibly already taxed component of your network. Other logging solutions could involve installing an IDS or some other type of sniffer on your network to monitor and log the type of traffic roaming about on your network segments. (A *sniffer* is a device that captures detailed packet information.) If you do a lot of logging on your router (with the log option appended to your access lists), you can set up or use an existing Syslog server on your network and redirect the log files to it. This way, you don't run into the space limitations of a router's onboard memory, and if you have more than one router, you can have all the routers' logs sent to one centralized location.

POSTED: No Trespassing—The Importance of Banners

When configuring a router, it is possible to configure a banner that will be displayed at the logon prompt when a user first accesses the router. The command to create such a login banner is `router(config)#banner login ,_scary approved message,.`

The commas in this command represent some (any) delimiter, and "scary approved message" represents a login message that your business has chosen to most effectively ward off evildoers. Posting a warning doesn't guarantee that if a bad person elects to trespass on your virtual property you will be able to capture and convict him, but it can help improve the chances and help demonstrate the interloper's intent. More than one electronic trespasser has escaped conviction with the claim "I didn't know I wasn't supposed to be there." It is a good idea to get counsel familiar with your area's legal specifics to help choose the wording for your banner to maximize its effectiveness. Don't include information about your site or its equipment because this can all be used against you.

Remember that a banner can work against you as well. Using a banner that reads "Top-Secret Government Site—DO NOT ENTER!" is just asking for trouble. Something along these lines might be preferable: "ALL ACTIVITY ON THIS DEVICE IS MONITORED AND WILL BE USED AS EVIDENCE IN THE EVENT OF PROSECU-TION." Gives you a funny feeling, doesn't it? Again, the banner might have to be tweaked for your environment and local laws, but it does three things:

- It keeps your site completely anonymous.
- It lets trespassers know (without threats) that they are being watched.
- It states up front that the owner of this device will prosecute people who shouldn't be there.

The end result is that it makes the visitor think twice, and if bad things happen, it is a strong indicator of an attacker's intent.

To configure a Cisco router to perform logging, make sure it is currently enabled with the command `router(config)#logging on`.

To send logging information to a local Syslog server, use the command `router (config)#logging ip address`, where `ip address` represents the IP address for the Syslog server in question.

After logging is successfully configured, the router sends its logging information to the Syslog server based on the "trap" level you configured. This is set using the command `router(config)# logging trap information level`, where `information level` is the informational level of the messages that will be sent to the Syslog server. (This command sends all messages of the listed level and lower.) The default level of the `trap` command is `informational`, which includes all message types except debugging information (which is generated by the Cisco debug commands). To log this information as well, change the trap level to `debugging`.

Tip

Keep in mind that the debug commands can generate quite a lot of information and can fill up log servers quickly.

After logging is properly configured, messages like this one should magically appear on your Syslog server:

```
138: 1d06h: %SEC-6-IPACCESSLOGP: list 112 permitted tcp 10.0.0.3(4766)
➥-> 192.168.219.25(80), 5 packets
```

The message is an example of a standard Cisco log entry as generated by an access list, including the log keyword (`access-list 112` to be exact). The ACL was a permit rule, so this is reported as matching the permit and is allowed to pass. Most of the rest of the entry is pretty intuitive—address, port source, and destination—except the cryptic Cisco labeling mechanisms. For more information on log files, take a look at Chapter 20.

For readability of log files and for sanity between multiple devices, it is a best practice to force all routers to use the same time zone or, if your company crosses more than one time zone, to use Greenwich Mean Time (GMT) as your standard. To do this on a Cisco router, use the following command:

```
enable clock timezone GMT 0
```

Here, GMT is a label for the time zone you are configuring and 0 is the offset from GMT.

Automatic Securing and Auditing of Cisco Routers

Due to the complexities of securing a Cisco router, several automated methods have been established to help ease the burden on network professionals when auditing and hardening router configurations. The two we will discuss in this section are Cisco's Auto Secure and the Router Audit Tool (RAT).

Securing Your Router with Cisco's Auto Secure Feature

As of IOS version 12.3(1), administrators can take advantage of a new security tool for Cisco routers. Cisco's Auto Secure option allows the automated securing of Cisco routers using best practices. It adds ingress filters and disables commonly exploited services while enabling security enhancements, all with little input from the end user. The syntax of the command is as follows:

```
auto secure
```

This command is typed in enable mode (*not* config mode) and will offer prompts to the end user. First, it will ask if the router is connected to the Internet. If the answer is yes, it will ask questions to determine the interfaces facing the Internet and apply ingress filters to them blocking IANA reserved addresses and RFC 1918 addresses.

Next, it will go on to disable Finger, service PAD, UDP and TCP small servers, CDP protocol, Bootp server, HTTP server, source routing, and gratuitous ARP. It will enable password encryption, `tcp-keepalives-in`, and `tcp-keepalives-out`.

It then asks if SNMP is used to manage the router. If the end user answers yes, it deletes the default RO and RW community strings and suggests the use of SNMPv3. If the end user answers no, it disables SNMP.

Then the command prompts the user with a sample banner and asks him to input a banner of his own. It then checks the enable password and forces it to be configured if it doesn't exist or if it is of insufficient length.

The command then configures local AAA authentication and applies local authentication, exec-timeout, and transport options for all available con, vty, and aux lines. It disables IP redirects, IP proxy ARP, IP unreachables, IP directed broadcasts, and IP mask replies on all interfaces. It enables Cisco Express Forwarding and enables Unicast RFP on all interfaces connected to the Internet. To see an example of a configuration created by Auto Secure, check out Appendix A, "Cisco Access List Sample Configurations."

Cisco Auto Secure, though no substitute for a security professional, is a great step in the right direction for Cisco router security.

Auditing Your Router with the Router Audit Tool (RAT)

The Router Audit Tool (RAT) is a freeware command-line program available from The Center for Internet Security at www.cisecurity.com. As its name implies, RAT allows the automated auditing of your Cisco router configurations (and more recently PIX configurations) for common security issues. It runs from a computer's command prompt and is available for both Windows and UNIX platforms. After installing RAT, you will need to load a copy of the Cisco router configuration you want to audit on to the station where you installed RAT. This can be accomplished by loading a TFTP server on your RAT station and issuing the command `copy running-config tftp` from the Cisco router. You will be prompted for the communication information of your TFTP server. After transferring the file to the download directory of your TFTP server software, you will need to move the configuration file to the `RAT/bin` directory. Then, simply go to a command prompt and run the following command from the `RAT/bin` directory:

```
RAT router-config
```

Here, `router-config` is the name of the router configuration file you copied to your host. RAT will go through and check your configuration against a plethora of security best practices, much like Auto Secure. However, the end result is not an updated router configuration, but instead a report in HTML format that documents all the security tests your router configuration has failed and why they are issues. Next, the report includes a rating of your router's security and a script (that will need some minor editing for your particular IP address information) to correct the vulnerabilities it has found. This script, once adjusted for your environment, can simply be pasted into the command-line interface of the Cisco router from which it was downloaded. Though there may be a few minor false positives and some user input required, RAT offers many more security tests than Cisco Auto Secure and produces a friendly audit report that helps educate the user. The Router Audit Tool is a powerful program to add to your security arsenal.

Summary

The router plays a significant role in the security of your network. It can be configured as a role player in defense in depth, helping protect your QoS, defending against DoS attacks, or just taking some of the burden off your existing firewall by handling egress or ingress filtering. Your router might also be acting as your primary firewall, using technologies such as CBAC, NAT, and ACLs. With CBAC, your router might be supporting you as a truly stateful firewall. With NAT, your router might be shielding your addressing scheme from prying eyes and helping protect your network from unsolicited entrance. Finally, with access lists, your router might be defending your network using packet-filtering technology.

In any case, the router performs important security duties and must be sufficiently armored. Be sure to disable unused features and block unused services, use adequate pass-wording and authentication, secure configuration channels and methods, prevent the propagation of unneeded network information, and use logging to audit your success. Tools such as Cisco's Auto Secure and the Router Audit Tool can assist in the automation of your router hardening. After all, a properly implemented and hardened router is the beginning of a secure network.

7

Virtual Private Networks

IN TODAY'S INTERCONNECTED WORLD, THE NEED TO move information from site to site is becoming common. Whether this move is from one end of town to the other or across the globe, the basic challenge is the same: How can we securely transport our data? For many years, this transportation was accomplished with expensive proprietary links that were leased from communication vendors so that companies had a "private" segment for such communications. The longer the distance, the more these connections cost, making wide area networks (WANs) a luxury that many firms could not afford. At the same time, many firms could not afford to go without them. As broadband Internet connections became staples for many firms, the concept of using the existing structure of the Internet as WAN cabling became an intriguing one. Costs could be greatly reduced using these already available public access points. The concern again was how to keep the data secure. Because we are sharing an international "party line" with anyone else who connects to the Internet, how can we be sure that our data is protected from eavesdroppers? The solution is Virtual Private Networking.

In this chapter, we discuss the basic concepts of how a Virtual Private Network (VPN) works and is configured, the basic encryption technologies that a VPN uses, details of Internet Protocol Security (IPSec) (a standard for VPN networking), as well as other popularly implemented protocols for virtual networking. We also show sample configurations that demonstrate practical applications for the theory we cover. This chapter also provides a foundation for understanding Chapter 16, "VPN Integration," which discusses how VPN technologies can be incorporated into the security perimeter.

VPN Basics

A VPN is a connection that is established over an existing "public" or shared infrastructure using encryption or authentication technologies to secure its payload. This creates a "virtual" segment between any two entities that have access. This might occur across the shared infrastructure of a local area network (LAN), WAN connections, or the Internet. In this chapter, we focus predominately on VPNs that traverse the Internet as a means to create a secure channel over its public infrastructure. Such channels make for an inexpensive and effective remote networking solution that anyone with Internet access can take advantage of.

VPNs can be categorized into three basic configuration types: host-to-host, host-to-gateway, and gateway-to-gateway. Any of these scenarios could be used with a VPN that is traversing the Internet, although host-to-host VPNs are also popularly used as a means to communicate privately on local network segments.

Regardless of which media the VPN uses, which type of configuration it represents, or what shared infrastructure it crosses, the VPN is a powerful tool that can be used in many different ways to create a secure communication channel.

Note

If you would like to brush up on cryptography fundamentals, take a look at Appendix B, "Crypto 101," where we review key topics in cryptography that you need to know to effectively plan and implement VPNs.

Basic VPN Methodology

The basic concept behind a VPN is securing a communication channel with encryption. Communication can be safeguarded through encryption at many different layers of the network, such as the following:

- Application
- Transport
- Network
- Data link

At the application layer, encryption can be applied with programs such as Pretty Good Privacy (PGP) or through channels such as Secure Shell (SSH). In addition, remote single-session programs such as pcAnywhere and multisession programs such as Terminal Server can be used with encryption to protect remote communications. Most of these programs work from host to host, meaning that they only offer protection for the packet's payload and not the packet. The exception is SSH, which can be used in a port-forwarding mode to create a tunnel. We will cover this in greater detail in Chapter 16.

At the transport layer, protocols such as Secure Sockets Layer (SSL) can be used to protect the contents of a specific communication between two parties. This is typically used via web browser communications. As with application layer protection, the contents of the communication are protected, but the IP packets that carry this information are available for inspection. SSL can also be used as a tunneling facilitator for other communication session types using a product called Stunnel (http://www.stunnel.org/). SSL and its use are covered in greater detail in Chapter 16.

At the network layer, protocols such as IPSec not only encrypt the payload of the packet, but they also encrypt the TCP/IP information. Although the IP address information for the parties that are encrypting and decrypting the packet is necessary to facilitate proper routing, higher-level information, including transport protocols and associated ports, can be completely obfuscated. Endpoint station IP address information can also be hidden if a gateway device such as a router, firewall, or concentrator is doing the encryption, using a concept called *tunneling*. We will cover IPSec's implementation, its inner workings, and sample configuration in detail in the "IPSec Basics" section, later in this chapter.

Layer 2 Tunneling Protocol (L2TP) is an addition to Point-to-Point Protocol (PPP), which allows the encryption of packets sent over PPP on the data link layer (Layer 2). We cover L2TP and its predecessor PPTP (Point-to-Point Tunneling Protocol) in greater detail later in this chapter, in the "Other VPN Protocols: PPTP and L2TP" section.

Despite the fact that these encryption technologies occur at many different network layers, they all could be part of a VPN. However, some might not be able to handle all the duties of a VPN without some help from other applications or protocols. In this chapter, we predominately discuss the use of network and data link layer encryption technology for VPNs.

What Is Tunneling?

Tunneling is the process of encapsulating one type of packet inside another to facilitate some sort of transport advantage. For example, tunneling could be used to send broadcast traffic across a routed environment or SNMP traffic across the Internet, or to secure IP packets with encryption. One effective demonstration of tunneling as a means of encryption can be illustrated by using a gateway-to-gateway VPN example. The two networks in Figure 7.1 are interconnected via a VPN that is terminated at either end by a firewall.

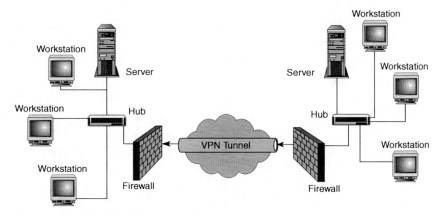

Figure 7.1   A virtual tunnel is formed across the Internet, connecting the two remote networks.

The firewall in our example translates any packet that is destined for the remote network into encrypted form, and it adds a new IP header to the resultant payload with its own

IP address as the source address and the remote firewall's address as the destination IP address of the packet. Encryption hides the actual IP information of the original packet. When the remote firewall receives the packet, it decrypts the packet back to its original form and passes it to the host for which it was originally intended. The virtual segment being created between the two gateway endpoints is called a *tunnel*. The hosts have no knowledge of the fact that the packets are being encrypted or that they are being sent over a public network. No special software or configuration is required for the hosts. When a host sends a packet that is destined for a host on the remote subnet, the VPN process is handled completely by the gateway devices.

When tunneling is used, even though host system IP addresses are masked from the outside world, they don't have complete anonymity. Because the IP addresses of the gateway devices are available, eavesdroppers can still determine who is communicating with whom. Maybe this won't give away communication streams on a host-to-host level, but it might on a network-to-network level, which could tell an outsider a lot. For example, what if it is rumored that Mr. X is a spy from Switzerland? The government immediately starts to monitor his Internet connection and determines that he is using a VPN. We can't tell what his communications are about. However, if we know Mr. X owns the source address and the destination is somewhere in Switzerland, we might want to investigate further.

Encryption, encapsulation, and tunneling do not make the packets that are being sent inaccessible. The packets can still be gathered and analyzed. However, if a properly implemented, adequately strong encryption algorithm is used, your payload should still be safe. In the next section, we take a closer look at what a gateway-to-gateway tunnel transaction looks like in packet form.

Packet-Level View of Tunneling

The concept of tunneling can be more clearly understood by taking a look at it at the packet level. The following code, which uses tcpdump, shows a packet as it would appear without going through an encrypted tunnel:

```
00:05:18.671517 192.168.44.129 > 172.16.1.128: AH(spi=580532459,seq=0x3):
➥1232 > 80: P 1:260(259) ack 1 win 17520 (DF)
```

This is actually an IPSec packet that uses the Authentication Header (AH) security protocol, which we will cover in greater detail in the IPSec section of this chapter. This packet is sent in a mode that does not require tunneling. The packet traverses directly from one host to the other, without being translated in any way by the gateway devices. Make note of the IP addresses. They represent the addresses of the two hosts. In addition, notice that the transport layer information is available and that this is an HTTP transaction, as signified by the use of TCP port 80. (It is actually the contacting of a web server.) Because the TCP flags are available, we can tell that this is actually the end of the three-way handshake. Host 192.168.44.129 is sending a lone ACK back to the web server at IP address 172.16.1.128.

The following code shows a similar packet that has been encapsulated. It is the same transaction as listed previously, but it is translated by a gateway-to-gateway VPN tunnel. Notice that the IP-level information appears much the same. Also note the lack of Layer 4 TCP information:

```
00:01:30.057912 192.168.44.1 > 172.16.1.1: ESP(spi=1302500357,seq=0x3) (DF)
```

The source and destination IP addresses changed from the previous packet to this one. This address switch is because the tunneled packet took on the addressing of the source and destination VPN gateways. Layer 4 information (in this case, TCP information) is missing because it, along with the original IP information and higher-level information, is actually encapsulated into the payload of this packet. All we have available is the IP information and the information of the protocol doing the encapsulation (ESP, the Encapsulating Security Payload protocol).

Advantages and Disadvantages of VPNs

When determining whether a VPN is the solution of choice for your organization's remote connectivity needs, you must consider many factors. What is the confidence level of the data you are sending? What value is placed on its secrecy? How important is it to know the source of the data? If the secrecy level is high enough, even a VPN that uses strong encryption might be inappropriate. Only a dedicated point-to-point connection might be suitable.

You can describe all forms of remote connectivity as three different types:

- Dedicated point-to-point connections, such as via a leased T1 line
- Standard unencrypted Internet communications
- Encrypted VPN Internet communications, which is a compromise between the first two types

Of the first two types, the security and performance advantages both go to a dedicated connection type. Why consider an alternative? The answer is that a third factor is involved: finances. Dedicated connections are expensive, especially when they cover great distances. To add to this expense, most sites are also already utilizing some sort of high-speed Internet connection. Because broadband Internet connections are becoming a common part of most networks, the ability to utilize such a high-speed connection as a means of remote connectivity is attractive for most businesses. The monthly expense of leased T1 lines can be a thing of the past.

However, the use of a shared medium such as the Internet makes security an even greater issue. Your data is literally traversing an infrastructure shared by millions of people around the world. The cost advantages of such public access connectivity must offset the value of your data's secrecy. Therefore, to be able to leverage the functionality of your existing Internet connection and increase the security level of your communications, the VPN is an excellent compromise. Encryption protects your data, but it adds a slight burden to your network and decreases bandwidth. Varying levels of encryption strength can add to the VPN's ability to protect your data, although greater encryption strength comes with a cost. More expensive hardware—or often, more expensive or additional software—might be required to use a stronger encryption algorithm. Because of the greater complexities of such an algorithm, additional overhead must be shouldered by the equipment you are using, thus decreasing overall bandwidth.

> **Note**
>
> Although some commercial VPN solutions might vary their prices based on the level of encryption you choose, it should be mentioned that some excellent free VPN solutions are available. Many free Linux variants have exceptional IPSec implementations, and freeware VPN applications provide adequate protection as well.

Benefits of a VPN

The main benefit of using a VPN for remote network access can be summed up as the price effectiveness of being able to utilize a public medium to transport private information as securely as possible. A VPN can supply many levels of security to a shared network medium, including improved confidentiality, integrity, and authentication. Because a VPN utilizes existing infrastructures, it can be implemented swiftly, without having to wait for the establishment of a line or other factors that commonly hold up such implementations. If VPNs are used for remote users, they can offer a secure and more cost-effective "road warrior" solution. That way, people who need remote access can take advantage of local Internet access wherever they are, instead of making costly long-distance calls. The combination of security, quick setup, and cost effectiveness can make a VPN an excellent communication solution.

Security

VPNs offer many security features that make them a powerful method for securing information traveling across insecure territory. These features can be customized depending on the "hostility level" of the environment. This security level must be balanced against the value of the data.

Lower-strength encryption might be adequate for remote connections for many companies; the information that is being transmitted might be of little value to others. For example, if you owned a car lot with two locations, you might want to share inventory and pricing information between them. For obvious reasons, it might be a little too tempting for your competitors if you transmit this information in the clear, making it possible for someone else to read it. On the other side of the coin, it is unlikely that your competition will go to great lengths to break your encrypted traffic; they could easily drive by to count the inventory in your lot, and probably have a good general idea of what you are paying for your inventory. Utilizing a low-strength encryption VPN might adequately protect your information.

However, what if you are sending a top-secret formula for an item that is a matter of national defense or possibly the whole reason your company is in business? That data might be valuable enough that some outsiders would be willing to go to great expense and effort to defeat your protection. Therefore, stronger encryption would be needed. In general, if the cost of using stronger encryption is not much greater than that for weaker encryption, carefully consider using stronger encryption. The security needs for the communications could increase over time without your knowledge, so it is safer to use the strongest available encryption.

Regardless of the strength of the chosen encryption technology used for your VPN, your VPN should still offer the requirements of a secure communication channel. The following three requirements are the most basic:

- *Confidentiality* is the guarantee that no one else is going to be able to peek at your information. The encryption algorithms that scramble your private data into meaningless segments of characters provide this for a VPN. If this encryption algorithm is not sufficiently strong enough to protect your data, your confidentiality can be compromised.

- *Data integrity* is the next issue that can be protected through encryption and VPN use. Integrity verifies that the information you are receiving is the same as it was when it was sent to you. Long ago, this was often accomplished by securing a document with a wax seal emblem of the party who was sending the message. If the seal was broken, you could not be sure that the message wasn't altered in transit. In today's world, this same integrity assurance can be accomplished with digital signatures and hashes. Both are discussed in greater detail in Appendix B.

- *Authentication* verifies that the information has come from whom it is supposed to and, in turn, that it is received by whom is supposed to receive it.

Deployment Advantages

Anyone who has had to wait for the phone company to terminate or activate a line knows that the waiting can be the hardest part. When you need to have something done today, filling out requests and waiting for outside parties are not things you want on your itinerary. Because VPNs can take advantage of existing infrastructure, many of these stumbling blocks can be avoided. Even in cases in which internal infrastructure needs to be patchworked, a VPN can shine. For example, imagine you are the network engineer at a college campus. You are told that the accounting office is having an audit tomorrow and you are responsible for setting up a place for the teams of auditors to work. The auditors have to be separate from the rest of the accounting office, and the only place you have for them to go is quite a distance away on the other side of the campus. Networks connect the whole campus, but none connect to the accounting office because it is on a separate segment from the rest of the campus. You could get out your handy spool of fiber-optic cable and trench digger and get ready to physically run the half-mile connection, or you could rely on securing the connection through existing infrastructure with VPN technology. This could either be accomplished by adding an additional hardware device and doing some fancy cable-patching to tie the remote location to the accounting office, or relying on an existing VPN device that the accounting office already uses for remote connection and some already available Internet connections across campus. The end result of going with the latter option is a lot less work, considerably less preparation time, and, most likely, a savings cost of infrastructure changes.

Cost Effectiveness

A VPN can save you money in many ways, most of which involve the VPN replacing some type of high-cost, dedicated WAN link. Often, high-speed Internet access is already in place at these same locations. When pitching broadband Internet, you should see a bean-counter's eyes light up when you explain that the monthly Internet access charges will be offset by the removal of the dedicated T1 link that the company is currently using to connect to its branch office. Usually, same-speed Internet access offsets the price of a similar speed point-to-point T1 within a year or two (this can vary greatly by region and location proximity), even considering the costs of additional firewall/VPN hardware.

VPNs can help pay for themselves in other ways as well. For instance, most VPN solutions can also offer an alternative to remote dial-in. This can add up to savings in long-distance bills for remote users who are accessing your network. It also removes the need for dedicated dial-in servers or modem pools for these same users, meaning lowered equipment cost, as well as a reduction in monthly dial-up phone charges. Regardless of the network setup, in most scenarios a VPN can give an excellent return on investment and add up to considerable savings in the long run.

Disadvantages of VPN

Despite all their positive points, VPNs are not all smiles and sunshine. You must consider the disadvantages before confirming that a VPN is suitable for your environment. The use of encryption brings about an additional processing burden, most likely to be handled by your existing gateway devices or by additional equipment that must be purchased. Fitting a VPN into an existing location can also be a challenge in some environments due to the additional packet overhead. A VPN has significant design issues that novices (as well as some intermediates) will most likely not want to tackle on their own, and troubleshooting traffic that is encapsulated can be a real challenge for even the most experienced practitioners.

Processing Overhead

Encryption, the backbone of the VPN, involves incredibly complex mathematical computations. These must occur for every packet that is sent across and received by a VPN gateway device. These complicated computations take their toll not only on the gateway device, but also on the overall bandwidth of the VPN connection. This speed reduction intensifies with stronger encryption algorithms, which in turn require more mathematical complexity and more processing bandwidth. This problem has become such an issue over time that special "offload cards" have been created to help absorb some of the additional processing burden of VPN encryption. These hardware acceleration devices can improve the detriment of lost processing power, but at a hefty price. In turn, it is important to make this processing burden a part of your hardware and bandwidth determination requirements when deciding on a VPN.

Packet Overhead

Another interesting disadvantage of implementing a VPN is the additional overhead that is added to every packet. Existing packets can be encapsulated, which requires the "wrapping" of the original packet in additional packet overhead. Even if you aren't using encapsulation, additional header information still adds to the packet size. In either case, this overhead, although not substantial, can be enough to become a design concern in some environments. In addition, adding size to every packet can negatively affect network bandwidth, not only due to sending larger packets, but also because each larger packet is more likely to need fragmentation as it journeys across various gateways and routers. This fragmentation will negatively affect network performance.

Implementation Issues

Implementation is a concern when making a VPN part of your existing network infrastructure. Some of these implementation issues include incompatibility with Network Address Translation (NAT), VPN passthrough usage, and maximum transmission unit (MTU) size and design issues. VPN design and implementation details are covered in greater detail in Chapter 16.

Troubleshooting and Control Issues

Troubleshooting a VPN can be a complicated process. Because the inner headers and payloads of encapsulated packets are unavailable until they are decrypted, you can't see what is happening while the packet travels between two gateway devices. Tools such as traceroute are ineffective when employed across a VPN tunnel. For more information on traceroute and VPN troubleshooting considerations, see Chapter 21, "Troubleshooting Defense Components."

Common means to examine the packet flow, such as network intrusion detection systems (IDSs), are less effective because the payload is unknown until after it passes through the perimeter VPN device. Not only can this make troubleshooting more difficult, but it also can punch a big hole in an otherwise secure network.

Note

Host-based intrusion detection offers one way to effectively monitor encrypted traffic, as we discuss in Chapter 10, "Host Defense Components." Because the traffic is decrypted either before reaching the host at a perimeter device (tunnel mode) or on the host (transport mode), the host-based IDS can check the packets after they are translated. Therefore, in high-security environments that use a VPN, it is wise to implement host-based IDS on mission-critical systems.

It becomes a security concern when you don't have controls on entities that are remotely connected by the VPN. For example, users who telecommute via a VPN might provide backdoors to your network due to a lack of security on their home PCs. Also,
smaller remote offices that lack an IT staff, or even extranet connections to customers or
vendors, could be the source of backdoor attacks or malicious code propagation.

Regardless of your environment, you must consider many issues when deciding the
effectiveness of a VPN solution as your remote communication choice. If all issues are
adequately considered beforehand, the outcome will be a correct decision and a smooth
implementation.

Internet Availability Issues

One final point that must be made about using the Internet as the backbone of your
wide area network (WAN) concerns the communication glitches that can occur
between you and your remote partners' networks. Technical problems at your Internet
service provider's (ISP's) level, denial of service (DoS) attacks, or other infrastructure
issues such as damage to outside cabling can cause outages to Internet service that most
of us have experienced at one time or another. Because the Internet is redundant by
design, hopefully these problems are few and far between. However, when your business
relies on remote communications, any such outage can become a major financial burden
and an unacceptable outcome. Designing in extra redundancy to your Internet connectivity can help alleviate such situations. Multiple Internet connections using multiple
ISPs can lessen the chance that a problem at a single ISP will create a system-down situation for you. This, combined with the incorporation of screening routers or like products that can help prevent DoS conditions, can maximize Internet availability for your
network. For more information on the use of such screening routers, check out Chapter
6, "The Role of a Router."

IPSec Basics

Even though IP has become the most-used communication protocol in the world and is
the backbone technology behind the Internet, it still has many flaws. Some of these
issues are address space limitations, no auto-configuration of hosts, and a lack of intrinsic
security. The main reason for these flaws is that IP wasn't designed for use by the masses.
It was actually designed for a much smaller, self-sufficient, contained environment.
Because IP has invaded most businesses and homes, many of these flaws have been
patched with other protocols and programs.

In an effort to move IP forward, a new version of the protocol, IPv6 (IP version 6),
was born, with built-in functionality that takes care of many of the issues of its predecessor. Because the adoption of a new version of IP in our constantly growing, current
Internet environment has been difficult, the security measures incorporated into IPv6
have also been ported to our current version of IP (version 4) as an optional protocol
suite. This set of protocols is known as the IPSec Protocol Suite.

IPSec Protocol Suite

IPSec's goal is to facilitate the confidentiality, integrity, and authentication of information communicated using IP. This is accomplished through the use of several protocols, including Internet Key Exchange (IKE), Encapsulating Security Payload (ESP), and Authentication Header (AH). These three protocols combine to allow the secure exchange of information without fear of outside eavesdropping or tampering. A second goal of the security suite is a means for multiple vendors to have a set of standards by which they can interoperate securely. Industrywide testing is being done to verify that the products of these vendors can all work together correctly to provide sound IPSec implementations. IPSec-based security starts with the forming of a security association (SA) between two communicating parties.

SA

An SA is basically an agreement between two entities on how they will securely transmit information. One of the exceptional things about IPSec is the openness of its standard to support not only multiple protocols and communication modes, but also various encryption algorithms and hash types. All these details must be prenegotiated before the secure exchange of user data can begin. The resultant agreement is an SA. Each communication session has two SAs—one for each communication partner. Each partner negotiates a new SA for every IPSec connection he makes.

Before an SA is negotiated, the particular settings that an IPSec partner is going to support must be configured for it locally. These settings are held in what is known as a *security policy database (SPD)*.

After the SA has been negotiated, it is contained in a security association database (SAD). This is necessary because different communication rules can be configured for each of the sessions that a host or device might initiate. For example, look at Figure 7.2. A Cisco PIX firewall can be set up to allow Data Encryption Standard (DES) or 3DES as the encryption algorithm for a VPN tunnel. When Host 1 connects, it might only support DES and would negotiate an SA with DES encryption. However, Host 2 behind another PIX might also attempt to create a tunnel with our PIX, and it might require a 3DES tunnel because of its own business and security requirements. In this case, only a 3DES tunnel could be negotiated. Each of these negotiated connections would require its own SA entry in the SAD, listing all the specific details of what was negotiated for each. These details will include such information as encryption algorithm negotiated (DES, 3DES, AES, and so on), VPN mode, security protocol negotiated (ESP or AH), and hash algorithm negotiated (MD5 or SHA-1).

Because multiple IPSec sessions are available per device (each with its own set of unique settings), for this process to function correctly, each SA session must have its own singular identifier. This identifier is made up of a unique security parameter index (SPI) that tells which SA database entry pertains to the connection in question, the destination address of the connection, and the protocol identifier for the ESP or AH protocol, whichever is being used for the connection.

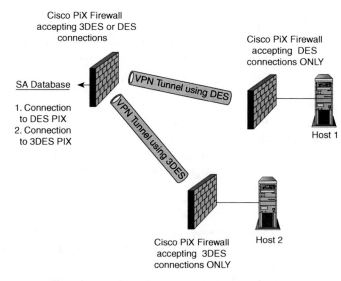

Figure 7.2   IPSec connection parameters negotiated
for VPN tunnels are maintained in the SAD.

Listing 7.1 is an excerpt from a Cisco router's SA database for an inbound ESP connection.

Listing 7.1   **Cisco Router SA Database**

```
inbound esp sas:
  spi: 0x71BB425D(1908097629)
  transform: esp-des esp-md5-hmac,
  in use settings ={Tunnel, }
  slot: 0, conn id: 2000, flow_id: 1, crypto map: mode
  sa timing: remaining key lifetime (k/sec):(4608000/3500)
  IV size: 8 bytes
  replay detection support: Y
```

This excerpt contains much information about this specific connection, such as the SPI number of the connection, the encryption and hash algorithms being used for this connection, the fact that it is working in tunnel mode, and the lifetime for this connection. This information is recorded in the SAD for each negotiated connection.

IPSec Tunnel and Transport Modes

An IPSec connection has two basic modes: transport and tunnel. Transport mode is a host-to-host form of communication and involves the encryption of a packet's payload only. Because of this host-to-host requirement, software needs to be loaded on all communicating hosts, which in large installations can be an administrative nightmare.

However, this VPN mode is well-suited for encrypted communications between hosts on the same network, or in situations where it is important to be able to differentiate hosts by their IP address information. Transport mode lacks a means to do gateway-to-gateway communication and the ability to conceal host IP information, which can be a major concern when your data is traversing a public medium such as the Internet. Transport mode communication can be coupled with other tunneling means for a more secure communication channel.

The other IPSec mode takes advantage of tunneling. Tunneling mode is the method of choice for most VPNs because it encrypts not only the payload but also the entire original packet, partially or completely obfuscating the source and destination addresses of the communicating systems. Also, tunneling mode can occur host-to-host, host-to-gateway, or gateway-to-gateway. Gateway-to-gateway operation is another reason that tunneling mode is well-suited for VPN operation; it allows simplified network-to-network communications setup. Gateway devices such as routers or firewalls need to be set up for VPN communication, but communicating hosts on the internal network need no special setup or additional software. Encryption of the entire packet and gateway-to-gateway setup combine to make tunnel mode an excellent choice for securing a communication channel. Most VPNs use tunnel mode and have at least one gateway device.

IKE

The IKE protocol is the authenticator and the negotiator of IPSec. It verifies that you (or, more typically, your system) should be allowed to start encrypted communication with the device in question, and then it negotiates the type of encryption that will be used. IKE is actually a combination of two protocols: Internet Security Association and Key Management Protocol (ISAKMP), which handles security negotiations, and Oakley (based on a variation of Diffie-Hellman), which is responsible for exchanging keys. Two phases of the IKE transaction support the creation of an SA between communication partners. In the following sections, we will explore these phases in greater detail.

Note

IKE is not the only key-management solution for IPSec, although it is the standard. Key management can be done manually or by using IKE alternatives such as Secure DNS, Photuris, or Simple Key Internet Protocol (SKIP).

IKE Phase 1

If a remote user wants to begin a session with a VPN gateway device, the process starts with IKE Phase 1. Phase 1 serves two functions: authenticating the remote user and exchanging the public key information that will be used for encryption in Phase 2.

IKE authentication can be done in several ways. The most common is with pre-shared keys or digital certificates. A *pre-shared key* simply means that some key value is preconfigured on all systems that want to communicate via the VPN. For an example of a Cisco router using a pre-shared key configuration, see the pre-shared key example in the "Cisco Router VPN Examples" section later in this chapter.

In smaller, low-risk environments, a pre-shared key can be an easy and effective way to quickly set up authentication with little extra administrative overhead. It is by far the easiest means to configure VPN authentication, but with this simplicity comes several drawbacks. Sometimes the same pre-shared key is used on all communicating devices. This is not necessary (and definitely not recommended unless another choice is not available), but it is the easiest way administratively speaking. Using such a configuration is common when planning for dial-up remote systems because it is difficult to predict the IP addresses they might use. The IP address could be anything, so a wildcard is used in place of an identifying address or hostname and in conjunction with the pre-shared key value. Therefore, all stations dialing in must use the same key. Because this key value is configured locally on the devices, if any of them is compromised, the VPN's security is compromised as well. Of course, a pre-shared key can be reconfigured at any time if a compromise is known. However, if a pre-shared key is successfully captured and the thief is clever enough not to tip off the owner, he could have a backdoor into your system as long as that particular key is in use.

Because the pre-shared key must be configured manually, regularly changing keys can be a headache that falls to the bottom of many busy administrators' lists. Using pre-shared keys with remote users is equivalent to giving them a password to your network. This is not a problem until they are no longer employed at your company. The effect is comparable to the re-keying of all the locks in a building when an employee who had a key leaves, but in this case you are the locksmith. Other key-management issues occur as well, such as remote site configuration. How do you send the key? Who at the remote site is trusted with keeping the value secret? Wouldn't it be nice if you could remotely manage keys for everyone who needs one on a connection-by-connection basis?

That brings us to a second popular way to authenticate users: digital certificates. Digital certificates can be assigned separately to each entity that connects to the VPN, and they can be remotely managed and administered by a centrally located Certificate Authority (CA). This can ease administration problems, although it also adds an extra piece with which an administrator has to be concerned.

The CA is the centerpiece of a greater structure known as *Public Key Infrastructure (PKI)*. The whole concept behind PKI is a publicly available structure to distribute public key information. A popular way to do this in the enterprise is to combine the PKI with existing network directory structures, such as Microsoft's Active Directory or Novell's Network Directory Services. This way, the existing base of user information can be combined with the user's public key information, preventing duplication of user information databases. For an example of VPN authentication through digital certificates and a CA, look at the CA example under the "Cisco Router VPN Examples" section later in this chapter.

Other than authenticating that the communicating parties are who they are supposed to be, the other function of the Phase 1 session is spent setting up the parameters for the communication session that will occur in Phase 2. Phase 2 is where the actual VPN SA's are negotiated. In other words, Phase 1's second purpose is the negotiation of the parameters for the connection (Phase 2) that will carry out the negotiation of the parameters for the actual VPN tunnel. This might sound redundant, but this is by design, to help ensure the security of the final VPN connection.

In Phase 1, two modes can be used when exchanging authentication information and security parameters for Phase 2: main mode and aggressive mode. The differences between them are in the number of packets exchanged and when the public key information is generated. Aggressive mode has lower packet overhead, but main mode is the more secure of the two and the more frequently used. Some VPN implementations don't support the use of aggressive mode. The important thing to remember is that the candidates who want to connect must both be using the same mode to negotiate successfully.

Annotated IKE Phase 1 Example

Now you will see what one of these exchanges actually looks like under the packet microscope. The following example demonstrates a common exchange when doing an IKE Phase 1 negotiation. We can see the order in which the packets are actually transmitted and when the authentication and key exchange processes actually occur. The listing is from a log file generated by a SafeNet VPN client connecting to a Cisco PIX firewall. It is using main mode, as can be seen by the MM listings throughout. We start by exchanging proposed parameters for our IKE SA as follows:

```
Initiating IKE Phase 1 (IP ADDR=<MY IP ADDRESS>)
SENDING>>>> ISAKMP OAK MM (SA)
RECEIVED<<< ISAKMP OAK MM (SA)
```

Next, we exchange key information and what is known as a *nonce*. A nonce is a random number that the initiator generates; the number is then digitally signed and sent back by the responder. The nonce is used to confirm that the key information is coming from whom it is supposed to be coming from. This IPSec implementation also includes a vendor ID (VID) that allows participants in cross-platform interactions to make determinations on the capabilities and configuration of their partners that might be of a different manufacturer. The exchange of key information looks like this:

```
SENDING>>>> ISAKMP OAK MM (KE, NON, VID, VID)
RECEIVED<<< ISAKMP OAK MM (KE, NON, VID)
```

In our final exchange confirming what we've negotiated, a hash is sent from each party to confirm that all are who they say they are. These are the first exchanges that are encrypted, using the negotiated information and keys exchanged in earlier messages. This is also where authentication of both parties finally takes place. The ID or identification value identifies the parties to each other. This value can be an IP address, hostname, and so on, as chosen when configuring the partners. Both hosts must use the same identification method or the connection will fail. The final exchange looks like this:

```
SENDING>>>> ISAKMP OAK MM *(ID, HASH, NOTIFY:STATUS_INITIAL_CONTACT)
RECEIVED<<< ISAKMP OAK MM *(ID, HASH)
Established IKE SA
```

The end result is an established IKE SA. This means that the two parties have agreed on the methods they will use during Phase 2 IKE to exchange parameters for the actual VPN connection.

> **Note**
>
> Phase 1 of the IKE exchange creates the IKE SA, not an IPSec SA. The IKE SA states the parameters for Phase 2 communications. The IPSec SA states the parameters for the actual VPN communication. The IPSec SA is negotiated in IKE Phase 2.

If this had been an aggressive mode transaction, it would have only taken three packets instead of six. The first packet is sent to the responder with keys, nonces, and SA suggestions all in one. The responder then returns a similar packet, but with a hash appended for authentication. Finally, the initiator responds back with its own hash to confirm the IKE SA negotiation. Although aggressive mode obviously offers a speed advantage in that fewer packets are exchanged, the lack of redundancy in the packet flow leaves it more open to exploitation than its main mode counterpart.

IKE Phase 2

In IKE Phase 2, we are specifically negotiating the parameters of the IPSec SA. The exchange is similar to the one in Phase 1 aggressive mode. After Phase 2 is complete, the IPSec SA is formed and we have a VPN connection! Actually, two unidirectional IPSec SAs are created, each protecting communications in a single direction.

Phase 2 has only one exchange mode selection: quick mode. Quick mode is a brief exchange involving three packets. The security precautions of the Phase 1 exchanges aren't needed because of the protection given by the established IKE SA. Because the previous IKE SA was established, all the exchanges in Phase 2 are encrypted using the negotiated protocols and encryption type. The only other protection is in the form of hashes and nonces that are included in the packets to confirm their origin.

Annotated IKE Phase 2 Example

Now that we have discussed the principles of the Phase 2 exchange, it's time to look at an actual example. Continuing the previous example, this is also from the log file of a SafeNet VPN client that is initiating a connection to a Cisco PIX firewall. This time, because only internal private range IP addresses are listed, they don't need to be sanitized.

The first packets exchanged include hashes and nonce information as well as the proposed SA parameters. The responder returns a similar respondent packet. Both contain ID values, identifying each participant, as originally labeled in Phase 1:

```
SENDING>>>> ISAKMP OAK QM *(HASH, SA, NON, ID, ID)
RECEIVED<<< ISAKMP OAK QM *(HASH, SA, NON, ID, ID, NOTIFY:STATUS_RESP_LIFETIME)
```

Finally, the initiator confirms the agreement with a final hash. Notice that these transactions also use ISAKMP and Oakley and that QM is used in the listings to represent quick mode (the only choice for Phase 2):

```
SENDING>>>> ISAKMP OAK QM *(HASH)
Loading IPSec SA (Message ID = 353EEA13 OUTBOUND SPI = B53E860B INBOUND
➥SPI = 3FAF771D)
```

An established IPSec SA and the creation of unique inbound and outbound SPI information earmark the successful exchange. This last line tells us that we have established a tunnel.

IPSec Security Protocols AH and ESP

Now that we have covered the creation of a security association using IKE, it's time to look at the security protocols. You have two security protocols from which to choose in the IPSec suite: AH and ESP. When building an IPSec-based VPN, you can elect to employ either one of these protocols or to use both AH and ESP at the same time. Each has its own functions, although in practical application, ESP is used much more frequently than AH. In the following sections, we examine the inner workings of AH and ESP and describe strengths and limitations of these protocols to help you design and set up an IPSec VPN that matches your needs.

AH Protocol

The AH protocol is IP protocol number 51. It offers packet authentication and integrity-checking capabilities, but it does not offer confidentiality for the packet's payload, thus limiting its effectiveness as a sole security method for most VPN implementations.

The AH protocol provides packet authentication and integrity protection by adding an additional header to each IP packet. This header contains a digital signature called an *integrity check value (ICV)* that is basically a hash value verifying that the packet hasn't been changed in transit. The IP information in the packet is guaranteed to be correct, but it is not hidden in any way. Because AH looks at the IP header when computing the digital signature, we can be sure that the source IP address on the packet is authentic and that the packet came from where it claims to. AH also supports the use of sequence numbers that help prevent replay attacks. Because communicating devices track the stream of conversation using these numbers, an intruder who is attempting to gain VPN access can't re-send a captured packet flow.

The fact that AH authenticates the packet using its IP address information makes it incompatible with the IP header changes that are brought about by NAT. Because AH's ICV would be computed before NAT changes the IP address for an outbound packet, the integrity check performed on the packet at its destination would fail.

On the other side of the coin, because AH offers no confidentiality for its packets, it does not possess the computational overhead of having to encrypt packets. Not only does the lack of payload encryption equate to smaller processing burden for the sending device, but it also means that the overall overhead of encapsulating packets is lighter. These factors combine to make AH a fine solution where only integrity and IP address authentication are needed and performance is highly valued.

Much can be learned about a protocol by taking a look at its packet header (see Figure 7.3). If a definitive source exists for what a protocol does or what information a packet carries, the header is it.

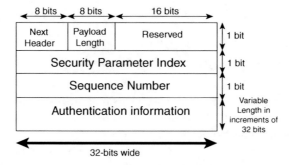

Figure 7.3 An AH packet header is composed of several fields.

The following are the fields of information contained in the packet header:

- The next header field contains an identifier that specifies the protocol type of the next packet header following the AH packet header.
- The payload length field specifies the length of the AH header information.
- The reserved field is an area for the possible future expansion of the AH protocol.
- The SPI value is listed next, showing of which SA's communication stream this packet is a part.
- The sequence number is the next field listed. It is simply a unique incrementing value that protects against replaying captured packets successfully. This type of assault is called a replay attack.
- The authentication information is listed last. This field contains the ICV and digital signature for authenticating the packet in question.

Now that you know more about the packet structure, let's look at an example of some AH packets. Listing 7.2 is a Tcpdump trace of AH traffic. It is actually an example of a user accessing a web page. Notice that the payload of the packets contains cleartext representations of the information they carry. (This is most noticeable in the last packet listed, `seq=0x3`.)

Listing 7.2 **AH Packet Trace**

```
00:05:18.645054 192.168.44.129 > 192.168.44.128:
➥AH(spi=580532459,seq=0x1): 1232 > 80: S 3631297390:3631297390(0)
➥win 16384 <mss 1460,nop,nop,sackOK> (DF)
0x0000    4500 0048 089a 4000 8033 1797 c0a8 2c81    E..H..@..3....,.
0x0010    c0a8 2c80 0604 0000 229a 38eb 0000 0001    ..,....."8.....
0x0020    c118 fc19 0124 3688 d1b7 3e13 04d0 0050    .....$6...>....P
```

Listing 7.2   **Continued**

```
0x0030     d871 336e 0000 0000 7002 4000 57cd 0000    .q3n....p.@.W...
0x0040     0204 05b4 0101 0402                         ........

00:05:18.655236 192.168.44.128 > 192.168.44.129:
➥AH(spi=3951698033,seq=0x1): 80 > 1232: S 2981983731:2981983731(0)
➥ack 3631297391 win 17520 <mss 1460,nop,nop,sackOK> (DF)
0x0000     4500 0048 0080 4000 8033 1fb1 c0a8 2c80    E..H..@..3....,.
0x0010     c0a8 2c81 0604 0000 eb8a 2071 0000 0001    ..,.......q....
0x0020     24db fdd4 aaa4 0c89 16cf c00c 0050 04d0    $............P..
0x0030     b1bd 75f3 d871 336f 7012 4470 2b9b 0000    ..u..q3op.Dp+...
0x0040     0204 05b4 0101 0402                         ........

00:05:18.659869 192.168.44.129 > 192.168.44.128:
➥AH(spi=580532459,seq=0x2): 1232 > 80: . ack 1 win 17520 (DF)
0x0000     4500 0040 08a1 4000 8033 1798 c0a8 2c81    E..@..@..3....,.
0x0010     c0a8 2c80 0604 0000 229a 38eb 0000 0002    ..,....."  .8.....
0x0020     cbf6 be88 73d7 97a6 a63b a092 04d0 0050    ....s....;.....P
0x0030     d871 336f b1bd 75f4 5010 4470 585f 0000    .q3o..u.P.DpX_..

00:05:18.671517 192.168.44.129 > 192.168.44.128:
➥AH(spi=580532459,seq=0x3): 1232 > 80: P 1:260(259) ack 1 win
➥17520 (DF)
0x0000     4500 0143 08a2 4000 8033 1694 c0a8 2c81    E..C..@..3....,.
0x0010     c0a8 2c80 0604 0000 229a 38eb 0000 0003    ..,....."  .8.....
0x0020     3521 0ef0 df8f 17db d87e 7477 04d0 0050    5!.......~tw...P
0x0030     d871 336f b1bd 75f4 5018 4470 0108 0000    .q3o..u.P.Dp....
0x0040     4745 5420 2f20 4854 5450 2f31 2e31 0d0a    GET./.HTTP/1.1..
0x0050     4163 6365 7074 3a20 696d 6167 652f 6769    Accept:.image/gi
0x0060     662c 2069 6d61 6765 2f78 2d78 6269 746d    f,.image/x-xbitm
0x0070     6170 2c20 696d 6167 652f 6a70 6567 2c20    ap,.image/jpeg,.
0x0080     696d 6167 652f 706a 7065 672c 202a 2f2a    image/pjpeg,.*/*
0x0090     0d0a 4163 6365 7074 2d4c 616e 6775 6167    ..Accept-Languag
0x00a0     > truncated for display purposes.
```

Not only is the payload of these packets in cleartext, but the Layer 4 (transport) information is also viewable. We can watch the three-way handshake as the user's workstation attempts to contact the remote web server. We can also see other flags, window size settings, and TCP ports used (80 for the web server and 1232 as the ephemeral port chosen by the workstation). SPI and sequencing information are also listed for each one-way connection.

ESP

The second security protocol that IPSec offers is ESP. The ESP protocol is IP protocol number 50. It offers full confidentiality by completely encrypting the payload of IP packets. ESP is modular in design and can use any number of available symmetric encryption algorithms to encrypt its payload. Popular choices include DES, 3DES, and AES.

The way that ESP works differs slightly depending on the IPSec mode that is being used. In transport mode, ESP simply adds its own header after the IP header and encrypts the rest of the packet information from Layer 4 up. If ESP's authentication service is specified during the initial negotiation of the IPSec connection, ESP then adds a trailer that contains ICV information to confirm packet integrity and authentication. However, unlike AH, ESP does not include IP header information when calculating the ICV.

In tunnel mode, ESP encapsulates the entire original packet, encrypting it fully and creating a new IP header and ESP header at the tunneling device. A trailer is also added for authentication purposes if ESP's authentication service is chosen.

In either mode, ESP offers sequence numbers in each packet that, like AH, provide protection against replay attacks.

ESP is often regarded as the IPSec protocol that works with NAT. Although this is usually the case for ESP used in tunnel mode, transport mode ESP and NAT do not work together because of changes that NAT makes to the packet's header information. When NAT translates the packet's IP information, it also needs to recalculate the checksum located in the TCP header. This is because the TCP checksum is calculated using information in the TCP header and the IP header, including the source and destination IP addresses of the packet. Therefore, NAT must recalculate the TCP header checksum to keep the packet from failing its integrity check. In transport mode ESP, the entire TCP header is encrypted, preventing the TCP checksum from being recalculated by the NAT device. (A similar problem occurs with UDP packets as well, when UDP checksums are used.) As a result, upon decryption the packet will fail its integrity check, keeping transport mode ESP from interoperating successfully with NAT. This issue can be avoided in rare cases where TCP checksums are not used or can be disabled.

In tunnel mode ESP, traffic can successfully pass NAT because the entire original packet, including both IP and Layer 4 information, is encapsulated and therefore untouched by NAT. Because the IP and Layer 4 information and checksums are unaltered in tunnel mode ESP, after the packet is decrypted it will still pass its TCP integrity check. However, even though ESP traffic in tunnel mode can pass through NAT, you may still encounter NAT-related problems when negotiating IPSec connection parameters. For instance, one-to-many NAT (frequently referred to as *Port Address Translation [PAT]*) will rewrite the source port of an outbound IKE packet, causing it not to have the expected value of 500, and resulting in the failure to re-key IPSec session parameters.[1]

One great point of contention is the authentication capabilities of ESP. ESP has authentication services that can be used, but the hash that is generated is based on the entire packet, with the exception of the IP header and authentication trailer. This is good in that any changes that might be made to the IP header (for example, by NAT) do not invalidate ESP's ICV value. However, this lack of IP header authentication is upsetting to some because it prevents the guarantee of identifying the originating IP address. In most implementations, however, the successful authentication of the packet's payload, as implemented by ESP, can be considered adequate proof that the packet actually came from the expected source.

Now that we have discussed the ESP protocol, let's take a closer look at the structure of its packet header (see Figure 7.4).

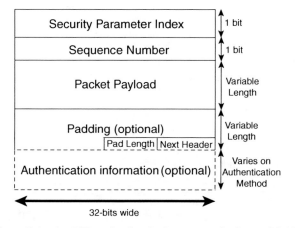

Figure 7.4   An ESP packet header is composed of several fields.

Here's an explanation of the individual fields in the ESP packet header:

- The SPI is the first field in this packet.

- The sequence number field follows it and is used, like the AH headers, to prevent replay attacks.

- The payload of the packet follows this information. This is where the encapsulated information is located.

- The pad length field tells how much padding, if any, was needed to make the payload, pad length, and next header fields fit appropriately into the packet's bit-length requirements.

- The next header shows the protocol number for the type of information encapsulated inside the ESP packet.

- The authentication information lists the optional ICV authentication option that is available for ESP packets.

Now that we have gone over the packet structure, let's look at a real-world example of ESP packets in transit. The following is a tcpdump trace of ESP-encrypted traffic. Notice that no identifiable commands or information exists in the payload of the packets because of the encryption of the packet's payload (in this particular case, with 3DES). Despite its obscure appearance, Listing 7.3 is actually an example of a user checking a standard web page, like the AH trace seen previously.

Listing 7.3 **ESP Packet Trace**

```
00:01:30.031 192.168.44.128 > 192.168.44.129: ESP(spi=1728941913,seq=0x1) (DF)
0x0000    4500 0050 0061 4000 8032 1fc9 c0a8 2c80    E..P.a@..2....,.
0x0010    c0a8 2c81 670d 8f59 0000 0001 0262 5e96    ...,.g..Y.....b^.
0x0020    d238 3af3 c90e c385 fca7 09cf 693a b6cc    .8:.........i:..
0x0030    6d88 5400 d417 a0c4 6f5b df7f 5e96 994f    m.T.....o[..^..O
0x0040    cb03 1624 6668 d10d cf89 f6b0 e4e7 46a9    ...$fh........F.

00:01:30.038 192.168.44.129 > 192.168.44.128: ESP(spi=1302500357,seq=0x2) (DF)
0x0000    4500 0048 06a7 4000 8032 198b c0a8 2c81    E..H..@..2....,.
0x0010    c0a8 2c80 4da2 9405 0000 0002 f22d 2ce7    ...,.M........-,.
0x0020    4dc6 ba58 11e3 333f 0cd5 8079 62d7 7128    M..X..3?...yb.q(
0x0030    0590 3056 085a dd96 3653 ef97 35e1 593c    ..0V.Z..6S..5.Y<
0x0040    8213 a0e7 2516 835b                        ....%..[

00:01:30.105 192.168.44.128 > 192.168.44.129: ESP(spi=1728941913,seq=0x2) (DF)
0x0000    4500 01a8 0062 4000 8032 1e70 c0a8 2c80    E....b@..2.p..,.
0x0010    c0a8 2c81 670d 8f59 0000 0002 5e96 994f    ..,.g..Y....^..O
0x0020    cb03 1624 7da5 0ecb 392f a703 6f53 aa21    ...$}...9/..oS.!
```

One point of interest on this ESP trace is the SPI numbers. The SPI numbers change depending on which partner initiates the communication, because each end of an IPSec connection has its own SPI value assigned. You might also notice that each packet has an incrementing sequence number to help prevent the use of replay-type attacks. Layer 4 (TCP or UDP) transport information is blatantly missing because any such information is encapsulated into the encrypted payload of this packet. Other than these points, this trace looks much like any other IP traffic exchange.

The existence of two IPSec protocols—AH and ESP—offers the flexibility of selecting the configuration that is appropriate for your security requirements and can operate under the constraints of the existing network infrastructure. AH is great at providing authentication and integrity services but does not protect the confidentiality of the packet's payload. ESP is more computationally expensive but is able to encrypt data while also offering limited authentication capabilities.

Combined Use of ESP and AH

If your environment requires the address authentication capabilities of AH and the confidentiality provided by ESP, the two protocols can be combined into a single IPSec implementation. In this configuration, not only are the strong points of both AH and ESP combined, but the weak points are as well. Therefore, you have a configuration that has all the NAT problems of AH and the additional processing burdens of ESP, which are added on the AH processing for an even greater overall workload. Such extra security comes at a high price, and in the real world such configurations are relatively uncommon.

IPSec Configuration Examples

Now that we have journeyed through the creation of an IPSec VPN, let's take a look at some practical examples of VPN configuration on some popularly used devices that you might even find on your own network.

Cisco Router VPN Examples

Most Cisco routers have the potential (with the correct IOS software version) to be a gateway device for a VPN. The only other consideration is the processing power of the router, which could become heavily taxed by the additional burden of traffic encryption and decryption.

Assuming that the router has the necessary power, it can be configured as part of a VPN in many ways. In this example, we allow the creation of a tunnel from one Cisco router to another, using ESP as the IPSec security protocol and SHA-1 as the hashing algorithm. A pre-shared key provides the authentication. This configuration and all commands are based on IOS version 12.3.

The first section of the code involves the ISAKMP settings for the IKE part of the VPN configuration, as follows:

```
crypto isakmp policy 10
authentication pre-share
crypto isakmp key s3cr3t! address 199.199.199.199
```

In the ISAKMP policy section, the authentication type is specified as using a pre-shared key, and the key (*s3cr3t!*) is set up for the address in question (199.199.199.199) in the line that follows it.

The next code shows all the security options that this router will require when negotiating an SA. In Cisco's world, these security configuration options are called a *transform set*:

```
crypto ipsec transform-set secure esp-3des esp-sha-hmac
```

The transform set `secure` is set up with the listed encryption capabilities. Other transform sets, using other unique names, can be set up as well, each defining other security options that the router would also accept during the negotiation process.

> **Note**
>
> A VPN device must be set up with security parameters that are acceptable to its communication partner; otherwise, a connection will not be established.

The next command is used to assign a crypto map to an interface:

```
crypto map cmap local-address Ethernet1
```

In this example, the crypto map name is `cmap`. A *crypto map* is a set of configuration information that defines traffic that should traverse the VPN and the details of how that connection can occur.

In the next section of the listing, we define the crypto map cmap from the last example:

```
crypto map cmap 10 ipsec-isakmp
set peer 200.200.200.200
set transform-set secure
match address 101
```

These statements tie together all the VPN configuration components. They give the peer address of the entity to which the tunnel will be constructed, list any transform sets that will be allowed, and specify an access list that will match any traffic that should be directed across the VPN.

The following access lists are the ones defined in the crypto map cmap:

```
access-list 101 permit ip 192.168.2.0 0.0.0.255 192.168.1.0 0.0.0.255
access-list 101 deny ip 192.168.2.0 0.0.0.255 any
```

They are specifically used to match the VPN traffic and, in turn, encrypt those packets and direct them to the VPN peer.

Now we will look at the interface configuration section of the router:

```
interface Ethernet1
description external interface
ip address x.x.x.x
crypto map cmap
```

The only setting that is specifically needed for a VPN configuration is the crypto map cmap command. With Cisco routers, it is necessary to apply a crypto map to the interface where the tunnel will be initiated.

The following line is typically used to configure NAT service on a router. It is listed here because a Cisco router that is running NAT must be explicitly configured to allow VPN traffic to bypass NAT translation:

```
ip nat inside source route-map nonat interface Ethernet1 overload
```

When you configure the route map that defines the traffic that should be NAT-translated, it should exclude VPN traffic. In this example, the route map is called nonat.

In this section, we define the route map nonat:

```
route-map nonat permit 10
 match ip address 102
```

This route map allows the traffic denied in the listed ACL to bypass NAT, while NATing the permitted traffic.

Following are the access lists defined in the previously listed route map nonat:

```
access-list 102 deny ip 192.168.2.0 0.0.0.255 192.168.1.0 0.0.0.255
access-list 102 permit ip 192.168.2.0 0.0.0.255 any
```

These access lists are used to bypass translation by NAT and allow the IPSec-related traf-fic that will initiate the VPN tunnel:

```
access-list 112 permit udp any any eq isakmp
access-list 112 permit esp any any
```

The access lists are configured to allow in the ISAKMP (UDP port 500) and ESP (IP protocol 50) traffic involved in the creation and use of the VPN tunnel. If you will be using the AH protocol (IP protocol 51), you will need an access list that allows it.

Cisco Router VPN and Access List Rules

When you're using a Cisco router as a VPN device, it is important to understand how the rules that apply to access lists work, specifically in a VPN environment. For example, after a VPN-encrypted packet initially passes through the access list that allows IKE, AH, or ESP traffic and is unencrypted, it will be tested a sec-ond time by the inbound access list. Creating an access list that allows traffic from the private IP address range used by the partner VPN to the private IP address used by the local network solves this issue. You should have no fear of this access list being a security hole; if someone fabricated traffic that would be able to pass it, the responses would be encrypted and sent to the VPN peer and would never be returned to the originator.

When traffic leaves the inside network, it is encapsulated in a new packet with a source address of the gateway device and a destination address of the peer gateway. This has to be considered when creating out-bound access lists on the external interface. For example, if you are creating an egress filter that is applied outbound on the outside interface, it typically reflects the inside IP address range. Encapsulated VPN traffic does not pass this egress filter. For this reason, egress filters work better inbound on the inside router inter-face.

Next, we provide an in-depth example of a Cisco router with certificate authentication. Using pre-shared keys appears to be such a simple solution that some questions exist on why you would choose an alternative. Setting up two VPN peers is as simple as typing in a few commands and a single secret piece of information. However, when your environ-ment grows from two peers to 2,000, the concept of a centralized key-handling authori-ty becomes more attractive. This concept becomes more appealing when you consider the scenario of having to change keys. Being able to make these changes through a cen-tralized CA is why PKI is a buzzword among the IT elite. To show the differences between a pre-shared key and a CA configuration, we will use the same Cisco router example we used previously, only changing settings that are needed for certificate authentication. All commands that remain the same will not be re-listed; we will only list new commands and commands that would need to be changed. This section will assume that you have an accessible CA already configured in your environment and available to you.

Let's start our look at CA authentication by seeing what must be changed from our previous configuration. Because we are discussing authentication specifically, we know that this falls into the IKE section of the VPN; therefore, only our ISAKMP settings will be affected. Crypto maps, transform sets, encryption types, and everything else will remain the same. We only need to change the authentication type under our ISAKMP policy and then make the changes necessary to prepare our router for such authentication.

The first statement in this section is identical to the one listed in the pre-shared key example:

```
crypto isakmp policy 10
authentication rsa-sig
```

The change is reflected in the second line of the section. The `authentication` command must reflect the use of RSA digital signatures, or `rsa-sig` for short.

Because a certificate-based authentication scheme requires the querying of an entity outside the router for its keys, key storage and CA accessibility become important issues. If the CA is inaccessible, your router might accept an expired certificate or you might suffer an offline condition on your VPN. Storing certificates locally can help offset this problem of downtime, but at the price of taking up some of the precious router NVRAM storage. To configure your Cisco router to request a certificate whenever necessary, use the following command:

```
MyRouter(config)# crypto ca certificate query
```

This command prevents the storage of certificates or certificate revocation lists (CRLs) from using any of your router's NVRAM. Because these items wouldn't be found in local NVRAM, the router must take a performance hit to make a request.

The next commands are probably already configured on your router. However, they are listed here because they are essential for operation with digital certificates:

```
MyRouter(config)# hostname MyRouter
MyRouter(config)# ip domain-name domain.com
```

Host and domain names must be present in the router configuration because certificates are named with a fully qualified domain name. This means that the certificate's name is actually the hostname of the router followed by its domain name. For example, in this example, our router's certificate would be named `MyRouter.domain.com`.

Before we go any further, we must generate the RSA key pair that we will use to request a certificate for our router. The following command is entered only once to generate the keys and is not a saved part of the configuration:

```
MyRouter(config)# crypto key generate rsa
```

To verify that your keys have been generated, you can use this command:

```
show crypto key mypubkey rsa.
```

Now we must configure the specifics so that our router knows where and how often to collect certificates:

```
MyRouter(config)# crypto ca identity CA.COM
```

This line specifies the domain name of the Certificate Authority and drops you into CA configuration mode.

The following line is the last required line in this section. The rest are optional or used only in some environments:

```
MyRouter(ca-identity)# enrollment url http://ca_4u
```

This line simply specifies the URL of the CA. In this example, it is *http://ca_4u*.

These next two lines are needed only in environments that use a Registration Authority (RA). An RA is an extra entity that caches certificates and CRLs in case the CA is down or otherwise unavailable.

```
MyRouter(ca-identity)# enrollment mode ra
MyRouter(ca-identity)# query url ldap_url
```

If you have an RA in your environment, specify the first command. The second is also only used in an RA environment, but one that also supports LDAP. `ldap_url` in this example is the URL of the LDAP server.

The next two optional lines specify how often, in minutes, the router will retry to get a certificate and how many times it will retry:

```
MyRouter(ca-identity)# enrollment retry period 5
MyRouter(ca-identity)# enrollment retry count 100
```

The default number of minutes for the first command is 1, and the default number of retries is infinite.

This last entry, which can be configured in the CA configuration mode, is regarding whether CRLs must be available to accept a certificate:

```
MyRouter(ca-identity)# crl optional
```

When this line is entered, if a given CRL is not available, the router still accepts the certificate in question. This could be a security concern because the certificate might have been previously revoked. However, it can keep authentication functioning even if the CA is temporarily unavailable.

Now we are ready to request the CA's certificate. This is done with the following command:

```
MyRouter(config)# crypto ca authenticate CA.COM
```

Requesting the CA's certificate is necessary for authentication before receiving a certificate for your router. As a best practice, you might want to manually confirm this certificate after downloading it from the CA. The information used in this command should match the information specified in the `crypto ca identity` command:

```
MyRouter(config)# crypto ca enroll name
```

The previous command is used to receive a certificate for your router. After this command has been issued, you should be ready to initiate a VPN connection.

The following are a couple of useful commands for auditing your router's CA capabilities:

```
MyRouter# show crypto key pubkey-chain rsa
```

The previous command shows details of available RSA public keys on your router.

The following command lists all certificates stored on your router if you are not using query mode, which disallows certificate storage:

```
MyRouter# show crypto ca certificates
```

It is plain to see that setting up the use of digital certificates is more complicated than using pre-shared keys in the short haul, but in the long run, the time spent can pay you back many times over, especially in a large environment.

Windows XP IPSec Configuration Example

Windows XP Professional and Windows XP Home Edition can also effectively handle IPSec duties if properly configured. Doing so requires the addition of the IP Security Policy Management snap-in to your Microsoft Management Console (MMC) and monitoring with the IP Security Monitor snap-in. This integrated capability lies at the operating system level, and Windows XP's prevalence in many businesses will most likely make it an important player in the future of VPNs. (Other versions of Windows, including Windows 2000 and 2003, also offer similar IPSec capabilities.)

IPSec VPN policy is configured on a Windows XP system using the IPSec snap-in for MMC. The console appears in Figure 7.5.

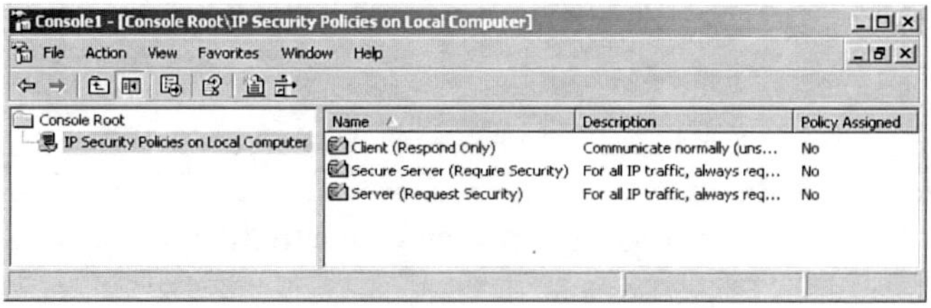

Figure 7.5   MMC can be used to configure local and remote Windows XP IPSec policies via the IP Security Policy Management snap-in.

As listed in the right pane, several default security policies can be used for quick setup of Windows XP system-to-system VPNs. However, to set up an IPSec policy that will work well with other VPN products, we need to create a custom policy. This is primarily because the default authentication used for these policies is the Windows Kerberos authentication protocol. To begin to create a new security policy, follow these steps:

1. Right-click the desired IP Security Policies object in the left pane of the window and then select Create IP Security Policy. This opens the IP Security Policy Wizard. Click Next to continue.

2. Name your security policy. You might also want to include a description of its purpose. When you are finished, click Next to continue.

3. On the following window, remove the check from the Activate the Default Response Rule check box. Click Next to continue.

4. Verify that the Edit Properties check box is selected because we will be customizing this policy. Then click Finish.

5. This brings up the Policy Properties box (see Figure 7.6), where *Policy* is the name of the policy you specified in step 2. Make sure the Use Add Wizard check box is checked and then click the Add button to continue. This opens the Security Rule Wizard. Click Next to continue.

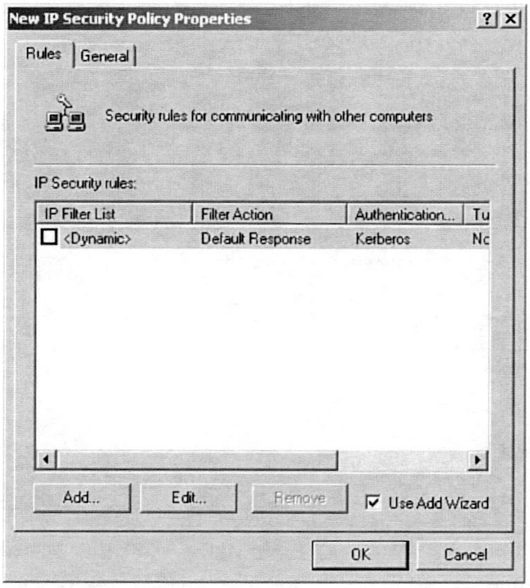

Figure 7.6   The New IP Security Policy Properties box is used to define IPSec rules for the currently selected policy.

The Security Rule Wizard walks you through the process of setting IPSec parameters, such as authentication settings and IP filter settings. (IP filters are discussed further in Chapter 10.) To define IPSec parameters, follow these steps:

1. Choose whether to use a tunnel. In this example, we will use a tunnel, so click the option button to specify the tunnel endpoint and type in its IP address. Click Next when you're finished.

2. Choose the type of network connections you want to affect (most likely All Network Connections) and click Next.

3. In the Authentication Method window, we pick the authentication we want to use: Kerberos, certificates, or a text string to use as a pre-shared key. If you are creating a connection to be used with another Windows XP system, you should probably use the default Kerberos authentication. Otherwise, for interoperability, you will most likely have to use certificates or pre-shared keys. For our example, we will use the latter. To use a pre-shared key, choose the appropriate option button and specify the pre-shared key value used in the text box below it (see Figure 7.7). Click Next to continue.

Note

Microsoft discourages the use of pre-shared keys for IPSec authentication on production systems, stating that it was implemented primarily to achieve RFC compliance. Furthermore, the confidentiality of the pre-shared key is difficult to protect because it can be viewed from the local computer.[2] Whenever possible, use Kerberos or certificate authentication methods for IPSec.

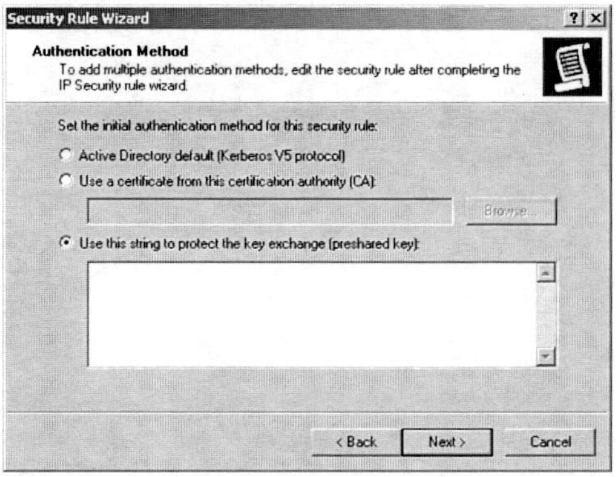

Figure 7.7   In the Authentication Method window, we specify which authentication method should be used for the IPSec policy.

4. In the IP Filter List tab, click the Add button. In the next window, make sure the Use Add Wizard box is checked, specify a name for the filter you are creating, and click the Add button. This opens the IP Filter Wizard. Click Next to continue.

5. For Source Address, choose My IP Address. This assumes that you are using this system directly to contact the peer VPN device and not using it as a gateway or proxy device. If you were using your Windows XP system as a gateway, you would most likely choose A Specific IP Subnet and specify the IP addresses and subnet mask settings. Click Next to continue.

6. For Destination Address, choose the appropriate type from the drop-down menu. A Specific IP Subnet is usually the correct selection for a VPN. Then specify the subnet range of the network that is protected by the gateway VPN device. Click Next when you're finished.

7. Unless you have a specific change needed, leave the protocol type as Any and click Next. With tunnel traffic, it would be inappropriate to specify a setting other than Any because tunnels can't filter on port information or protocol type.

8. Make sure the Edit Properties box is checked so that we can verify settings. Then click Finish. This ends the IP Filter Wizard.

9. Verify that the Mirrored check box is checked in the Filter Properties window, under the Addressing tab. The Mirrored check box ensures that the policy applies to both incoming and outgoing traffic. Click OK when you're finished.

10. Click OK on the IP Filter list screen.

After completing the IP filter configuration settings, the next step is to tie the filter to the policy and describe how the policy should be enforced. To do so, follow these steps:

1. Choose the filter list you just created from the ones listed and then click Next.

2. On the Filter Action screen, make sure the Use Add Wizard check box is checked and then click the Add button. This opens the Filter Action Wizard. Click the Next button to continue.

3. Create a new name and optionally a description for your filter action and then click Next.

4. Choose Negotiate Security for Standard IPSec Operation. Otherwise, you could create a specific Permit or Block rule in this section. When you're finished, click Next.

5. Check Do Not Communicate with Computers That Do Not Support IPSec to support only IPSec communications. Then click Next.

6. In the IP Traffic Security window, choose the security level you desire based on the settings of the peer device with which you are communicating. Using Custom allows you to set exactly the protocol (AH or ESP), encryption, and integrity algorithm combination you want to use. Click OK when you're finished and then click Next.

7. You have come to the end of the wizard. Verify that the Edit Properties check box is checked so that we can make final settings changes. Then click Finish.

8. This drops you into the Properties window for the action you just created. Be sure to uncheck the Accept Unsecured Communication, But Always Respond Using IPSec check box for highest security. You should end up with a screen similar to the one shown in Figure 7.8, but reflecting your security choices. When you are ready to proceed, click OK.

9. Choose the new filter action you just created on the Filter Action screen. Click Next.

10. Make sure the Edit Properties check box is unchecked because we are now done. Click Finish.

11. Click Close on the Policy Properties box, and your new policy should appear in the right pane of the window. Right-click the policy and choose Assign. This changes the Policy Assigned column from No to Yes. The policy is now active.

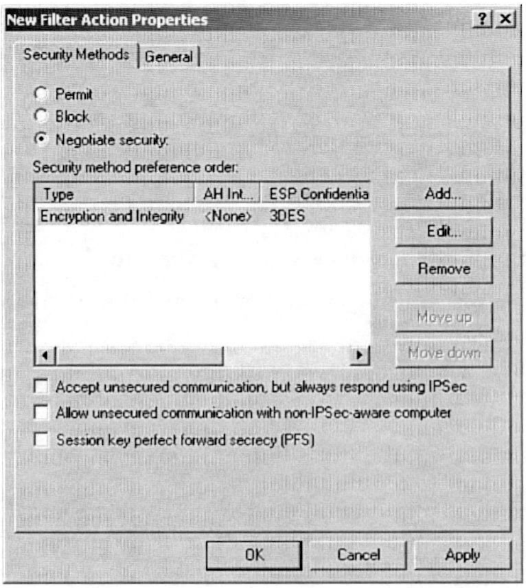

Figure 7.8   We use the New Filter Action Properties window to specify how IPSec properties should be negotiated for traffic that matches the current IP filter.

To test the settings, open a command prompt and try to ping a host on the remote subnet in question. After security is negotiated, the pings will get through if everything is configured correctly. This can be confirmed by checking the IP Security Monitor screen to show active security associations after the device is successfully pinged. Figure 7.9 shows the IP Security Statistics screen, which can be loaded by right-clicking a hostname in the IP Security Monitor and selecting Statistics. The IP Security Statistics screen contains many different counts related to IKE and IPSec activity, including several types of failures.

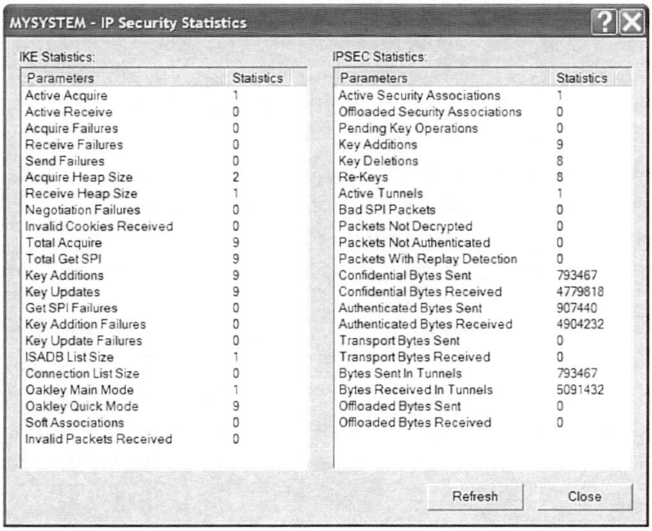

Figure 7.9   We can use IP Security Monitor to observe
statistics regarding the host's IPSec operations.

Other VPN Protocols: PPTP and L2TP

As stated previously, IPSec is not the only tunneling set of protocols that can offer VPN-type service. At Layer 2, PPTP and L2TP are both popularly implemented VPN protocols. The greatest reason for this is that both are included with Microsoft Windows operating systems, which enjoy the greatest distribution of any operating system to date. This means that a large portion of the deployed computer base has built-in VPN capabilities using PPTP and L2TP. For this reason (and because popular VPN software often goes for as much as $100 per seat), both protocols, especially the newer L2TP, can be effective for VPN solutions in Windows environments. An interesting thing to keep in mind is that neither has inherent encryption capabilities. Encryption must be added to make either a true VPN protocol. Let's take a look at each.

PPTP

PPTP is an outgrowth of PPP, which appeared in computers everywhere with the advent of dial-up Internet access. PPTP, although popularized by Microsoft, was actually designed by a consortium of computer technology vendors, including US Robotics, Ascend, and 3Com. Microsoft's original implementation of PPTP was highly criticized as being insecure by cryptography gurus industrywide, which left a bad taste in the mouths of many IT people. For encryption, PPTP relies on Microsoft Point-to-Point Encryption (MPPE), which uses the RC4 cipher. However, most of the security issues were due to the insecurity of its authentication method—the Microsoft authentication protocol Microsoft Challenge Handshake Authentication Protocol (MS-CHAP). PPTP has PPP's capability of user authentication using all associated protocols, such as MS-CHAP, Password Authentication Protocol (PAP), Challenge Handshake Authentication Protocol (CHAP), and Extensible Authentication Protocol (EAP). Later PPTP implementations from Microsoft that included MS-CHAP version 2 actually resolved most of the afore-mentioned security issues, making it a much safer bet (although not as well regarded as IPSec) as a VPN protocol.[3]

PPTP operates through two channels that work together. The first is a control chan-nel that operates on TCP port 1723. This channel sends back and forth all the com-mands that control the session management features for the connection. The second is an encapsulated data channel that uses a variant of the Generic Routing Encapsulation (GRE) protocol (IP protocol 47), which uses UDP as its transport protocol.[4] PPP frames are encapsulated and sent using this method. This is the "tunnel" of PPTP. An advantage of the GRE tunnel over a standard IPSec tunnel is that it can encapsulate and carry pro-tocols other than IP. For this reason, GRE tunnels can find their way into environments that are otherwise completely IPSec.

PPTP does have some interesting attributes that can make it useful in particular envi-ronments. First, it works without a hitch through NAT because NAT-related changes to the IP layer have no effect on Layer 2 PPTP. Second, it comes integrated with many hardware devices and is available in operating systems; with such high availability, it is more easily deployable in environments that use such products. However, on the down-side, because PPTP uses PPP to initiate communications, it can be vulnerable to spoof-ing and man-in-the-middle attacks.

L2TP

L2TP is defined by RFC 2661. As its name implies, it is a Layer 2 tunneling solution. L2TP is actually a hybrid of two previous tunneling protocols—Cisco's Layer Two Forwarding (L2F) protocol and PPTP—and combines the best attributes of both. It replaced PPTP as the Layer 2 VPN protocol of choice for Microsoft Windows operating systems as of Windows 2000.

Like PPTP, L2TP uses PPP's user authentication capacities (MS-CHAP, CHAP, EAP, PAP, and so on). Also like PPTP, L2TP has two communication method types: control messages and data transmission "tunnel" messages. The first bit in the PPTP header dif-ferentiates these message types (1 for a control message; 0 for a data message). Control messages are given precedence over data messages to ensure that important session administration information gets transmitted as effectively as possible. The concept behind L2TP's operation is similar to PPTP. A control connection is set up for the tunnel, which is then followed by the initiation of an L2TP session. After both are completed, informa-tion in the form of PPP frames can begin to traverse the tunnel.[5]

Comparison of PPTP, L2TP, and IPSec

L2TP most commonly uses UDP port 1701 as its transport medium for all its packets. Because UDP is a connectionless protocol, it can actually require less communication overhead (it doesn't require TCP's response traffic to confirm connection) than PPTP, which transports control messages (only) on connection-oriented TCP.

An advantage of L2TP over PPTP or IPSec alone is that it can create multiple tunnels between two hosts. However, its disadvantage is that it relies on PPP and can be victimized by spoofing and man-in-the-middle attacks. Also, like PPTP, it supports the transmission of non-IP protocols, which is an advantage over IPSec. However, unlike PPTP, it does not require IP and TCP as its transmitting protocols. It can use other options such as X.25, Frame Relay, and ATM.

Although L2TP lacks its own encryption capability, it has the potential as a Layer 2 protocol of working in conjunction with IPSec. L2TP can be used to provide a tunnel for transport-mode IPSec traffic. For example, Windows 2000 and Windows XP rely on IPSec as the encryption method for their L2TP tunnels. This combination of IPSec and L2TP can be mutually agreeable because it allows IPSec to supply packet authentication for L2TP control messages, which lack such protection. L2TP offers IPSec multiprotocol transmission capability and multiple tunnel support. Also, the advantage of L2TP's user authentication protocols can be applied to IPSec, which has no such ability of its own.

PPTP and L2TP Examples

Now that we've discussed the details of how PPTP and L2TP tunnels work, let's look at some practical examples of how the technologies can be implemented in common network devices: a Windows XP system and a Cisco PIX firewall.

Client Windows XP Setup

Because L2TP support is integrated by default in Windows XP, setting up client software to support an L2TP VPN is not difficult, as the following steps prove:

1. Double-click the Network Connections icon in Control Panel and click Create a New Connection to start the New Connection Wizard.

2. After receiving the splash screen, click Next to continue. For L2TP VPN client access configuration, you will choose the Connect to the Network at My Workplace option button. Click Next to continue.

3. In the Network Connection window, specify Virtual Private Network Connection. Click Next to continue.

4. In the Connection Name window, enter a name for the connection. Click Next to continue.

5. In the VPN Server Selection window, type the hostname or IP address of the entity to which you are connecting. Click Next to continue and then click Finish to save the configuration.

6. Windows XP should then display a Connect window. Click Properties to alter the default settings.

7. On the Options tab, select the Dial Another Connection First option if Windows XP needs to establish a dial-up connection before the VPN.

8. On the Networking tab, change the Type of VPN setting from Automatic to L2TP IPSec VPN. (The only other choice is PPTP VPN.)

9. The Advanced tab contains settings for Internet Connection Sharing, which allows you to specify that the system you are working on should act as a gateway for other network systems. That way, other systems can gain access to the entity you are connecting through your system. Unless you have a specific need for this type of sharing, do not check the check box.

10. Review all other settings, such as those for authentication, and confirm that they are appropriate for your needs and environment. When finished, click OK to save the configuration changes.

11. Windows XP will show the Connect screen again. This is where you will need to specify the logon and password information to authenticate with the L2TP device you are connecting to.

After your authentication information is entered, you are ready to connect. Simply click the Connect button, and the system will attempt to contact the remote system. If the connection fails, it returns an error and waits a predetermined time before redialing. This connection can be reached any time through the Network Connections screen.

Note

The VPN connections that are created, as explained in this section, are for PPTP or L2TP connections specifically. They do not necessarily support IPSec as listed. For IPSec support, see the example in the IPSec section.

Cisco PIX VPDN Setup for PPTP Traffic

In this example, we will specify the commands of interest in a Cisco PIX configuration that is running software version 5.1 or later. We will not go over all the standard configuration commands, just those that pertain to Virtual Private Dial-Up Network (VPDN) support for PPTP connections. VPDN is basically Cisco's way to support non-IPSec, dial-up-type protocols. The protocols are the most popular incarnations of PPP: PPTP, L2TP, and Point-to-Point Protocol over Ethernet (PPPoE), which is popularly used with DSL connections.

To begin our PIX configuration, we need to specify an access list to describe the traffic leaving our network that will need to bypass NAT. PIX firewalls have NAT integrated at the lowest level, and to keep VPN traffic from "breaking," we need to make sure it isn't translated. Here is the access list we will be matching:

```
access-list 101 permit ip 10.0.0.0 255.255.255.0 192.168.1.0 255.255.255.0
```

This access list simply says that it will match or allow any IP traffic that has a source address in the 10.0.0.x subnet and a destination address in the 192.168.1.x subnet.

The next section does not specifically relate to VPDN, but it's of interest because it lists our inside and outside interface addresses. This can shed some light on other IP address selections in the rest of this listing:

```
ip address outside 172.16.1.2 255.255.255.0
ip address inside 10.0.0.1 255.255.255.0
```

The outside address or external address in this case is 172.16.1.2 and is using a class C subnet mask. The inside address also uses a class C subnet and is 10.0.0.1.

Our next statement creates an address pool to assign all connecting PPTP clients:

```
ip local pool pool4pptp 192.168.1.1-192.168.1.50
```

The pool name is pool4pptp and the address range is 192.168.1.1-50.

Only one of the next lines is of consequence in our VPDN configuration. The lines contain the NAT settings that will be used on our PIX. The `global` command lists the range of external addresses that will be used for our NAT pool:

```
global (outside) 1 172.16.1.3-172.16.1.4
nat (inside) 0 access-list 101
nat (inside) 1 10.0.0.0 255.255.255.0 0 0
```

The `nat (inside) 1` command shows all IP addresses that should be NAT-translated. The command of interest is the `nat (inside) 0` command. This command shows what addresses should bypass NAT. In this case, the addresses are specified by the 101 access list that we looked at previously. Therefore, traffic that has the source address of our internal network and is sent to the addresses used by connected PPTP clients (as stated in our pool) should bypass NAT. Otherwise, if the source address is in our network address range (as stated in the `nat (inside) 1` command), NAT it.

The next command simply states that all PPTP traffic should be uniformly allowed access:

```
sysopt connection permit-pptp
```

VPDN will not work without this command.

The next group of settings shows specific configuration options for our VPDN clients. The first line shows the protocols we will allow access through our VPDN configuration. L2TP could also be specified:

```
vpdn group 1 accept dialin pptp
```

The next group of authentication settings shows acceptable protocols to use for PPTP authentication. Only specify the protocols you want to allow:

```
vpdn group 1 ppp authentication pap
vpdn group 1 ppp authentication chap
vpdn group 1 ppp authentication mschap
```

The next line is what assigns our IP address pool mentioned previously to the connecting PPTP clients:

```
vpdn group 1 client configuration address local pool4pptp
```

The following line chooses where the authentication information is held:

```
vpdn group 1 client authentication local
```

In the example, the PIX will use local authentication. This is not a best practice. Ideally, it is best to have authentication information held outside of the PIX on a separate authentication system such as a RADIUS or TACACS server.

The username line then specifies the local information we alluded to in the last statement:

```
vpdn username user password secret
```

Here, *user* refers to a username, as defined by the person configuring the PIX, and *secret* refers to a well-chosen password.

Finally, the `enable outside` command says that the outside interface can accept VPDN traffic. With this final statement, PPTP traffic will be allowed to traverse our PIX firewall:

```
vpdn enable outside
```

Summary

In this chapter, we discussed the basics behind how VPNs work and the process of tunneling. We discussed the advantages of VPNs, including security, deployment, and cost benefits. We also looked at some disadvantages, including bandwidth considerations, design and implementation issues, and troubleshooting and control issues.

We also covered the popular VPN protocols IPSec, L2TP, and PPTP. IPSec is a suite of security protocols that includes IKE, AH, and ESP. IKE is used in two phases to negotiate and authenticate VPN partners. Next, one or both AH and ESP protocols are used as the main security protocol for data transmission. AH is used to authenticate and verify integrity of data flow, whereas ESP completely encapsulates the packet or its payload (depending on SA mode), offering full confidentiality of data flow.

Finally, we covered L2TP and PPTP and saw the advantages of a Layer 2–based tunneling protocol, including the transmission of non-IP protocols, and its ability to pass NAT without issue. The downside is that because both protocols were built on PPP, they have communication session vulnerabilities that aren't found with IPSec.

Regardless of your choice of VPN hardware or tunneling protocol, the concepts of VPNs are universal. Correctly identifying and weighing the disadvantages and advantages for your particular environment is a necessary part of designing remote communications. After a VPN is decided upon as the choice communication for your situation, a full understanding of the principles of cryptography and their incorporation into the VPN will help facilitate a smooth implementation.

Understanding VPNs, IPSec, cryptography, and other tunneling protocols will be advantageous to anyone who is involved in the upkeep and implementation of network security.

References

1 Microsoft, Inc. "How to Configure an L2TP/IPSec Connection Using Pre-shared Key Authentication (Q240262)." http://support.microsoft.com/default.aspx?scid=kb;EN-US;q240262. September 2004.

2 Microsoft, Inc. "Mutual Authentication Methods Supported for L2TP/IPSec (Q248711)." http://support.microsoft.com/default.aspx?scid=kb;EN-US;q248711. September 2004.

3 Bruce Schneier and Mudge. "Cryptanalysis of Microsoft's PPTP Authentication Extensions (MS-CHAPv2)." August 1999. http://www.counterpane.com/pptpv2-paper.html. September 2004.

4 Kory Hamzeh, Gurdeep Singh Pall, et al. "RFC 2637 Point-to-Point Tunneling Protocol." July 1999. http://www.ietf.org/rfc/rfc2637.txt. September 2004.

5 W. Townsley, A. Valencia, et al. "RFC 2661—Layer Two Tunneling Protocol 'L2TP'." August 1999. http://www.ietf.org/rfc/rfc2661.txt. September 2004.

8

Network Intrusion Detection

A GOOD NETWORK INTRUSION DETECTION SYSTEM (IDS) can have an enormous positive impact on the overall security of your organization. The focus of intrusion detection is identifying attacks and security incidents, but in this chapter we see that intrusion detection can do so much more than that. After covering the basics of intrusion detection, we discuss the critical role that IDS plays in a perimeter defense. Much of this chapter is devoted to determining where IDS sensors should be deployed in various environments. By the end of this chapter, you will have a strong sense of how you can use network intrusion detection to strengthen your organization's defenses.

Network Intrusion Detection Basics

Network intrusion detection systems are designed to sniff network traffic and analyze it to identify threats in the forms of reconnaissance activities and attacks. By detecting malicious activity, network intrusion detection enables you to identify and react to threats against your environment, as well as threats that your hosts might be directing at hosts on other networks. (Many network IDSs today also offer intrusion prevention capabilities, which means they can stop detected attacks. See Chapter 11, "Intrusion Prevention Systems," for much more information on network-based intrusion prevention.)

Although the focus of this chapter is network IDS, there is also a related IDS technology known as *host-based intrusion detection*. Host-based IDS software focuses on detecting attacks against a particular host, such as a workstation or server, and is run from the host itself. There are several types of host-based IDS software products, including log analyzers and file integrity checkers. Log analyzers monitor operating system and application logs, looking for entries that might be related to attacks or security violations. File integrity checkers alert you if particular files are altered, which might indicate a successful attack. You can learn more about host-based intrusion detection products in Chapter 10, "Host Defense Components."

The Need for Intrusion Detection

Many people have heard of intrusion detection, but they might not realize why they need to deploy it in their environment. Without intrusion detection, you may be unaware of many attacks that occur. Because you don't have information about attacks, when a successful one occurs, you won't have the information you need to stop it from happening to that host again, or to other hosts. Most ominously, you may never know about an attack that doesn't damage your host, but simply extracts information, such as a password file. Without intrusion detection, you will be unaware of these events until it's much too late. This is why intrusion detection is beneficial in many environments.

Many attacks involve multiple steps or phases. For example, an attacker might start by launching a scan that sends a DNS query containing a `version.bind` request to each IP address in a range. Some DNS servers respond to such a query with their BIND version number. The goal of this scan is to identify which hosts are DNS servers and what versions of BIND they are using. Based on the results of the first scan, the attacker then sends a specially crafted DNS query to some of the DNS servers to exploit a buffer overflow vulnerability in a particular version of BIND. This second set of queries could occur hours or days after the first set—or it could occur within seconds. It depends on the tools being used and the attacker's methodology.

If any of the buffer overflow exploits are successful, the attacker might be able to perform unauthorized actions on one or more of the servers, potentially gaining administrator-level privileges. An attacker who gains privileged access to a server could do many things, including using that server to launch attacks against other hosts on the network and against external hosts. It is important to understand that this is not a hypothetical attack scenario we are describing. Various attack tools use this exact technique to scan, attack, and compromise servers; many worms also do this by spreading throughout the Internet on their own. Sometimes it only takes seconds from the initial scan until the vulnerable host is compromised.

If you are not using intrusion detection, how will you know when a successful attack has occurred? Some attacks are immediately visible, such as a website defacement; others are not. Perhaps you will look through a directory and see some strange files or directories. Perhaps your server's performance will decline and you will find many unknown processes running. Perhaps your server will crash and you won't be able to reboot it. Or perhaps no one will notice that anything has happened.

A properly configured, robust IDS can play more than one role in identifying typical attacks. An IDS can detect reconnaissance activity that may indicate future targets of particular interest. It also generates alerts for the subsequent attempts to breach host security. Alerts are usually generated through one of two methods. The first method, anomaly detection, relies on statistical analysis to identify traffic that falls outside the range normally seen in this environment, or it relies on protocol analysis to identify traffic that violates protocol standards or typical behavior. The second method, signature detection, identifies known attack signatures observed in traffic. Although most network IDS products throughout the years have been signature-based, anomaly-based products are growing in popularity as a complement to signature-based products. The following sections describe the anomaly and signature detection methods.

Anomaly Detection

Although there are various ways to detect anomalies in network traffic, many IDS products based on anomaly detection methodologies work by establishing baselines of normal network activity over a period of time, then detecting significant deviations from the baseline. For example, a product could monitor a network for two weeks to identify which network services are provided by each host, which hosts use each service, and what volume of activity occurs during different times of the day and days of the week. A month later, if the IDS sensor sees a high volume of traffic involving a previously unused service on a host, this could indicate a distributed denial of service (DDoS) attack against the host or a compromised host providing a new service. This class of product is sometimes known as a DDoS *attack mitigation system*, because it not only detects the DDoS attacks, but also acts to stop them through intrusion prevention techniques (as described in Chapter 11). Examples of DDoS attack mitigation systems include Captus IPS, Mazu Enforcer, and Top Layer Attack Mitigator.

One obvious drawback of this type of anomaly detection is that the baseline needs to be updated constantly to reflect authorized changes to the environment, such as the deployment of a new server or the addition of another service to an existing server. Some products permit the baseline to be updated manually, at least in terms of identifying which hosts are authorized to provide and use certain services. If the baseline can be kept current, or if the environment is quite static and the baseline changes rarely, anomaly detection can be extremely effective at identifying certain types of attacks and reconnaissance activities, such as port and host scans, network-based denial of service attacks, and malicious code (particularly worms). Unfortunately, this type of anomaly detection cannot identify most other types of attacks, so it is best used to complement other IDS technologies.

Many signature-based IDS products perform some type of protocol anomaly detection. This means that the IDS compares traffic to the expected characteristics for widely used protocols, such as HTTP, DNS, and SMTP. When a serious discrepancy is discovered—for example, a header field that contains hundreds of binary values instead of the expected small number of text characters—the IDS generates an alert that an anomaly has been discovered. This can be very effective at identifying certain previously unknown instances of attacks that a purely signature-based IDS could not identify.

One significant limitation of anomaly-based IDS is that generally it cannot determine the intent of an attack—just that something anomalous is occurring. Analysts need to study the data captured by the IDS to determine what has happened, validate the alerts, and react appropriately. However, because network and protocol anomaly detection–based methods can detect attacks that signature-based IDS cannot, a robust IDS solution for an enterprise should incorporate both anomaly-based and signature-based methods if resources permit.

Signature Detection

A network IDS signature is a pattern you are looking for in traffic. When a signature for an attack matches observed traffic, an alert is generated, or the event is otherwise recorded. A simple signature example is one that detects the Land attack; the source and destination IP addresses in a packet are the same (http://cve.mitre.org/cgi-bin/cvename.cgi?name=CVE-1999-0016). Some older operating systems could not properly handle such packets, which violate standards, so attackers would send crafted packets with the same source and destination addresses.

Although some network traffic signatures, such as ones for the Land attack, are quite simple, others are considerably more complicated. Many signatures are protocol or application specific; for example, many signatures pertain only to DNS traffic. Because DNS zone transfers traditionally use TCP port 53, a signature pertaining to a zone transfer vulnerability includes the TCP protocol and also needs to look for destination port 53. Each signature specifies other characteristics that help to identify the vulnerability that the attacker is trying to exploit. Some IDSs focus on long sequences of code from published exploits, whereas other IDSs actually perform full protocol analysis, examining and validating the header and payload values of each packet. Although full analysis is more resource intensive, it tends to produce a much more robust signature solution.

Most intrusion detection vendors release new sets of signatures regularly. If a major new vulnerability is discovered or an exploit is widely seen, intrusion detection vendors quickly research the exploit or vulnerability, create new signatures for it (or determine that existing signatures already match it), and release the signatures to their users as soon as possible. This process is similar to the process that antivirus software vendors follow when addressing threats from new viruses, worms, Trojans, and other types of malicious code. When a major new threat emerges suddenly, such as the Slammer and Netsky worm, IDS vendors typically have a signature available for their customers in a matter of hours.

How Signatures Work

Let's look at an example of a signature for the Nimda worm. Because the worm uses a common text-based protocol (HTTP) and uses a relatively simple exploitation technique, it's an ideal subject for understanding the basics of signatures. When the Nimda worm tries to infect a web server, it sends a set of HTTP requests, including this one:

```
GET /scripts/..%c0%af../winnt/system32/cmd.exe?/c+dir
```

The purpose of this particular request is to exploit a Unicode-related vulnerability in certain unpatched Microsoft IIS servers to gain unauthorized privileges. %c0%af is the Unicode equivalent of a slash, so this command is actually trying to traverse the root directory to exploit the vulnerability. Although no damage is done to the server, success at this point tells the worm that the server is vulnerable. The worm can now launch a damaging attack to this server.

You want your network intrusion detection sensors to notify you when they see this traffic. Many different possible signatures exist. A simple text-matching signature would look for /scripts/..%c0%af../ in a URL (more precisely, in the payload of a TCP packet that a client sends to a server's port 80). Because the Nimda worm issues several GET requests with slightly different values, you would need a separate signature for each one of them if you wanted to identify each attack attempt.

Some IDS sensors have a much more robust way of identifying these types of requests as attacks. Rather than doing simple text matching, they actually decode the request, substituting a slash for the %c0%af sequence, and then analyze the validity of the decoded URL. As a result of the analysis, the IDS sensor determines that the attacker is trying to go past the root directory, and it generates an alert. Although this method is more resource intensive, it provides a much better detection capability than the simple text-matching method because it actually examines traffic for the attack technique, not for specific known instances of that technique being used.

False Positives and False Negatives

Signature development is always a balancing act. A specific signature might be extremely accurate in identifying a particular attack, yet it might take many resources to do so. If an attacker slightly modifies the attack, the signature might not be able to identify it at all. On the other hand, a general signature might be much faster and require far fewer resources, and it might be better at finding new attacks and variants on existing ones. The downside of a general signature is that it also might cause many false positives— when a sensor classifies benign activity as an attack. Another factor is the original release date of the signature; over time, false positives are identified by the IDS vendor and corrected, leading to the release of higher-quality signatures. Brand-new signatures often generate high numbers of false positives.

Every intrusion detection system generates false positives. When you first look at an IDS console and see dozens or hundreds of alerts, you might think that your systems are under massive attack. But those alerts are much more likely to be false positives. By selecting a solid IDS product and tuning your sensors, you can reduce false positives, but you can't completely eliminate them. No matter how precisely a particular signature is written, there's still a chance that some benign traffic will accidentally match that signature. False positives are a headache for an intrusion analyst because you have to spend time and resources determining that they are, in fact, false.

The Intrusion Detection System Is Possessed!

I will never forget the first time I had to review and analyze intrusion detection alerts. I opened the IDS console to review the data, and my mouth dropped as I saw hundreds of alerts that all said "Devil." I scrolled through screen after screen of Devil alerts, and I started to wonder if the IDS was possessed! The Devil turned out to be an alert for the Devil Trojan. After several hours of research, I determined that the alerts were false positives caused by a poorly written signature.

A false negative occurs when a signature fails to generate an alert when its associated attack occurs. People tend to focus on false positives much more than false negatives, but each false negative is a legitimate attack or incident that IDS failed to notice. False negatives get less attention because you usually have no way of knowing that they have occurred. Sadly, you're most likely to identify a false negative when an attack is successful and wasn't noticed by the IDS, or when a different type of network IDS sensor or host-based IDS product notices it. In addition, if a signature generates many false positives, the analyst usually shuts off the signature altogether or ignores all the corresponding alerts. This means that the analyst doesn't review legitimate instances of the alert, and this also becomes a type of false negative. It's important to understand what causes false positives and negatives so that you can choose an IDS that minimizes them.

Developing Signatures That Minimize False Positives and Negatives

To better understand false positives and negatives, let's look at a simple example. Suppose that in your intrusion detection system, you write a signature that looks for `cmd.exe` anywhere in a URL. (`cmd.exe` is often used in root traversal exploits against IIS servers, such as the Nimda worm.) This is a general signature that matches many different attack attempts. Unfortunately, it also matches `cmd.exe-analysis.html`, a web page that contains an analysis of `cmd.exe` attacks. It matches against `nascmd.exe` as well, which is unrelated to these exploits. These are examples of false positives caused by an overly general signature.

Because of the false positives, you decide to rewrite your signature to use some contextual information as well. Now your signature is a URL that contains `/winnt/system32/cmd.exe`. Because this is a more specific signature, it triggers fewer false positives than the more general signature.

Unfortunately, reducing false positives often comes at the expense of increasing false negatives. If an attacker uses a URL that includes `/winnt/system32/../system32/cmd.exe`, the more specific signature misses it, causing a false negative to occur. However, the more general first signature would have sent an alert. And the more robust method described earlier, which decodes the entire URL and evaluates it for root traversals, would have sent an alert for both versions. More complex signatures are usually better than simple text-matching signatures, which are unable to identify most variations on attacks. In fact, some attackers purposely craft their attacks to avoid detection by simple signatures; this is known as *IDS evasion*.

Detecting IDS Evasion Techniques

As if developing an IDS signature that minimizes false positives and false negatives isn't difficult enough, you must also consider the effects of IDS evasion techniques on signature development. Attackers have many methods of altering their code to avoid IDS detection. Many are simple, such as the example discussed previously that obfuscated the path by including .. sequences. Another technique used in URLs is replacing a character with its hex or Unicode equivalent. Therefore, cmd.exe could become cmd.%65xe because %65 is the hex representation of e. Only IDS products that perform hex decoding before performing signature comparisons would determine that this string matches cmd.exe.

Some evasion techniques actually relate to the IDS sensor's core architecture, not specific signatures. One such technique is to fragment a packet so that it has a small initial fragment; the attacker hopes that the IDS examines only the first fragment, which looks benign, and ignores the remaining fragments, which contain malicious content. An IDS that does full-packet reassembly is not fooled by this evasion method.

Avoiding Unwanted Alerts

Besides false positives, you might also have alerts that address legitimate problems that you simply don't care about. Unwanted alerts seem to occur in just about every environment. For example, if your environment is an ISP or a wireless company, you are providing network services to customers. You probably have a lot of traffic passing on your networks between your customers and other outside hosts. If you are monitoring these networks with IDS sensors and you tune them to identify all possible scans and attacks, you are likely to be overwhelmed with a huge number of alerts that you honestly don't care about. Do you really want to know if one user sends another a FOOBAR.TXT.EXE file? This could trigger an alert because of the suspicious extension combination—and the alert would almost certainly be accurate—but the activity is outside the scope of your control.

> **Note**
> Tuning your sensors to produce only the information relevant in your environment is critical if you're going to get the best results from your IDS solution.

Alerting, Logging, and Reporting

When an intrusion detection system sees traffic that matches one of its signatures, it logs the pertinent aspects of the traffic or generates an alert, depending on the severity of the activity and the configuration of the IDS sensor. Alerts can be delivered to intrusion analysts in a variety of ways, including messages on the analyst console, emails, and SNMP traps, depending on the product being used.

Reporting is another key element of intrusion detection. If you have only one sensor, reporting should be simple. If you have dozens of sensors, you probably don't want separate reports from each of them. Instead, you want all data to be collected in one place because it's more convenient to view and easier to back up. It's also far easier to correlate events that all sensors see. Reporting formats vary widely among IDS products; most also permit sensor alerts and logs to be exported to other databases for further queries and reporting.

Review IDS Sensor Status Regularly

I was helping an intrusion analyst tune the dozens of network IDS sensors deployed in his environment. He told me he had noticed recently that the number of alerts he was seeing on his analyst console had dropped significantly. After a few days of this, he noticed that several sensors weren't generating alerts. Puzzled, he finally checked the sensor status reports and discovered that none of them were seeing packets. An investigation revealed that a co-worker had reconfigured the switches to which the sensors were connected.

Check the status of your sensors regularly. Most IDS sensors provide some sort of status report that indicates how the sensor is functioning and what volume of traffic it is seeing. If you notice unexpected drops in traffic levels, you need to investigate the situation as quickly as possible; your sensor might no longer be seeing traffic.

Intrusion Detection Software

Many different network IDSs are available, each with its own distinct features. Some of the best-known and most popular products include Cisco Secure IDS, Enterasys Dragon Network Sensor, ISS RealSecure Network Sensor, NFR Sentivist IDS, Snort, and Sourcefire Intrusion Management System. They all provide alerting, logging, and reporting capabilities. Signature sets are available through a variety of means, depending on the product. Users of some products have written their own signatures and made them publicly available. Other products must be purchased to get signatures; some vendors hide the signature details, whereas others allow users to view and even modify their signatures.

Network IDS sensors have other helpful features. For example, some systems can perform network monitoring and traffic analysis, collecting statistics on connections, protocols in use, and the like. This capability can be invaluable in identifying policy violations, such as unauthorized services in use, and traffic oddities in general. We will discuss policy violations later in this chapter. Another feature covered in more depth later is that of intrusion prevention, in which an IDS sensor works with other network devices or acts on its own to halt certain traffic from occurring. You can learn more about such features in Chapter 11.

Some IDS products provide tiered solutions, which typically involve deploying multiple IDS sensors on various network segments. Each sensor transmits its IDS data to a centralized server that stores all the data. The individual sensors or the centralized box, which is able to correlate events from all the sensors' data, can make alert decisions. Many IDS solutions also have separate analyst consoles that connect to the centralized system or the individual sensors; these enable analysts to view recorded data and alerts, as well as reconfigure the sensors and update signatures. Some software vendors, such as ArcSight, e-Security, GuardedNet, Intellitactics, and netForensics, offer console products that can process and correlate data from various brands of IDS sensors, firewalls, and other hosts; Chapter 20, "Network Log Analysis," discusses such products.

Intrusion-Related Services

Besides intrusion detection products, some intrusion detection–related services might be able to assist you with the analysis of your intrusion detection data. Some organizations choose to outsource the analysis of their IDS sensor data to specialized commercial monitoring services. Other organizations elect to do their own analysis, but also submit their data to free distributed IDS services for additional help.

Distributed IDS Services

As IDS products have become more popular, the use of free distributed IDS services has also grown significantly. The basic concept is that administrators from organizations all over the world submit logs to a distributed IDS service from their own IDS sensors, firewalls, and other devices. These services analyze the data from all the sites and perform correlations to identify likely attacks. Two of the best-known distributed IDS services are Symantec's DeepSight Analyzer, located at http://analyzer.symantec.com, and DShield, located at http://www.dshield.org.

Using a distributed IDS service has a few benefits. Because the service receives logs from many environments, it has a wealth of data to use for its intrusion analysis. A distributed IDS service finds patterns among all the attacks that individual sites cannot see. Another great feature of some distributed IDS services is that if they conclude that a host at a particular IP address attacked a substantial number of sites, they will email the technical contact for that domain so that the activity can be investigated. Distributed IDS services can reduce some of the burden placed on intrusion analysts by analyzing logs, correlating events, and following up on highly suspicious activity—essentially providing another tool that can help analysts.

Outsourced Intrusion Detection System Monitoring

Many companies, such as Counterpane, ISS, and Symantec, offer managed security services that include IDS monitoring capabilities. This generally entails 24-hour remote monitoring of your IDS sensors, analysis of IDS data, and rapid notification of your staff in case of serious attack or IDS failure. One advantage of using these services is staffing related; they can provide trained intrusion analysts to monitor your sensors at all times. Another advantage is that because these services collect data from so many networks, they can correlate attacks among them. The disadvantage is their lack of knowledge about your environment and their inability to correlate events unless they can access firewall and host log files in near real time. (In addition to outsourcing IDS monitoring, many organizations also outsource the monitoring of other security event sources, such as firewalls and antivirus servers; in such cases, correlation is generally not an issue.)

At best, outsourced IDS monitoring can identify serious attacks and help your organization respond to them quickly and appropriately. If your organization doesn't have the time or expertise to analyze its own IDS sensor data properly and promptly, outsourcing that work is important for maintaining a strong perimeter defense. At worst, such services add little or nothing to the existing IDS solution, while requiring substantial financial commitments. Because outsourced IDS monitoring is very resource-intensive, it can easily cost millions of dollars a year for larger organizations.

The Roles of Network IDS in a Perimeter Defense

IDS sensors serve several purposes in a good perimeter defense. In some cases, they are uniquely suited to the task they perform. Besides identifying attacks and suspicious activity, you can use IDS data to identify security weaknesses and vulnerabilities, including policy violations. IDS data is also an invaluable part of network forensics and incident-handling efforts. Network IDS complements other perimeter defense components by performing functions that they cannot, such as full protocol and payload analysis. IDS sensors can also work with other defense components to halt active attacks. Network IDS is valuable in most environments for creating and maintaining a strong overall security solution.

Identifying Weaknesses

It is absolutely crucial that you identify vulnerabilities and weaknesses and reduce or eliminate them. If you don't take care of them, attackers will most likely find and exploit them, and hosts might be compromised. If a host is compromised, an attacker is likely to use it as a jumping-off point for attacks against other hosts in your environment. By preventing that host from being compromised, or by being alerted immediately after it has been, you can achieve a much better outcome. You can use IDS proactively to find vulnerabilities and weaknesses and identify early stages of attacks, and you can use it reactively to detect attacks against hosts and log what occurs.

Security Auditing

Network IDS can assist in security auditing. You can use the IDS logs and alerts to identify weaknesses in network defenses. For example, if a sensor sends alerts about suspicious Telnet activity from an Internet-based host and your firewall is supposed to be blocking all incoming Telnet activity, either your firewall is not blocking the traffic properly or your network has an additional connection to the Internet that is not secured properly.

Policy Violations

Some IDSs enable you to receive alerts when certain protocols or well-known port numbers are used. For example, if your users are not permitted to use the Internet Relay Chat (IRC) protocol, you could tune your IDS to alert you whenever it sees IRC traffic on the network. Because many Trojans, such as Sdbot, and other malicious code use IRC for communication, IRC traffic on your network could indicate that an incident has occurred. It could also indicate a user who is violating your security policy. Either way, it's activity you're likely to want to know about.

Along the same lines, IDS sensors can be useful in finding misconfigured systems on your own networks, such as a host that isn't using your web proxy server and is reducing the overall security level of your environment. Sensors can also help you find rogue systems that unauthorized personnel are running; for example, a user might set up a web server for her consulting business on her corporate workstation. When reviewing your IDS logs, you would see port 80 traffic directed to this box. Identifying improperly configured hosts and addressing their problems is a key part of reducing the vulnerabilities in your environment.

Detecting Attacks from Your Own Hosts

Although network IDS sensors used to be thought of as only identifying suspicious activity that enters a network from the Internet, it's important to consider that you can also use IDS sensors to identify outgoing attacks. This use is particularly valuable in environments where outbound access is largely unrestricted. You certainly want to be aware of attacks that your internal hosts are performing on external entities; your users could be causing these attacks, or the attacks could signal that another party or a worm is using compromised machines to attack others.

In an environment where firewalls and packet filters are configured to let almost any activity out of your organization, an IDS is probably the only method you have of identifying such attacks. If your border devices place some restrictions on outbound activity, you might identify an attack by reviewing your firewall logs, but this is far less likely to happen because most firewalls have no signature capabilities and can't identify most attacks. Also, reviewing firewall logs is much more resource-intensive than reviewing the logs of an IDS sensor that checks outgoing traffic.

Incident Handling and Forensics

In an ideal world, your organization would have staff monitoring your IDS logs and alerts 24 hours a day and reacting immediately to suspicious activity. Although organizations are increasingly implementing 24-hour monitoring, it's more likely than not that yours has not. You probably receive a page when the most serious alerts occur, and you review your IDS alerts and logs as often as you can, given all your other duties. It's important that you review alerts as often as possible so that you can quickly identify serious attacks and react appropriately to them.

Even if you don't notice that an attack is occurring until the damage has been done, the IDS data can still be invaluable to you. It can show you which hosts were attacked and what attacks were used against them. This critical information can help you recover from incidents much more quickly and identify the likely source of an attack. It gives you the basic information you need when starting to handle an incident, and it indicates other hosts that might have related data, such as firewalls that the traffic passed through or other hosts that were attacked.

Along the same lines, many people do not consider the forensic uses of IDS. You can use IDS logs to investigate an incident. Also, some IDS products enable you to monitor and log specified types of traffic. For example, if you don't permit IRC to be used on your network, you might want to set your IDS to log all IRC traffic, which could then capture IRC communications between malware on one of your machines and a remote IRC server. Of course, you need to consider the privacy rights of your users before configuring your IDS this way; legitimate users might be chatting with each other using IRC, and the IDS might record their conversations.

Complementing Other Defense Components

Part of the purpose of network IDS is to correlate the activity that individual hosts might see. If 100 hosts each record one failed Telnet attempt, no one might notice; but if an IDS sensor records 100 failed Telnet attempts, it's much more likely to trigger an alert. IDS sensors may work with perimeter defense components to stop attacks in progress. IDS sensors can also perform functions that other perimeter defense components generally can't.

For example, firewalls and packet filters have limited capabilities to examine traffic. Typically, they do not look at the contents of packet payloads, although some might do some basic protocol analysis. Firewalls generally look at some of the most basic characteristics of traffic and accept, deny, or reject it accordingly. A firewall might try to stop certain services from passing through by blocking certain port numbers, but it generally does little or nothing to evaluate traffic that uses allowed port numbers. IDS sensors are designed to examine the contents of packets; some IDS sensors are even capable of doing full protocol analysis, which means that they can examine the contents of an entire session as it occurs and alert you if the traffic does not match its expectations, without matching the traffic against a known attack signature.

A simple example of this is the identification of applications that run on unexpected ports. For example, a Trojan that is installed on a host might use TCP port 21 (usually associated with FTP control connections) for all communications with its Trojan master. If your firewall is configured to let internal users FTP to external sites, the Trojan could initiate a connection to its master, and your firewall would respond as though it were an FTP connection and permit it. However, the IDS sensor would actually analyze the content of the packets and alert you that the traffic was not FTP. You could then review the IDS logs for more information and investigate the host in question.

A more complex example of the value of protocol analysis is the identification of various known and unknown attacks. One of the most commonly used attack techniques is the buffer overflow, in which the attacker sets various fields or arguments to overly large or long values to attempt to overwrite memory locations. By performing protocol analysis—for example, validating the header and payload values in a DNS query—the IDS can identify anomalous values that are possible signs of buffer overflow attempts. Although stateful firewalls might do some protocol analysis, they are usually poor logging tools and have no signature capabilities. Other types of firewalls generally don't do protocol analysis at all.

IDS Sensor Placement

Now that you're familiar with the basics of network intrusion detection, you're ready to consider how it fits into your environment from a network architecture standpoint. It can be difficult to balance your desire to monitor as much of your network as possible with financial and staffing limitations. This section looks at the need for having multiple IDS sensors and where they are typically placed in a network. We'll also discuss some issues that can affect sensor placement, as well as the advantages of implementing a separate IDS management network.

Deploying Multiple Network Sensors

In many environments, you should deploy multiple IDS sensors. Each sensor generally monitors a single network segment. In a small organization with a simple network architecture and limited traffic, a single sensor might be adequate, although more than one might still be advisable in high-security situations. In larger environments—particularly those with many network segments, those that offer substantial Internet-based services, and those with multiple Internet access points—multiple sensors are almost certainly needed to adequately monitor network traffic.

Deploying more intrusion detection sensors usually produces better results. By deploying sensors on various network segments, you can tune each of them to the traffic you typically see on that segment—the type of hosts that use it and the services and protocols that are traversing it. You would probably tune a sensor on an Internet-connected segment much differently than you would tune one that is monitoring traffic between two tightly secured internal portions of your network. If you deploy only one sensor, the amount of tuning you can do is generally quite limited. Of course, if you deploy multiple sensors, you need to be prepared to handle the increased number of alerts that will be generated. Placing additional sensors on the network is not very helpful if administrators do not have time to maintain and monitor them.

Another reason for using multiple sensors is the fault tolerance of your IDS. What if your single sensor fails, for any reason, or the network segment that it's monitoring is unexpectedly unavailable? If you have one sensor, you won't have a network intrusion detection capability until the failure is corrected. Having more than one sensor provides a more robust solution that can continue monitoring at least portions of your network during a sensor failure or partial network outage.

Placing Sensors Near Filtering Devices

Typically, you deploy IDS sensors, which are often paired with firewalls or packet filters, near Internet access points. Sometimes you place a sensor on one side of the filtering device, and sometimes on both sides. For example, an Internet firewall might have an IDS sensor on the external network segment to identify all suspicious activity, and a second IDS sensor on the internal network segment that can identify all suspicious activity that passes through the firewall from the outside.

If possible, deploy sensors on both sides of firewalls and packet filters. However, if financial or other resource constraints limit you to one sensor per filtering device, you have to decide on which side of the filtering device the sensor should be deployed. It's often recommended that the sensor be placed on the outside network so that it can detect all attacks, including those that don't get through the filtering.

However, in some cases, you might prefer to put the sensor on the inside network. Sensors on an outside network, particularly one that is connected to the Internet, are more likely to be attacked, and they're also going to process much more traffic than a sensor on an inside network. In addition, if your staff has limited time to perform intrusion analysis and can only address the most serious threats, putting the sensor on the inside network collects data and generates alerts only on attacks that get into the network. Another advantage to putting a sensor on the inside network is that it can help you determine whether your filtering device is misconfigured.

If you're limited to one sensor, your firewall policies might be relevant to its placement. We mentioned earlier that you should also consider issues involving outgoing traffic from compromised or malicious hosts within your own environment. If your firewall has a default deny policy for outgoing traffic, a sensor on the inside network is required to identify attacks that your internal hosts attempt against external hosts but that your firewall blocks. If your firewall has a default allow policy for outgoing traffic, the sensor's location is much less important (as long as there's one near your firewall).

Another factor in sensor deployment is the volume of data to be processed. If a network segment has an extremely high volume of data, you might want to deploy multiple sensors with different configurations to split the traffic. After a sensor starts dropping packets, you will almost certainly experience more false positives and negatives. If your external network sees extremely high volumes of traffic, consider putting a sensor outside the firewall that is tuned to identify only the most severe attacks, particularly flooding-type attacks meant to cause a denial of service for your Internet connectivity or firewall. Use a second sensor inside your firewall to do more detailed analysis; this sensor should see a significantly smaller volume of data than the first sensor.

Note

Wherever there is a link to the Internet or to other external networks or hosts, there should be an IDS sensor. This rule varies from environment to environment, of course. Another great place to put a sensor is where a filtering device should be but isn't.

Placing IDS Sensors on the Internal Network

In many environments, network IDS sensors are placed along the network perimeter only, typically around Internet firewalls and packet filters. However, some environments also benefit from the deployment of additional network IDS sensors. A classic example is a company's research and development division. The company might have established a firewall or packet filter that prevents users in other divisions from accessing the hosts in

R&D. Because the information on the R&D hosts is valuable to external attackers and malicious insiders, it would be prudent to deploy an IDS sensor near the firewall or packet filter.

Some companies are so security conscious that they deploy IDS sensors throughout their networks to monitor all traffic. Of course, this requires considerable financial and staffing resources, but it gives the intrusion analysts a great feel for what's happening throughout their environment. If you only look at the activity occurring on your borders, you're missing much of the picture. Remember that IDS sensors aren't limited to identifying attacks against servers; many can also find signs of worms and other malware attempting to spread through a network, sometimes before antivirus software can identify them.

Working with Encryption

When planning network IDS sensor placement, you must consider how to deal with encrypted network traffic, such as VPN connections. IDS sensors certainly don't have the capability to decrypt traffic, but that's a good thing! If all the traffic on a certain network segment is encrypted, it still might be valuable to deploy a sensor to examine packet headers and look for unencrypted traffic. To monitor the content of the traffic that was encrypted, you should deploy IDS sensors at the first point in the network where the decrypted traffic travels. In addition, you should put host-based IDS software on the host decrypting the traffic because it's a likely target for attacks.

Processing in High-traffic Situations

Consider the volume of network traffic. The amount of traffic that IDS sensors can process is dependent on many factors, including what product is being used, which protocols or applications are most commonly used, and for which signatures the sensors have been directed to look. Therefore, no simple answers exist as to what volume of traffic any particular product can handle. In general, IDS sensors reach their capacity before firewalls do, primarily because IDS sensors do much more examination of packets than other network devices do. Also, the field of IDS sensor and signature development and optimization is still fairly young, at least compared to other aspects of network security.

Configuring Switches

If portions of your network that you would like to monitor are switched, then ensure that you configured your IDS sensors and switches appropriately. Switches must have their spanning ports configured properly for network IDS sensors to see all the traffic passing through the switches. This critical configuration has adversely affected many IDS deployments. A sensor that tries to monitor traffic on an improperly configured switch might see no traffic at all—or it might see only parts of the traffic, such as only one side of two-way TCP connections, which is only marginally better than seeing nothing. Thoroughly test sensors in switched environments to confirm that they are seeing all the traffic properly.

> **Note**
> In some cases, it is not feasible for an IDS to use spanning ports to monitor network activity. Some switches stop sending some or all traffic to the spanning port under peak usage. Also, a spanning port may only be able to see traffic for a single VLAN on a switch. A better alternative may be to deploy a network tap. Taps are available from several vendors, including Finisar (previously known as Shomiti), Intrusion, Net Optics, and Network Critical.

Using an IDS Management Network

To improve the security of your network IDS sensors, you might want to create a separate management network to use strictly for communication among IDS sensors, a centralized IDS data collection box, and analyst consoles. In this model, each network IDS sensor has at least two network interface cards (NICs). One or more NICs sniff traffic from monitored networks as their sole function. These NICs do not transmit traffic. Instead, the last NIC is connected to a separate management network, which is only used for transferring IDS data and configuration updates. This is also known as performing out-of-band management of the network IDS.

By implementing such an architecture, you make it much more difficult for attackers to find and identify an IDS sensor because it will not answer requests directed toward its monitoring NICs. Because the management NIC is on an isolated network, attackers shouldn't be able to reach it. Also, most monitoring NICs are pure sniffers and do not use an IP address. If an IDS sensor uses an IP address and an attacker knows what that address is, the attacker could launch a DoS against it so that it couldn't see her attacks, or she could otherwise try to hide or obfuscate her traffic from the sensor.

Implementing a separate management network has other advantages. It isolates management traffic so that anyone else who is monitoring the same network doesn't see your sensors' communications. It also prevents the sensors from monitoring their own traffic. A separate network might also be a good way to deal with potential problems related to passing sensor data through firewalls and over unencrypted public networks.

Maintaining Sensor Security

One important item that hasn't been addressed yet is that of sensor security. It's critical that you harden your IDS sensors to make the risk of compromise as low as possible. If attackers gain control of your IDS, they could shut it off or reconfigure it so that it can't log or alert you about their activities. Attackers might also be able to use your IDS to launch attacks against other hosts. However, if attackers can get access to your IDS management network, they might be able to access all your sensors. Maintaining the security of your sensors is key to creating a stable and valuable IDS solution.

Note

Most IDS vendors offer IDS appliances that have already been hardened. Typically, appliances offer only the services necessary to support IDS functions, and they are configured to minimize the possibility that they will be compromised. Configuring and deploying an appliance-based sensor generally requires much less effort than building a sensor. However, when a new OS or service vulnerability occurs, it may not be possible to patch the appliance until the vendor releases updated software, because many appliances do not provide any OS access.

Case Studies

Now that we have discussed some of the factors that go into sensor placement, let's look at three different scenarios. Each one is shown through a simplified diagram of the relevant portions of the network. No right or wrong answers exist, only reasons why certain locations might be more beneficial than others.

Case Study 1: Simple Network Infrastructure

Figure 8.1 shows a network diagram for a small organization with a simple network infrastructure. It has only one connection point to the Internet. A firewall divides the network into three segments:

- An external DMZ segment that is connected to the Internet

- A screened subnet that contains servers that are directly accessed by Internet-based users or must directly access the Internet, such as email, web, web proxy, and external DNS servers

- An internal segment that contains servers that typically aren't directly connected to the Internet, as well as workstations, printers, and other host devices

In this environment, incoming connections from the Internet can only be made to hosts on the screened subnet; those hosts can then initiate connections to the internal network. Hosts on the internal network can initiate connections to hosts on the screened subnet or directly to Internet-based hosts. Although the firewall has a default deny policy for incoming traffic, it has a default allow policy for outgoing traffic. Little outgoing traffic is restricted.

IDS Deployment Recommendations

Figure 8.1 shows the IDS management network as a separate entity from the monitored networks. Each sensor contains two NICs: one sniffing packets on the monitored network, and the other transmitting IDS data on the management network. The management network is connected only to the sensors, a central IDS logging box, and the analyst workstations.

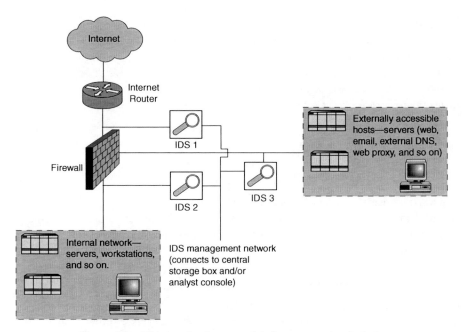

Figure 8.1   This is a simple network infrastructure that includes
IDS sensors and a separate IDS management network.

Ideally, all three network IDS sensors shown in Figure 8.1 should be deployed. IDS 1
(on the external segment) looks for any probes, scans, or attacks coming from the
Internet. IDS 2 (on the internal segment) shows you which malicious traffic got through
the firewall to your internal network. Both IDS 1 and IDS 2 can monitor outgoing traffic as well, looking for attacks from your internal hosts. IDS 3 focuses on identifying
attacks against your externally exposed boxes, which are the most likely targets of attackers. The same sensor is also able to monitor network activity between your external
servers that doesn't pass through the firewall. If one of your external hosts becomes compromised, this is the only sensor that could see attempts from it to compromise other
hosts on the same segment.

Case Study 2: Multiple External Access Points

Figure 8.2 shows a more complicated network. This environment has multiple external
points of access: a dedicated connection to the Internet, a dial-up modem bank for
remote users, and multiple frame relay connections to remote offices and business partners. Firewalls have been deployed at each access point to restrict the traffic that enters
the internal network.

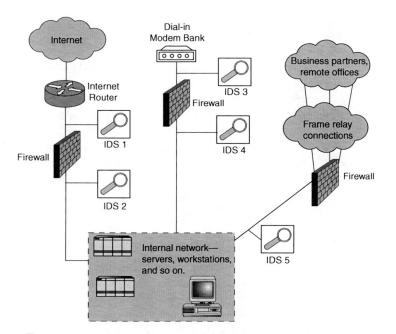

Figure 8.2   A more complex corporate network has multiple external points of access, which each need to be protected with IDS sensors.

IDS Deployment Recommendations

This scenario follows the same general rule as before: Whenever practical, deploy network IDS sensors on both sides of firewalls and packet filters. The most interesting area to consider is that of the external networks connected through the frame relay connections. You will notice that no sensors monitor the connections on the external side. If your budget permits, you can add sensors to those connections as well, although they might not be needed. It depends on what is on the other side of the connection and what your firewall is supposed to be doing.

You might feel that a remote office poses little threat and that a separate sensor to monitor its connection is not necessary. Of course, you could also deploy a sensor at the remote location, which would monitor traffic before it was sent over the frame relay connection. If the remote site is a business partner's network, you might want to be more cautious; however, your firewall might only be permitting a small, well-defined set of traffic to pass through. The risk might be small enough that you can't justify the expense of an additional sensor. Perhaps the connection to your business partner is largely unrestricted, in which case you would want to monitor it much more closely. If you decide to deploy sensors for the external links that enter the firewall, and the firewall has several interfaces on separate network segments, you would probably want to deploy a sensor for each segment. Each sensor can then be tuned for the nature of that particular connection.

Another item to consider is the risk that outgoing attacks and probes pose. If you are not restricting outbound traffic very much, then sensor placement shouldn't be affected by it. But if you do restrict outbound traffic—for example, you block all connection attempts from the internal network to the modem bank—then having the sensor on the inside is necessary to detect attempted attacks. The question is, how much do you care about that? In your environment, is it sufficient for the firewall to report that a connection attempt was blocked, or do you need to know what the nature of that attempt was? How important is the resource on the other side of the connection? What are the consequences if you fail to notice an attack from one of your hosts against your business partner's systems?

Case Study 3: Unrestricted Environment

Our final case study, shown in Figure 8.3, is a greatly simplified view of a university network with three main groups of hosts: students, faculty and staff, and administration (registrar, bursar, and so on). As is typical of many university environments, no firewalls restrict traffic. A small amount of packet filtering might occur at routers throughout the network, but otherwise, virtually any sort of traffic is permitted. The only exception is some machines in the administration network that contain sensitive information, such as student grades and financial information; these machines are somewhat protected through router packet filtering. Because of the open nature of most universities, faculty and student machines are usually vulnerable to exploitation, in part because just about any sort of traffic is permitted. In addition, many servers are run by students or faculty, not centralized IT staff, and are almost certainly not kept fully patched and secured.

We can expect many student and faculty machines to use modems or wireless network cards. We can also expect that some of these machines run software such as pcAnywhere to allow external hosts to dial in to them. In such an environment, it's impossible to define the border of your network. It's also likely that the university offers dial-in services for users. These services may require little or no authentication.

IDS Deployment Recommendations

As you might imagine, the security requirements of the groups of hosts shown in Figure 8.3 are quite different. In addition, staffing and financial resources are probably quite limited, so you need to focus on the most important areas. Your first priority is protecting the administrative computers, which are at high risk of being attacked. You want to monitor these systems as closely as possible, through a combination of IDS sensors deployed to the segments where the hosts reside, and host-based IDS software running on all of them. If you can do nothing else, you need to regularly monitor IDS alerts and logs related to these sensitive hosts.

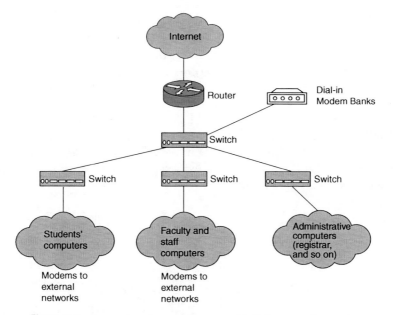

Figure 8.3   In a university environment with little network security, it is not easy to determine where to deploy IDS sensors.

Even if you have the resources to deploy and monitor additional sensors, will you have the resources to react to what you see? These environments might contain tens of thousands of largely unsecured machines that can be infected with viruses, Trojans, or other malware. This is a similar problem to that seen by Internet service providers (ISPs), which carry customer traffic but have little control over what their customers do. In fact, portions of a university network can be thought of as an ISP for students. If network IDS sensors are deployed, they need to be carefully tuned to only send alerts on the most severe attacks. If the sensor sends an alert every time a port scan or host scan occurs, the intrusion analyst will quickly be overwhelmed with alerts. Sensors might also be unable to keep up with the high volumes of traffic if they are performing too much analysis.

You might be asking yourself, "Why should I bother trying to monitor this traffic at all? If users are permitted to do almost anything they want to, why should I try to deploy sensors to the networks they use?" Here's a scenario that explains why some level of network intrusion detection should be performed. Suppose that hundreds of hosts throughout the university have been infected with the same Trojan and that these hosts are used to launch DDoS attacks against other sites. Given the lack of other defense devices, deploying an intrusion detection sensor to monitor outgoing traffic may be your best chance of quickly detecting such an attack and collecting enough information about it to identify the infected hosts.

Summary

In this chapter, you learned about the basics of network IDSs, particularly signatures and how they cause false positives and negatives. We took a close look at where IDS sensors and software can be located in various network environments and discussed the advantages and disadvantages of various deployment architectures. The goal of this chapter was not to teach you everything you will ever need to know about intrusion detection. Several good books focus on that topic, such as *Network Intrusion Detection: An Analyst's Handbook*, by Stephen Northcutt and Judy Novak, and *Intrusion Signatures and Analysis*, by Stephen Northcutt, Mark Cooper, Matt Fearnow, and Karen Frederick. Instead, we examined the role that IDS plays in a layered defense and how it has become a critical component of a good security solution.

9

Host Hardening

THE TERM *HOST HARDENING* REFERS TO TAKING a typical or default installation of an operating system (OS) and associated applications and then modifying the configuration to decrease the host's potential exposure to threats. The extent of hardening depends on the role the system performs. A properly locked-down host can act as an effective contributor toward a reliable network security perimeter.

This chapter presents core principles of the host-hardening process, with the goal of helping you devise standards and procedures for locking down system configurations in your organization. Rather than providing long checklists for every scenario and OS you might encounter, we focus on concepts that are common to most host-hardening scenarios, empowering you to customize publicly available checklists and guidelines for your purposes. With this in mind, we go over key steps involved in stripping the system of unnecessary OS components and tools as well as discuss the procedures for limiting user access to unnecessary files and programs. We also offer guidance regarding auditing issues and go over best practices related to applying patches. We complete the discussion of host hardening by offering pointers to additional hardening resources. The topic of host-level security continues in Chapter 10, "Host Defense Components," where we build on this chapter's guidelines by explaining how to use hosts to help detect and isolate attacks on the network security perimeter.

The Need for Host Hardening

Leaving the system in its default configuration provides attackers with too many opportunities for obtaining unauthorized access to the host. Even if there is a well-tuned firewall in front of the machine, it's hard to anticipate every way in which attackers may access the protected system. This is why the material in this chapter is so critical to ensuring the security of your infrastructure. When erecting a house, you want to make sure that high-quality concrete is used to provide a robust foundation for the structure built upon it so that the concrete will not crack under stress. In a network security system, each measure we take to lock down the host's configuration provides us with the basis for offering secure and reliable services to the system's users.

A significant issue in host-level security is the applications installed on the system. Of course, a host is typically useless without the applications and OS components necessary for it to fulfill its function. At the same time, any software enabled on a system may be exploited due to vulnerabilities in the application or the underlying OS. A configuration flaw or a coding error can provide the attacker with access to the underlying host, offering an internal "island" from which to conduct further attacks. For example, buffer overflow exploits against a vulnerable application can allow an attacker to execute privileged commands on the targeted system. Operating systems and applications contain vulnerabilities that attackers can exploit, even though some of these vulnerabilities might not have been discovered yet or have not been publicly announced.

The NNTP Vulnerability in Windows, Circa 2004

The MS04-036 security bulletin and the associated patch, which Microsoft released in October 2004, addressed a critical vulnerability in the Network News Transfer Protocol (NNTP) component of Windows operating systems. If exploited, the bug could allow a remote attacker to gain full control over the affected host. Of course, the vulnerability existed before it was publicly announced. If the attacker possessed a "private" version of the exploit, she could have accessed the vulnerable system with little effort. Organizations that removed or disabled the NNTP component from their hosts (if it was not needed) protected themselves against this attack vector even without knowing about the vulnerability.

From a security perspective, the most reliable way of locking down the host's configuration is to begin with a minimalist system—just the core OS (freshly patched, of course) with only administrative accounts and tightly restricted access rights. You would then add user accounts, install applications, and relax permissions only to the extent needed for the system to function properly. Unfortunately, the installation process of many operating systems and applications doesn't facilitate this process, installing unnecessary components with loose permissions in a default configuration. In such situations, you will need to carefully comb the system to disable, remove, and otherwise lock down components that unnecessarily increase the host's risk profile.

Keep in mind that as you increase the extent to which the system is locked down, you often end up decreasing the level of convenience it offers to its users. That might be one of the reasons systems are frequently shipped with too many features enabled by default. For example, Microsoft has, historically, shipped its products with user–friendly default settings for ease of setup and use, with little regard to security implications of having too many unnecessary components running on the system. With the release of Windows 2003 Server and Windows XP Service Pack 2, we have seen a shift toward tighter default configurations of Windows; however, system administrators still need to review the operating system's setup, tuning it to match their requirements.

When devising hardening procedures for hosts on your network, keep in mind the cost you incur from applying the hardening techniques and maintaining the systems that have been locked down. Not all hosts should be hardened to the same extent. If an end-user workstation, a web server, and a VPN server have different responsibilities on the network, their extent of appropriate hardening is different as well. You need to achieve the right balance between security and functionality to determine what exposure to threat is acceptable while still providing critical business services.

Securing Applications on the Host

Many of the principles discussed in this chapter in the context of OS hardening apply, to a large extent, to applications that run on top of the OS. Especially when dealing with more complicated applications such as databases and web servers, you will need to get rid of unnecessary software components and internal user accounts; establish access privileges; audit events; protect accounts, data, and configuration parameters; and so on.

Consult vendor documentation when installing an application, in case the vendor has provided best practices guidelines for locking down the program's configuration. Such recommendations may explain how to install the application so that it runs under a system account with limited privileges, and how to change the default passwords assigned to the application's internal users during the installation process. Keep in mind that you should not rely solely on the vendor's documentation—seek out books and guides that offer independent advice on setting up the application in a secure manner.

An essential aspect of host hardening is ensuring the secure configuration of the underlying OS. Securing the OS involves disabling or removing unnecessary services, daemons, libraries, and other extraneous components that find their way onto the system as part of the default OS installation.

Removing or Disabling of Unnecessary Programs

A modern operating system can provide a multitude of services, ranging from those applicable to end-user workstations to those designed for high-end servers. When installing Red Hat Linux, for example, you have the opportunity to pick a profile for the system you wish to build—in response to your selection the installer ensures that the resulting build contains the necessary program and configuration files. In Windows, you make a similar decision when selecting the flavor of the OS to install (Home, Professional, Server, and so on) as well as when configuring the machine after it boots up for the first time. Keep in mind that the profiles OS installers present to you are generic, and they only approximate the role the machine may play in your particular organization. As a result, it is up to you to remove or disable the OS components you do not need.

Controlling Network Services

You should pay particular attention to programs that may be invoked over the network. Attackers often scan networks in search of systems listening on commonly used ports, especially those associated with known vulnerabilities. Leaving unnecessary network services running on the host increases the risk that the system might be compromised. Even if the host is located behind a firewall, attackers can gain access to the services through ports that the firewall doesn't filter, or by finding ways to bypass the firewall altogether.

> **Note**
>
> It is often difficult to stop an attacker once she gains access. Therefore, it is crucial to be proactive to block the attacker from ever getting in.

You can use the `netstat -na` command on most operating systems to list the ports on which your system is listening. If this command presents you with a port number you do not recognize, search the Web for that port number using your favorite search engine and determine whether the associated application should remain running on your host. For example, if you determine that your host is listening on TCP port 80, the system is probably running a web server. If this is the desired behavior, great! Otherwise, be sure to disable the offending service before releasing the system into production.

On UNIX platforms, the `/etc/inetd.conf` or `/etc/xinetd.conf` files control a large number of network services, which are started by the Inetd process. You will need to edit these text files to deactivate unneeded daemons. You may also need to look though various files under the `/etc` directory to disable some services. The location of such files differs across UNIX flavors. Here are some of the directories to look into:

- `/etc/xinetd.d`
- `/etc/init.d/rc.d`
- `/etc/rc.d`

Under Windows, you can control many network services through Control Panel's applets such as Services and Network Connections. For example, to disable the NetBIOS protocol, which is ridden with legacy security weaknesses and is no longer needed in most environments that use Windows 2000 or higher, you'll need to perform the following steps:

1. Edit the properties of your Local Area Connection.
2. Select TCP/IP properties and click the Advanced button.
3. Select the WINS tab.
4. Activate the Disable NetBIOS over TCP/IP option.

This process is illustrated in Figure 9.1.

In most Windows 2000 and XP environments, you will still be able to access files and printers remotely through the built-in Server Message Block (SMB) protocol running directly over TCP/IP, even if you disabled the NetBIOS protocol. Older Windows operating systems, however, rely on NetBIOS for remote file and printer access.

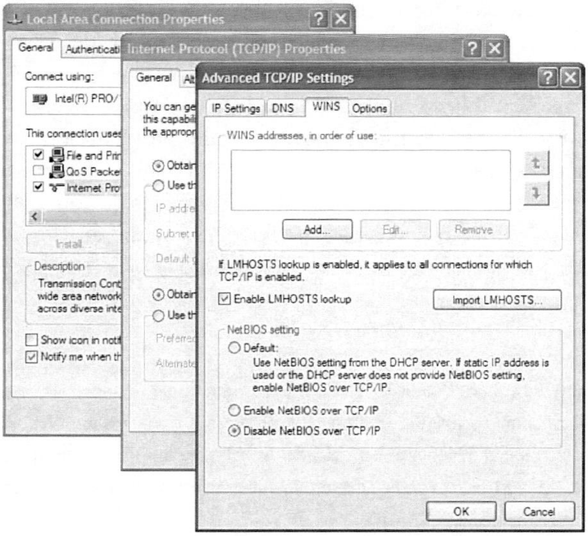

Figure 9.1   You can disable NetBIOS over TCP/IP in Windows 2000 or higher by modifying properties of your network connection.

Deactivating a network service decreases the likelihood that it will be used as a doorway into the system, but it might complicate the task of remotely administrating the host. For example, file-sharing services might not be directly related to a business function of an Internet-accessible web server, but they might be helpful for administrators when uploading or downloading the server's files. The more critical the system, the more likely you will be willing to forego some administrative convenience for the sake of hardening its configuration.

Let's take a look at some of the resource-sharing and remote access services you should consider disabling on Windows and UNIX hosts.

Resource-Sharing Services

Resource-sharing services, sometimes called "file and print" services, allow a remote user to access data on the host by connecting to it over the network. Sometimes default OS installations provide too many opportunities for such access, leaving it up to you to disable aspects of these services that you do not need.

Windows allows remote users to access files on a host using the SMB protocol through the Server service, which the OS enables by default. Consider disabling this service on your workstations if you do not require remote access to user workstations. The users will still be able to connect to file shares on your servers—such outgoing connections are established by the Workstation service. If the system's purpose requires that the Server service remain running, be sure to disable any unneeded file shares that the OS might activate by default. For instance, Windows NT and higher automatically establishes "hidden" administrative shares such as C$, ADMIN$, and PRINT$.

You can view, delete, and create hidden and regular Windows file shares through the Computer Management applet in the Administrative Tools folder of the host's Control Panel. For detailed information on managing Windows shares, take a look at Microsoft Knowledgebase articles 314984 and 318751 at http://support.microsoft.com.

File sharing on UNIX operating systems is usually performed through Network File System (NFS) services. It is a good idea to disable NFS-related daemons, such as nfsd and mountd if you do not require the use of their services. If you will use NFS for providing remote access to the system's file, carefully review the entries in the appropriate configuration files, such as `/etc/exports` (under Linux) or `/etc/dfs/dfstab` (under Solaris).

NFS and RPC Services

NFS expects Remote Procedure Call (RPC) services to be running on the host. On many critical UNIX systems, NFS may be the only service that requires RPC. Therefore, if you disable NFS altogether on your system, check whether you can deactivate RPC as well. Attackers often target RPC to obtain reconnaissance information about the host or to attempt exploiting vulnerabilities that have plagued many implementations of these services over the years.

Remote Access Services

In addition to providing resource-sharing services, modern operating systems often give administrators the ability to remotely configure the host as well as to execute commands on the machine without sitting directly in front of its console. Such services are attractive targets for attackers, because, if compromised, they can grant unrestrained access to the host.

Administrators can access Windows workstations remotely through Remote Desktop service, which is part of Windows XP or and higher. They can access Windows servers through Terminal Services, which run on Windows 2000 Server or higher. Although these services require that the user be authenticated before connecting to the host, they provide remote attackers with another network attack vector. If you will not use the Remote Desktop or Terminal Services, you should disable them on your hosts. (For additional information regarding Terminal Services, please see Chapter 10.)

In addition to providing full access to the remote system through Remote Desktop or Terminal Services, Windows offers the Remote Registry Service, which allows authenticated users to remotely manage the system's Registry. (Windows uses the Registry to store critical configuration data for the OS and its applications.) In the spirit of disabling network components that you do not need, you should deactivate this service unless you are actually going to use it to remotely maintain the machine.

UNIX platforms support numerous services that can be used for remotely accessing the host and that can be misused by an attacker. The most vulnerable of such programs are the so-called *r-commands*, which include rsh and rlogin. These two programs allow users to execute remote commands, but they do not encrypt the communications. Telnet is another popular mechanism for remotely accessing UNIX systems. Much like the r-commands, Telnet is gradually being phased out in favor of Secure Shell (SSH), which encrypts the session and provides stronger authentication options.

It is possible set up a trust relationship between UNIX systems so that a remote user can execute a command on another host without providing a password. Such trust relationships are useful and might be required for the system's business purpose. Most r-commands use IP addresses as the basis of verifying the identity of the trusted system; therefore, it is relatively easy to spoof the trusted host's identity. Remote access mechanisms, such as SSH, support the establishment of trust relationships based on cryptographic keys, which are much more dependable for authenticating users and systems. With all trust relationships, keep in mind that if it is easy for a legitimate user to jump from host to host, it is just as easy for an attacker who compromises just a single trusted host to do the same.

TCP Wrappers

TCP Wrappers (ftp://ftp.porcupine.org/pub/security) is a time-tested mechanism for letting a UNIX system restrict and log access to its network-accessible services. In basic terms, TCP Wrappers works by checking whether a remote system is allowed to connect to a specific service before the connection is passed to the application. Hosts that are allowed to connect are listed in the `hosts.allow` file, and hosts that should be blocked are specified in the `hosts.deny` file. In a way, this resembles the functionality of the host-centric firewalls we discuss in Chapter 10.

TCP Wrappers has been used primarily to control access to services launched through Inetd; however, TCP Wrappers functionality can also be compiled into many standalone daemons. For example, SSH servers from OpenSSH as well as from SSH Communications can be configured via a compile-time option to use TCP Wrappers libraries. (The SSH version of the daemon also supports the use of `AllowHosts` and `DenyHosts` tags in the server's configuration file.)

TCP Wrappers can provide access control functionality at a level that is independent of the application's internal authentication mechanism. As a result, TCP Wrappers can be used to block undesired networks or hosts before they have an opportunity to target the application. This functionality contributes to defense in depth by reinforcing the application's internal access control mechanisms.

In addition to controlling the host's network-accessible services, it is important to remove or disable other services and applications that the system does not require to fulfill its tasks.

Information Leakage

A network access mechanism that has serious implications for information leakage in Windows is known as a *null session*, which may allow remote users to anonymously access sensitive data. One of the legitimate uses of null sessions is to list users from another domain when granting them access to local resources. Some older third-party tools also use null sessions for similar purposes. Unfortunately, an attacker can use the same mechanism to query the remote system for usernames, shares, and services without authenticating to the host. Although environments based on Windows 2000 or higher often do not require null sessions for proper operation, they are commonly left enabled without regard to their security risk.

If you disable the Server service, null session connections will be disabled as well. If the Server service has to remain running, you can limit null session access through the Local Security Policy editor, which you can access through the Administrative Tools folder in Control Panel, or through Group Policy in environments that use Active Directory. The relevant policy entry is called "Additional restrictions for anonymous connections," illustrated in Figure 9.2. You will find this setting under Local Policies, Security Options. The most secure option is "No access without explicit anonymous permissions," which eliminates most risks associated with null sessions, but might break some legacy applications.

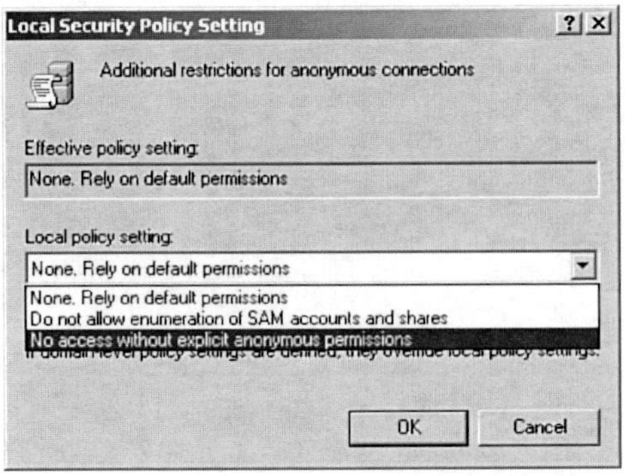

Figure 9.2 You can limit null session connections by restricting anonymous actions using the Local Security Policy editor or through Group Policy.

Another network service that often provides attackers with sensitive information is Simple Network Management Protocol (SNMP). As we discuss in Chapter 19, "Maintaining a Security Perimeter," administrators can use SNMP for remotely querying and modifying configuration parameters of a wide range of hosts and network devices. In most SNMP installations, SNMP-based access is restricted to those who know the proper passwords, which SNMP calls *community strings*. Unfortunately, community strings are often set to the words *private* and *public* in many default installations. If you cannot disable SNMP on your host, be sure to at least change its community strings. Numerous SNMP tools can be used to retrieve a wealth of information about the host running SNMP services, much more than the information leakage associated with null sessions on Windows systems.

Removing Extraneous Software Components

Removing extraneous software components, even if they are not network services, is important regardless whether you are installing an OS from scratch or locking down a system that has been already installed. For example, a C compiler such as GCC might be installed on a Linux-based web server by default, but it is rarely required for the web server to operate properly. When a system is compromised and a utility such as GCC is available to the attacker, it will be easier for her to compile additional attack tools or to install a backdoor to the system that will allow future access.

To remove unnecessary software components from Windows hosts, use the Add/Remove Programs applet in the Control Panel. Clicking the Add/Remove Windows Components tab will result in the window depicted in Figure 9.3. By removing unnecessary OS components in this manner, you will slow down the progress of an attacker should she find her way onto your system.

Figure 9.3 The Windows Component Wizard allows you to remove unnecessary software components from the host.

UNIX operating systems typically include package management tools that allow you to remove unnecessary software components with relative ease. For instance, many Linux distributions offer the rpm utility to remove unwanted packages that come with the OS, whereas Solaris comes with the pkgrm program, which can be used to fulfill the same purpose.

It is sometimes tricky to figure out which package to uninstall in order to get rid of a particular program. To make this determination, you can usually query the package management database on the host with the program's file path. For instance, in Linux you would use the following command to determine that gcc-3.2-7 is the package that "owns" the GCC program file:

```
# rpm -q -f /usr/bin/gcc
gcc-3.2-7
```

You should remove unnecessary administrative tools and OS components from critical servers, especially those that act as bastion hosts firewalls, VPNs, and other security services. You may encounter situations where removing a software component is too difficult: It may be embedded too deeply into the OS, or you may need to use it once in a while for administrative purposes. Whatever tools you elect to keep, be sure to modify file system permissions on their files to make it difficult for non-administrative users to get to them. You can usually accomplish this by setting the appropriate file system permissions so that only those authorized to use the tools will have access to the files.

Now that we've covered the principles behind disabling or removing unnecessary programs, let's take a look at the steps involved in limiting local access to sensitive data and configuration files.

Limiting Access to Data and Configuration Files

Should an attacker obtain remote access to the system through a non-administrative account, he will often look for ways to elevate his privileges to gain full control over the host and to access sensitive data or configuration files. By taking the time to set the appropriate access restrictions on such files, you can significantly impede the attacker's progress. In this section we take a brief look at defining file system–level permissions for UNIX and Windows, as well as limiting permissions to the Registry on Windows systems.

In order to implement file access restrictions, you need to make sure the host uses a file system that supports security permissions. Legacy file systems for DOS and Windows, such as FAT and FAT32, cannot restrict file access, granting all local users full control over any file on the host. Microsoft has since equipped Windows with a much more powerful file system, called NTFS, that allows administrators to control who can access a local file and what that user can do with it. At this point, NTFS and the associated management and recovery tools are sufficiently mature that situations where it would make sense to deploy a FAT-based file system, rather than NTFS, are very rare.

Like NTFS, UNIX-based file systems allow administrators to restrict file access based on the user's identity. Although UNIX platforms are typically more careful about granting file permissions than Windows, attackers may still exploit vulnerabilities because of loose file permissions on default installations of UNIX operating systems.

File Permissions and Race Conditions

One type of vulnerability often associated with incorrect file permissions, in conjunction with coding errors, is a *race condition*. In a common incarnation of this attack, during a brief window of opportunity, files are temporarily assigned file permissions that allow anyone to access them. Attackers can then manipulate these files to elevate their access on the host. For example, a race condition in FreeBSD's rmuser script allowed a local user to extract all password hashes from the system while the administrator removes a user (http://www.securityfocus.com/advisories/3544). This attack was possible because rmuser created a temporary file that was world-readable.

Default installations of both Windows and UNIX operating systems usually result in settings that are overly permissive. Host-hardening checklists, which we reference at the end of this chapter, offer detailed guidelines for protecting specific files and directories after installing the OS. The general idea behind such steps is to provide users with only the minimum access required to perform their tasks.

Be sure to carefully test the system's configuration after tightening its file system permissions to verify that the necessary applications continue to function. For example, if you restrict default permissions in the `%SystemRoot%` directory on Windows, this might create a problem when a user attempts to print. The `%SystemRoot%\system32\spool\printers` folder requires read and write access for users to be able to print successfully.

UNIX operating systems typically use files for storing OS and application-related configuration details. Limiting access to such data involves manipulating file system–level access restrictions. Although Windows also uses files for storing some configuration parameters, it increasingly relies on the Registry database for maintaining local system information. You can use the Regedit32 and Regedit utilities that come with Windows to set access control restrictions on Registry keys, just like you would set them on files. If your organization is using Active Directory, you can also distribute Registry permission settings through Group Policy.

Note
Applying file and Registry access restrictions can be a tedious task. You will be most effective at completing this step of the hardening process if you automate it, as we discuss in the "Automating Host-Hardening Steps" section later in this chapter.

The process of limiting access to powerful programs and sensitive files goes hand in hand with user and group management practices, which we cover in the following section.

Controlling User and Privileges

Attempting to gain access to user accounts on the targeted host is a step common to many network-based attacks. To protect the system against this attack vector, it is important to control user access through the following measures:

- Managing unattended accounts
- Protecting administrative accounts
- Enforcing strong passwords
- Controlling group membership

Let's begin this discussion by looking at the threats posed by unattended accounts.

Managing Unattended Accounts

Some of the most vulnerable accounts on a host are those assigned to the system's services, as opposed to human users. Such accounts are often left unattended, without a legitimate user available to notice attempts to misuse the account. Examples of unattended accounts in Windows that should be disabled, unless they are actually used, are Guest and IIS_*servername*, where *servername* is the name of the machine. UNIX platforms often come with unattended accounts that many hosts end up not using as well, such as sys, lp, and bin.

You should delete or disable unattended accounts if you do not need them. Deleting, rather than disabling, such accounts is often a more attractive option because it eliminates the likelihood that the account will be accidentally enabled. However, removing an account may result in orphan files owned by a UID that may get reassigned to another user by accident, particularly on UNIX platforms. Additionally, it is more difficult to restore an account that you deleted, rather than simply disabled, should you later find the need for using this account.

> **Note**
> It's important to verify regularly that unused user accounts are disabled or deleted to ensure that they are not accidentally reactivated.

If possible, unattended accounts should be deactivated in a way that logs any attempts to access them over the network. In UNIX you can easily accomplish this by setting the shell of the disabled account to noshell, which disconnects any user attempting to log in to the disabled account and creates an appropriate entry in the system's log. (The noshell utility is part of the Titan hardening package and can be downloaded free from http://www.fish.com/titan.)

Unattended accounts are often created with more privileges than they require or are assigned easy-to-guess passwords. You may need to leave some of these accounts on the system so that the applications that use them continue to function. In this case, you may still be able to limit access rights assigned to them and to change their password. Unattended accounts that remain on the system should be configured with the least necessary amount of privileges, and they should have complex passwords.

Protecting Administrative Accounts

Administrative accounts, such as root in UNIX and Administrator in Windows, may be even more attractive to attackers than unattended accounts. After all, administrative users are known to possess the greatest access level to the targeted host. You can protect administrative accounts by making them available to as few individuals in your organization as possible and by being careful about the actions these persons take while using such accounts.

Traditionally, UNIX systems have a single administrative user named root, which has a user identifier (UID) of 0. The root account is special because UNIX grants special privileges to any account that has UID 0. The Administrator account on Windows systems has a security identifier (SID) that ends with the suffix 500. This SID belongs to the Administrators group by default; any account you add to this group will have administrative privileges.

If the machine is maintained by multiple administrators, we recommend assigning dedicated nonprivileged accounts to these users. You should ask the administrators to use privileged accounts only when their actions require such access. They can accomplish this without logging out of their primary account by using the su utility in UNIX or the runas tool in Windows. Limiting the users of administrative accounts in this way will minimize the chance that these accounts will be compromised (for instance, when the administrator browses a malicious website while using a vulnerable browser). Using administrative accounts in this manner also helps provide an audit trail for detecting and investigating the compromise of such accounts.

> **Tip**
>
> Consider renaming the original root or Administrator account, and placing a dummy account in its place that has no privileges and a very long and complex password. A naïve attacker will attempt targeting this account, wasting time on an attack that is bound to fail. Creating a dummy administrative account and enabling auditing on it allows you to detect when someone is attempting to target your privileged accounts.

Enforcing Strong Passwords

Even a password for a nonprivileged account can act as an entry point for launching further attacks against the host as well as for accessing information available through the user's account. User accounts with poor passwords are one of the most commonly exploited security weaknesses. After an attacker obtains access to a user account, he often seeks to elevate the user's permissions to administrative permissions. The attacker gains full access to the system by taking advantage of a vulnerability in the OS or in one of the installed applications.

The system's users need to be educated to understand that they are responsible for safeguarding their passwords. Knowing that even security-conscious people have a tendency to select passwords that are easily guessable, administrators should implement mechanisms that enforce the desired password guidelines. On the one hand, a person may have a difficult time remembering cryptic passwords required by an organization that has unreasonable password strength requirements. On the other hand, increasing the complexity of a user's password makes it much harder for an attacker to "crack" the password with a tool that guesses passwords based on a dictionary file. Some of the tools attackers can use for this purpose are listed here:

- L0pht Crack (http://www.atstake.com/products/lc)
- Crack (ftp://ftp.cerias.purdue.edu/pub/tools/unix/pwdutils/crack)
- John the Ripper (http://www.openwall.com/john)

Just as the attackers can use these tools to locate accounts with weak passwords, so can you. In fact, you should routinely audit the strength of your users' passwords so that you have an opportunity to address the issue before attackers can take advantage of it. Before auditing system passwords, it is very important that you obtain documented authorization from your organization's management to perform this task. Jobs have been lost, and administrators have even gone to jail due to apparent misunderstandings over the purpose of their password-auditing activities.

Establishing an effective password policy and educating the users about proper ways to select and remember strong passwords goes a long way toward helping to prevent unauthorized system access. Another way to help ensure the integrity of the authentication process is to use tokens such as RSA's SecurID. SecurID is a small hardware device or a software module that generates a different access code approximately every minute and works in conjunction with RSA back-end software. When logging in, users are asked to supply a password that they remember as well as the temporary access code that the SecurID token has generated.

Another challenge in securing access to user accounts is the administrative complexity of assigning initial passwords to new user accounts. Many organizations use the same default password for all new users, and many individuals in the organization generally know this password. Using a random initial password is an effective way to protect new user accounts. Many attackers, especially insiders, attempt to compromise newly created accounts by trying typical first-time passwords such as "password," "test," or the username of the user. Other important password policies include a minimum password length of eight characters, password aging, password history, and account lockout after a certain number of consecutive failed login attempts.

> **Note**
>
> Enforcing the account lockout policy might open your organization to a denial of service (DoS) attack if attackers can attempt to log in to your system over the network as the user whom they want to lock out.

Password aging limits the amount of time a password is valid before the user must select another password. This option is critical for preventing an attacker who knows an account's password from being able to access the host months later because the user doesn't want to and doesn't have to change the password.

Maintaining password history is important because users often inadvertently circumvent security policies. Password history will remember the prior n number of passwords used for an account and prevent these passwords from being used again. Although password history is helpful, users can frequently bypass this restriction by incrementing the number that they add at the beginning or the end of the password. If possible, consider implementing mechanisms that require that a new password differ from the previous password by a certain number of characters.

> **Password Games Users Play**
>
> In some environments, password aging only sets the maximum age for a password, not a minimum age. A minimum age says that after a password has been set, a user cannot change it for a certain number of days. If you do not establish a minimum password age, but you require passwords to be changed regularly, some of your users will play a fun password game. For example, a user might change his password "raiders" to "newpass" and then immediately change it back from "newpass" to "raiders." If you have password history enabled, some users will rapidly change their password several times, then change it back to what it originally was. Change the rules of the game by implementing a minimum password age of at least a few days.

You can help prevent users from picking weak passwords by implementing password-filtering mechanisms that verify the strength of the password before allowing the user to set it. You can use the ntpassword tool to accomplish this on UNIX platforms (http://www.utexas.edu/cc/unix/software/npasswd). Windows 2000 and above come with such capabilities built in, whereas Windows NT requires you to install the passfilt.dll utility before you can enable this functionality (see Microsoft Knowledgebase article 225230).

A compromise of the password's confidentiality might grant a remote attacker local access to the system, whether the password belongs to a user or service account. Password-related issues can be mitigated through user awareness and through enforceable policies that encourage good password practices. By developing and implementing a password policy that balances security needs, business requirements, and human limitations, you can alleviate many of the risks associated with password misuse.

Controlling Group Membership

Another aspect of controlling user access involves examining groups that user accounts belong to and limiting access permissions assigned to those groups. One reason for assigning access permissions to groups instead of individual users is that group permissions automatically apply for each user in the group. By managing permissions for groups and assigning users to groups, administrators can keep much better control of security in their environments. You should grant groups the minimum access rights that the group's members need to fulfill required tasks.

A common configuration mistake when placing users into groups is having too many users assigned to highest-privilege groups. Although it's natural to think of placing users who need to perform certain administrative functions in the Domain Administrators group in Windows or in the root group in Linux, you should determine whether another administrative group has lesser permissions that are still adequate for performing the required tasks. For example, if you have to change the time on a host, what would be the preferred group membership? The recommended group for Windows would be Server Operators or Power Users. It's important to determine which group would provide the most restrictive level of permissions while still supporting the task.

UNIX groups such as sysadmin, sys, and root should also have a controlled membership. The permissions granted to these groups might allow their members to access sensitive files and executables. Instead of adding user accounts to these critical groups, consider using tools such as Sudo to allow specific users to execute privileged commands without having full root privileges (http://www.courtesan.com/sudo). Using Sudo is an effective security measure because it restricts administrative privileges and records the invocation of Sudo privileges into a log; this is terrific for determining accountability for restricted tasks.

Keeping an eye on how your administrative accounts and groups are used is an important aspect of protecting a host against attacks. You can quickly detect the misuse of user accounts, and investigate other security-related problems, if you maintain and monitor security logs as we discuss in the following section.

Maintaining Host Security Logs

Security logs are invaluable for verifying whether the host's defenses are operating properly. Another reason to maintain logs is to ensure that forensics evidence is available when you need to figure out what happened, even if you already determined that something went wrong. Of course, each security safeguard is only as good as the actions taken upon it. A log file is of minimal value if you never look at it. As we discuss in Chapter 10, it is often wise to utilize software, such as host-based intrusion detection systems (IDSs), that can automatically notify the administrator when a suspicious event occurs. This helps provide effective responses to potential security threats.

> **Note**
> A common alternative to having in-house staff monitor logs for signs of malicious activity is outsourcing this task to a company that provides security-monitoring services.

We devote Chapter 20, "Network Log Analysis," to the guidelines relevant to processing log entries from the network security device's perimeter. The following section looks at issues specific to Windows and UNIX hosts.

Windows Logging and Auditing

Windows offers built-in tools that help administrators capture security-related events and audit the resulting log files. By default, Windows logs only general system events aimed at resolving system and application faults. To capture security-related information, you must enable auditing through the Local Security Policy editor (on a standalone system) or Group Policy (when using Active Directory). You can use the Event Viewer program to examine security log entries collected by the Windows auditing facility.

Figure 9.4 illustrates reasonable settings for a Windows workstation, although the specifics of the configuration will depend on your organization's requirements. As you can see, Windows allows you to log successful and failed actions associated with several categories of events. The more event types you choose to log, the more thorough your understanding will be of what takes place on the system. On the other hand, excessive auditing can degrade the host's performance, fill up its file system, and overwhelm you with superfluous log entries. Striking the right balance for event logging may require several different settings until you achieve the desired configuration.

UNIX Logging and Auditing

Like Windows, UNIX can gather detailed information regarding security events on the system, such as logon and logoff times, occurrences of failed logons, the use of privileged accounts, and even the commands users execute. The configuration of UNIX logging facilities is flexible and varies across UNIX flavors. However, here are some of the more standard log files:

- **utmp**—Maintains a snapshot listing of users who are currently logged in. Viewable using the `who` and `users` commands.
- **wtmp**—Maintains a historical record of users' login and logout activity. Viewable using the `who` and `last` commands.
- **btmp**—Maintains a historical record for failed user logins. Viewable using the `lastb` command.

A UNIX system stores event records in these log files using a binary format. As a result, you need to use the appropriate tools, specified in the preceding list, to view their contents.

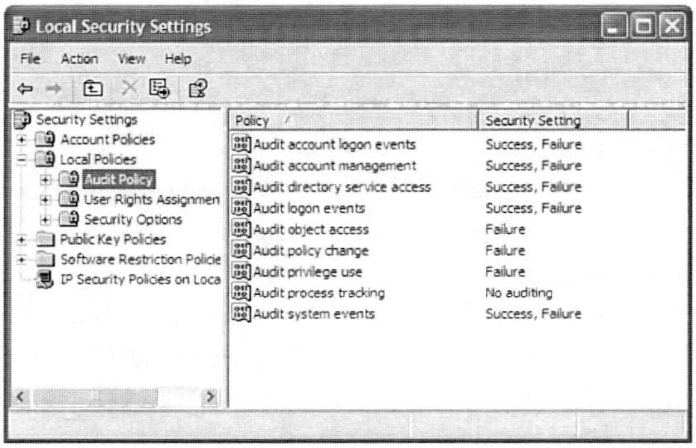

Figure 9.4   You can use the Local Security Policy editor or Group Policy to enable security auditing in Windows.

> **Note**
> Although the `utmp` and `wtmp` files exist by default on most UNIX platforms, you may need to explicitly create the `btmp` file for the system to log failed logon activity to that file.

In addition to maintaining the binary log files just mentioned, UNIX systems rely on the Syslog facility to centralize logging of security and other system events. Syslog typically uses the `/etc/syslog.conf` configuration file to determine what types of events to log and where to store the log files. Depending on how you configure it, Syslog can record messages from the kernel, user processes, the mail system, locally defined events, and so on. Syslog stores its records in text-based log files, which can be examined by regular text file viewers as well as through the use of the automated monitoring tools we mention in Chapter 10.

Following best practices when configuring the host's security logging mechanisms helps detect malicious activity during the early stages of an attack. This also allows administrators to determine what happened in the event of a successful compromise.

Another critical aspect of host hardening, which we discuss in the following section, involves installing patches to address security vulnerabilities.

Applying Patches

The never-ending probes that reach our systems in an attempt to bypass perimeter defenses have taught us, the hard way, that we must take extreme care in making sure the host's applications and the underlying OS are patched on a timely basis. Vendors routinely release software patches to address vulnerabilities discovered during the lifetime of their software products. Keeping up to date with patches can be time intensive, but it is necessary in order to address the vulnerabilities before an attacker exploits them. At times, a serious vulnerability may be known, but the patch may not be yet available; you must be prepared to compensate for this exposure by temporarily adjusting other components of your security perimeter.

> **Tracking a System's Survival Time**
>
> SANS Internet Storm Center (ISC) keeps track of the average time between probes directed at individual IP addresses (http://isc.sans.org). Many such connection requests are initiated by worms, as they scan the network in search for new victims. ISC calls the time between such probes the "survival time" of a system. If the OS or its applications are not patched, the probe is likely to lead to a successful compromise of the machine. The scary trend is that the survival time is rapidly decreasing. At the time of this writing, this interval is at 16 minutes, approximately half of what it was a year earlier.

When deploying a fresh system, it is a good idea to install its OS and applications on an isolated network segment. You should not release the system to production before it is fully patched up. Otherwise, you run the risk of having the host compromised even before you finish setting it up.

In order to apply patches in a timely manner, you need to monitor security announcement forums used to post notices about discovered vulnerabilities and released patches. Some of our favorite notification newsletters, which provide information in a concise format, are listed here:

- Subscribe to the Microsoft Security Notification Service at https://profile.microsoft.com/RegSysSubscriptionCnt.

- Subscribe to the Sun Customer Warning System by sending an email message to security-alert@sun.com with the subject "subscribe cws."

- Subscribe to the weekly bulletin SANS @RISK: The Consensus Security Alert, at http://www.sans.org/newsletters. This newsletter summarizes critical vulnerabilities and explains how to protect yourself from them.

- Subscribe to the Windows and Linux weekly newsletters at http://www.securityfocus.com/newsletters. These newsletters document notable security events of the week.

In addition to these resources are numerous other mailing lists that provide cutting-edge vulnerability information. The most notable of these announcement forums are Buqtraq (http://www.securityfocus.com) and Full-Disclosure (http://lists.netsys.com/mailman/listinfo/full-disclosure). When signing up for these mailing lists, keep in mind that they are highly volume intensive.

Patch installation resolves several key security concerns, but reckless patching practices can have disastrous consequences. Although a patch typically corrects the faulty OS or application code, resolving the security issue, a patch could have side effects that prevent your custom scripts or applications from working properly. As we discuss in Chapter 19, you should test any patches before applying them to your production systems. By testing in a controlled environment, you can verify that the patch will resolve your security issues without breaking critical functions.

Additional Hardening Guidelines

To conclude this chapter, let's look at some valuable resources that provide hardening guidelines and automation techniques. Such documents and tools can assist in implementing the hardening best practices described throughout this chapter. Using a checklist or a script to harden hosts helps ensure that they are built in a consistent manner every time and that the extent of hardening applied to the systems is properly documented.

Automating Host-Hardening Steps

If you expect to deploy more than one system in your organization, it often makes sense to automate the OS installation process, configuring the OS in a locked-down manner as part of the base build. You can accomplish this with Windows through the use of techniques such as Unattended Answer Files (UAF) and Remote Installation Services (RIS). A similar approach works with UNIX-based systems as well. For instance, the Sun Solaris "JumpStart" mechanism allows you to create a custom profile for the system that begins with Solaris Core System Support Software Group (abbreviated as SUNWCreq), along with any additional packages your host may require.

In situations where beginning with a minimalist OS build is impossible or impractical, you will have to remove unneeded programs, libraries, and configuration files after installing the OS. We suggest carefully documenting and, when possible, automating this procedure to ensure that you end up with a setup that is predictable, reliable, and consistent with your intentions.

A number of freely available tools can help you automate these host-hardening steps as well as those discussed throughout this chapter. The following list includes some of the more popular utilities of this nature that are available for free:

- Security Configuration and Analysis snap-in for the Microsoft Management Console (MMC)
- The Center for Internet Security's tools and benchmarks for tuning your host's configuration to industry best practices (http://www.cisecurity.org)

- Titan Security Toolkit, for Solaris, Linux, and Free BSD
  (http://www.fish.com/titan)
- Bastille Hardening System, for Linux, HP-UX, and Mac OS X
  (http://www.bastille-linux.org)
- Solaris Security Toolkit (JASS), for Solaris (http://wwws.sun.com/software/
  security/jass)

If a hardening toolkit does not meet your needs, you can replace or augment it with a
collection of your own scripts that perform the steps you would need to take if locking
down the host's configuration by hand.

Common Security Vulnerabilities

The SANS Top 20 Vulnerabilities list (http://www.sans.org/top20) provides a concise
and authoritative summary of the most often compromised vulnerabilities. The purpose
of creating this list was to help administrators start securing their hosts against the most
common threats, without feeling overwhelmed by the task. We recommend that you
review this list to verify that your hardening procedures account for the top 20 weaknesses and that your hosts' configurations do not match this "most wanted" list.
Understanding the vulnerabilities in the system's configuration goes a long way toward
helping to arm your hosts against them.

Hardening Checklists

Many great resources on the Internet contain detailed information on hardening various
operating systems. For example, numerous software vendors provide security guidelines
or step-by-step instructions on their websites. A general resource with many papers related to operating system, network, and application security is the SANS Reading Room,
located at http://www.sans.org/rr.

You can also find the following free OS hardening documents, helpful in defining
procedures for securing your own hosts:

- National Security Agency (NSA) publishes well-researched security configuration
  guides for a variety of operating systems, applications, and network devices
  (http://www.nsa.gov/snac).
- The Center for Internet Security offers several checklists and benchmarking tools
  to rate security of Windows and UNIX hosts (http://www.cisecurity.org).
- Microsoft offers a number of checklists and guides for hardening Windows-based
  systems (http://www.microsoft.com/technet/security/topics/hardsys).
- Sun provides a variety of guidelines for securing Solaris and Linux-based environ-
  ments (http://wwws.sun.com/software/security/blueprints).
- SANS Institute publishes several step-by-step guides for hardening Windows and
  UNIX-based hosts (http://store.sans.org).

Summary

Hardening the configuration of host computers allows us to reinforce the security of the network perimeter by following the principles of defense in depth. As with all components of a defense infrastructure, we rely on multiple security components to protect resources against attacks. This notion can be applied at the network and at the host level. The extent to which a system should be hardened depends on its role on the network and also accounts for the resources you have available to maintain the locked-down configuration. As we discussed in this chapter, default operating system installations rarely implement hardening best practices that allow us to build systems that are highly resistant to attacks. You can significantly improve the host's defenses if you take the time to disable or remove unnecessary services and applications, limit access to data, control user access and privileges, maintain logs, and apply patches.

10

Host Defense Components

THE HOST'S PERIMETER, OPERATING SYSTEM (OS), and applications are our last line of defense against network attacks. If an attacker manages to get through or around your firewall, or if you are defending against malicious code or an insider, it is up to the host to limit the scope of the potential compromise. In Chapter 9, "Host Hardening," we explained how to configure the system's OS and related applications to help the host withstand local and network-based attacks. We locked down the file system, disabled unnecessary accounts and services, enforced strong passwords, fine-tuned group membership, and applied patches. This chapter builds on the concepts of hardening by demonstrating how hosts can play an active role in protecting data and services. In a layered security architecture, hosts that are configured according to the risks they might face and to the tasks they need to fulfill reinforce perimeter components such as routers, firewalls, and network intrusion detection systems.

In this chapter, we explain how to use hosts to help detect and isolate attacks, and we discuss tools and approaches that will help you strengthen the system's defenses. We look at differences in needs of host categories and describe best-fit roles for antivirus software, host-based intrusion detection products, and other host-based tools. We also talk about host-based firewalls and how they compare to the gateway firewalls you have seen in the book so far. We examine the strengths and weaknesses of each type of host defense component to allow you to effectively incorporate any of them into the design of the overall network security perimeter.

Hosts and the Perimeter

Any system that is operating as part of a network infrastructure has the potential of falling victim to a remote attack. A successful compromise might come as the result of a system misconfiguration or vulnerabilities in the OS or installed applications. As you know, administrators can help mitigate the risks associated with known vulnerabilities by routinely applying software patches and ensuring that hosts are hardened sufficiently. To effectively protect systems against attacks that might yet be unknown to us, we have been using the defense-in-depth approach, relying on multiple layers in the defense perimeter's architecture to reinforce its resilience.

Red Hat and the WU-FTPD "File Globbing" Vulnerability

An unknown vulnerability and one that has been announced to the world are different. For example, Red Hat issued a security advisory about a bug in the Washington University File Transport Protocol Daemon (WU-FTPD).[1] The vulnerability could allow a remote attacker to obtain root access to the server running WU-FTPD, which is bundled with many Linux distributions. Unfortunately, the statement was erroneously published days before the date on which Linux vendors had agreed to issue the advisory and release appropriate patches. Red Hat's announcement accidentally undermined efforts to coordinate the announcement with the availability of the fix, leaving thousands of users of non–Red Hat distributions vulnerable.[2]

Of course, the WU-FTPD vulnerability existed before Red Hat's announcement; those who were aware of its technicalities might have been quietly exploiting it. The security advisory, albeit unfair to Red Hat's competitors, allowed administrators to consider ways to protect against the vulnerability, possibly by disabling the vulnerable daemon until the patch became available. On the other hand, by prematurely publicizing the information, Red Hat increased the chances that a skilled attacker could develop an exploit to take advantage of the vulnerability before administrators could protect their hosts against it.

The nature in which the system is being used impacts the risks it might need to be protected against and the ways in which the host's defense components need to be deployed and configured. To help you understand the applicability of host-based security software, we have classified systems into two general categories:

- Workstations
- Servers

Although the distinctions between these types of hosts are often intuitive, let's formalize the security challenges associated with each category to lay groundwork for subsequent discussions.

Workstation Considerations

Workstations, which include laptops and desktops, are used by end users to interactively run local applications and to access services on the network. Workstations routinely interact with potentially unsafe resources on the Internet as users connect to external sites that provide services such as web, file sharing, and instant messaging. Because of the unpredictable nature of human behavior, it is difficult to foresee the problems that might arise when a user connects to an external system that is not under your control. The same workstations are also used to connect to resources that are more trusted: internal file and mail servers, Human Resources systems, and other applications that are specific to your organization's business. Interactions with partner and supplier networks carry a degree of risk as well. In these cases, although you cannot directly control the security of third-party resources, you can often define accountability and liability through the use of legal agreements with your partners and suppliers, as well as by inquiring about their security posture when formalizing the business relationship.

In most companies, workstations—particularly laptops—are no longer just located behind the reinforced security perimeter of your network. Traveling and telecommuting users may reach the company's network by first connecting to the Internet through dial-up, broadband, or wireless hot spots. In these cases, the workstations are not protected by the company's central security components, such as network firewalls and intrusion detection systems (IDSs). Chapter 13, "Separating Resources," discusses the need to apply different degrees of protective measures to systems based on their roles, from LAN-connected desktops to wireless clients.

The Qaz Worm and Microsoft

Around October 2000, an attacker was able to gain unauthorized access to Microsoft's internal systems and, reportedly, view source code for upcoming product releases. Investigators surmised that the attacker succeeded at compromising Microsoft's perimeter defenses by first infecting an employee's home workstation with the Qaz worm by emailing him a Trojanized attachment.

Qaz propagates by scanning the subnet for Windows shares that are not password protected. When a vulnerable system is found, Qaz copies itself to the system's Windows directory via NetBIOS as `notepad.exe`, while renaming the original `notepad` to `note.com`. The worm also modifies the infected system's Registry key to ensure that the host automatically launches the worm upon startup. The worm also establishes a backdoor on TCP port 7597 on the infected system, allowing the attacker to run arbitrary commands, upload new files, or terminate the worm's program. To announce the IP address that the attacker can use to access the backdoor, the worm sends an email message to 202.106.185.107, which corresponds to a system located in China.[3]

The attacker probably used the backdoor the Trojan established to access Microsoft's systems when the employee connected to the company's internal network. If Microsoft's corporate firewall did not block inbound connections on TCP port 7597, the attacker also could have waited for Qaz to infect the company's internal systems and then connected to them directly.

One of the challenges in maintaining workstations is the sheer number of them, generally one per employee in a company. This makes it difficult to effectively monitor workstations for suspicious events, install OS and application patches, update virus definitions, and enforce security policies, in addition to other tasks.

A useful tool for determining the current patch level of systems distributed throughout your network is Microsoft Baseline Security Analyzer (MBSA), available as a free download from http://www.microsoft.com/technet/security/tools/mbsahome.mspx. For local or remote systems, MBSA can determine which patches are missing from several versions of Windows, as well as Internet Explorer, Exchange, SQL Server, Internet Information Server (IIS), and other common Windows components. By default, it operates by downloading from the Microsoft website a digitally signed file that contains information about available patches and then querying the Registry and the file system of the local system or remote machines to see whether the patches have been applied. It provides specific details on each issue, including its relative priority, corrective guidance, and pointers for more information, such as Microsoft Knowledge Base articles. Before using MBSA, you should first ensure that your environment supports its requirements.

For example, MBSA must be able to log on remotely with administrative rights to target systems, and the systems must be running certain services.[4]

Server Considerations

Server systems are typically dedicated to running services that are accessed by client systems over the network; they do not allow users to directly execute local processes. In such cases, only the server's administrators can log on to the system. This decreases the likelihood that a user who is logged on to the server will launch a local copy of Internet Explorer and start browsing through dubious websites. To further reduce that likelihood, your security policy should restrict the kind of actions administrators can take when maintaining such servers.

Dedicating a server to a particular task allows you to strip the system of many components, leaving only software that is required for the server to perform its business task. In this case, security of the local system can be improved because the usability of the server does not need to be as full featured as that of a workstation. For example, a Solaris 8 server with 64-bit support running Check Point FireWall-1 requires only 83 packages[5], out of hundreds that would be needed if the system were used as a workstation.

Multiuser hosts form another class of servers, because they allow multiple users to be simultaneously logged in to and running interactive processes on the system. For example, such servers can be implemented by deploying Windows Terminal Services or by creating multiple accounts on a UNIX system and allowing users to log in using SSH. Universities frequently offer such services to students and faculty by allowing them to log in to the multiuser server and run shell-based as well as X Window System applications.

When defending against vulnerabilities that can be exploited over the network, you can deploy multiple firewalls, fine-tune packet filters on your routers, and configure network IDSs to detect the attacks. These measures are not effective, however, at defending the multiuser server against a user who already has local access to the system. For instance, incorrect path usage by stmkfont under HP-UX B.11 could allow a local user to execute arbitrary code (http://cve.mitre.org/cgi-bin/cvename.cgi?name=CAN-2004-0965). This condition could not be directly exploited over the network without first obtaining local access to the server. System hardening, patch management, host-based intrusion detection, and security policy are probably your best bets for protecting multiuser servers.

Servers are usually considered to be more sensitive than individual workstations. Whether the attacker compromises a multiuser server or a dedicated server, she is likely to have an immediate impact on numerous users who rely on the services of that host. Consider the influence an attacker might have if she manages to compromise a domain controller in a Microsoft Windows Active Directory. Another prominent attack of this sort is a web server defacement that announces to the world that the company's public web server has been compromised. Attacks on the more sensitive servers located within a company are likely to inflict larger financial harm to the victim, but are generally not widely publicized.

Antivirus Software

Antivirus software is the most widespread mechanism for defending individual hosts against threats associated with malicious software, or *malware*. Malware threats take many forms, including viruses that are carried via infected files, worms that spread autonomously over the network, and humans who use malicious software as agents to remotely control or monitor victims' systems. Many established vendors, such as Symantec, McAfee, Sophos, Trend Micro, and F-Secure, offer products that detect and, in many cases, eradicate malware from the system. This is accomplished by monitoring the local host's boot sector, memory, and file system for signatures of known instances of malware. Another detection mechanism that is often used in conjunction with the database of malware signatures monitors programs for behavior patterns frequently associated with malware. When properly deployed, antivirus software can be effective at helping to establish an in-depth security architecture.

> **Note**
>
> Software for defending hosts against malicious software is called *antivirus* primarily for historical reasons, even though it protects the system against several categories of malware, including viruses, worms, Trojans, and malicious mobile code. Antivirus software can also detect some forms of spyware, particularly those that use traditional malware mechanisms.

Strengths of Antivirus Software

Antivirus software establishes a significant layer in a reinforced security perimeter. Just like all defense components, antivirus software has its strengths and weaknesses. Some of the core strengths of antivirus software are listed next:

- Antivirus software is effective at identifying numerous popular malware specimens—for most products, tens of thousands. Antivirus companies enjoy the benefit of significant research investments and can analyze malicious software relatively quickly to the extent that it allows them to produce a signature for a specific instance of malware.

- Antivirus software can monitor many client applications for malware activity, such as email clients, web browsers, instant messaging clients, and other common mechanisms for receiving and transmitting malware.

- Antivirus software is unobtrusive partly because it has a relatively low rate of false positives. Even when configured to operate in a "real-time" protection mode, antivirus software runs in the background, rarely drawing attention to an event that should not require the user's attention. As a result, end users do not mind having virus protection enabled on their workstations.

- Antivirus software is affordable and has been accepted as a necessity by many budgetary decision makers. It is not easy to find a person who is unaware of the dangers associated with malicious code. Antivirus software has been around long enough that it has become an accepted part of the corporate lifestyle.

> **The EICAR Test File: The Ultimate False Positive**
>
> Although antivirus software may be installed on systems, it may not be enabled or configured properly. Take care to verify that virus protection is active on your systems and that it operates as expected. One of the quickest ways to check this is through the use of the EICAR test file. Most antivirus products are programmed to recognize this file's content as a virus, even though it does not actually contain malicious code. The file, which can be downloaded from http://www.eicar.org/anti_virus_test_file.htm, consists of 68 ASCII characters. If saved with the .com extension, it actually executes on Windows platforms to print the message "EICAR-STANDARD-ANTIVIRUS-TEST-FILE" to standard output. Of course, if your antivirus software is active, it should not let you execute this file in the first place.

In addition to protecting individual hosts, antivirus software is effective when integrated with gateways that process network traffic for common application protocols such as SMTP, HTTP, and FTP. Most major antivirus vendors offer specific software products for these protocols that can be quite effective at removing known malware threats from network traffic before they reach individual hosts.

As you can see, malware protection can take place at several different locations on the network. You do not need to limit yourself to any one of these. In fact, it is generally advantageous to perform such scans on individual workstations, as well as on file servers and Internet gateways. If malware is a large concern for your business, consider deploying one vendor's antivirus product on your hosts and another vendor's product on the gateways. This configuration increases the likelihood that a malware specimen will be blocked. Such redundancy can be justified because antivirus software has many significant limitations that impact the design of the security perimeter.

Limitations of Antivirus Software

In most cases, the effectiveness of the antivirus product depends on the extensiveness of its malware signatures. When a major new worm emerges, it typically spreads so rapidly that most organizations are affected by it in a matter of hours, before antivirus vendors have time to analyze the worm and create, test, and distribute signatures. Even when a signature is available, not all companies are capable of automatically distributing the latest signatures to their hosts. As you might recall, we discussed some of the ways of preparing for such incidents at the end of Chapter 1, "Perimeter Security Fundamentals." As one of the measures, be sure to set up your systems to routinely poll the signature distribution server for updates. Most antivirus products allow you to configure the software to automatically download the latest signature database from the vendor's website or FTP site. Enterprise versions of such software allow you to distribute signature updates from your own server within the organization. This approach allows you to centrally monitor infection-related alerts across many systems and allows you to force remote hosts to retrieve the latest updates outside of the routine schedule, especially when you know about a worm outbreak.

Another limitation of current antivirus products focuses on their effectiveness at detecting mutations of known malware specimens. For instance, if you receive an email attachment with a known Trojan, your antivirus software is likely to detect it and display a warning. Unfortunately, it might be sufficient to modify a particular byte in the Trojan's executable using a plain text editor to prevent antivirus software from recognizing it as malicious. If you know what you are doing, this change would not affect the Trojan's core functionality. By modifying the executable in a relatively trivial manner, you might alter one of the characteristics that antivirus software uses for the Trojan's signature.

Another way of mutating a malware specimen is to use one of the many packers that compress and often encrypt the compiled executable. The encoded version of the executable is self-contained and contains a small decoding routine that is triggered during runtime to extract the original program into memory. For example, another way of mutating the Trojan without changing its functionality would be to use a freely available packer called UPX. When the Trojan's original executable is compressed, its size and content are altered. Antivirus software may no longer recognize the Trojan, and the compression may complicate the analysis of the Trojan's functionality.

Of course, individuals who possess the source code for malicious software have the luxury of modifying it directly with the specific goal of bypassing signature-matching antivirus engines. Malware mutations are not as effective against behavior-based scanners, but behavior-based techniques are not as accurate at identifying known threats as signature matching.

Packers for Executables

Many packers are available for compressing and possibly encrypting executables. Some of these allow you to reverse the packing process to recover the original executable; others purposefully do not make such a facility available. In some cases, antivirus software might be able to automatically reverse the encoding to compare the original version of the program to malware signatures. Some of the more popular packers include these:

- ASPack (http://www.aspack.com/)
- PECompact (http://www.collakesoftware.com/pecompact.htm)
- UPX (http://upx.sourceforge.net/)

Polymorphic malware, which changes itself on the fly, is another challenge that antivirus vendors have been working to overcome with a varying degree of success. One of the first mechanisms that facilitated the creation of polymorphic malicious code was created in 1993 under the name Dark Avenger's Mutation Engine (DAME).[6] Although modern antivirus products easily uncover the polymorphic tricks DAME performs, other techniques can significantly complicate the detection of malware. The evolution of malicious software is running its course in parallel with advancements in antivirus technologies. Ways to bypass controls enforced by antivirus software will probably always exist.

Antivirus applications, just like any other software, can have vulnerabilities that expose its host to attacks while helping to combat malware. For example, some versions of Norton AntiVirus allowed a remote attacker to perform denial of service (DoS) attacks against hosts (CAN-2004-0487, CAN-2004-0683) by creating a file containing many compressed directories. There are dozens of CVE entries for antivirus software vulnerabilities, many of which are common flaws that have affected several products.

Spyware

When spyware threats began growing exponentially, most antivirus products did not have spyware signatures or the capability to detect some forms of spyware. In part, this was because some spyware mechanisms, such as tracking cookies, do not use any malicious code, even though they have similar effects to malware-based spyware. Antivirus vendors are starting to make progress against spyware threats by adding new capabilities and signatures to their products. Also, several specialized spyware detection and removal utilities are freely available, including Ad-aware and Spybot—Search & Destroy, that can provide more protection against spyware.

Despite the limitations, antivirus software remains one of the most effective ways to control the spread of common malware specimens across multiple systems. Many instances of malware are difficult to block using traffic-filtering devices alone because they can enter the network through legitimate network channels, such as email and web browsing, as well as non-network means such as CDs, floppy disks, and flash drives. After malware is inside the organization, it can be programmed to communicate with its author via outbound connections that are often allowed to pass through the firewall unchallenged, whether to announce its presence via SMTP or to retrieve additional instructions through an HTTP request. An attacker can use malware as an agent working inside the targeted network, facilitating further, more directed attacks on internal resources. Host-based firewalls, deployed on systems throughout the network, are another part of an in-depth security architecture that can mitigate some of the risks network-based and host-based antivirus software doesn't cover.

Host-Based Firewalls

The firewalls we have been discussing in this book so far are network based. We placed them on the borders between subnets to regulate how network traffic crosses from one segment to another. Similar processes can be applied at the host level to control how packets enter and leave the system that the host-based firewall is protecting.

Most host-based firewalls enforce access policies bidirectionally by monitoring packets that enter and leave the system. Controlling network access at the host level is effective, whether the host is located behind layers of traffic-screening devices or is directly connected to the Internet. Host-based firewalls reinforce the system's defenses by addressing threats that antivirus products don't cover:

- Unrestricted access to the system's file shares
- Anonymous access to the system
- Undetected malicious code
- Port scans and other types of reconnaissance probes
- Vulnerable network services running on the system

Host-based firewalls are often referred to as *personal firewalls* because they aim to protect individual systems instead of whole networks. We would like to use the term *personal firewall* solely when discussing traffic-screening functionality on workstations. Although such software can be installed on servers, referring to it as "personal" might be misleading because server systems are rarely used just for personal computing.

In this section, we examine a number of popular host-based firewall software choices, some of which are available for free. To help you plan and deploy appropriate host-level defenses, we discuss the capabilities of firewalls that are optimized to run on workstations and compare them to the features of products that are more suited to protect individual servers.

Firewalls for Workstations

Host-based firewalls are often geared to run on workstations and are particularly critical for roaming laptops that do not always enjoy the protection of network firewalls and other network-based security controls. The number of products that fit into the category of such personal firewalls has been increasing, and in this section, we discuss only a few of them to illustrate important concepts. Some of the more popular products in this sector are listed next:

- ZoneAlarm (http://www.zonelabs.com/)
- Tiny Firewall (http://www.tinysoftware.com/)
- Norton Personal Firewall (http://www.symantec.com/)
- Sygate Personal Firewall Pro (http://www.sygate.com/)
- Windows Firewall (http://www.microsoft.com/windowsxp/using/security/internet/sp2_wfintro.mspx)

Many of these products are inexpensive, and ZoneAlarm is available free of charge for personal use. Also, Windows Firewall is provided as part of Windows XP starting with Service Pack 2. (Earlier versions of Windows XP offer the Internet Connection Firewall, which lacks many of the features of Windows Firewall.) Many other products provide host-based firewall functionality for the workstation. Some of these can be used on servers as well. For example, firewall functionality is often combined with host-based intrusion detection systems (IDSs), which we discuss in the "Host-Based Intrusion Detection" section of this chapter.

Most personal firewalls that run on Windows-based workstations are capable of imposing access restrictions based on the local application attempting to send or receive packets. Before an application is allowed to connect to another host, or before the application is allowed to accept a network connection from another host, the personal firewall must consult its rule set to determine whether access should be granted. Figure 10.1 shows an excerpt of the application rule configuration for Norton Personal Firewall. By default, the firewall uses the vendor's knowledge of applications to determine which actions should be permitted or denied. You may also override the default settings by manually setting the appropriate action for each application. As Figure 10.1 shows, the alternatives are to permit all, block all, or create custom settings.

Figure 10.1   Norton Personal Firewall allows users to define
permitted and denied activity for specific applications.

In addition to application-specific rules, many personal firewalls also allow you to define access restrictions using the same parameters as traditional network firewalls: protocol, destination IP, and port number. Figure 10.2 shows an excerpt of the default general rule set for Norton Personal Firewall, which includes dozens of types of network traffic. Note that each rule permits you to specify which network interfaces it applies to, and whether the rule should apply to inbound and/or outbound traffic.

Others products, such as ZoneAlarm Pro, take a different approach that might not be as intuitive for firewall administrators, but are aimed at simplifying firewall configuration for less tech-savvy users. As you can see in Figure 10.3, ZoneAlarm Pro allows users to group external systems into those that are trusted and those that are not. Each of the two zones can have its own set of access restrictions, which are applied depending on the remote host's category. For example, you can allow file and print protocols such as NetBIOS/SMB going to, and possibly from, systems in the Trusted zone. By placing the internal subnet into the Trusted zone, you allow the workstation to connect to Windows-based file and print services on the internal network. Other networks would be placed in the Internet zone, which is generally much more restrictive and does not allow NetBIOS connections.

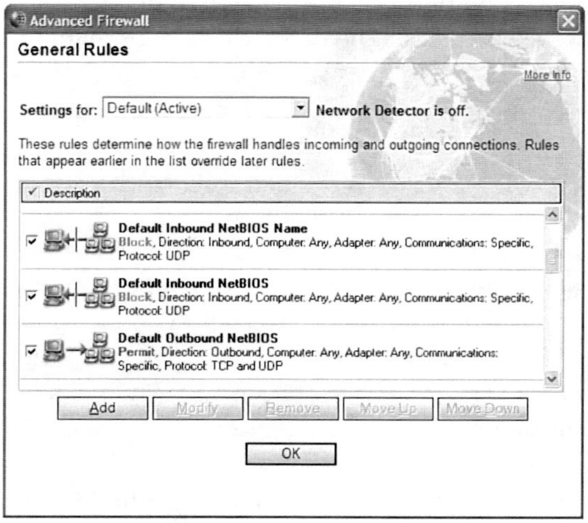

Figure 10.2   Norton Personal Firewall offers a default set of filter rules for network and application protocols.

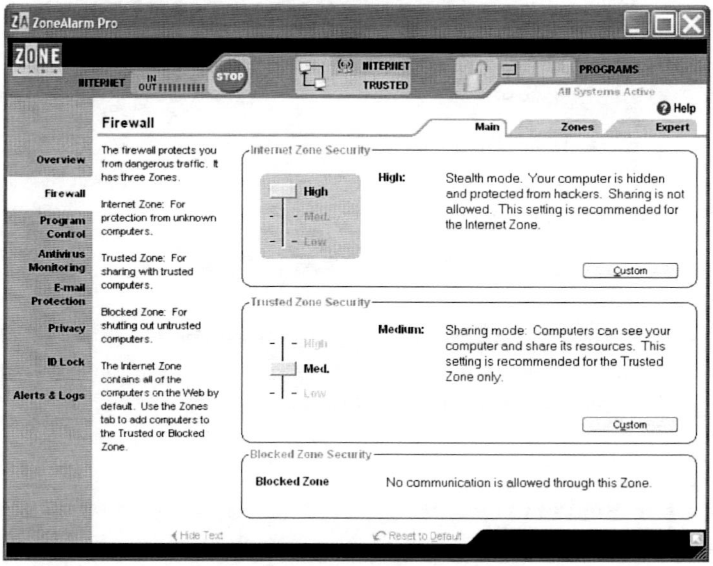

Figure 10.3   ZoneAlarm Pro groups network resources into two zones, depending on how trustworthy the resources are.

Most personal firewalls ship with a default rule set that improves the security of the workstation compared to its state without a firewall, but is still overly permissive. We suggest customizing the default firewall policy by backing it up and then clearing the original rule set. Personal firewalls that do not have a rule set usually default to prompting the user for every new communication attempt to or from the host. Figure 10.4 shows such a prompt as presented by Norton Personal Firewall, asking whether Mozilla Firefox should be allowed to access the Internet. This allows you to build the rule set by letting the firewall "remember" your responses to communication attempts. When going through the initial "learning" period, you might become frustrated by a seemingly unending stream of questions regarding applications that seem to want to initiate network connections. Don't worry; the rule set tends to reach a stable state after a couple of days.

Keep in mind that although you might be willing to answer the firewall's questions while it "gets to know" your system, other users at your organization might not be as patient or might not know how to answer some of the firewall's questions. Incorrect answers could inadvertently block legitimate activity or allow unauthorized activity to pass through the firewall. This is a major obstacle to the adoption of host-based firewalls by the general population of users. As we discuss in the section "Controlling Distributed Host Defense Components" at the end of this chapter, personal firewall vendors offer software that centralizes the creation and distribution of the firewall policy across the organization's workstations. Deploying host-based firewalls on servers is not as dependent on the product's user friendliness and carries its own set of advantages and challenges.

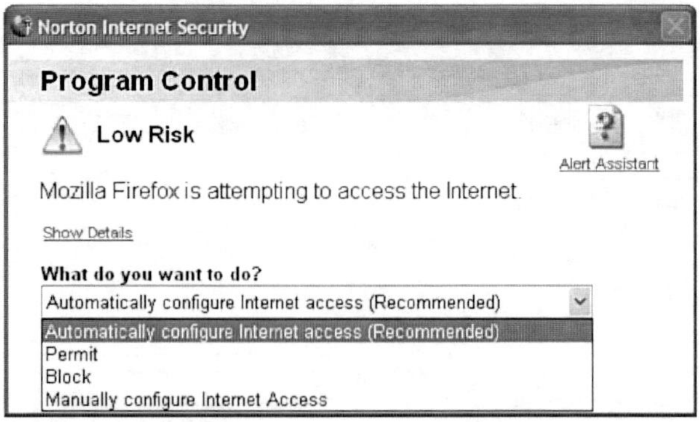

Figure 10.4   Norton Personal Firewall can be configured to prompt the user if an unfamiliar application attempts to initiate a network connection.

Firewalls for Servers

Host-based firewalls are also effective at helping to protect individual servers; they function similarly to firewalls that run on workstations. Although servers are often located behind traffic-screening devices, the critical nature of their data and services might warrant this additional layer of protection that does not usually come at a large expense. Host-based firewalls are also useful for protecting servers that cannot be located on a screened subnet or a DMZ, or that are at an increased risk of insider attacks. In many cases, the same software used to protect workstations could be used for servers. The major differences in requirements between firewalls for workstations and for servers are as follows:

- The performance impact of installing the host-based firewall is more critical for servers. Network latency is generally not as high of a concern on a workstation as it is on a server.

- The need to focus on inbound connections to the system is more critical for servers. Outbound connections made by servers are usually not as unpredictable as those exhibited by workstation users; in fact, many servers only initiate outbound connections for standard maintenance activities, such as downloading patches. Accordingly, it is typically much simpler to control outbound activity for servers on a per-application basis than workstations.

- The need to eliminate interactions between the firewall software and the system's user is more critical for servers. Host-based firewalls installed on servers cannot be expected to prompt the user with rule set questions or alerts because most of the time, no one is logged in to the server locally to answer the questions.

Because you have already seen host-based firewalls that are optimized to protect workstations, this section examines products that address server-specific requirements. Instead of focusing on protecting whole networks, host-based firewalls are tuned to provide protection for a single system. This section provides two examples of methods to protect individual servers: the PF firewall and packet filtering via IPSec on Windows.

As you may recall, in Chapter 9 we mentioned TCP Wrappers as one of the tools used for controlling inbound connections to individual systems. TCP Wrappers is an effective way to control access to the server's network services, especially those that were started through inetd. However, TCP Wrappers lacks some of the features available in full-fledged firewalls that we can install on the network as well as on a host. One such "true" firewall, which we discuss next, is PF. It is available for free and runs on numerous UNIX platforms.

PF

In Chapter 3, "Stateful Firewalls," we discussed IPTables, which is a stateful firewall designed for Linux hosts. Many BSD systems use a firewall with similar capabilities called PF (http://www.openbsd.org/faq/pf/). PF is an excellent firewall for protecting whole networks, as well as individual hosts. The syntax of PF is based on another popular firewall, IPFilter. Let us see how to use PF for implementing some of the tasks typical for host-centric firewalls that run on servers.

PF obtains its rule set from a plain-text configuration file, `pf.conf`. By default, PF reads through all entries in the file before making a final decision about whether to block a packet. This differs from the default behavior of most firewalls we encountered, which stop processing the rule set after locating the first rule applicable to the packet in question. To force PF to stop iterating through the rule set as soon as it makes a match, we need to use the `quick` keyword in the rule's definition. For example, when a system receives an undesired attempt to initiate an SMTP connection, PF stops processing the rule set after encountering the following rule:

```
block in quick proto tcp from any to any port 25
```

Like most modern firewall packages, PF is a stateful firewall. It can monitor the state of TCP sessions and, to a limited extent, the "state" of UDP and ICMP connections. Use the `keep state` keyword in the rule to specify that PF should keep track of a session's state. For example, when running PF on a web server, you could use the following statements to allow inbound HTTP and HTTPS traffic in a stateful manner:

```
pass in quick on fxp0 proto tcp from any to host.ip.addr port = 80 keep state
pass in quick on fxp0 proto tcp from any to host.ip.addr port = 443 keep state
```

In this case, `fxp0` is the server's NIC where inbound requests will be originating, and `host.ip.addr` represents the web server's IP address. Of course, these web server rules assume that at the end of the rule set, you have specified the following rule, which blocks (and probably logs) all traffic that has not matched any other rule in the policy:

```
block in quick on fxp0 log all
```

We can fine-tune HTTP and HTTPS rules presented previously by ensuring that PF creates a state table entry only for TCP packets that have a SYN flag set. Packets with any other TCP flags should not be allowed to initiate a connection, and they could constitute attempts to mangle the system's state table. To account for such packets, we would use the `flags` keyword like this:

```
pass in quick on fxp0 proto tcp from any to host.ip.addr port = 80
➥flags S keep state
pass in quick on fxp0 proto tcp from any to host.ip.addr port = 443
➥flags S keep state
```

If PF isconfigured to block and log all inbound packets that are not explicitly allowed, then the preceding web server rules can help detect port scans against the server that manipulate TCP flags in an attempt to avoid detection.

> ### Note
> PF offers "scrub" capabilities, which means that it can reassemble packet fragments and perform sanity checks on certain aspects of packets to identify anomalous ones. For more information on PF scrubbing, see the documentation at http://www.openbsd.org/faq/pf/scrub.html.

Even though UDP packet exchanges are effectively stateless, a UDP request is expected to have a reply with inverse port and IP address parameters. This can allow PF to offer basic stateful protection for UDP packets that are targeting a DNS server:

```
pass in quick on fxp0 proto udp from any to host.ip.addr port = 53 keep state
```

To control outbound connections made by the server, you could use the following rule, which blocks and logs outbound traffic that has not been explicitly allowed:

```
block out log quick on fxp0 all
```

Because inbound traffic is controlled through the use of stateful rules, it is wise to keep outbound connections made by the server to a minimum. This is more challenging on a workstation, which tends to make outbound connections much more often than it accepts inbound traffic. As a result, host-based firewalls that are optimized for workstation usage generally pay more attention to offering a granular and user-friendly approach to controlling outbound connections.

Responding to Ident Requests

By default, when blocking a connection, PF does not return a response to the sender to let it know that the packet was not allowed through. As mentioned in Chapter 3, this behavior is often advantageous for defending the system against reconnaissance probes. In some cases, however, lack of a response from your server might introduce delays as the peer's system waits for the timeout or attempts to re-send the packet. For example, if your server is configured to send outbound email, the recipient's mail server might try to connect back to your ident daemon in an attempt to confirm the identity of the user who is connecting from your system. If your server is hardened, it is probably not running the ident daemon and blocks all packets destined to ident's port 113. However, the delivery of your outbound email is likely to be suspended until the recipient's mail server's ident request times out.

To speed up this process, you could configure your server to respond with a TCP RST packet to all connection attempts to ident's TCP port, or with an ICMP "port-unreachable" packet to its UDP port. (UDP connections rely on ICMP for the equivalent of a TCP RST.) The following PF rules cause your server to block connections to TCP and UDP port 113 and respond with an appropriate "error" packet:

```
block return-rst in quick on fxp0 proto tcp from any
➡to host.ip.addr port = 113
block in quick on fxp0 return-icmp(port-unr) proto udp from any
➡to host.ip.addr port = 113
```

PF is effective at protecting networks when it is installed on a gateway system. When installed on an individual server, it offers robust protection against network-based attacks that target the individual host. This can also be said for other UNIX firewalls in PF's class, such as IPTables, which we covered in Chapter 3.

We have numerous choices when it comes to installing firewalls on servers. We can use products marketed for use on workstations, as well as software that is not as user friendly and is catered more toward the needs of a server. As the last mechanism in the discussion of host-based firewalls for servers, let's examine an inexpensive way of achieving packet-filtering functionality on Windows servers through the use of IPSec policies.

Packet Filtering via IPSec on Windows

One of the most powerful network security components built in to Windows servers is IPSec. In Chapter 7, "Virtual Private Networks," we described how to use IPSec to secure communications between remote systems. We used the Microsoft Management Console (MMC) to define IPSec policies on VPN endpoints. IPSec policies can also be configured to filter out unwanted network traffic that is targeting the Windows server. Built-in packet-filtering capabilities allow us to specify which local ports can be accessed without authentication and encryption, which should be limited to valid Authentication Header (AH) or Encapsulating Security Payload (ESP) peers, and which should be blocked altogether. This technique allows us to mimic basic functionality offered by many host-based firewalls for servers, without deploying additional products.

For example, we can use built-in IPSec filtering capabilities to permit administrative traffic from authenticated remote systems. We could create a new IPSec rule that accepts ESP-protected administration traffic from specific hosts. If worried about the added load on the server, we could use AH instead of ESP to remotely authenticate the host without encrypting the administrative traffic. Of course, we would need to configure IPSec policies on administrative workstations to match IPSec connection parameters on the hardened server. Environments that have deployed Active Directory can use Group Policy to centrally distribute IPSec policies, avoiding the time-consuming and error-prone process of manually configuring policies on numerous systems.

> **Tip**
>
> Remotely administrating a Windows-based bastion host is often a challenge because it frequently opens the server to attacks on native Windows protocols. One of the ways to address such concerns is to configure the Windows server to block all administrative connections that are not secured with ESP. This provides an easy way to tunnel traffic across the firewall without using native and potentially vulnerable Windows protocols if the server is located on a screened subnet.

IPSec-based filtering is based on basic packet filtering, and accordingly it is prone to similar limitations as other non-stateful traffic-filtering devices that we described in Chapter 2, "Packet Filtering." IPSec-based filtering should not be used as the only firewall protection for a system; instead, it can best be used to add an extra layer of defense to Windows servers with relative ease.

So far, we have discussed two primary defense components that we can use to reinforce the security of individual systems: antivirus software and host-based firewalls. As we have shown, each component category, as well as each tool within the categories, is optimized for different environments and is best at mitigating different risks. In the next section, we examine host-based IDS products, which are optimized for detecting and investigating malicious behavior on the host.

Host-Based Intrusion Detection

As you saw in the previous section, firewalls can be used to defend whole networks, as well as individual servers. Similarly, IDSs exist in two varieties: network-based and host-based. We introduced the notion of intrusion detection in Chapter 8, "Network Intrusion Detection," where we examined optimal uses of IDS components for monitoring a network for malicious events. We deployed network IDS sensors in a way that allowed us to sniff traffic going between hosts and network devices. Network IDS enabled us to apply certain criteria to captured traffic to single out events that were likely to be indicative of an attack.

Much like their network counterparts, host-based IDS products also exist primarily to detect and examine malicious activity at various stages of an attack, but they are optimized for monitoring individual hosts. Additionally, many host-based IDS products can be configured to integrate their findings, providing a unified view of multiple systems throughout the network. Some host-based IDS products also provide intrusion prevention capabilities, stopping attacks before they can cause damage; such products are described in Chapter 11, "Intrusion Prevention Systems." In this section, we examine key aspects of the host-based intrusion detection process and look at several categories of host-based IDS products.

The Role of Host-Based IDS

At its core, host-based intrusion detection involves monitoring the system's network activity, file system, log files, and user actions. (Most host-based IDS products typically monitor only one or a few of these categories, not all.) This allows a host-based IDS to identify activities that network-based IDS may not be able to see or understand, because the actions take place on the host itself. For example, a host-based IDS could alert if accounts such as guest or nobody suddenly possessed administrative privileges. Specifically, host-based IDS software has the following key advantages over its network counterparts:

- Host-based IDS software can monitor user-specific activity on the system. The software can observe the user's local activity because it has access to such host-specific information as process and service listings, local log files, and system calls. Network IDS sensors, on the other hand, have a hard time associating packets to specific users, especially when they need to determine whether commands in the traffic stream violate a specific user's access privileges.

- Host-based IDS programs can monitor data exchanges of encrypted network streams by tapping in at the connection's endpoint. Running on the VPN's endpoint allows host-based IDS to examine packets in their clear-text form, before the host encrypts outbound packets, or after it decrypts inbound packets. A network IDS sensor, on the other hand, cannot examine the payload of an IPSec packet or the contents of a packet that is part of an SSL session. The need to perform content analysis of network traffic at the hosts continues to increase as companies continue to deploy VPN solutions.

- Host-based IDS programs can detect attacks that utilize network IDS evasion techniques. As we discussed in Chapter 8, such techniques exploit inconsistencies in the way a network IDS interprets the packet's intentions from the effect that the packet might have on the targeted host.[7] For example, unusual packet fragmentation might confuse a network IDS sensor, but would have no effect on host-based IDS products.

Host-based intrusion detection is also useful for correlating attacks that are picked up by network sensors. If a network IDS sensor detected an attack that was directed at one of your hosts, how would you know whether the attack was successful? The host's IDS software can help you determine the effect of the attack on the targeted system. Of course, if the host is compromised, its logs might be altered or deleted. But if you are automatically relaying all host IDS data to a central, dedicated log server, you can use that data instead of the original IDS logs if they are unavailable or untrusted. From an incident-handling perspective, host-based IDS logs are also vitally important in reconstructing an attack or determining the severity of an incident.

Ideally, you would deploy host-based IDS software on every host in your organization. However, that might not be a viable option for your company, considering the amount of resources involved in deployment, maintenance, and monitoring. When deciding whether to deploy host-based IDS software on a system, consider the host's risk level. Critical servers that store sensitive data and are accessible from the Internet will surely benefit from the extra layer of protection that host-based IDS provides. You might consider deploying such products on workstations as well, depending on the nature of threats to which they are exposed.

Host-based IDS products can watch over the channels that need to remain open for the host to perform its business function. If a host needs to function as a public web server, its firewall cannot block inbound connection attempts to TCP port 80, but its host-based IDS can be tuned to monitor HTTP traffic or other host attributes for malicious activity. Additionally, some host-based IDS products can interact with host-based firewall software to shun the attacker if an intrusion attempt is detected.

Host–Based IDS Categories

Now that you understand the roles that host-based IDS plays when operating as part of a network's security perimeter, let's examine different types of host-based IDS solutions. As you know, multiple sources for data can be used to perform intrusion detection at the host level. The primary reason for wanting to look at the host's file system, log files, and network connections is because the malicious activity on a host can exhibit itself in multiple ways. Some commercial products, such as ISS Proventia Intrusion Detection and Enterasys Dragon Intrusion Defense System, can monitor several data sources on the host. Other products are optimized to perform host-based intrusion detection based on a specific data source:

- The host's file system: AIDE, OSIRIS, Samhain, Tripwire
- The host's network connections: BlackICE, PortSentry
- The host's log files: LANguard, Logcheck, OsHids, Swatch

Note

Chapter 11 describes host-based intrusion prevention products that monitor another type of data source: application behavior. Products such as Finjan SurfinGuard and Cisco Security Agent monitor the behavior of locally running programs to detect and block malicious actions. Some host-based antivirus and firewall products also offer limited application behavior controls, such as not allowing web browsers to run programs stored in temporary directories.

Checking the File System's Integrity

A category of host-based IDS tools known as *file integrity checkers* work by detecting unauthorized changes to the host's file system. They operate by taking a "snapshot" of the file system in a trusted state, when all the files are considered to be valid. During subsequent scans, these tools compare the system's files to the initial baseline and report noteworthy deviations. To tune the integrity checking mechanism so that it only monitors relevant aspects of files, you can specify what file attributes are allowed to change, or what files can be ignored altogether. For example, applications frequently create temporary files in `C:\WINNT\Temp` or `/tmp` directories; alerting the administrator every time a new file appears or disappears from these directories would generate too many false positives. On the other hand, contents of core system libraries rarely change, and it is normal for the host's log files to grow in size while retaining initial ownership and access permissions.

Note

The AIDE software we discuss in this chapter is a free integrity verification tool. This is different from the commercial AIDE software that carries the same name, but is an intrusion detection tool for correlating log information from different firewall and IDS products. Litton PRC developed the commercial AIDE program; it has no relation to the freeware AIDE utility discussed here.

Integrity checking tools are able to detect changes to a file's contents by calculating the file's checksum or cryptographic hash during the scan and comparing it to the file's "signature" that was obtained when creating the baseline. An alternative method, which is impractical in many situations due to space requirements, is to make an actual copy of each file to be monitored. Increasing the difficulty of tampering with the database of baseline signatures can be accomplished in several ways:

- Obfuscate the contents of the baseline database by using a proprietary binary format instead of plain text when saving the database to disk. Although this mechanism makes it more difficult to tamper with the database, it hardly prevents the attacker from discovering the obfuscation scheme or from using the integrity checker to update the baseline.

- Place the baseline database onto read-only media, such as a write-protected floppy disk or a CD-ROM. This method requires that the disk or the CD be accessible to the integrity checker when it performs the verification scan. This method is reliable and is most useful for hosts whose baseline does not need to be frequently updated. Keep in mind, though, that even if the attacker is unable to modify the baseline database, he might be able to change the integrity checker or modify its configuration to use an unauthorized baseline. Placing the checker onto the read-only media helps defend against some attacks of this nature, but having access to the host might allow the attacker to modify the system's kernel or file system drivers to conceal his presence on the host anyway.

- Digitally sign the baseline database. In this scenario, updating the program's baseline typically requires the administrator to present the appropriate cryptographic keys and supply the necessary passwords. This technique achieves a good balance between the first two approaches. It is frequently used in environments that need to be able to remotely update the baseline periodically, such as when installing system patches or otherwise updating the host's configuration.

Tripwire is the best-known file integrity checking utility. In many ways, Tripwire is a benchmark against which other tools in this category are measured. The original version of Tripwire was developed in 1992 at Purdue University in West Lafayette, Indiana, and it is still available free under the name Tripwire Academic Source Release (http://www.tripwire.com/products/tripwire_asr/). This version of Tripwire runs only on UNIX platforms. Despite its age, this version of Tripwire is still effective at detecting unauthorized changes to the host's files, although it is no longer being actively maintained. Full commercial versions of Tripwire for servers and network devices (http://www.tripwire.com/products/servers/) are not free, but they boast a number of improvements over the initial version:

- The commercial software Tripwire for Servers runs on both Windows and UNIX hosts. The Windows version of the tool can monitor the system's Registry in addition to the file system.

- The commercial software Tripwire for Network Devices can monitor the integrity of configuration files on routers and switches.

- Multiple hosts and devices monitored by the commercial versions of Tripwire can be controlled centrally through a unified configuration and reporting interface through Tripwire Manager.

Note

An open source version of Tripwire for Linux is available for free at http://www.tripwire.org. It is included with many Linux distributions, including Red Hat Linux. The open source version of Tripwire was derived from the commercial product, but it is not being actively maintained.

Tripwire Manager is a console available with the commercial version of Tripwire that offers the ability to centrally manage multiple Tripwire "agents" that are deployed on remote hosts and devices across different operating systems. Tripwire Manager is the key difference between the commercial version of Tripwire and free tools that exist in the same category of host-based IDS products. When you need to support many Tripwire instances, this feature alone can help justify purchasing Tripwire instead of using the freeware alternatives.

AIDE (http://sourceforge.net/projects/aide), which stands for Advanced Intrusion Detection Environment, is a free integrity checker with similar features to the academic release of Tripwire. Some of the key differences between AIDE and various Tripwire versions are listed next:

- AIDE is free, just like the academic version of Tripwire and the Linux version of Tripwire Open Source.

- AIDE is maintained through a steadier development cycle than the academic version of Tripwire, which is no longer maintained. At the same time, the commercial version of Tripwire is being developed much more actively.

- AIDE runs on a wide range of UNIX platforms but, unlike the commercial version of Tripwire, it does not run on Windows.

- AIDE does not cryptographically sign its baseline database, making it more difficult to ensure the integrity of its findings. (The academic version of Tripwire does not do this either.)

Overall, organizations that cannot justify paying for the commercial version of Tripwire will probably benefit from installing AIDE instead of the academic version of Tripwire. Another free alternative is Samhain (http:/samhain.sourceforge.net/), which offers file integrity checking capabilities for various versions of UNIX. Samhain provides the ability to cryptographically sign not only the baseline database, but also its configuration file. Samhain can be configured to monitor files for a single host or for a group of hosts through a secure log server. It also offers stealth capabilities, which assist in concealing the presence of Samhain from attackers.

Those who need to perform file system integrity verification for critical Windows systems will not find many robust alternatives to the commercial version of Tripwire, but they might consider taking advantage of similar features built in to some other host-based products, such as personal firewalls that monitor changes to executables. On older Windows platforms, the sysdiff utility from the Windows Resource Kit can be used to detect added or deleted files and changes to configuration files and Registry entries.

Sysdiff does not use cryptographic techniques enjoyed by tools such as AIDE and Tripwire, and it is not available starting with Windows XP. A more powerful alternative to the sysdiff tool is a relatively inexpensive monitoring utility for Windows called Winalysis (http://www.winalysis.com/). Winalysis has a graphical interface, supports the collection of SHA-1 digital signatures, and can be scheduled to observe remote hosts from a central location.

File integrity checking software typically relies on the administrator supplying a policy file that defines which attributes of which files need to be monitored for changes. One of the ways to go about defining this policy is to list a limited number of critical files on the system that you know are supposed to change infrequently. A more comprehensive approach, applicable primarily to hardened server systems, calls for monitoring all files on the host with the exception of those that change frequently. Defining such a policy is a time-consuming process because each server is configured slightly differently and can modify different files during normal operation.

When defining a comprehensive file monitoring policy, it is recommended that you start by specifying that the program should monitor all files and directories recursively from the root of the file system, with the exception of files that are expected to change constantly (such as swap files and logs). You can then run the integrity checker, see which attributes of which files changed during the system's normal operation, and modify the policy appropriately. After several iterations, you should be able to achieve a stable state that will save you from having to constantly update your policy and the baseline database, while monitoring as many aspects of the host's file system as possible.

Network Connection Monitors

Now that you know how to detect unauthorized changes to the host's file system, let's switch our attention to monitoring another critical aspect of the host's operation: its network connectivity. Specifically, we want to use available data about network connections that attempts to initiate or terminate on the host to detect malicious behavior. The impetus behind connection monitoring is similar to the one in network IDS products that run in promiscuous mode to examine network streams for multiple hosts and devices. A host-based IDS, however, can also associate network sockets with specific processes and users on the system, and it can be tuned to the exact characteristics of the host. Additionally, host-based network-monitoring software is unlikely to be overwhelmed by the voluminous network traffic that continues to push the limits of network IDS performance.

One popular host-based IDS product for monitoring the system's network connections is BlackICE (http://blackice.iss.net/), produced by Internet Security Systems (ISS). There are two versions of the software: BlackICE PC Protection runs on Windows-based operating systems and is optimized for protecting a workstation, whereas BlackICE Server Protection offers similar capabilities for servers.

Whenever BlackICE observes a suspicious network connection that targets its host, it creates a log for this event. A host-based firewall would typically create an individual record for each blocked packet. The IDS mechanism in BlackICE is able to group events associated with multiple offending packets into a single log entry that identifies the attack. For example, BlackICE can correlate several suspicious packets as being a single port scan. Instead of logging each packet that comprised the scan, BlackICE creates a single entry in the log. However, BlackICE can be configured to capture full packets that it identifies as belonging to an attack sequence and log them for future analysis. In addition to performing IDS services, BlackICE comes with a built-in host-based firewall that can block unauthorized inbound and outbound connections.

Host-based IDS products that monitor network connections frequently have the option of responding to detected attacks by blocking the attacker's host from accessing ports on the protected system. This capability is known as *intrusion prevention*, and we described it in the context of network IDS sensors in Chapter 8. Host-based IDS products, such as BlackICE, can perform intrusion prevention by automatically reconfiguring its host-based firewall component to shun the attacking IP address for some time period. This capability is useful for blocking an attack at an early stage, such as during a port scan, before it escalates into something more forceful, such as a buffer overflow attempt.

PortSentry (http://sourceforge.net/projects/sentrytools/) is another host-based IDS product that can detect port scans and other unauthorized connection attempts to the system. PortSentry is free and can run on most UNIX operating systems. When PortSentry detects a network-based attack, it can block the attacking host by automatically reconfiguring the compatible firewall on the local host or by placing an appropriate entry into the `hosts.deny` file used by TCP Wrappers. For example, the following are Syslog records that document PortSentry actions when it detects a port scan coming from 192.168.44.1:

```
Jan 19 10:35:57 localhost portsentry[1252]: attackalert: TCP SYN/Normal scan
➥from host: 192.168.44.1/192.168.44.1 to TCP port: 13
Jan 19 10:35:57 localhost portsentry[1252]: attackalert: Host 192.168.44.1
➥has been blocked via wrappers with string: "ALL: 192.168.44.1"
Jan 19 10:35:57 localhost portsentry[1252]: attackalert: TCP SYN/Normal scan
➥from host: 192.168.44.1/192.168.44.1 to TCP port: 21
Jan 19 10:35:57 localhost portsentry[1252]: attackalert: Host:
➥192.168.44.1/192.168.44.1 is already blocked Ignoring
```

In this example, PortSentry detected an unauthorized connection to TCP port 13 on the local host. It responded by reconfiguring TCP Wrappers in an attempt to block subsequent connections from the offender.

As useful as active response capabilities can be in a host-based network connection monitor, they are also dangerous because the supposed offender might get blocked based on a false positive. As a result, this functionality is much more appropriate for workstations than it is for servers. Workstations are usually not accessed via inbound connections as often as servers are, and they are less likely to receive a slew of benevolent inbound connections that look like a port scan.

Log File Monitors

So far, we have examined host-based intrusion detection techniques that involve examining the system's network connections and its file system. Another core data source for useful security information is the host's log files, which may include system, audit, authentication, and application events. Log file monitors observe the contents of logs and alert administrators when suspicious events are detected. One such host-based IDS product is called Swatch (its name stands for "simple watcher") and is available at http://swatch.sourceforge.net/. Swatch is free and runs on most UNIX operating systems. We could use Swatch, for example, to stay abreast of attacks that PortSentry detects. To set this up, we would configure Swatch to email the administrator when it locates a line with the string `attackalert` in a Syslog record.

Another free UNIX-based tool for monitoring log files is Logcheck (http://sourceforge.net/projects/sentrytools/). Unlike Swatch, Logcheck does not monitor logs in real time; it runs periodically and emails alerts in batches. This helps the administrator to limit the number of email messages that he receives, but it might also delay the administrator's response to an attack.

Log file monitoring utilities are available for Windows platforms as well. The following represent a couple of the products worth your look:

- TNT ELM Log Manager (http://www.tntsoftware.com/)
- LANguard Security Event Log Monitor (http://www.gfi.com/lanselm)

Log file monitors have the benefit of being able to observe events generated by multiple security components on the host. Moreover, in scenarios in which logs from several systems are submitted to a single host, log file monitors can perform intrusion detection based on data from multiple perimeter security hosts and devices. This is a powerful technique that transcends the boundaries of defense components of a single host, and we discuss it in greater detail in Chapter 19, "Maintaining a Security Perimeter," and in Chapter 20, "Network Log Analysis."

Challenges of Host Defense Components

We have examined host defense components that help provide defense in depth at the level of an individual host and allow us to treat the host as an active member of the overall security perimeter. We have discussed individual strengths and weaknesses of each component type. In this section, we look at major challenges that face host defense components as a unified product category. Some of these challenges, which impact the deployment of antivirus software, host-based firewalls, and host IDS components, are listed next:

- Ensuring the component's effectiveness and trustworthiness after a system is compromised
- Configuring and monitoring host defense components that run on systems

Let's take a closer look at these challenges so that we are prepared to adjust the design of the overall security perimeter accordingly.

Defense Components on Compromised Hosts

As you probably realize, systems that are protected by host defense components can still be compromised. The attacker can deploy a malicious agent that is not recognized by the antivirus software or can bypass the host's firewall protection via an open port or through another compromised route. As a result, an attacker can delete security logs, create new accounts, install backdoor programs, and disable locally installed security components. To minimize the likelihood that such an attack will succeed, we deploy multiple security components that work in unison, but we need to be prepared for the possibility that our controls will be bypassed.

The host-hardening procedures we discussed in Chapter 9 offer an effective way to limit the scope of the attacker's influence on the compromised host. A constraining mechanism that we mention in Chapter 13 calls for the use of `chroot` to create a "jail" around an application on a UNIX system. Additionally, a host-based firewall on the compromised host has not necessarily outlived its usefulness; it can still assist the administrator in detecting the compromise, and it can help restrict a host's access to other systems on the network.

Although these measures can help dampen the attacker's progress, the effectiveness of host defense components drastically decreases after the intruder has gained access to the system. Having access to the host gives that attacker the capability to target the system's defense components from within. Malware specimens, for example, have been known to proactively fortify their positions on the infected system. Many worms automatically kill processes of common antivirus products, personal firewalls, and other host-based security controls. These actions make it more difficult for the victim to determine that the system has been compromised, make it easier for the infection to spread to other systems, and allow attackers to use the system without the interference of host-based firewalls that would otherwise stop unauthorized incoming and outgoing activity.

Controlling Distributed Host Defense Components

Another challenge to the deployment of host defense components lies in the ability to centrally manage large numbers of them. Any participant of the security perimeter—whether it is a router, a firewall, or an IDS—needs to be watched over after it has been installed. This often involves fine-tuning its configuration, installing software updates, reviewing activity logs, and responding to alerts. The more security components we have to manage, the more challenging it is to do so effectively. Manually maintaining a limited number of servers is something that is possible with a relatively small staff, but the challenges increase as we consider deploying host defense components on workstations throughout the organization.

> **Note**
>
> Attackers have developed effective mechanisms for centrally controlling thousands of victimized computers in an efficient manner. Copies of the Leaves worm, for example, knew to retrieve encrypted instructions for operation from a network of publicly accessible websites. Instances of the SRVCP Trojan were programmed to log in to specific Internet Relay Chat (IRC) channels and sit there waiting for instructions from the attacker.

Antivirus products are the oldest among the host defense components we discussed in this chapter. As a result, their means of effectively operating in large numbers are the most mature. Nearly every antivirus product has the ability to automatically retrieve virus signature and antivirus software updates from the vendor's site, without special modifications to the organization's existing infrastructure. This helps ensure that antivirus software is up to date, but it does not really assist the company's system administrators in keeping an eye on the effectiveness of virus protection. Major antivirus vendors offer products that centrally manage distributed antivirus software installations. For example, Symantec System Center allows the administrator to use Microsoft Management Console to see what, if any, viruses were found on Norton AntiVirus installations throughout the company, obtain copies of infected files, and remotely install and update antivirus software on multiple hosts.

Makers of commercial host-based firewalls and IDS software also offer products for centrally managing their defense components that are installed on multiple hosts. These enterprise-centric products are typically structured to consist of the following major tiers:

- The policy enforcement agent, such as the host-based firewall or the host-based IDS sensor.

- The central management server, used by administrators to control remote instances of policy enforcement agents. This server pushes software and configuration updates to enforcement agents and collects events that enforcement agents report.

- The back-end database, used by the management server to archive events that enforcement agents submit to the server. Some products rely on a built-in data store for this functionality, whereas others can interoperate with external relational databases.

- A client application, such as a web browser, that the administrators can use to communicate with the management server.

Most of the commercial products we discussed in this chapter follow this architecture. Also, most commercial host-based products have been merging into host-based product suites. For example, Tiny Firewall originally offered only personal firewall capabilities; it has been expanded to provide file integrity protection, network traffic intrusion detection and prevention, and Windows-specific monitoring, such as file and Registry key access. The Norton Internet Security suite offers antivirus, personal firewall, pop-up blocking, spam and website filtering, and privacy protection for hosts. Using a single product suite that provides adequate host-based protection is much easier to administer than several separate products, each with its own configuration and maintenance needs.

Summary

In this chapter, we looked at reinforcing the security of the network perimeter by equipping hosts with defense components of three types: antivirus products, host-based firewalls, and host-based IDS software. We examined the strengths and weaknesses of each category of host defense components, and you learned to take them into account when designing and implementing a defense-in-depth architecture.

We rely on antivirus products to defend hosts against malicious software, with the understanding that they cannot detect every malware specimen that can find its way onto the system. We use host-based firewalls to protect the system from network attacks that are not blocked by traditional network firewalls. Host-based firewalls are configured based on the business requirements of the individual host on which they run, and they can usually block inbound as well as outbound network traffic. Some potentially vulnerable channels might need to remain open for the host to perform its function; these can be watched over with the use of a host-based IDS. Host-based intrusion detection further complements network IDS by monitoring the host's internal parameters, such as critical files, logs, and local user activity.

As a category of security tools, host defense components possess several limitations that need to be accounted for in the overall design of the network perimeter. We examined some of these at the end of the chapter. You learned what to expect from a host defense component running on a compromised system, as well as how to manage host defense components installed on systems throughout the organization. We will take advantage of our knowledge of the strengths and weaknesses of host and network defense components in Part III, "Designing a Secure Network Perimeter," where we concentrate on architecture considerations of the network security perimeter.

References

1 Red Hat. "Updated wu-ftpd Packages Are Available." November 20, 2001. http://www.redhat.com/support/errata/RHSA-2001-157.html. November 2004.

2 ARIS Incident Analyst Team Wu-Ftpd Report. "Wu-ftpd Incident Alert." November 28, 2001. http://aris.securityfocus.com/alerts/wuftpd/. November 2004.

3 McAfee Virus Information Library. "W32/QAZ.worm." October 27, 2000. http://us.mcafee.com/virusInfo/default.asp?id=description&virus_k=98775. November 2004.

4 Microsoft. "Microsoft Baseline Security Analyzer (MBSA) 1.2.1 Q&A." August 24, 2004. http://www.microsoft.com/technet/security/tools/mbsaqa.mspx. November 2004.

5 Lance Spitzner. "Armoring Solaris: II." July 20, 2002. http://www.spitzner.net/armoring2.html. November 2004.

6 Mikko Hypponen. "F-Secure Computer Virus Information Pages: DAME." http://www.europe.f-secure.com/v-descs/dame.shtml. November 2004.

7 Thomas H. Ptacek and Timothy N. Newsham. "Insertion, Evasion, and Denial of Service: Eluding Network Intrusion Detection." January 1998. http://secinf.net/info/ids/idspaper/idspaper.html. November 2004.

11

Intrusion Prevention Systems

Note

The material in this chapter is the basis for the "Intrusion Prevention System" chapter in the SANS Institute course, "SANS Security Leadership Essentials," and is used here with the permission of the SANS Institute.

Though *intrusion prevention system (IPS)* began life as a marketing term, IPS is one of the fastest changing areas in perimeter protection. As an active defense measure, IPS gives us more options in our primary Internet/intranet perimeter as well as the ability to extend perimeter defenses across the internal switches and host systems. In this chapter you will see how the IPS concepts we discussed in Chapter 1, "Perimeter Security Fundamentals," and Chapter 8, "Network Intrusion Detection," are becoming fully mature with products available from a number of vendors. We focus our attention on both emerging and fairly mature intrusion prevention technologies that hold a lot of promise for helping organizations defend against a variety of attacks.

Rapid Changes in the Marketplace

Until 2004, intrusion prevention was primarily hype. As recently as June 11, 2003, when the famous Gartner "IDS Is Dead" report was released, following its advice to give up on your IDS and trust in the latest generation of "intrusion prevention" firewalls was almost impossible because the IPS products were still too immature and firewalls were not sufficiently advanced to run within internal networks in a blind and unprotected manner. Although the criticisms of IDS were certainly true—they have a high false-positive rate and can be bandwidth challenged—that did not support the conclusion of investing in a better firewall.

However, no one can deny that this paper was the nexus of a lot of change, especially in the IDS industry. The most positive effect was a significant improvement in false-positive handling. NFR started working on a network intrusion prevention system (NIPS); SoureFire ditched Snorty the pig and became Realtime Network Awareness

(RNA), a passive sensor and visualization tool company in terms of primary internal focus. Symantec and Enterasys were quick to point out the Gartner report was simplistic; you really should buy both an IDS and an IPS, and you should buy both from them. And, of course, every firewall vendor, no matter how lame, immediately found a way to get intrusion prevention onto its home page somehow. The entire industry reformed itself in a year's time, but not always for the better.

The Classic Response to the Gartner "IDS Is Dead" Report

The Gartner report stirred up a considerable amount of anger, and there were some pretty steamy postings on newsgroups. My favorite is the tongue-in-cheek reply by the Chief Technology Officer of the intrusion detection company NFR (who now also has an IPS):

"How about the demise of current generation industry analysts by 2005. Reason? Excessive false positives and lack of corporate value. They will be supplanted next-gen analysts who will deliver outrageous claims with no loss of performance. After all, if you can make stuff up, why bother with thoughtful analysis. :-)

Andre Yee, NFR Security, Inc."

You can view Andre's report at http://seclists.org/lists/focus-ids/2003/Jun/0184.html.

The biggest problem with the "IDS Is Dead" report is that it ignores the value of sensors. We would never ask a pilot to fly in visual blackout conditions without instrumentation, nor would we ask a CFO to run a company's finances without up-to-date, validated financial information. If you agree with these examples, would you ask the Chief Security Officer of an organization with high-value intellectual property assets to turn off or minimize his IDS sensors? Scarcely a week after the Gartner report, The SANS Institute was receiving email from people being asked by senior management if they should still be running their IDS systems.

Today, we have an industry where everyone has a product labeled "intrusion prevention." However, there is no definition of what intrusion prevention is. It is no longer just hype; there are some powerful trends afoot, even though the functionality provided by industry products varies significantly. Therefore, as we work our way through the chapter, we will classify the products into two major groups:

- **Network intrusion prevention systems (NIPS)**—Devices that sit on the network and help prevent intrusions
- **Host-based intrusion prevention systems (HIPS)**—Software that runs on a host system and helps prevent intrusions

What Is IPS?

Simply stated, intrusion prevention technology adds an active layer of defensive technology. Intrusion detection technology generally only reports attacks against monitored systems, although since 1997 active responses have been available, such as forging resets to blow away TCP connections (the so-called *session sniping* or *reset kill*). Intrusion prevention technology, by contrast, will attempt to stop the attacks before they are successful.

As IPS continues to mature, it will probably evolve to be something more like a capability than a single product. For instance, consider the logic behind Cisco Secure IDS, CiscoWorks Management Center for firewalls and VPNs, and Cisco Security Agent (CSA). A suspicious packet enters the network and is perhaps detected with the Cisco Secure IDS technology. The attack is classified by the operating systems vulnerable to that attack. The CiscoWorks Security Information Management (SIM) console is consulted to see if the attack and the destination are a match. For instance, if the attack is a Solaris exploit and the target system is a Sun Microsystems workstation running that version of Solaris, it would constitute a match.

To double-check, an agent on the target can be consulted in case the console is out of date. If the attack does not match the target (for example, an SGI attack against a Windows XP box), the alert is deprecated.

However, if there is a match, the agent can be consulted to determine the potential for an active vulnerability. If the box is patched and not vulnerable, again, we can deprecate, or reduce the priority of the alert. If the box is vulnerable, we can test to see if a compromise has occurred. If the file system has changed, we can begin forensics and incident response.

To be sure, this doesn't sound like intrusion prevention; it is more like modern SIM-enabled intrusion detection. This capability—modern intrusion detection with strong multiproduct coordination features—is exactly what well-funded organizations across the globe are trying to implement using Intellitactics, netForensics, Huntsman, ArcSight, and other database-driven consoles. However, next we add the defensive layers based on the former Okena StormWatch product purchased by Cisco and renamed *Cisco Security Agent (CSA)*, a host intrusion prevention system (HIPS). CSA can stop the attack in the network, just like a personal firewall does. However, what if the user is surfing the web using Internet Explorer and malicious code compromises the system via an Internet Explorer vulnerability? CSA also has an operating system shim so that if the malicious code activates in the file system and misbehaves, CSA can detect and stop the application. Wrong behavior, as we discussed in Chapter 10, "Host Defense Components," could range from trying to initiate a network connection to making a call for interrupt 13H to make a direct write to the hard disk. You can expect to see similar console and agent capabilities from Symantec and possibly Guidance Software. Encase, by Guidance, is a fully capable incident-handling tool already; it gives you the ability to detect signatures of malicious activity and to quarantine a file.

Because both host-based and network-based intrusion prevention systems are active technologies in the sense they directly interact with packets and are extremely capable of causing denial of service conditions, we can easily deduce the requirements for a successful product:

- It has to be fast.
- It has to keep state.
- It has to have some knowledge of application protocol or application behavior.
- It has to be accurate and up to date.
- It has to nullify an attack.

Let's take a look at these requirements in greater detail.

An IPS Must Be Fast

Perhaps you remember the early days of routers and a company named Cisco that offered a router that operated at "wire speed." Once they had wire speed, nothing else would do. The same is true for a NIPS. If it starts adding latency, it becomes a denial of service device—and companies do not intentionally purchase denial of service devices. This likely means doing as much processing in hardware as possible and even better processing in parallel, which is going to add to the cost of the device. Cheaper, single-threaded NIPS may be able to perform much of their processing in kernel space to gain speed. Does a HIPS have to be fast? Certainly. Who would tolerate a security layer that slowed down his or her machine?

An IPS Must Keep State

The state of a communication flow affects the correct interpretation of a packet. This is fairly simple at the IP/TCP/UDP header level, but the IPS must be able to create state tables so that sufficient state is available to interpret packets. Perhaps you will recall that the original stateful firewalls—Check Point FireWall-1 and Cisco PIX—had gobs and gobs of problems with state. It is a lot harder than it sounds because various TCP stacks do not always perfectly implement RFCs, and state is not always easy to predict and requires lots of memory and processing.

Perhaps you have heard the marketing term *Deep Packet Inspection*. If such a thing exists, it stands to reason there must also be "Shallow Packet Inspection"—and there is. Shallow Packet Inspection is a field-by-field analysis of the IP/TCP/UDP header. Because all these fields are fixed length, we can do this very fast, and anomalous values can be detected with a high degree of accuracy. The craft of Shallow Packet Inspection was first created by Stephen Northcutt with the DoD Shadow team and brought to maturity by Judy Novak at the Army Research Laboratory. It's now incorporated by most network analysis tools. Deep Packet Inspection requires understanding of the protocol itself and dealing with fields that may not be fixed-length. The earliest significant work was the BRO freeware intrusion detection system by Vern Paxton. Although there are application-specific IPSs especially for web servers, as a general rule of thumb you can expect it will be several years until an IPS that can actually monitor a large number of protocols becomes available.

You can see the reason why we were careful to point out the hype in the intrusion prevention space. This is very hard stuff to do, and there are significant limitations that affect the performance possible at a given price point.

An IPS Must Be Accurate and Up to Date

Because it is an active device, an IPS runs the risk of creating a "self-inflicted" denial of service condition. Therefore, it must be nearly 100% accurate for the attack signature it takes an active role in defending. This difference may be one reason the pre-Gartner report IDS vendors were a bit sloppy with their signatures; if they were wrong, nothing broke. Clearly keeping state is a large part of that; knowing how the application is supposed to perform is also important. However, the accuracy of the signatures depends on far more than that. The signature language and rule-processing engine must be fully industrial strength. Also, they have to be up to date. The rule of IPS signatures is simple: The cycle time from the moment a vulnerability is announced to develop and distribute a new signature with a prescription must be less than the cycle time to develop a worm to take advantage of the vulnerability.

An IPS Must Have the Ability to Nullify an Attack

We realize this is a stretch, but there actually are products that meet the acid test requiring an IPS to be fast, keep state, know the application protocol or behavior, be accurate, and be up to date. Now we come to the core issue: Can an IPS reliably stop attacks? There are two basic methods: eliminate only the very awful packets and kill the stream. One approach, as you will learn later, is a "bump in the wire" approach to network-based intrusion prevention. For a NIPS to nullify an attack, all the packets to a segment of the network must pass through the network device—either a switch or a chokepoint next-generation firewall-type device. IPS must be fast, stateful, and hopefully accurate and up to date.

Ideally, IPS see the attack set up and drop only the payload of the buffer overflow or shell code. This approach has the minimum possible impact on network traffic yet keeps you safe. In contrast, there are NIPS and HIPS technologies that look for signatures of problems and, at the first sign of trouble, terminate (or refuse to pass) the communication stream. The classic example of this approach is the UNIX Sentry Tools (http://sourceforge.net/projects/sentrytools). PortSentry, one of the most employed HIPS ever, detects an attack, can disallow the attacking IP from making further connections, and can null-route the path back to the attacker. Both approaches are fine, but the bottom line is that to be truly considered an IPS, it must implement a far more robust active mechanism than a TCP reset kill.

Note

We mentioned PortSentry in Chapter 10 in the context of an IDS with active response capabilities and that one could classify it as an IPS as well.

IPS Limitations

One of the truly overused clichés of our industry is the line, "there is no such thing as a silver bullet." Possibly the reason that expression will not go away is that we really do need to keep reminding ourselves of that fact. Everyone who has deployed or managed a firewall has heard someone ask, "Why do we have to patch? We are behind a firewall." In this section of the chapter, we take some time to consider the things that an IPS cannot possibly do for you. As an informed technical professional, when you hear that an IPS must be a fast, keep state, know the application protocol or behavior, be accurate and up to date, and be able to nullify an attack, you understand there are discrete technical limits to the implementation. A NIPS might be able to defend against 800 different attacks well, but there could be thousands more it doesn't have a signature for. An IPS is a useful tool, but it is only one part of our overall defensive capability.

An Excuse to Ignore Sound Practice

A major focus of this book is sound practice. IPS technology is a step forward, which is good, but we are in a game of measures and countermeasures. You cannot employ IPS technology and fail to implement the guidance contained in the other chapters of this book. The attackers will likely find ways to circumvent the protections an IPS provides. The 1998 paper "Insertion, Evasion, and Denial of Service: Eluding Network Intrusion Detection," by Thomas Ptacek and Timothy Newsham, is still valuable as a reminder of the potential weaknesses NIPS may have. The paper is available at http://www.insecure.org/stf/secnet_ids/secnet_ids.html. In addition, worms such as Goner and Gokar directly targeted host security tools such as antivirus. It is clear attackers will attempt to circumvent or even directly attack our IPS tools, so we need to create an architecture that can survive even if the IPS fails.

An IPS Simply Buys You Time

Deploying an intrusion prevention system is not a replacement for patch management and system hardening. Instead, you are hoping it buys you a valuable asset: time in the race before the next worm is released. Organizations using IPSs are often able to extend the amount of time they have to deploy patches to resolve operating system and application flaws, potentially delaying the deployment of fixes until several patches have accumulated and a window for scheduled maintenance of equipment is available. And we need all the time we can get. What's more, sometimes patching is not possible.

Sometimes You Cannot Patch

Although patching is necessary, as we show in Chapter 19, "Maintaining a Security Perimeter," there are serious constraints to patching, and sometimes it can be a difficult problem. Dr. Marc Willebeek-LeMair, CTO of TippingPoint Technologies, points out, "It is important to understand what it takes to patch a vulnerable system." Here are some points to consider:

- Is a patch available? Vulnerabilities are often disclosed in advance of a vendor patch being available. Sometimes vendors don't bother creating patches for older versions of software.

- Are you aware of all systems to which the patch applies? Mobile systems, embedded software within bundled applications, and the sheer size of some organizations make it very difficult to identify all vulnerable systems. Telecommuters and trusted partner connections further complicates matters.

- Do you have access to all affected systems? Owners must often be contacted to apply a patch and some may not be available during the patching interval or their systems may be temporarily inaccessible.

- Is there an opportunity to bring down critical systems to apply the patch? Fully redundant systems are costly and not always possible. There is never a good time to bring down critical systems.

- After testing in the lab and on development systems, can you afford the risk to then test the patch on critical systems to verify that it works and does not adversely affect business-critical applications? Thorough testing can be very time consuming. Besides the fact that the patch may be faulty, custom applications may interact unfavorably with the new software patch.

- Should you wait until next week and apply multiple patches at the same time? The frequency of new vulnerabilities being discovered and patches being made available is so high that IT managers are challenged to keep up. They would rather batch fixes to minimize IT overhead and system downtime.

- Finally, do you have the resources to apply a patch? The number of patches multiplied by the number of machines multiplied by the time to patch each machine ("patch-hours" of work) may exceed IT capacity.

Like IDS, IPS is not a fire-and-forget technology. It requires significant maintenance and monitoring to be an effective defense tool. IPS is also not an inexpensive tool for enterprisewide deployment.

Next, we will consider the best known form of IPS, network-based IPS devices, or NIPS.

NIPS

In this section we will discuss NIPS technology. NIPS essentially breaks down into two categories:

- **Chokepoint devices**—These are conceptually similar to firewalls; you generally have one or more pairs of interfaces and you use these to segment traffic in a network. One common application of these devices is to place them in front of firewalls to keep common attacks from ever reaching them. They can also be used to segment internal LANs.

- **Intelligent switches**—These are the so-called "bump in the wire" solutions. You plug in your internal network to an intelligent switch and it stops attacks. For instance, two of the most common ways for worms to spread internally involve users double-clicking on attachments and laptops leaving the facility, getting infected at home, and then being plugged back into the corporate network. A "bump in the wire" solution helps moderate the damage from these sorts of worm infections.

In addition to these architectural classes, NIPS designers make a choice between two types of technology: general-purpose CPUs and application-specific integrated circuits (ASICs). General-purpose CPUs tend to be the easier choice from a development standpoint because you can build on a ready-to-deploy appliance such as the Nokia IP130. ASICs have the ability to support much higher performance because the chip can be optimized for a particular application. However, products built on ASICs require much more development. The good news is that a lot of the work has already been done; a number of off-the-shelf ASICs have been designed for TCP/IP processing. If a developer chooses an ASIC solution, he still needs to decide whether to implement a single ASIC "board-level" solution or a parallel implementation. If you can devote a processor to each IP flow, you have a massive speed and latency advantage. A single Adaptec TCP Offload Engine (TOE) ASIC can maintain sustained performance at rates above 900Mbps.

> **Note**
>
> ASIC-based devices still have general-purpose CPUs. The performance increases only apply when processing can be done on the ASIC. If you have to signal the bus to transfer the packet(s) to the general-purpose CPU(s), the NIPS will probably suffer a significant drop in performance.

How Chokepoint NIPS Work

A chokepoint NIPS could be located outside of your firewall or on your screened subnet in front of a device you want to protect, such as your web server. They will often be configured without an IP address on either of the chokepoint interfaces to minimize their impact on the network's architecture. Traffic that originates from the Internet is passed through the NIPS to your corporate firewall and beyond if it does not generate any alerts. In IPS mode, traffic that does generate an alert can be dropped or rejected by the NIPS and never delivered inside your network. These can also be run in IDS mode, where a report is generated but the packet is not dropped. These tend to either be a "firewall plus something" or an "IDS plus something."

Firewall Plus Something

Firewalls fall into three major categories, listed in increasing security protection: packet filter, stateful, and proxy or application gateway. The overwhelming majority of deployed firewalls are stateful. Firewalls are the original IPS; the first time you heard the term *intrusion prevention system* you were probably wondering if the person was talking about a firewall. To be credible as an IPS, the firewall needs to add additional functionality, such as the ability to run IDS-type rules. Stateful firewall inspection has been a very strong technology for many organizations. The next logical progression for many firewall vendors is to add intrusion detection capacity to their firewalls. Because the firewall is an inline network device, it is in an excellent position to identify malicious events on the network, performing analysis at the transport through application layers to identify attacks. Because the firewall must collect and retransmit each packet that flows through it, a logical advancement would be to allow policy to define whether traffic identified as malicious should generate an alert and be forwarded to the destination or whether it should generate an alert and be dropped, thereby preventing the attack from being successful.

> **Note**
>
> A fourth category of firewalls—circuit firewalls—has you authenticate once and then use a path through the firewall conceptually to nullify intrusion prevention. They were never widely deployed, so though it is doubtful you would find a large number of SOCKS protocol connections in your network, you might well find internal VPNs that are conceptually similar. It is okay to bypass a perimeter or chokepoint control as long as you have equivalent controls on both of the endpoints.

Vendors such as Cisco, Jupiter (Jupiter acquired NetScreen), and Check Point have been rapidly acquiring intrusion prevention technology for integration into their product lines, or they have been developing their own tools for the job. The resultant products are often classified as "smarter" firewalls instead of classic intrusion prevention devices, but we expect this trend to change as more organizations become comfortable with the term *intrusion prevention* as well as the benefits and limitations of the technology. Let's take a quick look at some of the firewall-plus-something implementations, including FireWall-1, Border Guard, and modwall.

Check Point FireWall-1 NG

Check Point's central product is FireWall-1, which is the best-known example of a "firewall plus something" positioned as a NIPS.

Check Point FireWall-1 NG has the following IPS features:

- Attack protection with "Application Intelligence," a rudimentary content-inspection capability that blocks many well-known, well-defined attacks.
- Access control based on stateful inspection, the capability this firewall is best known for.
- Choice of software and appliance deployments. The software is available on a number of platforms to balance needs versus costs. The high end is based on the high-performance, secure, and expensive Nokia appliance.

FireWall-1 protects network resources against attacks and unauthorized access at both the network and, increasingly, the application level. Enterprises attain this degree of security by defining and enforcing a single, comprehensive security policy. What makes Check Point stand out in the industry is the advantage of utilizing the Open Platform for Security (OPSEC), the most widely used application programming interface (API) of any security device. Instead of trying to be the best at everything, Check Point has focused well on partnering. Third-party products can access the Check Point security policy using the OPSEC Management Interface (OMI). Intrusion detection–style capabilities are available via the Suspicious Activity Monitoring Protocol (SAMP). Also, Check Point has been doing content inspection for years with the Content Vectoring Protocol (CVP) .

Check Point and OPSEC

The OPSEC Alliance was founded in April of 1997. OPSEC has since grown to over 350 partners, making it the leading platform alliance by far for integrated Internet security solutions. Programmers find the interface very workable, which is probably the reason for the large number of partners.

OPSEC has enabled FireWall-1 to be extended into a number of areas outside of Check Point's core competency, including the following:

- Authentication

- Authorization

- Content security

- Intrusion detection and protection

- Wireless

modwall

Modwall was developed by Bill Stearns and is available from http://www.stearns.org/modwall. Modwall is a set of firewall/IPS modules that can be inserted into an existing IPTables firewall on Linux. Rather than focusing on the normal "allow this kind of traffic from here to here" firewall rules, modwall focuses on illegal packet traffic, which includes invalid or unassigned source or destination IP addresses, invalid TCP flag combinations, and packets that have been intentionally fragmented. Modwall then allows the administrator to define what action to take, including dropping the traffic, logging it, and blocking traffic from the source for a limited amount of time. Let's use the -L (list rules) option of IPTables to examine the rules in the "address check" module (one of 38 modules in the package) as an example:

```
[root@sparrow modwall]# ./address start
Starting address
[root@sparrow modwall]# iptables -L address -n
Chain address (3 references)
target     prot opt source             destination
DROP       all  --  127.0.0.0/8        0.0.0.0/0
DROP       all  --  0.0.0.0/0          127.0.0.0/8
DROP       all  --  224.0.0.0/4        0.0.0.0/0
DROP       !udp --  0.0.0.0/0          224.0.0.0/4
DROP       all  --  240.0.0.0/4        0.0.0.0/0
DROP       all  --  0.0.0.0/0          240.0.0.0/4
DROP       all  --  255.255.255.255    0.0.0.0/0
```

After it is started using the command address start (like IPTables, modwall also supports start, stop, and restart command-line directives), the following default address checks are performed on all non-loopback traffic (that is, traffic on all real network interfaces). Note the keyword DROP, which means just what you think: If the packet matches the rule, it will be dropped.

The first and second DROP entries drop all traffic found on the real network with loopback addresses. Note that 0.0.0.0 simply means the default network, whereas 0.0.0.0/0 would match anything, essentially serving as a wildcard. The reason the first and second entries are paired is to manage traffic in both directions (that is, the first one in the case of 127 in the source address and the second in the destination address). However, there is a very remote possibility this rule pair could have unintended consequences because 0.0.0.0 could also indicate a legacy broadcast. (In the early days of the Internet, BSD UNIX systems used 0 for broadcast.) However, that would mean the machine is very old.

In the third and fourth rule pairs, DROP is for network 224, which is multicast. Before you filter out multicast internally, you might want to sniff for a while and make sure you are not using it (some enterprise backup systems rely on it). The reason for !udp (meaning *not* UDP) is that UDP might legally multicast, but TCP should never multicast. Therefore, a safer rule, one that is less likely to cause a self-inflicted denial of service, might be this:

```
DROP       tcp  --  0.0.0.0/0            224.0.0.0/
```

The fifth and sixth DROP rule pairs are for the IP addresses reserved for experimental applications (240).

The final rule is used to quench directed broadcasts.

The "firewall plus something" concept in intrusion prevention is here to stay. As time goes on, firewalls will continue to add packet-scrubbing functionality and decrease in latency as they benefit from Moore's law.

> **Note**
>
> Moore's law is based on an observation by Gordon Moore from Intel in 1965. He said that computer processing capability would double every 18 months or so. It has proven to be remarkably accurate, and most analysts believe it will continue to hold true at least until the end of the decade.

Next we will take a look at another category of the early intrusion prevention devices: IDS plus something.

IDS Plus Something

The "IDS plus something" classification for IPS products refers to those vendors who have traditionally had strong IDS tools and have added active functionality to stop the activity that generates an alert before it is delivered on the network or executed on a host. An IDS plus something–style IPS would generally be referred to as a NIPS, where blocking is done at the network level.

False-positive detects can be a nuisance with IDS technology, but they are a much more significant problem in IPS technology. A false positive from an IDS generates an alert that may be false, but the activity from the IDS is benign. A false positive from an IPS stops legitimate services from being delivered. This could be intended functionality of a production application on a database server or it could be a customer visiting your website. False positives in the IPS realm have a significant cost to the organization because they can ultimately lead to self-imposed denial of service on production resources.

IntruShield

IntruShield is an example of a commercial IDS plus something–style of NIPS. In 2002, McAfee (McAfee was formerly named Network Associates) acquired the IPS company Entercept for integration into its product line. The Entercept product line merged with the IDS products previously available from Network Associates to offer both NIPS appliances and a host-based IPS suite of products to protect desktops and servers.

IntruShield is a chokepoint architecture that uses classic IDS signature and anomaly techniques to identify attacks. The standard product is shipped with a base rule set that can be customized. You can enable or disable features to best meet the demands of your network. A lot of work has been put into the IntruShield user interface, and it is easy to switch between IDS (passive) mode and IPS (active) mode.

NFR Sentivist

A NIPS that is directly positioned against IntruShield is NFR's Sentivist appliance. Intrusion prevention is designed and built with a focus on three distinctive areas in this "IDS plus something" NIPS technology:

- NFR detection engine
- Fine-grained blocking
- Resistance to self-inflicted DoS

Sentivist's IPS leverages NFR's historical detection capability and advanced but difficult to customize signature engine to offer a combination of pattern-matching signatures, protocol anomaly detection, and heuristics. It is able to perform context-based detection of attacks via the use of OS or application fingerprinting techniques, a capability you should insist on seeing demonstrated before purchasing any NIPS.

Instead of blocking only by IP address or port, NFR Sentivist's IPS is able to block discrete attack traffic carried in the application layer. Fine-grained blocking should be enabled by attack type, by impact, or by a qualitative confidence score. Blocking by confidence score is critical because it allows the user to block attacks on the basis of a system's confidence that the detected event is truly an attack. Users can choose to calibrate the level of prevention appropriate to their risk tolerance.

NFR Sentivist provides resistance to self-inflicted DoS by using multiple techniques such as whitelisting and graceful session termination.

HogWash and Snort-Inline

HogWash was originally developed by Jed Haile and was the first to use Snort rules in a security gateway device. This development effort seems to have stalled, and the work is being continued by Snort-Inline. Rob Mcmillen was the next to lead the effort, hosted at http://snort-inline.sourceforge.net/.

With Snort 2.3, Snort-Inline became part of the Snort distribution. The huge new change is that Snort-Inline gets its packets from the kernel using IPTables instead of libpcap, just like modwall. The Snort rule language has been extended for three new types of rules: `drop` (standard IPTables drop and log), `sdrop` (silent drop, no logging), and `reject`, the noisiest rule (drop, log, forge a TCP reset or "ICMP Port Unreachable" message, as appropriate). Because it is open source and part of a wildly popular distribution, Snort-Inline will probably accelerate the understanding and acceptance of active response.

LaBrea Technologies Sentry

We end the discussion of external NIPS with a fascinating product that is neither a firewall or an IDS at its heart. Perhaps the best classification would be to call it a *deception device*. Sentry was developed by Tom Liston, author of the famous Code Red tarpit. At the time of this writing, this is primarily a proof of concept for an appliance that uses attempted connections to unused IP address space as an indicator of an attack. The logic is that any ARP request for an unassigned IP address can be considered hostile. Sentry responds by forging an ARP response, claiming Sentry is the IP address. It then uses a variety of techniques to tie the attacker up for as long as possible. It is fairly simple and would only cause a self-inflicted denial of service if its information about the unused address space is incorrect. Liston hopes to roll it out with an additional capability using an Internet Storm Center–like correlation database so that whenever one of the devices learns about an attacking address or attack pattern, that information can be passed to all Sentries.

Switch-Type NIPS

So far we have discussed chokepoint-style systems with roots as firewalls and similar devices with roots as IDS systems. We have also mentioned the use of a deception system. The fourth classification of NIPS is an intelligent switch you plug your network in to. This is probably the most effective of the NIPS products available on the market place today, making the best use of firewalls, IDS tools, and routers/switches, ideally in a single parallel-processing, high-performance, low-latency device.

These switches have enough processing power to do more than just enhance the performance of a network by preventing Ethernet collisions. Expect to see antivirus, traffic-shaping, load-balancing, and intrusion prevention in the network itself. Of course, this next generation of switches that use massive arrays of parallel ASICs to connect the internal and external segments of your network together are going to be expensive. By using many of the techniques employed by advanced NIDS tools, the NIPS device can identify events on the network that are hostile. Because of its position (inline with the traffic of your entire network), the NIPS device can stop the hostile activity from ever being delivered to the target system. This also strongly enhances anomaly detection and network learning because all the traffic passes through the switch.

Protocol Scrubbing, Rate Limiting, and Policy Enforcement

Sitting inline has some advantages that aren't always directly related to thwarting malicious attacks. In some cases, a NIPS device can be used to clean garbage from the traffic stream, thus reducing the overall network load. For example, a server that is attempting to close a connection with a workstation that has shut down may continue to send packets to the destination waiting for a response saying "I'm done." The NIPS tool can use intelligence to recognize that the conversation is finished and then either drop the traffic received from the server or send a spoofed packet to the server on behalf of the nonresponsive workstation to stop the traffic altogether.

Another feature of switch-type NIPS devices is the ability to use rate limiting to apply Quality of Service (QoS) mechanisms to network traffic. The administrator can identify traffic on the network that should receive higher or lower priority than other traffic, or he can limit the total amount of traffic from a particular network, host, or specific application. This feature is particularly useful when trying to manage throughput on Internet connections, where the administrator can limit the ability for a single application or host to consume all the available bandwidth for the organization.

Because the NIPS device is already classifying traffic based on application, administrators can use this functionality to enforce organizational policy to drop traffic from unauthorized applications. A common use of this feature is to stop the activity of peer-to-peer applications on the network. Because the switch type NIPS device already recognizes peer-to-peer applications, it doesn't require any additional processing requirements to apply the policy and drop the traffic, generating alerts to indicate the policy violation from a specific workstation.

Environmental Anomaly Analysis

What is anomalous with a given application or protocol in one environment may not be anomalous in the next environment. One organization may utilize a busy public web server farm, with hundreds of web requests per minute. Another organization may utilize a single internal-use-only web server for the finance department. If the finance department network receives hundreds of web requests per minute, that dramatic short-term change in network behavior would be considered anomalous for that environment, but not for the server farm.

One of the immediate benefits of this capability is the support of an active change control program. NIDS and NIPS tools alike can detect a new version of an operating system or application and raise an alert, or even modify the rule set to take the new information into account. This could help the operations administrators manage unauthorized change. Obviously, you can only process so many alerts, so this would be managed by the analyst or administrator to help determine where appropriate thresholds should be set. Because the NIPS device is simultaneously tracking connection state for thousands or even millions of connections, it can take a "broad perspective" view to detect anomalies that involve many connections across an entire enterprise.

NIPS Challenges

In order for NIPS devices to be deployed as reliable, effective devices, they must overcome several challenges:

- Detection capabilities
- Evasion resistance
- Stable performance
- High throughput
- Low-latency, built-in security
- The ability to passively determine operating systems and application versions

Let's examine each of these in turn.

Detection Capabilities and Evasion Resistance

NIPS devices must utilize the same techniques of traditional network IDS tools to reduce the risk of false negatives. At the same time, they have to be extraordinarily careful not to generate false positives on the network because these types of mistakes would lead to a denial of service condition. A NIPS device uses a combination of application analysis, anomaly analysis, and signature-based rules to identify events that are malicious on the network. Traffic that is identified as malicious is dropped and may also be logged for review by the analyst to ensure it should have been dropped. A switch-type, "bump in the wire" NIPS must also use many of the same evasion-resistance techniques, such as normalizing traffic employed by IDS to reduce the threat of attackers obfuscating data in an effort to bypass the NIPS's detection capability. After all, because the switch-based NIPS is going to see all the traffic, evasion techniques and attacks for which there are no signatures (zero day) are going to be the most successful tools for attackers. This is a significant challenge for the NIPS to overcome, and the end result is that for the near future it will not be possible for NIPS devices to have as many active signature as IDSs are able to employ in passive sniffing mode.

In order to detect the greatest number of attacks without false positives, effective NIPS tools use passive OS and vulnerability assessment, as you will see later in this chapter.

Stability Demands

Because the NIPS is inline with network traffic, it represents a single point of failure for the network. NIPS devices must be as stable as a firewall or switch to gain market acceptance. They must also be resistant to malformed traffic and cannot break existing network protocols. This is a very similar risk to that of false positives by the NIPS—if a NIPS cannot properly interpret traffic or should fail in any way, it causes a failure on the network and denies legitimate requests. These failures can be accidental (as in the case of hardware or software failures) or intentionally performed by an attacker executing a denial of service on a network. One of the critical design features to understand when considering the purchase of a NIPS is whether it is designed to fail open or fail closed, or if this is user configurable. If network availability is critical to your organization, you want to be pretty certain that if the NIPS application should crash, the switch part of the product continues to pass traffic.

Throughput Demands

NIPS devices must be able to keep up with the throughput of network traffic, and in modern networks that means Gigabit Ethernet speeds. It is important to understand how the device degrades when it reaches its limits. For instance, when switches reach their limits, they may simply cease to forward traffic to a spanning or monitoring port and concentrate their resources on their core function. With a NIPS, traffic forwarding may well be more important than monitoring or protecting.

Latency Requirements

Despite the requirements to use extensive analysis techniques on network traffic to identify attacks, the NIPS must also provide low latency for network traffic. Additional latency on traffic that is analyzed should be in the low millisecond range. In general, latency will prove to be the primary difference between higher priced solutions and more moderately priced solutions because the easiest way to reduce latency is by adding more ASICs in parallel.

Security

The NIPS device must be secured against compromise because a compromised NIPS would give an attacker the ability to establish a man-in-the-middle attack against all the traffic entering or leaving the network. This is typically performed by configuring the NIPS without IP or MAC addresses on data interfaces, using a hardened operating system that resists common attacks, and using a secured management interface that strictly defines who is permitted to connect to and administer the system. Attackers will seek opportunities to break NIPS, whether using denial of service or to circumvent the protection the NIPS provides, so the NIPS device must be able to withstand any direct attacks.

Although not specifically an innovative advancement through NIPS technology, many NIPS vendors are looking for ways to properly classify and identity malicious activity with fewer demands on system processing and memory capacity. One technique is the use of a rule classification scheme to quickly sort through traffic in order to rapidly identify malicious events. Some vendors have coined the term *multiresolution filtering* for this technique, where simple analysis tests are first applied to traffic. The simple tests represent a portion of the overall detection capacity of the NIPS device, where a packet that matches a simple test is then processed using the more thorough tests.

For example, a NIPS device may require traffic to have data on the payload of the device for analysis. If this simple test fails (overall length − packet header length = 0), the NIPS device does not attempt to further classify this packet and sends it onto the network. This way, the NIPS can reserve its available system resources for more complex analysis.

After applying the simple rules, the NIPS device proceeds to apply more rule sets of additional complexity, including the examination of packet header information, transport layer session state information, application layer session state information, context-sensitive string matches against the packet payload, application layer analysis, and, finally, complex regular expression matching. The NIPS device is able to quickly and effectively classify traffic using only the required processing to complete the analysis, thereby allowing itself to process additional traffic.

Passive Analysis

In order to help the NIPS identify false-positive traffic, vendors make use of passive analysis techniques to identify host operating systems, network architecture, and what vulnerabilities are present on the network. Three of the most well-known standalone tools for this purpose are P0f (available at http://www.stearns.org), RNA by SourceFire, and NeVO from Tenable Security, and they should be available to some extent on every NIPS. Figure 11.1 provides a sample analysis using the NeVO system. Once this information is gathered, the NIPS can use it to classify attacks against internal systems based on their operating system and vulnerabilities.

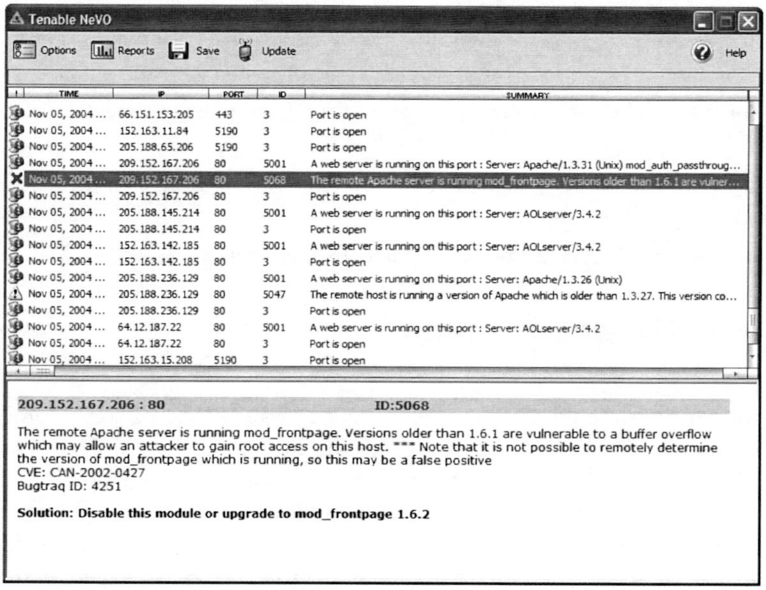

Figure 11.1   The screenshot shows the types of analysis data that can be captured and displayed by the NeVO system.

Increased Security Intelligence in the Switch Products

Switch-based, "bump in the wire" NIPS is a fast growing market segment, and there is no possible way to predict what all the players will do. By the time this book hits the marketplace, expect to see a large number of switch products with intelligence, ranging from antivirus and malware detection to network signature detection, from Symantec, TippingPoint, Enterasys, and Radware. All our efforts to get Cisco to share its plans have failed; however, between the existing Cisco Security Agent, the Network Admissions Program, and educational efforts to help network administrators get more security out of their existing IOS products, it seems certain Cisco will be a player. A subset of these products includes the true NIPS devices, which are categorized as wire-speed switches, have IPS capability, and, in general, are based on parallel ASICs. These products include TippingPoint's UnityOne IPS and TopLayer Attack Mitigator.

TippingPoint's UnityOne IPS

At the time this chapter was written, TippingPoint's UnityOne IPS product was currently the overwhelming market leader for a switch-type NIPS. It offers an inline NIDS that provides multigigabit performance, low latency, and multiple mechanisms to detect known and unknown attacks on the network. In addition to providing IPS features, UnityOne provides the ability to traffic-shape or rate-limit traffic for QoS measures. It also provides policy enforcement by blocking applications that are prohibited by your organization's acceptable-use policy (such as peer-to-peer apps, web mail, or instant messaging).

When the UnityOne device identifies malicious activity or activities that violate policy rules, the engine uses one of four available response mechanisms:

- **Monitor**—The UnityOne device monitors the activity, generating a log for later analysis.
- **Report**—The UnityOne device simply reports the event without detailed logging data.
- **Limit**—The UnityOne device restricts the throughput or rate of the malicious activity.
- **Block**—The UnityOne device simply drops the traffic before it is delivered to the destination.

Whenever you are speaking with a vendor and he says, "We are the only company in the space that can provide *X*," it is always a good lead in to ask, "Why are you the only company in the space?" If the vendor cannot provide a good answer, you know the company is either marketing fluff or it has put in some silly feature that no one else finds important. However, sometimes you learn the vendor you are talking with has a patent or other legal device so that it is very hard for others to effectively compete with the company he represents. This may prove to be the case with switch-based NIPS. 3Com (TippingPoint) has applied for patent on a technology it calls a "Threat Suppression Engine," which uses massively parallel ASIC hardware to perform packet inspection on traffic. If TippingPoint is granted this patent and it withstands the almost certain legal challenge, it could really change the future of the NIPS marketplace. One unique twist is that 3Com (TippingPoint) implements the "looks like a duck, walks like a duck, quacks, so it must be a duck" logic in hardware. The UnityOne uses "vulnerability filters" that identify attack behavior, not just specific exploits or vulnerabilities. This way, TippingPoint is able to identify and stop some attacks that exploit applications in an observable fashion—through buffer overflows, SQL injection, and other common exploitative techniques. TippingPoint sells a "Digital Vaccine" subscription service, similar to an antivirus subscription service, to its customers, who then receive regular updates for their UnityOne device so it can defend against emerging threats.

TopLayer Attack Mitigator

In the days before true gigabit IDS, TopLayer gained fame as the solution for high-bandwidth monitoring via load balancing. Like TippingPoint's product, this is a very fast box with high availability, hot-swappable components, parallel ASICs, and a price tag to match the performance. Attack Mitigator's roots are more from quelling distributed denial of service resource exhaustion and protocol anomaly attacks than a true IPS, but it certainly has the chassis to build on and, like FireWall-1, is very good at well-known, well-understood attacks. TopLayer calls its inspection technology TopInspect.

Switch NIPS Deployment Recommendations

Deploying a NIPS solution is a major project, and we recommend you begin planning for it now. Start off with reporting-only mode, study the false positives and negatives for your chosen solution carefully, invest the time in creating a sustainable process for configuration management, make sure Operations is a full partner in the process of NIPS deployment, and remember that your NIDS is still a valuable source of information.

Begin Budgeting Now

You will probably be strongly considering the next generation of switches with security intelligence sometime in the next two years. This is going to be expensive, so speak to your manager and see what can be done to plan for this expense in a technology refresh cycle.

Review Products in Report-Only Mode

Before you start using a NIPS device to start blocking attacks on your network, run the device in report-only mode. Use this information to identify what events the NIPS would have dropped on your network, and what the impact would have been to the network.

Work with Vendors Identifying Test Procedures for False Positives and False Negatives

Ask your vendor to detail its testing procedure for new rules and anomaly analysis techniques. Ensure the vendor uses a combination of "live" and "attack" scenarios at rates that are appropriate for your network environment before shipping you updates. Ask your vendor what techniques it uses to eliminate false-positive traffic, and how it exercises auditing to ensure it isn't missing attacks.

Be Wary of Absence of Auto-Update Mechanisms

In 2004, we saw a decrease in the time from a vulnerability announcement to the release of a worm. Instead of the month we were used to, the Witty worm was released three days after the vulnerability announcement. Because one of the main reasons an organization would consider the purchase of expensive switch NIPS is worm management, this makes being able to keep the device up to date with the latest signatures critical.

Be Wary of Auto-Update Mechanisms

The technology for automated analysis or signature database updates has been around for various products for a while, with NIPS vendors touting this feature for the ability to quickly respond to new threats. The ability to respond to new threats is certainly desirable, but with it comes the risk of poor traffic-identification patterns that lead to false positives on the network. Exercise caution when implementing such features, using organizational policy to dictate the tradeoff between the risks of new threats and the risks for dropped traffic.

Auto-update mechanisms ease the implementation and deployment of NIPS products but can assert a new set of challenges on your organization. Ask your vendor to support a mixed-reporting mechanism, where new rules are placed in report-only mode for a specified amount of time. This way, the organization can take advantage of existing functionality in the NIPS while the analyst has the ability to identify false-positive alerts or performance burdens that affect throughput and latency on the network.

Document a Change-Management Mechanism

Identify who should be responsible for managing updates to NIPS software, and how often the software should be updated. Include information about how the organization should react to updates based on new Internet threats, such as a new worm or other exploitative threat. Having this policy in place before a new threat emerges will define how well your organization will be able to leverage NIPS technology.

Expect the NIPS to Be Blamed for All Problems

Veterans of network security will remember that when they first installed a firewall, every time anyone had a problem, the firewall administrator's phone rang. A new product like a NIPS is potentially invasive toward network operations. At some point, someone in the organization is bound to experience a problem and cast blame on the NIPS device. The best way to mitigate this problem is to clearly document the use and functionality of the NIPS device and utilize the logging features that come with the NIPS to identify traffic that is dropped, shaped, or altered in any way. Over time, other people in the organization will come to understand the benefits and limitations of the technology, and they will accept the NIPS device as a critical security component for the network.

Use a Combination of NIPS and NIDS Where Appropriate

NIDS investments don't go out the window after a NIPS device is deployed. We can still leverage the technology of NIDS devices to aid in assessing threats, baselining attack statistics, and troubleshooting network problems with the addition of a NIPS device. After deploying a NIPS tool, many organizations focus their NIDS tools to monitor internal networks, to aid in identifying attacks that make it past the NIPS device, and to identify insider threats. We don't expect NIDS technology to go away anytime soon; instead, we expect the technology to continue to mature and add value to organizations that take full advantage of the functionality available.

Host–Based Intrusion Prevention Systems

We'll now investigate the technology supporting HIPS products in more detail. Essentially, they are an iterative improvement on personal firewalls. We expect most vendors that are offering personal firewalls or host-based intrusion detection systems (HIDSs) today to be offering HIPSs by 2005. One of the major benefits to HIPS technology is the ability to identify and stop known and unknown attacks, both at the network layer where personal firewalls operate and in the operating system. It is this functionality that lets enterprises have a wider window to deploy patches to systems, because already deployed HIPS software is able to prevent common attack techniques, including worm activity.

Currently, all commercial HIPS software uses a technique called *system call interception* (which is very similar to what antivirus vendors have been doing for many years). The HIPS software uses something called an *OS shim* to insert its own processes between applications, accessing resources on the host and the actual OS resources. This way, the HIPS software has the ability to deny or permit those requests based on whether the request is identified as malicious or benign. For instance, if Internet Explorer was to initiate interrupt call 13H to make a direct write to the boot sector of the hard drive, which is a signature of a boot sector virus, the HIPS would intercept the call. Another approach might be to implement HIPS via a device driver. The SANS Institute was testing Windows software based on this approach as early as 2002, but it is still not ready for commercial use as of this writing. Finally, Computer Associates' eTrust Access Control resembles a HIPS in that it offers server-based access control at a higher degree of granularity than most operating systems support.

HIPS tools use a combination of signature analysis and anomaly analysis to identify attacks—this is performed by monitoring traffic from network interfaces, the integrity of files, and application behavior. Let's take a detailed look at each of these functions as well as how each monitoring mechanism can stop common attack techniques.

Real-world Defense Scenarios

HIPS products such as Cisco Security Agent, Security Architect's Ozone, and Platform Logic's AppFire have been deployed in enough organizations to start getting some "real-world" experience in defending against attacks from worms and other exploits, including Blaster, Nachi/Welchia, Sobig, IIS WebDAV, and so on. The organizations that have deployed HIPS software have reported favorably about their vendor's ability to stop unknown attacks against systems. The best defenses in this area are from vendors that offer intrusion prevention that is not solely based on signature or rule-based analysis. Because rules have to be updated to detect and catch new exploits, organizations are in a race to deploy signature updates to the HIPS agents to defend against new attacks. Using application analysis techniques, the best-in-class vendors are able to stop attacks that have common exploit methods (such as buffer overflows) without requiring updates to the software.

Dynamic Rule Creation for Custom Applications

Another development in the HIPS market is being designed to support customers who are using applications that have not been thoroughly analyzed by the vendor for application analysis–detection techniques as well as those organizations using custom applications. HIPS vendors are readying tools that monitor how an application operates in a learning mode, identifying what files are opened, what Registry keys are accessed, what system calls are made, and so on. An organization using this technology would "train" the HIPS software in learning mode to recognize the traditional behavior of the production software and use the results of this training later in production to identify and stop anomalous events.

This functionality is helpful for both vendors and customers. Vendors can use this method of analyzing applications to reduce the amount of resources needed to add an application to their list of supported applications for monitoring, and customers can use this tool to monitor custom or unsupported applications. An organization using this technology should always use caution before wide-scale deployment, preferably starting with applications such as instant messaging and email before moving on to protecting ERP applications from misuse.

Monitoring File Integrity

Whereas traditional file integrity analysis tools use cryptographic hashes on files to determine if changes have been made (at a later date), HIPS software uses its operating system shim functionality to monitor any files that are opened as read/write or write-only on the operating system. When a program or process attempts to call a function that would change the contents of a file, such as `write()`, `fwrite()`, or `fsync()`, or use any other file-modification system calls, the operating system checks whether the file handle corresponds to a list of files that should be monitored for change. If the file is supposed to be monitored for change, the HIPS software then checks to determine if the user or application requesting the change is authorized to do so.

The lack of authorization to change the contents of a file causes the HIPS software to drop the request to write to the file and then to generate an alert. When authorization is granted to make changes to the file, the HIPS software honors the request by passing the necessary information to the requested operating system calls.

A significant advantage of HIPS software is the ability to define authorized users in real time for monitoring the integrity of files. For instance, you could utilize HIPS software on a web server to prevent unauthorized people from making changes to web pages (such as the user account running the web server, which is IUSR_HOSTNAME on Windows IIS servers), but permit your web developers to make changes when necessary.

Monitoring Application Behavior

Application behavior monitoring is a feature of HIPS software where a manufacturer selects a supported application and records the intended functionality of the application in normal use. For example, if a vendor has provided application behavior monitoring for Microsoft Word, it would record how Microsoft Word interacts with the operating system and other applications, identifying all the product functionality. After collecting all the data about how the application should work, the vendor creates a database that details the functionality of the application to feed to the HIPS software. Once installed, the HIPS software identifies and monitors the use of the supported application. If Microsoft Word were to open a file from the file system and print the document, the HIPS software would recognize this as intended functionality. If Microsoft Word started parsing through each contact in the Outlook Contact Book to send repeated email to each recipient, the HIPS software would recognize that as anomalous activity and shut down the application, generating an alert for the analyst.

Another example of application behavior monitoring involves a web server product such as the Apache web server. If the HIPS software sees the request GET /index.html, it would recognize this as intended functionality and let the web server respond to the request. If the HIPS software sees a request for ./././././././././././././././. repeated 100 times, it would recognize the request as unintended functionality for the application and stop the request from being delivered to the application.

In practice, application behavior monitoring is difficult to get right because applications are constantly changing functionality with updates and new releases. Most vendors are developing hybrid solutions that utilize a combination of application behavior monitoring and anomaly analysis, using a specified list of anomalous events that should not be allowed on the system.

It is important to remember that application behavior analysis only works for supported applications. If your vendor supports Microsoft Exchange and the Microsoft IIS web server, and you run the IIS SMTP engine, the HIPS software offers no protection for the SMTP engine.

HIPS Advantages

Now that you have a better understanding of how HIPS software functions and what it can do, let's take a look at the advantages of using HIPS.

HIPS software includes nearly all the capabilities of HIDS software. Identifying unauthorized change to files, monitoring network activity, and the ability to see the results of network-encrypted traffic are all advantages to using HIPS software as well. The added benefit for HIPS, of course, is the ability to stop attacks from being successful. This is a welcome advantage for many organizations that struggle with patch management challenges and the short window of time between when a vulnerability is announced and when it is actively being exploited. HIPS is one more tool that might help the problem of the so-called *zero-day exploit*, an attack that occurs before the vulnerability is published.

Organizations are further challenged with an expanding network perimeter. Years ago we only had to worry about attacks from our Internet connections; now attacks come from wireless networks, modems, VPN connections, malware introduced by traveling users to our networks, and more. HIPS software provides a better method of defending our perimeter when distributed throughout the enterprise than traditional tools allow.

HIPS Challenges

HIPS deployments have implementation and maintenance challenges that include testing updates, deploying updates, troubleshooting updates…all the joys of complex operational software. False positives are a major challenge in the IPS market as well, although they are slightly less significant with HIPS because a false positive is this risk, however, because the false positive you experience may be how your web server responds to HTTP requests, thus limiting your ability to serve pages to people on the Internet.

The ability to detect unknown attacks is a big advantage for IPS technology, but it is often tied to specific application functionality such as IIS, Apache, or Exchange. The ability to monitor for anomalous behavior from applications is limited to those applications selected by your vendor, with almost no support for protecting custom applications. Hardening operating systems and secure coding practices are still good ideas for protecting custom application software.

More HIPS Challenges

Despite the ability for HIPS software to identify and stop attacks, it is not a replacement for regular system patching or antivirus defenses. IPS software is still in an early stage of maturity, and it isn't yet clear what weaknesses attackers will discover and exploit in this technology. It is best to use HIPS software as another piece of defense for your organization's security.

With all the advantages and detection techniques offered by HIPS software comes the additional burden of processing requirements on servers and workstations. This will contribute to the total cost of ownership (TCO) of HIPS software, possibly reducing the life cycle of your current server and workstation investments. Expect HIPS software to utilize about 20MB of RAM and between 2% and 3% of available CPU power, depending on configuration and analysis options.

Finally, the need for a management console to oversee HIPS software throughout the organization is obvious, just as many organizations use it to manage antivirus software updates and signature data files. Vendors are struggling with the extensibility of managing large numbers of nodes from a management console. Though it is growing, version 4.5 of Cisco's management console is expected to support 100,000 agents. If you are planning a HIPS deployment larger than your console supports, expect to make multiple investments in management consoles and the labor to replicate the management burden across multiple HIPS groups.

HIPS Recommendations

This section contains recommendations to keep in mind when evaluating or planning a HIPS deployment. This is a major software rollout, so you must plan, test, and manage.

Document Requirements and Testing Procedures

Carefully evaluate vendor products in a lab and production environment to ensure they deliver the desired functionality without generating false-positive detects. If a vendor's product requires significant troubleshooting and tweaking to get it working properly, record the time spent on this effort and add it to the TCO calculation for each application you wish to use on hosts protected with the HIPS software.

Develop a Centrally Managed Policy for Controlling Updates

Strong configuration management practice can significantly reduce the risk of problems with the HIPS rollout. The lower the total number of repeatable-build operating systems deployed at your facility, the better suited you are for a HIPS solution. If every single operating system is different, you should be considering a NIPS solution, not a HIPS solution. Identify who should be responsible for managing updates to HIPS software, and how often the software should be updated. Include information about how the organization should react to updates based on new Internet threats, such as a new worm or other exploitative threat. Having this policy in place before a new worm threatens your organization will impact how well the organization will be able to leverage the HIPS technology.

Don't Blindly Install Software Updates

Despite the claims from manufacturers that they extensively test the updates to their products before deployment, they still can make mistakes and ship updates that render workstations and servers useless or severely impaired. Establish a test environment for the supported workstation and server images for your organization and thoroughly test product functionality before approving the distribution of software.

Don't Rely Solely on HIPS to Protect Systems

You should use HIPS software to augment defense-in-depth techniques. Exclusively relying on HIPS software to protect systems is not a wise choice. Instead, use the extra time from the defenses provided by HIPS to carefully test and plan the delivery of patches to ensure workstations are not vulnerable to the common exploits used by attackers.

Expect Your HIPS to Come Under Attack

The popularity of HIPS software has started to get the attention of the attacker community, looking for ways to circumvent this technology. Some groups are focusing their attention on attacking the management station and disabling HIPS software on clients throughout the organization centrally. Other groups are looking at how HIPS software examines system calls, and how the process might be circumvented. Because malware has been released into the wild that disables antivirus software and/or personal firewalls, you should expect attacks against the HIPS itself. To date, there have not been any public exploits or security advisories for HIPS software, but attackers will continue to research, looking for weaknesses in these tools and ways they can be exploited.

Summary

Marketing buzzwords are commonplace in the IPS field, and each vendor has a different opinion about what these buzzwords actually represent. This chapter has illustrated two major classifications of intrusion prevention products: host based and network based. Network-based IPS can be classified as external NIPS (point-defense devices that you put in front of an object you want to protect) and switch NIPS (devices you plug your network, or part of your network, in to).

External NIPS are primarily iterative improvements to firewalls or IDS systems. Firewall vendors are adopting additional intelligence in their products to stop attacks as they traverse the network for network-based IPS. A similar method of inline NIPS is to deploy a "switch-like" device between public and private networks that uses stateful packet inspection and IDS techniques to examine and drop malicious traffic. NIPS devices must be able to process traffic at high speeds with low latency while minimizing false negatives and eliminating false positives. False positives and dropped traffic by the NIPS results in a denial of service to your organization.

Antivirus vendors are adding more IPS protection to their host-based products by expanding their detection of malware and integrating the defensive tools from firewall software. Because they are masters of the art of OS calls, these vendors are well positioned to create HIPS products.

Other IDS vendors are developing personal firewalls and host-based IPS tools that combine system call interception, file-change monitoring, network monitoring, and application behavior analysis to detect known and unknown attacks. These tools have proved beneficial for many organizations, lengthening the window of opportunity for the deployment of software updates to resolve application and operating system vulnerabilities.

Finally, it is important to remember that IPS technology can only be fully utilized when it is used by trained analysts who clearly understand the technology's advantages and limitations. IPS is not a replacement for defense in depth, but it is a good way to strengthen the security posture of your organization.

III

Designing a Secure
Network Perimeter

12

Fundamentals of Secure
Perimeter Design

IF YOU ARE NOT CURRENTLY THE LEAD DESIGNER for your organization, we suspect that becoming one is one of your goals. You might be laying out a network from scratch, assessing the strength of an existing infrastructure, determining where to place a new security device, or deciding whether to deploy one at all. You know of many defense components you could incorporate into your security infrastructure, and you know of countless ways of arranging them. This chapter concentrates on the do's and don'ts of security perimeter design and covers some of the more common scenarios.

Before jumping into a design session, you need to have the right tools for making design-related decisions. In the world of network security architecture, these tools are bits of information about your environment and your business goals. You need to figure out the following:

- What resources need to be protected
- Who you are protecting against
- What your business needs and constraints are

In this chapter, we review the factors you need to consider when designing the network's perimeter. We analyze several building blocks that are useful for crafting more complex architectures. These scenarios will incorporate firewalls, routers, and VPN devices in various permutations.

Deciding on a particular defense architecture is a rewarding and complicated task that requires making tough choices in the world where functionality and security are often at odds with each other. It is understandable to want to delay making such decisions as long as possible. After all, it is easier to avoid confrontation than fight an uphill battle for budget and resources. Making security design decisions involves resolving conflicts that incorporate many aspects of the network and application infrastructure, such as usability, reliability, manageability, and cost. Principles that are presented in this chapter are meant to help you make hard decisions early in the process of setting up a security perimeter; that way, you can save sleep, time, and money in the implementation and maintenance phases of your deployment.

> **Tip**
>
> The later you make a decision that modifies your design, the harder it is to properly implement the change. You should put extraordinary effort into the design phases of your engagement to minimize the chance of making significant changes later in the process.

Gathering Design Requirements

Whether you are designing a new network or working with an existing infrastructure, it helps to treat components and requirements of your environment as elements of a unified perimeter security architecture. Doing so allows you to identify scenarios in which devices might be configured in an inconsistent or even conflicting manner, and lets you tune the design to match your needs. Based on specifics of your environment, you will decide, for instance, whether a single packet-filtering router on the edge of your network will provide sufficient protection, or whether you need to invest in multiple firewalls, set up one behind another, to properly segment your network. A good place to start designing your perimeter architecture is determining which resources need to be protected.

Determining Which Resources to Protect

In the realm of network security, we focus on ensuring confidentiality, integrity, and availability of information. However, the notion of information is too general and does not really help to make decisions that account for specifics in a particular situation. For some organizations, the information that needs to be protected is credit card and demographics data; for others, it might be legal agreements and client lists. Information can also take the form of application logic, especially for websites that rely on dynamically generated content. To decide what kind of network perimeter will offer adequate protection for your data, you need to look at where the information is stored and how it is accessed.

Servers

Modern computing environments tend to aggregate information on servers. This makes a lot of sense because it is much easier to keep an eye on data that is stored centrally; some of the problems plaguing peer-to-peer file-sharing systems such as Kazaa demonstrate difficulties in providing reliable access to information that is spread across many machines. Because all of us face limitations of overworked administrators and analysts, we often benefit from minimizing the number of resources that need to be set up, monitored, and secured.

The Case of the Missing Server

InformationWeek once published a story about a missing server that had been running without problems for four years. System administrators, unaware of the server's whereabouts, had to resort to manually tracing the network cable until it led them to a wall. Apparently, "the server had been mistakenly sealed behind drywall by maintenance workers."[1] (Alas, some claim that this is just an urban legend,[2] but there is some truth to all tales.) Do you know where your servers are?

Make sure you know what servers exist on your network, where they are located, what their network parameters are, and what operating systems, applications, and patches are installed. If you have sufficient spending power, you might consider taking advantage of enterprise system management software such as HP OpenView, Microsoft Systems Management Server (SMS), and CA Unicenter to help you with this task.

If the infrastructure you are protecting is hosting multitier applications, you need to understand the role of each tier, typically represented by web, middleware, and database servers, and their relationship to each other. In addition to documenting technical specifications for the server and its software, be sure to record contact information of the person who is responsible for the business task that the system is performing. You will probably need to contact him when responding to an incident associated with this system.

Workstations

End-user workstations serve as an interface between the technical infrastructure that powers the computing environment and the people who actually make the business run. No matter how tightly you might want to configure the network's perimeter, you need to let some traffic through so that these people can utilize resources on the Internet and function effectively in our web-dependent age. To create a perimeter architecture that adequately protects the organization while letting people do their work, you need to make sure that the design reflects the way in which the workstations are used and configured.

For example, if your Windows XP workstations never need to connect to Windows servers outside the organization's perimeter, you should be able to block outbound Server Message Block (SMB) traffic without further considerations. On the other hand, if your users need to access shares of a Windows server over the Internet, you should probably consider deploying a VPN link across the two sites.

Similarly, evaluating the likelihood that your system administrators will routinely patch the workstations might help you decide whether to segment your environment with internal firewalls. Organizations that can efficiently distribute OS and application updates to users' systems are less likely to be affected by an attacker gaining access to a workstation and then attacking other internal systems. At the same time, if the centralized control channel is compromised in this configuration, the attack could affect many systems.

When examining your workstations, look at the kind of applications and operating systems they are running and how patched they are. Is data stored only on your servers, or do users keep files on their desktops? Don't forget to take into consideration personal digital assistant (PDA) devices; corporate users don't hesitate to store sensitive information on their Palms, BlackBerries, Pocket PCs, and smartphones. You also need to make special provisions for traveling and telecommuting users; by going outside of your core network, telecommuters will unknowingly expand your defense perimeter.

Networking Gear

Bridges, switches, and routers interconnect your computing resources and link you to partners and customers. In earlier chapters, we talked about the role of the router and explained the need to secure its configuration. Modern high-end switches offer configuration complexities that often rival those of routers, and they should be secured in a similar manner. Moreover, Virtual LAN (VLAN) capabilities of such switches might require special considerations to make sure attackers cannot hop across VLANs by crafting specially tagged Ethernet frames.

> **Note**
> Is this process beginning to look like an audit of your environment? In many respects, it is. Given budget and time limitations, you need to know what you are protecting to determine how to best allocate your resources.

Make sure you know what devices are deployed on your network, what function they serve, and how they are configured. Hopefully, you will not keep finding devices you did not think existed on the network. It is not uncommon to see an organization with "legacy" systems that were set up by people who are long gone and that everyone is afraid to touch for fear of disrupting an existing process. Be mindful of network devices that terminate private or VPN connections to your customers or partners inside your network. You need to evaluate your level of trust with the third party on the other end of the link to determine the impact of such a device on your network's perimeter.

Modems

When looking for possible entry points into your network, don't forget about modems that might be connecting your servers or workstations to phone lines. Modems offer the attacker a chance to go around the border firewall, which is why many organizations are banishing modems from internal desktops in favor of VPN connections or centralized dial-out modem banks that desktops access over TCP/IP. With the increasing popularity of VPNs, the need to connect to the office over the phone is gradually decreasing. Yet it is common to find a rogue desktop running a remote control application such as pcAnywhere or Remote Desktop over a phone line.

Sometimes, a business need mandates having active modems on the network, and your security policy should thoroughly address how they should and should not be used. For example, modems that accept inbound connections might need to be installed in data centers to allow administrators out-of-band access to the environment. In such cases, your security architecture should take into account the possibility that the modem might provide backdoor access to your network. To mitigate this risk, pay attention to host hardening, consider deploying internal firewalls, and look into installing hardware authentication devices for controlling access to the modems. (Such devices are relatively inexpensive and block calls that do not present a proper authentication "key.")

Controlling Modem Connections

Several vendors offer devices that control access to telephone lines in a manner reminiscent of traditional firewalls. Instead of keeping track of protocols and IP addresses, telephone firewalls look at call type (voice, data, or fax) and phone numbers to determine whether to let the call through. Products in this category may also allow administrators to automatically disconnect workstations from the LAN when they establish modem connections. Examples of such products are SecureLogix TeleWall (http://www.securelogix.com) and CPS Basic Mini Firewall (http://www.cpscom.com).

Other Devices

When looking for devices that can be used to store sensitive data or provide access to information, private branch exchange (PBX) systems often slip people's minds. However, even back in the era when voice communications were completely out of band with IP networks, attackers knew to tap into organizations' voice mail systems over the phone, fishing for information and setting up unauthorized conference calls and mail boxes. With the growing popularity of IP-based telephony systems, the distinction between voice and data is beginning to fade. For instance, in a hybrid system offered by ShoreTel, traditional analog phones are employed, but the dialing process can be controlled using a desktop agent over TCP/IP, and voice mail messages are stored as .wav files on a Windows-based server.

Tip

If it can be accessed over the network, it should be accounted for in the design of the perimeter.

Don't forget to consider other devices that comprise your computing infrastructure, such as modern printers and copiers. Manufacturers of these systems often embed advanced services into these devices to ease management without regard for security. Don't be surprised if your Sharp AR-507 digital copier comes with built-in FTP, Telnet, SNMP, and HTTP servers, all with highly questionable authentication schemes.[3]

Indeed, modern networks are heterogeneous and support communications among a wide range of resources. We need to understand what servers, workstations, and various network-aware devices exist on the network to determine what defenses will provide us with adequate protection. Another factor that contributes toward a properly designed security architecture is the nature of threats we face. Potential attackers who could be viewed as a threat by one organization might not be of much significance to another. The next section is devoted to determining who it is we are protecting ourselves from, and it's meant to help you assess the threat level that is appropriate for your organization.

Determining Who the Potential Attackers Are

We think we know who our enemy is. We're fighting the bad guys, right? The perception of who is attacking Internet-based sites changes with time. Sometimes we look for attackers who are specifically targeting our sites, from inside as well as outside, to get at sensitive information. In other situations, we feel inundated with "script kiddy" scans where relatively inexperienced attackers are running canned scripts in an attempt to reach the "low hanging fruit" on the network. Lately, automated agents such as remote-controlled Trojans, bots, and worms have been making rounds and threatening our resources in new and imaginative ways that we will discuss in this section.

In reality, only you can decide what kind of attacker poses the greatest threat to your organization. Your decision will depend on the nature of your business, the habits and requirements of your users, and the value of the information stored on your systems.

Each category of attacker brings its own nuances to the design of the network's defenses. When operating under budget constraints, you will find yourself assigning priority to some components of your security infrastructure over others based on the perceived threat from attackers that worry you the most.

Determined Outsider

Why would anyone be targeting your network specifically? Presumably, you have something that the attacker wants, and in the world of computer security, your crown jewels tend to take the form of information. A determined outsider might be looking for ways to steal credit card numbers or other sensitive account information about your customers, obtain products at a cost different from what you are offering them for, or render your site useless by denying service to your legitimate customers. The threat of a denial of service (DoS) attack is especially high for companies with relatively high profiles.

An Attack on Authorize.Net

Authorize.Net, a popular Internet payment processing company, fell victim to a distributed denial of service (DDoS) attack in September 2004. The attack, which began after the company refused to meet extortion demands, led to service disruptions to approximately 90,000 of its customers. Roy Banks, the company's general manager, admitted that they were caught off guard by this attack. "We've invested heavily in defense, and we thought we were prepared," he said. "But the nature of this attack was something we had never experienced."[4] When planning your defense infrastructure, be sure to consider all attack vectors that may influence the availability of your service.

If your organization provides services accessible over the Internet, a determined outsider might be interested in obtaining unauthorized access to such services, instead of specifically targeting your information. In some cases, you might be concerned with corporate espionage, where your competitors would be attempting to obtain your trade secrets, important announcements that have not been released, your client lists, or your intellectual property. Such an attack is likely to have significant financing, and might even incorporate the help of an insider.

The difficulty of protecting against a determined outsider is that you have to assume that with sufficient money and time to spare, the attacker will be able to penetrate your defenses or cause significant service disruptions. To counteract such a threat, you need to estimate how much the potential attacker is likely to spend trying to penetrate your defenses, and build your perimeter with this threat profile in mind. Additionally, intrusion detection presents one of the most effective ways of protecting against a determined attacker because it offers a chance to discover an attack in its reconnaissance state, before it escalates into a critical incident. A properly configured intrusion detection system (IDS) also helps to determine the circumstances of an incident if an attacker succeeds at moving beyond the reconnaissance state.

Determined Insider

The threat of a determined insider is often difficult to counteract, partly because it is hard to admit that a person who is working for the organization might want to participate in malicious activity. Nonetheless, many high-profile criminal cases involve a person attacking the organization's systems from the inside. With a wave of layoffs hitting companies during economic downturns, disgruntled ex-employees have been causing something of a stir at companies that have not recognized this as a potential risk.

Insiders at Cisco

On August 20, 2001, two former Cisco accountants admitted to exploiting an internal "Sabrina" system, used by the company to manage stock options, to illegally issue themselves almost $8 million of Cisco shares. They used access to the system to "identify control numbers to track unauthorized stock option disbursals, created forged forms purporting to authorize disbursals of stock," and "directed that stock be placed in their personal brokerage accounts."[5]

The insider does not need to penetrate your external defense layers to get access to potentially sensitive systems. This makes a case for deploying internal firewalls in front of the more sensitive areas of your network, tightening configurations of corporate file and development servers, limiting access to files, and employing internal intrusion detection sensors. Note that because an internal attacker often knows your environment, it is much harder to detect an insider attack early on, as opposed to an attack from the outside.

Even without getting into the argument of whether insider attacks are more popular than the ones coming from the outside, the ability of an internal attacker to potentially have easy and unrestricted access to sensitive data makes this a threat not to be taken lightly.

Script Kiddy

The term *script kiddy* is at times controversial due to its derogatory nature. It typically refers to a relatively unsophisticated attacker who does not craft custom tools or techniques, but instead relies on easy-to-find scripts that exploit common vulnerabilities in Internet-based systems. In this case, the attacker is not targeting your organization specifically, but is sweeping through a large number of IP addresses in hopes of finding systems that are vulnerable to published exploits or that have a well-known backdoor already installed.

Scanning for SubSeven

In 2001, SubSeven was one of the most popularly probed for Trojan horse programs on the Internet. Knowing that SubSeven often listened on TCP port 27374 by default, attackers who were looking for easily exploitable computers scanned blocks of IP addresses in hopes of finding a computer with an already-installed instance of SubSeven. The scanning tool then tried to authenticate to the Trojan using common backdoor passwords built in to SubSeven. After the attacker was authenticated, he had virtually unrestricted access to the victim's system.

The nature of script kiddy attacks suggests that the most effective way of defending against them involves keeping your system's patches up to date, closing major holes in network and host configurations, and preventing Trojans from infecting your internal systems.

A hybrid variant of the "script kiddy" attack might incorporate some of the elements of a determined outsider threat and would involve an initial sweep across many network nodes from the outside. This activity would then be followed up by a set of scripted attacks against systems found to be vulnerable to canned exploits. In such scenarios, IDSs are often effective at alerting administrators when the initial exploratory phrase of the attack begins.

In one example of a hybrid script kiddy attack, Raphael Gray (a.k.a. "Curador") harvested tens of thousands of credit card numbers in 2000. He started the attack by using a search engine to locate potentially vulnerable commerce sites and then exploited a known vulnerability to gain unauthorized access to those sites. Referring to the attack, Raphael said, "A lot of crackers don't like what I did. They consider me to be a script kiddy, someone who can't program in any language, because I used an old exploit instead of creating a new one. But I've been programming since I was 11."[6] By the way, one of the credit card numbers Ralph obtained belonged to Bill Gates.

Automated Malicious Agents

The beginning of the century shifted the spotlight away from attacks performed directly by humans to those that were automated through the use of malicious agents. Fast-spreading worms such as Code Red and Nimda demonstrated the speed with which malicious software can infect systems throughout the Internet and our inability to analyze and respond to these threats early in the propagation process. By the time we had detected and analyzed the Nimda worm, it had infected an enormous number of personal and corporate systems. Persistent worms such as Beagle and NetSky have demonstrated the difficulty of eliminating worm infections on the Internet scale, even after they have exhibited their presence for months. The "success" of Beagle and NetSky is, in part, due to their email-based propagation mechanisms, which allowed malicious code to slip through many perimeter defenses.

Worms and Script Kiddies

The Nimda worm had several propagation vectors that allowed it to spread across a large portion of the Internet in a matter of hours. One such mechanism allowed the worm to scan Internet hosts for vulnerable IIS servers and infect machines it came across.

This technique closely resembles actions of a script kiddy because the worm was preprogrammed to scan for several well-known exploits and backdoors. The advantage that the worm had over a script kiddy is that by infecting a corporate system via one vector, it could continue spreading internally to hosts that were not accessible from the outside.

Maintaining a perimeter that is resilient against worm-based attacks requires keeping abreast of the latest vulnerabilities and applying patches as soon as they are released. To further limit the scope of the agent's potential influence, you should consider segmenting your infrastructure based on varying degrees of security levels of your resources. Antivirus products can also be quite effective at dampening the spread of malicious programs, but they are limited by their ability to recognize new malicious code. Unfortunately, as we have learned from the past worm experiences, virus pattern updates might not be released in time to prevent rapid infection of vulnerable systems.

Defining Your Business Requirements

When designing the perimeter defense infrastructure, we need to keep in mind that the purpose of addressing information security issues is to keep the business running. Considering that security is a means, not an end. The design must accommodate factors such as services provided to your users or customers, fault tolerance requirements, performance expectations, and budget constraints.

Cost

Cost is an ever-present factor in security-related decisions. How much are you willing to spend to protect yourself against a threat of an attack or to eliminate a single point of failure? For instance, SANS Institute spent three months and significant resources putting all their servers in a highly secure Network Operations Center (NOC). Then when the Code Red worm hit, they experienced 50 times more traffic in 24 hours than during any previous peak. They were secure against intrusions, but the architecture became a single point of failure.

How much should you spend? As we discussed earlier, this depends on the perceived value both for access and control of the resources you are protecting. Making informed choices regarding the need to spend less on one component of a defense infrastructure allows us to spend more on another layer that might require additional funding. When looking at the cost of a security component, we should examine the following cost factors:

- Initial hardware
- Initial software

- Initial deployment (time to deploy)
- Annual software support and updates
- Maintenance and monitoring of the component

Cost and Risk Mitigation

When considering whether to invest in a set of intrusion detection sensors at a relatively large organization, I had to present a detailed cost analysis report that included all factors outlined in the preceding list. Each sensor cost around $9,000 to obtain (software and hardware), $5,400 to deploy (let's say three days of work at the rate of $1,800 per day), and $2,000 per year for technical support and software upgrades. I also had to take into account the cost of having the device monitored and supported by in-house or outsourced analysts. Associating specific numbers with risk mitigation options allowed us to make an informed decision regarding our ability to purchase the IDS.

When calculating the cost of adding a perimeter security component, you might conclude that mitigating the risk that it would protect you against is not worth the money it would cost to deploy and maintain it. In that case, you might consider employing a less thorough but more affordable solution. For example, alternatives for purchasing a relatively expensive commercial IDS product might include obtaining open source packages such as Snort, an outsourced security monitoring solution, or an additional firewall. (An additional firewall might mitigate the same risk in a less expensive manner, depending on your environment.) Even when using "free" software such as Snort or an academic version of Tripwire, be sure to take into account the cost of the administrator's time that will be spent installing and maintaining the new system.

Business-Related Services

Of course, when setting up your network's perimeter, you need to know what services have to be provided to your users and customers. In a typical business, you will probably want to block all nonessential services at the network's border. In a university, you might find that unrestricted access is one of the "services" provided to the university's users. In that case, you will probably be unable to block traffic by default; instead, you will filter out only traffic that is most likely to threaten your environment.

Protecting your resources against threats that come through a channel that needs to be open for business use is not easy. For instance, if you decide to allow ICMP through your network for network troubleshooting purposes and are fighting an ICMP flood attack, blocking ICMP traffic at your ISP's upstream routers is likely to free up some bandwidth for services that absolutely must be accessible. If, on the other hand, you are being flooded with SYN packets or HTTP requests targeting TCP port 80 and you are a web-based e-commerce site, asking the ISP to block this traffic at their routers is probably not an option. (You can try blocking traffic from specific sources, but in a DDoS attack, you might have a hard time compiling a complete list of all attacking addresses.) Only a defense-in-depth architecture has a chance of protecting you from attacks that might come through legitimately open channels.

Performance

When analyzing your business requirements, you need to look at the expected performance levels for the site that are protected by the security infrastructure. As we add layers to perimeter defense, we are likely to impact the latency of packets because they might be traversing through multiple filtering engines, sanity checks, and encryption mechanisms. If performance is a serious consideration for your business, you might be able to justify spending money on equipment upgrades so that the impact of additional security layers is minimized. Alternatively, you might decide that your business hinges on fast response times and that your budget does not allow you to provision appropriately performing security hardware or software. In the latter case, you might need to accept the risk of decreased security for the sake of performance.

Establishing performance expectations in the design phase of your deployment, before the actual implementation takes place, is a difficult but necessary task. Indeed, it's often hard to estimate how much burden an IPSec encryption tunnel will put on your router, or how many milliseconds will be added to the response time if a proxy server is in place, instead of a stateful firewall. If your design goes over the top with the computing power required to provide adequate performance, you might not have much money left to keep the system (or the business) running. At the same time, not allocating proper resources to the system early on might require you to purchase costly upgrades later.

Inline Security Devices

Consider the architecture that incorporates multiple inline firewalls located one behind another. For a request to propagate to the server located the farthest from the Internet, the request might need to pass through the border router and several firewalls. Along the packet's path, each security enforcement device will need to make a decision about whether the packet should be allowed through. In some cases, you might decide that the security gained from such a configuration is not worth the performance loss. In others, you might be willing to accept the delay in response to achieve the level of security that is appropriate for your enterprise. Or you might devise alternative solutions, such as employing a single firewall, to provide you with a sufficient comfort level without employing inline firewalls.

The Use of Encryption

Other significant effects on performance are associated with the use of encryption due to the strain placed on the CPU of the device that needs to encrypt or decrypt data. You might be familiar with SSL and IPSec accelerator cards or devices that you can employ to transfer the encryption duties to a processor that is dedicated and optimized for such tasks. These devices are not cheap, and the business decision to purchase them must take into account the need to provide encryption, the desired performance, and the cost of purchasing the accelerators.

For example, most online banking applications require the use of SSL encryption to protect sensitive data as it travels between the user's browser and the bank's server. Usually, all aspects of the user's interaction with the banking application are encrypted,

presumably because the bank was able to justify the expense of purchasing the computing power to support SSL. Cost is a significant factor here because you need to spend
money on SSL accelerators to achieve the desired performance.

At the same time, you will probably notice that SSL encryption is not used when
browsing through the bank's public website. This is probably because the information
provided on the public site is not deemed to be sensitive enough to justify the use of
encryption.

Detailed Logging

Among other considerations relating to the site's performance is the system's ability to
handle large amounts of log data. Availability of detailed logs is important for performing
anomaly detection, as well as for tuning the system's performance parameters. At the
same time, enabling verbose logging might inundate a machine's I/O subsystem and
quickly fill up the file system. Similarly, you must balance the desire to capture detailed
log information with the amount of network bandwidth that will be consumed by logs
if you transport them to a centralized log archival system. This is an especially significant
issue for situations in which you need to routinely send log data across relatively slow
wide area network (WAN) links.

Fault Tolerance

The amount of fault tolerance that should be built in to your environment depends on
the nature of your business. The reason we discuss fault tolerance in an information
security book is because eliminating single points of failure is a complex task that strongly impacts the architecture of your network.

When designing fault tolerance of the infrastructure, you need to look at the configuration of individual systems, consider the ways in which these systems interact with each
other within the site, and, perhaps, offer geographic redundancy to your users.

Intrasystem Redundancy

Looking at a single machine, you examine its disk subsystem, number of processors,
redundancy of system boards and power supplies, and so on. You need to decide how
much you are willing to pay for the hardware such that if a disk or a system board fails,
the machine will continue to function. You will then weigh that amount against the likelihood this will happen and the extent of damage it will cause.

You might also ask yourself what the consequences will be of a critical process on
that system failing, and what is involved in mitigating that risk. The answer might be
monitoring the state of that process so that it is automatically restarted if it dies.
Alternatively, you might consider running a program that duplicates the tasks of the
process; for instance, you might want to run both LogSentry and Swatch to monitor
your log files. Keep in mind that many applications were not designed to share the host
with multiple instances of themselves. Moreover, running multiple instances of the application on the same system does not help when the host fails and eliminates all processes
that were supposed to offer redundancy. When running a duplicate process on the same

host is not appropriate or sufficient, look into duplicating the whole system to achieve the desired level of redundancy.

Intrasite Redundancy

Redundant components that are meant to fulfill the same business need are usually considered to be operating in a cluster. We might set up such clusters using hardware and software techniques for the most important systems in the environment, such as the database servers. Similarly, network and security devices can operate in a cluster, independently of how other components of your infrastructure are set up.

If a clustered component is actively performing its tasks, it is considered to be active; if the component is ready to take on the responsibility but is currently dormant, it is considered to be passive. Clusters in which all components are active at the same time provide a level of load balancing and offer performance improvements, albeit at a significant cost. For the purpose of achieving intrasite redundancy, it is often sufficient to deploy active-passive clusters where only a single component is active at one time.

Redundancy of the network is a significant aspect of intrasite redundancy. For example, if Internet connectivity is very important to your business, you may need to provision multiple lines linking the network to the Internet, possibly from different access providers. You may also decide to cluster border routers to help ensure that failure of one will not impact your connection to the Internet. Cisco routers usually accomplish this through the use of the Hot Standby Router Protocol (HSRP). With HSRP, multiple routers appear as a single "virtual" router.

Firewall Redundancy   Many commercial firewall and VPN products also provide clustering mechanisms that you can use to introduce high availability to that aspect of your perimeter, should your business justify the added cost. Check Point, for example, offers the ClusterXL add-on to provide automated failover and load-balancing services for its FireWall-1/VPN-1 products. A popular third-party solution for Check Point's products that achieves similar results is StoneBeat FullCluster. Nokia firewall/VPN appliances also offer their own failover and load-balancing solutions. Cisco PIX clusters can also ensure high availability of the firewall configuration, as well as active-active load-balancing clusters.

> **Note**
>
> When researching firewall clustering solutions, keep in mind the difference between technologies that provide failover and load-balancing capabilities, and those that only support failover. Failover mechanisms ensure high availability of the configuration, but they do not necessarily focus on improving its performance through load balancing.

For stateful firewalls to function as part of a unified cluster, one of the following needs to take place:

- Clustered devices need to share state table information.
- Packets that are part of the same network session need to flow through the same device.

If one of these requirements is not met, a stateful communication session may be interrupted by a firewall device that doesn't recognize a packet as belonging to an active session. Modern firewall clustering methods typically operate by sharing the state table between cluster members. This setup allows stateful failover to occur—if one of the clustered devices fails, the other will be able to process existing sessions without an interruption. Let's take a closer look at why sharing state information is vital to a firewall cluster.

Consider a situation where two FireWall-1 devices, set up as an active-active ClusterXL cluster, are processing an FTP connection. The cluster member the communication traveled through initially preserves FTP transaction information in its state table. Because ClusterXL can share state table information across the cluster, even if the returning FTP data channel connection came through the other cluster member, it would be processed correctly—the device would compare the connection to the state able, recognize that it is part of an active session, and allow it to pass. This process functions similarly in an active-passive cluster failover. When the formerly passive firewall receives the communication that is part of an active session, it can process this communication as if it was the cluster member that originally handled the session.

Another way to support stateful failover with redundant firewalls is to ensure that a given network session always goes through the same device in a pair of firewalls that are independent of each other, but act as if they are in a cluster. Before products that allow state table sharing were available, the only way to achieve redundancy with two active firewalls was to create a "firewall sandwich.," which refers to a design where two independent firewall devices are sandwiched between two sets of load balancers. In this case, the load balancers are responsible for making sure that a single session always flows through the same firewall device.

Whether you're using a firewall sandwich or a firewall solution that allows the sharing of state information, firewall redundancy is an important way to ensure availability in highly critical network environments.

Switch Redundancy   When planning for intrasite redundancy, also consider how the availability of your systems will be impacted if one of the internal switches goes down. Some organizations address this risk by purchasing a standby switch that they can use to manually replace the failed device. If the delay to perform this manually is too costly for your business, you may decide to invest in an automatic failover mechanism. High-end Cisco switches such as the Catalyst 6500 series can help to achieve redundancy in the switching fabric, although at a significant expense. They can be set up with redundant power supplies and supervisor modules, which provide the intelligence for the switch, in a single chassis.

For additional switch redundancy, consider adding an extra switch chassis to the design. In this scenario, the switches can be interconnected using trunks, and the hosts can be connected to both switches using *network card teaming*, a function of the network card software that allows several network cards to be virtually "linked" so that if one of the cards fails, the other can seamlessly take over communications. With each of the teamed network cards connected to one of the clustered switches, multiple failures need to occur to cause a connectivity outage. Clustering switches in this manner is a strong precautionary measure that may be appropriate for mission-critical infrastructure components.

Geographic Redundancy

Sometimes, achieving intrasite redundancy is not sufficient to mitigate risks of system unavailability. For example, a well-tuned DoS attack against a border's routers or the ISP's network equipment might not allow legitimate traffic to the site. Additionally, a disaster might affect the building where the systems are residing, damaging or temporarily disabling the equipment. To mitigate such risks, consider creating a copy of your data center in a geographically distinct location.

Much like clusters, the secondary data center could be always active, sharing the load with the primary site. Alternatively, it could be passive, activated either manually or automatically when it is needed. In addition to considering the costs associated with setting up the secondary data center, also look at the administrative efforts involved in supporting and monitoring additional systems. You might also need to accommodate data sharing between the two sites so that users have access to the same information no matter which site services their requests.

Design Elements for Perimeter Security

One of the reasons we have so many choices when architecting network perimeter defense is because resources differ in the sensitivity of their information and the likelihood that they will be successfully exploited. For example, a web server running Apache and hosting static HTML pages is generally subject to fewer risk factors than an Oracle database storing order information for the organization's customers.

> **Risk Versus Vulnerability**
>
> Risk that is associated with an event is a function of how likely an event is to occur and the extent of the damage it can cause. Vulnerability refers to the likelihood that the resource can be compromised. Risk takes into account vulnerability as well as the importance of the resource in question. Thus, a resource can be vulnerable but not risky if little is at stake.[7]

In a world where we are free to permute security components in any imaginable manner, some design elements are seen more often than others. We cover some of the more basic patterns here to put you in the right frame of mind, and we discuss more specialized architectures in subsequent chapters.

Firewall and Router

The firewall and the router are two of the most common perimeter security components. In Parts I and II of this book, we described different types of these devices and explained what roles they play in defending the network. In this section, we concentrate on the relationship between the router and the firewall and go over several configurations you are likely to encounter when setting up and securing your network.

Figure 12.1 illustrates one of the most common ways to deploy a router and a firewall together. The Corporate Subnet hosts "private" systems used by the organization's internal users, and the Screened Subnet hosts "public" servers that need to be accessible from the Internet. In this scenario, no internal server can be accessed from the Internet; for example, instead of opening TCP port 25 on the firewall to the internal mail server, we route SMTP traffic through mail relay that is hosted in the Screened Subnet.

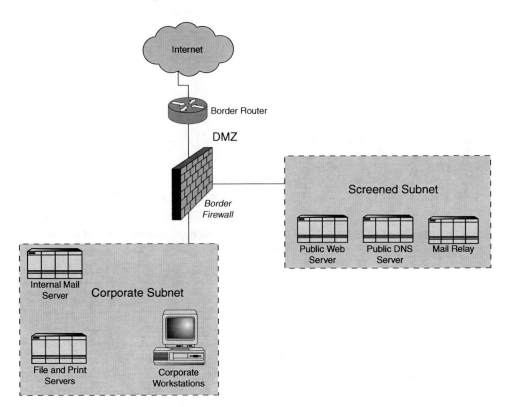

Figure 12.1 Deploy a router with a firewall behind it.

Basic Filtering

In the configuration described previously, the router is responsible for performing the routing functions it was designed for—it links the site to the Internet. It often makes sense to use the router's packet-filtering capabilities to filter out some of the "noise" that we might not care to see in the firewall's logs or that we want to stop at the very edge of the network. We described a similar setup in Chapter 2, "Packet Filtering," and Chapter 6, "The Role of a Router," where the router was configured to perform basic egress and ingress filtering as well as to disable dangerous routing options, control the flow of ICMP messages in and out of our network, and so on.

Generally, we do not want to block too much at the router because in this configuration, most of the monitoring efforts will be focused on the firewall. By blocking the majority of network traffic at the router, we might not have a complete view of the denied packets in the firewall's logs, and correlating events that are logged at the router and the firewall might be too draining for many organizations.

Access Control

In the scenario described previously, the firewall has primary access control responsibilities. This is where we will implement the policy of blocking all traffic by default and explicitly allowing only those protocols our business requires. In this case, the firewall becomes the manifestation of the business rules the security policy defines. By this point of the design, you should have a good understanding of what your business needs are (see the first half of this chapter if you are not sure), so implementing the firewall rule set should not be too daunting of a task.

> **Note**
>
> Even if your hosts are located in a screened subnet behind a firewall, they should be hardened to withstand attacks that the firewall might let through or that might be launched if the firewall is bypassed. The extent to which you need to tighten the systems' configuration depends on the sensitivity of their data and the likelihood that they will be compromised.

Note that in some cases, placing systems onto the Screened Subnet might not be appropriate. Perhaps this is because the firewall is too much of a bottleneck, or because the system is not trusted to be located on the same subnet as the servers in the Screened Subnet. In this case, you might consider placing this system into the DMZ, between the border router and the firewall. You will need to use the router's packet-filtering capabilities to control access to this system from the Internet. You will also need to configure the firewall to regulate communications between this system and the Corporate Subnet.

Router Under the ISP's Control

ISPs can provide you with an Ethernet connection to their networking equipment, eliminating the need to set up your own border router, but not giving you control over how their router is maintained and configured. You would then typically place your firewall behind the ISP's router. In some respects, this simplifies the task of setting up and administering your network because you have to maintain one fewer component. At the same time, you cannot trust that the ISP configured the router in the same way you would have configured it.

> **Note**
>
> Lack of control over the border router might conflict with the business requirements of your organization. In such cases, you might need to devise technical solutions or make business arrangements that give you greater control over the router's configuration.

This architecture is not very different from the one discussed previously. Not having control over the router simply means that you might not have the level of defense in depth you could have had if you had tightened the router's configuration yourself.

One of the major limitations of such a configuration could be lack of detailed information about blocked traffic. If the ISP relies on the router to block unwanted traffic, your firewall never gets a chance to log it. If this is the case, consider asking your ISP to relax access control restrictions that the router enforces or to share the router's logs with you.

Router Without the Firewall

In Chapter 6, we presented the configuration in which the border router was the only device that separated the internal network from the Internet. With firewalls becoming a staple of security best practices, this design is becoming less and less common. However, it might still be appropriate for organizations that decide that risks associated with the lack of the firewall are acceptable to their business. When properly configured, routers can be quite effective at blocking unwanted traffic, especially if they implement reflexive access lists or if they use the firewall feature set built in to high-end routers.

It is common to find routers at various other points on the internal network, not just at the border of the perimeter. After all, the router's primary purpose is to connect networks, and a company might need to connect to networks other than the Internet. For instance, if your organization has several geographically distinct sites, you will use routers to connect them. In such cases, the routers will probably be decoupled from the firewall.

Even when you are using routers with private WAN connections, such as T1s or frame relay links, lock down the devices, tightening their configuration by disabling unnecessary services and setting up required access control lists. This approach is compatible with the defense-in-depth methodology we've been discussing, and it helps protect the network against a multitude of threats we might not be aware of yet.

Firewall and VPN

Firewalls and VPNs are often discussed in the same context. Firewalls are generally responsible for controlling access to resources, and VPN devices are responsible for securing communication links between hosts or networks. Examining how VPNs interact with firewalls is important for several reasons:

- Network Address Translation (NAT) might be incompatible with some VPN implementations, depending on your network's architecture.
- VPNs might create tunnels through your perimeter that make it difficult for the firewall to enforce access restrictions on encrypted traffic.

- VPN endpoints have access to data in clear text because VPN devices are the ones that decrypt or authenticate it; this might warrant special considerations for protecting the VPN device.
- VPNs, by protecting confidentiality of the encrypted data, can be used to pass by IDSs undetected.

When deciding how to incorporate a VPN component into the network architecture, we have two high-level choices: maintaining the VPN module as its own device, external to the firewall, and integrating the VPN with the firewall so that both services are provided by the same system. Each approach has its intricacies, strengths, and weaknesses. We will present the general overview here, leaving a detailed discussion of VPN integration for Chapter 16, "VPN Integration."

Firewall with VPN as External Device

Many design choices allow us to set up a VPN endpoint as a device that is external to the firewall. Some of the placement options for VPN hardware include these:

- In the DMZ, between the firewall and the border router
- In the screened subnet, off the firewall's third network interface card
- On the internal network, behind the firewall
- In parallel with the firewall at the entry point to the internal network

NAT is the cause of some of the most frequently occurring problems when VPN equipment is deployed separately from the firewall. For example, outbound packets that pass through the VPN device before being NATed by the firewall might not pass the integrity check at the other end of the VPN connection if an authentication scheme is being used, such as IPSec's Authentication Header (AH). This is because AH takes into account the packet's headers when it calculates the message digest signature for the packet. Then the NAT device modifies the source address of the packet, causing the message digest verification to fail on the other end of the VPN connection.

Another issue with VPN devices located behind the firewall is address management; some VPN specifications require VPN devices to be assigned a legal IP address. For example, when authenticating VPN devices using X.509 certificates, the IKE phase of IPSec might fail if the certificates were bound to each gateway's IP addresses, which were then rewritten by NAT.[8]

Placing VPN hardware in front of the firewall, closer to the Internet, helps avoid potential NAT and address management problems, but it might introduce other concerns associated with all NAT deployments. As you probably know, many applications—such as those that use Microsoft's Distributed Component Model (DCOM) protocols—do not work with some NAT implementations. This is because generic NAT processors translate addresses only in the packet's header, even though some application-level protocols embed addressing information in packet payload as well.

Another disadvantage of placing VPN devices in front of the firewall is that they cannot enjoy the protection the firewall offers. If the system serving as the VPN endpoint is compromised, the attacker might gain access to information whose confidentiality is supposed to be protected by the VPN.

Firewall and VPN in One System

When deploying a device that integrates VPN and firewall functionality into a single system, you will most likely recognize some cost savings over the solutions in which the two devices are separated. Most of these savings will not come from the cost of initial deployment because VPN functionality on a firewall is likely to require additional software licenses and possibly a hardware upgrade. An integrated solution is generally less expensive to maintain, though, because you have fewer systems to watch over. Additionally, a commercial VPN solution such as Check Point VPN-1 integrates with the GUI used to manage Check Point's firewall. Most integrated solutions do not have the NAT-related problems discussed earlier, and they enjoy robust access control capabilities offered by the firewall component of the device.

One of the biggest drawbacks of an integrated solution is that you might be limited in the choices you can make with regard to optimally deploying your VPN and firewall components. Firewall products that match most closely to your business needs might not be as well suited to their VPN components. Similarly, under some situations, you will benefit from deploying an external specialized VPN device, and purchasing an integrated solution might lock you into having VPN and firewall components on the same system.

Hopefully, we've given you an idea of some of the choices and dilemmas you will face when integrating a VPN component into your perimeter architecture. Further discussion about VPN placement scenarios can be found in Chapter 16.

Multiple Firewalls

Some designs call for the use of multiple firewalls to protect the network. This makes sense when you want to provide different levels of protection for resources with different security needs. Such scenarios might involve deploying firewalls inline, one behind another, to segment resources with different security requirements. Firewalls can also be deployed in parallel, next to each other and equidistant from the Internet.

Using multiple firewalls provides the designer with the ability to control access to resources in a fine-grained manner. On the other hand, costs of setting up and maintaining your network increase dramatically as you add more firewalls. Some products, such as Check Point FireWall-1, provide an intuitive interface for controlling multiple firewalls from a single system. Others, such as NetFilter, might require more significant efforts for keeping firewall configurations in sync with the organization's security policy.

Inline Firewalls

Inline firewalls are deployed one behind another, and traffic coming to and from the Internet might be subjected to access control restrictions of multiple firewall devices.

This is not as unusual of a configuration as you might think. Consider the typical architecture in which a single firewall is located behind the border router. If you use the router's access list functionality to control access to resources instead of doing only basic packet filtering on it, the router is acting very much like a firewall. The idea here might be to have redundancy in your access enforcement points; that way, if one device doesn't stop malicious traffic, the one behind it might.

If locating one firewall-like device right behind another seems wasteful to you, another inline configuration, presented in Figure 12.2, might make more sense. Here, we take advantage of the subnets with different security levels created by multiple firewalls. The closer the subnet is to the Internet, the less secure it is. In such an architecture, we could place web servers behind the first firewall, while keeping more sensitive resources, such as database servers, behind the second firewall. The first firewall could be configured to allow traffic to hit web servers only, whereas the second firewall would only allow web servers to talk to the database servers.

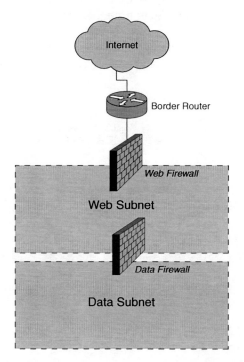

Figure 12.2   When multiple inline firewalls are employed, the most sensitive information should be kept behind the second firewall.

One of the biggest problems with environments incorporating inline firewalls is that of manageability. Not only do you need to set up, maintain, and monitor multiple firewalls, but you need to support multiple firewall policies. If, for example, you need to allow a system behind multiple firewalls to connect to the Internet, you need to remember to modify the rule sets of both firewalls. Commercial firewalls, such as Check Point FireWall-1 and Cisco PIX, provide software solutions for managing multiple firewalls from a single console, and they allow you to ensure that all inline firewalls are properly configured. If you determine that a device protected by inline firewalls needs to communicate directly with the Internet, you might also consider restructuring the network's design to minimize the number of firewalls to be traversed.

Firewalls in Parallel

Many times you might be compelled to set up firewalls in parallel with each other. We can design architectures that incorporate firewalls in parallel in many ways. In most such configurations, the firewalls protect resources with different security needs. When firewalls are set up inline, as discussed in the previous section, packets destined for the hosts deep within the organization's network might be delayed because they need to go through several access control devices. With parallel firewalls, this is not a significant concern because the firewalls are equidistant from the Internet.

In a parallel configuration, we can deploy firewalls that are each tuned specifically for the resources they are protecting. One such scenario is shown in Figure 12.3. Here, we use an application gateway and a stateful firewall, each protecting a different set of systems.

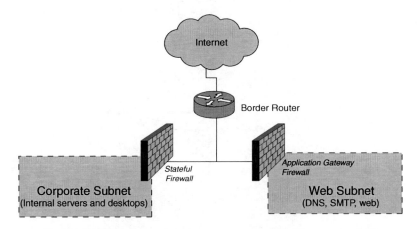

Figure 12.3   When parallel firewalls are employed, delays are avoided because the firewalls are equidistant from the Internet.

In this example, we assume that our business requires the use of robust proxy-level capabilities of an application gateway to protect Internet-accessible systems such as web, SMTP, and DNS servers. We are okay with the generally slower performance of the proxying firewall for this purpose. At the same time, we need the flexibility of a stateful firewall for the corporate network, which hosts internal workstations and servers. By deploying two different firewalls in parallel, we are able to take advantage of the best-of-breed functions offered by each type of device. At the same time, we do not have the luxury of placing a system behind multiple layers of firewalls, as would be the case with the inline configuration.

Summary

This concludes our discussion of the fundamentals of perimeter design. In the course of this chapter, we talked about the need to carefully examine our environment before jumping into design. Also, by spending time in the planning stages of the deployment, we minimize late changes to the network's architecture, thus saving time and money. Business needs drive all security requirements in the real world, and we must understand our goals and requirements before deciding what traffic should be blocked at the border and how many firewalls should be deployed. Recognizing that organizations differ in their business needs, we discussed several popular building block patterns and explained their advantages and disadvantages. We will use these principles in the upcoming chapters to empower you to create a robust network perimeter that meets your security and business needs.

References

1 John Rendleman. "Server 54, Where Are You?" InformationWeek. http://www. informationweek.com/story/IWK20010409S0001. October 2004.

2 Sun Microsystems. "University of North Carolina Denies They Are Looking for Solaris 'Server 54'." http://www.sun.com/smi/Press/sunflash/200105/sunflash.20010521.3.html. October 2004.

3 Kevin Smith. "Do You Copy? Security Issues with Digital Copiers." September 16, 2000. http:// www.giac.org/practical/Kevin_Smith_GSEC.DOC. October 2004.

4 Security Wire Perspectives, Vol. 6, No. 74, September 27, 2004.

5 U.S. Department of Justice. "Former Cisco Accountants Plead Guilty to Wire Fraud via Unauthorized Access to Cisco Stock." August 20, 2001. http://www.usdoj.gov/criminal/cybercrime/OsowskiPlea.htm. October 2004.

6 "The Hacker Who Sent Viagra to Bill Gates." July 12, 2001. BBC News. http://news.bbc.co.uk/hi/english/uk/newsid_1434000/1434530.stm. October 2004.

7 Bruce Schneier. Crypto-Gram Newsletter. September 15, 2001. http://www.schneier.com/crypto-gram-0109.html. October 2004.

8 Craig Biggerstaff. VPN Frequently Asked Questions. "How Does IPsec Work with Network Address Translation (NAT)?" http://vpn.shmoo.com/vpn/FAQ.html. October 2004.

13

Separating Resources

RESOURCE SEPARATION IS ONE OF THE CORE network defense principles, and it is evident in many security-conscious designs. Grouping resources based on similarities in security-related attributes allows us to limit the attacker's area of influence if he gains access to a system inside the perimeter. The way that you group resources depends on their sensitivity, on the likelihood that they will be compromised, or on whatever criterion you choose as the designer.

We have applied the principle of resource separation throughout this book, perhaps without formally stating so. For example, we used screened subnets to host servers that were accessible from the Internet, presumably because their sensitivity and acceptable exposure differed from systems on the internal network. In addition to segmenting the network, resource separation can be accomplished by dedicating servers to specific tasks, and even by splitting the site into geographically distinct hosting centers. Resource separation also influences the design of software architecture, as we demonstrate in Chapter 15, "Software Architecture."

By the end of this chapter, you will understand practical means of achieving the desired extent of segregation on your network. We present several ways to separate resources within servers and networks as well as explore examples that incorporate such separation. We also discuss chroot, mail relays, split DNS, and wireless networks, and we examine the merits and dangers of using VLANs when implementing security zones.

Security Zones

As you have already witnessed in one of the basic network design patterns, we might place external web servers onto the same network as public DNS servers and mail relays. This makes sense because we want to limit which resources an attacker can access directly if he succeeds at compromising one of the systems. We can use many techniques to achieve resource segmentation on different layers of defense, all of which share the underlying principle of security zones.

A *security zone* is a logical grouping of resources, such as systems, networks, or processes, that are similar in the degree of acceptable risk. For instance, we might place web servers in the same security zone as public DNS and mail relay servers because all these systems have to be accessible from the Internet and are not expected to store sensitive information. If, on the other hand, we use the mail server to host data that is more sensitive than what is stored on the public web and DNS servers, we would consider placing it into a separate network, thus forming another security zone. It is a common best practice for organizations to place critical systems, such as a company's Human Resources servers or a university's grade databases, behind internal firewalls.

The notion of a security zone is not limited to networks. It can be implemented to some extent by setting up servers dedicated to hosting similar applications. To create an effective design, we need to understand how to group resources into appropriate security zones. This approach mimics the design of a large ship that is split into multiple watertight compartments to resist flooding. If one of the sections is compromised, other areas retain a chance of maintaining their integrity.

A Single Subnet

Let's look at how we can create security zones within a single subnet by using servers that are dedicated to particular tasks as well as those that are shared among multiple applications. In an attempt to minimize the number of systems that need to be set up and maintained, designers are often tempted to create servers that aggregate hosting of multiple services. This configuration is often effective from a cost-saving perspective, but it creates an environment that is more vulnerable to intrusion or hardware failure than if each service were running on a dedicated server.

Consider a scenario in which a single Internet-accessible Linux box is used to provide DNS and email services. Because both of these services are running on the same server, an exploit against one of them could compromise security of the other. For example, if we were using BIND 8.2.2, an unpatched "nxt overflow vulnerability" would allow a remote attacker to execute arbitrary code on the server with the privileges of the BIND process (http://cve.mitre.org/cgi-bin/cvename.cgi?name= CVE-1999-0833).

Hopefully, in this scenario, we already configured the BIND server to run as the limited user nobody; that way, the attacker would not directly gain root privileges through the exploit. Having local access to the system gives the attacker an opportunity to exploit a whole new class of vulnerabilities that would not be triggered remotely. For instance, if the mail-processing part of our server relies on Procmail, the attacker might be able to exploit the locally triggered "unsafe signal handling" vulnerability in Procmail 3.10 to gain root-level access to the server (http://www.securityfocus.com/bid/3071). If the vulnerable BIND application were not on this system, however, the attacker would not be able to take advantage of the Procmail vulnerability because only a local user can exploit it.

Security Zones Within a Server

What should you do if you do not have the budget to purchase servers that are dedicated to performing only one task each? In the previous example, the organization segments BIND from the rest of the server in a primitive manner by running BIND as the user nobody instead of root. That is a good start because it doesn't allow the attacker to immediately obtain administrative access to the system by compromising BIND. This technique of dedicating limited access accounts to applications is appropriate in many circumstances on UNIX as well as Windows-based systems.

A more robust way of separating a daemon such as BIND from the rest of the system involves the use of the chroot facility, which is available on most UNIX operating systems. In a way, chroot allows us to set up multiple security zones within a single server by creating isolated subsystems within the server, known as *chroot jails*.

How Chroot Works

Relative isolation of the chroot jail is accomplished by changing the perspective of the "jailed" process on what its root directory is. Most applications that run on the server locate files with respect to the system's root file system, identified as /. A chroot-ed process considers its / to be the root directory of the jail and will not be able to access files above the jail's root directory. For example, BIND's core executable often resides in `/usr/local/sbin/named` and loads its configuration file from `/etc/named.conf`. If BIND is set up to operate in a chroot jail, located in `/usr/local/bind-chroot`, the named process will be started from `/usr/local/bind-chroot/usr/local/sbin/named`. This process will think it is accessing `/etc/named.conf` to load its configuration, although, in reality, it will be accessing `/usr/local/bind-chroot/etc/named.conf`.

A chroot-ed application is typically not aware that it is operating in an isolated environment. For the application to function properly, we need to copy the required system libraries and devices into the chroot jail because the application will not have access to OS components outside the jail. An attacker who exploits a chroot-ed process will have a hard time accessing resources outside the chroot jail because file system access will be severely limited, and the environment will not have most of the tools necessary to cause serious damage. Procedures for setting up chroot are available throughout the Web and are often specific to the application you are trying to isolate.

Some applications rely on too many OS components to make setting up a chroot jail for them practical or beneficial. Additionally, in numerous documented cases, problems with the implementation or the configuration of a chroot-ed environment have allowed an attacker to break out of the chroot jail. For examples of such vulnerabilities, search for "chroot" in the Common Vulnerabilities and Exposures (CVE) database at http://cve.mitre.org.

Finally, not all operating systems provide chroot facilities. Such caveats make it difficult to set up fault-proof isolation for security zones within a single server. However, dedicated system accounts and chroot-like facilities are effective at complementing other zoning techniques on the server and network levels.

Security Zones via Dedicated Servers

A more effective method of reliably separating one application from another involves dedicating a server to each application. (This technique is often considered to be among information security's best practices.) As in most designs that incorporate security zones, the purpose of dedicated servers is to help ensure that a compromise of one infrastructure component does not breach the security of the other. If an attacker exploits a vulnerability on one server, either in an application or an OS module, the other server still has a chance of withstanding an attack. This configuration slows down the attacker's progress, giving the system's administrator more time to detect and respond to the attack.

For example, many organizations need to maintain web and mail servers that are accessible from the Internet. Such web servers are often used to host the company's public website, which typically combines static and dynamically generated content. The mail server is generally used to accept email messages via SMTP, which are then delivered to the company's internal users. Many companies use web servers like the one in this example primarily for marketing purposes and do not store confidential information on the web server's file system. The mail server, on the other hand, might store confidential data in the form of sensitive email messages from the company's partners and clients. Therefore, it makes sense to split the two services into separate security zones to provide a degree of isolation for applications that differ in their degree of acceptable risk. In many cases, business needs might allow us to purchase multiple servers but prohibit us from placing them on separate networks because of budget constraints. Setting up an additional network costs money and time that some organizations cannot justify spending.

Even if the company does not consider the mail service to be more confidential than the web service, it can justify splitting them into separate servers because web services tend to be more vulnerable than mail services. Functionality offered by web server applications tends to be more feature rich and less predictable than the functionality of mail applications. As a result, history shows that web services are exploited more frequently than mail services.

> **Note**
>
> As you might recall from Chapter 12, "Fundamentals of Secure Perimeter Design," risk is a function of the resource's data sensitivity and of the likelihood that it will be compromised. Because risk is the primary driving force behind the need for security zones, we must look at both sensitivity and vulnerability when deciding how to separate resources. Even if the data sensitivity of two services is the same, differences in the likelihood of a compromise can warrant placing them into different security zones.

Providing resource isolation solely through the use of dedicated servers is often sufficient when differences in acceptable risk of resources are not significant. Under more varying conditions, however, we might need to increase the extent of isolation the design provides. In the next section, we explore situations in which the nature of the resources, along with business needs, require us to separate systems by using multiple subnets.

Multiple Subnets

Using multiple subnets provides a reliable means of separating resources because communications between systems on different subnets are regulated by devices that connect the subnets. Tools and expertise for implementing such segmentation are widely available. After all, much of perimeter defense concentrates on using routers and firewalls to control how traffic passes from one subnet to another.

In addition to creating security zones by enforcing access control restrictions on traffic across subnets, routers and firewalls limit the scope of network broadcast communications. Broadcasts can have significant effects on network performance as well as on resource security.

Broadcast Domains

A *broadcast domain* is a collection of network nodes that receives broadcast packets and typically matches the boundaries of a subnet. Subnets can be used in network design to limit the size of network broadcast domains. Splitting a network into two or more subnets decreases the number of hosts that receive network broadcasts because routing devices are not expected to forward broadcast packets. Broadcasts have security implications because they are received by all local hosts. Decreasing the size of a broadcast domain also brings significant performance advantages because network chatter is localized to a particular subnet, and fewer hosts per broadcast domain means fewer broadcasts.

A Doomed Network?

When the PC game Doom first came out, it quickly showed up on LANs throughout the world, from corporate networks to college computer labs. Doom was one of the earliest multiplayer shoot-'em-up games. The game allowed players to easily establish game sessions over the network. Network administrators quickly discovered detrimental effects that Doom v1.1 had on a LAN's performance. It turned out that, probably in an unbridled enthusiasm to release the first version of Doom, its coders programmed the game to use broadcasts for all communications among players. In tests (yes, someone performed such tests), a four-player Doom session was shown to generate an average of 100 packets per second and increase the network load by 4%.[1] If administrators couldn't ban Doom from the network, they had to rely on broadcast domain boundaries to prevent Doom communications from engulfing the whole network.

We mentioned network broadcasts in Chapter 6, "The Role of a Router," in the context of disabling propagation of broadcasts through a router. This was done primarily to prevent Smurf-type attacks, which could use a single packet sent to a broadcast address to elicit replies from multiple hosts on the network. ARP uses the ability of broadcasts to deliver packets to all hosts in the broadcast domain when a system on the Ethernet segment does not know the MAC address of the host to which it wants to send an Ethernet frame. In this case, the sender typically issues an ARP request to the MAC address ff:ff:ff:ff:ff:ff, which is always the Ethernet broadcast address. The Ethernet media delivers this discovery packet to all hosts on the segment; the exception is that the system that holds the sought-after IP address replies with its MAC address.

Because ARP traffic travels without restraints within a broadcast domain, a malicious system could manipulate MAC-to-IP-address mappings of another host with relative ease. Most ARP implementations update their cache of MAC-to-IP-address mappings whenever they receive ARP requests or replies. As illustrated in Figure 13.1, an attacker who is on the broadcast domain could poison system A's cache by sending it a crafted ARP packet that maps host B's IP address to the attacker's MAC address. As a result, all traffic that system A tries to send using host B's IP address is redirected to the attacker. Tools such as Dsniff (http://www.monkey.org/~dugsong/dsniff/) and Ettercap (http://ettercap.sourceforge.net/) are available for free and are effective at automating such attacks. One way to defend against ARP cache poisoning is to enforce proper authentication using higher-level protocols, such as Secure Shell (SSH). Controlling the size of broadcast domains also limits a site's exposure to such attacks.

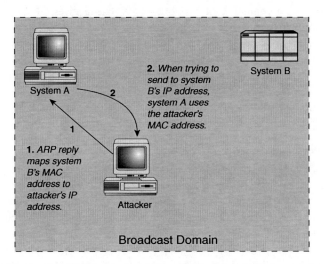

Figure 13.1 When performing an ARP cache poisoning attack, the attacker convinces system A to use the attacker's MAC address instead of system B's MAC address.

As you can see, IP communication in Ethernet environments is closely tied to MAC addresses. Systems can send network layer broadcasts by destining IP datagrams to broadcast addresses such as 255.255.255.255, NET.ADDR.255.255, and so on. In this case, the underlying data link layer, such as the Ethernet, is responsible for delivering the datagram to all hosts in the broadcast domain. Ethernet accomplishes this by setting the destination address of the Ethernet frame to ff:ff:ff:ff:ff:ff.

Note

On Ethernet-based TCP/IP networks, IP broadcasts are translated into Ethernet broadcasts to the ff:ff:ff:ff:ff:ff MAC address. As a result, all hosts in the broadcast domain receive broadcast datagrams, regardless of the operating system or the application that generated them.

Network layer broadcasts are frequently seen in environments that host Windows systems because Windows often relies on broadcasts to discover services on the network.

> **Note**
>
> To quiet a chatty windows NetBIOS network, you can disable broadcasts by configuring a WINS server. In Windows 2000 (and after) network, the NetBIOS protocol can be disabled and DNS can be used as the sole means of name resolution. For information on NetBIOS name resolution, configuring WINS, or disabling NetBIOS functionality in Windows 2000 and later operating systems, take a look at http://www.microsoft.com/resources/documentation/Windows/2000/server/reskit/en-us/prork/prcc_tcp_gclb.asp.

The following network trace demonstrates such NetBIOS-over-TCP/IP (NBT) packets directed at all hosts on the local subnet 192.168.1.0 (tcpdump was used to capture this traffic):

```
192.168.1.142.netbios-ns > 192.168.1.255.netbios-ns:NBT UDP PACKET(137):
➥QUERY; REQUEST; BROADCAST
192.168.1.142.netbios-ns > 192.168.1.255.netbios-ns:NBT UDP PACKET(137):
➥QUERY; REQUEST; BROADCAST
192.168.1.142.netbios-ns > 192.168.1.255.netbios-ns:NBT UDP PACKET(137):
➥QUERY; REQUEST; BROADCAST
```

If you fire up a network sniffer even on a relatively small subnet that hosts Windows systems, you are likely to see similar NBT broadcast datagrams at the rate of at least one per second. Because all nodes in the broadcast domain must process such datagrams, a system devotes CPU resources to processing broadcasts whether it needs to or not. We talk more about performance implications of network broadcasts in Chapter 17, "Tuning the Design for Performance." From a security perspective, broadcast communications are likely to leak information about the application that generated them because all hosts in the broadcast domain will be "tuned in." One purpose of splitting networks into smaller subnets is to limit the amount of traffic that each node processes due to broadcasts.

Security Zones via Subnets

In perimeter security, the most powerful devices for enforcing network traffic restrictions are located at subnet entry points and usually take the form of firewalls and routers. As a result, we frequently use subnets to create different security zones on the network. In such configurations, communications that need to be tightly controlled are most likely to cross subnets and be bound by a firewall's or a router's restrictions.

Consider the example illustrated in Figure 13.2. We separated the network into three security zones, each defined by a dedicated subnet.

In this scenario, we group resources based on their primary purpose because that maps directly to the sensitivity levels of the data the system maintains. The border firewall and the internal router allow us to control access to and from network resources based on the business requirements for each zone. The zones are defined as follows:

- The Public Servers zone contains servers that provide information to the general public and can be accessed from the Internet. These servers should never initiate connections to the Internet, but specific servers might initiate connections to the Corporate Servers zone using approved protocols and ports.

- The Corporate Servers zone contains the company's internal servers that internal users can access from the Corporate Workstations zone. The firewall should severely restrict the servers' ability to initiate connections to other zones.

- The Corporate Workstations zone contains internal desktops and laptops that can browse the Internet using approved protocols and ports and can connect to the Corporate Servers zone primarily for file and print services.

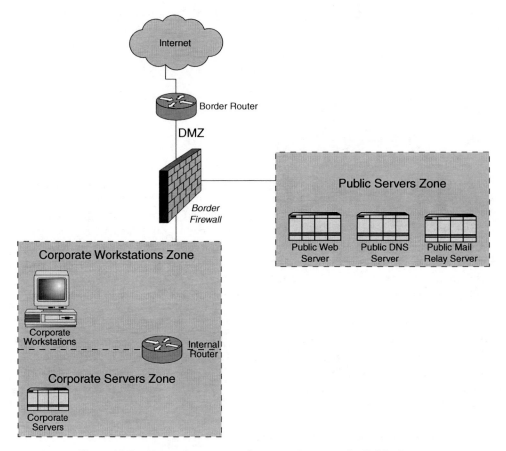

Figure 13.2   Here, subnets create three security zones: the Public Servers zone, the Corporate Workstations zone, and the Corporate Servers zone.

Access control lists (ACLs) on the internal router are set up to let only Windows network traffic from corporate workstations access the servers. (In this example, the servers are Windows based. For UNIX, you would allow Network File System (NFS), Line Printer (LPR), and related protocols.) In this scenario, we do not have business requirements for the corporate servers to initiate connections to the Internet. If the servers have peering relationships with external partner sites, the router's ACLs need to be tuned appropriately. Additionally, the organization's security policy in this example does not allow servers to download OS and software patches from external sites. Instead, patches are retrieved and verified in the Corporate Workstation zone before they are applied to relevant servers.

The firewall is configured to allow from the Internet only inbound traffic destined for systems in the Public Server zone on HTTP, DNS, and SMTP ports. These servers are not allowed to initiate connections that cross security zone boundaries except when relaying mail to the internal mail server.

Systems on the Corporate Workstations zone are allowed to browse the Web using approved protocols, such as HTTP, HTTPS, FTP, and so on. (For tighter control, we might want to set up a proxy server to help enforce restrictions on outbound traffic.) Corporate users can also connect to the Corporate Server zone in a manner controlled by the internal router. The workstations can connect to hosts in the Public Servers zone for remote administration using the SSH protocol.

So far, this example has focused on the high-level requirements for defining security zones and associated access control rules. Some additional details need to be addressed before you implement this design. Specifically, you need to pay close attention to how corporate and public systems resolve domain names and how inbound and outbound email relaying is configured.

What would happen if we hosted all corporate and publicly accessible systems on a single subnet, without defining multiple security zones? We would still be able to control how traffic traverses to and from the Internet because the Internet is considered a security zone, and we know that we have control over traffic that crosses zone boundaries. However, we would have a hard time controlling how internal systems interact with each other, primarily because internal traffic would not be crossing zone boundaries. (You can control intrazone traffic if the subnet is implemented as a VLAN, which we discuss in the "Private VLANs" section of this chapter.)

The reality is that setting up multiple security zones on the network is expensive. It requires additional networking gear, such as routers and switches, and it significantly complicates ACL maintenance on all access enforcement devices. That is partly why we are rarely able to provision a dedicated subnet for each core server of the infrastructure.

Also, it is generally much easier to justify separating publicly accessible servers from internal systems than splitting internal systems into workstation- and server-specific zones. In terms of risk, public servers are accessible to everyone on the Internet and are more likely to be compromised than internal servers. This difference in vulnerability levels often serves as the primary factor for separating public and internal resources into different security zones. The distinction between internal servers and workstations is often not as clear cut, but it still exists because workstations are more likely to be infected with malicious software as a result of a user's actions. Each organization must decide how much it is willing to invest into resource separation given its budget and business objectives.

Common Design Elements

We would like to spend a few pages discussing design elements that are not only commonly used, but are also representative of architectures that take into account resource separation. This section talks about setting up a mail relay to help you secure your organization's email link to the Internet. We also explore a DNS configuration known as *Split DNS*, which is very useful for mitigating risks associated with running a publicly accessible DNS server. Finally, we discuss ways of applying resource separation techniques to secure client stations. These scenarios are meant to demonstrate practical uses of resource separation. They will help you make decisions regarding the extent of separation that is appropriate and feasible for your organization.

Mail Relay

A mail relay is one means to help secure your environment's email functionality. Mail can be passed into your environment using a properly configured external mail relay server to forward inbound messages to a separate internal mail system. To accomplish this, you install mail-relaying software on a bastion host that is accessible from the Internet. You then configure the relay to forward all inbound messages to the internal mail server, which, in turn, delivers them to the organization's internal users. Splitting the mail server into two components allows you to place them into separate security zones.

Justifying Mail Server Separation

Instead of implementing a store-and-forward configuration to separate mail functions into two components, we could have used a single mail server to attend to internal users and accept email from the Internet. This setup eliminates the cost of deploying and maintaining an additional host, but it increases the risk that an external attacker might get access to the company's sensitive information. As we have seen throughout this chapter, it often makes sense to separate public systems from the internal ones to sandbox an attacker who gains access to an Internet-accessible server. Additionally, modern mail systems such as Microsoft Exchange, which are commonly used within a company, are complex and feature rich. Hardening such software so that it is robust enough to be accessible from the Internet is often difficult.

Splitting the public-facing component of the server from the internal mail distribution system allows us to place these resources into separate security zones. This offers many benefits over a configuration that integrates the two components into a single system:

- We can use different software for each component in a manner that is optimized for the component's tasks and risk factors.
- We can isolate the most vulnerable component in a way that limits the extent of a potential compromise.

- We can have higher confidence that we tightened the relay's configuration appropriately because its software is relatively straightforward.

- We can allow ourselves granular control over how tightly each component is configured and how it can be accessed over the network.

Implementing a Mail Relay

A common configuration for implementing a mail relay is illustrated in Figure 13.3. As you can see, we have placed the mail-forwarding agent into the Public Servers zone, which was set up as a screened subnet. The internal mail server was placed on the Corporate zone to be used by internal users when sending and receiving email messages. To ensure that messages from the Internet are delivered to the mail relay server, the organization's DNS server set the mail exchange (MX) record for the company's network to point to the relay server.

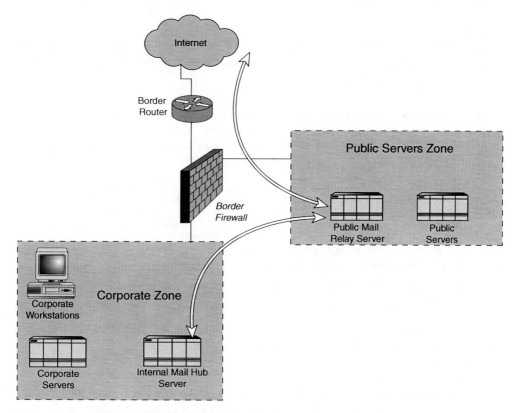

Figure 13.3   When you are implementing a mail relay, you can place the mail-forwarding agent in the Public Servers zone.

The primary function of the mail relay is to receive messages from the outside and forward them to the internal mail server. To further isolate the internal mail server from the Internet, you might want to route outbound messages through the mail relay as well. Making outbound connections is not as risky as accepting inbound ones, but fully separating the internal server from the outside helps decrease the likelihood that it will be adversely affected by a system on the Internet. In this configuration, the internal mail server accepts messages from internal workstations and servers and forwards those that are Internet-bound to the mail relay in the Public Servers zone.

One of the advantages of splitting Internet-facing mail functionality away from the internal mail server is that it allows us to use different software packages for each component of the mail infrastructure. For instance, a Microsoft Exchange server might have the desired functionality for an internal server, but you might consider it too feature loaded for a simple mail-forwarding agent. In that case, you might want to use software you feel more comfortable locking down, such as Sendmail, Postfix, or Qmail, to implement the mail relay.

Note

Using products from different vendors for public and internal servers decreases the chances that a vulnerability in one product affects all systems. At the same time, it increases the number of software packages you need to maintain and monitor.

Specifics for configuring a mail relay to forward inbound messages to the internal server and outbound messages to the appropriate system on the Internet differ with each software vendor. In most cases, you need to specify the following parameters on the mail relay:

- The name of the domain for which the forwarder is relaying mail. If you don't specify this, the mail relay might reject inbound messages, thinking they are destined for somebody else's domain.

- The name or addresses of internal systems from which you accept outbound mail messages. To prevent internal SMTP clients from accessing the relay directly, you should consider limiting this to include only your internal mail server.

- The name or address of the internal mail server to which inbound messages will be forwarded.

You should also consider implementing masquerading features on the relay server, especially if multiple internal servers need to send outbound mail through the relay. Mail masquerading rewrites headers of outbound messages to remove the name of the originating host, leaving just the organization's domain name in the From field.

The Enterprise editions of the Microsoft Exchange 2000 and Windows 2003 Server support a distributed topology that allows you to set up a front-end server that acts as a relay for mail-related communications and forwards them to the back-end server that actually maintains users' mailboxes. Specifying that the Exchange server should be a front-end server is a matter of going into Properties in the desired server object in Exchange System Manager and selecting the This Is a Front-End Server option.

Microsoft recommends that the front-end server be fully configured before placing it into the DMZ or a screened subnet:

> "Configuring settings on the front-end server in Exchange System Manager requires the System Attendant (MSExchangeSA) service to be running so that the configuration information can replicate to the metabase. The MSExchangeSA service requires RPC access to the back-end servers, and RPCs often are not allowed across an intranet firewall in a perimeter network."[2]

Future changes to the front-end server might, therefore, require temporary changes to the firewall's policy to allow RPC traffic for the period when the front-end server is being reconfigured. Alternatively, you can set up an IPSec channel between the administrative workstations and the front-end server to tunnel the RPC traffic in a secure manner.

Tip
If you are setting up an Exchange front-end server, be sure to follow the Exchange lockdown instructions described at http://www.microsoft.com/technet/prodtechnol/exchange/2003/library/febetop.mspx.

If you are interested only in relaying SMTP and do not require POP, IMAP, and Outlook Web Access (OWA) functionality of Microsoft Exchange, you could use the SMTP Virtual Server built in to Microsoft's Internet Information Services (IIS) as the mail relay. Such configuration will generally cost less to deploy because you are not required to purchase the Enterprise Edition of Microsoft Exchange 2003 Server. As shown in Figure 13.4, the SMTP component of IIS offers highly configurable mail-relaying functionality, and it can be set up with most of the other functionality built in to IIS disabled. (Be sure to lock down IIS appropriately; it has a history of security compromises.)

Administrators who are not experienced in hardening Windows-based servers will probably prefer to use a UNIX system as the mail relay server. However, if you specialize in setting up and maintaining Microsoft Windows servers, you will probably benefit from using the operating system you know best. You need to strike a balance between using software that you know and deploying software from multiple suppliers across your security zones. If your organization is relatively small, you will probably benefit from not overloading your support staff with maintaining mail software from multiple vendors. Larger enterprises are more likely to benefit from using specialized software for different components of the mail system.

Splitting email functionality into two servers allows you to apply different levels of hardening to each system. The mail relay should be configured as a bastion host, stripped of all OS components and applications not required for forwarding SMTP messages. The internal mail server does not need to be hardened to the same degree because it does not communicate with hosts on the Internet. This is often advantageous. The internal mail server might need to integrate with the internal user management system, such as Microsoft Active Directory, whereas the mail relay does not need to be aware of any such nuances of internal infrastructure.

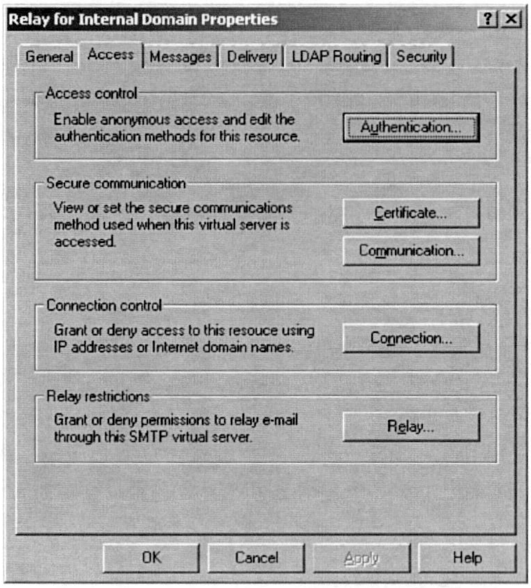

Figure 13.4   When configuring an IIS SMTP virtual server, you can set options that specify how the system relays mail, authenticates users, and communicates with other network components.

Split DNS

The DNS service, which maps hostnames to IP addresses, and vice versa, is a principal component of many networks. In this section, we examine a Split DNS configuration, which is also sometimes called *Split Horizon DNS*. This is a relatively common design pattern that calls for separating the DNS service into two components: one that is available to external Internet users, and another that is used internally within the organization.

One of the purposes of Split DNS is to limit what information about the network's internal infrastructure is available to external users. If an Internet-accessible DNS server hosts your public and internal records, an external attacker might be able to query the server for hostnames, addresses, and related DNS information of your internal systems. The attacker can issue targeted lookup requests for a specific domain, hostname, or IP address, or attempt to retrieve the complete DNS database through a zone transfer.

Another purpose of Split DNS is to decrease the likelihood that critical internal resources will be affected by a compromised DNS server. Earlier in the chapter, we looked at how buffer overflow vulnerability allowed an attacker to gain shell access on a server running BIND. Many such attacks have been found in DNS software over the past few years, as evidenced by postings to vulnerability forums and databases.

BIND and the Lion Worm

The Lion worm, which spread across vulnerable UNIX servers in early 2001, exploited the TSIG vulnerability in BIND 8.2.x (http://cve.mitre.org/cgi-bin/cvename.cgi?name=CVE-2001-0010). The buffer overflow vulnerability in the portion of BIND's code that handled transaction signatures allowed Lion to execute its payload with the privileges of the user who was running the BIND daemon (http://www.securityfocus.com/bid/2302). If the worm succeeded at exploiting the TSIG vulnerability, it attempted to download a copy of itself from a website at coollion.51.net.[3]

After Lion infected the server, it attempted to replace many frequently used programs and set up a shell listening for inbound connections as a backdoor into the system. It also emailed the contents of local `/etc/passwd` and `/etc/shadow` files to `huckit@china.com`. The worm continued to spread by scanning random IP addresses for vulnerable BIND servers until the site from which it was hard-coded to download itself was disabled.[4]

Justifying DNS Server Separation

When deciding where to place DNS servers and whether to split DNS servers into multiple security zones, consider two primary types of users of DNS services:

- Users on the Internet who need to be able to obtain DNS information of publicly accessible systems hosted on your network. In addition to being able to resolve hostnames of your public systems, external hosts use DNS to obtain the name and address of the MX server.

- Internal users within your network perimeter who need to be able to obtain DNS information of hosts on the Internet as well as of hosts on the intranet. If a DNS server does not know the answer to the internal user's query, it can connect to external DNS servers to find out the answer; this action is known as a *recursive query*. Alternatively, the DNS server can simply forward the request to a predefined DNS server that will perform the necessary recursive queries and return the final answer to the initial DNS server.

DNS servers catering to different audiences vary in the sensitivity of data they require for useful operation. Specifically, publicly accessible DNS servers do not have to be aware of the hostname-to-IP mappings of systems that cannot be reached from the Internet. Also, DNS servers differ in the likelihood that they will be compromised, depending on whether they can be accessed from the Internet. Differences in risks associated with different types of DNS servers point to the need to separate DNS resources into multiple security zones.

DNS Spoofing Attacks

DNS is an attractive target for spoofing, or poisoning attacks through which attackers attempt to propagate incorrect hostname-to-IP-address mappings to the DNS server. Such attacks, in various forms, have been known to affect DNS software from most vendors.

Because DNS queries are typically submitted over UDP, servers cannot rely on the transport protocol to maintain the state of the DNS connection. Therefore, to determine which response matches to which query, DNS servers embed a numeric query ID into the DNS payload of the packet. If an attacker is able to predict the query ID the DNS server used when directing a recursive query to another DNS server, the attacker can craft a spoofed response that might get to the asking server before the real one does. The DNS server usually believes the first response it receives, discarding the second one as a duplicate. Consequently, the host that uses the DNS server to look up the spoofed domain record is directed to the IP address of the attacker's choice. Predicting DNS query IDs was relatively easy in older versions of DNS software because it tended to simply increment the IDs by one after each query.

Another variation of the DNS spoofing attack is effective against servers that happily cache a DNS mapping even if they received it as additional information in response to a query that was completely unrelated to the spoofed record. By default, DNS server software that comes with Windows NT and 2000 is vulnerable to this attack unless you explicitly set the following Registry key to the REG_WORD value of 1: HKEY_LOCAL_MACHINE\System_CurrentControlSet\Services\DNS\Parameters\ SecureResponses.[5] On Windows 2000 and 2003, this Registry value also can be defined using the DNS Management Console by checking the Secure Cache Against Pollution check box in properties of the server's object.[6] As shown in Figure 13.5, this check box is not set by default in Windows 2000 (though it is in 2003). Microsoft DNS is not the only software that might be vulnerable to such attacks; older versions of BIND were vulnerable to such spoofing attacks as well.

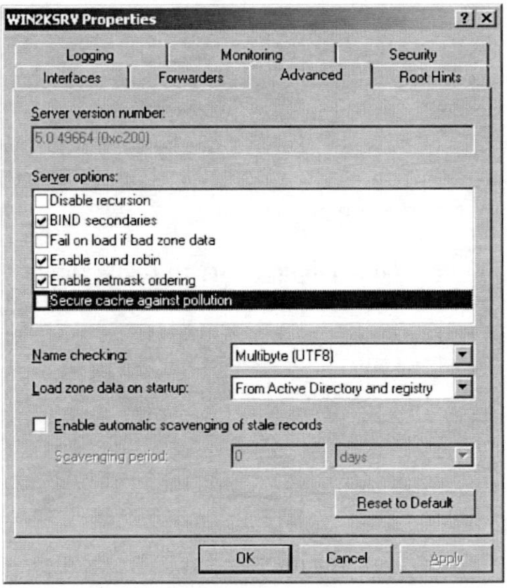

Figure 13.5   The Secure Cache Against Pollution check box
(shown in Windows 2000) is not enabled by default.

Implementing Split DNS

The implementation of Split DNS is relatively straightforward when it comes to servicing inbound DNS requests from the Internet. As shown in Figure 13.6, the external DNS server is located in the Public Servers zone, which is typically set up as a screened subnet or a DMZ. The external server's database only contains information on domains and systems of which the outside world should be aware. Records that need to be accessible only by internal users are stored on the internal DNS server. This design decreases the possibility that an attacker can obtain sensitive information by querying or compromising the external DNS server.

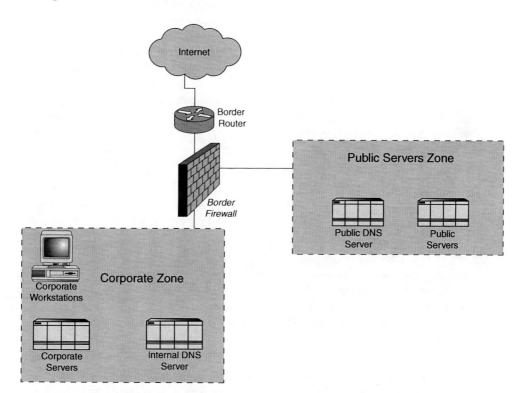

Figure 13.6   In Split DNS configurations, public and internal DNS records are hosted using two servers, each located in different security zones.

The internal DNS server, in addition to maintaining authoritative records for internal systems, needs to handle requests from internal hosts for DNS information about systems on the Internet. How does the internal server answer queries about external systems for which it does not have authoritative information? We can configure the internal server to forward such queries to another DNS server that performs the recursive query.

Frequently, the DNS server located in the Public Servers zone plays this role. Alternatively, we can configure the internal DNS server to perform recursive queries.

Consider a scenario in which the internal DNS server forwards queries for Internet records to our external server. In this case, the internal DNS server is maximally isolated from the Internet because, in addition to never accepting connections from external hosts, it never initiates connections to systems on the Internet. The external DNS server, of course, needs to be configured to accept recursive queries only if they come from the internal DNS server. Unfortunately, in this scenario, the internal server relies on the server in the Public Servers zone to handle such requests. That is the same server we deem to be under increased risk because it accepts DNS requests from external hosts. If an attacker compromises the external DNS server or manages to spoof its DNS records, the internal DNS server might receive fabricated answers to its queries.

An alternative configuration permits the internal DNS server to perform recursive queries, in which case it initiates DNS connections to hosts on the Internet. In this scenario, the queries do not have to go through a server in the Public Servers zone, which bypasses a potentially weak link in the DNS resolution process. Unfortunately, by allowing the internal server to make connections to systems on the Internet, we increase the possibility that the internal server is directly affected by an external system. For example, a malicious DNS server could exploit a buffer overflow condition by carefully crafting a response to a DNS query. An attacker could use the server's ability to initiate connections to the Internet to establish a covert channel for communicating across the network's perimeter.

> **Note**
>
> The server that makes outbound connection requests is under the increased risk that it will be directly affected by an attack. Besides exploiting vulnerabilities such as buffer overflows, attackers could exploit DNS-specific weaknesses of the server (for example, by poisoning the server's DNS cache in response to a query). You can protect yourself against known vulnerabilities of this sort by staying updated with the latest version of your DNS software and by configuring it in accordance with the vendor's and industry's best practices. You also need to ensure that additional defense mechanisms are in place to mitigate the risks associated with unknown attacks.

If you use a server in the Public Servers zone to process outbound DNS requests, you are not protected against attacks such as DNS cache poisoning because spoofed information might be propagated to the internal DNS server. After all, a DNS server in the Public Servers zone is more likely to be compromised because it accepts requests from external hosts and is located on a subnet with other publicly accessible servers.

If you are willing to accept the risk that a compromise to the external DNS server might impact the ability of your internal users to resolve Internet hostnames, consider relaying outbound DNS requests through the server in the Public Servers zone. In a best-case scenario, you would actually use three DNS servers: one for servicing external users, one for answering queries for internal domains, and one for performing recursive queries about Internet systems. Unfortunately, this alternative is relatively expensive to set up and maintain and is quite uncommon.

Client Separation

As we mentioned previously, resources should be placed together based on their level of acceptable risk. One example of a set of resources in most business environments that share a similar acceptable risk is the client network, where end-user workstations and their ilk reside. When local area networks (LANs) first started springing up, it was not uncommon for servers and clients to share the same flat network structure. However, as networks became more and more complicated and businesses had a need for outside users to contact their servers, it became apparent that in most environments, servers needed to be split off into their own security zones. Now, in a world filled with Internet worms, mail-transported viruses, and the like, it is often more likely for a client to propagate a virus than a server. Because this places clients at a similar level of acceptable risk, it makes sense that they all share a security zone of their own. Clients differ in their level of insecurity, ranging from LAN-connected desktops, wandering laptops, VPN and dialup remote connectors, and, finally, wireless clients. In this section, we will discuss the advantages of separating these client types into their own zones for the benefit of your organization.

LAN-Connected Desktops

LAN-connected desktops usually have the lowest risk of any of our network's clients. Although most such clients have Internet access and the potential to propagate viruses and the like, at least we as administrators have the capability to force these stations to subscribe to our organization's security policy. We can verify that they are properly patched, with up-to-date virus definitions, and locked down to the best of our abilities, even creating automated processes that verify that all is well on a daily basis.

Despite all our efforts as administrators, the client PC can still be a liability to our network's security. By keeping clients in a separate security zone from internal and/or Internet available servers, we limit the chances of having our clients affect the availability of our server networks. Although having a firewall between our clients and servers requires additional administration to upkeep the firewall policy, it facilitates a "choke-point" to control communications between them and to help mitigate client risks.

Wandering Laptops, VPN and Dialup Users

A more complicated challenge in many network environments is the client we can't control. Whether physically located at our site or connecting in through a dialup connection or the Internet, it can be very difficult to force these hosts to subscribe to our security policy. It is a best practice to segregate all remote users into their own security zone, preferably behind a firewall. This will prevent these hosts from contacting resources they shouldn't, while logging their access to resources they should. Though dividing these clients into a separate security zone affords an additional level of protection, it does not confirm that the hosts follow your security policy. How can you be sure that the sales rep who is plugging in to a conference room network jack has the latest virus updates? Or that a VPN or dialup user has carefully patched all known vulnerabilities for her version of operating system? One answer is an initiative like Cisco's Self-Defending Network, as mentioned in Chapter 24, "A Unified Security Perimeter: The Importance of Defense in Depth." It uses Network Admission Control to confirm that *any* host that connects to your network meets certain criteria (patched, up-to-date virus definitions, certain version of the OS, and so on) before allowing access. This can even be applied to a host plugging in to a random jack in your office. For more information on NAC and the Self-Defending Network, check out Chapter 10, "Host Defense Components."

The Wireless Client

The wireless client is by far the most vulnerable of the clients in this section. It has all the vulnerabilities and concerns of other clients, plus is exposed to possible anonymous connection without physical access being necessary. Depending on your requirements, you might consider limiting the way every wireless node communicates with each other. Alternatively, in a more cost-effective manner, you might group wireless nodes with similar security risks into their own security zones. As shown in Figure 13.7, we group all wireless laptops into a single security zone because for the purposes of this example, our laptops do not significantly differ in acceptable risk exposure. (For this example, each laptop is as likely to be compromised as the other because of its use and configuration, and each laptop contains data of similar sensitivity.) At the same time, we consider wireless nodes to be more vulnerable to attacks than hosts on the wired segment and therefore decide to separate wireless and wired systems by placing them into different security zones.

In this scenario, wireless and wired machines are hosted on different subnets—one representing the Corporate zone, and another representing the Wireless zone. We use an internal firewall to control the way that traffic passes between the two subnets. The firewall ensures that even if an attacker is able to gain Layer 2 access to the Wireless zone or its hosts, her access to the Corporate zone will be restrained by the firewall's rule set. (Additional defense mechanisms will still need to be in place to protect against attacks that use protocols the firewall doesn't block.) Even traffic that passes the firewall will be logged, giving us an audit trail of any attempted attacks. We could have used a router instead of a firewall, which would also segregate broadcast domains and dampen the attacker's ability to perform attacks against systems in the Corporate zone. We elected to use a firewall because its access restriction mechanisms are generally more granular than those of a router; however, if your budget does not allow you to deploy an internal firewall, a properly configured router might provide a sufficient level of segmentation. As always, this decision depends on the requirements and capabilities of your organization.

This separation is imperative, not only because of the client issues of the laptops themselves, but also the vulnerabilities inherent in wireless technology. Wireless is the first Layer 2 network medium to which we need to worry about attackers having remote anonymous access. Having wireless connectivity available outside of your physical perimeter is like having a live network jack outside of your building! Hence, the call for all the additional security mechanisms employed with wireless networks. In any event, by dividing all wireless connectivity into its own zone—a "wireless DMZ"—Layer 3 access controls can be applied to wireless hosts connecting to your wired network. With new security concerns such as wireless DoS threatening us on the horizon, adding a chokepoint between your wireless connectivity and the rest of your network is crucial to a secure network.

Note that wireless access points typically have hub-like characteristics. This means that any wireless node that gains Layer 2 access to the access point might be able to promiscuously monitor network traffic on all ports of the access point. Placing a firewall between wireless and wired hosts does not protect you against such attacks because the firewall can only control traffic that crosses security zones you defined. To mitigate risks of wireless-to-wireless attacks, you would probably need to employ personal firewalls—coupled with robust VPN solutions such as IPSec to encrypt and authenticate wireless traffic—in a manner similar to protecting wired traffic that travels across potentially hostile networks. For more information on wireless security, refer to Chapter 14, "Wireless Network Security."

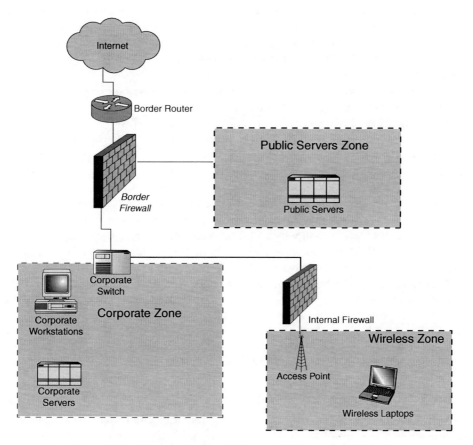

Figure 13.7   To accommodate differences in risk, we isolate wireless systems by placing them into a dedicated security zone.

VLAN-Based Separation

VLANs were created with the primary purpose of allowing network administrators to define broadcast domains flexibly across multiple switches. VLANs are a useful isolation tool, especially for the purpose of improving the network's performance. Using VLANs to implement security zones carries additional security risks that we will examine in this section.

From a performance perspective, it makes sense to place devices that frequently communicate with each other into the same broadcast domain, especially if the systems rely on broadcast-rich protocols such as NetBIOS or IPX's SAP advertisements. Often, systems that are physically separated from each other should logically belong to the same subnet; for example, your Accounting users might be sitting on different floors but accessing the same file and print servers. VLANs allow you to logically group devices into broadcast domains without tying the domain's boundaries to a particular switch, or in some cases to a single geographic location. Properly configured VLANs can also help you group resources according to their risk exposure and function, even if the systems in question are located on different floors of the building and cannot be interconnected using a single switch.

In server farm deployments, where servers tend to be in close proximity to each other, VLANs are increasingly used to define multiple virtual switches within a single high-end switch. A VLAN-enabled switch can host multiple VLANs, each representing a specific broadcast domain. Using VLANs to structure subnets is often enticing because it frees administrators from deploying dedicated switches for each subnet and allows them to add ports to VLANs by simply reconfiguring the master switch without purchasing additional hardware. Using only one physical switch to represent multiple subnets also minimizes the number of devices that need to be maintained and monitored. Also, hundreds of networks can get the benefit of hardware redundancy with as little as two switches. The flexible nature in which VLANs can be configured, as well as the slew of intra- and inter-VLAN communication options available in high-end VLAN implementations, makes VLANs an attractive tool for network administrators.

Unfortunately, virtual network divisions do not afford the comfort level that a physically disparate box does. Improperly configured VLANs can result in a vulnerability that would allow a savvy attacker to "jump" across VLAN boundaries. In the next few pages, we discuss the risks associated with VLAN deployments. Along with the potential dangers, we examine security-enhancing features of VLANs that could allow you to control how traffic travels within a single VLAN.

VLAN Boundaries

Even though subnets that are defined by VLANs might be considered virtual, they still require a router to forward network traffic from one VLAN to another. Intra-VLAN routing can be performed using a traditional router and can be controlled via ACLs, much like traffic that is crossing regular subnets. Vendors of high-end switches, notably Cisco, also offer hardware modules for their VLAN-enabled switches that can perform inter-VLAN routing at high speeds within the switch. For example, Cisco's high-end Catalyst switches support multilayer switching (MLS) through the use of add-on cards, which function like virtual routers within the switch and can route traffic across VLANs. MLS supports access lists that we can use to control how network traffic crosses VLAN boundaries.

> **Note**
>
> The ability to perform routing within a switch is sometimes called *Layer 3 switching*. Cisco implements this using MLS-enabled cards such as the Multilayer Switch Feature Card (MSFC) for Catalyst 6500 switches.[7] Practically, Layer 3 switching is different from traditional routing only in implementation; instructions to perform Layer 3 switching are hardwired into the dedicated module that is part of the switch, whereas traditional routing is implemented in software that runs using the router's CPU. Because Layer 3 switching is hardware assisted, it tends to be faster than traditional routing.

Because VLANs are meant to create isolated broadcast domains, we could use VLANs within a single switch to implement the security zone subnets shown in the network designs presented throughout this chapter. As with physical LANs, we would rely on routers (or their MLS equivalents) and firewalls to transport packets across subnet boundaries in a controlled manner. For this implementation to work, we would need to ensure that the switch that hosts the VLANs does not allow an attacker to "jump" across misconfigured VLANs and avoid the router or firewall.

Jumping Across VLANs

According to the IEEE 802.1q standard, Ethernet frames traversing through VLAN-enabled switches can be identified as belonging to a particular VLAN through the use of a tag header inserted into the frame immediately following the source MAC address field.[8] Frame tagging is used when multiple switches are "trunked" together to function as a single switch that can host multiple VLANs. Tag headers defined in the 802.1q standard carry identifying VLAN information across trunked switches and identify a frame as belonging to a particular VLAN.

> **Note**
>
> Switch trunking requires the configuration of trunking ports used when wiring participating switches together.

If the switch is not configured correctly, it might be possible to craft custom 802.1q frames that the switch will direct to the desired VLAN, thus avoiding the Layer 3 routing mechanism generally required for intra-VLAN communications. Specifically, Cisco Catalyst 2900 switches were found vulnerable to such attack when multiple VLAN switches were trunked together.[9] For this attack to work, the attacker needs to have access to the VLAN that contains an active trunking port (http://cve.mitre.org/cgi-bin/cvename.cgi?name=CAN-1999-1129). By connecting to a VLAN that contains a trunking port, the attacker could craft Ethernet frames destined for arbitrary VLANs on the other switch.

> **Tip**
>
> To decrease the risk of VLAN-hopping attacks in trunked environments, place trunking ports onto dedicated VLANs.

The vulnerability described in the previous paragraph has been carefully researched, and it resulted in a specific recommendation for mitigating the risk associated with trunking configuration options. If correctly configured using best practices, VLANs cannot be jumped. Independent security assessments by the highly respected security consulting firm @Stake "clearly demonstrate that VLANs on Cisco Catalyst switches, when configured according to best-practice guidelines, can be effectively deployed as security mechanisms."[10]

It is easy to understand why administrators would want to use VLANs to represent security zone subnets, especially in enterprise environments that have already deployed high-end switches and only require a configuration change to create a new "virtual" subnet. When deciding whether to use VLANs, consider the likelihood and the implications of a compromise to the VLAN boundary on Layer 1 or 2. For high-security environments, you may want to consider employing dedicated switches to represent each security zone. By not relying on VLANs, you physically ensure security. Though physical security can be compromised with something as simple as an improperly run network cable bridging dedicated switch security zones, with dedicated switches you do not have to worry about the configuration intricacies of trunking, or risk other misconfigurations that might result in the switch ignoring VLAN boundary restrictions.

> **Tip**
>
> You might be able to justify using VLAN-enabled switches to segment the internal network, where the convenience of VLANs outweighs the risk of deploying them in a relatively low-threat environment. You might then consider using dedicated switches for high-threat segments, such as the DMZ or the screened subnet.

It is a good rule of thumb to have sets of switches dedicated to a particular security zone (such as an internal zone, screened subnet, or DMZ) and then to use VLANs to segment networks that fall within that security zone. All networks on those switches should share a similar risk level. It is *not* recommended that you have security zones with disparate levels of risk (such as a DMZ and a Internal High-Security zone) sharing a physical switch. No matter how secure *anything* is today, there are always new vulnerabilities about to be discovered. However, a properly configured VLAN affords a good security boundary for segments with a similar risk level.

Firewalls and VLANs

As mentioned earlier in this chapter, VLANs need to be connected, like physical network segments, with a routing device. Security between VLANs can be quite a task. Typically the only security devices available for a router are access control lists. Though they are effective, managing access lists can be considerably more complicated and cumbersome than the interface of a commercial firewall solution. Also, logging and stateful handling of protocols may be missing or not as feature rich as a firewall solution. Recently, firewall vendors have started to offer solutions that take advantage of VLAN and trunking technologies. Both Cisco and Check Point currently have firewall solutions that allow the securing of communication between VLANs on the same switch.

Cisco's FWSM (mentioned in Chapter 3, "Stateful Firewalls") is a blade installed into 6500 series Catalyst switches. The Firewall Services Module (FWSM) uses the VLAN interfaces on the switch as its firewall interfaces. This way, policies can be created protecting hundreds of VLANS from each other with the full granularity of a PIX firewall.

Check Point has a solution called the Virtual System Extension (VSX). The VSX is a powerful Check Point FireWall-1 server with extras. A switch can be plugged in to it via a trunk, allowing multiple VLANs per trunk to appear as virtual interfaces on the firewall. The VSX can support as many trunks as it has available interfaces, so it can scale to handle the requirements of the most demanding environments. Up to 250 virtual firewalls can be created for the interfaces in question, allowing separate security policies (if required due to complexity or for management considerations) for the attached VLAN interfaces. Keep in mind that configuring the VSX as your VLAN's gateway means that it will be doing the routing for all VLANs so configured.

No matter what your need, advanced firewall technologies can be successfully employed to facilitate strong security between same-switch VLANs, making communications between your VLANs as secure as any physical LAN environment.

Private VLANs

The appeal of modern high-end switches makes it increasingly difficult to resist using VLANs to define subnet boundaries. VLAN implementations are becoming more robust, and network engineers are becoming more familiar with the configuration and maintenance of VLANs. Some Cisco switches support an attractive VLAN security feature called *private VLANs* (or *PVLANs*), which you should weigh against the risks associated with VLAN deployments. A private VLAN is a grouping of ports specially configured to be isolated from other ports on the same VLAN.

Private VLANs can help you restrict how hosts communicate with each other within the primary VLAN. As we discussed earlier in this chapter, firewalls and routers allow you to control network traffic only when it crosses subnet boundaries. Private VLANs are helpful for isolating systems within the subnet, without the lost addresses due to splitting the address range into multiple subnets. The ability to enforce such restrictions is most relevant in server farm deployments, where servers are frequently placed on the same subnet but rarely require unrestrained access to each other. If you are able to justify the use of VLANs in your environment, private VLANs will improve your design by adding another layer of security to the network's defenses.

When configuring ports that belong to a private VLAN, you can specify whether the device connected to a particular port can communicate with other ports of the private

VLAN. *Promiscuous ports* have the ability to communicate with all other ports and are typically assigned to the gateway for the VLAN in question, such as a router or firewall. *Isolated ports* are completely shielded from all other ports of the private VLAN, except promiscuous ports. *Community ports* can communicate among themselves and with the promiscuous ports.[11]

Despite features that enhance Layer 2 security, private VLANs can be subverted if they are not properly secured. Private VLAN restrictions can be bypassed by passing intra-VLAN traffic up to the gateway router connected to the VLAN and back down to the target host. Normally, hosts located on the same VLAN communicate with each other directly because they are on the same subnet. An attacker with access to one host on the private VLAN could purposefully route packets to a neighboring system through the gateway. All he would have to do is send the traffic (via a static host route) to the gateway of the VLAN. Because the gateway needs to be a promiscuous port, it will also be able to communicate with the target host. When the router receives the packet, it will realize that it needs to go back to the target host and forward the packet on, despite the Layer 2 isolation the private VLAN creates. To prevent this from happening, you can configure Layer 2 ACLs (or VACLs) on the primary VLAN to deny traffic with the source and destination of the same subnet.[12] This will not affect normal traffic because standard behavior dictates that any traffic between hosts on a subnet should never be forwarded to that subnet's gateway. However, it prevents the routing of traffic between PVLANs on the same subnet.

As you can see, VLANs offer numerous features that allow network designers to separate network resources in a very flexible manner. At the same time, VLAN-based subnet boundaries are more likely to be compromised due to misconfiguration than if they were implemented using simpler, physically separate switches. At this point, we hesitate to recommend using VLANs for defining disparate high-risk security zones in the same physical switch, especially those that are in close proximity to the Internet. However, administrative advantages that VLAN-capable switches offer might justify using VLANs to segment internal network segments and those with similar risk levels or those that are in the same security zone, depending on the security requirements and VLAN expertise of your organization.

Summary

This brings us to the end of the chapter on separating resources. Our discussion focused on ways to isolate systems and processes based on their security requirements, while taking into account the budgetary and administrative overhead of segmenting resources in an overly granular manner. In the process, we discussed the advantages of limiting how resources interact with each other when crossing security zone boundaries. This approach to the design of the security perimeter allowed us to limit the scope of the influence an attacker would have if the network were compromised. We also examined some of the merits and disadvantages of employing VLANs to segregate systems. As you have seen, resource separation is an important technique for fortifying the layers of your defense-in-depth strategy. The extent of the appropriate isolation depends on your goals and capabilities, which are articulated when assessing your business needs and documented as part of your security policy.

References

1 Laura Chappell and Roger Spicer. "Is Your Network Doomed?" NetWare Connection. http://www.nwconnection.com/jan-feb.96/doomed/. December 2001.

2 Microsoft Corporation. "Exchange Server 2003 and Exchange 2000 Front-End and Back-End Topology." July 29, 2004. http://www.microsoft.com/technet/prodtechnol/exchange/2003/library/febetop.mspx. August 25, 2004.

3 National Infrastructure Protection Center. "Lion Internet Worm DDoS Targeting Unix Systems." Advisory 01-005. March 23, 2001. http://www.nipc.gov/warnings/advisories/_2001/01-005.htm. December 2001.

4 Global Incident Analysis Center. "Lion Worm." April 18, 2001. http://www.sans.org/_y2k/lion.htm. December 2001.

5 CERT Coordination Center. "Microsoft Windows NT and 2000 Domain Name Servers Allow Nonauthoritative RRs to Be Cached by Default." Vulnerability Note VU#109475. http://www.kb.cert.org/vuls/id/109475. December 2001.

6 Microsoft Corporation. "How to Prevent DNS Cache Pollution (Q241352)." September 10, 1999. http://support.microsoft.com/support/kb/articles/Q241/3/52.ASP. December 2001.

7 Cisco. "System Requirements to Implement MLS." http://www.cisco.com/warp/public/_473/55.html. December 2001.

8 IEEE. "IEEE Standards for Local and Metropolitan Area Networks: Virtual Bridged Local Area Networks." IEEE Standard 802.1Q-1998. http://standards.ieee.org/reading/ieee/std/_lanman/802.1Q-1998.pdf. December 2001.

9 David Taylor. "Are There Vulnerabilities in VLAN Implementations?" July 12, 2001. http://www.sans.org/newlook/resources/IDFAQ/vlan.htm. December 2001.

10 David Pollino and Mike Schiffman. "Secure Use of VLANs: An @stake Security Assessment." @Stake. August, 2002. http://www.cisco.com/application/pdf/en/us/guest/products/ps708/c1697/ccmigration_09186a008012ed31.pdf.

11 Cisco Systems, Inc. "Configuring VLANs." June 1, 2001. http://www.cisco.com/univercd/cc/_td/doc/product/lan/cat4000/rel6_2/config/vlans.htm. December 2001.

12 Cisco Systems, Inc. "Securing Networks with Private VLANs and VLAN Access Control Lists." http://www.cisco.com/warp/public/473/90.shtml. December 2001.

14

Wireless Network Security

WIRELESS 802.11 NETWORKS ARE BECOMING MORE and more popular as a means to augment traditional wire-based LANs within companies. The pervasive nature of wireless communications forces a security perimeter designer to reexamine some of the underlying principles of traditional network architectures. In a wireless world, we can no longer assume that physical infrastructure (walls, doors, guards, and so on) will reliably protect the network against unauthorized external access on Layer 2 (media access) and Layer 1 (physical). To access wireless resources, the attacker only has to be in the proximity of the wireless network, often without even having to enter the building of the potential victim. In this chapter we will briefly examine the fundamental 802.11 wireless technologies, go over popular wireless network encryption protocols and important techniques used to secure wireless networks from attack, look at tools and methods used to audit our secure wireless infrastructure, and then finally review an example of a secure wireless deployment.

802.11 Fundamentals

802.11 is a family of specifications adopted by the Institute of Electrical and Electronics Engineers (IEEE) for implementing wireless LANs. 802.11 is similar to the IEEE 802.3 Ethernet standard in that it maps to Layer 2 and Layer 1 protocols and services.[1] With Ethernet CSMA/CD technology, wireless nodes address each other using MAC addresses, which are embedded into the compatible network cards. However, 802.11 does not rely on wires for carrying signals on Layer 1. This means that 802.11-compliant nodes can wirelessly communicate with each other within a range defined by the specifications and supported by their wireless equipment. Because the wireless aspect of communications is limited to the media access and physical layers, higher-level protocols such as IP, TCP, and UDP do not need to be aware that datagrams are transported without wires.

802.11 networks that are most frequently deployed within companies require the use of one or more access points (APs). An AP is a device that facilitates wireless communications between 802.11 nodes and bridges the organization's wireless and wired networks. In this configuration, known as *infrastructure mode,* wireless nodes must go through the AP when communicating with each other and with nodes on the wired network. Alternatively, wireless networks can be deployed using an *ad hoc* topology, in which case participating 802.11 nodes communicate directly with each other on a peer-to-peer basis.[2]

Three main types of 802.11 networks are in use today:

- **802.11b**—This was the first standard to really catch on for wireless networking. It runs at 11Mbps, uses a wireless frequency of 2.4GHz, and has a range of up to 300 feet. It is also the most common 802.11 network type. A need for transfer speeds greater than 11Mbps created demand for 802.11a equipment.

- **802.11a**—802.11a network components run at an improved bandwidth of 56Mbps and use a broadened frequency range of 5GHz, which causes fewer conflicts with typical appliances such as cordless phones and microwaves. The 802.11a specification allows for up to 12 simultaneous communication channels, as opposed to the three channels of the 2.4GHz standards, thus equaling support of a greater number of stations per wireless network. However, because it uses a different frequency range, 802.11a offers no built-in compatibility with already deployed 802.11b equipment. Also, 802.11a equipment is much pricier and has a decreased range over its 2.4GHz counterparts (about 50 feet at the full 54Mbps).

- **802.11g**—Many people have waited to fulfill their wireless bandwidth requirements with the 802.11g standard. With a speed of 56Mbps and using the 2.4GHz frequency range, 802.11g equipment is backward compatible with the more popular 802.11b standard and offers a similar distance range of up to 300 feet, allowing full 54Mbps speeds at as far as about 100 feet. 802.11g equipment offers the speed of 802.11a, at a more competitive price and with backward compatibility with 802.11b, making for a much easier and inexpensive upgrade path.

Securing Wireless Networks

Despite all the conveniences supplied by 802.11 networks, the fact that wireless network traffic knows no physical boundaries and travels freely through the air makes it inherently insecure. In this section we will discuss ways to effectively secure wireless networks. All the elements that go into making a wired network secure can be applied in a wireless environment as well. In the upcoming pages we will discuss the best way to design a wireless network to keep it secure, the use of wireless encryption for confidentiality and authentication, the hardening of APs to ward off attacks, and the use of mechanisms outside the wireless technology domain for additional defense-in-depth security.

Network Design

The most important aspects to securing a wireless network are the way it is designed and the way it interfaces to your wired network. No matter what features you use to secure your wireless infrastructure, there will always be ways to defeat them. By utilizing a solid network design strategy, you can make it harder for attackers to reach your wireless network. This can also add more controls to your wireless segments and protect your wired network from its wireless counterparts. In this section we will examine the use of firewalls and routers to exact the same kind of controls on wireless networks that you can on wired networks and to prevent signal leakage through proper AP placement and wireless signal dampening.

Separation via Network Control Mechanisms

Because an AP typically connects wireless and wired networks, nodes that are located on networks on both sides of an AP participate in the same broadcast domain. Under such circumstances, a wireless attacker can use techniques that apply to wire-based networks, including attacks such as ARP cache poisoning, thus exploiting the loquacious nature of broadcast domains.[3] Such an attack would impact other wireless nodes that are connected to the access point, as well as devices on the wired side of it.

Because of the number of vulnerabilities associated with and the nature of wireless deployments, it makes sense to treat 802.11 networks as more vulnerable than an isolated wired network. The justification for separating wire-based and wireless resources is further reinforced by unrestrained Layer 2 access that a wireless node might have to wired hosts on the other side of the access point. As stated in Chapter 13, "Separating Resources," it is a good practice to divide the wireless part of your network from the wired part using a control mechanism, such as a router or firewall. This way, Layer 3 and higher access controls can be applied, rather than dealing with the standard problems associated with the fact that wireless communications transpire at Layer 2 and below.

A common, but flawed design that is utilized in many environments is the connection of an AP directly to a production switch (see Figure 14.1). Though this option is easily configured, it allows all wireless nodes direct Layer 2 access to any of the resources on that same production switch. At a minimum, placing the AP in its own isolated VLAN on the production switch and securing it using Layer 3 mechanisms is suggested.

A better design to consider is the concept of a "wireless DMZ," as eluded to in Chapter 13. By placing the APs into a dedicated security zone, additional Layer 3 and greater access controls (such as a firewall) can be applied. For example, by connecting all our APs to a single switch (or two switches for redundancy) and then connecting the switch to a firewall that connects to the production switch (see Figure 14.2), we have a chokepoint or Layer 3+ control between the APs and our production network.

If someone compromises a wireless node or an AP, he is now limited to only the services we are allowing across our firewall to the production network. Additionally, all traffic can be logged at the firewall, so we have an audit trail and a greater chance of detecting an attack.

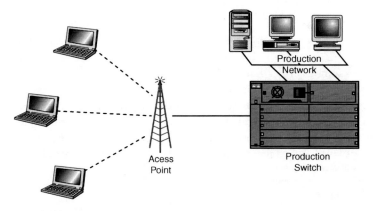

Figure 14.1   It is not uncommon to find an AP connected directly to a production switch. What this gains us in convenience, it lacks in control.

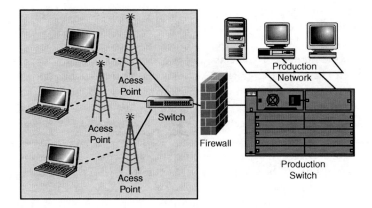

Figure 14.2   A wireless DMZ allows Layer 3 controls in the form of a firewall between our wireless and production network.

Finally, in cases where the APs themselves fall into different risk levels, it is possible to separate each of them into its own security zone, on a multileg firewall or multiple interface router (see Figure 14.3) .

A design like the one pictured in Figure 14.3 may be useful in environments such as college campuses, where instructors and students might have very different rights to production resources.

As enterprise class APs are developed, more and more of the same important security features incorporated into wired network switches are being integrated into APs. Access points have been produced that support the configuration of Quality of Service (QoS) and VLANs on the AP itself! This way, the AP can help control the QoS considerations for connected wireless clients and can group the traffic into security zones with different levels of risk using VLAN technologies. This is a major improvement over past APs, which basically acted like "dumb hubs." With a multi-VLAN AP, an important design consideration is how it will be integrated into your wired network. The connection between it and your production switch will most likely be an 802.1q trunk, which can propagate the same poor design considerations as demonstrated in the example in Figure 14.1. Placement of a firewall that supports 802.1q trunking between the AP and the switch would be recommended for exacting Layer 3+ controls on your wired networks. At the minimum, Layer 3 controls can be forced by configuring unique VLANs to support the wireless networks on the attached wired switches, forcing wireless traffic to go through a Layer 3 device for access to the rest of the wired network (see Figure 14.4). For more information on the separation of the network into security zones and the use of trunking, refer to Chapter 13.

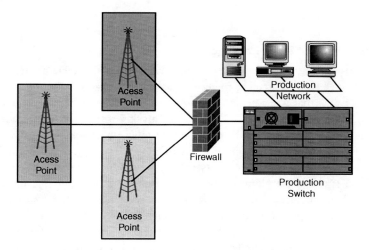

Figure 14.3   By segmenting the APs into their own security zones, we protect our wireless resources from each other.

Note
You can find information on trunking, the Cisco Firewall Services Module (FWSM), and the Check Point VSX in Chapter 13.

No matter which of these wireless network designs suits your business needs best, an important point to take away from this section is that adding Layer 3+ controls at the edge of your wireless network provides the type of control you take for granted between your wired network security zones.

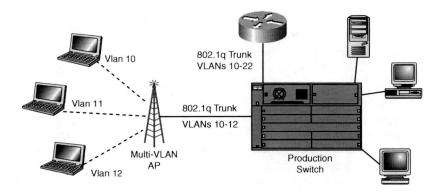

Figure 14.4   By using unique VLANs for wireless networks, communications between wireless and wired networks are forced through a Layer 3 access device.

Protecting Against Signal Leakage

Wireless infrastructure components have historically been vulnerable to attacks that could allow a determined attacker to access data on the wireless network as well as on the wired network that is connected through its access point. Such attacks have an increased threat level because 802.11 allows the attacker to connect to the wireless network at the media access layer without having to infiltrate the organization's physical facility. All that is needed to communicate with an 802.11 network is a compliant network card and the appropriate proximity to the target. One of the best ways to help alleviate such issues is by controlling wireless signal leakage. By carefully placing APs and the direction of their antennas, you can limit the amount of signal that is available outside of your building or campus. Insulating materials (such as thermally insulated windows and metallic paint and window tint) can be used to help deaden signals before they leave the areas you physically control. The less access that the public has to your network, the better. Also, choosing the areas where signal leakage occurs can also work to your advantage. If your wireless network is accessible from a public parking lot, you are at a greater risk than if your network is accessible via a secured parking lot that is monitored by cameras. Having your wireless network range mesh with your physical security, though often not possible, is a solid step toward good network security.

Defending Against Wireless Denial of Service (DoS)

There is a lot of conjecture about a new threat to networks everywhere—the wireless DoS. Though the range from which a wireless DoS can be executed must be much closer than a standard Internet DoS, the threat still has a very dangerous potential. A wireless DoS can slow down or even bring your wireless network to a halt, and depending on your network design, it could even spill over into your wired network. Most businesses do not have the equipment to be able to track down a device that could be causing a wireless DoS, though commercial packages to track down wireless transmitters (and more) are now available, such as Airmagnet (www.airmagnet.com).

The main defense against wireless denial of service (short of triangulating the source and tracking it down) is again the use of solid design fundamentals, such as those we have discussed in the last two sections. Being able to segregate the DoS away from your production network via a firewall or other control devices is ideal. QoS controls can also be implemented at the edge of the wireless DMZ. Network intrusion detection sensors can be placed at the point where your wireless and wired networks join. Finally, all the means used to keep signal leakage in can also help keep the wireless DoS out. Though no foolproof method of defense is available for wireless DoS, a proper design can go a long way toward threat mitigation.

Wireless Encryption

Although wired Ethernet-based networks do not incorporate encryption at the media access and physical layers, 802.11 designers developed specifications for encryption mechanisms to allow authentication and encryption of communications between wireless nodes on Layers 1 and 2. Wireless encryption is meant to guard against eavesdropping and limit access to the wireless infrastructure, thus protecting against the inherently "public" nature of wireless communications that allows them to pass through walls and other physical barriers.[4] An attacker is much more likely to gain access to the wireless network if the organization has not enabled an encryption method or related access-control mechanisms in its 802.11 deployment. An inexpensive reconnaissance experiment in 2001 by security enthusiasts in the Boston area detected hundreds of 802.11 access points, only 44% of which had encryption enabled.[5] Remember that any encryption is better than no encryption. Many wireless attackers are simply looking for a jumping-off point from which they can launch further attacks. If an attacker finds a network with poor encryption and one with no encryption, it is very likely he will attack the network with no encryption. After all, why bother going through all the work to crack weak encryption when he can immediately access the unprotected network?

Wired Equivalent Privacy (WEP)

An important part of securing a wireless network is using an adequate encryption algorithm to protect your airborne data. In this section we will discuss the first security protocol for wireless networks and some of the inherent weaknesses that led to its replacement.

When the 802.11 specification was created, the individuals developing it realized that eavesdropping was a major concern for wireless networking. When your precious data, personal information, and passwords are traveling through the air, confidentiality becomes paramount. With this in mind, Wired Equivalent Privacy (WEP) was created to allow secure communications between wireless network cards and access points. The original version of WEP supported a 40-bit or 64-bit pre-shared key, with a later implementation (WEP2) offering a 128-bit key. It uses the RC4 algorithm for encryption.

The paper "Weaknesses in the Key Scheduling Algorithm of RC4," by Scott Fluhrer, Itsik Mantin, and Adi Shamir, discuss flaws with RC4 in great detail, including issues with the way RC4 is implemented in WEP. The authors state that "when the same secret part of the key is used with numerous different exposed values, an attacker can rederive the secret part by analyzing the initial word of the keystreams with relatively little work."[6] In turn, countless programs have been developed to exploit this weakness in WEP, including WEPCrack and AirSnort, both of which will be covered later in this chapter. For more information on the vulnerabilities of WEP and RC4, check out "Weaknesses in the Key Scheduling Algorithm of RC4," which is available all over the Internet.

Note

The fact that some implementations of RC4 are weak does not mean that RC4 itself is broken. Properly implemented, RC4 is considered secure. For more information, checkout "RSA Security Response to Weaknesses in Key Scheduling Algorithm of RC4" at http://www.rsasecurity.com/rsalabs/node.asp?id=2009.

Despite the inherent weaknesses in WEP, it is still deployed today. If WEP is your only choice, it is better than no encryption at all. However, you should consider WEP to be broken and should replace it if at all possible.[7] Some vendors have strengthened WEP by incorporating an authentication protocol such as LEAP into their products.

Extensible Authentication Protocols: PEAP/LEAP/EAP-TLS

One of the major weaknesses of WEP was that it used a pre-shared key. Any time a static pre-shared key is used, it is unlikely it will be changed regularly, if at all. This makes it very vulnerable to attack because exploits can be run on it again and again. Also, there are no usernames to be determined, so just one item needs to be cracked—the key itself. If multiple parties need to gain access to the network, the pre-shared key needs to be disseminated in some form, which leads to issues in keeping the key secured as it is passed around. One means to mitigate these issues is by using a protocol that supports authentication. Using a centralized authentication server (such as RADIUS or TACACS) means that there are multiple usernames and passwords, all which are centrally managed and can be controlled via a strict password policy forcing complexity and regular password changes.

Protected Extensible Authentication Protocol (PEAP), Lightweight Extensible Authentication Protocol (LEAP), and EAP-TLS are all examples of authentication protocols used with wireless networks. These protocols incorporate the use of authentication servers (for example, RADIUS) instead of using a pre-shared key. They supply not only an additional level of security, but also a centralized means to share credentials across multiple APs and other network devices that can utilize RADIUS technology.

LEAP is a proprietary protocol created by Cisco systems. It uses Microsoft Challenge Authentication Protocol version 2 (MS-CHAPv2) to authenticate against an authentication server. In its original implementation it used transient WEP keys to protect information flows (though it can also be used with other encryption standards such as WPA).

Though these benefits help negate all the exploitable negatives with WEP deployments, there has still been a lot of talk recently about the security of LEAP. At DEFCON in August of 2003, Joshua Wright revealed weaknesses in LEAP to dictionary attacks.[8] This is due to limitations that can be found in the MS-CHAP implementation, including the facts that user credentials travel in the clear (immediately giving up half of what an attacker needs) and that its hashes do not use salts.

What Is a Salt?

A *salt* is a random piece of information that is added to data before it is hashed, preventing two identical pieces of data from having the same hash. You can determine the value of a password that was hashed without a salt by using the same hashing algorithm against password guesses and comparing the resultant hashes against the original password hash. When the hashes match, you have successfully guessed the password!

The LEAP dictionary attack makes an excellent case for the necessity of a strong password policy. This attack only works well when the password guesses can be easily generated via a source such as a predefined password dictionary. If complex passwords are used, this assault will not work, and it is very unlikely that a brute force attack using the same methodology would give timely results.

Note

For more information on the LEAP dictionary attack vulnerability, check out "Weaknesses in LEAP Challenge/Response" (http://home.jwu.edu/jwright/presentations/asleap-defcon.pdf) and "Cisco Response to Dictionary Attacks on Cisco LEAP" (http://www.cisco.com/en/US/products/hw/wireless/ps430/prod_bulletin09186a00801cc901.html).

Another authentication protocol choice is PEAP. It was created by a consortium of vendors, including Microsoft, Cisco, and RSA Security. Though similar to LEAP, using an authentication server and MS-CHAPv2, it adds enhanced security by offering additional authentication options and forcing this authentication to take place in an encrypted Transport Layer Security (TLS) tunnel. TLS is the planned replacement for SSL and offers similar functionality. The additional security provided by the TLS tunnel has the positive effect of removing the concerns previously expressed for LEAP. However, the negative side effect is that a digital certificate is required for the authentication server.

TinyPEAP

Now that a known offline dictionary attack is available against the pre-shared key version of the new industry wireless security standard WPA, implementing an authentication server to defend your wireless environment is more important than ever. One interesting option is called TinyPEAP (www.tinypeap.com). It embeds a simple RADIUS server into firmware that can be added to Linksys WRT54G/GS model wireless routers. Though most likely only an ideal solution for home and small-office networks, it's a novel idea nonetheless! Perhaps one day all APs will come with integrated RADIUS servers.

EAP-TLS is the new standard for wireless authentication set forth in the newly adopted IEEE 802.11i security standard. It is similar to the other EAP protocols we mentioned; however, it requires digital certificates on both wireless clients and authentication servers, demanding the implementation of Public Key Infrastructure (PKI) for digital certificate management. This makes EAP-TLS the most secure of the EAP standards in this section and the most costly and complicated to deploy and manage.

Wi-Fi Protected Access (WPA)

Due to all the shortcomings in WEP, a new implementation of encryption protocol for wireless networks had to be developed. The answer: Wi-Fi Protected Access (WPA) Protocol. WPA integrates an improved choice of encryption algorithms with an almost infinite number of dynamically generated keys, with proven EAP authentication protocols and additional integrity checking for a rock-solid replacement for the former WEP standard.

The initial implementation of WPA used the Temporal Key Integrity Protocol (TKIP) encryption algorithm with 128-bit dynamic session keys. The second version of WPA (WPAv2) was enhanced to meet the IEEE 802.11i security standard by using Advanced Encryption Standard (AES) 128-, 192-, and 256-bit keys. The two modes of operation with either version of WPA are Personal (also called WPA-PSK) and Enterprise. Personal uses a pre-shared key (for which there has been an attack offered against—see the sidebar "WPA Pre-shared Key Passive Dictionary Attack," later in this section) whereas Enterprise supports an authentication server (such as RADIUS) and EAP methods such as EAP-TLS and PEAP.

The Wi-Fi Alliance states the following about WPA, with its improved encryption algorithms and security mechanisms: "Cryptographers have reviewed Wi-Fi Protected Access and have verified that it meets its claims to close all known WEP vulnerabilities and provides an effective deterrent against known attacks."[9] Both versions of WPA integrate a capability to verify the validity of packets with its Message Integrity Check (MIC). The WPA and WPAv2 standards are making wireless networks an easier security decision for IT managers everywhere.

WPA Pre-shared Key Passive Dictionary Attack

Just when you thought all your answers to wireless security had been answered with WPA, an attack is revealed by the folks who invented TinyPEAP, which puts poor WPA pre-shared keys (or passphrases) at risk. The attack tool takes a small network trace and runs a dictionary attack against it offline. This makes for an efficient attack because a small network trace can be run pretty quickly and then the actual dictionary processing can be run at a remote location and take as long as the attacker would like. A whitepaper and sample attack code are both available at www.tinypeap.com. This vulnerability does not mean that WPA is compromised. It does, however, reinforce that high-security environments should not be running the pre-shared key version of WPA, instead using a RADIUS server for authentication. Also, in environments with WPA using pre-shared keys, you should make sure your passphrase is not made up of standard dictionary words and that it is long (20 characters or longer was suggested by Robert Moskowitz, who originally warned of this vulnerability in WPA-PSK).[10]

Remember these points when implementing encryption on your wireless network:

- It is a good idea to use the strongest encryption your environment can support.
- A proven algorithm and suitably large key (128+ bit) makes for good security.
- Use user authentication methods to augment security. In highly secure environments, two-factor authentication is a major plus.
- Be sure to load firmware updates and security updates for wireless hardware and drivers when they become available.

Keep these points in mind when determining which technology is the best security fit for your environment and when deploying the technology, to maximize your environment's protection.

Hardening Access Points

Just as the border router is the entranceway to your wired network from the Internet, the AP is the entranceway between your wireless and wired networks. In turn, it must be locked down as much as possible to prevent it from being infiltrated. Several major issues must be considered when hardening your AP. Shutting down SSID broadcasts, locking down MAC addresses, disabling unused services, and using strong passwording are all important aspects of securing the access point.

Disabling SSID Broadcasts

One of the things that makes wireless networks great is how easy it is to connect to them. Of course, this is also one of the things that makes securing wireless networks very difficult. By default, most access points are configured to broadcast the Service Set Identifier (SSID), a configurable label on the AP that identifies itself to the wireless client and lets the client know it is an access point.

Extended and Basic Service Sets

You may hear the terms *ESSID* (Extended Service Set Identifier) and *SSID* used interchangeably. The SSID value that is assigned to the access points taking part in an Extended Service Set (ESS) is also known as the ESSID. The other type of SSID is the BSSID, or Basic Service Set Identifier, identifying the communication hub of a Basic Service Set (BSS). The ESS is all APs and clients making up an infrastructure mode wireless LAN. An ESS can be made up of one or more Basic Service Sets. When an ESS uses multiple APs, each individual AP and its support clients is a BSS. The BSSID for each of those APs would not be its assigned SSID but the MAC address for the individual AP. An ad hoc network is another type of BSS. In an ad hoc BSS, clients work together to act as an AP and use a virtual Ethernet address as the BSSID.

The wireless networking client in Windows XP will pop up a list of available networks when a wireless host is first connecting to a network. These networks are discovered by the SSID broadcasts sent by their access points. In the early days of wireless, many uninformed network practitioners thought that changing the SSID to something other than the manufacturer's default was a "hardening technique." However, client scanning shows all SSID broadcasts in the area. The only benefit that changing the SSID provides is the prevention of the instant identification of the AP vendor.

Despite the ease of administration broadcasting SSIDs offers, a good way to improve security is to disable SSID broadcasts on all wireless access points. This will help prevent outsiders from easily discovering your access points. On the downside, this means that all wireless clients will need to be manually configured with the SSID of the network they are a part of.

Wardriving

Wardriving is the term for searching out wireless access points, mostly ones that have no or poor security. It takes its name from the process "wardialing," which hackers used in the years of dial-up connectivity and modems. Hackers would program wardialing programs to dial up hundreds of phone numbers looking for modems and PBXs that could be compromised. Wardriving involves a similar process by which attackers drive around with a laptop or PDA with wireless capabilities and attempt to locate APs using detection tools such as Netstumbler and Mini-Stumbler. These tools search for SSIDs being broadcasted from the wireless access points. After finding APs, attackers sometimes draw symbols with chalk on the pavement near where the APs were found. This is called *warchalking*. Silencing SSID broadcasts may prevent you from being a victim of wardriving. Remember, your users are not the only people trying to connect to your AP!

It is important to keep in mind that locking down SSID broadcasts, though a good security step, does not guarantee a secure access point. Attackers with wireless sniffers can still examine communication flows between clients and APs and determine SSID information, even with broadcasts disabled. However, it does prevent your wireless clients from accidentally logging in to the wrong AP, and it prevents outsiders and attackers from accidentally logging on to yours.

However, the use of strong authentication and encryption methods goes a long way to help mitigate the issues caused by SSID broadcasts. It does not matter that an attacker knows your wireless network is there if there are no exploits to run against it and your authentication methods are solid.

FakeAP

FakeAP is a Linux-based program that can thwart wardrivers by creating the appearance of thousands of APs on AP-detection tools such as Netstumbler. Attackers won't know which of the thousands of access points are legitimate and which are "ghosts" generated by FakeAP. Check it out at http://www.blackalchemy.to/project/fakeap/.

MAC Address Lockdown

Another technique that has helped many a network administrator sleep easier at night is the ability to lock down MAC addresses on wireless access points. Some access points include the capability to configure a list of MAC addresses for wireless clients that are allowed to communicate with the AP. At first glance this seems like an almost foolproof way to prevent outsiders from gaining access to your wireless network. However, this unfortunately is not entirely true. Again, this is a good step toward a strong security posture, but with the right equipment this defense can easily be bypassed. All an attacker needs to do is use a wireless sniffer to watch communication flows between a client and AP. Once the attacker records the MAC address of an allowed client, he can easily spoof the MAC address in question and begin communicating with the locked-down AP. He may need to run a DoS (or the like) against the original owner of the MAC address to keep it from interrupting his communications, or he may need to wait for that client to disconnect from the network.

MAC Address Spoofing in Windows

Many users are familiar with operating systems such as Linux or Solaris that offer an easy means to change or spoof the MAC address on any installed network card. You may have also seen network cards whose drivers support the manual reconfiguration of MAC addresses themselves. However, how can an end user running an operating system such as Windows change the MAC address of his wireless network card? The answer is surprisingly *much* easier than you would think. An undocumented Windows Registry entry can be added under the key for the active network adapter, allowing the assignment of a new MAC address to the card! (Warning: Use Regedit at your own risk!) Using Regedit, browse through to `HKEY_LOCAL_MACHINE\SYSTEM\CurrentControlSet\Control\Class\{4D36E972-E325-11CE-BFC1-08002BE10318}`. Beneath this key will be a number of subkeys numbered 0000 and up, representing any network adapters (physical or virtual) that have been installed in your system. Browse down through them using the driver description (`DriverDesc`) to determine which one is the NIC you want to alter. Finally, add a string value under this key called `"NetworkAddress"` (watch the case and do not enter any spaces). Finally, edit this newly added string and add value data equaling the 12-digit MAC address you want to spoof. It must be in hexadecimal format, with no spaces or other symbols. Now to activate your new MAC address, you simply need to disable and then enable your NIC. You can check to verify the new MAC address has been properly assigned to your NIC using `ipconfig /all` from a command prompt.

Having to lock down the MAC addresses for all the wireless nodes in a large network is an administrative nightmare. However, in environments where security needs to be maximized, locking down the MAC addresses of nodes adds an additional layer of complexity that an attacker needs to bypass. The more steps an attacker needs to take to compromise your security, the more likely he is to give up.

Miscellaneous AP Hardening

Many additional steps can be taken to help lock down your wireless access point against attacks. First and foremost, *always* change the default password on the AP before putting it into production. Be sure to follow best practices for a complex password. Also, try to lock down AP management mechanisms as much as possible. Try to disable web management via wireless devices and lock down wired management as much as your AP will allow. If an out-of-band management method is available for your AP, it is highly recommended that you take advantage of it.

Many APs have the ability to bridge themselves to other APs. It is a good idea in a single AP environment to disable this capability. In a multi-AP environment, lock down your APs' intercommunication by MAC address. This can be overcome, as mentioned in the section on MAC address lockdown, but it's still worthy of completion.

As previously eluded to, make sure that up-to-date firmware is installed on a newly purchased AP. Also, track firmware updates that repair security vulnerabilities. Newer firmware versions will support additional security features, more robust and cutting-edge encryption algorithms, and new industry security standards.

Proper passwording, secured management, and up-to-date firmware are all important parts of locking down your access point. Hardening your AP is a key in securing your wireless network.

Defense in Depth for Wireless Networks

Some of the most effective approaches to securing a wireless network don't have anything to do with wireless technologies at all. Many defense-in-depth techniques used in the wired world can be applied with great success with wireless networks. In the following sections we will discuss some important technologies that can take your wireless network's security to the next level.

VPN/IPSec

When it was originally discovered that WEP was broken, many security analysts suggested implementing VPN technologies or host-to-host IPSec on wireless clients. This added an additional layer of confidentiality and authentication between wireless hosts and destination resources. All traffic is encrypted from the client to the destination (including across the wired network) without fear of WEP being cracked. Configuring transport mode IPSec is easily done for all traffic between hosts or just for certain protocols. Also, this requires an additional level of authentication for the client and server to communicate. For more information on IPSec or configuring it for transport mode operation, check out Chapter 7, "Virtual Private Networks."

Host Defenses

Many of the host-based defenses in Chapter 10, "Host Defense Components," are very beneficial for the wandering wireless client. Wireless networking technologies expose our clients at Layer 2 and below to assaults from anyone within range. Using host IDS and a firewall on a wireless client are excellent steps to prevent airborne attacks. Both will help you be aware of and defend against an attempted attack, whether you are connected to your office wireless network or on the road. Also, both act as additional "sensors" for your wireless network's security. Hosts may pick up wireless DoS or other attacks before they get to your wired network defenses. Strong host defenses are an important part of keeping your wireless environment secure.

Auditing Wireless Security

As in the wired world of networking, one of the most important parts of securing an environment is "checking your work." Auditing makes sure the security measures you have in place are working as you expected them to. It is a good practice when auditing security to make a list of your defenses and then write down some tests to prove that the defenses are working, followed by a list of expected outcomes and finally a place to describe what the outcome of the audit actually was. When the audit is complete, this will provide an excellent tool to refer back to in a "lessons learned" meeting if you ever face a successful intrusion or attack. It will help you determine if an issue was introduced after the initial design implementation that enabled the incident or perhaps help you discover flaws in your own auditing techniques. Auditing is sufficiently important that we have an entire chapter dedicated to it (Chapter 22, "Assessment Techniques"), where we go into the process of network security auditing in great detail. However, this section will provide information specifically dealing with the tools and techniques used for the auditing of wireless networks only.

A number of software programs allow network professionals to audit the security of their wireless networks, including wireless sniffers, encryption-cracking tools, and AP detectors. In the following sections we will discuss some of the more useful of these tools and describe techniques that can be used to verify the security of a wireless network.

Auditing the Wireless Network Design

Despite the best laid plans of mice and men, network security holes still happen. You can lay out the ultimate network design on paper, but one mistake while implementing a firewall rule can bring your whole network to its knees. That is why running audits against what your design should secure is an important part of the design itself.

Auditing Network Controls

No matter what design methodology you use to separate your wireless and wired networks (even the absence of separation is a design decision), it is imperative to determine what resources an attacker would be able to gain access to once he is connected to your wireless network. To verify this connectivity, make a list of critical resources you would not want an attacker to be able to contact. Then, using one of your wireless clients, run tests using common wired network security tools, such as port scanners, firewalk, and vulnerability scanners. If you can access your critical resources, a motivated attacker will be able to as well. Use the information gleaned from the audits to bolster your network design's security.

Auditing Signal Leakage

For this audit you are going for a walk, literally. Grab your favorite laptop and load it up with tools to see what's going on in the atmosphere around your workplace. It is advisable that you wield an external antenna, similar to the ones an attacker would use, to increase your range. The small omni-directional antennas that are integrated into most wireless PC cards have a fraction of the range of a directional antenna such as a Yagi. A chart of wireless coverage for an omni-directional antenna is almost spherical, whereas a Yagi directional antenna is more like a column stretching many times the distance of the "omni" in the direction the antenna is being pointed.

> **Warning**
>
> Remember that a wireless signal can be affected by interference, reflection, and outside factors. Though you may not be able to access your network from the parking lot today, you may be able to hit it from beyond there next week. Perform regular audits with varying equipment and tools, but don't rely on signal control as your sole defense mechanism.

Start by walking the perimeter of your environment with a tool such as Netstumbler (http://www.netstumbler.com) or, even better, Kismet (http://www.kismetwireless.net), which can find any valid access points you are using. Netstumbler is easy to load, easier to use, and can be run on popular handheld devices (Mini-Stumbler) as well as the ever-pervasive Windows operating systems. However, it relies on the passive reception of SSID broadcasts to detect APs and does not look beyond them. Do not rely on Netstumbler as your sole auditing tool because you'll gain a false sense of security with your results. Other programs such as Kismet are proactive and search out wireless packets to find APs and wireless networks. Kismet, however, is currently only available for Linux. In any case, either program may be used by an attacker looking for your network. When walking the grounds with either tool, take note of which APs can be located from public areas, including lobbies, restrooms, and other publicly accessible areas in your building. Finally, take a walk through your building and pay particular attention to SSIDs you don't recognize. A major security hole can be added to the most secure network when an end user deploys his own access point or configures a wireless NIC to be part of its own ad hoc environment. Believe it or not, this happens more often than you would expect. An executive feels tethered to his desk by a network cable, so he plugs in an AP (running without encryption, of course) and pops a wireless NIC in to his laptop. Talk about an attacker's dream!

Another good practice is running a sniffer capable of examining wireless traffic—such as Airmagnet, Ethereal (http://www.ethereal.com), or the like—and examining the information you are sending in the clear. You might be interested to find out what information an attacker can see even when your network is properly protected by MAC address lockdown, disabled SSID broadcasts, and strong encryption. Also confirm that the encryption protocols running on your network are the ones you deployed. Knowing your weaknesses is the first step in buttressing your fortress!

Auditing Encryption

Once you are confident the information being sent through the air in your environment is all encrypted, it is a good idea to run any available cracking tools to confirm that your encryption implementation is sound. Running searches on the Internet and exploiting websites such as http://www.packetstormsecurity.org should provide you with plenty of material to try. Here is a list of popular tools for various encryption types:

- **WEPCrack**—The first open source WEP cracking tool (http://wepcrack.sourceforge.net)
- **AirSnort**—A wireless sniffer that guesses WEP keys (http://sourceforge.net/projects/airsnort)
- **WEP Wedgie**—A tool used to inject traffic into a WEP conversation to speed the cracking of WEP (http://sourceforge.net/projects/wepwedgie/)
- **AirCrack**—A fast WEP-cracking tool (http://freshmeat.net/projects/aircrack/)
- **BSD Airtools**—A variety of wireless auditing tools for BSD, including a WEP cracker (www.dachb0den.com/projects/bsd-airtools.html)
- **Asleap**—A dictionary-based password attack on the LEAP protocol (http://asleap.sourceforge.net/)
- **WPACrack**—A tool that runs offline dictionary attacks against WPA implemented with pre-shared keys (http://www.tinypeap.com/page8.html)

AirSnort

AirSnort is a freeware Linux-based sniffer that intercepts and decodes WEP-encrypted packets (it has also recently been ported to Windows XP). AirSnort can be used by promiscuously capturing wireless packets. After approximately 100MB–1GB of wireless data has been gathered, AirSnort can "guess the encryption password in under a second."[11] AirSnort accomplishes this by exploiting a vulnerability in the key scheduling algorithm of RC4, discovered by Scott Fluhrer, Itsik Mantin, and Adi Shamir (as discussed in the section on WEP encryption, earlier in this chapter).

AirSnort needs to collect wireless packets before cracking the WEP password because, according to the program's documentation, out of 16 million 128-bit WEP keys that wireless cards can generate, about 3,000 are considered "weak." After the program gathers enough "weak" WEP key packets, it is able to decipher the WEP password and decode WEP-protected packets.

Do not consider this list as exhaustive. New vulnerabilities may appear at any time, and you need to update your auditing tools as regularly as your attackers will.

Case Study: Effective Wireless Architecture

Now that we have discussed the means to create a secure wireless architecture, let's put what you have learned to use by looking at a good wireless network design.

The sample organization is a small university that wants to add wireless for students, faculty, and visitors, as well as a small wireless network for executive administrators. The requirements are as follows:

- The Visitors network is unsecured and unencrypted.
- The Student, Faculty, and Admin networks are all to be encrypted with WPAv2 Enterprise, with the Admin network using its own RADIUS server.
- The Student and Faculty networks will access very different production network resources.
- Wireless service must be available for the Visitor, Student, and Faculty networks anywhere on the campus.
- The Admin network needs to be highly secure and efforts should be made to prevent its existence from being known.

Based on these basic requirements and the secure design elements we have discussed in this chapter, our proposed design is illustrated in Figure 14.5.

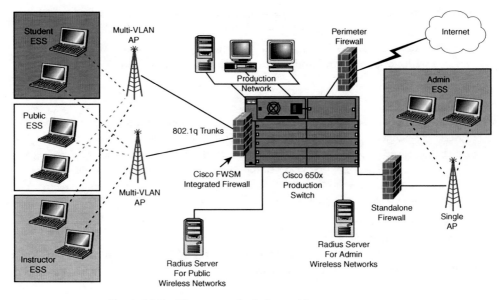

Figure 14.5 The proposed wireless architecture uses many of the defenses we discussed in this chapter.

The key to this design is the functionality of the Cisco Aironet 1200 series access point that is used for the public wireless networks—that is, the Faculty, Student, and Visitor networks. The Aironet 1200 supports multiple VLANs and a unique security policy on each VLAN. Each of the wireless networks is deployed as its own Extended Service Set (ESS), or basically as its own separate wireless network, with each being configured as an independent VLAN on the Aironet. Two APs are deployed to extend the range to cover the required service area of the campus. However, with this added coverage comes added exposure, which is why security is paramount. Both Aironets are trunked to the central

650x Series switch, which has a Firewall Services Module (FWSM) installed in it. The FWSM allows the trunked VLANs to be firewalled from each other as well as the rest of the wired network.

From a security perspective, each of the three networks is configured differently. The Visitor VLAN security policy is configured to support no encryption, as specified in the network requirements. MAC address authentication is disabled because anyone should be able to access the Visitor ESS. No authentication is required, but connections are logged and the FWSM is configured to only allow the Visitor network access to the Internet and certain public resources at the university.

The Student VLAN security policy is configured to support WPAv2 Enterprise and uses a RADIUS server that is protected by the FWSM. This strong security algorithm is critical in the campus environment to protect outside access to critical university resources. Because the university grounds are basically an unsecured public space, an interloper with a laptop could wander right into range without drawing any suspicion. Therefore, a secure protection algorithm combined with strong authentication can greatly increase the security of the university network. Also, specific firewall rules are added for the Student VLAN to only allow access to student resources. SSID broadcasts are enabled because we will not be able to configure all of the students' laptops and MAC address authentication is disabled. RADIUS authentication will be used for student access, which will steer the students to the correct VLAN using a special feature of the Aironet AP that forces authenticated clients to the appropriate ESS.

The Faculty ESS VLAN security policy is also configured to support WPAv2 Enterprise and uses the same protected RADIUS server. This strong protection protocol and authentication method is vital not to only protect the faculty resources from outside attackers, but also to protect them from curious students who may want to take a closer look at their grades. Again, the FWSM is used to allow only access to faculty resources and defend the wired network from the wireless network. Broadcasts are not required in this case, but due to the fact that we have RADIUS configured to assign clients to the correct VLAN, we can save ourselves a lot of administrative work by keeping broadcasts enabled. MAC address authentication will be enabled for the Faculty VLAN to add an additional level of security.

Faculty laptops are deployed using host-hardening best practices and installed with host-based defense components. Not only will this help protect the Faculty network from direct wireless attacks, it will help the university be aware of events occurring on the wireless network.

Finally, the Admin network is configured quite differently from the public wireless network. Though in a highly secure environment wired connectivity would be strongly suggested over wireless, sometimes business requirements force the use of inherently less-secure solutions. In this case, the administrators are the ones making the decisions and they want the flexibility of wireless networking in the administration area. With this in mind, the highest level of wireless networking security must be applied to the administrators' network. The center of the design is a single AP deployed in a carefully chosen point in the administration office area, thus minimizing access from the outside (as demonstrated in Figure 14.6).

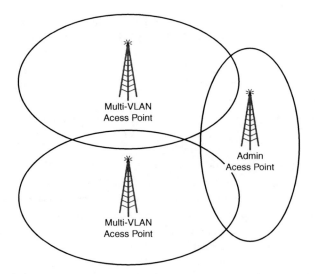

Multi-VLAN
Acess Point

Admin
Acess Point

Multi-VLAN
Acess Point

Figure 14.6 Whereas the main publicly accessible multi-VLAN
APs are available all over campus, controls are used to limit
the range of the Admin AP as much as possible.

Signal leakage will be minimized by using signal-limiting window tint on all offices.
Also, because redecorating is not allowed in the admin area, the ceilings below their
second-floor offices will be painted with signal-limiting metallic-based paint. The Admin
AP will be a different manufacturer than the public APs to help enable additional
defense in depth. However, with this decision comes additional administrative costs,
because support personnel need to be trained on more than one product type. Broadcasts
will be disabled and MAC address authentication will be configured. WPAv2 Enterprise
is enabled and a separate RADIUS server is used for authentication.

Host-hardening best practices are used and the same host-defense components are
installed on the administrators' laptops. Also, because security is paramount in their environment, the administrators' laptops are configured to use transport mode AH IPSec
connectivity to critical resources they need to access, such as student grades, confidential
employee information, and business information that is not publicly available. We have
chosen AH because it has less overhead than ESP, and because we have implemented
WPAv2 using AES encryption, we are not terribly concerned about the confidentiality
being breached in the Admin network. When the traffic is unencrypted after it has left
the AP, it is subject to IDS scans and content inspection because AH is unencrypted.
However, AH adds another level of authentication that needs to be passed to gain access
to critical resources.

An additional firewall is deployed between the Admin wireless network and the production network to control access to production wired resources.

This design employs many of the security options we have covered in this chapter. A strong network design is the foundation of this plan. Despite the fact that wireless may not be ideal for parts of this network, business requirements justify the security tradeoff. Therefore, maximizing the security posture through the use of all means available is paramount. Defense-in-depth methodologies are used throughout and a proven encryption algorithm enhances the network's security. Finally, all devices are properly hardened using best practices and the design is continually audited as a means of ongoing verification.

Summary

Many concerns are involved in securing wireless networks. A solid network design with proper Layer 3+ controls and controlled signal leakage are all part of an important start. Using proper, proven encryption algorithms and authentication, disabling SSID broadcasts, locking down MAC addresses, and hardening your access point are all vital in the proper security of your wireless network. Employing defense in depth with host-based security mechanisms and IPSec round out the network's security. Auditing the design with popular AP detection tools, wireless sniffers, and encryption-cracking tools validates your work.

Although no one suggestion in this section is a foolproof defense for wireless security, using the combination of these security techniques will help keep your network off the attacker's radar and make compromising it a much more difficult task. Because undefended wireless networks are in such great number at this time, the more protected your wireless network is, the less likely an attacker will waste his time pursuing it. The reality of network security is that in environments that need to be highly secure, wired networking should be deployed. It is less expensive and easier to lock down than its wireless counterpart. However, when business needs dictate that wireless networking is to be used in your environment, deploying solid wireless network security methods, as covered in this chapter, will prove invaluable to your organization.

References

1 Intelligraphics. "Introduction to IEEE 802.11." http://www.intelligraphics.com/articles/80211_article.html. December 2001.

2 Jim Zyren and Al Petrick. "IEEE 802.11 Tutorial." http://www.packetnexus.com/docs/IEEE_80211_Primer.pdf. December 2001.

3 Bob Fleck and Jordan Dimov. "Wireless Access Points and ARP Poisoning." http://www.cigitallabs.com/resources/papers/download/arppoison.pdf. December 2001.

4 Wireless Ethernet Compatibility Alliance. "802.11b Wired Equivalent Privacy (WEP) Security." February 19, 2001. http://www.wi-fi.net/pdf/Wi-FiWEPSecurity.pdf. December 2001.

5 Craig Ellison. "Exploiting and Protecting 802.11b Wireless Networks." ExtremeTech. September 4, 2001. http://www.extremetech.com/print_article/ 0,3428,a%253D13880,00.asp. December 2001.

6 Scott Fluhrer, Itsik Mantin, and Adi Shamir. "Weaknesses in the Key Scheduling Algorithm of RC4." August 2001.

7 Ronald L. Rivest. "RSA Security Response to Weaknesses in Key Scheduling Algorithm of RC4." http://www.rsasecurity.com/rsalabs/node.asp?id=2009 2001.

8 Joshua Wright. "Weaknesses in LEAP Challenge/Response." http://home.jwu.edu/jwright/ presentations/asleap-defcon.pdf. 2003.

9 Wi-Fi Alliance. "Wi-Fi Protected Access: Strong, standards-based, interoperable security for today's Wi-Fi networks" http://www.wi-fi.net/OpenSection/pdf/Whitepaper_Wi-Fi_ Security4-29-03.pdf. April 29, 2003.

10 Robert Moskowitz. "Weakness in Passphrase Choice in WPA Interface." http://wifinetnews.com/archives/002452.html. November 4, 2003.

11 AirSnort home page. http://airsnort.sourceforge.net/. December 2001.

15

Software Architecture

SOFTWARE ARCHITECTURE IS A CRITICAL CONCEPT that is frequently overlooked in discussions about network security. In the context of perimeter defense, the term *software architecture* refers to the manner in which the components of an application should be deployed to make it as secure as possible while preserving its usability and maintainability. Many people are unaware that functionality and security issues are often related to where application components are deployed on a network. If these issues are not addressed, the application is at increased risk of encountering serious functionality or security-related problems, which could also impact other infrastructure components important to the organization. In this chapter, we review various software architecture issues, focusing on the effects that software architecture and network defense components, such as firewalls and routers, have on each other.

After examining the fundamentals of software architecture, we review several issues involving configuring software to be more secure. One of the features of this chapter is an extensive discussion of what characteristics to look for when purchasing or designing software. We also talk about the importance of testing software in a secure environment before deployment and about designing your security perimeter in a way that will make future application deployments easier. Finally, we look at case studies of two application deployments to see how they can be made more secure by following the principles of robust software architecture.

Software Architecture and Network Defense

When we speak of software architecture, we are talking about where each component of an application should be deployed on a network. Application components include user interfaces, databases, and middleware, which can be thought of as the back end of the application, providing functionality behind the user interface and connecting the user interface and the database. Application users can be considered another "component" of the application. In this chapter, we focus on applications whose users connect to them over the Internet hosts. Such applications are often at high risk of being attacked because, by definition, they must be accessible from the Internet. These applications often contain sensitive data, such as credit card numbers, that attackers want to access.

The Importance of Software Architecture

To clarify what software architecture does and doesn't involve, let's consider a simple example. You work for a company that wants to deploy a web-based application so that customers can buy widgets online. The users of this application access it from various hosts on the Internet. The application has a web interface for the users, which interacts with a database server through a middleware component. When you are planning the deployment of this application, you must consider where to place the web interface, middleware, and database on your network so that business needs for functionality and security are met. This is the core of software architecture.

Deciding where to deploy software components is a much more complicated issue than you might realize. Some applications may not work properly when you pass their traffic through firewalls; for example, a common problem is that an application is incompatible with Network Address Translation (NAT). Applications may also fail to provide adequate encryption for sensitive network traffic. Some applications require extensive network defense changes to be made in order to run properly and securely, depending on how you deploy them and how insecure their design is. When applications need to interact with hosts on the Internet, software architecture and network defense components are often at odds with each other. Two viewpoints must be considered:

- Many applications are not designed to follow best security practices and, in fact, might not work properly if you try to secure them. For example, an application might require root privileges to run properly on a host. You will be required to weaken your network and host defenses in order to use the application; therefore, applications that cannot be secured adequately should not be used.

- The whole purpose of having the network is to meet business needs, and network defenses should not "get in the way" of providing needed services and functionality to users. Security measures should be flexible and robust enough to provide adequate protection without hampering application functionality.

So which point of view is correct? Both are. The purpose of security is to support business needs by allowing access to applications and data while protecting them against unauthorized activity. If your network defenses are so rigid that they cannot accommodate a new, critical application, you should reconsider your perimeter design. It does no good to have a secure network if it can't meet your organization's needs. On the other hand, if an application is so insecure that it is prohibitively difficult or expensive to secure properly, it's likely in the best interest of your organization not to implement it. Your decisions should be based on a combination of your organization's needs and your security policy.

The Need to Evaluate Application Security

If you considered security-related issues in the beginning of the software-selection process, you could mitigate many conflicts between software characteristics and network defense. However, it's far more typical for security to be largely ignored until well after the software has been purchased. Often business users in the organization who know nothing about networks, security, or computing in general are the ones who choose the software. These users know what business needs must be met, and they choose the software solution they feel best meets those requirements. Unfortunately, the business users are unaware that the solution they are choosing might be completely insecure, violate your security policies, and, in some cases, be impossible to run with your present network defenses and configuration.

The Value of Assisting with Software Evaluations

I worked at a large company where well-meaning people from various business units were selecting applications without considering security and then were upset when the IT department raised objections to deploying these applications. We found an easy solution for this problem: A few of us who were knowledgeable in security and application deployment approached the business units and offered to attend meetings with the business unit employees and software vendors. We watched the product demonstrations and had the opportunity to ask various security questions. We then evaluated the products and documented our security concerns with each product. The business unit employees used our reports as one factor when deciding which solution was the best.

Of course, we would be happiest if they chose the product we felt had the best security. But even if the product with the most serious security shortcomings was the one chosen, we would have adequate time to plan how to compensate for these shortcomings and already know what the potential issues would be. We strongly felt that our participation in product selection was a win-win situation—the business unit employees and IT staff would have far fewer headaches and surprises to deal with.

How Software Architecture Affects Network Defense

In the course of planning or deploying a software solution, you often have to make adjustments or changes to your network defense. Firewall and packet-filtering policies are often affected by new applications, particularly those that use more than one static port. Issues with network configurations and architectures also occur frequently, including poor reliability and performance. Ensuring that connections carrying sensitive data are encrypted is very important too. Finally, you might have to face an application that uses an operating system that isn't usually deployed in your environment. The following section considers all these potential problems.

Firewall and Packet-Filtering Changes

Probably the most common issue involving software architecture and network defense is that of changing firewall rule sets and router ACLs. Many applications that either are accessed through the Internet or access the Internet themselves might need to pass traffic through your firewalls or routers. In many cases, these applications use protocols or port numbers that you normally do not permit to pass through your firewall. Although on the surface it sounds like it should be easy to just open the required port on the firewall, it's a much more complex issue than that.

Many applications require more than one port to be opened; in fact, some applications require several. This might be because the application uses more than one service; in such a case, it might be acceptable to open each of those ports on your firewall. Unfortunately, some applications or protocols require a range of ports to be opened—sometimes dozens or hundreds of port numbers. Examples of this include many instant messenger programs, games, and multimedia and streaming protocols, such as RealAudio. As if that isn't bad enough, some applications assign ports dynamically and use any one of hundreds or thousands of possible port numbers at any time.

If your organization requires the use of these types of applications, you do not have many options. Certain firewalls, such as Sidewinder, provide proxy services for commonly used protocols, particularly multimedia-related ones. As we discuss in Chapter 4, "Proxy Firewalls," these proxies can be extremely helpful in handling application ports securely. Some applications also enable you to restrict the number of ports they use—for example, opening only a small range of ports instead of hundreds. If you have no other option but to open many firewall ports, be sure to strictly limit which internal hosts can be accessed through those ports and, of course, harden those hosts as strongly as possible to limit the risk posed by attacks on them.

Handling Unexpected IP Protocols

It's always possible that an application might use an IP protocol other than TCP, UDP, or ICMP. I was once testing a VPN client application, but my co-worker and I could not get it to work. When we realized that the firewall was blocking the traffic, we were confused because we thought the rule set should be allowing the traffic. We banged our heads on our desks for a while until we found a casual reference in the application manual to the fact that the application used the Generic Route Encapsulation (GRE) protocol, IP protocol 47. Then we did some research on our firewall and found out that although it blocked GRE packets by default, this was not shown in the firewall rule set. After we learned about the GRE protocol, decided it was acceptable to use, and reconfigured the firewall to accept GRE packets, the application was able to communicate properly.

Web Services and Interapplication Communications

Many applications deployed on our networks are designed to interact with human end-users. Another type of software architecture, aptly named Service-Oriented Architecture (SOA), is increasing in popularity and aims at supporting network-based communications between applications. Techniques allowing applications to interact over the Web using standards-based protocols are often called *Web Services*. For example, Amazon.com allows software developers to use its Web Services interface to programmatically access Amazon.com's systems.

Various protocols exist to facilitate interapplication interactions over the network. For example, Simple Object Access Protocol (SOAP) is an XML-based protocol used in many Web Services implementations. SOAP allows diverse application components to exchange data among each other, even if they were written in different languages and run on different operating systems. A list of interapplication communication protocols also includes the Distributed Component Object Model (DCOM) and the Common Object Request Broker Architecture (CORBA). Unfortunately, the use of these protocols may conflict with network security practices and network configurations.

Although DCOM is a somewhat dated technology at this point, it is still in use on many networks. Created by Microsoft, DCOM dynamically assigns a TCP or (optionally) a UDP port at runtime to each DCOM process. In order for clients to connect to the correct process, they must first connect to the DCOM Service Control Manager (SCM) at port 135 to get the dynamic ports for the process. If this sounds like RPC, that's because DCOM is based on RPC. By default, DCOM uses any available ports for communications, although this can be restricted. Additionally, DCOM does not work in environments using Network Address Translation (NAT) or proxying.

Microsoft is encouraging software developers to move away from DCOM-based architectures toward the Web Services model implemented as part of its .NET platform. .NET uses SOAP, in conjunction with other complementary protocols, to allow distributed applications to communicate with each other over the Web. SOAP is designed make it easy to carry messages over the HTTP protocol, which makes it easy to support SOAP-based interactions that cross a firewall. As a result, you may not have to change your firewall configuration to support a SOAP-based application. On the other hand, because many firewalls allow HTTP traffic to pass with relative ease, you may find it difficult to control what SOAP-based messages are being tunneled in and out of your network.

Note

Although HTTP is the most frequently used protocol for transporting SOAP messages, SOAP could be also transported via other protocols, such as SMTP and FTP.[1]

Web Services communications can be encrypted using a protocol such as IPSec or SSL to protect them in transit against unauthorized modification and eavesdropping. For example, an SSL-protected SOAP message can be conveniently tunneled over HTTPS without requiring the developers to implement many application-level security functions. Additionally, a variety of application-level protocols exist for protecting and authenticating Web Services messages if it is not practical to carry them over an HTTP tunnel; examples of such technologies are WS-Security, Security Assertion Markup Language (SAML), and XML DSig.

In addition to DCOM and SOAP, CORBA offers another way of building distributed applications. Internet Inter-ORB Protocol (IIOP) is part of the CORBA standard that was created to ease the implementation of CORBA-based solutions over the Web.[2] IIOP does not have a fixed port number, and various implementations of IIOP use different port numbers. It is difficult to characterize the issues in deploying an IIOP-based application. However, IIOP is known to have problems with NAT. Also, many IIOP-based applications often require connections to be implemented from client to server and from server to client. This is unusual compared to most application protocols, which make unidirectional connections.

> **Note**
>
> You might be wondering why one web application would use HTTP and another would use a protocol such as IIOP. HTTP, in its purest form, is designed to transfer text only; IIOP is more effective at transferring many types of data other than text, such as arrays.

Fortunately, some firewalls have proxying capabilities for protocols such as IIOP, as well as NAT implementations that can handle them properly. Such firewalls are able to process the application traffic securely by accommodating dynamic port assignments and compensating for NAT-related issues. Newer protocols such as SOAP provide similar functionality to DCOM and IIOP while working within HTTP. By using HTTP as a transport mechanism, application components can communicate with each other using TCP port 80.

If you only consider firewall port numbers, then tunneling applications over HTTP might sound like a great idea because you are probably already permitting port 80 traffic through your firewall. However, doing this has definite disadvantages. Port 80 is intended to carry HTTP traffic for web page access; this application protocol is embedding itself inside HTTP so it can be carried by it. Now you have multiple types of traffic being sent using the same port number. As this trend continues and more applications use HTTP as a transport mechanism, port 80 traffic might become a jumble of applications and protocols that's extremely difficult to monitor and control properly.

Conflicts with Network Configuration

Another problem that occurs with some applications is that they may not work properly with your existing network configuration. A typical example of this is that some applications are incompatible with NAT. We've already mentioned that DCOM and IIOP have problems with NAT; many VPN solutions also encounter similar issues.

So why do many applications have problems with NAT? Applications and application protocols frequently embed the client's actual IP address and port within their data. Remember that with NAT, the IP address and port that the client is actually using are different from the IP address and port that the server sees. In addition, the client's IP address is often a "private" reserved address, such as 10.1.2.3. Some applications insist on sending data to the client's real IP address, rather than the NAT address assigned by the firewall. When the Internet-based application server tries to communicate with your host at 10.1.2.3, instead of the NAT address, it will be unable to do so.

Application Incompatibilities with NAT

One of my former colleagues was involved in the deployment of a business-to-business e-commerce application. The application worked great until it was tested in the production environment, where it wouldn't work properly at all. After several conversations with technical support, she finally reached a support engineer who was able to diagnose the problem: The application was incompatible with NAT. (The application vendor had previously assured her that the software worked just fine with NAT.) The deployment was delayed for weeks while additional network hardware was deployed and new subnets that did not use NAT were created. After much additional work, the application was transferred to the new network addresses, and it was able to work properly.

You may run into compatibility problems between applications and other network components, such as firewalls. These are issues to be particularly cautious about; if the application conflicts with key aspects of your security perimeter, you might need to drastically modify parts of your infrastructure in order to accommodate the application. A great example is a firewall that is not able to handle a particular IP protocol that your application uses. Can you imagine what would happen if a critical application that was about to be deployed in your environment failed to work because your firewall couldn't support the protocol? The earlier in the application deployment process you find out about such compatibility issues, the easier it will be to address them.

Tip

Make sure to document the components of your network infrastructure and review them with the vendor for potential trouble areas before deploying the software.

Encrypting Connections

Many applications do not encrypt the data sent between the user and the application server. The significance of this depends on your organization's security policy. Generally, if the application is running on an internal network and the data is not sensitive, the lack of encryption is not usually a problem. However, if the application carries sensitive data and uses public networks, your policy will probably require the use of encryption. If the application can't encrypt the data, you need to consider using VPN tunnels, such as those that support SSL, to encrypt the connections.

Although it's important to protect connections between users and servers, it's also important to make sure that traffic between servers is protected. For example, you might have a publicly accessible server that accepts information from users and then transmits that information to a database server. The application designers might have assumed that both servers would be on a private network and didn't encrypt the data going between them. If you are deploying a multitier application, be sure to consider the need to secure data connections between the tiers.

Performance and Reliability

An important issue related to software architecture is the effect that network security can have on application performance and reliability. For example, firewalls, especially proxies, can add considerable delay to connections. Encrypting traffic usually adds substantial performance overhead as well. In many cases, these delays won't drastically affect the usability of the application, but they could. As we describe in Chapter 17, "Tuning the Design for Performance," performance and security are often inversely related.

Reliability is another important aspect of software architecture. In many cases, the more components that participate in the application's functionality, the less reliable the application will tend to be. This is because each host or a device represents another component that may fail. For example, if you are deploying a multitier application and have put each tier on a separate host, each separated by firewalls, you need to consider how reliable the overall solution will be. This is not to say you should use as few devices as possible; rather, you should ensure that proper redundancy and fault-tolerance measures are implemented as needed to keep the overall reliability at an acceptable level. For more information on dividing components among hosts, see Chapter 13, "Separating Resources."

Atypical Operating System

Most environments tend to support a few operating systems, such as certain versions of Windows, Solaris, and Linux. Some applications might require the use of a particular operating system that is not normally used in your environment. Of course, the biggest issue is probably that of support: How will your organization be able to support and maintain this operating system?

Another important issue is that of host security. If the application requires the use of an operating system with which your staff is not familiar, the staff isn't likely to have much knowledge of how to secure and maintain it properly. Substantial financial and personnel resources will be required in order to gain and maintain such knowledge; in many cases, these resources are unavailable. Such an operating system is likely to be excluded from standard security maintenance measures due to lack of expertise, making it much more vulnerable to attacks. Whenever possible, it's a good idea for support and security reasons to stick with operating systems with which your technical staff is familiar.

Software Component Placement

At the heart of software architecture are issues involving where to deploy various components of each application. The architecture will vary greatly depending on whether the application and its data must reside on a single system or whether they can be run on multiple systems. We will discuss this in more detail as we look at single-system and multitier applications, including those used by internal users only. We will also look at issues surrounding administrator access to application components.

Single-System Applications

An application and its associated data are often designed to reside on a single host, and it might be impossible or impractical to split them among multiple hosts. In this situation, your major design decision is where the system should be located. Assuming that the system has external users, you will want to put it either on a screened subnet or possibly on your internal network and deploy a proxy server for it on a screened subnet. In both cases, external users are connecting to the system on your screened subnet and are unable to establish a connection directly to your internal network. You will just need to alter your firewall rules to allow external hosts to initiate a connection to only the screened subnet host using only the necessary port numbers.

Multitier Applications

Multitier applications present much more complex design issues than single-system applications. A multitier application consists of distributed components that can sometimes reside on the same system, but usually reside on separate systems. Multitier applications often have a user interface component (sometimes called the *presentation* component), a middleware component, and a database component. Sometimes the middleware and database components are combined, and sometimes several tiers exist. The considerations that impact the design of a secure architecture for multitier applications are often related to defining proper security zones, as we discuss in Chapter 13, "Separating Resources."

Generally, with multitier applications, the most sensitive tier is the one that contains the data, such as financial or personal information. This is the tier that should be the most isolated from users. If the application is designed with security in mind, users should never access the data directly; instead, they should interact with an intermediary application tier that accesses the data on their behalf. Therefore, avoid placing servers that contain data on publicly accessible networks. Instead, such servers should be located on private networks, and access to them should be tightly restricted.

Likewise, the tier that contains the user interface is the one that the users directly contact. This tier should be on a screened subnet (which is close to the external network), or perhaps accessible only by a proxying firewall. In any case, it's important to separate the top tier, with which the users interact, from the lower tiers, which contain the data and middleware. By keeping the tiers on separate security zones, you greatly reduce the risk that data will be compromised or that middleware code will be accessible if the top tier is compromised.

Administrator Access to Systems

Another important thing to keep in mind when designing software architecture is that others beside users will need to access your application's functionality and data. Database administrators, software developers, backup operators, and technical support personnel will all likely need to have some access to components of the application. Therefore, you will need to consider their needs when designing your application architecture.

User-Unfriendly Security

If you create a security architecture that becomes too unwieldy, IT staff members, just like regular application users, may try to circumvent security. Human nature is to do things easily and quickly. If you make tasks too complicated and time-consuming, people will look for ways to do them differently. Unfortunately, the alternative methods are likely to be less secure. Educating your staff about why the security measures are necessary should help. Always consider usability versus the risks in your environment.

Too Much Security Can Be a Bad Thing

Here's a simple example of how too much security can be a bad thing. I've seen instances in which web developers needed to follow several steps to update a single page. In some environments, the standard way to update a web page is to log on to a staging server and transfer the code to that box. Then you can initiate an additional connection from that box to the production box and transfer the code again, one file at a time. The purpose of doing this is to have the intermediate server log all connections and page updates.

The web developers quickly grew tired of having to do all of these logins and remember the complex passwords, so they instead copied their code onto a floppy, walked into the server room, and copied the code from the floppy to the server. By implementing a solution that was great from a network security standpoint but lousy from a usability standpoint, the solution failed to provide the level of security that the network administrator had been seeking.

External Administrative Access to Applications

Another problem that is difficult to handle is that of people from other companies who need administrative access to your application. In many cases, this is a developer or technical support person from your application vendor. This person can create a whole new set of security concerns. You will have to find a way to give this person access to your systems. This person might be using completely different protocols or accessing different hosts than those used by your application's users.

Although the application might be on a screened subnet that is directly accessible from the Internet, the development or staging systems that external personnel might need to access are traditionally located on your internal network. You might want to think of alternative ways to give access to external personnel, rather than permitting them to enter your internal network from the Internet. An example is a modem connection that gives outsiders access to limited resources on a single development server and no network access at all.

Applications for Internal Users Only

Throughout this chapter, we have focused on applications whose users were connecting to them over the Internet. However, you should keep a separate category of applications in mind: those that are used exclusively by internal users. Although most of these applications do not have any connectivity to external networks such as the Internet, some of them do. A good example would be an application that downloads weather data from a site on the Internet, stores it locally, and presents it to users on the internal network. Another example is the SETI@Home screensaver, which downloads data from the SETI project's servers at UC Berkeley and uploads results back to that server. Although such applications can certainly present a security risk, generally that risk is lower than that of applications that external users access.

Many of the security principles we discuss throughout this chapter still apply to applications that only internal users use. However, there are usually very few architectural decisions to make with such applications. They will normally be deployed to your internal network. The biggest architectural item to consider is whether the application can "pull" updates by initiating connections to the Internet host, or whether it is forced to accept "push" updates initiated by the Internet host. In the latter case, you should seriously consider placing the application on a screened subnet so that the external host can't establish a direct connection to your internal network. It's almost always safer to pull updates rather than to push them because you are in control of the operations when you're pulling. If you need to get updates for internal users, it's best to push or pull the updates to an intermediate box on your network; users can then interact with the intermediate box.

Identifying Potential Software Architecture Issues

To avoid a range of potential problems when implementing an application, it's a great idea to be proactive and evaluate the security of an application before it's purchased or written. A key aspect of this process is to talk to vendors at length about their products so that you can do a thorough evaluation of them and make solid recommendations to the potential application owners as to which product would be the best from a network configuration and security standpoint. The trick is knowing what information to get from the vendors and how to get it.

Software Evaluation Checklist

Many people who work in information security are involved in the process of choosing enterprise software solutions. When you are talking with software vendors or application developers, you might be unsure what questions you should be asking. Following is a list of questions that can help you evaluate the security of application architectures. Besides these general questions, ask specific questions related to your environment and security policy:

- How will this application interact with the rest of your environment? With what other resources on your network, or other networks, will it work? Do special requirements exist that have security implications; for example, does the application's host need to be a member of the same Windows domain as other servers?

- Who will be using this application: external or internal users or both? Who will be administering or updating this application: external or internal users or both?

- What network protocols will be used, and what ports will need to be open? In which direction will the traffic flow, and which components will initiate the connections?

- If network traffic should be encrypted, does the application perform that encryption? If so, what encryption algorithm choices are available? Are these industry standards or proprietary methods? If encryption is not available, can the traffic easily be "wrapped" in a VPN-style application or protocol that can provide adequate encryption?

- Does this application work with your current network security and network configuration (that is, proxy servers, firewalls, NAT)?

- Does security seem to be a fundamental part of the product or an afterthought? Does the vendor incorporate good security practices into its product design? When a security flaw is found, does the vendor act quickly to inform its customers and release a patch?

- Does the vendor have security-related deployment recommendations? Does the vendor supply default architecture recommendations? Will the vendor support the application if you deploy it in a different architecture than what is recommended?

- Is this application consistent with your network security policies?

Sources of Application Information

It's often helpful to test a working demo copy of the product. Sometimes this is not possible due to the complexity of the application, but in some cases it's trivial. If possible, install a demo of the product and look at its behavior. Another option is to talk to other organizations running the software to find out what problems they have encountered involving security or application architecture. This can give you a different point of view and provide valuable information that you cannot find elsewhere.

When you are attempting to evaluate the security of a product that you don't have access to, you have to rely primarily on the vendor for information. Don't be afraid to ask detailed technical questions and demand specific answers, preferably in writing. Don't settle for a general assurance that an application will work in any environment, because this simply isn't true. Every environment is different, and vendors certainly can't be expected to create a product that is going to work in each one. In addition, look for other sources of information on the security of the product—reviews, security advisories, and the like.

Just the Facts, Please

I've been in many meetings with vendors where I asked fairly simple technical questions and received very vague answers. For example, during a product demonstration, I asked a vendor which firewall ports would need to be opened. The vendor said that some would need to be and that we could work all that out during final implementation. Obviously, that is not an acceptable answer. Insist on getting specific answers to your questions to prevent problems for both sides in the future.

How to Handle an Unsecurable Application

At times, an application's characteristics are such that you feel it cannot be deployed with sufficient security in your environment, or it clearly violates your organization's security policy. You have a few options at this point: replacing the application, modifying it, or deploying it with less than ideal security. In the latter case, you and the application owners will need to discuss the severity of the security issues and the risks of deploying the application.

If the application owners are considering replacing or changing the application, they need to consider the time and resources necessary to make that happen. Of course, they should also consider security more strongly during product selection or modification so that other security or network problems do not occur again.

Software Testing

Time and time again, applications have worked great in a test or staging environment, but failed miserably when deployed in the production environment. Usually this is because the testing environment and production environment are often configured differently, especially with respect to network and host security.

Host Security

The application might have been tested on a server that had not been secured or hardened at all, and it broke in production when it couldn't perform the same actions on the hardened system that it could on the unsecured test server. When you are testing an application, do so on a server that is as close to the production configuration as is possible. The application and associated services should run with the correct privilege levels, and file and directory rights should be set properly. Many, many applications aren't designed or intended to run following your security standards; this sort of testing might be the only way to identify those problems before putting the application into production.

Too often, applications are tested successfully on a test system with full administrator privileges, and then the application support person is surprised that the application does not function properly when it runs with limited privileges. It is amazing how much software is written to require privileged access, such as root or Administrator, when running. Although it's normal for applications to require many privileges during installation, nearly all should run with reduced privileges. If an application such as DNS runs as root or Administrator in production and it is compromised, an attacker could potentially gain administrative access to your server through the vulnerability in that application. Other applications require wide-open file-sharing rights, or files set to Full Control privileges on Windows boxes, for example.

In some cases, you can coerce an application that expects such privileges into working properly without them. You might be able to get the application to run with limited administrator rights. Alternatively, you might be able to set directory rights that are more restrictive than the application supposedly requires, but less restrictive than what you would normally use. Just because the manual for an application claims to need certain privileges doesn't mean it really does. For example, an application might need Full Control to a directory on a Windows workstation, but only for one function that the users didn't need. Hopefully, the application can be deployed with limited rights while still giving the users the functionality they need. Unfortunately, this isn't always possible.

Ultimately, you and the application owners must decide whether the application is so critical to meeting business needs that it's necessary to deploy it even though it introduces substantial vulnerabilities. You should implement additional network security measures to further monitor activity and restrict access to the machine in question. If the application has multiple tiers and the security weakness exists in a single tier, you might be able to isolate that particular tier so that only the other tiers of the application can access that box and no other host can contact it directly. It's vitally important to do everything you can to protect this box.

Network Configuration and Security

Another problem that happens repeatedly is that applications are tested without production network security measures in place. During testing, all the components of the software solution are often on servers on the same subnet; firewalls or packet filters aren't involved. Then the application is transferred to a production environment, and the application owner quickly discovers that the network configuration and security measures prevent the application from working.

In an ideal world, the production environment would be duplicated in the test environment; however, this is typically not done due to financial limitations. Still, it can be costly not to discover a major architecture problem until the application is deployed to production. Delaying the rollout of a system for days or weeks while a firewall is upgraded or replaced, or the software architecture is otherwise redesigned, could cost a company substantial revenue. In such situations, it's certainly advisable to test in advance with a duplicate of your production firewall and other perimeter security components. Perhaps you can justify the purchase of spare equipment to your organization because that equipment can be used both for application testing and for a spare should your production equipment experience a failure.

If your organization simply cannot afford additional network equipment, another option is to do application testing using the production equipment. A separate screened subnet can be established for the test servers to shield them from all but your test traffic. This is a reasonable solution in some cases, particularly with applications that you fully expect to work, without making changes to your network configuration. However, if you test the application and discover it's not working in your production network environment, how easily will you be able to troubleshoot the problem and adjust your network? For example, changing rules on the production firewall on the fly to fix such a problem can be extremely dangerous. Such work should be done only in a test environment.

Network Defense Design Recommendations

Establishing a network defense that can handle the needs of applications in a secure manner is important. It's one thing to design a defense that meets your current needs, but it's quite another to design one that can handle future needs. Obviously, you can't anticipate everything, but you can take some proactive steps:

- Choose firewalls and border routers that are sophisticated and robust enough to securely support various types of applications. For example, some devices have built-in capabilities to support multimedia protocols, dynamic port allocation, multicasting, and other methods that applications might use. If you choose a firewall that cannot support multicasting, for example, what will you do when your business requires an application that uses it?

- Business needs often occur unexpectedly, especially from the perspective of IT staff. It's a good idea to have extra interfaces in your firewalls, not only so you can quickly recover from an interface failure, but also so you can create additional subnets quickly if an application requires them. In addition, plan for future growth.

- Understand the basics of various areas of security—including host, network, application, and database security—well enough to evaluate a design, identify the security weaknesses, and recommend ways to reduce or eliminate them. Staying current with the latest security technologies and products is also very important.

If you will need to make major changes to your network defense to accommodate an application, you should answer the following questions and present them to the application owners for consideration:

- What impact will these changes have on the security of this application? On the security of other applications? On overall network security?

- How will these changes affect application performance, reliability, and usability?

- What is the cost of making these changes, in terms of time and resources?

Case Study: Customer Feedback System

Now that you have learned about software architecture, let's examine a case study that shows how software architecture and network security fit together. Company Z wants to deploy a simple web-based application that allows its external customers to fill out a series of forms in order to provide feedback on its new line of widgets. None of the data is particularly confidential or sensitive. The feedback is supposed to be anonymous; therefore, no username, email address, or other data that might be sensitive from a privacy standpoint is transmitted or stored.

The perimeter network configuration at Company Z is pretty simple; it is shown in Figure 15.1. The configuration has a border firewall with three interfaces. One interface connects to the Internet, and a second interface connects to the internal corporate network. The third interface connects to a screened subnet that external users can access; it provides external email connectivity, DNS resolution, and web-based applications. The firewall does not perform NAT, and no proxy servers are in use.

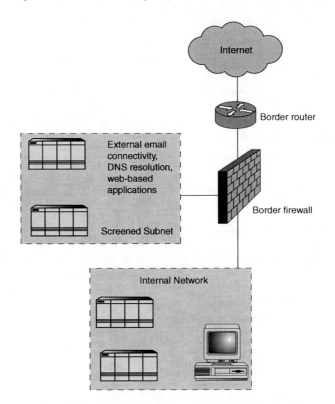

Figure 15.1   This perimeter network is simple; a border firewall passes packets between the Internet, the hosts on a screened subnet, and the internal network hosts.

Company Z has selected an application that meets its business requirements. All components of the software must run on the same host, and the data must be located on that host as well. You have been asked to recommend where in the network the application should be deployed, and what adjustments or changes need to be made to network security in order to implement it securely.

Deployment Locations

In this case, the application could be placed in a few possible locations. Let's consider the benefits and drawbacks of each of them:

- **Using the existing screened subnet**—Because other services accessed by external users are located on the existing screened subnet, it is a logical place to add another host that offers services to external hosts. The firewall rule set would need to be slightly adjusted to permit the appropriate traffic to and from this host. Deploying the application to this location would require the least work of the three options.

- **Deploying a new screened subnet**—If an evaluation of risk indicates that this application requires a different level of security than hosts on the existing screened subnet, a new screened subnet can be created for it. This requires using an additional interface on the firewall and creating new firewall rules.

- **Using the internal network**—If the Internet firewall does not have strong proxying capabilities, you could consider deploying a reverse proxy server to a screened subnet and only allowing that server to contact the application. This directly limits connections from external hosts that enter the internal network and might provide better host protection. However, unlike the first two solutions, using the internal network might require an additional host to be created and secured if a suitable proxy server isn't already deployed.

Architecture Recommendation

Because this is a one-system application, your primary areas of concern should be potential conflicts between the application and the border firewall and router as well as anything that contradicts your organization's security policy. But in general, any of these options should provide an adequate solution. Because the organization does not consider the data sensitive, the consequences of an application compromise are not as high as they would be for many other applications.

This is not to say that you shouldn't be concerned about security, but that you should keep in mind that security is only one factor in creating a design. A proxy-based solution might be somewhat more secure, but the additional costs and resources required for it might be unreasonable given the nature of this application. Performance and reliability might also become unacceptable due to certain network security components. Although it's good from a security standpoint to deploy the host on the new dedicated screened subnet, you will need to consider business needs and resources when choosing the best solution for your environment.

Case Study: Web-Based Online Billing Application

Company X has decided to deploy a web-based online billing application so that its customers can view and pay their bills through the Internet. This application must be able to use the data in the existing billing database so that the company continues to have one source of billing information. Because customers will be providing their credit card or checking account numbers as part of the payment process, the company is particularly concerned about protecting that information as well as respecting the privacy of its customers.

The perimeter network configuration at Company X is somewhat complex. As shown in Figure 15.2, Company X has an Internet firewall with four interfaces. One interface connects to the Internet, and a second one connects to the internal corporate network and provides NAT capabilities for all internal addresses. The third interface connects to a screened subnet that both internal and external users frequently access. That subnet provides external email connectivity, DNS resolution, and web-based applications; it also hosts web proxy servers used by internal hosts that want to access Internet websites and reverse proxy servers used by external hosts that want to access internal web resources. The fourth and final interface connects to another screened subnet that provides VPN capabilities for telecommuting employees.

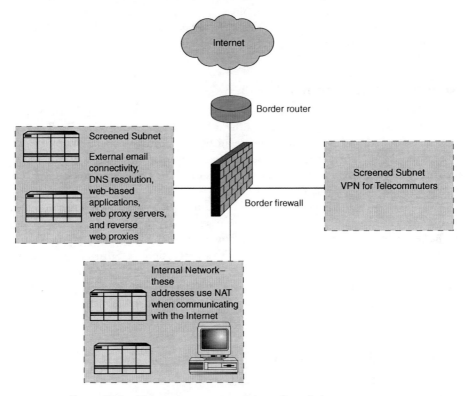

Figure 15.2   This perimeter network has a firewall that connects two screened subnets with the Internet and internal network; it also provides NAT capabilities for internal hosts that access the Internet.

Company X has completed the software selection process based on its business require-ments and has chosen an application to be deployed as quickly as possible. The applica-tion has three components: a web-based user interface, the application server to run the core components of the application, and a database. Because the company wants to use its existing online billing database, it wants to modify and expand this database rather than establish a new one.

You have been asked to research the application and determine how it can be deployed smoothly into the Company X environment. You should be most interested in identifying any potential network defense changes and problems that the application might pose to the current network configuration.

Deployment Locations

You have several options for where to put each component of the application. You want to use the existing database, which is currently located on the internal network; conceiv-ably, you could move this host, but the company doesn't want to move it unless it's absolutely necessary. Because you want to keep the lower tiers (containing data) on pro-tected networks, you might choose to keep the database on the internal network. Let's think about where the other systems could be deployed and what the strengths and weaknesses of each architecture are.

Web Interface on Existing Screened Subnet

Company X already has a screened subnet established for hosting services used by exter-nal hosts. You could locate the web interface on this subnet, perhaps on an existing serv-er that already delivers web pages. Users would connect to this server. The server would then make requests on their behalf to the application and database servers, which would be located on the internal network. Potential problems with this architecture are as follows:

- The firewall might not be able to handle the protocols used between the web server and the application server.
- The data that is passed between the web server and application server might need to be encrypted because it is passing on a publicly accessible network.
- External hosts would directly access the web server.

Web Interface and Application on the Same Screened Subnet

Another option is to deploy the web interface and the application server to the same screened subnet and leave the database server on the internal network. Although it is certainly preferable to leave the application server on an internal network if users do not need to contact it directly, it might be necessary to have the web server and application server on the same subnet if the firewall cannot securely and efficiently pass traffic between them.

If sensitive data is passed between the web and application servers and it is prohibitively difficult to encrypt this data, you can largely circumvent this problem. You can create a separate screened subnet, deploy only these two servers to it, and use strong network security measures to tightly restrict access to this subnet.

All Components on the Internal Network

The web interface, application server, and database server could all be located on the internal network. As mentioned in the previous case study, in this case, you would want a reverse proxy server on a screened subnet that handles web requests on behalf of the web interface. If that's not feasible, external users could potentially be allowed to enter the internal network, but that creates a much higher level of risk.

Architecture Recommendation

Of the options presented here, you should probably recommend placing the web server on a screened subnet and the application and database servers on the internal network as the best overall solution. This solution is the least expensive and the least resource-intensive, while providing a good level of network security.

If it were impossible to separate the web and application servers due to protocol or firewall issues, then placing them on separate hosts on the existing subnet or a new subnet would be an acceptable alternative. Avoid deploying all components to the internal network unless all other alternatives have been eliminated.

Summary

In this chapter, we examined many issues surrounding software architecture design and deployment. The goal of this chapter was to give you the knowledge to evaluate applications and determine how they can be deployed in your environment with their functionality intact and their code and data safeguarded from malicious activity. Although software architecture and perimeter defenses are sometimes in conflict with each other, in most cases you can design and deploy software in such a way that it and your perimeter defenses both maintain a proper level of security. However, in many cases, issues between software and network and host defenses are not discovered until the application is already placed into production because software architecture design is not evaluated properly in advance. By being proactive and reasonably aggressive in terms of software architecture evaluation, you can help your co-workers design and deploy solutions much more easily, efficiently, and securely.

References

1 Ethan Cerami. Web Services Essentials. February 2002. O'Reilly.
   http://proquest.safaribooksonline.com/0596002246/webservess-CHP-3-SECT-4.

2 Object Management Group. "CORBA/IIOP Specification." September 2001.
   http://www.omg.org/technology/documents/formal/corba_iiop.htm. December 2001.

16

VPN Integration

IN CHAPTER 7, "VIRTUAL PRIVATE NETWORKS," we addressed the basics of VPN technologies. This chapter discusses VPN integration, which refers to how these VPN technologies can be incorporated into the security perimeter. VPN integration is a complex subject because so many types of VPN solutions are available, and each one has many potential implementation issues. Without a good understanding of VPN integration, you will be ill-prepared to design or deploy VPN in your environment.

In this chapter, we look at several VPN options:

- Standard SSH connections and SSH tunnels
- Standard SSL connections, SSL tunnels, and SSL proxy servers
- Single-session and multiple-session remote desktop software
- IPSec

For each type of VPN, we examine the following:

- What services it can provide
- Under which circumstances it is most useful
- How it should be installed and configured
- How it can be integrated with other defense components

We also discuss other advanced VPN integration topics. Finally, we look in depth at a case study that presents a real-world scenario and demonstrates the advantages and disadvantages of three potential solutions.

Secure Shell

The first VPN method we examine in this chapter is Secure Shell (SSH). It has become a popular replacement for Telnet, rlogin, and other inherently insecure remote utilities. SSH can be used to provide strong encryption for remote shell access, file transfers, and other application usage. Another nice feature of SSH is that it offers multiple authentication methods, including username/password and public key based. In this section, we look at the two main types of SSH usage: standard SSH connections and SSH tunneling.

Standard SSH Connections

The most popular use of SSH is to provide a strongly encrypted connection to a remote server in order to gain shell or command-line access on that server, to transfer files between the client and server, or to remotely execute commands. We refer to these types of usage as *standard connections*.

SSH Client Integration

Installing SSH client software is simple. Actually, in nearly every UNIX operating system, installing SSH is not necessary because it's already included in the default OS install. If it's not, then downloading, building, and installing freely available SSH client code, such as OpenSSH (http://www.openssh.org/), is easy. However, Windows boxes do not include SSH client software, so you need to download SSH client software and install it. One of the most popular free Windows SSH clients is PuTTY, available at http://www.chiark.greenend.org.uk/~sgtatham/putty/. OpenSSH has also been ported to Windows (http://sshwindows.sourceforge.net/). There are also Java-based SSH clients, such as MindTerm (http://www.appgate.com/products/80_MindTerm/index.php), that are platform independent and can run within a web browser. Installing just about any SSH client should be easy because it is typically a simple software package that does not make changes to a machine's network configuration. The process is as simple as installing the SSH client and running it.

SSH Server Integration

SSH server software installations are also straightforward. Many UNIX systems have an SSH server daemon (sshd) installed by default. If not, it's usually simple to install sshd by compiling it from the source code. The only special note is that you may need to set sshd to start automatically so that it's available after a server reboot. Of course, it's important to keep all sshd installations and their servers' operating systems current with patches and upgrades.

Each SSH server implementation has its own default configuration. Many different SSH server configuration options are available, and it's highly likely that you will want to change some of the options to fit the needs of your environment. These settings not only affect the security of your installation, but may also impact the functionality of your SSH solution. The exact options you set are based on several factors, including the capabilities of your sshd implementation, the characteristics of your environment, your security needs, and the capabilities and characteristics of the SSH clients. Examples of options you should carefully consider include the following:

- How many failed logins should be allowed in a single session
- Which SSH protocols to allow: SSH1 or SSH2
- Which types of authentication to permit

The Dangers of SSH

You should be aware that, like any other program, SSH can be dangerous if it is not deployed, maintained, and upgraded properly. Multiple serious vulnerabilities exist in various implementations of SSH servers and clients; for example, a vulnerability in PuTTY in late 2004 allowed malicious SSH servers to execute arbitrary code on clients (http://cve.mitre.org/cgi-bin/cvename.cgi?name=CAN-2004-1008) in a man-in-the-middle attack. Also, weaknesses have been identified in the SSH1 protocol. If you are going to use SSH in your environment, be sure to use the latest software versions and to keep it current with all patches. Also, configure your SSH servers to only permit the use of the SSH2 protocol, instead of SSH1, unless a specific need exists for backward compatibility. SSH servers have become popular targets for attackers, so you must take great care to protect and harden such servers as much as possible.

SSH Perimeter Defense Adjustments

Minimal changes need to be made to most perimeter defenses in order to accommodate standard SSH connections. SSH servers typically listen on TCP port 22 only; this means that perimeter defenses only need to be adjusted to permit traffic to the SSH server's TCP port 22. Where in your environment should SSH servers be deployed? You may have many servers to which you want to enable external users to SSH, and it's both logical and easy to set up SSH server daemons on each of those servers. From a perimeter defense perspective, however, it's unwise to allow external users to directly SSH to each of those servers. You are opening too many holes in your perimeter and allowing unauthorized external users to have access to too many internal hosts.

From a security perspective, it would be much better to have an SSH server deployed on a screened subnet at the edge of your perimeter and to permit external users to initiate an SSH connection to only that server. After external users have successfully authenticated to that server, they can then SSH from that box to other SSH-enabled hosts on your internal network. This does require external users to perform an extra step in order to access the internal hosts, but it provides much greater control over your perimeter defenses and provides a much more secure solution.

The Hidden Value of Using SSH for File Transfers

As mentioned earlier, SSH has file-transfer capabilities. One major advantage of using SSH instead of FTP is that whereas FTP establishes one connection as a control channel and an additional connection for each data transfer, SSH only needs a single connection for all control functions and data transfers. SSH not only provides encryption for file transfers, but it also has much less of an effect on perimeter defenses than FTP.

When to Use Standard SSH Connections

Standard SSH connections have a well-defined usage: to facilitate remote shell access, remote command execution, and file transfers. Each connection provides access to a single host; therefore, if a user needs to access several hosts at a time, he needs to establish several separate connections. Standard SSH connections are handy for external users who simply need SSH access to particular internal hosts. However, for more sophisticated or complex needs, other VPN methods should be considered because a standard SSH connection has limited capabilities. One alternative that may provide a good solution is SSH tunnels.

SSH Tunnels

SSH has a powerful capability called *port forwarding*. In port forwarding, an arbitrary local port is chosen and linked by an SSH connection to a particular remote host and remote port. After the connection is established, the SSH client listens for traffic on the specified local port. Any traffic that is sent to that port is then sent through the tunnel to the remote SSH server. This technique is known as *SSH tunneling*.

Tunneling can be used for many services and applications; however, it's important to realize that because tunnels are remote-port specific, you need a separate tunnel for each remote host/port combination to which you want to tunnel traffic. For example, if you want to tunnel HTTP and IMAP traffic to and from host X, you need to establish a tunnel to host X's port 80 and another tunnel to its port 143. If you need to use six different protocols, you need to establish at least six tunnels—or possibly more than that if a particular protocol uses more than one port number. Another limitation of SSH tunnels is that they can only transfer TCP packets; therefore, packets for other protocols such as UDP cannot be carried by SSH tunnels.

SSH Tunnel Client Integration

The same SSH client software that is used for standard SSH connections can often be used for tunneling as well, although not all SSH clients support tunneling. If you want to do SSH tunneling, verify that your client supports it. The installation and configuration procedures for preparing for SSH tunneling are nearly identical to those for standard SSH connections, with one important exception: If you are configuring tunneling, you usually want to tell the SSH client to accept local connections only. This means that other hosts cannot connect to your local port that is being used for port forwarding and then pass traffic through your tunnel. If your SSH client accepts connections, attackers can contact your local port and gain access to the remote network.

Figure 16.1 shows an example of configuring an SSH client, SecureCRT, to perform local port forwarding for POP3 traffic. After you have configured your SSH client, you must reconfigure all the software packages on your local host that need to utilize the tunnel. For example, you would set your system's POP3 client to contact the local port you have configured to perform SSH port forwarding to the remote server's TCP port 110, instead of trying to directly contact the remote server's TCP port 110. When you ask your POP3 client to retrieve your mail, it contacts your local port, which then forwards the request through the tunnel to the remote mail server. The mail would then be returned through the tunnel to the local port and given to the POP3 client.

SSH Tunnel Server Integration

Setting up an SSH server for tunneling is nearly identical to setting it up for standard connections. The only difference is that most SSH servers have some sort of configuration setting that allows tunneling to be enabled or disabled. Of course, you would need to set this to enable tunneling. The exact details of the setting are server-dependent, so consult your SSH server's documentation for information on how to configure tunneling.

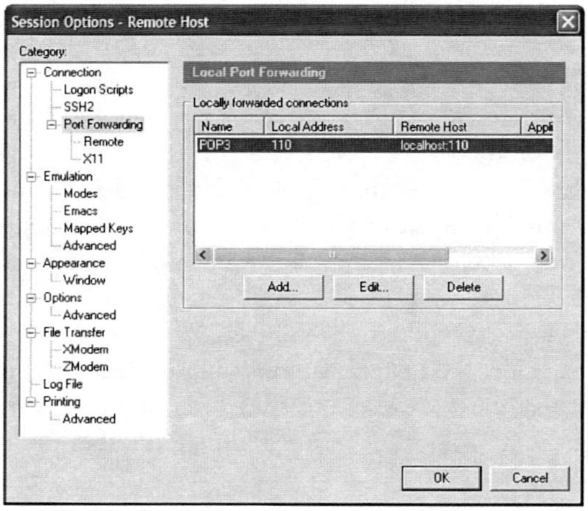

Figure 16.1 SSH clients can be configured to provide a tunnel for POP3 traffic.

SSH Tunnel Perimeter Defense Adjustments

Unlike standard SSH connections, which require minimal perimeter defense changes, SSH tunneling can require many perimeter changes to be made. Remember that each connection within the tunnel may have a different ultimate destination port; therefore, if external users are using tunnels for traffic destined to a variety of ports on many internal hosts, perimeter security can become a nightmare. Depending on the placement of the SSH server and the internal hosts, such a scenario can open far too many holes, allowing external users to attack many different internal hosts and their services. However, it's easy to eliminate this problem.

One nice feature of SSH tunnels is that you can put a tunnel within another tunnel. To implement this securely, you place an SSH server on a screened subnet on your perimeter, just as is recommended for standard SSH connections. After a user establishes a tunnel from her local host to this SSH server, she could then establish additional tunnels that pass through this tunnel to connect to other hosts on the remote network. In this scenario, the perimeter configuration needs to be modified to permit tunnels to be established to this single server and then to pass additional tunnels between that server and other hosts. Although this still weakens the perimeter somewhat, it is more secure than permitting dozens or hundreds of different tunneling connections to be made directly between external hosts and various internal hosts.

> **Note**
> When you place an SSH tunnel inside another SSH tunnel, you suffer a performance impact due to the two layers of SSH processing required and keying. Depending on the bandwidth available to users, the overhead involved in running a tunnel inside another tunnel may be significant.

When to Use SSH Tunnels

SSH tunneling can provide an inexpensive solution for remote users who need to run one or more insecure protocols over public networks in a secure manner. A major advantage of tunneling over most other VPN methods is that it can generally be deployed extremely quickly and at minimal cost. However, configuring and using tunneling requires a certain level of technical knowledge that many end users might not have. Also, because a separate tunnel needs to be established for each port, it can become cumbersome to establish several different tunnels, one or more for each protocol. Another factor is that some SSH clients do not support tunneling; therefore, users might have to find a client that does. For these reasons, SSH tunneling is recommended for technically proficient users who want to use a limited number of protocols.

Secure Sockets Layer

The Secure Sockets Layer (SSL) protocol and its successor, the Transport Layer Security (TLS) protocol, can be used to provide strong encryption for transmitted data. In this section, we will generically refer to both protocols as SSL. Like SSH, SSL-based solutions can use standard connections, which provide protection for a single SSL-enabled application, and tunnels, which allow one or more applications, SSL-enabled or not, to be passed through public networks securely. (TLS proxy servers are another alternative discussed later in this chapter.) Although SSH and SSL-based solutions have some similarities, you shall see that SSL is far different from SSH.

SSL Standard Connections

Without a doubt, the most widely used VPN method is web-based SSL. Countless websites use SSL to provide secure connections between web browsers and web servers. Most users are unaware of SSL other than seeing a little lock or other "secure" symbol at the bottom of their browser window. All major web browsers, such as Microsoft Internet Explorer, Mozilla Firefox, and Netscape Communicator, are SSL-enabled. SSL has become the standard method of providing encryption for web communications. Standard HTTP traffic uses TCP port 80; SSL-encrypted HTTP (better known as HTTPS) uses TCP port 443.

Although SSL is most commonly associated with HTTP, it can be used to provide encryption for other protocols. In fact, default port numbers have been assigned to various protocols that can be performed over SSL, such as SMTP over TLS/SSL (SMTPS), NNTP over TLS/SSL (NNTPS), LDAP over TLS/SSL (LDAPS), IMAP over TLS/SSL

(IMAPS), and POP3 over TLS/SSL (POP3S). (More information on these assignments is available at http://www.iana.org/assignments/port-numbers.)

> **Note**
>
> Many standard desktop applications also have web-based versions that are easily integrated with SSL to provide secure connections. A classic example is web-based email, which allows remote employees from anywhere on the Internet to get secure email access through an SSL-enabled web browser. However, as we'll discuss later, deploying such applications securely is more complicated than it might first appear.

SSL Client Integration

SSL is easy to enable on a client if the software that needs to use it is SSL-enabled. For example, nearly all web browsers are SSL-enabled by default. Although most browsers also allow users to configure certain SSL settings, such as using only certain SSL versions, users who leave the settings at the defaults should be able to use web-based SSL without problems.

Other applications that support SSL tend to require some basic configuration changes to enable SSL. For example, an email client, such as Eudora, is probably set by default not to use SSL because most email users do not need to. However, Eudora can be set to either require SSL to be used or to use SSL only if it is supported by the email server and to connect without SSL otherwise. Configuring an SSL-enabled client to use SSL is generally a fairly simple process. If an off-the-shelf program does not provide SSL support, however, it is probably prohibitively difficult to try to integrate that application with SSL. An alternative method, such as SSL tunneling, could be used instead.

SSL Server Integration

Enabling SSL support on an SSL-capable server program, such as a web server, is a fairly straightforward task. SSL uses a signed digital certificate on the server, so the major task in establishing SSL on a server is usually getting the proper certificate created and installed. Many SSL-capable server programs make this process fairly easy. First, the administrator is prompted to enter passwords or pass phrases, and the program generates a public key pair and a certificate-signing request (CSR), which contains the public key. Next, the administrator sends the CSR to a reputable Certificate Authority (CA), who reviews the CSR and supporting information to confirm that the request is legitimate. The CA generates a digital certificate by signing the public key and sends the certificate to the administrator. Finally, the administrator installs the certificate by following the directions for that particular server program. Now the server software is SSL-enabled.

> **Note**
>
> Administrators are free to use any CA they would like, or even to establish their own CA. The value of a certificate is largely dependent on how it has been signed. If SSL is needed for an application that external customers will use, you will want to use a well-known and dependable CA; if you just need SSL for an internal-only application, then creating and using your own CA might be a better option.

When setting up SSL for a server, you should keep in mind several configuration issues. Although configuration options vary among programs, one issue you should consider is what level of encryption to require. Recent web browsers support 128-bit strength or greater encryption for SSL by default, but old browsers may only support 40-bit or 56-bit encryption. On most SSL-enabled servers, you can require a minimum encryption level. If your users will be transferring sensitive data, you should be using at least 128-bit encryption. However, if you configure your server to require that encryption level, users with old browsers will be unable to use your application. In most cases, this situation does not occur, but you should always keep in mind what capabilities your users have.

Along the same lines, it is important to remember that in most cases, you will not have control over your external users or their hosts. Assume that your clients will act as insecurely as possible, and establish your SSL security accordingly. If you don't establish a sufficiently strong minimum encryption level, or if you don't require users to run SSL, you can be sure that some connections will be made with less-than-desirable security. Carefully consider your organization's security policies when determining what levels of encryption your systems should support and require.

SSL Perimeter Defense Adjustments

Adding SSL-enabled services to your environment usually requires some perimeter changes, depending on which services are being used. Because SSL-enabled services use different ports from their standard equivalents, firewalls and other filtering devices need to be modified to allow traffic involving those ports to be passed through. You also can choose to implement web proxy services, either on a firewall or on a separate dedicated proxy server. It might be possible to put a digital certificate on that device and have it provide SSL capabilities for web-based applications. Of course, you probably want to place these proxies on your perimeter, not on your internal network. See Chapter 15, "Software Architecture," for more information on where to deploy application servers, particularly web interfaces.

When to Use SSL

The most obvious case of when to use SSL is to provide encryption for HTTP sessions. However, this concept can be extended to make web-based SSL even more useful. For example, the Microsoft Outlook email client has a web-based equivalent: Outlook Web Access (OWA). If SSL support is added to a server that provides OWA, VPN-based email can be provided for remote users. Web-based SSL might be able to facilitate various applications being delivered securely—both web-native applications and those with alternative web-based interfaces. And you're usually pretty safe in assuming that your end users have web browsers with 128-bit encryption capabilities already installed. Web-based SSL is often transparent to users.

> ### A Note of Caution on SSL and Outlook Web Access
>
> Be cautious when implementing web-based SSL solutions. You might want to just enable SSL on servers and call it a solution, but always consider perimeter defenses. For example, if you utilize Microsoft Outlook and Exchange, OWA users might need to be authenticated to the corporate domain. Assuming that you deploy your OWA server to a screened subnet and put it in its own domain, you need to implement a trust relationship between that server and internal domains. Carefully consider the perimeter defense implications of your designs; don't be tempted just to enable SSL on servers and consider the architecture complete and sound.

Choosing to implement SSL for non–web–based traffic, such as POP or IMAP, is a more difficult decision. Although many POP and IMAP clients support SSL, some do not. In general, client programs that support SSL do not automatically use it; settings and options need to be adjusted to facilitate this. For example, as shown in Figure 16.2, Microsoft Outlook has options that can be enabled to use SSL to protect IMAP and SMTP traffic. Still, these changes are minor and only need to occur during initial client configuration. SSL can provide an easy way to give clients VPN capabilities for certain applications or protocols without requiring major client changes to be made.

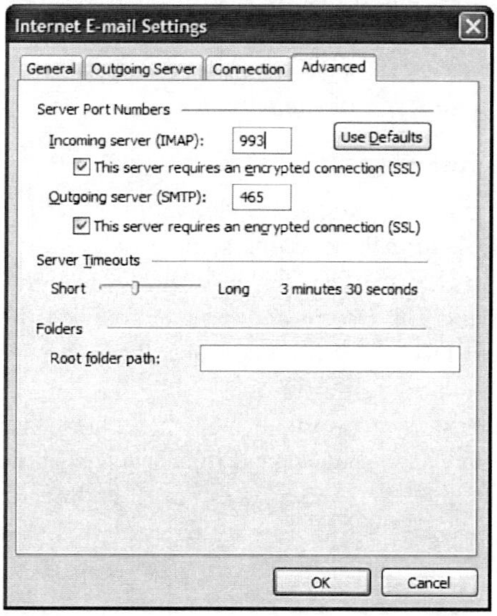

Figure 16.2   Microsoft Outlook has options for enabling
SSL protection for IMAP and SMTP traffic.

SSL Tunnels

A lesser-known way of utilizing SSL is by generating an SSL tunnel, which is similar to an SSH tunnel. After an SSL tunnel has been established, many other protocols can be sent through that tunnel. To use SSL tunneling, an SSL tunnel server must be set up, and SSL tunneling software must be installed on each client. The best-known software for SSL tunneling is Stunnel. More information on Stunnel, including directions on its installation and configuration, is available from http://www.stunnel.org/. SSL tunneling utilizes the same port-forwarding methodology as SSH tunneling: Stunnel clients designate a local port to listen for traffic and forward it through the tunnel to a particular port on the remote server. Applications on the client are reconfigured to point to the local port. The Stunnel server software runs on the same server as the remote application and listens at a particular port. When the server receives traffic through the tunnel, it decrypts the traffic and forwards it to the local port where the remote application is listening.

SSL Tunnel Perimeter Defense Adjustments

Like SSH tunneling, SSL tunneling might require many perimeter defense changes because connections carried within SSL tunnels can be established to many hosts and multiple ports on those hosts. This can severely degrade the integrity of your perimeter defenses. A better alternative is to create an SSL tunneling server and have users generate a tunnel to it, then generate additional tunnels inside that tunnel. This method limits the impact of tunneling on the perimeter defenses, although it makes tunneling more complicated and also has a negative impact on performance because of the overhead in running all traffic through two levels of tunneling.

When to Use SSL Tunnels

Overall, SSL tunneling provides similar functionality to SSH tunneling. The most significant difference is that SSL tunneling can be somewhat more expensive and not deployed as rapidly if you need an external Certificate Authority to sign digital certificates for the servers. On the other hand, this also provides a hierarchical trust capability that SSH tunneling does not. Another factor is that certain operating systems might not have an SSL tunneling client available, although most do.

Generally, SSL tunneling is recommended in the same scenarios as SSH tunneling: for a group of technically savvy users who need to access a small number of protocols remotely. Although SSH and SSL tunneling can both be beneficial, they can also be misused by attackers to conceal malicious activity, particularly outbound communications from a compromised internal machine. Because many organizations are more likely to permit outbound SSL activity than SSH, SSL tunneling might be favored by attackers who want to hide their activity from detection.

> **Note**
> Many other tunneling solutions are available besides the ones mentioned in this chapter. Although some products might work great in your environment, others might have serious issues, such as poor performance and instability. Thoroughly test any tunneling software before deploying it to users, and when in doubt, go with a well-known, proven solution.

SSL Proxy Servers

Using SSL proxy servers, also known as SSL VPNs, has become an increasingly popular way to provide secure communications for many applications through a single method. Despite the name, SSL proxy servers actually function as reverse proxy servers. (See Chapter 4, "Proxy Firewalls," for additional information on reverse proxy servers.) Users typically use a web browser to establish an SSL-protected HTTP session to the proxy server and then provide a username and password as authentication. Assuming that the authentication is valid, the user can then run applications through the proxy server, which acts as an intermediary. Based on the user's requests, the proxy server establishes connections between itself and the necessary application servers (usually web servers). These connections may or may not be protected, depending on the sensitivity of the communications and the threats the environment faces.

Although SSL proxy servers originally served only HTTP-based applications, some SSL proxy servers can now provide access to non–HTTP-based applications by tunneling their communications through SSL. However, this requires special software to be installed and configured on the client system. One of the primary advantages of an SSL VPN over an IPSec VPN is that an SSL VPN user can sit down at any computer with a web browser, type in the VPN's URL, and get connected; an IPSec VPN requires client software to be configured (and, of course, installed first if necessary). If SSL VPN users have to install and configure special software before using non-HTTP applications, the portability advantage of SSL VPNs is reduced or negated altogether.

SSL Proxy Server Perimeter Defense Adjustments

The use of an SSL proxy server requires minimal perimeter defense adjustments. Because users access all the applications on one server through one protocol, the perimeter only needs to allow incoming HTTPS connections to the proxy server. The perimeter should also be configured to restrict outgoing connections from the proxy server to only the appropriate ports on the necessary application servers. Of course, the proxy server's security is critical to the security of the whole solution, so the proxy server must be hardened as much as possible and maintained carefully.

When to Use SSL Proxy Servers

SSL proxy servers provide a relatively fast and inexpensive way to protect communications for many applications at once, when compared to the effort in adding protection to each individual application. Having only the proxy server directly accessible by users reduces the number of targets that attackers can attempt to compromise. SSL proxy servers are best suited to protecting web-based applications; when applications use a variety of protocols, SSL proxy servers are not nearly as advantageous.

Remote Desktop Solutions

A class of VPN-like methods utilizes remote desktop software to provide remote users with some of the same capabilities as local workstation users. Remote desktop software allows an external user to have access through the Internet to an internal host's graphical interface, such as a Windows XP Professional workstation. A remote user can access applications, files, and other host and network resources through the remote desktop software. Although not a pure VPN solution, the software offers protection for data traversing networks. Remote desktop software packages fall into two general categories: single session for one user at a time, and multiple session for concurrent users.

Single Session

Single-session remote desktop software allows one user at a time to have access to the GUI of a particular host. The best-known single-session software is Remote Desktop, which is built into Windows XP Professional, and pcAnywhere, a third-party product, although many different remote desktop products are available. Many people do not think of software such as pcAnywhere as a VPN option, but it can easily be configured to provide useful host-to-host VPN capabilities. Most remote desktop software packages can provide a strongly encrypted "wrapper" through which many applications can be run, files can be transferred, and other resources can be utilized. Other remote desktop software does not natively provide encryption but could possibly be run through an SSH or SSL tunnel to provide VPN capabilities. For example, VNC (http://www.realvnc.com/) does not provide encryption in its client software, and it recommends that tunneling methods be used to protect connections.

The Risks of Do-It-Yourself Remote Desktops

For many years, users have covertly installed packages, such as pcAnywhere, onto their corporate workstations to remotely access them from their home computers. Originally, this was done primarily through modem connections, but this has increasingly changed to Internet-based connections. In many cases, connections made with these applications are not strongly encrypted, or not encrypted at all. Remote desktop software might not even be configured to require authentication!

Don't permit remote desktop packages to be implemented for usage between internal and external hosts if you do not have the utmost confidence in the security of both the internal and external hosts. Do not permit users to implement and configure their own solutions because that is just an accident waiting to happen. Block traffic that is used by such packages at your firewall, and only permit such traffic to particular internal hosts whose security you can verify and maintain.

Single-Session Remote Desktop Client Integration

The appropriate remote desktop client software that corresponds to the remote desktop server software must be installed on the end users' workstations. Most products, such as pcAnywhere, can only be installed on Windows hosts. The Remote Desktop service built in to Windows XP Professional can be accessed remotely from various flavors of Windows and non-Windows systems, as long as they are running the Remote Desktop Connection client[1] or using Internet Explorer with the Remote Desktop Web Connection client.[2] Remote desktop products usually install like any other software and do not make changes to the network configuration of the host.

Single-Session Remote Desktop Server Integration

As mentioned previously, the same brand of remote desktop software must be installed on the client and the server. In general, you want to configure an internal host to have any necessary applications or resources, and you want to install the remote desktop server software onto that host. Of course, you want to harden this host strongly to reduce the risk of it being compromised, because external users will be connecting directly to it. You also want to take prudent measures to authenticate users properly, such as by requiring strong passwords to be provided for authentication and, in the case of pcAnywhere, by using a shared secret–like mechanism between the client and server software to further authenticate the external host. pcAnywhere also can be configured to only accept connections from certain IP addresses or subnets, which is helpful in certain situations.

It is absolutely critical that the server software be configured to require a sufficiently high level of encryption and to use a cryptographically strong encryption protocol. For example, the standard and web-based Remote Desktop clients offer 40-, 56-, and 128-bit encryption using the RC4 algorithm for their communications. Avoid using proprietary encryption methods because their cryptographic strength has usually not been verified through peer reviews and research. Proprietary methods often turn out to be flawed, which means that your traffic could be decrypted much more easily than you expect. For example, pcAnywhere 11.0 offers three encryption levels: symmetric encryption, public key encryption, and pcAnywhere Encoding (a proprietary method that provides a weak level of encryption). Thoroughly research the available encryption options for all remote desktop products; do not assume that just because the product offers encryption, the encryption is sufficiently strong for your needs.

Single-Session Remote Desktop Perimeter Defense Adjustments

Each remote desktop software package uses one or more specific TCP or UDP ports for its communications. Perimeter defenses need to be modified to permit traffic for these ports to pass. Determining where to deploy the remote desktop host can be difficult, depending on the purpose of the host. For example, if this solution is needed so that a particular user can access his corporate workstation from home, it's unlikely you would move that user's workstation to a screened subnet; you would leave the workstation on the internal corporate network. However, this means you would have to allow external traffic to directly contact the internal host. Host security, particularly host-based intrusion detection and firewalls, is important in such a situation because external parties could target the host.

One way around this is to use SSH tunneling to connect the external host to an SSH server on a screened subnet and then tunnel the remote desktop software traffic through it. Another possibility is to use a product that can be proxied by a firewall, which adds at least a better degree of perimeter security than just allowing a pure direct connection between an external host and an internal host. The applications and protocols that can be proxied vary widely among firewalls, so make sure to verify your firewall's capabilities.

When to Use Single-Session Remote Desktop Software

A VPN-like solution based on remote desktop software provides a capability that no pure VPN method can offer. When a user needs to run graphical applications that cannot be installed on the client system or needs to interface graphically with an application that manipulates huge amounts of data (too much to transfer from the server to the client), remote desktop software might provide the only feasible protection option.

Obviously, single-session remote desktop software is not very scalable. Multiple session products, discussed in the next section, provide a more robust implementation. But for an isolated use—one external user who absolutely needs VPN-like capabilities to a particular host on the network—such a solution is inexpensive and easy to deploy. Note that single session connections might be slow due to the amount of graphics being transmitted over the public network. However, when a graphical application must be run on an internal host and have its results sent to an external host, nothing can be done to alleviate the problem.

Multiple Session

Multiple-session remote desktop software is more commonly referred to as a *terminal server*. A terminal server, such as Citrix MetaFrame or Windows Terminal Services, establishes a desktop standard and allows multiple users to receive virtual copies of the same host desktop at the same time. Because a terminal server grants access to virtual interfaces, not the server's actual interface, none of its users has access to the others' sessions or data. Terminal servers provide a much more robust and scalable solution than single-session software. In addition, most terminal servers offer 128-bit encryption, often SSL-based, for its users' sessions. This section uses Citrix MetaFrame as an example, but other products, such as Windows Terminal Services, have similar capabilities and requirements.

Multiple Remote Desktop Client Integration

To use a terminal server, each host must have the appropriate client software installed. The Citrix MetaFrame client is called ICA Client; it is available for many operating systems, including several versions of Windows and UNIX, Macintosh OSs, PDAs, and even some types of cell phones. There is also a Java ICA Client applet that can be loaded onto a web server, which users can then access through a web browser. ICA Clients are free of charge and available from the Citrix website at http://www.citrix.com.

Multiple Remote Desktop Server Integration

A terminal server should have its own dedicated host. The host should be strongly hardened to reduce the risk of system compromise, of course; this is particularly important because external users will be connecting to this server, so it will be directly exposed to attacks from the outside. After the terminal software has been installed, it should be configured to require all clients to connect using sufficiently strong encryption and strong passwords. Then all desired user applications should be installed on the terminal server.

Multiple Remote Desktop Perimeter Defense Adjustments

Some terminal servers require multiple TCP or UDP ports to be used, whereas others only use a single port. Some firewalls have proxying capabilities for particular terminal services, but many do not. In most cases, you will probably just have to open holes in firewalls and packet filters to allow such traffic through. Of course, you should place your terminal server on a secured subnet, not your internal network, if at all possible.

When to Use Terminal Server Software

Terminal server software can provide a reasonable VPN-like solution for certain situations. Because the only traffic that is passing between the terminal client and server is graphics, keystrokes, and mouse movements, a terminal server can handle virtually any application and any protocol because the applications and protocols are not passing their traffic across the connection. Unlike the VPN methods we have discussed, which could not handle UDP-based applications, a terminal server-based solution would not know or care that UDP was being used on the internal network.

Any time you have graphical applications that must run on a host but be accessed by remote users, particularly over low-bandwidth connections, terminal servers should be strongly considered. Many applications might not be portable due to resource issues, platform requirements, data volumes, software licensing issues, or excessive costs, among other reasons. The only feasible way to access these applications remotely and securely is by implementing a remote desktop solution.

However, if you want to use a terminal server–based VPN across the Internet, you should consider the risks associated with doing that. The terminal server's native encryption might not be strong enough, or the encryption implementation might contain serious security flaws. In addition, terminal servers might have authentication issues. Remember that a terminal server is designed primarily to provide remote application usage on a local network, not to secure data that is traversing public networks. Consequently, you might find that to achieve a sufficiently secure solution for Internet usage, you will need to tunnel terminal server traffic inside a standard VPN solution, such as IPSec, rather than rely solely on the terminal server's encryption and authentication mechanisms.

IPSec

In Chapter 7, we discussed many of the characteristics of IPSec. Before we examine how IPSec can be implemented optimally, let's review the three types of IPSec architectures:

- **Host-to-host**—The entire connection between the client and the server is encrypted. This is comparable to the encryption that standard SSH or SSL connections provide.
- **Host-to-gateway**—The entire connection is encrypted except for the portion between the gateway and the remote server. The gateway is usually located on the perimeter. Host-to-gateway provides protection similar to SSH or SSL tunneling from a host to a remote SSH or SSL server or similar to using an SSL proxy server.

- **Gateway-to-gateway**—The connection between the two gateways is encrypted, but the connections from the client to the client-side gateway and from the server to the server-side gateway are unencrypted. Both gateways are typically located on their respective network perimeters. A gateway-to-gateway IPSec VPN provides similar encryption to SSH or SSL tunneling between a client gateway and a remote SSH or SSL server.

What's the difference between using SSH or SSL and using IPSec? Although SSH, SSL, and IPSec might provide similar encryption capabilities, they are different from a functional standpoint. For every additional application you use through SSH or SSL, you have to establish additional connections and tunnels. IPSec makes one connection from a client to the remote VPN gateway or host, and it tunnels all application traffic through that one connection. Certain IPSec architectures can also conceal IP addresses, which is a significant security consideration in some environments. From a perimeter defense perspective and from a usability perspective, implementing VPNs using IPSec instead of SSH or SSL has many advantages. Let's look at how IPSec-based VPNs fit into perimeter defenses.

IPSec Client Integration

Most operating systems in use today include native IPSec clients, although some still require a separate IPSec client program to be acquired, installed, and configured. Some organizations also choose to use IPSec clients other than those built in to their systems; this is most often done to take advantage of additional features offered by the clients or to achieve full interoperability with a certain IPSec gateway (that is, using the same vendor for both the IPSec clients and IPSec gateway). Besides the additional time and resources needed to deploy third-party IPSec clients, such software also modifies the operating system's networking functions, which can cause operational problems.

On Windows systems, most nonnative IPSec clients fall into one of two categories:

- Clients based on shim technologies actually add a new layer between the existing network adapter and the TCP/IP protocol that is normally bound directly to the network adapter. This new layer is responsible for processing all traffic and implementing IPSec for all appropriate traffic. Because the shim is part of the existing network configuration, no routing changes are necessary for it to work properly.

- Clients that create a new network adapter, in addition to existing network adapters. Because this IPSec-specific network adapter is separate from the regular network components, the host requires routing changes so that traffic that needs IPSec processing goes through the new adapter and non-IPSec traffic goes through the other adapter.

For UNIX-based IPSec clients, multiple implementation methods are available. IPSec support can be added directly to the kernel, added as a new device driver that is recompiled into the kernel, or added as a loadable kernel module. Examples of free UNIX-based IPSec clients include Openswan (http://www.openswan.org/) and strongSwan (http://www.strongswan.org/).

As already mentioned, IPSec clients sometimes require routing changes to be made on the host. This is particularly true when a client needs to contact internal hosts and external hosts; only the traffic destined for the internal hosts must be handled using IPSec, although all the traffic could be. This isn't just because of the way the client software works; often it is due to the organization's security policy. It might be desirable to route all traffic through the VPN connection and then permit the remote VPN gateway to route traffic to external or internal hosts as appropriate. Of course, this causes a significant performance hit as compared to allowing the VPN client to make direct requests to other external hosts without utilizing the VPN connection to do so.

There is one other important point to know regarding IPSec client software. If you are making a connection between a single external host and a VPN gateway, you should configure the client software so that other hosts cannot use the tunnel. If you want to connect a remote network to your VPN gateway, you have to configure the IPSec software on the client side as a gateway, of course, to pass through traffic only from the authorized hosts on that local network.

IPSec Server Integration

IPSec servers can be deployed to different types of devices. Chapter 12, "Fundamentals of Secure Perimeter Design," contains a good discussion of VPN basics. To quickly review, the three most commonly used systems are as follows:

- **VPN concentrators**—These dedicated boxes are used solely for VPN functions. Besides handling the establishment, maintenance, and termination of VPN connections, they might also perform functions such as firewalling, packet filtering, and Network Address Translation (NAT). The advantage of using a concentrator is that it is a single-function device, dedicated to VPN.

- **Firewalls**—Many firewalls also provide support for IPSec. Using a firewall for VPN functionality is possible as long as the VPN overhead does not adversely affect the firewall's other operations. This solution is generally less expensive than a dedicated VPN concentrator.

- **Routers**—Some routers have IPSec capabilities. The advantage of this is that a VPN can be established between two IPSec-capable routers, which provides an inexpensive gateway-to-gateway VPN.

Note

Although most devices implement IPSec according to standards, some have proprietary IPSec implementations that deviate from standards. If a VPN server runs a proprietary IPSec implementation, its users might be required to use a particular IPSec client, particularly in order to take advantage of proprietary features.

IPSec Perimeter Defense Adjustments

IPSec requires some interesting changes to perimeter defenses. Encapsulating Security Payload (ESP) mode uses IP protocol 50, whereas Authentication Header (AH) mode uses IP protocol 51. The Internet Key Exchange (IKE) negotiation uses UDP port 500. However, IPSec implementation can result in other things as well. NAT is often incompatible with IPSec. Because AH mode makes authentication value calculations based on the entire packet, which includes the source and destination IP addresses, any NAT must occur before IPSec is used on the packets. ESP mode does not have the same problem because it does not include the entire header when it makes its authentication value calculations. In general, if you want to use NAT, you should use ESP to provide authentication instead of ESP. However, there are still cases where ESP and NAT do not work well together, such as when a NAT mapping times out, causing the port used by IKE to change.

This becomes more complicated when Port Address Translation (PAT) is used instead of NAT. PAT relies on the use of port numbers. Remember, these are TCP and UDP port numbers, stored within the TCP or UDP payload portion of the packets. If the payload is encrypted, the port numbers are encrypted too, and the PAT devices are unable to process the packets because they cannot access the port number. Even if the payload is not encrypted, the structure of IPSec packets is different from that of non-IPSec packets, and many PAT devices can't correctly parse the IPSec packet structure.

To resolve conflicts between IPSec and address translation, some IPSec implementations now support a feature called NAT Traversal (NAT-T). If both endpoints state during the IKE negotiation that they support NAT-T, they next check to see if a NAT or PAT device between them is altering either of their IP addresses or source ports. If address translation is in use, the endpoints move their IKE negotiations from UDP port 500 to 4500 and wrap all their ESP packets within UDP packets. Known as *UDP encapsulation*, this separates the IPSec information from the new outer UDP header, which is subsequently manipulated by the NAT or PAT device without any impact to the IPSec headers. Unfortunately, because standards for NAT-T are still not finalized, there may be interoperability problems between different types of endpoints.

Note

VPN passthrough refers to the concept of successfully allowing VPN traffic to go through a perimeter defense device, even when that device performs NAT, PAT, or other actions that could adversely affect VPN traffic. VPN passthrough is often achieved by allowing VPN traffic to bypass functions such as NAT.

Whether you are implementing IPSec services on a VPN concentrator, a firewall, or a router, you have several options on where to place the IPSec services. This is discussed in detail in Chapter 12. Likely places for standalone VPN servers are on your perimeter, such as your DMZ or a screened subnet, and in parallel with your Internet firewall. Your design decision also depends on which IPSec architecture you want to implement.

IPSec Architectures

As we discussed earlier in this chapter, three types of IPSec architectures exist. Each is appropriate to meet certain types of needs.

- Host-to-host is most appropriate when external users need to access a single host. This requires software installation and configuration on the target host as well as each client that needs to access that host. Of course, installation is not necessary if the host operating systems have built-in IPSec support.

- Host-to-gateway is the best option for remote access, when many external users need to access a variety of internal hosts and resources. Each user's system must be IPSec-enabled (if it is not already) and configured appropriately. On the remote network, only the gateway needs to be configured; no changes are necessary for each host on the network that the external users will contact.

- Gateway-to-gateway is most commonly used to provide VPNs between separate external networks, such as two business partners, or to provide VPN capabilities within a single network, also known as an *intranet VPN*. The biggest advantage of this architecture is that no changes need to be made to the VPN clients or the hosts they contact.

Other VPN Considerations

We have already discussed several aspects of VPN integration. Other VPN issues also need to be considered when designing a VPN architecture. Two items that are particularly important are the usage of proprietary VPN systems and issues caused by compromised or malicious VPN clients.

Proprietary VPN Implementations

In the "IPSec Server Integration" section, we mentioned that some IPSec implementations do not strictly adhere to the IPSec standard and might be considered proprietary. In addition, some VPN solutions implement proprietary VPN protocols or proprietary versions of standard VPN protocols. Such solutions require users to install a particular VPN client on their workstations. You must be particularly careful when evaluating a proprietary VPN product to ensure that it has client software available for all the operating systems your users might utilize. Also, keep in mind that as new versions of operating systems are released, a significant lag might be present before the proprietary client software is available for that operating system.

Warning

Be cautious about using products with proprietary VPN protocols; such protocols are likely to have been tested and reviewed less thoroughly than standard VPN protocols and therefore are more likely to have vulnerabilities and other weaknesses.

Compromised or Malicious VPN Clients

Because VPN client hosts are usually external and are typically not under the control of your organization, your environment might be at serious risk if one or more of the client hosts is compromised or is acting maliciously. When a VPN connection is established between a client and your network, you can consider that client to be on an extended portion of your network. If Trojans have compromised the client hosts, remote attackers might be able to connect to a host and pass through the VPN connection onto your network. Depending on your VPN architecture and perimeter defenses, attackers might be able to enter your internal network and do serious damage to your resources.

To make this situation even worse, VPNs complicate the monitoring of network activity. Because by definition VPNs encrypt traffic, they can interfere with the normal operation of network intrusion detection systems (IDSs), antivirus software, content monitoring software, and other network security measures. When you are planning a VPN implementation, you should pay particular attention to where your network security systems currently reside. Your VPN should be designed so that decrypted traffic from it passes through your regular network security systems. Alternatively, you might have to move or add network security measures so that the traffic is monitored. For example, an additional network IDS sensor might need to be deployed, or host IDS software might need to be added. If you do not monitor the traffic that has been sent through the VPN, you greatly increase the risk of incidents from external clients occurring through your VPN.

VPN Design Case Study

Now that we have examined many different aspects of VPN integration, let's tie all the VPN concepts together by reviewing a case study. By analyzing a real-world situation, you will gain a much better understanding of the importance of VPN integration issues. We start with a list of requirements and business needs, and then we describe and critique various potential VPN architectures. This gives you some great examples of how to evaluate the strengths and weaknesses of a VPN design.

Case Study: Home Users and Multiple Applications

A network engineer at your organization has designed a VPN architecture. The purpose of the VPN is to provide limited access to a few corporate applications from employees' home computers. The expectation is that the solution will be used for occasional access primarily on nights and weekends. The user community for this VPN has been fairly well defined, as follows:

- Approximately 500 remote users exist, who will have an estimated maximum of 50 concurrent connections.

- Users will access the VPN from their personal computers only, not from corporate computers.

- The majority of the users will connect to the Internet through broadband access or other high-speed methods, with the remainder using dial-up.

Management has determined which applications and resources must be accessible through the VPN, as follows:

- The corporate intranet server, which includes many static web pages, as well as several web-based applications. The web pages and some of the applications do not utilize sensitive data, but a few of the applications contain information on personnel and operations that must remain confidential.

- Microsoft Exchange email, which is accessed through a Microsoft Outlook interface. All users have received training on Microsoft Outlook; therefore, management has mandated that Outlook is the only permitted email client. Because many emails between internal employees contain sensitive, unencrypted data, it is vital that the content of these emails does not pass across the Internet in plain-text format. Also, it is desirable that end users not be able to easily download and store corporate emails on their home computers, primarily for data retention and liability reasons.

- The corporate mainframe, to which users connect using TN3270 emulation. Only a small percentage of the remote users need mainframe access; however, the data that they will be accessing is sensitive.

Now that we have reviewed the user community characteristics and the business requirements, let's look at a few designs that attempt to meet these needs.

Terminal Server

Using a terminal server for VPN-like services has some advantages:

- Because users need secure access to a variety of applications—Microsoft Outlook, plus multiple web-based and mainframe-based applications—a terminal server would provide a single method of accessing all these resources, without requiring changes to the resources.

- Because all application components are available through the terminal server, users do not need to install business applications, such as mainframe terminal emulators or email clients, on their home computers.

- A few terminal servers could meet the needs of 50 concurrent users during peak times and provide redundancy in case a single terminal server became unavailable.

- External users would only directly connect to the terminal server. The terminal server would then initiate its own connections to other hosts as needed.

However, the terminal server–based design does have some disadvantages:

- Because users' home computers are being used, the chosen terminal server would need to have clients for several different operating system types and versions. In most cases, the users would have to install terminal server client programs on their home computers, which could require major technical support resources, not to mention the possibility of significant software licensing expenditures.

- Performance for these users, who are primarily connected to the Internet through dial-up connections, is likely to be sluggish at best and unacceptably slow at worst. Because the screen graphics are transmitted from the server to the client, users with slow network connectivity are likely to become frustrated at times with the performance.

- Network communications may not be protected adequately if the terminal server permits the usage of weak encryption protocols and too-small encryption key lengths.

Although a terminal server could be used to create a VPN-like solution, some significant issues are associated with it. Let's look at another likely option: an IPSec-based VPN.

IPSec

An IPSec-based design has several positive features:

- One IPSec-enabled firewall, or a dedicated IPSec concentrator, should have no problem handling 50 concurrent VPN sessions.

- External users would be directly connecting to the IPSec-enabled server. Decrypted traffic would then be passed from that host to other hosts. This allows direct connections to internal hosts through the VPN only; therefore, non-VPN users cannot make such connections.

- Compared to a terminal server solution, performance for IPSec users should be much better over slow connections.

However, IPSec also has some definite disadvantages:

- As with the terminal server solution, multiple issues are possible with users' home computers. Although many or most of the client hosts may already have IPSec clients installed, the clients still need to be configured on all of the hosts. This is not a trivial undertaking.

- Users need to have access to the client interfaces for all applications they use. The web-based applications should be easy because virtually every computer has a web browser installed, but the other applications will be considerably more difficult. If users can utilize OWA instead of the full Microsoft Outlook client, they will not need to install Microsoft Outlook on their home computers. However, OWA only has some of Microsoft Outlook's functionality, so more information is required before making a decision. Finally, the users who need mainframe access will have no choice but to install and configure terminal emulator software.

Microsoft Outlook Email Security

Over the years, many vulnerabilities in the Microsoft Outlook email client have been well publicized. Countless viruses have taken advantage of these vulnerabilities, sometimes with disastrous results. An alternative to using the full Outlook email program is deploying OWA instead. You can think of OWA as "Outlook Lite." It provides the core Outlook functionality, yet it is a separate program that is completely web based.

Therefore, the vulnerabilities that Outlook has generally do not apply to OWA, although it has vulnerabilities of its own. Viruses for Outlook are usually targeted at the full client and not at OWA.

Another, less obvious advantage exists for using OWA instead of Outlook for remote users. I used to work at a company that had stringent data-retention policies. All email was automatically deleted from corporate systems after a certain number of days. Also, employees were forbidden by corporate policy from downloading email or any other corporate data to noncorporate workstations. If users were permitted to connect to corporate Exchange servers using the full Outlook client, they would have been downloading emails to their personal computers' hard drives. By using OWA, they were able to retrieve their emails, but because OWA is web based, there was no easy way to download the emails onto their workstations. OWA was helpful to us in supporting corporate data-retention requirements.

From a purely technical perspective, IPSec is an elegant, robust, and efficient VPN method that definitely meets the needs and requirements as outlined at the beginning of the case study. However, when you consider the potential user and support-related issues, an IPSec-based design might be resource intensive to deploy and maintain. If one of your goals is to minimize user interaction and technical support costs, you might want to consider an alternative VPN method, such as SSL.

SSL-Enabled Applications

It is obvious that SSL could be used to provide encryption for the web applications and pages on the corporate intranet server. And as previously mentioned, Microsoft's OWA is available to provide a web-based interface to Outlook. OWA traffic can easily be encrypted using SSL because it is based on HTTP. But what about the mainframe access? Well, a little research on the Internet turned up dozens of Java-based TN3270 emulators, several of which have SSL support built in. You can set up a dedicated server that acts as an SSL-enabled TN3270 proxy; users connect to it and are forced to authenticate themselves before then being connected through the proxy to the mainframe.

As we did with the first two designs, let's look at the advantages and disadvantages of relying on SSL-enabled applications:

- The cost of SSL-enabling a server is low, especially when compared with the cost of deploying a terminal server or a VPN concentrator.

- The performance of the applications should be good—certainly much better than with a terminal server.

- To provide sufficient encryption, a small number of users may need to upgrade their web browsers to versions that use 128-bit encryption.

- Besides a few browser updates, no other installations or configuration should be necessary, with the exception of the small group of users who require mainframe access. Limited resources will be needed to assist them with downloading and configuring the chosen TN3270 emulator.

- Various changes would need to be made to the required resources. The corporate intranet server would need to be SSL-enabled. More significantly, OWA would need to be deployed, which can be a major project. The TN3270 proxy would also need to be set up, requiring a significant effort.

- External users would be directly connecting to the intranet and OWA servers. One potential workaround for this is the implementation of a reverse proxy server, which would add at least some degree of separation between external users and internal resources.

The most important unanswered issue at this point is how to authenticate users. If we are allowing users to connect to the intranet server and other resources using SSL, how are we authenticating them? One possibility is to issue digital certificates to all home-based users and then activate checks for SSL client-side certificates, but that might be complex and difficult to support. However, after a user has been authenticated to a particular server through a client-side certificate, the user can run multiple applications on that particular server, if you have configured the server to permit that. This solution provides SSL-based authentication while being relatively convenient for users.

Case Study Conclusion

Of the three options we have reviewed (terminal server, IPSec, and SSL), which is the best? Although all three can provide the required functionality and meet the identified needs, each has serious weaknesses that must be carefully considered. The best method in this case really depends on what the organization's security policies are, how much risk the organization is willing to incur, and how much money and time it is willing to spend on deploying and maintaining a solution. Unfortunately, there is no "magic answer" as to which method is clearly the right choice.

Summary

In this chapter, we examined the topic of VPN integration, and you learned how VPN technologies can be integrated with other defense components. The potential VPN methods we reviewed include standard SSH and SSL connections, SSH and SSL tunneling, SSL proxy servers, remote desktop software, and IPSec. Each of these types has advantages and disadvantages, of course, and each is best suited to certain types of usage. To choose the best solution, you must consider several factors, including the characteristics of end users and their systems, which applications will be used, and what effect everything will have on perimeter defenses. By gathering and evaluating all the pertinent information on the need for a VPN, you can choose an optimal method that secures your organization's data and resources.

References

1 Microsoft. "Get Started Using Remote Desktop." August 25, 2004. http://www.microsoft.com/windowsxp/using/mobility/getstarted/remoteintro.mspx. November 2004.

2 Microsoft. "Windows XP Remote Desktop Web Connection Overview." August 22, 2002. http://www.microsoft.com/windowsxp/using/mobility/getstarted/webconoverview.mspx. November 2004.

## 17

Tuning the Design for Performance

As we discussed in Chapter 12, "Fundamentals of Secure Perimeter Design," performance is an important element to include in the design of a network. Networks that do not offer acceptable performance to their users are frequently not used. It is also important to consider performance when designing the security infrastructure for a network because many techniques that are used to protect networks have performance impacts. Managing these impacts in your design is essential if you hope to deliver a secure network that is acceptable to its users. This can be difficult because performance issues can be hard to quantify prior to implementation, and adding security might decrease performance. This chapter discusses performance issues as they apply to security. We provide you with guidance on how different elements of your security infrastructure can contribute to performance problems and how you can reduce or eliminate the performance impacts of your design decisions.

Performance and Security

Performance and security are not necessarily directly competing design goals. Although many of the steps you must perform to secure a network do have performance costs, it is your job to identify the design elements that add the required security while allowing the network to meet its performance goals.

Defining Performance

When your users complain of poor network performance, they could be referring to several distinct problems. For example, they could be experiencing long download times from their favorite FTP site, or they might be experiencing slow processing of their commands on a remote server. Different types of performance issues can cause each of these problems. Therefore, we begin our discussion of performance with a few definitions.

Network Bandwidth and Latency

Network bandwidth is a measure of how fast information can flow across a network segment. It is typically measured in bits per second (bps). A network that can transfer 500KB of information in 16 seconds would have a bandwidth of 256Kbps (500 * 1024 * 8 / 16). This is a measure of how much information "fits" in the network in a given second. Bandwidth is shared among the different devices that are hooked up to a network segment. Wide area network (WAN) links are normally limited to two devices, which means that all the bandwidth is available to transfer data between them; however, LANs can have hundreds of hosts competing for the network's bandwidth. On a LAN, the available bandwidth between two hosts might be much lower than the total network bandwidth if many other hosts are trying to transfer data at the same time. Fortunately, LAN bandwidth is cheap. Common LAN technologies have large bandwidth capacities. 100BASE-T Ethernet networks are extremely common, and they are rated for 100Mbps. This is in direct contrast to WAN links. A T1 circuit is relatively slow (1.544Mbps) compared to 100BASE-T Ethernet, and it can cost thousands per month.

> **Tip**
>
> Because bandwidth is shared between the devices that need to communicate across a network, when you're determining bandwidth requirements, it is important to factor in the number of simultaneous network conversations that will be occurring. The easiest way to control this is by limiting the total number of computers attached to the network.

Network latency is a measure of how long it takes for a packet to travel from one point in a network to another. It is frequently measured by sending a test packet to a host, which the host then returns to the sender. The roundtrip time is then calculated to determine the latency. Several contributing factors can add latency to a packet:

- **Propagation**—This is the time it takes for the packet to travel from the start to the end of a particular transmission medium and is largely a function of distance. For example, neglecting other factors, a packet traveling from New York to California is going to have a larger propagation delay than a packet traveling from Manhattan to Queens.

- **Gateway processing**—This is the time taken by each device between the transmitter and the receiver that must process the packet. As a packet travels between network segments, it might have to pass through routers, switches, firewalls, network address translations (NATs), VPNs, and other types of network devices. Each of these devices takes time to process the packet.

- **Available bandwidth**—A packet might have to travel across many network segments to reach its destination. The time it takes for the packet to travel across each segment is directly affected by each network segment's available bandwidth.

- **Packet size**—Larger packets take longer to transmit than smaller packets. This time becomes more pronounced when available bandwidth is low or when a gateway-processing device is required to examine the entire packet.

Note

The ping command is frequently used to measure network performance, but it is important to note that it is a measure of latency and not bandwidth. By default, ping transmits a small packet and then waits to receive it back from the destination device. This correctly determines the roundtrip time between the two devices, but it does not tell you anything about the bandwidth between the two devices. Correctly measuring bandwidth requires that a much larger amount of data be transmitted between the two devices to attempt to completely use up all available bandwidth between them. Ping can be told to transmit larger packets, but this is still insufficient to reach the transmission rates that are normally necessary to saturate the network. Other available tools, such as ttcp, are specifically designed to test network bandwidth. Cisco IOS 11.2 and above implement a version of ttcp that is available as a privileged command. The tool ttcp is also available free on many UNIX distributions.

Response Time

Response time is the amount of time it takes a response to be received after a request is made. Response time is a function of the latency between the requester and the responder plus the processing time needed by the responder to calculate the response. Interactive protocols that require frequent bidirectional conversations, such as Telnet, are affected by response time. Response time is primarily what determines whether users perceive a service to be fast or slow. Because of this, when a request is received that will take a long time to calculate, some services immediately return an intermediate response to the user to indicate that they are working on the problem.

Throughput

Throughput is the measure of how much information can be reliably transmitted between two devices on a network. Throughput is principally a function of bandwidth, but it also is affected by protocol overhead. Protocols that are required to transmit large amounts of data in a timely manner are more affected by throughput restrictions. These include applications such as file transfer protocols, video-conferencing, and Voice over IP (VoIP).

Understanding the Importance of Performance in Security

It is worth spending some time discussing why we should care about performance when designing our security infrastructure. Remember, for a network to be secure, it must maintain confidentiality, integrity, and availability to its users. When performance is too low, the network fails to maintain availability. This can be true even when the service is still responding to requests. The performance of network services can directly impact the acceptability of those services. If we offer services securely, but at a service level below the users' tolerance, the services will not be used. Can we really consider the services secure when the users cannot or will not use them?

Of course, different applications have different performance requirements. It is an important part of the security-design process to identify the acceptable performance levels for the services on the network. This requires that you establish metrics to use to measure performance and that you determine acceptable values for each of these metrics. The following are some commonly used metrics:

- Response time
- Throughput
- Maximum simultaneous users
- Minimum availability (for example, 24×7×365)
- Maximum downtime
- Mean time between failure (MTBF)

Keep in mind that acceptable levels for each of your metrics will vary depending on the type and context of the request. For example, it is a commonly held rule of e-business that a visitor typically waits no longer than eight seconds for a web page to download. However, when placing an order, visitors are frequently willing to wait much longer than eight seconds to receive an order confirmation.

Network Security Design Elements That Impact Performance

Almost every decision you make concerning a network's security infrastructure impacts its performance. From the choice of which firewall to field, to the architecture of the network, many factors combine (sometimes in complex ways) to affect the network's overall performance. When designing your network, you need to understand what the individual performance impact of each design element is so that you can predict what the cumulative impact will be for the resulting network.

The Performance Impacts of Network Filters

Because perimeter defense relies so heavily on packet filters and firewalls to protect networks, it makes sense to start our performance discussion with them. Network filters perform the important job of determining which packets should be allowed to enter our networks. The process they go through to make this decision takes time, and the amount of time taken directly impacts the latency of the packet. Assuming similarly performing hardware, the more complex the decision that needs to be made, the longer it will take to reach the decision. From a performance point of view, we should prefer algorithms that can make simple, quick decisions. However, substantial security advantages result from performing more complex analysis of incoming packets. The following four filtering techniques demonstrate this security/performance tradeoff:

- Packet filters
- Stateful firewalls
- Proxy firewalls
- Content filters

Packet Filters

As we discussed back in Chapter 2, "Packet Filtering," packet filters are one of the most basic forms of network filters. All decisions are made based on the contents of the packet header with no reference back to previous packets that have been received. The most common fields on which to filter are source IP address, source port, destination IP address, destination port, and status flags. A typical filter rule might be to allow connections to TCP port 80 on a web server. Assuming the web server is at IP address 192.168.1.5, the Cisco ACL would look like this:

```
access-list 110 permit tcp any host 192.168.1.5 port 80
```

To make the filtering decision, the packet filter need only examine the packet's header for the destination IP address (192.168.1.5) and destination port (80). No other information is required. This is a simple operation that takes little processing time to complete, resulting in little added latency to the packet. Be careful when adding access lists to routers that already have high CPU utilization. The added load, minor as it might be, could cause the router to start dropping packets.

Tip

Apply access lists on incoming interfaces to minimize the performance impact. When they are applied on an incoming interface, the router does not need to make redundant routing decisions on packets that are being rejected.

When security decisions can be made based on small amounts of information, performance impacts are small. Unfortunately, as we explained in Chapter 2, several problems exist with packet filters, including problems protecting against spoofed packets and difficulties allowing return traffic back into the network without opening up unintended holes in the filter. To address these deficiencies, the filtering device must perform additional work.

Stateful Firewalls

Stateful firewalls (covered in Chapter 3, "Stateful Firewalls") address some of packet filtering's shortcomings by introducing a memory to the packet filter in the form of an ongoing connections table. Performance is impacted due to two additional tasks that the firewall must perform on this table. First, when a new packet is allowed through the firewall, the firewall determines whether the packet is the start of a new network conversation. If it is, an entry is added to the ongoing connections table. Second, when the firewall receives the return packet, a lookup must be performed to find the corresponding entry in the ongoing connections table before access can be granted. As you could imagine, on a busy firewall, this table can grow large. As the table grows, the time necessary to locate entries also grows, increasing the time necessary to make the access decision. Stateful firewall vendors employ hash algorithms to attempt to reduce this overhead, but it cannot be completely eliminated.

> **Tip**
>
> Most stateful firewall vendors allow you to tune the firewall by increasing the size of the connection table and corresponding hash table. Increasing these settings can noticeably increase performance and is recommended if your firewall can support the increased memory requirements.

If performance is still unacceptable, some products allow you to disable the memory feature on a per-rule basis. Using this feature increases performance, but at the cost of reduced security.

Proxy Firewalls

Proxy firewalls have the potential to make the best security decisions, but they are the worst performing of the three types of network filters we have discussed. Why use them? As we described in Chapter 4, "Proxy Firewalls," proxy firewalls place themselves in the middle of network conversations. Clients connect first to the proxy firewall, and the proxy firewall makes the request to the server on the client's behalf. To accomplish this, the proxy firewall must maintain two network connections for every ongoing network conversation. Every ongoing connection requires its own data record that records the source and destination of the connection and the current protocol state. When a packet is received, the proxy must examine the data portion of the packet and determine whether it is making a valid request based on that protocol state. This enables the proxy to deny requests that are invalid or out of sequence for the current protocol. For instance, according to RFC 921 (the RFC for Internet mail), during an SMTP session, a `mail from:` command should precede a `rcpt to:` command. By understanding the normal states that a protocol should support, the proxy can reject requests that would break the state model of the protocol—in this case, by rejecting any `rcpt to:` commands that are issued prior to a `mail from:` command being received. Although this approach has a substantial security benefit, it comes at the expense of high memory and CPU requirements. Careful consideration should be given to the choice of the firewall's hardware platform, especially when filtering high-bandwidth traffic.

Content Filters

Content filters protect a network by attempting to detect malicious activity in the content of a packet. Email filters are the most common type of content filters, but they also exist for other types of network traffic. As described in Chapter 10, "Host Defense Components," most of these tools are signature based. They contain a large database of malicious activity signatures. When a new message is received, the content filter must search the message to determine whether it contains malicious signatures. The amount of time this takes is dependent on the size of the signature database, the size of the message, and the speed of the computer performing the filtering.

Signature databases are guaranteed to grow over time. Little benefit would result from removing signatures from these databases. The outcome would be known attacks that the filter would not be able to detect. As the size of the signature database increases, performance of the content filter decreases. It is important to remember this when determining the appropriate hardware on which to host your content filter.

Another important factor to consider is the percentage of malicious traffic to normal traffic. When a malicious message is detected, most content filters need to perform additional work, such as sending out an alert or writing a log entry. This extra work is not an issue when most messages are normal. However, when the number of malicious messages becomes large, this extra work can undermine the ability of the content filter to function. It is possible for an attacker to exploit this problem by sending a large volume of malicious messages to induce a denial of service.

Network Architecture

Because a network that starts out slow will only become slower if we add security devices, it is useful to discuss ways that network design affects network performance. The following four network design issues, which can directly impact the overall performance of a network, are discussed in depth in the subsequent sections:

- Broadcast domains
- WAN links
- TCP/IP tuning
- Routing protocols

Broadcast Domains

Broadcast messages are the most expensive type of packet in terms of performance that can be transmitted on a network. Two reasons explain this. First, when a normal packet is sent out on a network, most hosts can ignore the packet if it is not being sent to them. However, every host in the same broadcast domain must process a broadcast packet, even if the packet is not relevant to it. As discussed in Chapter 13, "Separating Resources," each host in the same broadcast group must take a small performance hit for every broadcast packet received. Second, broadcast messages consume some of the network bandwidth from every host in the same broadcast domain, even when the network is implemented using network switches. Normally, network switches are able to intelligently direct packets to the intended recipient without consuming network bandwidth from other connected hosts. However, this is not possible with broadcast packets because they are supposed to be sent to all hosts.

> **Tip**
> To minimize the performance impact of broadcast messages, keep the number of hosts in a broadcast group as small as practical and try to eliminate or replace protocols that generate many broadcast messages.

WAN Links

WAN links allow geographically distributed networks to be connected. They are normally implemented using circuits that are provided by common carriers such as telephone companies, which charge a recurring fee to provide the WAN service. WAN services are sold in a wide variety of capacities, and the fee for service can grow large for high-bandwidth connections. Table 17.1 lists some of the most common circuit types.

Table 17.1 **Bandwidths for Common Circuit Types**

Circuit Type	Bandwidth
Dial-up modem	9.6–56Kbps
Switch 56	56Kbps
ISDN BRI	128Kbps
Cable modem	Approximately 1Mbps
Digital Subscriber Line (DSL)	256–768Kbps
T1	1.544Mbps
T3	45Mbps
OC3	155Mbps
OC12	622Mbps
OC48	2.45Gbps

When establishing a WAN connection, it is essential that you carefully analyze the bandwidth requirements for the connection. If you order too small a circuit, the network performs unacceptably. If you order too large a circuit, you waste your company's money. Finding an appropriate balance can be tricky, especially when large price increases exist between levels of service. If circuit prices are reasonable in your area, always opt for more bandwidth than you think you will need. You will always find a use for it later. If larger circuits are too expensive, though, you will need to make a careful price-versus-performance analysis that will require a detailed understanding of your WAN performance requirements.

After the appropriate circuit has been set up, it is important not to waste bandwidth over the connection. Following are some tips to help you avoid unnecessary WAN usage:

- Do not bridge the networks because this forces all broadcast traffic on both networks to flow over the WAN link. Route between them instead.

- Do not make one network reliant on the other for basic network services. For example, if you are running a Windows network, place a domain controller on each side of the circuit.

- Use network filters to restrict WAN traffic to essential connections.

- Cache frequently referenced materials locally. Just as Internet providers use web caches to improve performance, any frequently referenced materials should be cached locally to prevent redundant WAN usage to retrieve the same information.

- Try to schedule batch jobs that send large amounts of data over the WAN link for periods of low activity.

TCP/IP Tuning

Many TCP/IP stacks are not set up to perform optimally by default. To get the most performance possible, examine some of the specific controls available for your servers to optimize TCP/IP performance for your environment. Following are some specific issues for which you should look:

- **Maximum transmission units (MTUs)**—If you transmit a packet with too large an MTU, it might have to be fragmented to reach its destination. This adds substantial latency to the packet, and in some cases, it might prevent delivery. To address this, many manufacturers set the MTU to the smaller of 576 and the MTU of the outbound interface. This is normally small enough to avoid fragmentation, but it can significantly reduce transfer efficiency. RFC 1191 describes a method to dynamically discover the MTU. It works by sending out packets with the Do Not Fragment bit set. When a compliant router receives one of these packets but cannot forward the packet because the next link has a smaller MTU, it sends back an Internet Control Message Protocol (ICMP) error message that includes a new recommended MTU size. This allows the transmitting host to reduce the MTU to the largest value that will still permit the packet to reach its destination without being fragmented. Most manufacturers support RFC 1191, but it might not be turned on by default.

Note
Some networks block all ICMP messages at the network's border. This can break several TCP/IP protocols, including the mechanism on which RFC 1191 relies to function. For an RFC 1191–compliant operating system to determine a correct MTU, it must be able to receive ICMP type 3 (Destination Unreachable) and code 4 (Fragmentation Needed and Don't Fragment Was Set) packets. If all ICMP messages are filtered, the sending host assumes that the current MTU is supported, which might cause unnecessary packet fragmentation. In some implementations, it might disable communications entirely if the Do Not Fragment bit is set on all outgoing packets. For this reason, it is important to carefully consider what types of ICMP messages should be allowed into and out of your network instead of just creating a generic "deny all" ICMP rule.

- **Window size**—The TCP window value determines how much TCP data a host can transmit prior to receiving an acknowledgement. This is part of TCP's error-correction mechanism. When the value is small, errors in transmission are quickly detected. This is good if the circuit is unreliable. For reliable circuits, a larger TCP window size is more appropriate. TCP is designed to dynamically vary the window size to adjust for circuit quality. This mechanism works well for reasonably high-performance circuits. When circuit speeds are extremely high (greater than 800Mbps), the maximum window size is exceeded and performance suffers. To address this, RFC 1323 was proposed. RFC 1323 adds extensions to TCP to support extremely high-performance networks, including an increase in the maximum window size.

> **Tip**
>
> When working with extremely high-performance networks, you should use operating environments that support the RFC 1323 extension. Examples of operating systems that support RFC 1323 include AIX 4.1, HP-UX, Linux (kernels 2.1.90 or later), Microsoft Windows (2000 and above), and Sun Solaris (versions 2.6 and above).

- **Socket buffer size**—The send and receive socket buffers hold data during transmission until an acknowledgment for the data has reached the transmitting host. At this point, the acknowledged data can be flushed from the buffer, allowing new data to be transmitted. When these buffers are too small, performance suffers because the connection between the two hosts cannot be filled up completely with data. The amount of data that will fit between two hosts is directly related to the bandwidth and latency between the hosts. It can be calculated by the following formula:

  amount of data = bandwidth $\star$ roundtrip time delay

  The resulting value is the optimum size for the transmit and receive buffers for communication between the two hosts. Of course, different values would be obtained for conversations between different hosts. Currently, TCP does not support calculating this value dynamically, so a reasonable maximum should be chosen. Some applications allow the users to specify the buffer sizes, but this is uncommon. For most applications, the only way to increase the buffer sizes is to increase the system-level defaults. This should be done with care because it causes all network applications to use additional system memory that they might not require. Keep in mind that you will only gain a performance increase if both hosts are using sufficiently sized buffers.

Routing Protocols: RIP Versus OSPF

Routing is the process of deciding how to deliver a packet from one network to another. To deliver a packet, each router between the source and destination devices must know the correct next-hop router to which to send the packet. Routers maintain routing tables to make these decisions. These tables can be configured in one of two ways: by manually entering routing information into each router or by using a routing protocol. Routing protocols are designed to automatically determine the correct routes through a network by exchanging routing information with neighboring routers.

Two of the most common routing protocols in use on LANs are Routing Information Protocol (RIP) and Open Shortest Path First (OSPF). RIP is included as a standard routing protocol on most routers and was the first major routing protocol for TCP/IP. RIP is easily implemented and normally works just by turning it on. For this reason, many manufacturers use it as the default routing protocol. This is unfortunate because RIP suffers from many deficiencies, including substantial performance problems.

RIP has two major performance problems. First, it cannot make routing decisions based on bandwidth. RIP uses hop-count as its metric to determine the shortest path between two networks. Paths with lower hop-counts are preferred over paths with higher hop-counts, even if the bandwidth of the lower hop-count path is much lower. For an extreme example, see Figure 17.1. Router A has a 100Mbps connection to Router B, which has a 100Mbps connection to Router C. In addition, Router A has a 128Kbps connection to Router C. If Host 1 attempts to send a packet to Host 2, the preferred path from a performance standpoint would be A-B-C, but RIP would choose A-C, forcing the packet to travel across the extremely slow link.

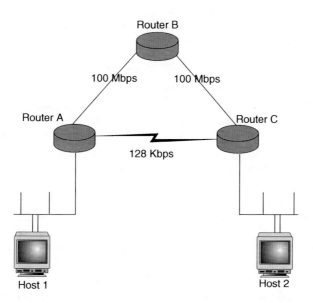

Figure 17.1   RIP networks occasionally make poor routing choices.

RIP's second problem is that it has an inefficient method of sharing routing information across a network. Every 30 seconds, routers that are running RIP must broadcast their entire routing table to each neighboring router. On large networks, these tables are big and can consume a substantial amount of network bandwidth. If the network includes slow network links, this route information can bring performance across the link to a crawl. In addition, RIP has other deficiencies that can make it a poor choice as your routing protocol. The most significant of these is that it takes a relatively long time for RIP routes to propagate throughout the network. In some cases, this can mean that RIP might not stabilize when routes are changing rapidly.

OSPF was created to provide a nonproprietary routing protocol that addressed the deficiencies of earlier routing protocols, such as RIP. OSPF includes the ability to represent a cost for each interface, which allows it to make decisions based on the bandwidth differences between paths. OSPF is significantly more efficient when sharing routing information across the network. It transmits routing changes only when they occur instead of broadcasting them at fixed intervals. The improvements that OSPF brings do come at the cost of implementation complexity. OSPF networks are more difficult to implement than RIP networks.

Case Studies to Illustrate the Performance Impact of Network Security Design Elements

Following are two case studies to illustrate some of the concepts covered so far. In the first, we examine performance issues that might occur when connecting a field office to corporate headquarters. In the second, we examine performance problems that can crop up when packet latency becomes high.

Case Study 1: Two Networks Connected Using 128K ISDN

The network presented in Figure 17.2 is a classic example of a field office connection to corporate headquarters. This office is responsible for processing sales orders for its local region, and its network has been connected to corporate headquarters over an ISDN BRI WAN circuit. The network's main resource is a file server. It contains product information, customer lists, and other materials that the field office uses to sell the company's products to its clients. Most of the sales transactions can be performed locally; however, when a new sale is processed, real-time inventory quantities must be queried from a server at corporate headquarters. Every hour, collected sales order information is uploaded to the corporate database. The field office network is modest and is organized as a single network subnet, which contains a dozen PCs, three network printers, and the file server. The network used to be a collection of different operating systems, including Windows 95, Windows NT, NetWare 4, and Mac OS 7. This changed when all systems, including the file server, were swapped out for Windows 2003 systems. The corporate headquarters network is large with dozens of subnets. It is mainly a TCP/IP network, but IPX is also in use due to some infrequently used Novell file servers. In addition, the marketing department has a few Mac OS X systems configured to run AppleTalk. This was the simplest method the marketing staff could find to enable continued access to the printers when it upgraded from earlier Macintosh systems.

The field office has been complaining for months about sporadic performance problems on its network. The workers are concerned with slow response time when checking inventory levels because it makes it difficult for them to respond appropriately to their customers. This problem is intermittent, but it is frequent enough to affect business. The company has asked you to determine what is causing the performance problem.

Given this information, what type of questions should you ask? You should focus your attention on several clues. The field office has a small-bandwidth connection back to corporate headquarters. It would not take much unnecessary traffic to affect performance. What could some of the sources of unnecessary traffic be? Look for unnecessary protocols. In addition to TCP/IP, the corporate network is running IPX and AppleTalk.

Because the field office used to have NetWare and Mac OS systems, it is possible that IPX and AppleTalk were once in use. It is reasonable to assume that the routers might be configured to pass this traffic. Now that the field office has standardized on Windows 2003, these extraneous protocols are no longer needed. Reconfiguration of systems relying on legacy protocols can significantly reduce network traffic and improve performance.

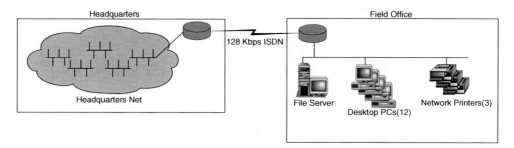

Figure 17.2   Case study 1 discusses the performance
issues in low-bandwidth WAN connections.

Another potential source of traffic is the routing protocol. The example did not mention which was being used, but it is highly possible that the office is using RIP. Because corporate headquarters has a large number of networks, RIP routing announcement packets will be large. Should you have the field office switch to something more efficient, such as OSPF? In this case, that might be overkill. Because the field office router has only two possible places to send packets, it might be better to use a static route.

Why is the problem sporadic? Could it be the hourly transmission of sales information to corporate headquarters? If this information does not need to be available immediately, perhaps it would be better to hold off transmission of the sales information until after business hours.

The last issue you might look at is the size of the circuit. Perhaps the office has outgrown its current bandwidth. In this case, the best course of action would be to purchase additional circuits or to upgrade to a faster type of circuit.

Case Study 2: Satellite-Based Network

The network shown in Figure 17.3 collects weather data at several remote sites across the continental United States. These data-collection sites have been in place for many years. Each uses an old Solaris 2.5 workstation connected serially to a weather data collection unit as well as a router connected to a satellite radio. The workstations send data on weather conditions whenever a change from the last transmitted value is detected. When conditions are stable, the rate of transmission is low. However, when conditions are variable, the data rate can be high. The equivalent of T1-sized circuits has been purchased to address this problem. However, even with the large satellite circuits, the scientist working on the project still experiences packet loss during rapidly changing weather conditions. You have been asked to determine what the problem is. Where do you begin?

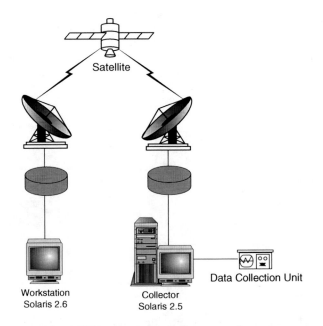

Figure 17.3   Case study 2 discusses performance
issues with large latency applications.

One of the major attributes of a satellite-based network circuit is that it has high latency.
It takes a long time for a signal to travel the distance up to geosync orbit (45,000 kilo-
meters) and then return to Earth. Even when bandwidth is high, this added time could
cause performance problems if the network protocol is not set up to handle the added
delay. If TCP is the protocol being used to transmit the data, it is possible that the packet
buffers are too small or the maximum window size has been reached. Either or both of
these issues could cause reduced performance.

To determine this, we must calculate the amount of data needed to fill our satellite
pipe. Based on the given circuit speed bandwidth of 1.544Mbps and the roundtrip time of
1 second for a satellite circuit, our bandwidth×delay product is 1544Kb, or close to
200KB. It turns out that Solaris 2.5's default packet buffer size is 256KB. This is large
enough to prevent delays; however, Solaris 2.5 is not RFC 1323 compliant. The maximum
window size for non-RFC-1323 systems is 64KB. This is more than likely the problem
because it would prevent us from making maximum use of the bandwidth of our circuit.
To address the problem, we would need to upgrade our Solaris system to a version that
does support RFC 1323. Solaris systems from 2.6 on are RFC 1323 compliant.

Impact of Encryption

Encryption provides powerful security advantages when used appropriately. It is also one
of the most computationally expensive protection measures available in our security
toolkit. In this section, we will discuss cryptography from a performance standpoint,

including the differences in ability and performance between public key and symmetric key cryptographic systems.

> **Note**
> If you would like to learn more about cryptographic services, see Appendix B, "Crypto 101." It provides a basic introduction to the subject and its terminology.

We will also discuss performance characteristics of network cryptographic protocols at the network layer, such as IPSec, and transport layer, such as SSL.

Cryptographic Services

As discussed in Chapter 7, "Virtual Private Networks," cryptography is often used to provide four important security services: confidentiality, integrity, authentication, and nonrepudiation.

Each of these services uses particular cryptographic techniques, and each has varying impacts on the performance of your systems. Confidentiality and integrity services affect performance for as long as they are in use. Because of this, they are normally provided using symmetric key cryptography. Efficient symmetric key algorithms exist that allow high-performance systems to be built using relatively low-end equipment. Public key cryptography can also be used in theory to provide confidentiality and integrity services, but this is not common because public key cryptography requires significantly more work and time to encrypt and decrypt data than symmetric key cryptography.

Public key cryptography makes up for its performance problems by offering the ability to authenticate users and uniquely identify the creator of a message. Because authentication and nonrepudiation are typically only performed once per session, the additional work needed for the public key algorithm does not unduly affect the performance of the entire session. Protocol developers frequently combine the best aspects of both types of cryptography when designing their protocols. It is common for public key techniques to be used to authenticate users and then exchange session details, including a shared secret. This shared secret is then used to generate a key used to encrypt the rest of the conversation using symmetric key cryptography. In this way, the strengths of both techniques are maximized while their weaknesses are minimized.

Understanding Encryption at the Network and Transport Layers

Cryptographic services can be added to almost any layer of the network stack. The decision of which layer to implement your cryptographic services on is dependent on the specific security goal you are trying to accomplish. In the following sections, we will discuss cryptography at the network and the transport layers.

Network Layer Cryptography

Network layer cryptography allows private conversations to occur across untrusted networks. They can be organized as network-to-network, network-to-host, or host-to-host links. The major cryptographic service offered is confidentiality. Performance impacts are driven primarily by the increased CPU utilization of the sending and receiving devices. This impact grows with traffic volume; high-bandwidth circuits use more CPU cycles than low-bandwidth circuits.

Assuming sufficient network bandwidth, performance of a VPN is mainly determined by the choice of algorithm and the hardware platform. A variety of popular algorithms are in common use, including Digital Encryption Standard (DES), Triple DES (3DES), Advanced Encryption Standard (AES), and Twofish. However, the choices available to you will be limited by those supported by your VPN device. In general, algorithms that use larger keys are more secure, but they also perform significantly worse. Table 17.2 shows some common algorithms and the key sizes they support.

Table 17.2 **Symmetric Key Algorithm Key Sizes**

Algorithm	Key Size
RC4	40 bits
FWZ-1 4	8 bits
DES 4	0 or 56 bits
3DES	112 bits
Twofish	128 bits
AES	Variable in 32-bit increments; typically 128, 192, or 256 bits

Even though algorithms with key sizes of 56 bits or lower, such as DES, have been decrypted using brute-force methods, you should not immediately discard their use. If immediate discovery of the contents of your messages is your primary concern, a 56-bit key algorithm might be more than enough to provide the necessary security while allowing you to use much higher performing encryption algorithms.

The speed of the hardware platform is the other major determinant of VPN performance. Encryption is a CPU-intensive operation. Because of this, platforms with faster processors perform better. Some hardware vendors also support hardware cryptographic accelerators. These are coprocessors that are optimized to perform cryptographic operations.

Tip
Be wary of manufacturer performance claims. Performance claims are often highly optimistic. If possible, test the performance of a device in your environment prior to committing to it.

When implementing a VPN in your environment, it is tempting to use preexisting equipment to implement the VPN service. Most firewalls and routers offer this ability either as a standard feature or as a low-cost option. The major performance impact of network layer encryption is CPU utilization on the encrypting and decrypting devices. You should be careful when adding a VPN to an existing router or firewall. If the CPU utilization is already high, then adding the VPN might cripple the device's ability to perform its other duties.

Tip

If CPU utilization is too high but a hardware upgrade is not possible, consider reducing the amount of network traffic being encrypted. Most VPN devices allow you to set filters that specify a subset of the network traffic to encrypt. Using this feature can dramatically reduce CPU load.

Transport Layer Security (TLS)

Transport Layer Security (TLS) is an important protocol for providing confidentiality, integrity, and authentication services, and it is in widespread use across the Internet. It was originally named Secure Sockets Layer (SSL) and was created by Netscape. SSL version 3 was the foundation used by the Internet Engineering Task Force to create TLS.

TLS is most commonly used for sensitive web connections, and it can also be used to protect other application protocols such as SMTP. Because of TLS's popularity, it is important to discuss some of its performance characteristics. TLS is composed of two different protocols: the record protocol and the handshake protocol. The record protocol carries the traffic of the TLS connection and can support several encryption protocols, including RC4, DES, 3DES, and Fortezza. The actual encryption used is chosen during the negotiations that occur at the start of a TLS session. These negotiations are handled by the handshake protocol, which authenticates the server to the client, optionally authenticates the client to the server and then negotiates session details, including the exchange of a master secret that will be used to generate the symmetric keys used by the record protocol.

The SSL performance cost is a combination of the one-time session setup costs performed by the handshake protocol, followed by the continuous cost of the record protocol as it encrypts the session traffic using the chosen encryption protocol. Of the two, the record protocol would seem to be the more dominate because its performance impact lasts for the entire session, whereas the handshake protocol's impact is limited to once per session. This turns out not to be true. There are two main reasons for this. First, web sessions tend to be short, with an average data transfer of approximately 4,000 bytes. This limits the amount of time over which the handshake costs can be amortized. Second, the SSL handshake, at least from the point of view of the server, turns out to be an expensive operation.

During the SSL handshake, both the client and the server are asked to perform public key cryptographic operations. However, the server performs the majority of the work. During the handshake, the client receives the server's certificate, which it uses to extract the server's public key. It uses this key to encrypt a secret, which the server eventually uses to generate the shared secret on which the record protocol relies. Before the server can make use of this secret, it must decrypt it. This decryption operation requires roughly two to three times more work than the encryption operation. During a typical SSL web transaction, the server might have to perform 100 times more work to negotiate the session than it would use to encrypt the data to be transferred.

The designers of SSL were aware of this problem. To help alleviate this, they included the ability to cache session details so that subsequent SSL sessions could resume the previous session without performing any of the public key operations. During the initial communication between client and server, the client can present a session ID that it received during the previous handshake. If the session details are still in the cache, the session can be resumed. Performance improvements as cache hits increase are impressive. Netscape reports the ability to handle 2.5 times more operations per second when session reuse is at 100%.[1]

> **Tip**
>
> If SSL performance is low, try increasing the size of the session cache and the length of the session timeout. This increases the chances of cache hits.
>
> If performance is still too low, try limiting the sections of the website that require SSL protection. Most e-commerce sites do not switch to SSL protection until a financial transaction is about to occur. This limits the amount of SSL sessions the site must accommodate.

Using Hardware Accelerators to Improve Performance

Another method you can use to boost performance is to offload the CPU workload to a coprocessor that is specifically designed to perform cryptographic operations. This provides two performance benefits. First, it significantly reduces the load on the main CPU. Because the main CPU does not have to perform the cryptographic operation, its time can be spent performing its normal activities. Second, because hardware accelerators are designed specifically to perform the mathematical operations that cryptography requires, they can perform cryptographic operations more efficiently than general-purpose computers.

Hardware accelerators are available for a wide variety of platforms, including Cisco PIX firewalls, HP-UX servers, Sun Solaris servers, Windows servers, and Linux servers, and a variety of protocols, including SSL and IPSec. When considering the purchase of one of these devices, keep the following details in mind:

- Support for the appropriate protocol (IPSec, SSL).
- Support for your hardware platform.
- Performance when executing session encryption.
- Performance when negotiating a session. This is especially important for SSL accelerators.
- Cost.

> **Accelerator Cards and Performance Bottlenecks**
>
> Be sure you understand what an accelerator accelerates before you purchase one. In a site where I worked, a CryptoSwift eCommerce Accelerator card was added to an underperforming secure web server. It made a noticeable improvement in the use of the secure website. The page had many hits from many different users, obviously generating a new session negotiation for every visitor. When the same card was added to another secure website, the performance didn't improve. In this case, only five to six users were on the website at a time, causing few key negotiations. The performance issue in this case turned out to be problems in the back-end database.

Whether you should consider a hardware accelerator depends on your performance goals and the availability of a product that supports your environment and your budget. The price of hardware accelerators can be high. If your current hardware can support the workload, hardware acceleration is wasted money.

Case Studies to Illustrate the Performance Impact of Encryption

These two case studies illustrate some of the cryptographic performance concepts we have covered so far. The first case study examines link encryption performance between two networks. The second case study looks at the performance of web servers when encrypting HTTP sessions.

Case Study 3: Link Encrypting Between Two Routers

A large organization (ALO) has purchased a 768Kbps frame-relay connection between its main headquarters and one of its business partner's field offices (BFO). A Cisco router, as shown in Figure 17.4, terminates each side of the connection. The ALO side has a Cisco 3640 router, and the BFO side has a Cisco 2611 router. Because ALO is not in control of the security policy of the BFO network, it has placed a firewall between its network and its Cisco 3640 router. Rules have been established on the firewall to prevent unauthorized network traffic from entering the ALO network. In addition, due to the sensitivity of the information that needs to be sent between the two networks, an IPSec encrypted tunnel has been set up between the two edge routers. Cisco's documentation shows that the 2611 router would not be able to provide sufficient performance when using the 3DES algorithm. DES performance, however, looks acceptable. Because of this, a business decision has been made to use the less secure but faster 56-bit DES algorithm. Performance between the two networks is acceptable, but it is slower than expected given the relatively large bandwidth connection that was purchased. The ALO management has asked you to look into the problem.

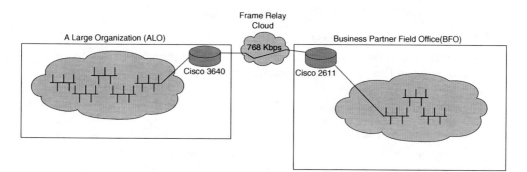

Figure 17.4   Case study 3 examines the link encryption performance issues.

In this case, the problem is more than likely the performance hit from the encrypted tunnel. Running a tool such as ttcp between the two sites can verify the actual available bandwidth.

> **Tip**
>
> Never run ttcp during normal production hours. To measure the bandwidth, ttcp has to consume it all. Not only would running ttcp during business hours cause its results to be wrong, but it would also bring the network to its knees while ttcp was running.

In this case, ttcp reports performance in the 260Kbps range. This is far below the bandwidth of the WAN link, so we need to look further into our configuration to determine the problem. An examination of the CPU utilization of both routers taken during the ttcp test will reveal the problem. The Cisco 3640 will more than likely be reporting CPU utilization rates at or below 50%. This will not be the case of the Cisco 2611. This router has a much slower CPU and will likely be reporting utilization rates above 85%. At this level, packet-forwarding performance is affected, increasing latency and potentially causing packets to be dropped. With encryption, the weakest link sets the overall performance—in this case, the Cisco 2611.

Now that we have identified the likely cause of the problem, what can we do about it? Because performance is acceptable, the easiest answer might simply be to ignore it. This is somewhat unsatisfactory, though, because ALO is paying for WAN bandwidth of which it is not able to take advantage. Reducing the bandwidth of the circuit—if it substantially reduced the price—might be a compensation for this. However, we need to be careful not to reduce the bandwidth too low or it will become the bottleneck. Another solution might be to reduce the key size of the encryption protocol. Forty-bit DES might reduce the load sufficiently to allow full performance to be achieved, although this would come at the expense of a substantial weakening of the confidentiality of the connection. An alternative solution might be to look at another tunneling protocol. Cisco routers support a proprietary tunneling protocol called Cisco Encryption Technology (CET). CET performs better than IPSec, so when your VPN consists entirely of Cisco products, CET might be a viable option. Your last option is to upgrade the hardware. If you have the budget, you could solve the problem by upgrading the Cisco 2611 router or adding a crypto accelerator card to it.

Case Study 4: SSL Web Server

A company maintains a server that has a website it uses to provide private company information to its large traveling sales force. After a recent embarrassing defacement of the company's public website, it became much more security conscious and has configured an SSL version of the website on the server. Client certificates have been installed on all the sales force laptops, and the website has been configured to require client-side SSL authentication. Almost as soon as the SSL website went online, the complaints started to come in. The sales force stated that the website was almost unreachable, and when it did respond, it took forever for a page to download. You have been asked to help eliminate the performance problems while still maintaining the security of the site.

By reusing the existing server, it is likely that the company did not consider the additional load that the SSL protocol would add to the server. CPU performance is more than likely the cause of the problem, and CPU utilization measurements bear this out. To reduce the load, you might look at SSL session reuse. If the session timeout values or session cache sizes are too low, the server performs unnecessary full SSL handshakes. Increasing these values might reduce the magnitude of the problem. If performance is still too slow, a hardware upgrade might be appropriate. Assuming that the budget is available, a faster computer or an SSL accelerator could be used to decrease the performance hit that SSL is causing. If this is not possible, the only remaining option is to limit the required number of SSL sessions. If some data on the site were less sensitive than other data, then removing it from the SSL side of the web server would reduce the work that the server needs to perform.

Using Load Balancing to Improve Performance

Sometimes the amount of work that must be performed exceeds the capabilities of any single device available to us. In this case, the only way to increase performance is to divide the work between multiple devices. By dividing the work in such a way that many devices can tackle it, we create a much more scalable and potentially reliable solution. These benefits come at the expense of added complexity and cost. When deciding to use load balancing, you will have to weigh the need for performance against the added costs in equipment, staff, and time needed to build and maintain the system.

Load balancers use various methods to direct requests to a pool of mirrored servers. One of the simplest methods to distribute the workload is DNS round-robin. This system works by having the DNS server provide the IP address of a different server from the pool every time a DNS request is made. Although simple, this solution does not work well for high-performance systems. This is due to many factors, but the largest is the problem of client networks caching the results of the first DNS query for the server. This causes all clients on a network to send their requests to a single server in the pool. If the number of users on the network is large, this can completely undermine DNS round-robin's ability to balance the traffic.

More sophisticated solutions such as F5's Big IP Controller and Cisco's Local Director rely on a dispatch controller to distribute the requests to the pool as they arrive. These products perform two important functions. First, when a dispatcher receives a packet that is the start of a new network conversation, it must deliver the packet to a server in the pool that has the capacity to handle the new request. Second, when a packet arrives at the dispatcher that is part of an ongoing conversation, the dispatcher must have the intelligence to deliver the packet to the server that has been previously assigned to handle the request. The sophistication used to make the first decision is the major difference between the various products on the market.

Load balancing can also be used to increase availability. If one of the devices in the group breaks down, the other systems can take up the load and continue operation. If you are going to rely on this to maintain availability, keep in mind the loss of performance your solution will experience when it loses a system. You will need to make sure a minimum number of systems is always available, even if one of the systems fails. Also, if you are truly concerned about redundancy, don't forget to have a redundant load balancer. Without one, a load balancer failure will bring down the entire system.

Problems with Load Balancing

Load balancing does not improve all situations. Certain types of problems are difficult to divide among various servers. If a problem cannot be divided or if the work necessary to divide it would exceed the performance gained from distributing it, then load balancing will not help. Another problem with load balancing occurs if the handoff of a request from one server to another requires the second server to perform expensive setup operations. SSL is a classic example of this. As we discussed earlier, SSL handshakes are so expensive that the SSL servers cache session details so that new sessions do not have to go through the entire handshake. When using some load-balancing systems, it's not guaranteed that a returning client will be redirected back to the server that handled the previous request. This might actually result in performance lower than before the load-balancing solution because almost every request will be forced to make a full SSL handshake. More sophisticated load-balancing devices include the ability to redirect SSL session requests back to the original server. This is accomplished by tracking the session ID in the header of the packet and sending successive packets from a client (with the same session ID) to the same back-end server. In addition, some products support the ability to off-load all SSL functions, freeing up significant processing overhead on the web servers.

Layer 4 Dispatchers

Two major types of dispatcher products are on the market: Layer 4 dispatchers, such as the previously mentioned F5 Big IP Controller, and Layer 7 dispatchers, such as Radware's Web Server Director. The layer numbers are taken from the Open System Interconnection (OSI) reference model.

Layer 4 dispatchers make delivery decisions based on information contained within the Layer 4 (transport) header and Layer 3 (network) header of the TCP/IP packet. This information includes the source and destination IP addresses, source and destination protocol addresses (ports), and other session information, such as whether the packet is the start of a session or a continuation. Because the different pieces of information in the header of the packets are always in the same locations within the packets, Layer 4 dispatchers do not have to perform much work to locate the information on which they will make their delivery decision. This enables fast decisions and fast switching.

When a packet arrives at a Layer 4 dispatcher, the dispatcher determines whether the packet is the start of a new session or the continuation of a previously started session. If it is a new session, the dispatcher chooses a server to handle the new connection and forwards the packet to it. The way this decision is made varies depending on the load-sharing algorithms the dispatcher supports. Common algorithms include round-robin, weighted round-robin, least connections, least load, and fastest response. If the packet is a continuation of a session, the dispatcher looks up the connection details and forwards the packet on to the server handling the session.

Layer 7 Dispatchers

Layer 7 dispatchers look above the transport layer into the application data (OSI Layer 7) to make their delivery decisions. This allows them to make more intelligent decisions when delivering packets. One major advantage with Layer 7 dispatching of web servers is that different web servers in the pool can serve different types of content. Layer 4 dispatchers are unable to make decisions based on content. This means that when a Layer 4 dispatcher is used, all servers in the pool must have identical content. This is not a major issue if your site is fairly static. However, it is a major issue if your site content is changed dynamically. Keeping all your servers up to date can be a major undertaking, requiring significant network, storage, and computational resources. Having a shared file system eliminates the synchronization problems, but it introduces significant load on the servers. The servers must fetch a copy of the requested information from the common file server before the page can be returned to the client.

Content-based (Layer 7) dispatching provides an alternative to full replication or common file systems by making use of information that is contained within the HTTP request to route the packet. The dispatcher can look inside the web request to determine what URL has been requested and then use that information to choose the appropriate server.

The cost of this ability is a significant increase in the complexity and required resources for each delivery decision. Because the application data is pretty freeform and not structured into the rigid fields typified by the packet header, a substantially more expensive search must be conducted within the application data to locate the information from which the delivery decision will be made. Because of this, high-performance Layer 7 dispatchers tend to be more expensive than similarly performing Layer 4 solutions.

Mitigating the Effects of DoS Attacks

As we stated at the beginning of this chapter, performance is an important requirement for a secure network. This includes maintaining performance during network attacks. Denial of service (DoS) attacks have become common on the Internet and can be devastating to unprepared organizations. To consider your network properly protected, you need to include DoS protection as part of your perimeter.

An attacker can use many methods to launch a DoS attack against your site. Most are either based on bandwidth consumption or resource consumption. In a bandwidth consumption attack, the attacker continuously sends a large volume of spoofed packets into your network, filling up your WAN connections and potentially overwhelming the routers and firewalls that the traffic needs to pass through. A resource consumption attack, on the other hand, attempts to consume vital resources on the servers that make up your network. Any resource that, if exhausted, will stop the server from functioning can be targeted. This includes resources such as CPU cycles, hard disk space, and the TCP half-open connections buffer.

The type of defense needed to protect your network will vary based on the type of attack. To illustrate this, we are going to cover a couple classic DoS attacks and provide advice on how you can defend against them. The attacks we will cover are ICMP flooding and SYN flooding.

ICMP Flooding

ICMP flooding is a type of bandwidth consumption attack where a large amount of ICMP packets is sent to your network in an attempt to consume all your network bandwidth. The ease at which this can be done is dependent on how big your network circuits are. There are two main methods attackers use to create ICMP floods. The first uses distributed denial of service (DDoS) techniques. With DDoS, the attacker gains the ability to control a large number of computer systems on the Internet. These are referred to as *zombie* systems. All the zombies can be controlled simultaneously by the attacker. To launch the ICMP flood, the attacker instructs all the zombies to begin sending spoofed ICMP packets to the target (see Figure 17.5). If the attacker has enough zombies, this can cause a devastatingly large amount of traffic to reach the target network. DDoS attacks have been responsible for taking down the largest sites on the Internet, including eBay and Yahoo! They can be used for many types of DoS attacks, not just ICMP floods.

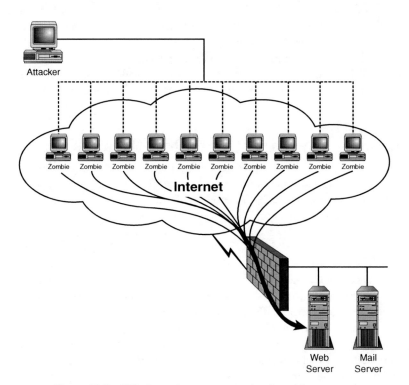

Figure 17.5   DDoS attacks use a network of zombie servers to send overwhelming volumes of packets to a target network.

The second common ICMP flooding technique is called *smurfing*. This method, named after the first tool to popularize the technique, relies on spoofing and TCP/IP broadcast addresses.

If you send a ping packet to the broadcast address of many networks, the packet will be received by every host on the network. Many operating systems will reply to these broadcast pings. Put another way, for the cost of one ICMP packet to a broadcast address, you may receive many reply ICMP packets. To use this in an attack, all the attacker needs to do is find a network where many hosts respond to a broadcast ping. He then spoofs a stream of pings destined to the broadcast address of this network using the target's IP address as the source address (see Figure 17.6). The result will be a much larger stream of ping packets heading toward the target. It is not that hard to find a network that contains hundreds of hosts that reply to the broadcast ping. Assume the attacker is using a 56K dial-up line to send the broadcast pings. The typical maximum upload transfer speed for 56K modems is around 4Kbps, but for highly compressible data, the speed can get as high as 10Kbps. Also assume that the attacker has found a broadcast network that has 200 responding hosts. The attacker can create an ICMP flood at a rate of 2000Kbps (2Mbps). This is sufficient to take down a site that is being serviced by a single T1 line.

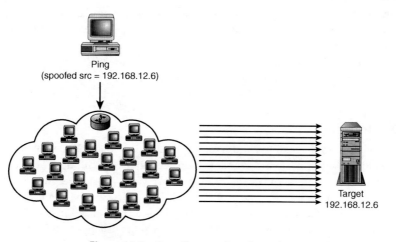

Figure 17.6   Smurfing uses broadcast pings
to amplify the attacker's bandwidth.

So, how do we defend against the flood? A good start is to make sure you are not a potential source of an ICMP flood. As we discussed in Chapter 6, "The Role of a Router," you should make sure you have disabled directed broadcasts. This will prevent your site from participating in a Smurf attack.

If you are the recipient of the flood, you need to be able to stop it before it reaches the circuit that will become saturated. For many sites, this will be the WAN circuit to their ISP. This presents you with a problem. You could perfectly filter out the extraneous

ICMP packets at your perimeter router, but still be down because all your WAN circuit bandwidth has already been consumed. This means that it will be your ISP, not you, who will need to take action. This makes having a responsive ISP an important part of your network's perimeter security.

The type of filter your ISP will need to install depends on the type of flood. Smurf attacks can often be handled by filtering out all packets coming from the source network being used by the attacker to launch the attack. This assumes that the source network is not one that you need to communicate with! DDoS attacks though can be harder to defend against than Smurf attacks.

In a DDoS attack, all the packet source addresses will likely be random, making it impossible to use source address as our filter criteria. We may still be able to use a filter, though, if we don't need the packet type that is being used to attack us or if there is some other unique aspect to the attack packets that would allow us to differentiate them from our normal traffic. For example, most networks do not absolutely need to support ping traffic. If all the DoS packets are pings, we can safely block ping packets to bring the attack under control. If the DoS packets are a type we must accept (such as HTTP packets heading toward your public web servers or SMTP packets heading toward your mail servers), there may be some other unique feature of the packets we can use to discriminate them from normal traffic (such as excessive size).

If the DoS traffic is a type we must support, and we can not easily discriminate it from normal traffic, our next best defense is rate limiting. With rate limiting, we instruct the filtering router to only allow so much bandwidth to a particular category of traffic (for example, ICMP). Any traffic above this limit is discarded. This prevents the traffic category from consuming all the available bandwidth. Although you will likely be throwing out some good traffic with the bad, at least your network will be back up.

SYN Flooding

SYN flooding uses the session handshake required to set up a TCP connection against us. As we discussed in Chapter 2, three packets are required to set up a TCP connection. These are the SYN, SYN-ACK, and ACK packets. When a server receives a SYN packet from a client, it needs to have a way of remembering that it has been asked to establish a connection to the client while waiting for the client to respond to its SYN-ACK packet. The server does this by recording the SYN request in its half-open connections buffer. Normally requests are cleared from the half-open connections buffer when the server receives the ACK packet from the client, thus finishing the three-way handshake. If no ACK is received, the server will eventually time out the connection and remove the entry. As a last option, a TCP reset packet is sent to the server to clear the entry.

The half-open connections buffer has a limited size and, when it fills up, the server is no longer able to accept new connections. The SYN flood attack abuses this feature by sending SYN packets to the server with no intention of finishing the handshake. As long as the attacker can send SYN packets faster than the server times out the half-open connections, the buffer will quickly fill up and the server will be unable to respond to new requests.

Two methods are commonly used to protect against SYN flood attacks: TCP half-open connection monitoring and TCP establishment proxying. With TCP half-open connection monitoring, your firewall (or router) watches the amount and/or age of half-open connections received by internal servers. When a preconfigured threshold is exceeded, the firewall begins sending TCP resets to the server to clear the half-open connections from the buffer. This frees up new slots in the buffer, allowing the server to continue receiving requests. Even though some of the half-open connections that will be cleared are going to be for valid connections, this is better than being completely offline.

A more sophisticated answer, though, is available in TCP establishment proxying. With this solution, the firewall responds to all SYN packets for internal servers by sending out a SYN-ACK packet on behalf of the server. If an ACK packet is eventually received from the client, indicating a normal three-way handshake, the firewall creates a connection to the server on behalf of the client and then binds the two connections together. If no ACK packet is received, the firewall will eventually drop the SYN packet, thus preventing the server from ever seeing the connection. As long as the firewall has sufficient memory to hold all the half-open connections, this is a very effective strategy for protecting against SYN floods.

Firewalls are not the only devices used to prevent DoS attacks, though. As we discussed in Chapter 11, "Intrusion Prevention Systems," IPS is becoming more popular and more powerful. Vendors such as Juniper, Radware, TippingPoint, and Top Layer Networks offer system that are very effective at blocking SYN floods and other types of DoS attacks.

Summary

This chapter highlighted some of the more important issues involved in performance-tuning your perimeter security. Performance and security often seem at odds with each other, but careful design can help minimize the impact that security has on performance. Remember that almost any security feature you want to implement will come with varying levels of performance impacts. You should be especially careful when implementing encryption in your design. Cryptographic techniques offer tremendous security advantages, but they are expensive from a performance standpoint. Try to identify as early as possible the performance requirements of your network, prior to building or revising your network structure. Performing this initial analysis will help you choose appropriate security measures that permit the security policy to be enforced while still allowing the network users sufficient performance to carry out their work efficiently. Security and performance must be in balance for the ultimate objectives of the network to be met.

References

1 Netscape Corporation. Performance Tuning, Scaling, and Sizing Guide, Netscape Enterprise Server, p. 80. http://enterprise.netscape.com/docs/enterprise/60/perf/perf60.pdf.

18

Sample Designs

Lᴇᴛ's ᴘᴜᴛ ᴛᴏɢᴇᴛʜᴇʀ ᴀʟʟ ᴛʜᴇ ꜱᴇᴄᴜʀɪᴛʏ ᴅᴇꜱɪɢɴ information presented in Part III, "Designing a Secure Network Perimeter." Each chapter has presented a substantial amount of material you must incorporate into your designs to ensure they reflect the needs of your organization. As we have discussed, designing a secure network perimeter requires you to achieve a balance between conflicting factors, such as security, performance, and usability. For example, deciding to use 3DES encryption on a VPN implemented using low-end routers might provide the best protection for the connection, but the performance impact caused by the encryption might reduce performance unacceptably. In other instances, it might be difficult to determine when to follow a particular piece of design advice. To help integrate all this material, this chapter provides case studies to illustrate how network designs vary depending on the unique needs of the organization. The case studies were chosen to highlight several distinct design situations:

- A telecommuter who is using a broadband connection to access the corporate network via the Internet
- A business that has only a basic Internet presence
- A small e-commerce site that has a corporate network as well as several systems accessible from the Internet

As an example of a more complex architecture, we also discuss a multizone design that was presented by a candidate for a GIAC Certified Firewall Analyst (GCFW) certification. This design was submitted as part of a GCFW practical assignment that received an honors status. We begin with a review of core design criteria for a network security perimeter.

Review of Security Design Criteria

Before we start our discussion of the case studies, let's review what we have covered so far in the design section of this book. In Chapter 12, "Fundamentals of Secure Perimeter

Design," we described the factors that must be considered when designing your network's perimeter. Put simply, this means you must incorporate the answers for each of the following three questions in every design you create:

- What needs to be protected?
- What are the threats?
- What are the business requirements?

Before embarking on the design of the perimeter, you must establish what it is you are protecting. At one level, this will be the servers, workstations, databases, and other network devices located on the network. At a deeper level, though, it is the information contained on the network along with the services the network must offer. To begin your design, you must determine what will compose your network. If you are starting from scratch, this is relatively easy, but when adding security to an existing network, the discovery process can be difficult. This is especially true when the network is large and not well documented.

Where Does This Wire Go?

During an assignment to add a private WAN link between two government organizations, I discovered an unlabeled T1 line in one of the network closets that was connected directly to the first organization's backbone network. No one in the organization seemed to know what it was being used for. The management of this organization was concerned with security and had spent a small fortune on the installation of firewalls and other perimeter security devices, so I was a bit surprised they allowed this line to exist. When I asked the IT group why they allowed the connection, they told me it had been installed before any of them had joined the organization, and they were afraid that if they disconnected it, someone might complain. For the record, they did eventually unplug the line, and no one ever complained.

Next, you need to determine what threats you should be concerned about. All networks attached to the Internet need to worry about external attack. Whether the attack is from a script kiddy or malicious code, you can be guaranteed that if you're hooked up to the Internet, you are under attack. Some organizations, though, need to consider more directed attacks. If your organization is famous in any way (or has a name that is close to someone who is) or has information that would be useful to an attacker (such as credit card data), you will almost certainly come under attack from determined outsiders. These attackers will spend significant time analyzing the security of your network. Protecting against these attackers requires significantly more effort than preventing access by amateurs. Even more difficult to protect against is the determined *insider*. Preventing individuals who have been already granted some access to your network from gaining more can be extremely difficult and requires you to consider considerably more internal security controls than you would need to defend against purely external attacks.

> ### Extortion Is a Common Motive for Attack
>
> In the early days of the Internet, computer attackers were in it for the challenge, the glory, or just simply malicious intent. That is rapidly changing as criminal elements have started to learn how to make money off of the Internet. Consider the case of Authorize.Net, a large Internet-based credit card processing service. In the fall of 2004, it began receiving extortion requests. It did not pay the extortionists, so starting on September 15th, the extortionists began a crippling distributed denial of service (DDoS) attack. This attack prevented Authorize.Net from processing thousands of credit card transactions for its customers, causing an untold amount of financial loss. Given this type of result, it's no wonder that many victims decide to pay. However, extortionists rarely disappear once they've found a willing participant. It is much better to be fully prepared for these attacks, which is how Authorize.Net has responded. The company has redoubled its security efforts to create a network it feels is ironclad against future DDoS attacks.

When designing the security perimeter, you must also determine what the business requirements for the network are. As we have emphasized throughout the book, network security is a means to an end, not an end to itself. It is important that the business reasons and business constraints are taken into account as you design your security architecture. To begin with, you need to know what services need to be provided to your users and customers. You also need to determine how reliable and accessible these services need to be. A network that provides a basic website describing a company's services might not need to be as reliable and fast as a network that hosts an e-commerce site that processes all the sales requests for a large company.

You must also consider the amount of resources in terms of money and time that should reasonably be spent to secure the network. We would like every network we build to have every security control we can think of, but we must always be cognizant that the purpose of the network is to support the business. A network design that is unaffordable but securely designed will never be implemented.

As we go through the case studies that follow, try to keep in mind these three basic design criteria. To focus your attention, ask yourself the following questions as you review each design:

- Does the design sufficiently protect the major resources of the network?
- Does the design place the emphasis on protecting the right resources?
- Does the design sufficiently account for the likely ways it might be attacked?
- Does the design support the business goals, or are the security controls likely to impact business operations negatively?

Case Studies

Presented next are four security designs to address four different business situations. Each was chosen to illustrate the need to vary your designs based on the specific business needs of an organization.

Case Study 1: Telecommuter Who Is Using a Broadband Connection

The situation presented in Figure 18.1 shows an increasingly common way for users to access private corporate network resources. The user has subscribed to a cable company's broadband Internet service and is using this connection to work from home. These types of connections are becoming increasingly popular and represent a significantly different security problem from the slow dial-up connections they are replacing.

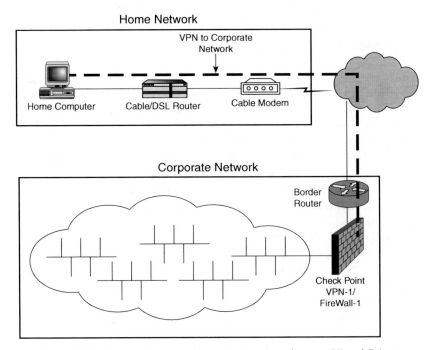

Figure 18.1   In this design, a telecommuting user relies on a Virtual Private Network (VPN) to tunnel across the Internet to reach the corporate network.

Previously, home computer users had limited exposure to Internet attacks because they were only accessible while they were dialed-in to the Internet. A potential attacker would need to time his attack to coincide with the time the user was using the Internet. This is not true with broadband services, such as cable and DSL. These types of connections, much like typical office Internet connections, are always on, making it much easier for the attacker to access the home computer.

Because of this problem, combined with the low security awareness of the typical home computer user, broadband-connected home computers have become a frequent target of computer attackers, which has resulted in many home user systems becoming compromised. These systems have then been used to commit other acts of cyberattack, including participating in denial of service (DoS) attacks.

The problem of home computer security has become important to companies as they begin to allow their employees to access private network resources from home. If home computers become compromised, the attacker can use them to circumvent the network's perimeter security.

The user's company—in this case, Big Company, Inc.—is concerned about these security problems but wants to allow the employee the flexibility of working from home on a high-speed connection. The company has asked us to create a secure home network design for the user.

The following is the design criteria the company provided to us:

- The user's home computer is the primary resource that must be protected.

- The company is specifically worried about the outsider threat. It recognizes that by allowing the home user to log in remotely, it is extending its security perimeter to include the home user's computer system. If the user's computer becomes compromised, it could be used to access the corporate network.

- From a business need perspective, this company views this service as a nice-to-have but not a business essential. High redundancy is not needed, and the solution must be reasonably inexpensive.

The company is also specifically worried about the following issues:

- The always-on connection subjects the home computer to direct network attack.

- Malicious code could be introduced onto the home computer through the receipt of an email attachment or the downloading of software that contains malicious code.

- The user's browser might contain vulnerabilities that are exploitable if the user visits a malicious website.

- The user's connection to the corporate network might be monitored or altered as it travels across the Internet.

To address these concerns, this design uses several perimeter security techniques to secure the home network. To start, a cable modem/DSL router has been placed between the home computer and the cable modem. These devices have become popular because they allow multiple home computers to share a broadband account, but most also include basic firewall functionality. For this case study, a Linksys Etherfast cable/DSL router has been chosen. Note that this device does not include wireless LAN capability. This was intentional because the company did not want to take on the additional risk of wireless networks at its employees' homes.

Because this home network is only used to access the Internet and does not host public network services, no externally initiated connections are needed. This enables us to use the default configuration of the cable/DSL router, which only allows connections initiated from the internal network to proceed. This defense measure prevents a broad range of attacks from proceeding. Some employees, though, may be tempted to modify this configuration to support peer-to-peer file sharing programs, which require an open port to work efficiently. Employees who use this service will need to be specifically cautioned against it because it would significantly weaken the security of the solution.

In addition to the cable/DSL router, the design also calls for a personal firewall product to be installed on the user's home computer. Personal firewalls such as BlackICE (http://www.iss.net), ZoneAlarm (http://www.zonelabs.com), and Tiny (http://www.tinysoftware.com) enable you to specify which applications are allowed to send and receive information over the network. For instance, we can tell the personal firewall to only allow connections destined to hosts on port 80 from Internet Explorer or Netscape Communicator.

To enable the home user to securely access private corporate resources, the Check Point SecuRemote client is installed on the user's home computer and is configured to establish an AES-based IPSec VPN connection to the corporate firewall whenever a packet needs to be sent to the corporate network. Basic username/password authentication is used whenever the VPN is established. The SecuRemote client supports stronger, certificate-based authentication but requires a Public Key Infrastructure (PKI).

The last element of this security architecture is the installation of an antivirus product such as Symantec Norton AntiVirus on the home computer. With the cable/DSL router and personal firewall products preventing most forms of direct attack, the next most likely way of gaining access to the home computer is the introduction of some form of malicious code. If the user downloads a program from the Internet that contains a Trojan horse or receives an email with a virus attached, the computer can still become compromised. To help prevent this, the AntiVirus tool has been configured to scan each downloaded file and each received email message for known malicious code patterns. Because these types of products are only as good as the content of their malicious code signature database, the antivirus tool has also been configured to check for new malicious code signatures on a daily basis.

As you can see from this description, even with small networks, you still need to consider all the design criteria when building the security perimeter. Understanding what you need to protect, how it might be attacked, and how much effort you should spend to secure it are fundamental issues that affect every design you create. In this network, what we needed to protect was narrow and consisted of a single workstation. We were specifically concerned with a direct attack from the Internet, plus the indirect attack from malicious code. Because our budget was small, we had to limit ourselves to inexpensive measures. Given these constraints, we were still able to come up with a design that should be highly effective at protecting the user's home computer while allowing secure access to the corporate network.

Case Study 2: A Small Business That Has a Basic Internet Presence

In this case study, a small sales company wants to set up an Internet connection but does not intend to sell products directly over the Internet. The owner of the business has read several horror stories about companies being taken over by attackers and has specifically asked for as secure a design as possible, but he does not have a large budget. Following are the specific design requirements and business needs the company has established:

- The workstations and Windows servers are the primary resources that must be protected. The company needs to establish an information website for its customers, but the site is not considered essential to the business operations.

- The company does not know of any individuals or organizations that would specifically want to do them harm, but the company does store customer information, including credit card data, on Windows servers.

- Employees must be able to send and receive email.

- Employees must be able to browse their suppliers' websites.

- The company website is not expected to get a large volume of traffic.

- The design must be secure, but the budget for security devices and software must be kept as low as possible.

- The external connection that has been arranged with the ISP is a burstable T1 line provisioned for a continuous usage of 256Kbps.

> **Note**
> Burstable T1 lines allow the full 1.544Mbps of a T1 line to be used some of the time, but the ISP only guarantees the continuous bandwidth level that has been agreed upon.

The resulting design is shown in Figure 18.2. The IT resources of the company are limited to a dozen PCs running Windows, two Windows servers acting as primary and backup domain controllers, and a network printer. The following features have been added to the network to meet the design requirements:

- A Nokia IP350 device has been added to act as both the border router and the external firewall.

- A web cache proxy, located in a screened subnet, is being used to control and protect the users' web sessions.

- A network intrusion detection system (IDS) is monitoring the local network.

- The website and email services have been outsourced to a web hosting company.

The first line of defense for the network is the Nokia IP350, which runs a version of the Check Point Next Generation (NG) FireWall software. We have installed a T1 card in the Nokia to allow it to act as both the border router and the external firewall. Of course, if the Nokia were to become compromised, the entire network would be exposed to the Internet. This is a design compromise that has been made to reduce cost; the money that would have been spent on the router can now be spent on a more sophisticated firewall. Other security measures, such as the IDS, will be counted on to provide the defense in depth necessary to back up the Nokia. The rulebase for the Nokia is shown in Table 18.1.

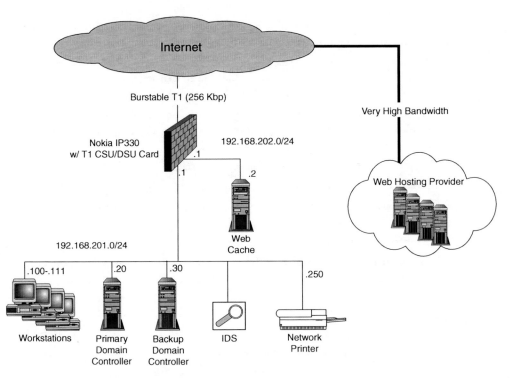

Figure 18.2 In this design, a small business outsources the hosting of Internet-accessible services to a third party.

Table 18.1 **Rulebase for the Nokia IP350**

Source	Destination	Service	Action
Workstations	Web cache server	HTTP, HTTPS, FTP in service	Allow
Web cache server	Internet	HTTP, HTTPS, FTP, DNS	Allow
Firewall	All	All	Deny, Log
All	Firewall	All	Deny, Log
Local network, web cache server	All	Ping	Allow
Any	Any	Any	Deny, Log

This rulebase has three main features. First, there are no rules with the Internet as a source, which prevents external attackers from initiating a connection to the company's internal computers. Second, all web and FTP connections from the LAN must be proxied through the web cache server before they can reach the Internet, which allows us to configure the web cache server to restrict which websites the employees can visit and provides the additional security benefit of terminating the external website connection at the web cache server instead of a workstation's browser, thereby preventing some malicious website attacks. Last, the rulebase makes no allowance for remote management or monitoring for any of the security devices. This network is sufficiently small, so a decision has been made to administer and monitor each system from its respective console.

The next device that needs to be discussed is the web cache server. To keep the cost down, this server has been implemented entirely from open source products. A PC that is running a hardened version of Red Hat Linux server hosts the open source Squid Web Cache Proxy software (http://www.squid-cache.org). This process is the only one running on the server that is listening to network ports.

Squid supports proxying of HTTP, HTTPS, and FTP connections and can limit by IP address the computers that are able to make use of its services. In this case, the proxy has been configured to allow hosts in the IP range of the workstations to connect to it. Squid also can limit which web and FTP sites users can visit. Currently, this company's users are allowed to surf to any site, but the company has reserved the right to block access to any sites it deems inappropriate or unsafe. In addition to the workstations, the IDS has been allowed to use the web cache server, but Squid has been configured to allow it to connect to only the Snort website (http://www.snort.org) and the company's website.

The last specific security device to talk about is the IDS. Like the web cache server, the IDS is implemented using only open source software. Red Hat Linux is again used as the operating system to host the Snort IDS software. Snort is a highly capable IDS, especially when its signature database is kept up to date. Luckily, the Snort community is active, and it continually updates the Snort signatures. It is not uncommon for a new Snort signature to be available for a new attack before any of the commercial providers has been able to update its signature databases. The reason the web cache has been configured to allow the IDS to connect to the Snort website is to allow the latest Snort signatures to be conveniently downloaded.

You might notice that no web, mail, or DNS servers are on the network. All these services have been outsourced to NTT/Verio, a web hosting company. For a small monthly fee, NTT/Verio provides space on one of its web servers to host the company's website. Administration of the website is performed using Microsoft FrontPage. In addition to the website, NTT/Verio provides WebMail, a web-based email system, which allows employees to send and receive email using their web browsers. By outsourcing these services, the design eliminates the need to handle externally originated connections, reducing the risk of network compromise substantially. However, it does require that the company trust NTT/Verio to secure the web and email services. To provide one additional level of protection, a small shell script has been placed on the IDS sensor that checks whether the home page of the website has been modified. If it has, the shell script generates an alert, providing a limited amount of protection should the NTT/Verio-maintained website become corrupted.

This case study shows some of the compromises you might have to make due to the business needs of the organization. Not every site requires three layers of firewalls with a full-time security administrator. In this case, it made more sense to outsource the harder elements to secure. It is unlikely that this company would dedicate the effort to properly administer the security of its public services. Outsourcing these services to a firm that provides them full time was a more secure solution. Always remember that each design must be attentive to the needs of the situation.

Case Study 3: A Small E-Commerce Site

In this case study, a small organization has decided that it could dramatically boost sales by accepting orders over the Internet. At the same time, it is concerned with some of the news reports about cybercrime and the possibility that private customer data might be stolen, opening up the potential for lawsuits. The company has asked us to create a design that allows it to sell products over the Internet while protecting customer data. It has provided a reasonable but not overly large budget for the design. These are the design guidelines the company has established for the assignment:

- The primary resource that must be protected is customer data, but the design must provide reasonable protection for the other devices on the network, such as user workstations.
- It is important that the site be available to customers, but a highly redundant design has been rejected as too expensive.
- The company is specifically concerned with an attack from determined outsiders.
- The company expects only a moderate number of visitors and estimates approximately 1,000 visitors per day with fewer than 5% of these visitors actually ordering anything.
- The company wants to maintain control of all equipment and has rejected the idea of outsourcing any part of its network.
- Employees need to be able to send and receive email.
- Employees need to be able to access external websites.

The resulting design is shown in Figure 18.3 and shows a fairly classic network security design, although certain security design features are not visible from the diagram.

Here is a quick description of the major features of the design:

- A border router connects the network to the Internet and provides some basic filtering.
- Just behind the router, a firewall enforces the majority of the access control for the network.
- Public services and private services have been separated by being placed on different network segments that are separated by the firewall. The firewall also maintains a special segment for management systems.
- The web server holds only transaction data for a short period of time. Periodically, the order server removes all current transactions from the web server for processing.

- Inbound email is cached on the email relay server until the Internal email server retrieves it.

- Split DNS is being used. The public DNS server provides name resolution for public services only. The private DNS server contains records for all systems, but external users cannot access it.

- Intrusion detection sensors are located on the public, private, and management network segments to watch for unusual activity.

- The workstations located on the "Internal" network can connect to the proxy firewall to gain access to external web and FTP servers. No other internal systems are allowed to connect to the outside.

- All security log entries are sent to the log server, which generates alerts when suspicious activity is detected.

- All configuration of security devices is performed from the management console.

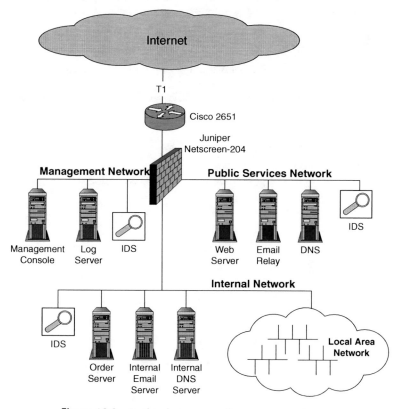

Figure 18.3   In this design, a small e-commerce site uses
several defensive measures to protect customer data.

Traffic that is entering the network must first pass through the border router; therefore, it is the first device we can use to enforce access control for the network. A thorough discussion of how to securely configure routers is included in Chapter 6, "The Role of a Router," so we will not go into depth about how this router should be configured. However, it is worth mentioning that ingress filters have been installed on the router to block packets that have illegal addresses. In addition to the ingress filters, an egress filter has been put in place to block outbound packets if they do not have a valid source IP address. The purpose of this egress filter is to make it harder for the site to be used to attack other sites should one of the servers be compromised.

The primary security device for this network is the Juniper NetScreen-204 firewall appliance. The NetScreen-204 comes with four Fast Ethernet interfaces, which we have used to create four security zones for this network:

- The Internet zone connects the network to the Internet and is completely untrusted.

- The Public Services network holds all servers that must provide service to users from the Internet.

- The internal network holds private servers and workstations that external users do not need to directly access.

- The Management network holds the log server and the management console.

The rulebase on the firewall controls what traffic can flow between each of these zones. Table 18.2 shows the rules we are using to secure the network.

Table 18.2 **NetScreen Rulebase**

Incoming Zone	Outgoing Zone	Source	Destination	Service	Action
Internet	Public	Any	Web Server	HTTP, HTTPS	Allow
Internet	Public	Any	Mail Relay	SMTP	Allow
Internet	Public	Any	DNS Server	DNS	Allow
Internal	Public	Order Server	Web Server	SSH	Allow
Internal	Public	Int. Mail Server	Mail Relay	SSH	Allow
Internal	Internet	Int. Mail Server	Any	SMTP	Allow
Internal	Internet	Int. DNS Server	Any	DNS	Allow
Internal	Internet	Workstations	Any	HTTP, HTTPS, FTP	Allow

Table 18.2 **Continued**

Incoming Zone	Outgoing Zone	Source	Destination	Service	Action
ALL	Management	All Devices Group	Log Server	Syslog	Allow
Management	Any	Management Console	Security Devices Group	SSH	Allow, Log
Management	Internet	Management Console	snort.org	HTTP, HTTPS	Allow
Any	Any	Any	Any	Any	Deny, Log

A lot is going on in this rulebase, so let's go over it step by step. The first three rules are designed to allow the public to access the public servers. The fourth rule allows the order server to retrieve customer transactions from the website. The company has built a custom e-commerce application that takes the following steps to protect customer information. When the web server accepts a customer transaction, it writes the details of the transaction to a file, which it then places in a special directory. This directory is only accessible to two accounts on the web server: the account that the web software is running as, and an account created for the order server. The web server is running a Secure Shell (SSH) daemon to allow the order server to periodically log in and retrieve the customer transaction files. In this way, the customer details are swept off the more exposed web server to the order server where they can be better protected. Using this arrangement, even if an attacker did gain control of the web server, he would only be able to capture a few customer transactions.

The fifth rule on the firewall allows the internal email server to retrieve inbound mail messages from the mail relay server. Normally, a mail relay server would use Simple Mail Transfer Protocol (SMTP) to transfer inbound messages to an internal mail server, but a security decision was made not to allow traffic to originate from the Public Services network to the internal network, which should block an attacker from accessing the internal network, even if she manages to compromise one of the public servers. Still, we need to allow the network's users to receive mail. To accomplish this, the internal email server periodically retrieves queued messages from the mail relay server using the same method that the order server uses to retrieve information from the web server. It logs on to the mail relay server using the SSH protocol and downloads the queued messages.

To enable outbound email, the sixth rule allows the internal mail server to send SMTP information to the Internet. In some situations, this might open up the internal mail server to attack from a malicious mail server. However, in this case, the risk is minimized due to our choice of firewall. The NetScreen-204 includes advanced packet inspection techniques such as malformed packet protection and protocol anomaly detection. These features should limit (though not eliminate) the ability for an attacker to compromise the mail server.

The seventh rule allows the internal DNS server to resolve DNS requests for external sites. Just like with SMTP, the NetScreen-204's packet inspection techniques will be needed to protect this network conversation.

The eighth rule allows the workstations to access web and FTP services on the Internet. Again, the NetScreen-204's packet inspection capabilities will provide the protection necessary to protect the workstations as they go out on the Internet.

The ninth rule allows any device on the network to send Syslog traffic to the log server. This rule allows all security log entries to be consolidated on a single server and is especially important for consolidating the log entries for the multiple IDS sensors deployed on the network. Consolidating the logs simplifies their analysis and makes it easier to defend against log modification. When an attacker gains control of a server, one of the first things he will do is modify the log files to erase evidence of his attack. Moving the log entries to the log server prevents this from happening. It also makes it easier to detect malicious activity. By centralizing all the log entries, it becomes possible to look for attack behavior across systems. A special process runs on the log server to look at the incoming log entries for these signs of attack. The log server has a modem attached to allow it to dial a beeper service to notify administrators when an attack has been detected.

The tenth rule allows the management console to log in to all the security devices on the network, including the IDS systems and the border router using the SSH protocol; this, in turn, allows each of these systems to be remotely administered. The firewall can also be remotely administered using SSH.

The last rule is the standard "deny all" rule. If none of the other rules match, this rule denies and logs the traffic. This rule enforces the design concept of least privilege.

The firewall and router do a good job of limiting access to the network, but they cannot prevent access to the public services on the network. Public services such as web, mail, and DNS must be provided to allow customers to place their Internet orders. This also allows attackers to communicate with these services. In acknowledgment of the additional risk that the public servers are exposed to, two additional security controls have been established for this zone. First, an aggressive patch management program has been instituted for all publicly accessible servers. Whenever a patch is released to correct a serious vulnerability in any software running on these servers, it is expeditiously tested and then deployed as soon as possible. If testing determines that the patch does not work properly though, other mitigating controls will need to be developed on a case-by-case basis. The second control is the installation of Cisco's Security Agent, a host-based intrusion prevention system, on each of the public servers. As we discussed in Chapter 11, "Intrusion Prevention Systems," host-based IPS systems can often detect and prevent attacks that are imperceptible to firewalls and network-based IDS tools. Although they can be expensive, both to purchase and to maintain, their use here on the servers most likely to come under direct attack is justified.

The public zone is not the only area of the network that we must protect. To provide additional security to the entire network, each network segment has an IDS installed on it. As with the previous case study, we have opted to use Snort as our IDS. This is the purpose for the rule just before the deny all rule. The management console needs to be able to download the latest signatures for the Snort sensors on a regular basis. In addition to the standard signatures, we are also adding a few custom signatures to detect traffic that is specifically unusual to our network, instead of relying purely on the default signatures.

To understand how this might be useful, let's look at the sensor located on the management network. Only a limited amount of traffic should be traveling across this network segment. By deciding which traffic is allowed, we can set up signatures to look for traffic that is abnormal. If we limit our discussion to TCP traffic, the following packets should be allowed:

- TCP packets that are leaving the Management network use only HTTP, HTTPS, and SSH.

- TCP packets that are entering the Management network are replies to previous Management Console requests.

- TCP traffic that is local to the Management network is only the Management Console logging in to the Log Server or the IDS using SSH.

Any traffic that does not match one of these conditions is invalid and might indicate that an attacker has gotten past our other defense measures. To detect this, we can add custom signatures to our Management network Snort sensor. For example, to detect invalid TCP packets leaving the Management network, we add the following rules to the sensor (assume that the Management network has been allocated the IP range 192.168.10.0/24):

```
var MgmtNet 192.168.10.0/24
alert tcp $MgmtNet any -> any 1:21 (msg: "Invalid TCP Packet destination on
➥Management Network";)
alert tcp $MgmtNet any -> any 23:79 (msg: "Invalid TCP Packet destination on
➥Management Network";)
alert tcp $MgmtNet any -> any 81:417 (msg: "Invalid TCP Packet destination on
➥Management Network";)
alert tcp $MgmtNet any -> any 419:442 (msg: "Invalid TCP Packet destination on
➥Management Network";)
alert tcp $MgmtNet any -> any 444: (msg: "Invalid TCP Packet destination on
➥Management Network";)
```

The combination of these five signatures triggers if any TCP packet is sent out of the management network that is not destined to an HTTP, HTTPS, or SSH server. Additional rules would need to be added to alert on unauthorized UDP and ICMP traffic.

These types of signatures would produce many false positives if placed on a typical network. However, in the special case of the Management network, if any of these rules were to trigger, it would be possible that an attacker had gotten past the firewall. This idea can be extended to any network segment where it is convenient to enumerate legitimate traffic.

Unlike our previous case study, this organization made the decision to rely heavily on e-business. Breaches in security could easily put the company out of business, which justified a larger investment in security but still did not free us up to spend money on security indiscriminately. We had to address the need to protect the network resources (especially the customer data) while keeping the need for security in balance with the other business requirements. The design that resulted provides defense in depth for the critical elements while keeping the overall expense of the design to a minimum.

Case Study 4: A Complex E-Commerce Site

In this last case study, we review the design produced by Rita Will as part of the requirements for her GCFW certification. As part of a practical assignment, GCFW students were asked to create a secure network architecture for a fictitious entity named GIAC Enterprises (GIACE), which is in the business of selling fortune cookie sayings. The requirements for the assignment included the following details:

- The business will be run entirely over the Internet.
- Expected sales are $200 million per year.
- Three classes of external users must be accommodated: customers who purchase the sayings, suppliers who provide the sayings, and business partners who translate and resell the sayings for the foreign market.
- GIACE management considers security a fundamental requirement of its business. It is willing to spend significant funds to ensure that a secure system is developed.

Reading a bit into the assignment, we can extract the following design criteria:

- The most important resources this network must protect are the fortunes, which constitute GIACE's intellectual capital, and the customer, supplier, and business partner records that GIACE must maintain.
- All GIACE revenue is generated from its website. Due to this, it is essential that the website be up 24×7.
- Suppliers must be able to securely provide new fortunes.
- Business partners must be able to securely access fortunes.
- The network must protect itself against determined outsiders. In addition, there is some concern about attacks launched by business partners and suppliers.
- Based on the sales projections, GIACE expects to be a high-volume site, which must be accounted for in the design.

The design that Rita submitted to meet these requirements was awarded honors by the GCFW Advisory Board and is shown in Figure 18.4. It can be downloaded at http://www.giac.org/practical/Rita_Will_GCFW.zip. It is a good design for securing the proposed network, but it is by no means the only way the network could have been secured. You need only look at the hundreds of student practicals posted at

http://www.giac.org/GCFW.php to see just how many different ways this problem can
be approached.

Rita's design uses two firewalls to break the network into five major security zones.
These are the Internet, the DMZ, the proxy layer, the security network, and the internal
network. As a way of organizing this discussion, we describe the security features of each
zone security separately.

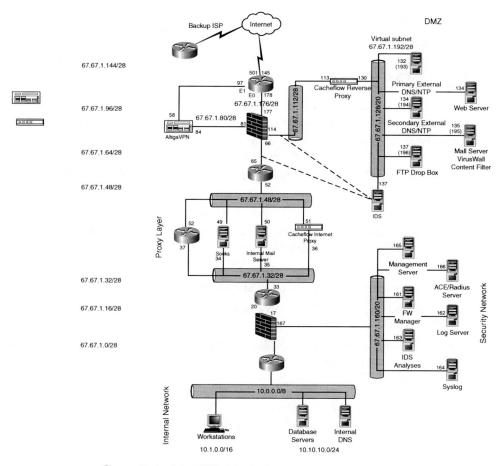

Figure 18.4   Rita Will's GCFW design uses several security
zones to enforce security across the network.

The Internet

This zone is unlabeled on the diagram, but it is the network formed between the border
routers and the external firewall. Access to the Internet is provided by a pair of Cisco

routers, which are using the Hot Standby Routing Protocol (HSRP) to allow one of the routers to take over for the other, should one of them fail. This is the first example of the redundancy features that have been included to make sure availability of the network is high. The routers are also being used to provide some packet filtering, including ingress and egress filters similar to the ones described in the previous case study.

Located just in front of the routers are the border firewalls and two Cisco VPN concentrators. The concentrators allow suppliers, vendors, and employees to establish secure VPN connections to the network from the Internet and have been set up to fail over to each other should one stop working. The concentrators can use hardware accelerator cards to provide high performance and support several authentications systems. For this design, the token-based RSA SecurID system is being used to authenticate users prior to granting access.

The border firewalls are a pair of Nokia firewall appliances that are also set up to fail over to each other. Like the Nokia appliance chosen in our second case study, these appliances run Check Point FireWall-1. The firewalls provide the first major access restrictions for the network. The size of the rulebase is largely due to the complexity of the design, so we will not go over it in detail. Here are the highpoints:

- Allow external visitors to browse to the cacheflow reverse proxy. This rule allows visitors to access the GIACE public website.
- Allow the public websites to connect to the internal database servers.
- Allow the Internet proxy to connect to external websites. This allows internal users to browse websites on the Internet.
- Allow mail into and out of the external mail server.
- Allow DNS queries between the DMZ and the Internet.
- Allow the suppliers, partners, and employees who have established VPNs with the Cisco VPN concentrator to reach the FTP drop box server.
- Allow employees who have established VPNs with the Cisco VPN concentrator to reach the internal GIACE network.
- Drop all other unnecessary traffic.

Using this rulebase, the firewalls effectively block all but the bare essential traffic from entering the GIACE network. This is a good implementation of the design concept least privilege.

The DMZ

Strictly speaking, this zone should be referred to as a *screened subnet* because it is a network segment protected by a firewall; however, it is not an insecure area located between two secure areas. As Chapter 1, "Perimeter Security Fundamentals," mentions, these two terms are often used interchangeably.

The zone holds all the servers that are accessible to external users. This includes the cacheflow reverse proxies, the public web servers, the external DNS servers, the external mail server, and the FTP drop box server. Each of these servers plays a public role for the GIACE network.

This zone is considered a high-risk network segment. Because of this, extra security precautions have been implemented. To start with, all servers have been hardened by removing all unnecessary services and making sure that all the remaining services are as up to date as possible. Also, although not specifically mentioned in Rita's practical, presumably good vulnerability scanning and patch management practices are being performed on all the servers in this zone. This is to ensure that exploitable vulnerabilities are detected and eliminated as quickly as possible to reduce the window of opportunity available to attackers if vulnerabilities are discovered in any publicly accessible services.

Next, a Snort IDS sensor has been located in the zone to watch for suspicious activity. If an attacker manages to circumvent some of the security controls in place, it is hoped that this sensor will provide a sufficient warning for the onsite staff to respond appropriately.

The most important servers in the zone are the web servers. The web servers provide the primary interface between GIACE customers and GIACE. All sales transactions are conducted on these systems and then recorded on the internal network database servers. To enable the web servers to keep up with the expected volume of traffic, all external web requests first pass through one of the cacheflow servers.

Blue Coat cacheflow servers are being used as reverse proxies for all connections from the Internet to the public websites. Cacheflow servers are designed to protect web servers while accelerating SSL connections. Because of the reverse proxies, external users never directly access the public web servers. Because many attacks against web servers require a direct TCP connection to the web server, placing the proxy between the Internet and the web server provides a substantial security improvement. By using the cacheflow servers, this design maximizes the performance and availability of the GIACE public website.

Other servers on the network include the DNS, mail, and FTP servers. Each has some specific security controls worth mentioning.

The DNS servers provide name resolution for external users. This network uses the split DNS concept, so these servers only contain records for publicly accessible servers.

The external mail server sends and receives email from the Internet. It is implemented using a Sun Solaris server running Sendmail. To prevent malicious code from entering the network via email, the server runs Trend InterScan's VirusWall software. This software scans each incoming or outgoing email message for viruses. Scanning incoming mail for viruses is a powerful way of protecting the network from malicious code. Keep in mind, though, that scanners are only as good as their signature databases.

The last server on the DMZ is the FTP drop box server. Suppliers, partners, and employees use this system to exchange files. Due to the rules in place on the border firewalls, this server is only accessible to internal users or to users who have established VPNs through the Cisco VPN concentrator. In addition, username/password authentication is required, adding a second layer of defense to protect the server.

The Proxy Layer

The proxy layer protects internal and security network systems while allowing these systems to access network services located on other networks. Because this layer is directly on the path to the rest of the GIACE network, another Snort IDS sensor has been placed in front of it to watch for suspicious traffic. This provides some extra defense should an attacker get by the border firewalls.

The proxy layer uses four devices to form a kind of proxy firewall. These include a cacheflow server, the internal mail server, a SOCKS server, and a bypass router. Each device allows different types of communications.

Probably the most used from a traffic volume point of view is the cacheflow server. Similar to the cacheflow server used on the DMZ, this server proxies web requests for the internal and security network zones. Any internal system that needs to communicate with a web server must pass the request through the cacheflow server, which allows GIACE to restrict the websites that employees can access while protecting the requesting system from malicious websites.

The internal mail server passes email into and out of the internal networks. By allowing only this system to send and receive email from the external mail server, this design limits the server's exposure to attack.

In addition to the web proxy that the cacheflow servers provide, two SOCKS servers have been used to provide proxy services for SOCKS-aware applications. SOCKS is a standards-based protocol that performs network layer proxies at the transport layer. It is used in this design to provide external access for some proxy-aware applications, such as RealAudio.

The last device is a Cisco 3660 router that allows network traffic that SOCKS or cacheflow servers cannot proxy.

Located just behind the proxy layer is the internal firewall, which creates the remaining two security zones. Following is a summary of the proxy layer's rulebase:

- Allow the internal network to make use of the cacheflow web proxies.
- Allow the internal network to send and receive email from the internal mail server.
- Allow website maintainers to log in to systems in the DMZ. This requires that the maintainer authenticate to the firewall to prove his identity.
- Allow the internal network to FTP to the FTP drop box server.
- Allow remote employees who have VPNed into the Cisco VPN concentrator to gain access to the internal network.
- Allow systems on the security network to manage the security devices located throughout the network.

This rulebase puts in place the access restrictions that form the two remaining security zones: the internal network and the security network.

The Internal Network

The internal network holds all the internal systems, including employee workstations and GIACE databases. This network contains a broad amount of information that is valuable to GIACE. This is why it has been protected with so many layers of defense.

The Security Network

The security network contains the systems that manage and monitor the security of the network. Two servers on the network manage the GIACE security devices. These servers must be carefully protected because they would grant an attacker the ability to circumvent almost all security controls on the network if one of them were to be compromised.

Another system on the security network is the RSA ACE server, which provides the authentication service for the SecurID tokens. The ACE server is accessed when users VPN in to the Cisco VPN concentrator. It is also used by the internal firewall to authenticate the website maintainers prior to allowing them to log in to the DMZ.

Next, this network holds a system that analyzes the results from the Snort IDS sensors. All alerts that the sensors generate are forwarded to this system. When a critical alert is received, the security network alerts a security administrator.

The last two servers on the security network centralize and protect all security log data generated on the network. As we mentioned in the third case study, attackers like nothing better than to erase the evidence of their attacks. By moving log data into a protected place, we can prevent attackers from erasing their footprints.

This design is pretty involved, so it is somewhat difficult to get your hands around all its security features. To recap, let's summarize some of the design's better qualities:

- Extensive redundancy is used throughout the network. No single point of failure will bring down a critical network service.

- Performance and security concerns at the web servers are addressed using a reverse proxy server to accelerate SSL content while protecting the web servers from direct Internet attack.

- Multiple layers of firewalls create distinct security zones. These zones group systems at similar risk levels. This makes it easier to enforce appropriate security controls in each zone.

- Mail is virus scanned before it enters or leaves the network. Assuming the virus signatures are kept up to date, this is a powerful way to prevent network compromise.

- VPN technology allows partners, suppliers, and employees to gain remote access to appropriate internal resources. This, in combination with the firewalls, allows appropriate individuals into the network while restricting them to just the set of services they should get access to.

- All remote access is strongly authenticated through the use of SecurID tokens. This is a substantial improvement over username/password authentication and provides a high level of confidence that you know the identity of the person to whom you are granting access.

Summary

In this chapter, we provided four security designs for you to review. The first three were chosen to highlight the requirement to match the needs of the business with the design of the perimeter security. In each case, we started with a description of the business needs for the network and moved from there to a design to meet those needs.

We followed these case studies with an example pulled from the practical assignment of a GCFW honors student. This example was substantially more complicated than the previous case studies and provided an interesting assortment of security techniques. Studying other professional's designs is one of the best ways to discover new ways to protect the networks you are responsible for.

Now that you have learned how to design secure networks, it's time to learn how to administer, test, and improve them. The next and final part of this book is on perimeter assessment. In it, you will learn how to maintain your security perimeter, monitor it for unusual activity, troubleshoot it when problems crop up, and test it to make sure it is functioning. Chapter 23, "Design Under Fire," builds on the principles of creating and maintaining a security perimeter by presenting a lesson on improving the security of the network through adversarial review. This chapter uses two more GCFW practicals to demonstrate how even good security designs can be improved by looking at them through the eyes of an attacker.

IV

Maintaining and Monitoring Perimeter Security

19

Maintaining a Security Perimeter

Welcome to Part IV, "Maintaining and Monitoring Perimeter Security." In Part I, "The Essentials of Network Perimeter Security," and Part II, "Fortifying the Security Perimeter," we talked about the primary components of the defense perimeter, such as firewalls, routers, hosts, intrusion detection systems (IDSs), intrusion prevention systems (IPSs), Virtual Private Networks (VPNs), and policies. In Part III, "Designing a Secure Network Perimeter," you learned how to deploy these elements according to their strengths while taking into account their weaknesses to create a unified defense architecture. After your security perimeter has been set up, two processes must continuously take place: administration of the perimeter's components and evaluation of its effectiveness. Mastering these concepts is the final step on the path to defense in depth.

This chapter discusses core principles of maintaining a security perimeter. One of the requirements for effective perimeter maintenance is awareness of the operating environment, which is why we begin with a section on system and network monitoring. In this chapter, you learn how to gather monitoring requirements and see how to implement them using free or relatively inexpensive software. We build on the monitoring processes by examining ways to respond to system fault events and malicious incidents. We also talk about the process of managing changes to the infrastructure throughout the evolution of the security perimeter so that the infrastructure's components stay effective in the face of changing threats and business requirements.

System and Network Monitoring

In the context of perimeter security, the primary goal of system and network monitoring is to provide administrators with the awareness of the state of a protected environment. We discussed monitoring in the context of intrusion detection in Chapter 8, "Network Intrusion Detection," and Chapter 10, "Host Defense Components," where we tuned IDS sensors to automatically detect events that are frequently indicative of misuse. System and network monitoring also involve anomaly detection but concentrate on availability and performance parameters of the resources. Security professionals should be interested in seemingly mundane issues, such as server uptime, network utilization, and disk space availability for numerous reasons:

- Monitoring helps detect interruptions in availability of the services that the security perimeter is meant to protect. A host's partition might have filled up, a critical process might have died, or a denial of service attack might have taken a system offline. Ensuring availability, as you might recall, is one of the key objectives of information security.

- Monitoring helps detect changes in the performance and availability of the system, which might be indicative of misuse. Administrators who routinely monitor their systems are able to sense even the slightest change in the behavior of the host or device and are wonderful intrusion detection sensors.

- Monitoring helps detect bottlenecks and shifts in performance of the infrastructure, which might indicate that the design or the implementation of the security perimeter is not properly tuned. For example, a web-based application might function too slowly over HTTPS if its servers cannot cope with the load that SSL imposes on them. Monitoring can help determine which aspects of the security perimeter need to be fine-tuned and in what way.

- Monitoring helps detect unexpected changes in the environment that might adversely impact the effectiveness of the security perimeter. For example, a new server might have been brought online without proper hardening, or hasty changes to the firewall rule set might have unintentionally blocked access to a critical service.

A well-defined monitoring process allows administrators to detect problems at an early stage—hopefully before the problems escalate into critical incidents. One of the most powerful ways to increase effectiveness of this process is to perform monitoring centrally, which generally involves configuring a server—or a cluster of unified servers—to observe multiple resources throughout the network. A centralized monitoring infrastructure often benefits from the use of client modules that report to the central server information gathered from remotely monitored systems. You should already be familiar with such a configuration because it is frequently used to manage multiple firewalls, VPN nodes, or IDS sensors centrally.

In this section, we look at a typical way of implementing a centralized monitoring infrastructure. To illustrate monitoring concepts, we use a popular monitoring application called Big Brother; however, the same monitoring principles apply to other applications of this nature.

Big Brother Fundamentals

Big Brother is a flexible software tool for performing network- and system-monitoring functions (http://www.bb4.org). Numerous products can fulfill monitoring needs; a small sample of these includes BMC PATROL (http://www.bmc.com), HP OpenView (http://openview.hp.com), IBM Tivoli (http://www.ibm.com/software/tivoli), and

Nagios (http://www.nagios.org). Unlike several other contenders, Big Brother focuses solely on monitoring aspects of system and network maintenance, without offering features to remotely manage devices. This makes it a lightweight application that is particularly well suited for demonstrating monitoring concepts. As a result, we use Big Brother in the examples throughout this section for many of the reasons we would consider using it on our networks:

- It is free for noncommercial use.
- It is relatively inexpensive for commercial use.
- It runs on Windows and UNIX-based operating systems.
- It is relatively easy to set up and maintain.
- It supports a wide range of monitoring and alerting requirements.
- It is expandable through the use of custom scripts.
- It has been around since late 1996 and has established itself as a trustworthy monitoring tool.

Big Brother is able to track the status of remote nodes by attempting to connect to monitored systems over the network. In this role, Big Brother can detect the availability of a system via ping packets, as well as by attempting to elicit an expected response from specific TCP services. Big Brother also supports the use of agent modules that run on remote nodes as Big Brother clients and gather local information, such as CPU performance, disk space utilization, and process status.

> **Note**
> The commercial version of Big Brother, called Big Brother Professional Edition, supports several enhancements to the free version. In particular, the Professional Edition offers a simplified installation routine and point-to-point encryption. You can purchase the commercial version from Quest Software (http://www.quest.com/bigbrother).

Big Brother's architecture consists of four core components that are integrated into a unified application. These components, described in the following list, can run on distributed systems to achieve the desired extent of scalability or can coexist on a single server:

- The BBNET host probes remote systems to determine the availability of monitored network services.
- The remote client agent runs on a monitored system and gathers performance and resource availability data local to its host.
- The BBDISPLAY host generates and displays web pages that administrators can look at to determine the status of monitored devices, services, and processes.
- The BBPAGER host issues notification alerts and processes event-escalation measures.

If Big Brother determines that a monitored parameter has exceeded an acceptable threshold, it alerts administrators by displaying a warning on the BBDISPLAY's web page. Figure 19.1 shows how Big Brother consolidates status information regarding multiple systems onto a single summary page. Icons on Big Brother's summary matrix represent the current status of monitored parameters for each system. A green square represents the normal state of the system, which is the case for most services in this figure. A flashing star icon for the HTTP service on "lemon" indicates that Big Brother experienced problems connecting to the web server on "lemon" over the network. Administrators can obtain additional information regarding the problem by clicking the icon. Additionally, Big Brother can send the alert via email, pager, Short Message Service (SMS), or a custom script.

Now that you know a little about fundamental capabilities of monitoring software, the next section covers how to determine which resources should be observed in the first place and how to set up such monitoring.

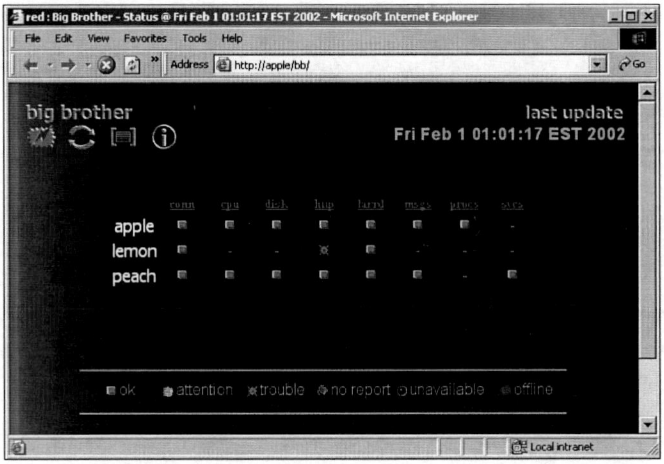

Figure 19.1   Big Brother presents a unified view of monitored resources by using icons to represent the status of observed attributes.

The Capabilities of HP OpenView

Of course, Big Brother isn't the only game in town when it comes to monitoring networks and systems. A wide variety of offerings are available to suit different requirements and budgets. HP OpenView is a product at the higher end of the price and functionality spectrum. The foundation of the OpenView family of products is the OpenView Network Node Manager (NNM). This application provides the framework for performing basic monitoring and discovery functions by using Simple Network Management Protocol (SNMP), ping, and other network probes, as well as for collecting historical data and handling event notification.

An extension of NNM, which is more full featured and expensive, is a product called OpenView Operations. This application is aimed at enterprises that require more extensive managing and monitoring features, along with native support for additional devices and applications. OpenView Operations also supports programmable actions that can respond to system events, such as by automatically restarting a crashed process. A core component in OpenView Operations, called Service Navigator, allows administrators to "teach" OpenView about relationships between particular services distributed throughout the network. For example, if a router goes down, Service Navigator (if appropriately configured) can flag all the services this event might affect, such as email or a mission-critical database. This functionality can help to assess the event's impact, determine its root cause, and assist in the troubleshooting process.

HP OpenView isn't for everyone due to its high price and significant implementation complexities. However, if a particular feature is important to your business and slimmer or less expensive tools do not support it, you should look into enterprise-centric solutions such as HP OpenView.

Establishing Monitoring Procedures

Be sure to define your goals and priorities before rolling out a monitoring solution. For example, if you are maintaining an e-commerce site that makes a significant portion of its revenue via the Internet, you might be interested in focusing on the following data points:

- Bandwidth utilization
- Server load
- Where your hits are coming from
- What percentage of site visitors purchase a product

Considering that most of us operate under the constraints of limited staff, it is impractical to treat all changes in the state of the environment with the same urgency. Moreover, monitoring all aspects of performance and availability on each system is likely to produce so many alerts that those that are truly important will be drowned out by the noise of inconsequential events. Knowing when a firewall process dies is likely to be more important than receiving notifications every time a user's workstation is rebooted.

We have been using risk analysis to define the extent of hardening and segregation for security perimeter components throughout the book. Similarly, we can define monitoring requirements based on the resource's importance and the likelihood that its availability might be disrupted. For example, if email communications are a critical business function for your company, you might consider monitoring numerous aspects of the mail server's availability and performance, such as the accessibility of the host over the network, the status of the mailer's processes, and the state of file system utilization. If that same mail server has been acting flaky, you might be interested in adjusting monitoring criteria to help track down the cause of the problem or to enable yourself to react to problems more quickly. In that case, it might help to adjust the thresholds for alerts or to monitor additional attributes, such as auxiliary system processes, as well as CPU and memory utilization.

> **Note**
>
> Monitoring and alerting go hand in hand. It is not uncommon to monitor more devices and attributes than we want to be alerted about. We then configure alerting thresholds so that we are notified of events that warrant immediate attention. Events that are less critical might not require a real-time response. Additionally, historical information that is collected through the monitoring process will be available for when we need to troubleshoot problems or to determine the relationship between events that we were alerted about.

Monitoring applications, such as Big Brother, can keep track of multiple attributes for resources throughout the network and offer you the flexibility to drill down into specific parameters of individual systems that need to be observed. Let's see how to establish monitoring procedures to track aspects of the environment that are most likely to require a watchful eye:

- Hosts and devices
- Accessibility of network services
- Local system attributes

Hosts and Devices

One of the first steps in setting up a monitoring system is to define which hosts and devices should be watched over. As we discussed a few paragraphs earlier, you need to strike the balance between your ability to handle information and the number of systems that warrant your attention at this stage. So that you see what's involved in configuring core aspects of a monitoring system, let's take a look at how to accomplish this with Big Brother. Big Brother uses a text file called bb-hosts to list the systems it should observe. The bb-hosts file follows the format of the regular hosts file, with the addition of directives that are specific to Big Brother.

For every system that you want to monitor, you can specify which attributes should be observed. A good starting point is ensuring that the host or device is accessible over the network. This can be defined for Big Brother by using a bare-bones bb-hosts file like this:

```
#
# THE BIG BROTHER HOSTS FILE
#
192.168.214.132 apple    # BBPAGER BBNET BBDISPLAY
192.168.214.17  lemon    #
192.168.214.97  peach    #
```

In this bb-hosts file, we defined `apple` as the host that houses Big Brother components that centrally monitor other systems. (Note that the `apple` host will be monitored as well.) Because we did not define directives for `lemon` and `peach`, Big Brother only checks whether it can access them over the network via an ICMP echo request (ping).

Specifying IP addresses for hosts, as we did in the bb-hosts file, makes the monitoring system more self-contained and decreases the possibility that a domain name resolution problem will skew monitoring results. However, maintaining IP address–to-hostname mappings specifically for the monitoring system creates additional administrative overhead. Furthermore, defining IP addresses within the monitoring system might be impractical when observing hosts that dynamically obtain IP addresses from a DHCP server. To address this, you can configure Big Brother to use the host's native domain name resolution mechanisms, such as DNS or its hosts file. You can accomplish this by simply specifying 0.0.0.0 for IP addresses in the bb-hosts file.

Some systems are configured not to respond to ICMP echo requests, or a firewall between the monitored system and the monitoring host will not let such traffic through. You can use the noping directive to prevent Big Brother from performing the ping test. In such cases, you will probably want to check the accessibility of specific services on the monitored host instead.

Accessibility of Network Services

One of the most useful features of monitoring programs is the ability to determine whether a remote service is accessible over the network. After all, a service might have crashed or have gotten disabled even if its host maintains network connectivity. You can use one of two primary methods to determine the accessibility of a TCP-based service:

- Check whether the monitored port is open by initiating a plain TCP connection with the service without exchanging data. You can do this with a half-connect, in which the monitoring server does not complete a three-way TCP handshake. Most monitoring systems, however, complete the handshake and close the connection as soon as it is established.

- Attempt to initiate a conversation with the remote service using the application-level protocol that is appropriate for the monitored service. For example, we could check the accessibility of a POP service by actually attempting to access a mailbox.

Port probes that are based on plain TCP connections obtain information without requiring us to program the monitoring system with knowledge of the protocol specific to the observed service. However, this technique does not help us detect problems with remote applications that accept TCP connections but do not respond properly. By programming the monitoring system to know the application-level protocol of the monitored service, we allow it to detect problems with greater accuracy and granularity. Another advantage of the application-level approach is that it can work with TCP- and UDP-based services.

Monitoring systems usually come with built-in support for determining accessibility of popular network services, such as SMTP, Telnet, FTP, POP, SSH, and IMAP. For example, the following line in Big Brother's bb-hosts file can be used to determine whether SMTP and SSH services run on the remote system plum:

```
192.168.214.101 plum    # smtp ssh
```

Big Brother usually attempts to evoke a response from the application when testing its availability, instead of simply verifying that it can establish a TCP connection. In most cases, Big Brother accomplishes this by sending the string `quit` to the remote service. Big Brother can handle some services in a slightly more intelligent manner by attempting to follow their protocols to make the test less obtrusive. For example, it sends `ABC123 LOGOUT` to IMAP services and sends an identifying string with the prefix `Big-Brother-Monitor` when connecting to the SSH service.

Tip

Sometimes, it makes sense to check whether a particular service is *not* running on a remote system. For example, if you transfer files only through Secure Shell (SSH), you might want to be alerted if a particular host suddenly starts accepting FTP connections. You can set up Big Brother to do this by using an exclamation mark (!) prefix when specifying directives in bb-hosts, like so:

```
192.168.214.101 plum   # smtp ssh !ftp
```

When testing accessibility of remote services, do not be surprised to see error messages in logs on the systems being observed. Monitoring tools often do not bother exercising all options of the remote service; they close the connection as soon as they receive some data in return or without exchanging data at all. For example, the Sendmail daemon may record a message such as the following one whenever Big Brother verifies accessibility of the SMTP service:

```
Feb 24 16:50:02 apple sendmail[23130]: NOQUEUE: apple [192.168.214.129]
➥did not issue MAIL/EXPN/VRFY/ETRN during connection to MTA
```

Big Brother has provisions for verifying service accessibility through plain TCP-based connections instead of exchanging data through a simplistic application check. To configure Big Brother to perform such probes, you can append `:s` (which stands for "silent") to the applicable directive in bb-hosts, like this:

```
192.168.214.101 plum   # smtp:s ssh
```

Unfortunately, this approach does not eliminate spurious log messages in many cases because Big Brother often confuses the monitored service by establishing a full TCP connection and not exchanging meaningful data. For example, using the `:s` suffix to test the SMTP service may not prevent Sendmail from issuing the alarming message shown previously. However, using `:s` might be effective for eliminating errors in the logs for certain software, so you might want to give this option a shot if the need arises.

Logging Incomplete OpenSSH Connections

The OpenSSH daemon may create the following log entry when a client initiates a connection to its port and closes the socket without going through the full SSH connection negotiation process:

```
Feb 24 16:51:03 apple sshd[19925]: Did not receive ident string from
➥192.168.214.129.
```

This message might indicate that a monitoring system is configured to observe the SSH service via plain TCP connections. The message is different when the system attempts to exchange data with the remote SSH service. Here's an example:

```
Feb 24 16:52:46 apple sshd[1295]: Bad protocol version identification
➥'Big-Brother-Monitor-1.9e' from 192.168.214.129
```

Of course, similar messages might appear in the logs when the SSH server is subjected to a port scan, so be careful not to blindly disregard these messages when examining the logs.

Monitoring web servers often warrants special considerations because web-based services are ubiquitous and are frequently critical to company operations. As a result, monitoring applications frequently offer you the ability to retrieve specific web pages. To set this up with Big Brother, you can use the bb-hosts file to specify which URLs to monitor:

```
192.168.214.17  lemon   # https://lemon/cart/order.jsp
192.168.214.97  peach   # http://peach/
```

The preceding configuration lines set up Big Brother to verify the availability of the /cart/order.jsp page on server lemon via HTTPS and to check the root page on server peach via HTTP. Clicking the HTTP icon on Big Brother's summary page enables you to see details of the established HTTP connection, as shown in Figure 19.2.

By monitoring applications, you can determine the accessibility of network services without installing additional software on monitored systems. However, obtaining detailed information about local attributes of the monitored resources often requires the further cooperation from the monitored system.

Figure 19.2   Big Brother can capture details of the HTTP response when connecting to the desired URL (in this case, to http://peach/).

Local System Attributes

Several attributes that are local to the monitored host might warrant your attention not only because they are critical to the host's function, but also because they can serve as an early warning system. Detecting the following conditions might help you discover problems before a host's network service stops being accessible over the network:

- File system is almost full.
- CPU utilization has exceeded an acceptable threshold.
- Critical processes are failing to run.

One of the most effective ways to observe these attributes is through the use of a monitoring agent that reports its findings to a monitoring server. Figure 19.3 shows a configuration screen of such an agent for Big Brother, with the client module running under Windows. Typical of such configurations is the need to define the central server to which notifications will be sent (in this case, 192.168.214.132).

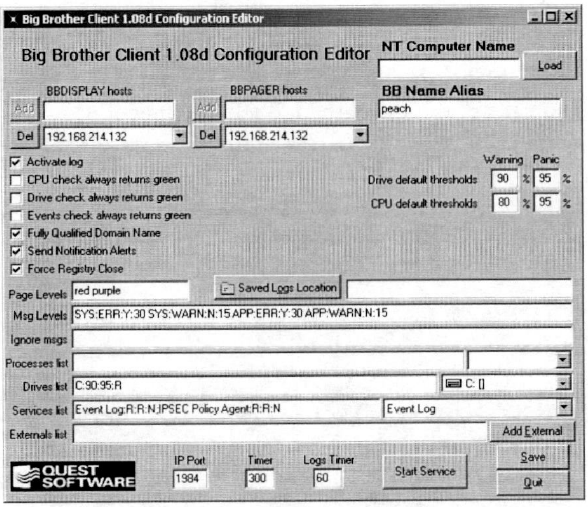

Figure 19.3   A GUI-based configuration utility defines monitoring settings for Big Brother clients that are running under Windows.

In this example, we set up the Big Brother client to monitor the state of two local services: Event Log and IPSec Policy Agent. Also, the client is set to issue a warning-level alert when the C: partition becomes 90% full and a panic-level alert when the partition's utilization reaches 95%. Even when the system is functioning normally, you can obtain useful information about the state of its resources. For instance, Figure 19.4 shows a status page displayed on Big Brother's central server when the remote host's file system utilization is below alarming thresholds. Status green means everything is OK with this particular attribute of the monitored host.

Figure 19.4   Monitoring systems can offer useful diagnostics information even when remote nodes operate below alarming thresholds.

Another way to obtain detailed information about a monitored system is via SNMP. The use of the application-specific monitoring agents we've discussed so far requires that client software be deployed on systems that need to be observed. One of the biggest advantages of using SNMP is that it is already built in to numerous devices and applications. An SNMP-compatible monitoring server can periodically poll remote SNMP agents for performance and availability attributes, such as configuration parameters, network statistics, and process details. For instance, here are some of the many attributes that Cisco routers natively expose via SNMP:

- MAC and IP address accounting
- CPU utilization
- Memory availability
- Startup and running configuration
- Network interface status

> **Note**
>
> Universal support for SNMP is one of the biggest advantages of this protocol, as well as a potential weakness. The SNMP vulnerability announced in February 2002, which we mentioned in Chapter 6, "The Role of a Router," simultaneously affected SNMP implementations of numerous vendors. Don't assume that an implementation of an established protocol is bug free. Even if the software has been around for years, you never know what dormant vulnerabilities lie within.

SNMP agents can also issue alerts to the monitoring system when a predefined condition occurs on the local device. These traps are generated asynchronously, regardless of the regular polling schedule the monitoring system implements. Traps can notify the monitoring system of an event that threatens performance or availability of the device. You can use the following command to enable all supported SNMP traps on a Cisco router (you will also need to use the `snmp-server host` command to specify where the traps should be sent):

```
router(config)#snmp-server enable traps snmp
```

One of the notifications that is enabled by using this command is the authentication trap, which alerts administrators when a remote host fails to properly authenticate when attempting to access the SNMP agent. This notification can help detect SNMP network scans and brute force attacks targeting the device over SNMP. If you are not interested in enabling all SNMP traps that the router supports, consider activating at least the authentication trap using the following command:

```
router(config)#snmp-server enable traps snmp authentication
```

> **Tip**
>
> Big Brother offers limited support for SNMP polling and trap handling through the use of add-on modules that can be downloaded from http://www.deadcat.net.au.

> **Versions of SNMP**
>
> SNMP has been around since 1988 and has been exposed to scrutiny by standards bodies, network engineers, and system administrators. As a result, numerous revisions have been made to the original SNMP protocol, but some of them failed to gain the community's acceptance and were phased away. One of the more popular phased-out SNMP provisions was the party-based authentication specification of SNMPv2 (now called *SNMPv2p* or *SNMPv2 classic*), which attempted to provide a more secure alternative to SNMPv1's community string authentication. Cisco routers used to support party-based authentication through the use of the `snmp-server party` command but stopped supporting it after release 11.2 of IOS.[1] Instead, Cisco followed the example of many other vendors in limiting itself to handling only the SNMPv1-style community string authentication defined by SNMPv2c.
>
> Additionally, Cisco adopted a full implementation of SNMPv3, which includes a rich set of cryptographic security mechanisms. One of the few major vendors that still supports the enhanced security framework of the SNMPv2 generation is Sun, which uses user-based authentication mechanisms defined by SNMPv2u in its Sun Management Center product. (Sun sometimes refers to this protocol as *SNMPv2usec*.)[2]

Another method of obtaining detailed information about remote system attributes is available, in addition to using SNMP or custom monitoring agents. This third method involves remotely executing commands that are native to the monitored host. For example, Mercury SiteScope (http://www.mercury.com) can obtain data from remote Windows machines through the PerfMon API, which Microsoft designed to gather performance-related information. To obtain detailed information from UNIX hosts,

SiteScope executes commands such as `ps` and `uptime` on the remote system via Telnet or SSH. When it comes to remotely executing commands or obtaining potentially sensitive information from the observed systems, you must take care to prevent attackers from exploiting the monitoring channel. We examine such considerations in the next section.

Security Considerations for Remote Monitoring

Attackers can exploit monitoring mechanisms, just like any other service operating on the network, to obtain sensitive information or to gain unauthorized access to remote systems. When selecting and configuring a monitoring solution, consider the following factors relating to its defenses:

- How sensitive are the monitoring communications that traverse the network, and should they be encrypted? You might not be concerned about the confidentiality of CPU statistics carried across the internal network, but you might not want to use clear-text SNMP to retrieve a router's running configuration across the Internet.

- How strong is the authentication scheme that prevents unauthorized entities from accessing monitored resources? Many monitoring solutions rely solely on IP addresses for access control. Additionally, SNMPv1 and SNMPv2c support only the use of community strings, which can be intercepted over the network or brute-forced via tools such as SolarWinds (http://www.solarwinds.net).

- Do monitoring mechanisms provide write access to observed resources? Even though we have been focusing on read-only aspects of system monitoring, SNMP can also be used to modify settings on remote devices. For example, an attacker with write access to a resource might be able to manipulate a router's ARP table or otherwise change the configuration of the system.

- Can the monitoring infrastructure be exploited to grant attackers elevated access to the systems? For example, a vulnerability in Big Brother allowed execution of arbitrary commands on the monitoring server with the privileges of the Big Brother user (http://cve.mitre.org/cgi-bin/cvename.cgi?name=CAN-2000-0450). Even if the server were restricted to accept status information from only specific IP addresses, systems hosting Big Brother agents could have been used to obtain access to the monitoring server.

Unauthorized access from monitoring agents to the central server is a particularly significant concern because the server is often located in a more secure area than the agents. Consider the configuration in Figure 19.5, where the server on the internal network collects performance and availability information from hosts on the screened subnet. If this scenario were implemented using Big Brother, client modules that run on public servers would be sending notifications to the monitoring server's TCP port 1984 and could exploit the CAN-2000-0450 vulnerability described earlier. (IANA officially assigned port 1984 for Big Brother's client-to-server communications.)

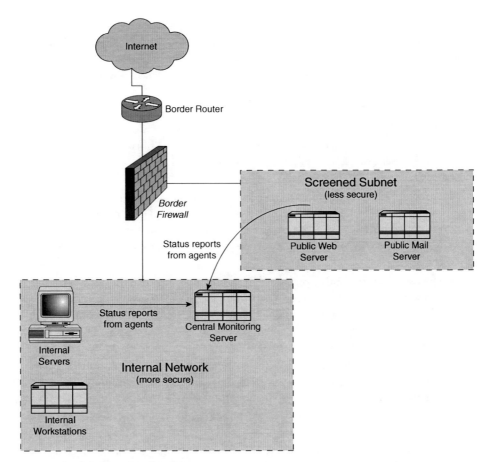

Figure 19.5 The central monitoring server could be exposed
to attacks coming from a host on the screened subnet if
agents can initiate connections to the server.

To minimize the risk of such attacks, run monitoring services as user accounts with constrained access. Big Brother, for instance, should be set up as a dedicated user without administrative privileges. If possible, also configure the hosts so that connections are initiated from the more secure subnet to limit the possibility of privilege escalation across network security zones. In the case of SNMP, for example, this would involve using the polling mechanisms when observing hosts across subnets as well as limiting trap communications to a single subnet. Monitoring applications might allow you to set up dedicated servers in each subnet for collecting status reports and then link them together; this way, the amount of traffic crossing subnet boundaries is minimized.

Perhaps one of the safest ways to monitor devices is by remotely probing their ports from the central server, as we discussed in the "Accessibility of Network Services" section. This method does not provide detailed information about the local state of the observed machines, but it also does not require that additional software be enabled on remote systems. Moreover, monitoring services that need to be accessible over the network, such as HTTP, DNS, and SMTP, often can be tested over channels that are already open. When a packet-filtering device blocks access to remote services from the network where the monitoring server is located, be sure to open access only to and from IP addresses that are required for monitoring to take place.

Monitoring products out of the box rarely provide many options when it comes to restricting which systems can obtain status information from a remote agent or who can submit status reports to the central server. Most products support restrictions based on IP addresses. To set this up in Big Brother, for example, you need to edit its security file to list addresses of hosts that should be able to communicate with the monitoring server.

Note
Monitoring products can provide supplementary modules that enhance the security of communications between the monitoring components. For example, you can purchase an add-on to HP OpenView Operations, called Advanced Security, to support encryption and cryptographic authentication.

IP-based restrictions form a useful layer for improving the security of the monitoring infrastructure and are most effective when combined with strong authentication in client-to-server communications. Cryptographic authentication is supported in SNMPv3; you should take advantage of it when setting up your monitoring infrastructure. SNMPv3 can also encrypt its messages, which helps to protect their confidentiality. As SNMP agents are beginning to adopt the security mechanisms of SNMPv3, it is becoming easier to find a monitoring system that can support them. Here is a list of some of the products able to securely communicate with SNMPv3 agent modules:

- HP OpenView and IBM Tivoli, with the help of an add-on called SNMP Security Pack (http://www.snmp.com/products/snmpsecpack.html)
- Castle Rock SNMPc Network Manager (http://www.castlerock.com)
- AdventNet SNMP API for implementing SNMP support in Java-based applications (http://www.adventnet.com/products/snmp)
- MG-SOFT SNMP management software (http://www.mg-soft.com)
- Net-SNMP, a popular set of free SNMP utilities for UNIX, utilized by applications such as Big Brother (http://net-snmp.sourceforge.net)

By this point in the chapter, we have discussed the fundamental principles of setting up system and network monitoring in a secure and reliable manner. After such infrastructure is in place, administrators can connect to a central server to view the status of the network's hosts and devices. The next step in maintaining a security perimeter is ensuring that administrators are alerted when critical conditions occur and empowering administrators to quickly respond to such events.

Incident Response

An *incident*, in the context of this chapter, is an anomalous event that can impact the confidentiality, integrity, or availability of the infrastructure. The anomaly might be malicious, or it might be an indicator of a system fault. In either case, we need to know how to set up alerts that warn us about a potentially threatening condition. Both IDS and system-monitoring mechanisms are useful for detecting suspicious events, but they are not of much help if administrators are not actually aware of conditions that these systems observe.

One way to remain apprised of the state of your resources is to periodically check the status screens of the monitoring system or the IDS console. Relying solely on this approach, however, does not allow detection and reaction to problems as soon as they occur. This is an especially significant concern for organizations that need to respond to incidents around the clock but cannot afford to hire personnel to observe the alert screen of the monitoring system 24 hours a day. Configuring IDS and monitoring systems to send out alerts and knowing how to respond to alarm conditions is an integral part of effective security perimeter maintenance. In this section, we discuss how to configure notification options in a way that is consistent with your security policy and monitoring requirements. Additionally, we examine considerations for responding to detected system faults and malicious events.

Note

Relying solely on automation of IDS or of the monitoring systems to detect all suspicious events in real time is dangerous. We illustrated limitations of this approach in Chapter 8 in the discussion of false positives and false negatives. Therefore, be sure to combine automated alerting with manual examination of data that such systems collect.

Notification Options

An old slogan of a New York telephone company reminded people that "We're all connected." Accessibility of system administrators, wherever they are, allows systems to get in touch with them in close to real time whenever a device requires attention. When evaluating or deploying an IDS or a monitoring system, consider the following aspects of its notification functionality:

- What means of alert notification do you require? Some of the more popular options are email, pager, and SMS-based messages. It might also be possible to integrate the notification mechanism with other applications already in use in your organization.

- What alert acknowledgement options do you find useful? If a critical alert is sent to multiple administrators, you might want to have the ability to let your colleagues know that you are working on the problem so that your efforts do not overlap.

- How configurable is the notification logic? You might want to send alerts to different people depending on the day of the week or the time of the day, or issue alerts to different devices depending on the event's severity. Also, plan for outages in your notification scheme because the primary notification mechanism might fall victim to a system fault or an attack.

> **Tip**
>
> Keep in mind that some of the cheaper paging devices, especially those that are purely numeric, do not guarantee a message will be delivered. To ensure that an alert eventually reaches the administrator when he is back in the communications range, you might want to subscribe to paging services that can queue messages to guarantee their delivery. Alternatively, or in conjunction with this, consider configuring the monitoring system to periodically reissue alerts until one of them is acknowledged.

One of the advantages of having a centralized alerting configuration is that only a single host needs to have the ability to generate alerts destined for the mailboxes or pagers of system administrators. This eliminates the need to set up dial-out modems on every observed system for dialing a numeric pager or the need to enable each server to send email when its business purpose does not require such functionality. In Big Brother, for example, a central server consolidates performance and availability information, and only the host that is designated as BBPAGER issues notification alerts. To eliminate a single point of failure, you might consider setting up multiple alert-generating systems or configuring them to operate in a failover mode.

General Response Guidelines

Make sure your company's policies and procedures clearly explain what an administrator should do when responding to an alert. Creating and distributing a document that answers the following questions will help you make sure problems are resolved in a consistent and thought-out manner that has the support of management and technical personnel:

- Who is responsible for responding to alerts? Defining this in advance helps ensure that the qualified staff members are available, according to relevant policies and business requirements. Also, this helps prevent administrators from failing to respond because they think somebody else will react to the alert.

- Whom should the administrator notify of the problem? As we already discussed, it is often worthwhile to let other administrators know that someone is responding to the alert. Additionally, the company's management should probably be notified of severe or prolonged conditions.

- What troubleshooting and investigative steps should the administrator take when resolving a problem? Consider creating a document that explains how to handle problems common to your infrastructure. (Chapter 21, "Troubleshooting Defense Components," addresses this aspect of perimeter maintenance.)

- How should the administrator connect to the troubled system? VPN access might come in handy when the administrator is away from the hosting facility. You might also want to define transportation options if she needs to travel to the hosting facility.

- When should the administrator call for help? It's possible that the person who is responding to an alert might not be the best person to resolve a particular problem. Specifying in advance when to involve a colleague, or even an external vendor, and empowering the administrator to do so even during off-hours helps to expediently resolve problems.

- How should the administrator document the cause of the problem and its resolution in a way that might help the company learn from this experience?

It is not uncommon for the administrator who is responding to the alert to perform a preliminary examination and then to call in the heavy artillery for in-depth troubleshooting. One such scenario, perhaps most relevant to this book, is when the administrator suspects that the event is malicious in nature. Your security policy should account for the need to investigate such situations and define the roles and responsibilities for the staff involved in responding to malicious incidents.

Responding to Malicious Incidents

Any anomaly, whether reported by an IDS or a monitoring system or recognized by a human, might turn out to be a malicious incident. After the event is deemed to be malicious, the specialized procedures created for handling such situations should guide your staff's response. These procedures can be broken into several phases, as defined in *Computer Security Incident Handling Step by Step*, published by the SANS Institute.[3] The following list presents a high-level overview of these phases:

1. **Preparation**—Tasks in this phase need to take place before an actual response to a malicious incident. They involve formalizing policies and procedures, training team members, and preparing communication channels for contacting people inside and outside your organization.

2. **Identification**—In this phase, a primary handler is assigned to the incident. He begins the investigation by determining whether the incident is, indeed, malicious. If it is, he assesses its scope, establishes a chain of custody for collected evidence, and notifies appropriate personnel.

3. **Containment**—The purpose of this phase is to set the stage for further analysis while preventing the incident from escalating. Here, the handler creates a backup of the affected systems to make sure that pristine evidence is available for later use. He also assesses the risk of continuing operations by reviewing logs, interviewing observers, and consulting with system owners. Determining the extent of the compromise and either taking appropriate systems offline or attempting to otherwise block the attackers' access achieves containment.

4. **Eradication**—At this point in the response effort, the handler determines the cause of the malicious incident, reinforces the system's defenses, and closes any vulnerabilities that might have allowed the attack to succeed.

5. **Recovery**—This phase is devoted to restoring and validating affected systems, returning to business as normal, and continuing to closely monitor systems that were compromised. At this point, the organization needs to decide whether it is ready to resume operations.

6. **Follow up**—In this phase, the incident handler creates a report that consolidates the team's experiences that relate to the incident. This "lessons learned" process helps improve the organization's defenses by addressing factors that allowed the compromise to occur. At this stage, the team implements the follow-up actions management approved.

As you can see, responding to alerts, whether they relate to a system fault or a malicious event, is no easy matter. As we discuss in the following section, you might be able to automate responses to some of the simpler events that require immediate action and that can be addressed without directly involving the administrator.

Automating Event Responses

Automating responses to events that are unlikely to be false alarms helps to expedite problem resolution. For instance, a monitoring system might detect that a critical process on the observed host died, issue an alert to the administrator, and automatically start a new instance of the process. When configuring such functionality, you might want to set limits on the number of times the system attempts to take corrective action in a given time period. If the process repeatedly dies soon after being restarted, chances are good that the automated recovery mechanism cannot help in this situation, in which case an administrator should become directly involved. Even if the fault was automatically resolved, the administrator should still follow up to assess the scope of the problem, determine its cause, verify that the corrective action was acceptable, and attempt to prevent the fault from reoccurring.

Another type of automated response can take place when an intrusion detection system or an intrusion prevention system detects a malicious event. Such products may allow you to automatically respond to the attack—for instance, by resetting the offending network stream or dynamically reconfiguring the firewall to block the attack. As we discussed in Chapter 8, "Network Intrusion Detection," and Chapter 11, "Intrusion Prevention Systems," such automated response carries the advantage of shunning the attacker as soon as malicious actions are observed, but it is often dangerous because it might deny service to a legitimate user. When deciding whether to enable such intrusion prevention functionality, weigh the risk of mistakenly blocking an authorized user against the risk of not blocking a particular attack right away.

In our discussion about maintaining a security perimeter, so far we have looked at monitoring the infrastructure for faults and malicious events and discussed how to efficiently respond to alarming conditions. An effective way of decreasing the rate at which anomalies occur in the first place is to ensure that perimeter components are updated in a controlled manner. We examine the process of managing changes to the environment in the following section.

Accommodating Change

The reality of maintaining a security perimeter built perfectly in tune with the organization's business needs is that at some point it will need to change to accommodate new requirements and emerging threats. The ability of the infrastructure to handle change in a controlled manner is one of the main attestations to the quality of its design, implementation, and maintenance. This section discusses rolling out patches, reconfiguring systems, and detecting environment changes without compromising the security of your network.

Fundamentals of Change Management

The general concept of *change management* refers to the ability to handle changes in business or technical areas of the organization. In the confines of this chapter, we focus on processes that support changes to network infrastructure and applications. One example of a process that might require change management is the rollout of a critical patch to web server software that needs to take place without causing prolonged downtime, crippling its applications, or exposing new security weaknesses. Similarly, a change to a firewall's rule set should take place without inadvertently denying authorized traffic or exposing internal systems to new threats. To accommodate such adjustments to the infrastructure, a robust change-management process should incorporate the following elements:

- Buy-in from management and technical personnel
- Communications regarding proposed changes
- Prevention and detection of unauthorized changes
- Ability to test changes before deployment
- Procedures to verify proper system operation
- Ability to roll back undesired changes

The majority of change-management situations benefit from a process that incorporates these steps. However, the extent of each phase might differ, depending on how complicated or risky the change is. For example, migrating a mail server from Microsoft Exchange to Lotus Notes is likely to require more planning and testing than adding a routine security patch to a server. Next, we examine these elements in greater detail so that you are better positioned to set up a change-management program that matches your needs.

Obtaining Buy-in from Relevant Personnel

You should obtain buy-in from relevant parties regarding the reasons for implementing the change before rolling it out. For instance, you might have valid reasons for wanting to block all outbound SMTP access from your screened subnet, but you might not realize that several servers hosted there have valid business reasons for generating email. We recommend formalizing the change-approval process so that management and technical personnel have a chance to voice objections to upcoming modifications. This procedure helps prevent making rushed choices that cause adverse side effects. The process should also define individuals who are authorized to make final decisions regarding proposed changes; this eliminates unending discussions and resolves potential conflicts.

Communicating Proposed Changes

You should keep business and technical personnel apprised of proposed modifications so that they are not caught off guard when the change occurs. Establish a procedure for notifying appropriate parties of scheduled changes and verify that all relevant parties have a way of obtaining necessary information. Also, do not forget to notify end users that systems might be inaccessible for a certain time period. To help alleviate inconvenience caused to end users by potential service disruptions, consider scheduling the change to take place during off-time hours.

> **Tip**
>
> To make notification to relevant personnel of planned service disruptions easier, consider preparing template documents that describe some of the more common downtime scenarios. The templates should explain when the event will occur, which services will be impacted, and when systems are scheduled to resume normal operation. You might also want to explain how users or the organization will benefit from upcoming changes so that they are more supportive of your plans.

Preventing and Detecting Unauthorized Changes

You are probably well versed in enforcing access controls by this point in the book. Implementing such controls will help prevent unauthorized or inadvertent changes to your systems. Also, integrity-assessment tools, such as Tripwire, are useful for detecting unapproved changes or for tracking authorized changes that mold your system during its lifespan. To prevent unpleasant situations in which administrators' actions are second-guessed, your security policy should clearly define who is authorized to make changes and what approval and communication process they need to follow.

Testing Changes Before Deployment

All changes to be introduced into a production environment should be tested first on a separate, staging network. Granted, you might not be able to afford to create a full replica of your production infrastructure for this purpose. However, you might still be able to introduce the proposed change into a scaled-down laboratory environment to help you assess the risk of rolling it out to production. When testing, be sure to go through the process of regression testing, which tests the new environment for all bugs. Often, by fixing an open problem, you might reopen an issue that was fixed previously. Regression testing will help you find these problems before they are reintroduced into the production environment. Your effort in testing a change before deployment should be proportional to the impact that the change is likely to have on the production environment. In most cases, adding an entry to a system's hosts file is likely to require less testing than upgrading the version of the firewall software.

Verifying Proper System Operation

Having a detailed plan for verifying that the infrastructure functions properly after the change is rolled out allows you to limit the impact of problems and makes it easier to track down their causes. The plan should incorporate a standard suite of tests that are performed after any change and should include specific tests to verify that the intended change has been implemented. Be sure to test access to relevant services and exercise core aspects of applications after upgrading software, reconfiguring hosts, or tweaking access control rules.

Rolling Back Undesired Changes

Even after all the planning and testing, your change might cause problems that you are unable to correct right away; in that case, you will need to roll back to the previous configuration. You save yourself and those around you a lot of anguish by preparing (and testing) a rollback plan before implementing the change. A time-tested method of reversing the effects of a change to a system is to restore it from the most recent backup. Of course, be sure to verify that such a backup exists and that you are able to restore data from it before implementing the change. A tape backup might come in handy even if you are applying a patch that has an uninstall function because such rollback mechanisms have been known to fail. If the scope of your change is relatively narrow (for instance, if you are just modifying a configuration file), a rollback plan might be simply a matter of creating a copy of the file before editing it.

When making changes to the infrastructure, you are often faced with making tough choices, even if your change-management process incorporates the principles mentioned earlier. In the next section, we go over several mechanisms that can help you make such decisions.

Implementing Change-Management Controls

The process of change management, described in the previous section, focuses on making sure that changes to the environment happen in a controlled and deterministic fashion. The cornerstone of this process is a documented change-management procedure that explains how things should be done, when, and by whom. There are also techniques that can make it easier for your organization to follow this procedure. In this section, we examine two essential ways of using tools and procedures to assist in implementing change-management practices:

- Applying patches
- Discovering new services and devices

Let's start by looking at an age-long problem that you've most likely faced in your career already: applying patches.

Applying Patches

On numerous occasions throughout this book, we've emphasized the need for regularly patching your OS and applications to prevent attackers from exploiting known software vulnerabilities. Unfortunately, sometimes this is easier said than done. It is not always easy to keep track of patches that vendors release for all the products you need to maintain. More importantly, some of the more urgent patches do not undergo regression testing, so the vendor does not guarantee that they will work well in all permutations of system configurations.

To make it harder to forget applying necessary patches, clearly designate individuals who are responsible for monitoring patch and vulnerability announcement forums. It often makes sense to assign this responsibility to system administrators who maintain the respective products, but do not assume that they are already subscribed to the relevant mailing lists. Consider handing out a list of applicable announcement forums. As a security professional, you should monitor them as well to help ensure a vulnerability does not go by unnoticed.

As a stream of vulnerability announcements flows through your mailbox, you need to decide whether they apply to your environment and how urgent it is for you to react. You need to weigh the risk of delaying a patch rollout, perhaps to perform more thorough testing, against the risk of having a vulnerable network resource. For instance, if a patch prevents an exploitable compromise of your DNS server, you might want to deploy the fix as soon as it comes out. A patch that is, perhaps, less urgent might be one that aims to correct a theoretical vulnerability in a print server deep within your network. If the print server is not your most critical resource, you might decide to wait until the vendor provides a more comprehensive upgrade or until your peers share their experiences pertaining to this patch. In some cases, patches might not be available or might be too risky to apply, and you will need to consider other workarounds to address critical vulnerabilities.

Whatever decisions you make regarding applying, testing, or delaying the installation of a patch or a workaround, be sure to document them. Such journals will help you remember reasons for making certain decisions, and if you chose not to apply the patch, the journals will allow you to revisit the decision at a later date. We suggest including the following fields in each journal entry:

- The date the patch or the vulnerability was announced
- The list and description of systems to which the patch or the vulnerability applies
- The decisions made regarding the patch or vulnerability
- The names of persons who made the decision

- If corrective action was deemed necessary, who is responsible for implementing it
- The date on which the decision was made, or when the corrective action was taken

In large environments, it might be difficult to know versions of applications that are installed throughout your organization, or even which services are running on remotely accessible systems. The next section focuses on techniques for keeping track of new systems and services that come online on your network.

Discovering New Services and Devices

You need to know which systems and services are available on your network to be able to assess risks and correct potential vulnerabilities. To help achieve this awareness, you might establish a policy that new network services have to be registered with and, possibly, approved by information security personnel. However, environments change quickly, and before too long, your network is likely to contain resources that you were not notified about. One of the most effective ways to discover the presence of unauthorized or inadvertent network resources on your network is to compare periodic snapshots of the state of your network.

We already described one mechanism for discovering which services are offered by your systems in Chapter 9, "Host Hardening." There, we mentioned the `netstat -na` command, which lists ports that the system listens on. Consider scheduling this command to run on regular intervals so that you can discover when a critical system begins listening on unexpected ports. You can then create a script that compares the output of each successive run by using tools such as `fc.exe` under Windows or `diff` in UNIX. This technique focuses on individual systems, but it might not be practical for monitoring the state of workstations, servers, and devices on a mid-to-large-size network.

Network and vulnerability scanners, which we describe in greater detail in Chapter 22, "Assessment Techniques," offer a way to remotely test for the existence of network services. To locate newly set up systems or unauthorized port listeners, you would compare the output of successive network scans and flag the differences. Nessus, a popular vulnerability scanner, and Nmap, one of the most powerful network scanners, make this a relatively painless task.

Nessus, freely available from http://www.nessus.org, does a great job of scanning networks for accessible hosts or open ports, and it specializes at probing systems for known vulnerabilities. One of the ways to detect changes in your environment is to regularly scan your network with Nessus and compare the results.

If you are not interested in scanning for vulnerabilities or you prefer to use a tool other than Nessus, you can take advantage of the scanning capabilities of Nmap. Nmap (http://www.nmap.org) is a wonderful tool for locating hosts and open ports, and it's invaluable for performing security assessments. You can also schedule Nmap to periodically scan your network and compare differences in the network's state. To perform such *differential scans* with Nmap, you can compare the results of your scans using a tool such as `fc.exe` or `diff`, or you can use an add-on utility called NDiff, available for free from http://www.vinecorp.com/ndiff.

To use NDiff, you first scan your network with Nmap and then save the output into a file by using an -m option, like this:

```
# nmap -m snapshot.nm 192.168.1.0/24
```

In this example, Nmap port-scans all hosts on the 192.168.1.0/24 network and saves the output into a file called snapshot.nm. The next time you run Nmap, you would save its output into a different file—say, newsnapshot.nm. You would then use NDiff to compare contents of the two files, like this:

```
# ndiff -b snapshot.nm -o newsnapshot.nm -format minimal
new hosts:
192.168.1.100

missing hosts:

changed hosts:
192.168.1.204
80/tcp/http (unknown -> open)
443/tcp/https (unknown -> open)
```

In this example, NDiff detects that a new host appears on the network and that another host begins listening for HTTP and HTTPS connections. To simplify the task of running Nmap, storing its output, and then comparing the results of the scan, NDiff comes with a wrapper utility called nrun.

Using differential scanning, you might detect services that should not be present on your network and react by disabling them. On the other hand, your investigation might show that a new service has a legitimate need, in which case you will need to understand what it is about in order to determine how it should be configured. In Chapter 15, "Software Architecture," we presented a software evaluation checklist with questions that you can ask when assessing how an application fits in with the rest of the security perimeter. We suggest asking such questions not only of your third-party providers, but also of your colleagues. Understanding the application's technical and business requirements will help you assess its risks and devise appropriate mitigations.

Summary

In this chapter we discussed the core principles of maintaining a security perimeter and examined the fundamentals of system and network monitoring, incident response, and change management. A reliable monitoring process is essential to knowing the state of your infrastructure and allows you to rapidly detect problems and react accordingly. We also covered considerations for centrally monitoring remote resources without exposing them to additional vulnerabilities.

Next, we examined incident response procedures to prepare you for responding to alerts generated by monitoring and intrusion detection systems. We emphasized the need to define a detailed plan for handling malicious and fault-related incidents so that you can focus on investigating and eliminating the problem when the need arises.

Recognizing that even the most thought-out infrastructure is bound to evolve along with the organization, we described the significance of sound change-management practices. This aspect of perimeter maintenance focused on applying patches, deploying new applications, enforcing controls, and detecting infrastructure changes in a deterministic manner.

The next chapters are meant to help you apply some of the practices discussed in this chapter while incorporating design concepts from earlier parts of the book. We also examine the process of assessing the effectiveness of the architecture and the implementation of the security perimeter. Stay tuned!

References

1 Cisco Systems, Inc. "Configuring SNMP Support." 1998. http://www.cisco.com/univercd/cc/td/doc/product/software/ios121/121cgcr/fun_c/fcprt3/fcd301.htm. February 2002.

2 Sun Microsystems, Inc. "Sun Management Center 3.0: General FAQ." http://www.sun.com/solaris/sunmanagementcenter/faq/faq-general.html. February 2002.

3 Stephen Northcutt. *Computer Security Incident Handling Step by Step*. SANS Institute. 1998.

20

Network Log Analysis

O NE OF THE MOST CHALLENGING, YET REWARDING, aspects of perimeter security is network log file analysis. This process involves trying to identify intrusions and intrusion attempts through vigilant monitoring and analysis of various log files and then correlating events among those files. There are many different types of network log files to review, from network firewalls, routers, and packet filters to host-based firewalls and intrusion detection systems (IDSs). Although analyzing log files might sound a bit tedious to you, the techniques presented in this chapter can help you to gain a great deal of value from your files in a short amount of time.

This chapter discusses several important topics that demonstrate why log file analysis is so critical to establishing and maintaining a strong perimeter defense:

- Purpose of and characteristics of log files
- Basics of log file analysis, particularly how to automate as much of the analysis as possible
- Examples of how to analyze router, packet filter, network firewall, host-based firewall, and host-based IDS logs

By the end of this chapter, you should be well prepared to perform your own analysis of network log files in your environment to accurately identify suspicious and malicious activity and to respond to it quickly. As a first step toward that goal, let's talk about why you should care about log files and what they can tell you if you listen.

The Importance of Network Log Files

In many environments, system administrators largely ignore network log files; the administrators are constantly putting out fires and don't have time to devote to log file review. Actually, it's more accurate to say that the files are ignored until a major incident occurs. Then there's a mad scramble to find out what happened, which typically includes a check of log files, often done by an administrator who isn't very familiar with the log file format or the proper procedures and steps for performing good log file analysis.

Sometimes the administrator discovers that detailed logging was not enabled, so no record of the event exists. After the crisis has ended, the log files are again ignored until the next catastrophe occurs.

Log files have many things to tell you, if you only stop to listen to them. Log files have several purposes of which you might not be aware, which will be reviewed in the "Purposes of Log Files" section later in this chapter. They are incredibly helpful in meeting a range of needs, such as intrusion detection, incident handling, event correlation, and troubleshooting. Each log file contains many pieces of information that can be invaluable if you know how to read them and, more importantly, if you know how to analyze the data from a perimeter defense viewpoint to identify scans, intrusion attempts, misconfigured equipment, and other noteworthy items. Before you can learn how to analyze the data, you first have to understand what sort of data you will likely have.

Characteristics of Log Files

Many different types of log files exist, and they are generated by various sources. Most operating systems, including all flavors of UNIX and most versions of Windows, are capable of performing extensive logging of events as they occur. Also, many applications log events of significance, such as authentication attempts, application errors, and configuration changes. For our purposes, we are most interested in analyzing network log files; to understand the events that occur on a network, you want to focus on log files that record network-related events, such as successful and failed connections. Many other logs (such as operating system log files) also contain valuable information that can be used to correlate the network activities, although the primary focus in this chapter is the examination of network logs. Devices such as firewalls, routers, and network IDS generate network logs.

> **Note**
>
> Although operating systems and many applications have great logging capabilities, they are often disabled by default. System administrators must take care to ensure that logging is enabled and that the logs are sufficiently detailed.

If you have ever looked at log files from several different devices or applications, you have surely noticed that the logs are typically in completely different formats. Later in this chapter, starting with the "Analyzing Router Logs" section, we will review some of the most commonly encountered log formats. Although it's important to realize that log formats differ, it's far more important to understand that different devices and applications might log very different information. Some logs contain little useful data, perhaps only a timestamp and the source and destination addresses and ports, whereas others contain just about everything you would possibly want to know about the event in question. Some logs record virtually every characteristic of traffic, plus an interpretation of the significance of that traffic. The two main factors—various log formats and different log information—are what make network log analysis a bit intimidating at first. Let's work through that by examining what data you might find in network log files.

Information That Log Files Usually Record

Most systems that utilize network log files record several core pieces of information about each connection or packet that they deem to be of interest:

- Timestamp, which typically includes the date, as well as the time (in seconds or fractions of a second) when the event occurred or when the event was recorded to the log

- Basic IP characteristics, such as source address, destination address, and IP protocol (TCP, UDP, ICMP, and so on)

- TCP or UDP source and destination ports, or ICMP type and code

Additionally, most log entries contain some sort of reason why the event was logged. However, this varies widely among log formats:

- Descriptive text explanation

- Rule number that matched traffic

- Action that was performed, such as accepting, dropping, or rejecting a connection

Although this might not seem like much data, you can do a lot with just this information. For example, you can analyze it to identify port scans, host scans, or other failed connection attempts. You can also do basic traffic analysis, but with just these elements, the amount of analysis you can do is quite limited. You need more data on events to perform a more in-depth analysis.

Information That Log Files Sometimes Record

Many network logs do record more information than just the core items. Other types of data that might appear include these:

- Other IP characteristics, particularly the IP identification number and the time to live (TTL)

- More TCP-specific characteristics, such as flags (SYN, ACK, and the like), TCP window values, and TCP sequence numbers

- The interface that saw the event

- The beginning of the payload's content, although this is much more the exception than the rule

These additional fields can be beneficial in terms of log analysis. For example, the time to live and TCP window values can be used to perform OS fingerprinting to determine the likely OS of the attacker (although attackers can modify telltale values such as the TTL). TCP flags might indicate the intent of an attacker; certain flag combinations tend to mean that the packets are trying to evade firewalls or IDSs. Some of these extra fields can also help determine what tool or malware is generating the attack. Many tools have a unique signature, and these data elements can help you to find that signature so that you know exactly what the attacker is trying to do. Unfortunately, even with this extra information, you still might not have enough data to perform as detailed of an analysis as you would like to do.

Information That Log Files Rarely Record

Most devices that perform network logging do not closely examine or even record the full payloads of the traffic they see. Doing so is generally outside the capabilities of the device, and it is incredibly resource-intensive. Most network logging is based on examining the core characteristics of the packets and connections and making decisions based on those characteristics alone. There's little need, from the perspective of that device, to examine or record all the packets in a connection.

However, it's often beneficial to have more information on traffic and to be able to do more careful evaluations of payloads. It's often useful to record full packet headers as well to capture all the pertinent information, not just the header values stored in the log. If full packets are recorded for connections or packets that are deemed suspicious, you could then perform a deeper examination as needed and have all the packets' information available. Unfortunately, many logs do not support packet recording; in these cases, you might be able to set up a dedicated packet sniffer or use a program such as Tcpdump to perform packet captures. However, in most environments, the volume of traffic and required storage space will be too high to record all packets, and organizational policies might forbid the recording of all traffic for privacy or liability reasons.

Most devices that perform network logging do not also perform protocol decoding at the application layer. A good example of this would be a DNS request. A network log might report that host 10.20.30.40 sent a packet to UDP port 53 on host 172.30.128.12. You see port 53 and think "DNS," but you really have no idea whether this was a DNS request. Even if it were a DNS request, you have no information about the request. With the exception of a proxying firewall, devices that perform network logging usually don't do protocol decoding or verification. You must rely on network intrusion detection and prevention systems, as well as proxies, to perform protocol verification.

Note

One great feature of proxying firewalls is that a web proxy can log URLs. If a new worm that exploits HTTP is spreading, other perimeter devices may log port 80 connection attempts, but the web proxy will actually log the URL that the worm uses, which can be invaluable in determining what is occurring.

Purposes of Log Files

Now that you have looked at the types of data that log files record, let's step back for a minute and think about the purposes that log files serve. Of course, the main purpose of a log file is to record events of significance or interest. But what you would really like to know is how these records can be useful to you and your organization. As you will see, log files have several important roles to play and can assist you in such areas as incident handling, intrusion detection, event correlation, and general troubleshooting.

Incident Handling

Probably the most obvious use of network log files is to provide data that can be used for incident handling. For example, if a network administrator receives a report that a device has been compromised, she might use network log files to determine which host or hosts might have been responsible for the attack and what methods of attack might have been used. When a web page is defaced, the system administrators are likely to consult the web server's logs, but also the logs of other devices through which the malicious traffic might have passed, which could provide additional information about the attack and the attacker. Network log files are an invaluable component of incident handling.

During incident handling, you will need to preserve evidence should you want to perform disciplinary actions against someone within an organization or pursue legal actions against an external party. Under those circumstances, log files are extremely important for forensic purposes. When properly preserved, network log files provide evidence of activity—evidence that might be admissible in legal proceedings. The procedures you need to follow for evidence handling vary widely depending on where you are located, but a general guideline is that the original, unaltered log files should be preserved, preferably both electronically and on paper. Contact your local law enforcement agency for advice on how to preserve log file evidence. For additional information on incident handling, see Chapter 19, "Maintaining a Security Perimeter."

Intrusion Detection

Although log files are invaluable during the handling of many incidents, this is a purely reactive use of log files. A related proactive use is that of intrusion detection. By automatically and continuously monitoring log file entries, you can be notified when someone is scanning your network or performing reconnaissance, or when an actual incident is in progress. This will also help with incident handling; when a significant intrusion is detected and reported to you, you already have much of the data you will need to perform incident handling for that event.

Note

Even the simplest firewall and router logs can be used for some basic intrusion detection. For example, blocked packets or connections can be counted by source or destination IP address or by destination port, which is useful in identifying scans, probes, and other reconnaissance attempts.

Event Correlation

Event correlation is useful in performing both incident handling and intrusion detection. When we speak of event correlation, we mean that it's possible to use multiple logs from various devices or applications together. Event correlation can be done to confirm what has occurred. For example, you see a suspicious entry on an internal router's log that involves an external host, and you search the logs of the Internet firewall for entries that provide more information on the action. Another use of event correlation is to relate events to each other. If your email server is compromised, you would search through various network logs from routers, firewalls, and other devices to look for any evidence relating to the compromise, such as other connection attempts made to the email server, or other hosts on your network that have been targeted by the same attacker.

General Troubleshooting

A final use of network log files is to assist in general troubleshooting, particularly involving connectivity issues. For example, a user complains that application XYZ can't download data from an external server. By getting the IP address of the user's machine and finding out what time he tried to use the application, you could quickly search your firewall's logs to look for denied attempts to make the required connection. If your firewall also logs all permitted connections, you could look for a valid connection to the remote site, which would indicate that the problem most likely involves the remote server or the application, not your perimeter defense configuration. More information on troubleshooting is presented in Chapter 21, "Troubleshooting Defense Components."

> **Note**
>
> In most environments, configuring your firewall to log all permitted connections is not possible due to the negative impact on performance and resources. However, temporarily configuring your firewall to log all connections is often helpful when troubleshooting a problem.

Log Analysis Basics

Now that we've discussed the basics of network log files, let's dig in to the really interesting material—how to analyze the log files after you have them. Log file analysis is an incredibly important area of network security that is often overlooked. If network log analysis is not being performed regularly and thoroughly in your environment, your organization's perimeter defenses are significantly weakened because you and other administrators are missing a large part of the overall security picture.

Getting Started with Log Analysis

When you're just starting to perform log analysis, you might find it difficult. Let's be honest—looking at page after page of cryptic log entries probably isn't how you want to spend your time. You have many other tasks to do, and most of those tasks are attached to people who are calling you, wanting to know when you're going to be taking care of them. Log files don't yell at you or beg for your attention, so it's easy to ignore them or forget about them altogether. And when you first start analyzing your logs, it's bound to take a significant amount of your time.

But after you have been reviewing your logs on a regular basis for a while and you have automated the log analysis (as described in the "Automating Log Analysis" section later in this chapter), you will find that it doesn't take as much of your time as you might think, and it can actually save you time and headaches down the road. The hardest part is getting started. Here are some tips that will help you start analyzing your logs:

- Establish a set time each day to review your logs, and stick to that schedule. Preferably, you can do your review at a time of the day when you will have minimal interruptions. If you start making excuses for skipping your log file review, you will most likely stop reviewing them altogether. Just hang in there—it will become easier and faster over time.

- Choose a reasonable length of time to do your daily log review and analysis session. Of course, this is highly dependent on how many log entries you will be reviewing and the security needs in your environment. An hour a day is probably a good starting point; adjust accordingly as needed. Of course, if you find that the amount of time doesn't work for you, you can always change it later.

- Decide in how much depth you want to analyze your logs. There is value in doing an overall review of all the log files, but also in doing an in-depth analysis of log excerpts. When you're starting, it's probably good to try both techniques to get a better "feel" for your log files.

> **Note**
>
> One method that might help you to "break the ice" and start analyzing your logs is to do searches on them using keywords such as "blocked," "denied," and "refused." With many log files, this is a quick-and-easy way to identify log entries that might need further review.

This brings up a critical point: the concept of "feel." Much of the motivation for reviewing your log files regularly is that you will get a feel for what your log files normally look like. The only way to achieve this is through regular reviews. After you have a sense of the baseline, it should be easy for you to spot most deviations from that baseline in the future. If you know what entries are normally recorded in your logs, and one day you see an entry that you have never seen before, you will naturally target that as something to be investigated further. If you didn't have that feel for your logs, you probably wouldn't even notice such an entry. That's the hidden value in performing regular analysis—the ability to sense when something unusual has occurred. After you have that feel, you can increasingly rely on automation to perform the basic log analysis for you, selecting only those items that are of particular interest to you.

> **Fun with Log Files?**
>
> You might think that reviewing log files is not the most exciting way to spend your time. Personally, I find log analysis to be a fascinating area of network security, and it's actually become a hobby of mine. Honest! When I am reviewing a potential incident, I think of log file analysis as a jigsaw puzzle, with some pieces that don't look like they fit at all, and other pieces that seem to be missing. Each piece has something to contribute to the picture, and figuring out how they all fit together is really quite addictive.
>
> When I first started doing log analysis, I found it to be rather boring and difficult. I didn't understand most of the log formats, and I usually didn't realize the significance of the data I was reviewing. Over time, my knowledge grew, and trying to decipher the activity behind the log entries became a welcome challenge. Try log file analysis—you might be surprised at how much you like it.

Automating Log Analysis

After you have been manually reviewing and analyzing your log files for a while, you will be able to glance at many log entries and immediately understand their significance. Most log entries will probably be of little or no interest to you. Over time, you will notice that fewer of the entries merit your attention. This is where automated log analysis becomes so helpful to you. By now, you know what log entries you really want to see—or, more correctly, you know what log entries you really don't want to see. By automating parts of the log analysis process, you can generate a report of only the unusual activities that you would like to investigate further, which will save you a great deal of time.

Log analysis automation can be a bit tricky, depending on the format of the log files. Many log files are in a text format, which means they are typically easy to review using automated techniques. However, other log files are in binary or proprietary formats that cannot be automatically reviewed in their native form. In some cases, you can export the log file to a text file, either through the application that recorded the log file or through a separate log conversion utility. In other cases, you might not be able to access the log file information unless you use a viewer that the application provides; in this example, you probably can't automate the review of that log file. Whenever possible, it is best to handle log files that are in some sort of text file format, such as tab-delimited or comma-separated values (CSV). This will make the rest of the automation process far easier.

Another potentially difficult aspect of log analysis automation is handling the volume of the logs. Depending on the amount of traffic being monitored and what events are being logged, a single log could contain millions of entries a day. Remember, you might be reviewing dozens, hundreds, or even thousands of logs, depending on the size and composition of your environment. In such a case, you will need to choose an automation method that not only can process that number of entries in a timely manner, but also has adequate storage space. Some of the possible automation methods are discussed in the next section, "Getting the Right Data from Log Files."

As you do network log analysis, you will discover that reviewing the "bad" log entries is often insufficient. Sometimes you will also want to look through the original log file to see other entries from the same source IP address, for example, or to look for other activity that occurred immediately before or after the event in question. If you save only "bad" log entries and do not preserve the raw logs, you lose the ability to analyze such events. Raw logs are sometimes required for evidentiary purposes, so saving them is often important.

Getting the Right Data from Log Files

As mentioned earlier, it's best to convert your binary log files to a text format such as tab-delimited or comma-separated values. After you have your log files in a suitable format, you want to find the pertinent log entries and generate a report. You can do this in two ways:

- Use a searching utility such as grep or sed to look through a log file for records that match or do not match particular strings or patterns.

- Import some or all of the data from the log files into a database and then search and analyze the data.

Determining which method to use depends on several factors, including your own preferences. Performance is a major consideration; if you have to process enormous numbers of records, you need to choose a method that can handle it. This is dependent on the number of log entries, the complexity of the searches and analysis you want to perform, and the tools and databases available to you. Databases have a distinct advantage because you can import logs into a database, store the data there, and run reports over days, weeks, or even months of data and significant events. This can identify suspicious activity that occurs over long periods of time, which might never be found by processing a day's worth of data at a time. It is also invaluable when performing incident handling because you can review previously logged events involving particular hosts or protocols.

Many different tools can be used to assist in log file processing. grep and sed are two useful text-searching tools from the UNIX world that have Windows equivalents. Programming languages such as Perl can be extremely powerful in parsing log files, selecting entries, and generating reports. If you have a small volume of logs, you might be able to import them in a spreadsheet and analyze them through macros, sorts, and searches. Microsoft Excel has a feature called AutoFilter that allows you to quickly sift through numerous rows of data. For larger volumes of logs or more complex logs, a full-fledged database might provide a robust and powerful solution that can analyze log entries and generate reports of suspicious activities.

Note

If you are a UNIX administrator who needs to perform log analysis on Windows systems, you might find that the task is much easier if you use a collection of cross-platform tools such as Cygwin (http://www.cygwin.com/), which provides a simulated UNIX environment, complete with many UNIX utilities, for Windows machines.

Be aware that it might take considerable time and resources to create a log analysis automation solution. You might need to write programs or scripts to perform the analysis and to generate reports based on the results of that analysis. For every hour you spend creating and testing a strong automation solution, you will save yourself many more hours in analysis time, and you will be able to react much more quickly when an incident occurs.

Automating Check Point FireWall-1 Log Analysis

After spending hours each day looking through FireWall-1 logs, I realized the need for a system to automate some of the mundane tasks of correlating and flagging suspicious records. Unfortunately, we did not have the budget to purchase a commercial log analysis solution, so I decided to do what I could with a custom Perl script. The script I wrote operated as follows:

- It extracted records from FireWall-1 log files.
- It parsed each entry to pull out relevant fields for all blocked packets.
- It counted the number of log entries for each source IP address, destination IP address, and destination port.
- It added record counts to numbers saved from previous runs.
- It generated a report that specified the top 20 addresses and ports the firewall blocked.

This relatively simple script made it easier for me to get a quick sense for the activity present in each day's logs, and it helped me detect low and slow scans that would not have come to my attention without maintaining a historical record of events.

Designing Reports

This might seem to be a silly question, but what do you want to report? Of course, you want to know what suspicious activity is occurring. But in many cases, it's ineffective to generate a single report of all suspicious activity. Some events are going to be much more significant than others in your environment by default, so you might want to emphasize them in your report and summarize the less interesting events. For example, if your daily logs typically include entries for a thousand port scans and two or three DNS exploit attempts, you probably want to see some details on the DNS attacks but only a summary of the port scan activity.

A key issue to consider is who will be receiving the report. If the report is just for you, then by all means, design it however you would like to. Perhaps, however, you are designing reports that will list suspicious activity for all of your organization's firewalls. Some system administrators might like a report of all events that involve their hosts that were logged by the firewall. The person who is responsible for web server security might like a report of suspicious web-related activity. It would also be nice to be able to do custom reports on demand, such as quickly generating a report of all events that were logged in the past two weeks involving a particular IP address. Such a capability would be extremely helpful when investigating an incident.

Using a Third-Party Analysis Product

Writing programs or scripts to analyze log files and generate reports might sound like a lot of work. Many times, it is, although it does give you a highly tailored solution. If creating your own automation system is not feasible, you might want to consider using a third-party product that will perform some log analysis and reporting for you. Or you might want to combine your own custom scripts with third-party products to create a solution.

Vendors such as ArcSight, e-Security, GuardedNet, Intellitactics, and NetForensics offer products called *security information management (SIM)* software that can be of great assistance to you in automating network log analysis. These products are designed to accept logs from various sources, including many brands of firewalls, intrusion detection systems, antivirus software, and operating systems. They can also accept generic text-based logs, such as ones you might create for other products with your own custom scripts. The SIM processes the log entries from all the sources to normalize the data into a consistent format and then performs event correlation and identifies likely intrusion attempts. SIM products offer other useful features, such as log archiving and extensive reporting functionality. You can save yourself many hours by using a SIM product as the heart of your network log analysis solution, but be warned that SIM products involve major software and hardware expenses.

Timestamps

The importance of timestamps in log files cannot be emphasized strongly enough. If an incident ever requires legal action and the timestamps in your log files are out of sync with the actual time, you might have difficulty proving that the incident occurred at a particular time. In many courts, you must be able to prove that your time source is reliable. A much more frequent problem is that you will have a difficult time correlating activities among different log files if all the log files are not synchronized to the same time. It's easy to compensate for this if two boxes are in adjacent time zones and are synched to be exactly an hour apart, but if you are dealing with 20 devices that are each seconds or minutes apart from each other, it becomes nearly impossible to correlate events effectively between any two logs, much less several of them.

The Network Time Protocol (NTP) can be used to perform time synchronization between many different devices on a network, as well as synchronizing the clocks on a network with a highly accurate NTP public time server. A detailed discussion of NTP is outside the scope of this book, but more information on it is available at many sites on the Internet, with the primary page at http://www.ntp.org/.

Hopefully, the logs you will be working with will have synchronized timestamps. However, if you are forced to work with logs that have unsynchronized timestamps, you can make the necessary adjustments to manually synchronize the logs. For example, you might be able to write a script that requests the current time from each logging device at the same time. It could then determine with a reasonable degree of accuracy (a few seconds) how far out of sync each box is. When the log files for that day are analyzed, the timestamps could be adjusted as necessary to bring all log entries to within a few seconds of being correctly synchronized. Of course, if you have a device that is drifting badly out of sync on a daily basis, you should probably be more concerned about taking care of its clock issues than synchronizing its log timestamps!

Note

It is generally recommended that if your organization's systems cover multiple time zones, you configure your systems to log everything using Greenwich Mean Time (GMT) to avoid confusion.

So far in this chapter, you have learned about the basics of log files and some of the fundamental concepts of log analysis. Now it's time to look at some real-world analysis examples. For the rest of this chapter, you will examine classes of devices: routers, network firewalls and packet filters, and host-based firewalls and intrusion detection systems. We will go through several log examples by studying a particular log type's format, reviewing a real example of that log format, and explaining how it can be analyzed. By the time you reach the end of the chapter, you will have a great exposure to how to analyze logs and identify suspicious and malicious activity. Let's start our journey by looking at router logs.

Analyzing Router Logs

Compared to other log files you will look at in this chapter, router logs tend to contain only the most basic information about network traffic. That makes sense because routers are typically processing high volumes of traffic and only examine the most basic characteristics of packets and connections when making routing decisions. However, this doesn't mean that router logs are not valuable; on the contrary, they can be extremely helpful in identifying certain types of activity, such as unauthorized connection attempts and port scans. Although the focus in this section will be on Cisco router logs, we will also briefly look at what information other routers log, which tends to be roughly the same.

Cisco Router Logs

In Chapter 2, "Packet Filtering," we discussed Cisco routers in depth, including how their logging capabilities can be configured. All Cisco routers use the same basic log file format. The following is an entry from a Cisco router log:

```
Jan 28 03:15:26 [10.20.30.40] 265114: %SEC-6-IPACCESSLOGP: list 105 denied
➡tcp 172.30.128.12(1947) -> 10.20.1.6(80), 1 packet
```

The format of the log entries requires a bit of explanation. After starting with a date and timestamp, the entry lists the router IP address and the message sequence number. The next entry, `%SEC-6-IPACCESSLOGP`, requires a bit more explanation. The `SEC-6` indicates that this is a security-related entry of severity level 6; the `IPACCESSLOGP` refers to the specific message type. The remaining fields are the ACL that matched this activity, the action performed, the IP protocol, the source IP address, the TCP source port, the destination IP address, the TCP destination port, and the number of packets. (Cisco routers use a similar format for UDP and ICMP packets.)

> **Note**
>
> If you're already familiar with Cisco router logs, you might look at this example and think that the format doesn't match your Cisco router's logs. That's entirely possible; aspects of the log format are configurable. For example, many logs contain an additional time value that indicates the router uptime. Some logs also have a GMT offset value at the end of each entry.

As you can see, only the most basic information is logged. In this example, you know the IP addresses and the TCP ports that were used, but that's about it. This entry tells us that an attempt to initiate a connection to port 80 on host 10.20.1.6 was blocked. Port 80 is most commonly used for HTTP.

By itself, this router log entry doesn't give us much information, just that someone probably tried to connect to the host for HTTP and that the router blocked the connection. However, think about what it would mean if you saw thousands of entries like this one in your router log, each one targeting TCP port 80 on a different destination host. Then, based on these log entries alone, you would have strong reason to believe that someone was scanning your entire network, looking for web servers.

Other Router Logs

Other brands of routers tend to log approximately the same information that Cisco routers do. Some routers may also log a few additional fields that are helpful in performing analysis, such as the size of each packet and the TCP flags that were set (if applicable). In most cases, though, you will not have that additional information in router logs—just the most fundamental characteristics of the packets.

Although all your router logs will contain important information, the most significant logs to check are probably from your border routers. If a border router denies a request from an external host, only that router can contain a corresponding log entry; devices that are further inside your network will never see the traffic. Therefore, that router's log is the only place you can see evidence of the denied request. Border router logs are a rich source of information on failed scans, probes, and attacks that never reach other areas of your network. Your network firewall logs are another great source of intrusion data.

Analyzing Network Firewall Logs

Dozens of different network firewall solutions are available, each with a unique logging format. Some such devices log little information about traffic—approximately the same information that most routers log. Other firewalls are capable of recording a great deal of detail about the traffic they monitor. As you will see in the examples that follow, the variety in the amount of information logged has a large impact on how deeply you can analyze incidents and suspicious activity. We have chosen to review the log formats of some of the firewalls that were discussed in Chapter 3, "Stateful Firewalls": the Cisco PIX, Check Point FireWall-1, and IPTables.

Cisco PIX Logs

The Cisco PIX firewall logs events of interest in the following format:

```
Jan 28 03:10:04 [10.20.30.50] %PIX-2-106001: Inbound TCP connection denied from
➥172.30.128.12/1938 to 10.20.12.34/53 flags SYN on interface outside
```

Take a moment to compare the format of this entry with that of the Cisco routers. Although the two have some similarities, they are different in certain ways as well. Whereas the Cisco router logs simply refer to the rule number that caused the entry to be logged, the Cisco PIX provides a detailed text-based explanation as to why this traffic was recorded. Also, note that the Cisco PIX records the TCP flags in its log entry, but the Cisco router does not. Because you're already familiar with the Cisco router log format, the rest of the Cisco PIX log format should be self-explanatory.

Let's practice log analysis a little more formally by examining the Cisco PIX log entry excerpt. What can be determined about the nature of this event based solely on the log entry? Of course, you know what date and time the event occurred. You can see which of your hosts was the target of the event and what the IP address of the potential attacker is. You know which firewall logged the activity, which might be helpful in determining why the traffic was blocked because you can examine that particular firewall's rule set. In addition, the log shows that the traffic was blocked trying to enter the firewall from an external interface. All this information helps you investigate the event and correlate it with logs on other devices.

One of the reasons that correlation is so important is that it's difficult to determine the nature of this event based on just this log entry. You can see that the blocked connection attempt had a destination of TCP port 53, which is typically associated with DNS traffic. Attackers often target TCP port 53 to get information from DNS servers or to attack vulnerabilities in those servers. However, there's not enough data here to make that assumption; a misconfiguration or another benign reason could cause this activity. By correlating this log entry with other logs—particularly a network intrusion detection sensor that saw this attempt—you can make a better determination as to the significance of this event.

Check Point FireWall-1 Logs

Check Point's FireWall-1 is another popular network firewall product. Check Point has a utility called SmartView Tracker that can be used to review logs from several security products, including FireWall-1. SmartView Tracker provides a GUI interface that displays the log entries in a table format. Some of the fields included in FireWall-1 log entries are listed next:

- The log entry number
- The date
- The time
- The interface that saw the activity
- The device that saw this activity
- The type of log entry
- The action that was performed (such as "block")

- The destination port number or service name
- The source IP address or hostname
- The destination IP address or hostname
- The protocol of the logged packet (such as "udp")
- The rule in the firewall's rule base that is associated with the log entry
- The source port number or service name
- Additional information that might be applicable to the log entry

You might look at the order of these fields and think that it's rather peculiar. Most devices list the source IP address and port together and then the destination IP address and port together; the FireWall-1 format is quite different. However, there's a good reason for this. Think of what information you, as a log analyst, are typically most interested in. You want to know what the target was; that is listed in the destination address and port, which in most cases will correspond to a particular protocol, such as HTTP or DNS. From an analyst's point of view, it makes a great deal of sense to pair the action with the destination service because they are often related. The source port, which is often not a factor when analyzing traffic, is not listed with the more pertinent data. Although this arrangement might be confusing at first, at least now you understand why it might be done that way.

IPTables Logs

In Chapter 3, we discussed IPTables. As you will see, IPTables logs more comprehensively than the other firewalls reviewed in this section:

```
Jan 28 03:09:31 mybox kernel: Packet log: IN=ppp0 OUT=
➥MAC=xx:xx:xx:xx:xx:xx:xx:xx:xx:xx:xx:xx:xx:xx SRC=172.30.128.12
➥DST=10.20.1.121 LEN=80 TOS=0x00 PREC=0x00 TTL=55 ID=13492
➥PROTO=UDP SPT=1907 DPT=27374 LEN=60
```

Here's a quick interpretation of the fields in this log entry: date, time, IPTables hostname, Syslog level, incoming and outgoing interfaces, MAC addresses, source IP address, destination IP address, packet length (LEN), type of service (TOS), TOS precedence (PREC), time to live (TTL), IP identification number (ID), IP protocol, source port, destination port, and IP payload length (LEN). You may have noticed that the outgoing interface value is blank; this indicates that the packet was received locally.

Not only does IPTables log all the information that the Cisco PIX and Check Point FireWall-1 do, but it also logs several other fields that are helpful in performing advanced log analysis. If you are highly experienced with network intrusion detection, you probably already know how valuable this data can be when identifying the nature of an attack, as well as the characteristics of the attacker.

Analyzing Host-Based Firewall and IDS Logs

So far, we have discussed performing analysis on logs from network firewalls and routers. These devices are monitoring connections to and from many different hosts. Now let's turn our attention to host-based firewalls and intrusion detection systems, which also record suspicious network activity, but only involve a single host. Such systems are most often installed on workstations. They are discussed in Chapter 10, "Host Defense Components."

Host-based firewall and IDS software often records activity that is otherwise unnoticed by network devices. For example, a firewall that only logs denied or rejected traffic won't keep a record of a connection that it permits to an internal host. In such a case, the internal host is the only device that might record the activity if it is using a firewall and/or IDS that is configured to reject and log such an attempt. Also, in many environments, few restrictions are placed on connections between hosts on the internal network; host-based network logs might be the only way that some malicious activity between internal hosts is recorded.

ZoneAlarm

The format of ZoneAlarm logs is easy to understand. By default, ZoneAlarm records all its information in a comma-separated value format in a text file called `ZAlog.txt`. (ZoneAlarm can also generate tab- and semicolon-separated log files.) Following are sample log entries for blocked TCP, UDP, and ICMP activity, respectively:

```
FWIN,2004/11/28,03:47:43 -6:00 GMT,172.30.128.23:15384,10.20.84.167:80,TCP
➥(flags:S)
FWIN,2004/11/28,03:57:46 -6:00 GMT,172.30.128.23:3283,10.20.84.167:3283,UDP
FWIN,2004/11/28,04:06:30 -6:00 GMT,172.30.128.23:0,10.20.84.167:0,ICMP
➥(type:8/subtype:0)
```

By now, this format should be pretty easy for you to decipher. The first address and port number are for the source; the second pair is for the destination. The FWIN label indicates that the firewall blocked traffic in the entry and that it was incoming. Lines that begin with FWOUT indicate that outgoing traffic was blocked. Finally, lines that start with PE indicate that the ZoneAlarm user has permitted a particular application's traffic to pass through the firewall.

Although you don't see much detailed information in each entry, remember that these entries are being recorded on a particular host. If ZoneAlarm is being run on a user's workstation, odds are good that the workstation offers few or no services and that there are only a few ports on which it might legitimately be contacted. ZoneAlarm should be configured to permit those connections and to reject and record any other incoming connection attempts, which are almost certainly caused by misconfigured or unauthorized equipment or software, mistakes such as a typo in an address, or malicious activity.

Each ZoneAlarm log by itself can contain valuable information. These logs become much more useful when they are gathered together from many different hosts. If most or all of your workstations are using host-based firewalls and you can monitor all of their firewall logs, you can get a great picture of what suspicious activities are occurring within your network. Check Point, the manufacturer of ZoneAlarm, sells a product called Integrity (http://www.checkpoint.com/products/integrity/) that facilitates centralized logging and has other features that are extremely helpful to analysts. There are also free utilities available for performing intrusion analysis and report generation with ZoneAlarm log data; examples include VisualZone (http://www. visualizesoftware.com/) and ZoneLog Analyser (http://zonelog.co.uk/).

Here's an interesting entry from a ZoneAlarm log:

```
FWIN,2004/12/01,22:30:51 -5:00 GMT,172.30.128.198:22,10.20.84.94:22,TCP
➡(flags:SF)
```

You can see that this blocked connection was intended to target TCP port 22 on host 10.20.84.94. SSH usually utilizes this port, so this looks like an attempt to find or use an SSH server. Can you tell whether this is a benign or malicious activity?

There are two telltale signs in this log entry. The more obvious one is that the SYN and FIN flags are both set, which is a classic sign of malicious activity. The less obvious one is that the source port is also set to 22. In a normal SSH connection, you should see a high source port and destination port 22. Because the source port is also set to 22, this is almost certainly crafted traffic that is malicious in nature. Just through this single log entry, you can determine that an attacker is hoping to exploit SSH vulnerabilities on this host.

Norton Personal Firewall

Norton Personal Firewall records information similar to ZoneAlarm. However, like several other personal firewalls, Norton Personal Firewall does not automatically log to a text file. Instead, it provides a GUI log viewer that displays events and permits administrators to export logs to text files. The text files have a simple comma-separated format: date, user, message, and details. The log excerpt shown next is easy to understand without additional explanation. It records an attempt to connect to port 27374 on the local workstation, which is not an available port on this host:

```
12/4/2004 4:02:26 PM,Supervisor,"Rule ""Default Block Backdoor/SubSeven
➡Trojan horse"" blocked (172.30.128.23,27374).",
➡"Rule ""Default Block Backdoor/SubSeven Trojan horse"" blocked
➡(172.30.128.101,27374).  Inbound TCP connection
➡Local address,service is (MYSYSTEM(172.30.128.23),27374)
➡Remote address,service is (172.30.128.101,1380)
➡Process name is ""N/A"""
```

Here's a great example of a potential incident that has been recorded in a Norton Personal Firewall log. Take a few minutes to review these entries and to get as much information about the incident from them as you can:

```
12/4/2004 4:13:50 PM,Supervisor,Unused port blocking has blocked
➥communications.,"Unused port blocking has blocked communications.
➥Inbound TCP connection   Remote address,local service is
➥(172.30.128.101,http-proxy(8080))"

12/4/2004 4:13:50 PM,Supervisor,Unused port blocking has blocked
➥communications.,"Unused port blocking has blocked communications.
➥Inbound TCP connection   Remote address,local service is
➥(172.30.128.101,http(80))"

12/4/2004 4:13:50 PM,Supervisor,Unused port blocking has blocked
➥communications.,"Unused port blocking has blocked communications.
➥Inbound TCP connection   Remote address,local service is
➥(172.30.128.101,3128)"

12/4/2004 4:13:50 PM,Supervisor,Unused port blocking has blocked
➥communications.,"Unused port blocking has blocked communications.
➥Inbound TCP connection   Remote address,local service is
➥(172.30.128.101,socks(1080))"
```

Are you finished with your review? Let's take another look at the log entries to see what they're trying to tell us. Here are the key pieces of information and their significance:

- All four log entries show the same source IP address. If you saw one attempt from the source address, it could be an accident; however, four separate attempts are much more likely to be malicious activity than an accident.

- All four connection attempts occurred within the same second. This indicates that the activity was almost certainly automated or scripted. It also gives you more proof that this activity is purposeful, not accidental.

- The destination ports—8080, 80, 3128, and 1080—might not all look familiar to you. Fortunately, Norton Personal Firewall tries to assist your analysis by listing the name of the service typically found at each common port. The three identified services are all web related, and a quick check of any good ports list shows that the fourth port, 3128, is also often used for web-related services.

Based on these three points, it appears that this log has recorded a scan by a single host for web-related services. If the source address is external, you might want to consider restricting incoming traffic to block such attempts in the future, only permitting incoming traffic on the necessary ports to those hosts that are authorized to provide web services to external hosts. It's also likely that other hosts on your network were scanned; therefore, correlating this activity by checking your other network log files for similar events is highly recommended.

Initially, most host-based firewalls had minimal IDS capabilities, if any. Host-based firewalls logged blocked connections, but they didn't do any analysis of the activity that they saw, and couldn't determine the likely intent of a connection attempt or packet. As host-based firewalls have evolved, they have incorporated basic intrusion detection principles to attempt to identify the intent of apparently unwanted connection attempts.

The IDS capabilities of host-based firewalls can save you time when you perform an analysis. For example, by listing the service most often associated with a certain port, host-based firewalls reduce the need to look up port numbers. The text descriptions that explain why the event was logged also facilitate easy searching and log automation. From an analysis standpoint, it's definitely advantageous to have intrusion detection capability built in to host-based firewalls.

Summary

Throughout this chapter, you learned of the many valuable roles that network file log analysis plays in a strong perimeter defense. By automating most of the log analysis and reviewing the reports generated by the automation, you can quickly gain insight into activity on your network and respond much more quickly to events that have just occurred or are in progress. Network log analysis can be of great assistance in such diverse areas as intrusion detection, incident handling, and problem troubleshooting. With an initial investment of time to familiarize yourself with typical log entries and to establish log analysis automation, you can make network log analysis an integral part of your perimeter defenses.

21

Troubleshooting Defense Components

BAD THINGS HAPPEN. IT DOESN'T MATTER HOW much time and effort your team has spent researching, designing, implementing, and maintaining your network security architecture; something is going to break. That's why having a strong troubleshooting methodology is important to your success as a network security practitioner.

Troubleshooting is simply a diagnostic process that is applied to a problem to fix it. "Symptoms" are gathered to determine the cause and solution for network security problems. These symptoms usually start out at a very general level ("Why can't I connect to a server?") and progress to more specific symptoms ("Why can I connect to other servers and not this one?") until the root cause of the problem is discovered and fixed.

Instead of trying to cover a selection of network security products and hoping they apply to your environment, in this chapter we focus on general troubleshooting techniques in the context of sample problems. Much of this chapter is spent applying a set of basic tools to gather the necessary input for your troubleshooting progression. We apply a hands-on approach to help you develop a methodology and toolkit that will work effectively in any environment.

The Process of Troubleshooting

Troubleshooting is a problem-solving process that many find rewarding. In general, it revolves around proving or disproving hypotheses. The following steps are all part of the troubleshooting process:

1. Collect symptoms.
2. Review recent changes.
3. Form a hypothesis.
4. Test the hypothesis.
5. Analyze the results.
6. Repeat if necessary.

You probably already apply some form of this process whenever you sit down to solve a problem. You gather information and formulate a hypothesis, whether consciously or not, by simply thinking of a pertinent question to ask. The answer either strengthens or weakens the proof and helps you move on to the next question.

Let's consider these steps in the context of an example in which Internet users can no longer access their company website. You have learned of this issue via a call to the company helpdesk from an outside user complaining that she can no longer remotely connect to the site. It's time to gather some facts to see if we can get to the root of the problem.

Collecting Symptoms

Collecting symptoms seems like an obvious step in the troubleshooting process, but sometimes it's easy to jump into solving a problem before you really understand what the problem is. You can often save a lot of time by slowing down the process and confirming the symptoms before proceeding further. Try to re-create the problem (unless the results are catastrophic, of course). If you can re-create the problem, you will have an easier time later determining whether your solution actually fixes it. Also, check whether your client or server software includes debug options that might help you collect more specific symptoms.

After talking to the outside user, we now know that the main symptom for the website problem is that the browser times out after a while and presents a message saying that the server is unavailable. Other calls have also been received from outside users, so this isn't a contained problem for one user. To verify this symptom, we try to connect to the troubled server from the outside as well, using a dial-up Internet connection. We are also unable to connect to the site, so this appears to be a problem that affects all outside users. In addition, we try to access the server locally. It works fine, which suggests that this is probably not a server problem. Because the symptoms haven't given us a definitive answer yet, let's consider things that might have recently changed in our environment that could shed some light on the situation.

Reviewing Recent Changes

Reviewing recent changes is included as a separate step in the troubleshooting process, because the cause of so many problems can be traced back to a recent change to the environment. Obviously, recent changes must be considered if they coincide with the problem timeframe. In fact, you should consider these changes even if they don't at first seem to relate to the problem. Often, a change uncovers problems that existed before, but didn't manifest themselves. A popular example of this is a server change that doesn't present itself until the first time the server is rebooted. Depending on the circumstances and your environment, you may be able to remove the change immediately and worry about understanding the real cause later. As far as our sample problem goes, we do some research and determine that a firewall protecting the web server's network segment was replaced with a new firewall about the time the problem started. We need more information before we can fix it. To get more information, we need to formulate a hypothesis to pursue.

Forming a Hypothesis

If you like puzzles, you might enjoy this part of troubleshooting—that is, unless you are under severe pressure to fix the problem. This is where the troubleshooting gurus really shine. Your mission is to combine all your observations, experience, intuition, and prayers to come up with a fix for the problem. You do this by first hypothesizing the cause of the problem and then working to prove it. If you can't guess a specific cause, try the reverse approach. Form a hypothesis and then work to disprove it. This is a good way to collect additional symptoms or other pertinent information.

Let's continue with the example in which our users can't access the website after a firewall upgrade. An obvious hypothesis is that we somehow configured the firewall rule set incorrectly, and it's blocking inbound HTTP access to our web server. The next step is to test that hypothesis.

Testing the Hypothesis

Ideally, you test your hypothesis by implementing a fix for the problem, which is the most direct way to prove or disprove it. However, you might still be working to narrow the possible causes of the problem, in which case a fix is not yet apparent. In that event, you might design and execute a series of tests to gather information until a specific fix presents itself or until you're forced to try a different hypothesis.

Our firewall problem isn't in the "fix-it" stage yet because we're still investigating whether the firewall rule set is the problem. Perhaps the easiest way to test that hypothesis is to look at the firewall configuration and logs to see whether the traffic is being blocked. A quick check shows that the configuration is correct, and the log shows that HTTP traffic is being allowed through.

Analyzing the Results

After you have executed your test, the next step is to analyze the results. If your test involved implementing a fix, such as rearranging the firewall's rule set, then all you need to do is check whether the problem is resolved. This process will be much easier if you are able to reproduce the problem. If the problem isn't fixed yet, you will need to analyze the test results to determine what to do next.

We tested our hypothesis that our firewall rule set was incorrect and found that it was not blocking HTTP traffic to the server. We might not have completely disproved the hypothesis, but we should look at other possibilities. We will have to continue troubleshooting the problem to get to its root cause and fix it.

Repeating If Necessary

If the problem is solved, your work is done. Otherwise, you will have to perform another iteration of the process. If your test disproved your hypothesis, you must continue by forming and testing another hypothesis. Otherwise, you will have to design another test whose results you can analyze to further narrow the possible causes. This is the nature of most problems, which aren't often solved by the first pass through the troubleshooting process.

We have completed one iteration for our sample firewall problem without solving it. Maybe you would have started with another hypothesis, or you already have another test in mind for gathering more information. To learn whether you're right, however, you have to read more of the chapter to finish the diagnosis!

Troubleshooting Rules of Thumb

Before moving on to describe troubleshooting tools, we want to present a few important rules of thumb to keep in mind while working on a problem. Utilizing proven techniques keeps your troubleshooting process on track and prevents it from resulting in false positives or incorrect results. The concepts we cover in this section will help keep your hypotheses focused on the problem and you on track.

Make Only One Change at a Time

This is perhaps the most important rule, and it can be the hardest to follow when you're in a hurry. You can refer to as many sources of information as you like, but don't make multiple changes at the same time. Otherwise, you will end up not knowing for sure which change fixed the problem. Worse, you might mask the solution with another problem.

While troubleshooting our sample firewall problem, we moved the client station between external and internal locations, and although we examined the firewall configuration, we didn't make any changes to it. As a result, we know that the problem depends on the client location. If we had changed the firewall rule set while moving our client's test location, we might have incorrectly deduced that the problem was related to a change we made in our rule set and not the location of the client.

Keep an Open Mind

We can't overstress the importance of keeping an open mind when working on a tough problem. Most people, especially experienced troubleshooters, tend to reason through many problem aspects at an almost unconscious level. Have you ever had trouble explaining a conclusion to someone who is trying to understand how you arrived at it? Sometimes those conclusions are sound, born of past experiences that aren't easily recalled, but have been internalized in your own rules of thumb. Sometimes, though, these conclusions are influenced by inaccurate perceptions, false assumptions, personal motivations, and a host of other human traits. If you believe you made no mistakes configuring the firewall—a natural assumption—you might not do a good job of examining the configuration. If you can, work with another troubleshooter to give each other a fresh perspective.

Get a Second Opinion

Sometimes when you can't see the solution to a problem, you need a second set of eyes. Bouncing a situation off of a peer can be a great help when you think that you hit a dead end while troubleshooting a problem. Just the process of methodically explaining to someone else the steps you have gone through can be enough to help you find holes in your own troubleshooting methodology. In any case, brainstorming can be a powerful troubleshooting tool, and it is indispensable when a solution is difficult to find.

Stay Focused on Fixing the Problem

If you subscribe to our philosophy, a problem isn't truly fixed until you understand what caused it. If you don't understand a problem, it's likely to reappear in the future. Obviously, the way that you apply this philosophy should be based on the context of the situation. It's often easier to fix a problem than explain how it happened. If the problem is causing your users pain, fix it and finish debugging it later.

We might easily fix the firewall problem, for example, by hooking back up the original firewall. If the outside caller was a paying customer who was complaining about the web server being inaccessible, we would certainly choose that route. In that case, the quick fix would justify the extra difficulty we might face in trying to finish the diagnosis offline or with a different network configuration.

Don't Implement a Fix That Further Compromises Your Security

This is usually worth some thought. Hopefully, you wouldn't diagnose a fiber-optic problem by staring at the end of the cable. Also, the pain associated with a fix doesn't always arrive immediately, especially when you're fixing security problems. All too often, in an effort to get something working, security is put on the back burner. In the long run, this can be a greater liability than the original issue was. For example, you shouldn't fix a firewall problem by installing a "permit everything" at the top of the rule set. When something is broken and Service Level Agreements (SLAs) are in jeopardy—or worse, your job security is looming in the balance—it can be easy to implement a fix that compromises your company's security. Always be sure to consider the security implications of any fix that you apply and consider ways to mitigate any security concerns it may introduce to your environment. For example, if you need to add a firewall rule to allow access that wasn't previously allowed, enable logging on the rule and audit activity for that rule regularly after it is implemented.

The Obvious Problems Are Often Overlooked

How much time have you wasted diagnosing connectivity problems, finding the source to be the improper use of a crossover cable? Start with the simplest hypotheses first and work your way up to the most complex.

Document, Document, Document!

Finally, one of the most important things you can do to improve your success as a troubleshooter is to document fixes and causes of your problems in a personal "knowledgebase." How many times are you faced with a problem and have a peculiar feeling of déjà vu? You know that you have seen this issue before, but you just can't seem to remember what the cause was—or more importantly, what you did to fix it. By recording problems, their solutions, and causes in a searchable database, you may save yourself a lot of time.

Ideally, knowledgebase entries should not only include the description of the problem and cause, but also a step-by-step explanation of the solution, covering in great detail all the information needed to recover from the problem successfully. Also, facts should be included that will help identify the initial incident, such as location, involved products, the time when it occurred, and the party who logged the knowledgebase entry. You should make an effort to enter any facts that will help in the search for the problem when you face it again. With that in mind, if possible make all these information fields searchable. Although this can make for slow searches and a lot of space used by index files, it will be easier to track down an event by the most minute of remembered details.

No matter what methods you rely on, it is important to develop a troubleshooting methodology that works for you. Your methodology will depend on your own responsibilities, strengths, and weaknesses. We have provided some food for thought to help you develop or improve your personal methodology, but so far we have omitted a core component: the tools. We will spend the next section covering popular tools that you can utilize to help make your troubleshooting process more efficient.

The Troubleshooter's Toolbox

In this section, we present some of our favorite tools and techniques for troubleshooting security-related and network problems.

The tools in this section are organized by the TCP/IP layers to which they apply; that way, you can pick and choose between them depending on the kind of problem you are addressing. You will see that some of the tools apply to multiple layers, which represents the nature of most troubleshooting efforts. You will also learn how the tools can help you zero in on a particular layer, depending on the problem symptoms.

UNIX vs. Windows Tools

Many of the tools we examine in this chapter are available for Windows as well as UNIX-based operating systems. When tools aren't included in a default installation, we include URLs where you can download them.

If you see a UNIX tool that you do not think exists under Windows, don't despair; open source UNIX environments are available for Windows. One of the most popular ones is Cygwin, which was developed by Red Hat and uses a DLL to provide a UNIX emulation layer with substantial UNIX API functionality. You can download Cygwin from http://www.cygwin.com. A user guide is provided at http://www.cygwin.com/cygwin-ug-net/cygwin-ug-net.html. You will find many useful tools have been ported to Cygwin that would otherwise be unavailable under Windows.

Another popular way to take advantage of the power of UNIX-based tools in non-UNIX environments is through the use of self-booting UNIX CD-ROM or floppy disks. There are *many* selections available, with quite a few featuring very useful networking and security tools. These include the following:

- Trinux (http://trinux.sourceforge.net/)
- F.I.R.E. (http://fire.dmzs.com/)
- PHLAK (http://www.phlak.org)
- ThePacketMaster (http://www.thepacketmaster.com/)

All these tools are self-contained on a CD-ROM or floppy disk and require no installation. Simply boot from the disk and you will be running a total Linux environment loaded with a full array of precompiled network and security tools.

You no longer have to be a UNIX guru to take advantage of the power of UNIX-based troubleshooting tools!

Application Layer Troubleshooting

First, let's look at some tools that can assist with troubleshooting problems at the application layer. This layer primarily addresses issues that arise on the local machine, such as configuration file locations and missing link libraries. Another area that can be problematic is the Domain Name System (DNS). Applications query DNS to resolve hostnames to IP addresses; therefore, if the DNS server isn't responding for some reason, applications that use hostnames as opposed to IP addresses cannot function.

Often the client software used for the applications can be useful in debugging problems. Most email clients, for example, include menu items to view all the message headers, which can be invaluable in determining where an email came from, to whom it was addressed, and so on. You might use a client combined with other tools to dig into the actual network traffic that is associated with the application. A couple tool classes that are especially worth mentioning are DNS query tools and system call trace utilities. Nslookup is a common DNS query tool, whereas common trace utilities include strace, ktrace, and truss. A couple other useful tools in this category are strings and ldd.

Nslookup

Many application communication problems are associated with DNS. Applications query DNS through the resolver, which normally occurs transparently to the end user of the application. DNS is always a good place to start troubleshooting when your application can't connect to a remote host by its name. First, make sure that IP address connectivity is successful and then verify that the hostname you are attempting to contact maps to the IP address it is supposed to. You can do this by using a tool to query the DNS. Perhaps the most common DNS query tool is nslookup, which is available on both UNIX and Windows NT and higher. It can be most helpful in diagnosing application layer connectivity problems involving your secure network architecture.

> **Note**
>
> Although we focus on the cross-platform tool nslookup in this section, UNIX platforms offer another tool—dig. Dig provides more information with fewer keystrokes after you get used to its syntax, and it's a fine substitute for nslookup if it's available.

UNIX-based operating systems provide a Network Name Switch (NSS), whereby the functions used to query the resolver can first check a local file before issuing a DNS query. The search order is configurable on most UNIX variants through the use of the `/etc/nsswitch.conf` file, and the local file is in `/etc/hosts` by default. You must consider this when you're doing DNS troubleshooting.

Windows does not have a configurable NSS capability. The local file is always searched before DNS. The local file is located in `%SystemRoot%\hosts` on Windows 9x and in `%SystemRoot%\system32\drivers\etc\hosts` on Windows NT and higher. For new installs, you will find a `hosts.sam` (sample) file at that location, which you will have to rename or copy to `hosts` (without the extension). Don't edit the `hosts.sam` file and expect it to work!

For example, suppose you're trying to use SSH to access an external server by name, and the command simply hangs without establishing a connection. This could indicate a problem with DNS or with your NSS configuration. You can use nslookup to bypass the NSS and query DNS directly, as follows:

```
$ ssh www.extdom.org
never connects, no error messages, nothing
^C
$ nslookup www.extdom.org
Server:        192.168.1.2
Address:       192.168.1.2

Non-authoritative answer:
Name:   www.extdom.org
Address: 192.168.2.100
```

The nslookup query puts www.extdom.org at 192.168.2.100, which in this case is correct.

If you're working from a UNIX host, check `/etc/nsswitch.conf`, as follows, to determine which name resolution facility the host uses:

```
$ grep hosts /etc/nsswitch.conf
hosts:    files nisplus nis dns
```

The `hosts` line indicates that local files are checked before other name services, including DNS. This means that if an entry exists in `/etc/hosts` for www.extdom.org, it will be used in preference to DNS. Check `/etc/hosts`, as follows:

```
$ grep www.extdom.org /etc/hosts
192.168.2.111          www.extdom.org
```

Because the entry doesn't match the DNS information we obtained earlier, we clearly have the wrong address in the `/etc/hosts` file. The administrator might have switched the web server to a different host, justifiably thinking that he could notify the world of the change through DNS. Although you could modify `/etc/nsswitch.conf` to change the NSS search order, it's often handy to override name resolution through local files. The best fix for this problem is probably to delete the entry in `/etc/hosts`.

> **Tip**
>
> A quick way to determine which address an application is using, without examining the `/etc/`
> `nsswitch.conf` and `/etc/hosts` files, is to ping the target host. Ping does not query DNS directly
> like nslookup does, so it goes through the NSS to get the destination IP address and then prints this to the
> screen, even if a firewall blocks its packets. If you're executing it on Solaris, you will have to specify the `-n`
> switch to see the IP address. Also, remember that NSS operates differently on Windows, where it checks the
> local file and DNS and then tries to resolve the NetBIOS name.

System Call Trace Utilities

System call trace utilities monitor the OS calls that an application executes and print the
details to the console or a specified output file. This can be a great way to find out
where an application looks for its configuration files. Suppose that you install the binary
OpenSSH distribution for Solaris from http://www.sunfreeware.com and can't find in
the documentation where it hides its `sshd_config` file. Just run truss on the sshd executable:

```
# truss -o sshd.truss sshd
# grep conf sshd.truss
open("/usr/local/etc/sshd_config", O_RDONLY) = 3
open("/etc/netconfig", O_RDONLY)       = 3
open("/etc/nsswitch.conf", O_RDONLY)    = 3
```

Here, we saved the truss output (which is usually voluminous) to `sshd.truss` and then
searched for anything that looks like a configuration name. This example shows sshd trying to open the file at `/usr/local/etc/sshd_config`. If you browse the truss output,
you will see a wealth of other information about the application.

> **Tip**
>
> SGI IRIX includes the par utility, which produces system call activity. For similar functionality, HPUX admins
> can download the tusc program at ftp://ftp.cup.hp.com/dist/networking/tools/.

For non-Solaris operating systems, you can get the same type of information from the
strace and ktrace tools. Strace is usually distributed with Linux, and ktrace with BSD.

> **Tip**
>
> Look for an open source version of strace for Windows NT and higher at
> http://www.bindview.com/support/Razor/Utilities/. Take note of its shortcomings, however. To install strace,
> copy the `strace.exe` and `strace.sys` files from the zip archive to `%SystemRoot%`.

Other Useful Utilities

Other useful utilities for debugging problems at the application layer include the strings
and ldd utilities for UNIX. Strings outputs everything from a binary file that looks like a
printable string, which enables you to browse or search for interesting stuff. For example,

the following command executed on a Linux machine shows the Sendmail version to be 8.11.0. (We use the sed utility to filter out lines before the version.c string and after the next line beginning with @.) Tricks like this one can let you quickly gain access to information that you might have otherwise had to spend a considerably longer time researching.

```
# strings /usr/sbin/sendmail | sed -e '/version.c/,/^@/!d'
@(#)$Id: version.c,v 8.43.4.11 2000/07/19 20:40:59 gshapiro Exp $
8.11.0
@(#)$Id: debug.c,v 8.2 1999/07/26 04:04:09 gshapiro Exp $
```

Note

BinText is a Windows-based tool that does pretty much the same thing as the UNIX strings utility. It's free and can be downloaded from http://www.foundstone.com.

The ldd command prints shared library dependencies, which can come in handy when you're installing or copying executables. The following output shows all library dependencies are met for the TCP Wrappers daemon on an IRIX 6.5 machine:

```
$ ldd /usr/freeware/bin/tcpd
    libwrap.so.7 =>     /usr/freeware/lib32/libwrap.so.7
    libc.so.1 =>  /usr/lib32/libc.so.1
```

Troubleshooting Check Point FireWall-1 with FW Monitor

Like many firewalls, Check Point FireWall-1 only logs the initiating packet of any given network transaction. Because of this, there may be times when you want to see what FireWall-1 is doing with packets other then those that initiate a connection, or when you need to track down packets that are not showing up in the logs for some other reason. FireWall-1 has an integrated function to show all packets as they enter and leave any of its interfaces called FW Monitor. FW Monitor is run from the FireWall-1 enforcement point's command prompt. Simply type in fw monitor, followed by -e *expression*, where *expression* represents a capture filter that will cause only the specific traffic you are interested in seeing to be logged. It is advisable to use a capture filter on heavily used production firewalls to prevent the monitor process from overwhelming the firewall. Output of this command is very similar to Tcpdump, but with each line preceded by the interface the packet came in on and then a single letter—either i, I, o, or o. The i means that the packet is inbound before being processed by the FireWall-1 kernel, whereas I means the packet is inbound after passing through the FireWall-1 kernel. The o means the packet is outbound before the FireWall-1 kernel, and o means it is outbound after leaving the FireWall-1 kernel.[1] These additional pieces of information can be invaluable when troubleshooting dropped packets on your FireWall-1. For more information on FW Monitor, and specifics on how to build its capture filters, check out the article "How to use fw monitor," available at http://www.checkpoint.com/techsupport/downloads/html/ethereal/fw_monitor_rev1_01.pdf.

Case Study: Troubleshooting Check Point FireWall-1 SMTP Security Server

I once worked for a company that implemented a Check Point FireWall-1 as its main perimeter security device. Sometimes, taking advantage of the full potential of such a powerful piece of equipment can have a real learning curve! Check Point FireWall-1 includes an SMTP Security Server that enables firewall administrators to filter incoming mail or pass it off to a virus checker. The SMTP Security Server acts as a proxy, and it is invoked by defining a resource and rule to associate TCP port 25 (SMTP) traffic with the host that handles email. It offers a powerful mechanism for screening email messages and attachments before they enter your network.

At the time, I was not completely familiar with FireWall-1, and I simply defined a rule that allowed SMTP connections to our publicly accessible mail server. Later, I decided to define a resource and do some filtering on inbound mail. This worked fine. Then I decided to hide the publicly accessible server by changing the associated rule to accept SMTP connections to the firewall's external interface. Unfortunately, the firewall started blocking all inbound SMTP when we implemented the change. The reason was immediately apparent. I forgot to consider the DNS MX record for the domain. Here's how you can query an MX record with nslookup:

```
$ nslookup
> set type=mx
> zilchco.com
Server:  ns.s3cur3.com
Address:  192.168.111.1

zilchco.com ..., mail exchanger = mail-dmz.zilchco.com
> exit
```

Here, nslookup operates in interactive mode, allowing the user to set the query type for MX records. We see that the domain MX record points to mail-dmz.zilcho.com, which is the original email server. This means that everyone on the Internet will continue to send email for zilcho.com to the old server, which the firewall will now block. The solution is to add an A record for the external firewall interface and point the domain MX record to it. I chose to name it mail-gw, as shown in the following example:

```
$ nslookup
> set type=mx
> zilchco.com
Server:  ns.s3cur3.com
Address:  192.168.111.1

zilchco.com ..., mail exchanger = mail-gw.zilchco.com
> exit
```

Transport Layer Troubleshooting

The transport layer encompasses many of the problems with which you're likely to deal. The transport layer directly addresses connectivity issues associated with network services. In this section, we will describe the following tools:

- Telnet
- Netcat
- netstat
- lsof
- Fport and Active Ports
- hping
- Tcpdump

Our goal is to show you how to effectively use these tools to troubleshoot problems at the transport layer. As a result, most of the tools in this category test transport layer connectivity. A few of the tools display connection information for the host on which they are run. We have selected these tools because their value will likely lead you to use them over and over again.

Telnet

Telnet and its underlying protocol were developed so that local users could start a shell session on a remote host. Telnet uses TCP port 23 by default, but it's incredibly handy simply because it takes an optional command-line argument to specify the remote TCP port you want to connect to. In addition, the Telnet client is available on almost every platform, including many routers, making it an excellent troubleshooting tool to test TCP connectivity and service availability.

> **Note**
>
> Telnet is a TCP application and can only be used to test TCP connectivity and availability on hosts. If you need to troubleshoot services running on UDP, you will need to rely on another tool, such as Netcat or hping (covered later in this section).

The behavior of Telnet clients typically varies by OS. Whereas most Telnet versions that come with UNIX-type operating systems print an escape character message after the connection is established, followed by any header information that the server cares to return, Windows Telnet versions display a blank screen followed by the application-returned header information. Though the escape character (Ctrl+]) is not displayed after connection with the Windows version of client, it still works to terminate communications sessions. In either case, this provides a quick way to check whether the remote service is accessible. For example, suppose you're having trouble connecting with SSH to a remote server. To test whether the service is available, you can Telnet to port 22 on the server:

```
# telnet mail-dmz.zilchco.com 22
Trying 192.168.1.20...
Connected to mail-dmz.zilchco.com (192.168.1.20).
Escape character is '^]'.
```

```
SSH-2.0-OpenSSH_2.9
^]
telnet> quit
```

After the `Escape character is '^]'` message appears, you know that the connection is established, which is useful for services that don't return greetings.

> **Note**
>
> All examples of Telnet in this chapter will use a UNIX version that displays an escape character message after a connection is established. It is important that you understand the differences in expected output when troubleshooting with various distributions of Telnet clients.

In this case, a banner announces some details about the secure shell server. To break the connection, type `^]` (Ctrl+]) to get a `telnet>` prompt, from which you can end the session gracefully by typing `quit`. Now let's see how Telnet behaves when the remote service isn't available:

```
$ telnet mail-dmz.zilchco.com 21
Trying 192.168.1.20...
telnet: Unable to connect to remote host: Connection refused
```

FTP (port 21) is obviously not running on the server. Now for one more example; we have been going into all this detail for the grand finale, for which we pose the following puzzle:

```
# telnet mail-dmz.zilchco.com 143
Trying 192.168.1.20...
Connected to mail-dmz.zilchco.com (192.168.1.20).
Escape character is '^]'.
Connection closed by foreign host.
```

What is the meaning of this output? We established a connection to the IMAP service on port 143, but we never got a greeting before the connection terminated. This is almost always indicative of a service that is protected by TCP Wrappers. The tcpd daemon accepts the connection and then validates the client IP address against the `/etc/hosts.allow` and `/etc/hosts.deny` files to determine whether it's allowed to connect. If it's not, the tcpd daemon terminates the TCP session.

As you have seen in this section, Telnet makes an excellent troubleshooting tool. Realize that this functionality can be applied in two different ways:

- To verify service availability on a local or remote host
- To verify connectivity across a firewall or another access control device to an available service

It is important to realize that both components need to be tested for a solid troubleshooting methodology when testing connectivity across a firewall. For example, if you wanted to see if SQL was running on a host on the other side of a firewall from the host you were testing from, not only would connectivity need to be opened on the firewall, but SQL would need to be running on the remote host. Both of these points should be considered when troubleshooting a network connection. If a developer contacted you and complained that one of his web servers could not connect to its SQL back-end server across the firewall, your Telnet troubleshooting should be two-fold. First, you could attempt to access the SQL port (TCP 1433) of the back-end SQL server from a host that resides on the same segment. If this test doesn't work, you could conclude (because there are no access control devices between the two hosts) that the problem is on the back-end SQL server itself and your troubleshooting should continue there. If the Telnet test works, this proves that SQL is running properly and is available on the server. You could then attempt the same access from the web server experiencing the issue on the other side of the firewall. If the connectivity fails, you could infer that the traffic is being prevented in some way by the firewall. Taking advantage of both these techniques is an invaluable aid when troubleshooting Layer 3 connectivity.

Firewalls and Telnet Connection Testing

It is important to apply your knowledge of the way TCP/IP functions when you're using Telnet to troubleshoot Layer 3 connectivity across access control devices such as firewalls. If you attempt to connect with Telnet to a host on a given port and are rapidly returned a "connection refused" message, it is very likely that the service is not running on the host. However, if the "connection refused" response takes a while to be returned, it is very likely that the connectivity is being blocked by a firewall or the like. The reasons for these behaviors are easily explained if you have an understanding of standard TCP/IP communications. When a server receives a request for connection to a port that it is not "listening" on, it will immediately send back a reset packet to the originating host. This is the cause for the quick "connection refused" response. When a firewall is intercepting the traffic, its default behavior is to silently drop the packet and not send back any response. The originating host will try to re-send the packet several more times (as many as specified by its TCP implementation) until finally giving up. This is why the "connection refused" message takes so long to occur when the traffic is being dropped at a firewall.

Netcat

We doubt you will ever see a TCP/IP network troubleshooting discussion that doesn't include Netcat. The Netcat program, usually named *nc*, has several capabilities, but its core feature is probably the most useful—the ability to open a socket and then redirect standard input and standard output though it. Standard input is sent through the socket to the remote service. Anything that the socket receives is redirected to standard output. This simple capability is unbelievably useful, as we will show you in a moment. For now, you can become familiar with Netcat's other options by executing the command `nc -h`. You will see a source port option (`-p`), a listener option (`-l`), and a UDP option (`-u`).

You might also try connecting to a TCP service by executing `nc -v remotehostip port`. This allows Netcat to be used for service availability and connectivity testing, as was shown with Telnet earlier in this section. Note that you break a Netcat connection with Ctrl+C rather than Ctrl+]. Also, take notice of Netcat's support for UDP, making it a more complete troubleshooting solution. However, Netcat does not come with every operating system distribution like Telnet does. Also, Netcat employs additional capabilities that we will go over later in this section.

> **Note**
>
> Although Netcat started out as a UNIX tool, it has been ported to Windows. Netcat is included with most Linux and BSD distributions, but it might not be installed by default. You can download Netcat from http://www.securityfocus.com/tools/139.

Let's consider a situation in which an administrator is unable to query an external DNS server while troubleshooting another problem. You decide to investigate. You know that the organization uses a router to restrict Internet traffic, and you hypothesize that it has been configured to accept only DNS queries that originate from port 53. How do you find out? You choose a test case based on Netcat.

> **Note**
>
> DNS servers are sometimes configured to forward queries from source port 53, so router filters can be constructed to allow query responses without opening inbound UDP to all nonprivileged ports. Instead, only traffic destined for the DNS server IP address on UDP port 53 from the source port UDP 53 would be allowed. Otherwise, you would need to allow all UDP traffic with a port greater than 1023 to your DNS server. Of course, this wouldn't be necessary if the router supported reflexive ACLs, as described in Chapter 2, "Packet Filtering."

Most DNS queries are encapsulated in UDP datagrams. UDP, being a stateless transport protocol, does little validation of received datagrams and simply passes them on to the application. This means that the application must decide whether to respond to datagrams that don't make sense. DNS silently drops most such datagrams. We have to send a valid DNS query to receive a response and prove that source port 53 filtering is in place. Nslookup can't use source port 53, so we have to find another way. First, capture a query using Netcat and save it in a file:

> **Note**
>
> If you're running UNIX, as in the following example, you have to be logged in as root to bind port 53.

```
()
# nc -u -l -p 53 >dnsq &
# nslookup -timeout=5 www.yahoo.com localhost
^C
# kill %1
```

The background Netcat command listens on UDP port 53 (we assume this isn't a DNS server, which would already have port 53 bound) and redirects anything that is received to a file named dnsq. Then, Nslookup directs a query to localhost, so it's intercepted by

Netcat and written to the file named dnsq. Press Ctrl+C before the specified 5-second timeout to terminate Nslookup before it issues a second query. Then kill the background Netcat, which causes it to print the `punt!` message. If you have a hex editor, the contents of file `dnsq` should look something like this:

```
00000000    00 43 01 00   00 01 00 00   00 00 00 00   03 77 77 77   .C..........www
00000010    05 79 61 68   6F 6F 03 63   6F 6D 00 00   01 00 01      .yahoo.com.....
```

Finally, execute Netcat again to send the captured query using source port 53 to the remote DNS server and save any response to another file:

```
#nc -u -p 53 -w 10 dns_server 53 <dnsq >dnsr
```

The `-w` option specifies a timeout of 10 seconds; therefore, you don't have to terminate Netcat manually. If a response is received, the `dnsr` file will have a nonzero size and you will know that your hypothesis is correct: The router allows outbound DNS queries if the source port is 53.

Netstat

If you aren't already familiar with it, you will find the netstat utility invaluable in debugging several types of connectivity problems. It is distributed with all UNIX and Windows variants, but unfortunately its command-line options vary greatly. For additional information on netstat and its switches on your platform, look at the UNIX man page or `netstat /?` from the command line in Windows.

Use netstat to display information about transport layer services that are running on your machine and about active TCP sessions. This way, we can corroborate or disprove the information we gathered with Telnet regarding connectivity or service availability. We will also demonstrate other uses for netstat in subsequent sections. To display active connections and listening ports, use the `-a` switch and the `-n` switch to prevent hostname resolution and display IP addresses. With UNIX, you might also want to use the `-f inet` switch to restrict the display to TCP/IP sockets. As an example, here's the output from a hardened OpenBSD web server:

```
$ netstat -anf inet
Active Internet connections (including servers)
Proto Recv-Q Send-Q  Local Address           Foreign Address     (state)
tcp        0      0  192.168.111.99.22       192.168.111.88.33104     ESTABLISHED
tcp        0      0  192.168.111.99.22       *.*     LISTEN
tcp        0      0  192.168.111.99.80       *.*     LISTEN
tcp        0      0  192.168.111.99.443      *.*     LISTEN
```

We see the TCP and UDP port numbers displayed as the final "dot field" (for example, .22) in the Local Address column. Only three TCP services are running on the machine, as identified by the LISTEN state: SSH on TCP port 22, HTTP on TCP port 80, and HTTPS on TCP port 443. The SSH session has been established from 192.168.111.88.

The output from the command `netstat -a -n` looks a little different on a Windows XP system:

```
Active Connections

  Proto  Local Address         Foreign Address      State
  TCP    0.0.0.0:135           0.0.0.0:0            LISTENING
  TCP    0.0.0.0:445           0.0.0.0:0            LISTENING
  TCP    10.0.0.24:139         0.0.0.0:0            LISTENING
  TCP    10.0.0.24:2670        10.0.0.3:139         ESTABLISHED
  TCP    127.0.0.1:1025        0.0.0.0:0            LISTENING
  TCP    127.0.0.1:1027        0.0.0.0:0            LISTENING
  TCP    127.0.0.1:1032        0.0.0.0:0            LISTENING
  UDP    0.0.0.0:445           *:*
  UDP    0.0.0.0:500           *:*
  UDP    0.0.0.0:1026          *:*
  UDP    0.0.0.0:1204          *:*
  UDP    0.0.0.0:4500          *:*
  UDP    10.0.0.24:123         *:*
  UDP    10.0.0.24:137         *:*
  UDP    10.0.0.24:138         *:*
  UDP    10.0.0.24:1900        *:*
  UDP    127.0.0.1:123         *:*
  UDP    127.0.0.1:1900        *:*
  UDP    127.0.0.1:1966        *:*
```

Here the ports are listed after the colon following the local addresses. Otherwise, the display is pretty similar.

The Linux netstat command-line options are significantly different from those of most other UNIX variants. For example, you use `--inet` instead of `-f inet`. Windows doesn't include an `inet` option because that's the only address family its netstat can display.

As you can see, netstat is a powerful troubleshooting tool. It can be used in conjunction with a tool such as Telnet to confirm or disprove troubleshooting hypotheses. For example, let's say that, as in the last section, you attempt a Telnet connection across a firewall from a web server in the DMZ to a SQL server on your inside network and it fails. This would insinuate either that the service is not running on the server or that the firewall is blocking the connection. After logging in to the SQL server and running the `netstat -a -n` command, you receive the following output:

```
  Proto  Local Address        Foreign Address      State
  TCP    0.0.0.0:1433         0.0.0.0:0            LISTENING
```

This shows that the server is listening on TCP port 1433 (Microsoft SQL Server protocol) and is waiting for a connection. More then likely, the traffic is being blocked on its way in by the firewall. Firewall logs could be used to corroborate that hypothesis. However, what if you had received the following `netstat -a -n` output instead?

```
  Proto  Local Address        Foreign Address      State
  TCP    0.0.0.0:1433         0.0.0.0:0            LISTENING
  TCP    10.0.0.1:1433        172.16.1.3:1490      ESTABLISHED
```

This tells us that not only are we running the SQL service, but we are receiving SQL connection traffic from the host at address 172.16.1.3. If this was the "troubled" web host that could not connect, either some access control mechanism is blocking the return traffic or there is a routing issue from the SQL server to the web host that we need to investigate. If the listed host is another host that could connect successfully to the SQL server, the firewall may still be blocking traffic from our "troubled" web host. Learning how to combine the information gathered from multiple sources such as these is vital in the development of strong troubleshooting skills.

Lsof

The UNIX lsof utility can display everything covered by netstat, and much more. Unfortunately, lsof isn't part of most distributions.

If you can't find a trusted lsof binary distribution for your platform, you can get the source at ftp://vic.cc.purdue.edu/pub/tools/UNIX/lsof/. Lsof is included in our toolbox primarily because of its capability to list the process ID (PID) and command name associated with a socket. This is useful if you're investigating a possible break-in on your machine or verifying that a service is running on it. (The Linux version of netstat can provide the same information using its -p option, and Windows XP Service Pack 2 can provide the same with the -b option.) For example, here's the output of lsof running on a Linux machine:

```
# lsof -i -n -V -P
COMMAND      PID    USER    FD   TYPE   DEVICE SIZE NODE NAME
portmap      1209   root    3u   IPv4   18068       UDP  *:111
portmap      1209   root    4u   IPv4   18069       TCP  *:111 (LISTEN)
rpc.statd    1264   root    4u   IPv4   18120       UDP  *:1016
rpc.statd    1264   root    5u   IPv4   18143       UDP  *:32768
rpc.statd    1264   root    6u   IPv4   18146       TCP  *:32768 (LISTEN)
ntpd         1401   root    4u   IPv4   18595       UDP  *:123
ntpd         1401   root    5u   IPv4   18596       UDP  127.0.0.1:123
ntpd         1401   root    6u   IPv4   18597       UDP  129.174.142.77:123
X            2290   root    1u   IPv4   23042       TCP  *:6000 (LISTEN)
sshd         7005   root    3u   IPv4   143123      TCP  *:22 (LISTEN)
```

The lsof utility, by name, lists all the open files on a system. (As you might have guessed, lsof stands for *list open files*.) With the -i command-line switch appended, lsof lists only open files of the type IP (version 4 or 6), which basically give us a list of files that are running IP processes. The -n option removes the listing of hostnames, and the -v option guarantees a verbose output. -P is used to force lsof to display port numbers, rather than the popular service name for the port in question. The result of the command is a list of running programs that have a TCP or UDP port open. Listings with (LISTEN) following them are actually accepting traffic on the port in question. Anyone who has ever tried to figure out whether a backdoor service is installed on his machine can recognize the value in this! Of course, lsof won't magically find a backdoor if the attacker has taken advanced steps to hide it, such as replacing the lsof utility with a Trojan version or installing a cloaking kernel module.

Fport and Active Ports

Foundstone's Fport, available at http://www.foundstone.com, is a tool for Windows NT and higher that reports open TCP and UDP ports and maps them to the owning process, similarly to lsof. Listing 21.1 shows the output from running Fport on a Windows 2000 machine (edited slightly to shorten the length of a couple lines).

Listing 21.1   Running Fport on Windows 2000

```
C:\>fport
FPort v1.33 - TCP/IP Process to Port Mapper
Copyright 2000 by Foundstone, Inc.
http://www.foundstone.com

Pid    Process          Port    Proto Path
392    svchost      ->  135     TCP   C:\WINNT\system32\svchost.exe
8      System       ->  139     TCP
8      System       ->  445     TCP
588    MSTask       ->  1025    TCP   C:\WINNT\system32\MSTask.exe
8      System       ->  1031    TCP
8      System       ->  1033    TCP
920    mozilla      ->  1090    TCP   ...\Mozilla\mozilla.exe
920    mozilla      ->  1091    TCP   ...\Mozilla\mozilla.exe
420    spoolsv      ->  1283    TCP   C:\WINNT\system32\spoolsv.exe
392    svchost      ->  135     UDP   C:\WINNT\system32\svchost.exe
8      System       ->  137     UDP
8      System       ->  138     UDP
8      System       ->  445     UDP
220    lsass        ->  500     UDP   C:\WINNT\system32\lsass.exe
208    services     ->  1027    UDP   C:\WINNT\system32\services.exe
872    MsFgSys      ->  38037 UDP C:\WINNT\System32\MsgSys.EXE
```

You can see a number of NetBIOS and other services running on the machine. You might consider eliminating some of them if you're hardening the system. You can also use Fport when you're investigating a possible break-in or verifying that a service is running.

The Active Ports freeware program offers similar functionality on Windows NT and higher platforms and is available from SmartLine's website at http://www.protect-me.com/freeware.htm. Using a user-friendly GUI, Active Ports displays the program name that is running, its PID, the local and remote IP and port using the process, whether it is listening, the protocol it is running on, and the path where the file can be located (see Figure 21.1).

By clicking the Query Names button, you can translate IP addresses to their associated DNS names. Another very useful feature of Active Ports is its ability to terminate any of the listed processes. Simply select any of the listed processes with a single mouse click and click the Terminate Process button. If it is possible, the process will be shut down.

This does not guarantee the process will not restart the next time you reboot the system, but it does allow for an easy way to shut down currently running processes when you're troubleshooting.

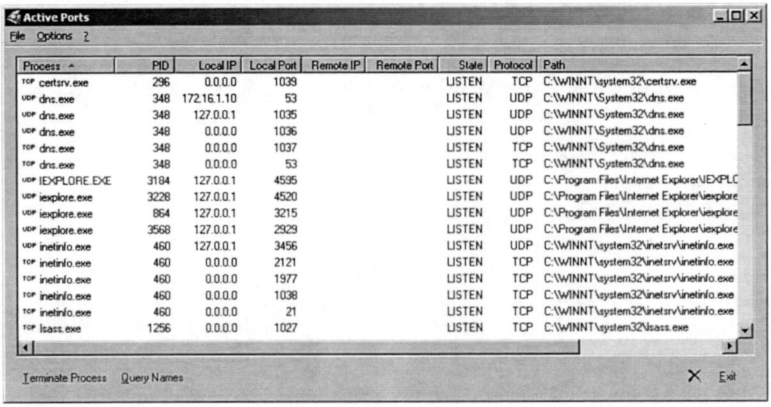

Figure 21.1 The Active Ports tool from Smartline offers similar functionality to lsof and Fport for Windows through an easy-to-read GUI interface.

Hping

The UNIX program hping has several capabilities, some of which we will touch on later in this chapter. With hping, you can generate almost any type of packet you can imagine, allowing you to choose the protocol, source and destination addresses, ports, flags, and what options are set in packets that you want to send to a target host.

> **Note**
>
> For similar functionality for Windows systems, download PacketCrafter from http://www.komodia.com/ tools.htm. Though not quite as feature rich as hping, it does offer many of the same packet-constructing capabilities in a Windows freeware package, with an easy-to-use GUI interface.

You can generate a packet with the SYN flag set and send it to a target host to determine whether a TCP port is open on that system, as shown in Listing 21.2.

Listing 21.2 **Checking Firewall TCP Rules with Hping SYN Packets**

```
# hping --count 1 --syn --destport 80 www.extdom.org
eth0 default routing interface selected (according to /proc)
HPING www.extdom.org (eth0 192.168.2.100): S set, 40 headers + 0 data bytes
46 bytes from 192.168.2.100: flags=SA seq=0 ttl=53 id=24080 win=16384 rtt=17.0 ms

--- www.extdom.org hping statistic ---
1 packets transmitted, 1 packets received, 0% packet loss
round-trip min/avg/max = 24.8/24.8/24.8 ms
```

Listing 21.2   **Continued**

```
# hping --count 1 --syn --destport 443 www.extdom.org
eth0 default routing interface selected (according to /proc)
HPING www.extdom.org (eth0 192.168.2.100): S set, 40 headers + 0 data bytes
46 bytes from 192.168.2.100: flags=RA seq=0 ttl=53 id=42810 win=0 rtt=20.2 ms

--- www.extdom.org hping statistic ---
1 packets transmitted, 1 packets received, 0% packet loss
round-trip min/avg/max = 20.2/20.2/20.2 ms
```

We sent a SYN packet to port 80. We can see that HTTP is open because the server returns a SYN+ACK (flags=SA). However, a similar packet that was sent to port 443 returns an RST+ACK (flags=RA) packet, which means that HTTPS is not open.

> **Note**
>
> Although it doesn't show it, hping sends an RST packet when it receives a SYN+ACK response. That way, we can't accidentally cause a SYN flood denial of service!

Hping's control over individual flags makes it particularly useful for testing firewall filtering capabilities and configuration. Consider the following output, where we send two SYN packets to a randomly chosen destination port:

```
# hping -count 2 --syn --destport 3243 www.extom.org
eth0 default routing interface selected (according to /proc)
HPING www.extom.org (eth0 192.168.2.100): S set, 40 headers + 0 data bytes
--- www.extom.org hping statistic ---
2 packets transmitted, 0 packets received, 100% packet loss
round-trip min/avg/max = 0.0/0.0/0.0 ms
```

We don't receive responses to the SYN packets, so we know the firewall silently drops disallowed traffic. We can verify that by looking at the firewall logs. Now look at the results in Listing 21.3, where we send ACK packets instead of SYN packets.

Listing 21.3   **Checking Firewall TCP Rules with Hping ACK Packets**

```
# hping -count 2 --ack --destport 3243 www.extom.org
eth0 default routing interface selected (according to /proc)
HPING www.extom.org (eth0 192.168.2.100): A set, 40 headers + 0 data bytes
46 bytes from 192.168.2.100: flags=R seq=0 ttl=53 id=8060 win=0 rtt=17.1 ms
46 bytes from 192.168.2.100: flags=R seq=0 ttl=53 id=2472 win=0 rtt=17.3 ms

--- www.extom.org hping statistic ---
2 packets transmitted, 2 packets received, 0% packet loss
round-trip min/avg/max = 17.1/17.1/17.1 ms
```

The firewall allows ACK packets to come through! This firewall most likely does not support stateful filtering and is configured to allow outbound TCP connections;

otherwise, this simulated response packet would have been silently dropped like the SYN flagged packet was. Allowing unsolicited ACK packets can be exploited as a reconnaissance method or as a means to successfully mount a denial of service (DoS) attack.

Tcpdump

Tcpdump is one of the most commonly used sniffer programs; it has many uses, including diagnosing transport layer issues. We have used Tcpdump throughout this book to look at network traffic. This freeware program came out of the BSD environment and has been ported to other platforms, including Linux, Solaris, and Windows. It is a critical component for debugging almost any network problem, and many experienced troubleshooters begin with it unless they're obviously not dealing with a network problem.

Try a Graphical Alternative to Tcpdump

Although Tcpdump is a command-line tool, other programs that are more graphical use the same programming interfaces and file formats, so you can get the best of both worlds. One of our favorite graphical sniffers is Ethereal, which is available for many UNIX variants and Windows at http://www.ethereal.com. One of the benefits of using a tool such as Ethereal is that it depicts both the raw data and a context-sensitive translation of header fields, such as flags, port numbers, and so on. In other words, this tool is closer to a protocol analyzer, so it's more user friendly. On the other hand, it's hard to wrap Ethereal in a shell script or run it on a machine that doesn't run a GUI like Windows or X, which is where Tcpdump comes in.

You will probably run Tcpdump often as you realize the power it gives you. The ability to see whether traffic is even being transmitted is often enough to solve a problem or at least isolate it. For example, suppose a client at a small company is complaining that he is unable to connect to websites on the Internet. You watch him attempt a connection and, sure enough, his Internet Explorer just hangs whenever he types in a URL. Many factors—DNS issues, a routing problem, or problems with the website—could cause this behavior. You could spend a lot of time working through this list, or you can fire up a laptop and run Tcpdump.

Problems with Network Traces in Switched Environments

In this chapter we discuss using Tcpdump to troubleshoot network security problems. However, because today almost all network environments are switched, simply hooking up a laptop to an available switch port will seldom yield the results you will need to examine problem traffic flow. In a switched environment, a packet trace tool such as Tcpdump would only be able to see traffic sourced from or destined to the host it is running on. There are several ways to deploy a network trace tool to overcome this issue.

First, you can deploy the tool on one of the problem systems. This can also yield additional insight into communication issues that you may not be able to glean from a network view. However, as mentioned later in this chapter, deploying a network trace program on a production server also has its own risks.

Another way the problem of switched networks can be overcome is by using monitor ports (also referred to as *SPAN ports*) on intermediary switches. Monitor ports allow the redirection of traffic from a single port or list of ports, or from an entire VLAN to a single monitor port, where a host running a network trace program can be connected. This allows visibility to the traffic to and from as many hosts as you would like on that switch. If your hosts exist on more than one switch, for a complete picture of your traffic flow, you might require a monitor port to be configured and a host running a network trace program on each switch. Depending on the complexity of your environment, similarly connected hosts may need to be at multiple intermediary points in the communication flow as well.

Yet another way to examine communications between two hosts in a switched environment is using an ARP cache poisoning tool such as Dsniff or Ettercap. For more information on how such tools can be used to examine traffic in a switched environment, take a look at the "Broadcast Domains" section of Chapter 13, "Separating Resources."

A final way to bypass the issues with switched traffic is by placing a hub at one of the troubled endpoint hosts. Many consultants who have to go onsite to troubleshoot a problem employ a solution like this. This will require a brief interruption to the network service for the troubled host, unless it offers a teamed NIC configuration (in which case this solution can be placed inline on the standby NIC while traffic continues on the active NIC, and then you can disconnect the active NIC and let it fail over to the standby). To use this solution, unplug the network cable currently going to the troubled host and plug the cable into a small hub. Be careful! If the hub does not have auto-configuring crossover ports or if it does not have a manual crossover port to plug into, you will need to connect a coupler and a crossover cable to the existing network cable before plugging into the hub. Next, take an additional standard network cable to connect the troubled host to the hub. Finally, plug your laptop running a network trace program into the hub. This way, you will be able to see all traffic destined to or sourced from the troubled host. This makes a strong case for any traveling network/security consultant to carry a laptop with a network trace program, a small hub, extra crossover and standard network patch cables, and couplers in his bag of tricks.

In this case, you might see something like the following when the user tries to access http://www.yahoo.com (the ellipses indicate where we truncated the long lines):

```
# tcpdump -i eth0 -n host 192.168.11.88 and tcp port 80
tcpdump: listening on eth0
17:59:26.390890 192.168.11.88.33130 > 64.58.77.195.80: S ...
17:59:29.385734 192.168.11.88.33130 > 64.58.77.195.80: S ...
17:59:35.385368 192.168.11.88.33130 > 64.58.77.195.80: S ...
```

Now we know that the user's machine is transmitting the SYN packets successfully (which means that it already has successfully queried DNS for the remote IP address), but it isn't receiving responses. We now hypothesize that something is filtering the responses, so we pursue that by connecting the laptop outside the border router. Now Tcpdump prints something like the following:

```
# tcpdump -i eth0 -n tcp port 80
tcpdump: listening on eth0
18:28:10.964249 external_if.53153 > 64.58.77.195.80: S ...
18:28:10.985383 64.58.77.195.80 > external_if.53153: S ... ack ...
18:28:10.991414 external_if.53162 > 64.56.177.94.80: S ...
18:28:11.159151 64.56.177.94.80 > external_if.53162: S ... ack ...
```

The router is performing Network Address Translation (NAT), so `external_if` represents the router's external IP address. The remote site is responding, but the SYN+ACK responses aren't making it through the router; otherwise, we would have seen some in the previous output. This is indicative of a filtering problem on the router. You might hypothesize that someone modified the ACLs incorrectly, and you could test your theory by looking at the router configuration. Imagine how long we might have spent isolating this problem without Tcpdump!

Revisiting the Sample Firewall Problem with Transport Layer Techniques

We have verified that something is blocking the HTTP traffic over our dial-up laptop connection to the web server because we installed a new firewall. We wonder whether the traffic is even making it to the firewall. We run Tcpdump on the web server and see no HTTP traffic. We run Tcpdump on another machine that is connected to an external network outside of our firewall and see the remote Internet user's SYN packets addressed to the web server coming into the network; however, we don't see response packets coming back from the web server. Now we wonder if the firewall is blocking HTTP traffic, despite what we found in our earlier examination of its configuration and logs. From the external machine, we Telnet to port 80 on the web server and discover that it works fine. Therefore, the firewall is not blocking HTTP from the external machine. However, the firewall doesn't seem to receive HTTP packets from the Internet at all; we would see log messages if they were blocked, and we would see response packets from the server if they weren't blocked.

Network Layer Troubleshooting

Security device problems at the network layer usually fall into one of the following categories:

- Routing
- Firewall
- NAT
- Virtual Private Network (VPN)

We will show you some tools to help troubleshoot problems in each of these areas.

NAT Has a History of Breaking Some Protocols

We discussed that NAT breaks some VPN implementations in Chapter 16, "VPN Integration." VPN is not the only application that NAT has broken in the past. This was usually because the associated protocols embedded transport or network layer information in their payloads. Perhaps the most notable of these was H.323, which is used in videoconferencing applications, such as Microsoft NetMeeting. NAT devices change IP and Transport layer header information, but in the past they have known nothing about what ports are stored in the application payload for a remote peer to work with. To make a long story short, such protocols simply would not work through NAT devices unless they had proxy support. However, some more recent NAT implementations have been incorporating content checking that will change the imbedded IP address values in H.323 and other protocols that would have been previously broken by NAT. So keep in mind when you're troubleshooting a NAT-related issue that there have been issues with certain applications and NAT in the past. Also, confirm compatibility between the implemented version of NAT and the problem protocol.

You have already seen some of the tools we present at this layer, but here we show how to use them for network layer problems. Some display information on the host, and some test network connectivity. Many have multiple uses and were introduced earlier.

Ifconfig and Ipconfig

Both ifconfig and ipconfig utilities display host information that helps you verify that the IP address, subnet mask, and broadcast address are configured correctly. There's nothing magic here, but it's probably one of the things you'll check most often.

The UNIX ifconfig utility configures network interfaces and displays network interface details. Use the -a option to display all interfaces when you don't know the name of the interface you're trying to look at. The -v option might show additional information, such as the speed and duplex of the interface, as in the following display from an SGI IRIX box:

```
# ifconfig -av
ef0: flags=415c43<UP,BROADCAST,RUNNING,FILTMULTI,MULTICAST,
¬CKSUM,DRVRLOCK,LINK0,IPALIAS>
inet 192.168.114.50 netmask 0xffffff00 broadcast 192.168.114.255
speed 100.00 Mbit/s full-duplex
lo0: flags=1849<UP,LOOPBACK,RUNNING,MULTICAST,CKSUM>
inet 127.0.0.1 netmask 0xff000000
```

The ipconfig utility for Windows NT and higher primarily displays IP configuration information, although you can also use it to release and renew DHCP configurations. Use the -all option to print the IP address, subnet mask, and broadcast address of each interface. The ipconfig -all command also displays the IP addresses of the DNS servers and, if applicable, the DHCP and WINS servers that are configured on the host. Windows 9x users also have access to ipconfig's functionality via the winipcfg GUI program. Listing 21.4 shows the type of information you get from ipconfig.

Listing 21.4   **Sample Ipconfig Output**

```
C:\> ipconfig -all

Windows IP Configuration

        Host Name . . . . . . . . . : TELLUS.intdom.org
        DNS Servers . . . . . . . . : 192.168.111.2
        Node Type . . . . . . . . . : Broadcast
        NetBIOS Scope ID. . . . . . :
        IP Routing Enabled. . . . . : No
        WINS Proxy Enabled. . . . . : No
        NetBIOS Resolution Uses DNS : Yes

0 Ethernet adapter :

        Description . . . . . . . . : Novell 2000 Adapter.
        Physical Address. . . . . . : 18-18-A8-72-58-00
```

Listing 21.4 **Continued**

```
DHCP Enabled. . . . . . . . : Yes
IP Address. . . . . . . . . : 192.168.111.130
Subnet Mask . . . . . . . . : 255.255.255.0
Default Gateway . . . . . . : 192.168.111.1
DHCP Server . . . . . . . . : 192.168.111.1
Primary WINS Server . . . . :
Secondary WINS Server . . . :
Lease Obtained. . . . . . . : 12 19 01 4:09:39 PM
Lease Expires . . . . . . . : 12 20 01 4:09:39 AM
```

From a security device troubleshooting perspective, you will most often focus on a few items in this output. The DNS server IP address in the Configuration section can help you diagnose some application layer problems. The IP address and default gateway addresses, in the Ethernet Adapter section, are useful for routing or other connectivity problems. The DHCP server and lease information might also be useful for troubleshooting connectivity problems. The other lines might be of interest for troubleshooting Windows domain or workgroup issues, such as file sharing or network neighborhood problems.

Netstat

As we mentioned in the section "Transport Layer Troubleshooting," the netstat utility exists in all UNIX and Windows distributions. Its -r option can be used for network layer troubleshooting to display the host routing table.

> **Note**
>
> You can also get this information on a Windows system via the route print command or on a UNIX system using the route command.

Most of the time we're looking for the default gateway, which is displayed with a destination IP and subnet mask of 0.0.0.0. The following Linux output shows two networks, 10.0.0.0 and 129.174.142.0, accessible through the vmnet1 and eth0 interfaces, respectively. Both are class C–sized, with a subnet mask of 255.255.255.0. The default gateway is 129.174.142.1. Almost all TCP/IP devices include a loopback interface, named lo in this case, serving network 127.0.0.0:

```
$ netstat -rn
Kernel IP routing table
Destination     Gateway          Genmask          Flags Iface
10.0.0.0        0.0.0.0          255.255.255.0    U     vmnet1
129.174.142.0   0.0.0.0          255.255.255.0    U     eth0
127.0.0.0       0.0.0.0          255.0.0.0        U     lo
0.0.0.0         129.174.142.1    0.0.0.0          UG    eth0
```

When troubleshooting network layer issues, you will usually focus on the default gateway line in netstat output. Many routing problems are caused by missing or incorrect gateway entries in the routing table. Every TCP/IP device, unless you're working on a standalone LAN or a core Internet router, should have at least a default gateway entry.

The routing tables can become large when you're running a routing protocol, such as the Routing Information Protocol (RIP), on your network. However, routing updates are automatic in such environments, which could eliminate the need to troubleshoot routing information with netstat.

Ping

The venerable ping utility, which is included in all UNIX and Windows distributions, employs the Internet Control Message Protocol (ICMP) to test whether a remote host is reachable. It sends an ICMP echo request packet and listens for the ICMP echo reply from the remote host. This is a great test of end-to-end connectivity at the network layer; however, unfortunately today most firewalls block ICMP. The protocol has been used one too many times in ICMP flood and other attacks. If you want to test end-to-end connectivity, you might have to move up a layer and use the hping or Telnet utility, described in the section "Transport Layer Troubleshooting."

Traceroute

Traceroute is another classic utility that is available on all UNIX and Windows machines, although the command is abbreviated as tracert in Windows. It manipulates the IP header time-to-live (TTL) field to coerce the gateways between your machine and the destination into sending back ICMP messages. Each gateway decrements the TTL and, if it's zero, returns an ICMP time-exceeded message to the sender. By starting with a TTL of 1 and incrementing it, traceroute detects the IP address of each router along the way by examining the source addresses of the time-exceeded messages. Traceroute also inserts a timestamp in each packet so that it can compute the roundtrip time, in milliseconds, when it gets a response. This is possible because the ICMP response messages include the original packet in their payloads. These capabilities make traceroute an excellent tool to help determine where traffic fails as it traverses the Internet.

Traceroute is also useful in diagnosing performance problems. If you see the route change frequently, you might hypothesize that you have a route-flapping problem somewhere. Unfortunately, proving that might be impossible because the loci of such problems are usually on the Internet, outside of your jurisdiction.

By default, UNIX traceroute sends a UDP datagram to a high-numbered port on the destination. The port is almost always closed on the destination. Therefore, an ICMP port-unreachable message is sent back when a packet finally makes it all the way, which tells traceroute when to stop.

Unfortunately, this won't work when your firewall blocks the outbound UDP packets or when the high port is actually open on the destination (in which case it will probably be discarded, with no response). Traceroute also breaks when the target organization blocks inbound UDP (for UNIX traceroute) or inbound ICMP (for Windows trace-route). Windows uses ICMP echo request packets instead of UDP. Many UNIX distributions now support the -I option to use ICMP instead of UDP.

Of course, traceroute also won't work if your firewall blocks outbound UDP or ICMP echo request messages (as the case may be) or inbound ICMP time-exceeded messages. One way to overcome these issues is by using hping. The hping command includes --ttl and --traceroute options to specify a starting TTL value, which is incremented like the actual traceroute command. Applying these options to an HTTP SYN packet, for example, will get the outbound packets through your firewall. However, if your firewall blocks inbound ICMP, you will never see the time-exceeded messages sent back by external gateways.

The output in Listing 21.5 shows a typical traceroute. You can see that three packets are sent for each TTL value. No packets were lost in this example (we don't see any * values in place of the roundtrip times), and all response times appear to be reasonable, so we don't see performance problems on this route.

Listing 21.5 **Sample Traceroute Output**

```
# traceroute -n www.yahoo.com
traceroute: Warning: www.yahoo.com has multiple addresses; using 64.58.76.224
traceroute to www.yahoo.akadns.net (64.58.76.224), 30 hops max, 38 byte packets
 1  63.212.11.177  0.675 ms  0.474 ms  0.489 ms
 2  63.212.11.161  1.848 ms  1.640 ms  1.636 ms
 3  172.20.0.1  26.460 ms  17.865 ms  40.310 ms
 4  63.212.0.81  24.412 ms  24.835 ms  24.488 ms
 5  198.32.187.119  33.586 ms  26.997 ms  26.715 ms
 6  216.109.66.4  33.570 ms  26.690 ms  27.066 ms
 7  209.185.9.1  33.576 ms  26.932 ms  26.811 ms
 8  216.33.96.161  20.107 ms  20.097 ms  20.181 ms
 9  216.33.98.18  24.637 ms  26.843 ms  26.901 ms
10  216.35.210.122  35.771 ms  28.881 ms  27.052 ms
11 64.58.76.224  33.452 ms  26.696 ms  27.020 ms
```

Tcpdump

We have to include Tcpdump at this layer, at least to help debug VPN problems. The latest versions print a lot of useful information about the Internet Key Exchange (IKE) service (UDP port 500), which establishes and maintains IPSec authentication and encryption keys. Tcpdump also prints some information about the IPSec Encapsulation Security Payload (ESP) and Authentication Header (AH) protocols—IP protocols 50 and 51, respectively (these are protocol numbers, not port numbers).

If you have users who are unable to establish an IPSec tunnel with a device that you are administering, you could successfully troubleshoot possible issues by tracing the traffic arriving at the device in question with Tcpdump. You can verify that IKE exchanges are occurring correctly and that the proper ESP traffic is getting to the device in question.

This is especially helpful because IPSec lacks good logging facilities of its own. As you might have noticed by now, Tcpdump is one of our favorite tools. It can put you on a fast track to solving almost any network problem, and many experienced troubleshooters will go straight to it rather than trying to understand all the problem symptoms, eyeball configuration files, and so on.

Hardships of Troubleshooting Performance

Performance issues represent one of the hardest classes of problems on which to get a handle. One time, I was at a client's office when she happened to complain that logging in on her Windows 2000 desktop took forever. She attributed this to a lack of available bandwidth on the network because everyone had the same problem. She was unconvinced when I pointed out that it would be hard for the 30 or so users on her Windows domain to exhaust the bandwidth of the corporation's 100Mbps switched network. I pulled out my laptop, connected both machines to the network through a hub I always carry, and ran a Tcpdump while she logged in. The Tcpdump output immediately pointed to a DNS problem. Her machine was issuing many queries for a nonexistent DNS domain. It turned out the local admin, still unfamiliar with Windows 2000, had configured her machine identity properties with membership to a nonexistent domain, apparently without realizing the DNS relationship. A quick test with my laptop acting as the DNS server for her machine convinced her that network bandwidth constraint was not the problem.

We have presented a few tools for network layer troubleshooting and have provided a few examples of their use. NAT and VPN problems probably represent the bulk of the problems you're likely to deal with in this layer. Next, we will move down to the bottom of the TCP/IP reference model: the link layer.

Link Layer Troubleshooting

This layer can present you with some of your toughest problems. These problems will be a lot easier to solve if you master a couple key topics:

- The Address Resolution Protocol (ARP)
- The differences between nonswitched and switched networks

ARP is the link layer protocol that TCP/IP devices use to match another device's Media Access Control (MAC) address with its IP address. MAC addresses, not IP addresses, are used to communicate with other devices on the same network segment. When a device determines that a given IP address resides on the same segment that it does (by examining the address and its own subnet mask), the device uses ARP to discover the associated MAC address. Basically, the device sends a link-level broadcast asking who has the IP address. Every device on the segment examines the request, and the one that uses the enclosed IP address responds. The original device stores the source MAC address of the response in its ARP table; that way, subsequent transmissions don't require the broadcast process. ARP table entries eventually expire, which necessitates periodic rebroadcasts. This ARP table expiration is necessary to facilitate the moving of IP addresses between devices (for example, DHCP) without the manual reconfiguration of all the other devices on the network segment.

In a nonswitched network, a network segment usually maps directly to the physical network medium. In a switched network, a network segment's boundaries become a little vague because the switches might be configured to break the physical network into logical segments at the link layer. In general, the set of devices that can see each others' ARP broadcasts delineates a network segment.

You can find out more about these topics and their security ramifications in Chapter 13 and on the Internet at http://www.sans.org/resources/idfaq/switched_network.php. With an understanding of these subjects under your belt, all you need are a couple tools to diagnose almost any problem at the link layer.

You will find link layer tools are similar to those used at the other network layers. Most of them display host information. Once again, you will find Tcpdump useful for displaying what's happening on the network, this time at Layer 2.

Ifconfig and Ipconfig

We already covered these tools in the "Network Layer Troubleshooting" section, but you might not have noticed that they can also display the MAC address associated with the link layer. Look back at the `ipconfig -all` output and you will see the MAC address displayed as the Physical address. On UNIX machines, the method for determining the address varies greatly. On Linux and FreeBSD machines, ifconfig shows the address by default, as seen in the following Linux output, as the `HWaddr`:

```
# ifconfig eth0
eth0      Link encap:Ethernet   HWaddr 00:10:5A:26:FD:41
...
```

Try one of the following methods to display the MAC address for your system:[2]

- Solaris: `arp ` hostname ``
- OpenBSD: `netstat -ai`
- IRIX: `netstat -ai`

ARP

The arp utility, naturally, displays information that pertains to the ARP protocol and ARP table. It exists in all UNIX and Windows distributions, and it is most often executed with the `-a` option to display the ARP table, as follows:

```
# arp -a
? (123.123.123.123) at 00:02:E3:09:D1:08 [ether] on eth0
? (192.168.126.88) at 00:D0:09:DE:FE:81 [ether] PERM on eth0
? (192.168.126.130) at 00:D0:09:DE:FE:81 [ether] on eth0
? (192.168.126.127) at 00:10:4B:F6:F5:CE [ether] PERM on eth0
? (192.168.126.1) at 00:A0:CC:7B:9C:21 [ether] PERM on eth0
```

You can glean a lot of information from this table, in which ARP stores its IP/MAC pairs. It shows static entries (tagged with PERM) that were added manually with the arp

-s option. These can help mitigate vulnerability to some devastating link layer attacks. The ARP protocol discovered the other entries and added them dynamically. You can also see that two logical networks are accessed via the eth0 interface and that this is probably a Linux box, given the interface name. In case the other methods we showed you to determine your MAC address failed, you can always use SSH to connect to another machine on the same LAN to see your own MAC address.

> **Note**
>
> Windows NT and 9x versions have trouble maintaining static ARP entries (see
> http://www.securityfocus.com/bid/1406). For a quick introduction to ARP and link layer attacks, such as ARP
> spoofing, refer to Chapter 13.

If your system can't connect to a host outside your local network segment, try pinging your default gateway's IP address (not its hostname) and then looking at your ARP table. If you don't see your gateway's MAC address, you probably have a link layer problem. Otherwise, the problem is at a higher layer. You can also apply this same logic on your gateway device. Check the ARP table on it to see what entry it contains for your source system. An incorrect, sticky, or static ARP entry could be the source of your problem. If no ARP entry is found in the table, you are most likely facing a physical layer issue (network card or cabling).

When troubleshooting connectivity issues between devices on the same network segment, ping the device you cannot connect to and check your ARP table to see if you receive an entry for the IP address you are trying to ping. If you do not, you have a link or physical layer issue, such as a stale ARP table entry on another host, a bad network card, bad cabling, or the like. If you do receive an ARP entry, you are most likely fighting a Layer 3 or above filtering issue, such as port filtering, a host-based firewall, or a restrictive IPSec policy on the target system.

Tcpdump

It's no surprise that we use Tcpdump at this layer, too! Tcpdump can help debug some insidious problems. For example, consider a workstation that can't access the Internet, although other workstations on the same hub have no trouble. We can ping the other workstations, but we can't ping the gateway router. If we run Tcpdump and ping the router again, we see the following:

```
# tcpdump -n host 192.168.1.130
12:17:56.782702 192.168.1.130 > 192.168.1.1: icmp: echo request
12:17:56.783309 192.168.1.1 > 192.168.1.130: icmp: echo reply
12:17:57.805290 192.168.1.130 > 192.168.1.1: icmp: echo request
12:17:57.805823 192.168.1.1 > 192.168.1.130: icmp: echo reply
```

The router (192.168.1.1) is actually replying to our pings! We try running Tcpdump again, this time with the -e switch to print the MAC addresses:

```
# tcpdump -en host 192.168.1.130
tcpdump: listening on eth0
10:27:03.650625 0:d0:09:de:fe:81 0:a0:cc:7b:9c:21 0800 98: 192.168.1.130 >
➥192.168.1.1: icmp: echo request (DF)
10:27:03.651260 0:a0:cc:7b:9c:21 0:10:5a:26:fd:41 0800 98: 192.168.1.1 >
➥192.168.1.130: icmp: echo reply (DF)
```

Note the source MAC address on the echo request our machine sent and the destination MAC address on the reply the router sent. They don't match. We check the router configuration and find an old static ARP entry in its cache. Deleting the entry fixes the problem.

Revisiting the Sample Firewall Problem with Link Layer Techniques

If you read the previous Tcpdump example, you're probably close to solving the sample firewall problem we have highlighted throughout this chapter. We have successfully accessed the web server from a workstation that is connected just outside the firewall, so the firewall rules are most likely correct. However, we still cannot access the web server from the Internet. A border router separates us from the Internet. Also, recall that the firewall was replaced with a new machine just before the problems started. We execute `tcpdump -en` to look at the MAC addresses, and we discover that the router is sending HTTP traffic to the wrong MAC address for the firewall. We check the router configuration, discover a static ARP entry for the old firewall machine, and change the entry to fix the problem.

Summary

We can't overstress the importance of fostering good troubleshooting habits by developing and practicing your own methodology, as we described at the beginning of the chapter. Follow the logical steps in the process of troubleshooting closely—collect symptoms, review recent changes, form a hypothesis, test the hypothesis, analyze the results, and repeat if necessary.

Also, don't forget to apply the rules of thumb when following these steps. Don't make multiple changes at one time as the actual solution for a problem can become unclear. Always keep an open mind when working on issues, let your troubleshooting process rule things out for you. When you get stuck, ask for a second opinion. Talking the problem out with someone else can help you find mistakes in your troubleshooting. Try to stay focused on the issue at hand. Don't implement a quick fix that may be more hazardous in the long run then the original problem. Remember not to overlook the obvious when considering the cause of your issue. Finally, try to keep strong documentation of your problems and their solutions so you don't have to "re-create the wheel" if you run into a similar issue in the future.

With those skills in place, however, your success will depend on knowing which tools to apply for a given problem. That's why we focused so heavily, in the remainder of the chapter, on describing some of our favorite tools and providing examples of their use.

Use the knowledge you have gained of these tools, information on the layers that they apply to and the way they can be utilized to troubleshoot any networking security issue to your advantage when working through scenarios in your own environment. The combination of solid troubleshooting skills and the right tools for the job result in success at finding the right answers for any security problem scenario.

References

1 Bernd Ochsmann and Udo Schneider. "How to use fw monitor." http://www.checkpoint.com/techsupport/downloads/html/ethereal/fw_monitor_rev1_01. pdf. July 10, 2003.

2 University of Washington Department of Computer Science and Engineering. "Determining Your Ethernet Address." http://www.cs.washington.edu/lab/sw/_wireless/yourmac.html. January 2002.

## 22

Assessment Techniques

THROUGHOUT THIS BOOK, WE HAVE DISCUSSED various methods of incorporating security into the network. You have learned how to apply recommended security concepts to perimeter components such as routers, firewalls, VPNs, and host systems. This chapter changes your focus from a defensive approach to an offensive one, as we examine how to assess your environment for possible security holes.

A terrific network security design is worthless if it is not faithfully implemented. Unfortunately, many organizations do not test their networks to verify how well they have achieved their security goals. This chapter is designed to show you how to plan an assessment to determine whether your security perimeter is operating according to your expectations. Many of the techniques we will discuss are similar to techniques in common use by network attackers. This includes information-gathering techniques that attackers use to fingerprint and enumerate your network, vulnerability-discovery efforts to determine potential holes in your network, and exploitation techniques that may demonstrate insecurities in your security perimeter. Going through the process of assessing the effectiveness of your security infrastructure helps improve the resiliency of your security perimeter and allows you to locate weaknesses before attackers can exploit them.

Roadmap for Assessing the Security of Your Network

Your network may expose vulnerabilities to attackers in many ways. A key area is information exposure. Many details about your organization that an attacker can gather can be used to assist in an attack. This includes technical data, such as what public services you offer, as well as nontechnical items, such as who your business partners are. The next area of importance is connectivity. Can attackers send and receive information to the systems within your network? This is dominated by the impact your firewalls (and filtering routers) have on connectivity into your network, but it can also be affected by the controls you have in place to allow workstations and notebook computers to connect to your internal network. The last major area that needs to be examined is whether the services your network relies on contain exploitable vulnerabilities.

To prepare you for performing your assessment, we present a roadmap for exploring each of these areas to ensure that you locate your exploitable vulnerabilities. Attackers often follow the same techniques when attempting to penetrate your defenses, which is why performing regular security assessments is a critical step in fortifying your network. An assessment consists of the following core phases:

1. **Planning**—Determine the scope of your assessment. Decide how you will conduct it. Develop written rules of engagement to control the assessment and, most important, gain proper written approval to perform it. Assemble your toolkit to perform the assessment.

2. **Reconnaissance**—Obtain technical and nontechnical information on the organization and known public hosts, such as mail, web, and DNS servers. This information may be used to focus cyber-attacks as well as reveal information useful for social engineering.

3. **Network service discovery**—Determine which hosts and network devices can be accessed from the outside. For each of these systems, determine what services are running on them.

4. **Vulnerability discovery**—Probe externally accessible systems and remote services to determine whether they expose known vulnerabilities to the outside. Analyze initial results to eliminate false positives.

5. **Verification of perimeter devices**—Evaluate firewall and router configurations to ensure that they are well configured. Verify that firewalls do not pass traffic that should be blocked. Verify that anti-discovery and anti-DoS controls are in place and work as expected. Test intrusion detection/prevention sensors to ensure that they detect, log, and alert on suspicious activity.

6. **Remote access**—Verify security controls of known remote access systems, including remote access servers, wireless access points, and VPNs. Search for unauthorized (rogue) modems and wireless access points.

7. **Exploitation (optional)**—Attempt to use exploitation techniques against the discovered vulnerabilities. Based on the goals of the test, this may be an iterative activity. Successful exploitation may lead to additional access on the network, which may open the opportunity up for further exploitation.

8. **Results analysis and documentation**—Analyze discovered vulnerabilities to determine their overall effect on the level of risk to the network's security. This is normally based on the vulnerabilities' impact to the affected system, the criticality of the system, the likelihood that the vulnerabilities will be exploited, and the effort required to remediate the vulnerabilities. Produce an assessment report that provides a list of prioritized vulnerabilities by level of risk and provides recommended steps to resolve the individual and root causes for the vulnerabilities.

For the remainder of this chapter, we will provide detailed guidance on the tools and techniques necessary to perform each of these steps. Assessments should always start with careful planning, so that is where we will begin.

Planning

Have you heard the old saying, "If you fail to plan, you plan to fail"? This saying rings true when you perform a security assessment. You must choose the appropriate time to execute the assessment, evaluate possible risks, determine costs, and obtain management's approval. That sounds like a lot of preparation to determine the strength of your defenses, but remember, hindsight is 20-20.

The first issue that needs to be addressed at the beginning of an assessment is determining your scope. This should include developing a list of the target computer systems and network devices that you will include in the assessment and what techniques are you allowed to use against them during the assessment. Listing valid targets may be as simple as stating that all computer systems that are part of your organization are in scope, but be careful. Are there any other organizations that have equipment attached to your network? Do you have agreements in place that allow you to audit their computer systems? You will need to determine that you have the right to include these systems in your assessment prior to firing packets at them! There may be other systems that are part of your network that you are not authorized to test. All these systems should be identified and placed in a do-not-test list.

The other issue to address for scope is to determine which test techniques will be used during the assessment. Some assessment activities are safer than others. You should be clear which techniques you will be using and what controls you will employ to reduce the organizational risk for the more dangerous techniques. Table 22.1 shows a list of common assessment techniques and the level of risk generally associated with each.

Table 22.1 **Different Assessment Techniques and the Different Levels of Risk**

Assessment Technique	Risk Level
Initial reconnaissance	Very Low
NETWORK SERVICE DISCOVERY	
Host discovery	Low
Port discovery	Low
Service detection	Low
VULNERABILITY DISCOVERY	
Automated vulnerability scanning (e.g., Nessus)	Medium
Wardialing	Low
Wardriving	Very Low
Online password brute force	Medium
Exploitation of detected vulnerabilities	Medium to High

As part of this step, you will also need to plan the logistics of the assessment, including determining what the valid test hours of operation are, the start and end dates for the assessment, and the administrative and management points of contact for in-scope systems. Keep in mind that performing a vulnerability assessment carries with it the inherent risk of disrupting service through crashing target systems or generating excessive network traffic. Therefore, administrators should be available during your assessment to deal with any issues that might arise. Because of this, access to the appropriate administrators will be an important consideration as you decide what your hours of operation will be.

Tip

When deciding on a time to perform the assessment, be sure to account for differences in time zones across the organization.

Finally, all the planning decisions need to be documented in a written rules-of-engagement document that must be signed by management before the assessment commences. Written approval has saved the careers of many people when critical systems went down as a result of simple scanning. In general, communication is one of the most important aspects of planning the assessment. You need to verify that all parties involved in supporting the targeted systems, as well as management, have been informed (as appropriate) of your activities. Keep communication and risk awareness in your thoughts as you plan and perform the assessment.

Testing Without Written Authorization Can Have Serious Consequences

For a concrete example of what can happen to you if you do not gain written approval for your assessments, look up the story of Randall Schwartz (http://www.lightlink.com/spacenka/fors). Randall found himself convicted of multiple felonies for basically conducting a much needed security assessment but without gaining proper approval. Remember, in the law's eyes, the difference between a hacker and a security professional is permission!

Once you have your scope determined and have gained approval to proceed, you will need to make sure you've got the test resources assembled to complete all the tests you have agreed to perform. Often this will require creating more than one test system, each running a different operating system and configured with test tools appropriate for that operating system. At a minimum, you will probably want to have both Windows and UNIX systems available to utilize the plethora of OS-dependent utilities each contains. Later in the chapter we will be discussing specific utilities you may want to use.

Tip

If you do not have extra computers lying around to run multiple operating systems, check out VMware (http://www.vmware.com/). VMware software enables you to run an OS within another OS. For example, if you use Windows 2000 Professional, you could use VMware Workstation on it, which would enable you to run Red Hat Linux at the same time on the same machine. Note that you might have to increase your system's RAM or disk space for proper performance.

Assuming you've determined your scope, gained written approval, and assembled your test systems, you can now move on to the reconnaissance step of your assessment.

Reconnaissance

The heart of the reconnaissance stage is to gather publicly available information about the organization without actually probing targeted systems directly. This often includes general business information as well as the organization's IP address ranges and the names and IP addresses of its public services, such as DNS, web, and mail. We also want to gather nontechnical information that might be used in a social-engineering attack.

A key starting place is determining what IP address ranges are associated with your organization. You can get this information by querying the ARIN database at http://www.arin.net. Query instructions are available on its website, but a basic query you'll want to include is ">*YOURORG*★" (for example, ">George Mason University★"). This will return a list of matching resource records from the ARIN database and show the net blocks associated with each. An example of this is shown in Figure 22.1. You will want to compare this information with the IP ranges you gathered during the planning stage to see if any address ranges got left out. If you discover new address ranges that you feel should be included, you will need to modify your rules-of-engagement document to include the new addresses.

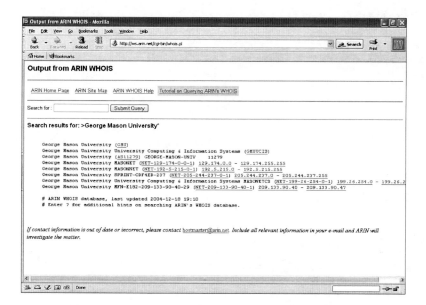

Figure 22.1 ARIN can be used to locate the IP address ranges associated with a particular organization.

You can also find out useful information by querying the various whois databases for any domain names you have registered. A good site to use for this is Allwhois.com. This site provides a single interface for searching many different registration databases. Whois queries can reveal several useful facts about an Internet site. Whois will give you two main types of information. First, it reveals the DNS names and IP addresses of the name servers. You can use this information in the next step when we attempt to collect DNS information. In addition, whois will often show contact information, including names, addresses, and phone numbers for people within the organization who are responsible in some way for the Internet site. This information can be very useful for social engineering. The following is an example of the type of result you may receive from a whois search:

```
Domain Name: GMU.EDU

Registrant:
   George Mason University
   4400 University Drive
   Fairfax, VA 22030
   UNITED STATES

Contacts:

   Administrative Contact:
   Tracy Holt
   George Mason University
   ITU Thompson Hall
   4400 University Drive
   Fairfax, VA 22030
   UNITED STATES
   (703) 993-3356
   holt@gmu.edu


   Technical Contact:
   Same as above

Name Servers:
   PORTAL-0-8.GMU.EDU       129.174.0.8
   THALASSA.GMU.EDU         129.174.1.3
   UVAARPA.VIRGINIA.EDU     128.143.2.7

Domain record activated:    14-Oct-1987
Domain record last updated: 05-Mar-2002
```

> **Tip**
>
> For an informative description of social-engineering techniques, take a look at the "Social Engineering Fundamentals" article by Sarah Granger at http://www.securityfocus.com/infocus/1527.

Once you've finished your ARIN and whois searches, it is time to start gathering DNS information. Nslookup is a tool included with most operating systems that can be used to determine DNS-related information. Some DNS servers may also allow you to obtain a listing of all registered names and addresses via a technique referred to as a *zone transfer*. A zone transfer is a complete transfer of all domain information that the DNS server contains. Zone transfers are included in the DNS standard to allow DNS servers within a domain to stay synchronized. Previously, it was common for DNS servers to allow anyone to initiate a zone transfer. Now, most sites have configured their DNS servers to reject anonymous DNS zone transfer requests. It is still worth verifying that your site does not allow zone transfers from every DNS server you maintain.

Various websites and utilities are available to make many aspects of the initial reconnaissance phase almost effortless. One such site is http://www.all-nettools.com/toolbox, which provides web-based access to tools, such as whois and nslookup. You can also use utilities such as NetScanTools Pro that run on your workstation and incorporate miscellaneous investigative tools into a single interface (http://www.nwpsw.com/). Figure 22.2 shows the GUI interface of NetScanTools Pro performing a DNS lookup.

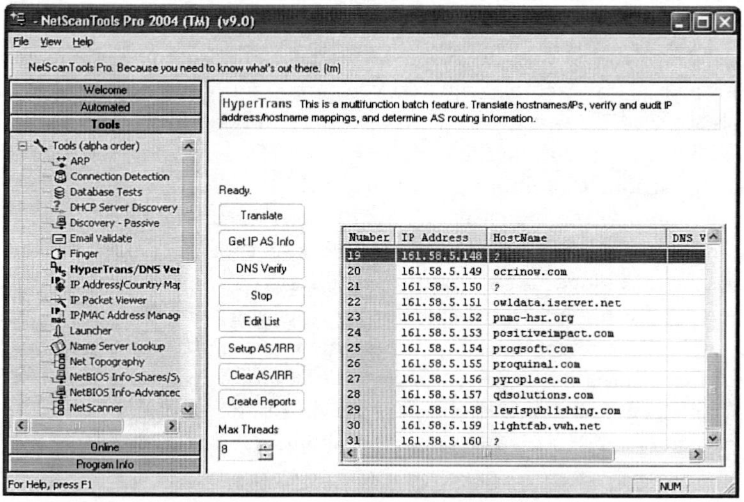

Figure 22.2 NetScanTools can be used to obtain detailed DNS information about the organization.

DNS discovery can also be performed using the `nslookup` command; however, it is much easier to point and click than to issue hundreds of commands via the command line. This example shows how the same investigative steps would look when using `nslookup` from the command line. The bold text indicates commands, and the rest indicates displayed output.

```
>nslookup
Default Server:  dns.xyz.com
Address:  192.168.200.250

> set type=any
> 12.142.174.129.in-addr.arpa.
Server:  dns.xyz.com
Address:  192.168.200.250

Non-authoritative answer:
12.142.174.129.in-addr.arpa        name = megalon.ise.gmu.edu

142.174.129.in-addr.arpa        nameserver = ite.gmu.edu
142.174.129.in-addr.arpa        nameserver = portal.gmu.edu
ite.gmu.edu      internet address = 129.174.40.84
```

In addition to standard DNS queries, you'll want to perform reverse lookups. Instead of resolving names to IP addresses, reverse lookups resolve IP addresses to names. Many DNS names are descriptive and can provide valuable information about the purpose of the host, as well as its location, because many organizations use geographic information in their hostnames. For example, what do you think londonfw.example.com could be? Many tools are available that can be used to exhaustively perform a reverse lookup of every IP address in a given range, including NetScanTools Pro.

Another great source of information you should include in your initial reconnaissance is your organization's web presence. Organization's often unknowingly publish private information to the Internet, such as usernames and corporate contact information. A tool such as BlackWidow (http://www.softbytelabs.com) can be used to crawl through your websites gathering information, and it provides you with the ability to quickly search through the resultant data. Figure 22.3 shows a sample session of BlackWidow. A couple freeware alternatives are wget (http://www.gnu.org/software/wget/wget.html), a command-line tool included with many Linux distributions, and HTTrack (http://www.httrack.com), an open source tool with GUI that works on both Linux and Windows.

Regardless of which tool you use, you will want to search for sensitive information in the pages you gather. Many types of information may be exposed on a website. For instance, backup copies of the programs that implement the website may be accessible, or you may have accidentally placed sensitive corporate documents within the site. Table 22.2 shows some good search terms you may want to include in your analysis.

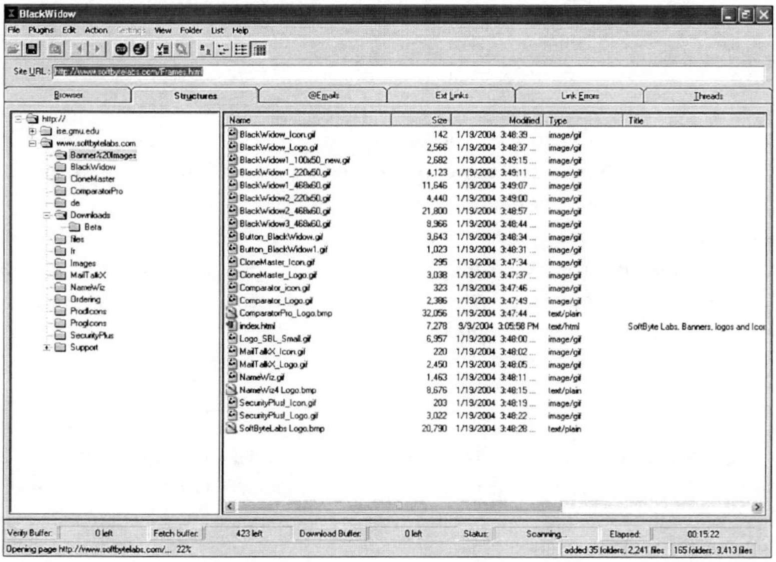

Figure 22.3 BlackWidow can be used to download an entire website.

Table 22.2 Sample Search Terms for Finding Sensitive Information from Your Websites

Search Terms	Purpose
.asp, .php, .cgi, .cfm	Find web programs
.asp~, .php~, .cgi~, .cfm~, .bak	Find backups of web programs
password, pass, pwd, shadow, secret	Find passwords
username, user, usr	Find user accounts
.mdb, .db	Find databases

You may also want to use terms based on data specific to your organization. For example, if you work for a pharmaceutical company, you may want to search on terms related to any proprietary drug research the company is conducting. More generically, you should search for IT and security-related items, such as network diagrams and firewall policies. You'd be surprised how often this technique reveals breaches in data confidentiality.

In addition to searching your websites, you may want to see what web search engines have archived from your sites. Web search engines regularly crawl Internet-accessible websites, including yours. Once they do this, anyone can query the search engine to gather information about you. A whole subcategory of hacking has grown up around search engines. It is often referred to as *Google hacking* because of the popularity of using Google to perform this type of attack.

Two Google search extensions you will find useful (if you're using Google during your assessments) are `inurl` and `link`. `Inurl` allows you to limit Google's search to pages related to your site. For example, to search only on SANS Institute–related websites, you could specify `inurl:sans.org` as one of your search terms.

`Link` can be used to see all the web pages that link to a particular page. Normally, some type of relationship exists between organizations that link to each other's sites. Some of these relationships concern business operations. For instance, a company that sells your products may provide a link on its site to yours. Also, it's not uncommon to discover that employees (or ex-employees) have set up personal websites that contain sensitive information about your organization. Because these sites often contain links back to your main web page, Google's `link` feature allows you to find them easily.

> **Tip**
>
> The site http://johnny.ihackstuff.com/ contains a large database of Google search terms you can use to discover sensitive information that has leaked out of your websites. This includes searches to find particular web software, locate login portals, and even reveal passwords. You can take the examples provided on the site and combine them with the `inurl` search syntax to determine whether your site is revealing information it shouldn't.

You have now completed the reconnaissance phase of the assessment. At this point, you should have some general knowledge about your organization, its IP address range, and addresses of at least a few publicly accessible servers (such as DNS, web, and mail). Given that these systems are available in some capacity directly from the Internet, they are the most likely systems to be attacked; therefore, you should pay special attention to them. After the initial reconnaissance phase is done, you need to continue by gathering more in-depth information about the targeted network.

Network Service Discovery

In this step of the assessment, you use host and port scanners to actively examine the network ranges you discovered during the reconnaissance step. This will reveal the existence of servers and services running on those servers. Some of the information you discover during this step you will already have uncovered during the initial reconnaissance. However, it is likely that you will uncover a large population of systems that you were previously unaware of. All the information you collect in this step will feed into the next, where you will probe discovered systems to determine their potential vulnerabilities.

System Enumeration

The two main aspects of network service discovery are system enumeration and service discovery. System enumeration combines discovery and analysis techniques to locate systems that can be used as access points into the network. Once you have located these systems, you then move on to service discovery, where you attempt to determine what network services are available on the discovered computer systems. We'll first start by showing you how to perform system enumeration.

Network Scanners

The standard method to discover devices on a network is to perform an ICMP scan, which simply issues ICMP echo request messages in hopes of receiving ICMP echo replies (for example, ping). You have a huge number of tools to choose from to perform your scan. SuperScan, available from http://www.foundstone.com/, is a free Windows utility that, in addition to supporting other techniques, can perform ICMP scans. Some of the many ICMP scanners for UNIX systems include fping (http://www.fping.com/) and pinger (http://packetstorm.widexs.nl/groups/rhino9/).

Figure 22.4 illustrates hosts and devices that are discovered when performing an ICMP scan using SuperScan. Keep in mind that results of an ICMP scan are not always exhaustive because routers and firewalls often block ICMP traffic, effectively hiding internal systems from ICMP scans. This is why we employ several network-scanning techniques—to determine the presence of network devices and hosts that might be invisible to a particular scanner.

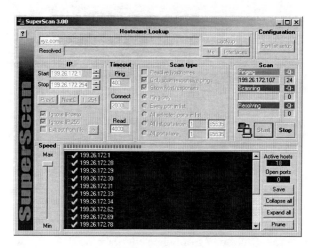

Figure 22.4   SuperScan can perform ICMP scans to detect systems that are available on the targeted network.

Tip

When you're performing the assessment, a good rule of thumb is to start small by scanning one subnet at a time. Performing scans in smaller increments allows for the assessment of a large network to become a more manageable task. Additionally, controlling the rate and breadth of network scans aids in the prevention of network saturation and possible failure.

Even if ICMP traffic is blocked at the border of your network, you can still locate remotely accessible hosts by performing scans using TCP or UDP packets. In this case, you would use a network scanner, such as SuperScan or Nmap, to probe all IP addresses in the targeted address range on commonly open ports. Figure 22.5 shows the results of a network scan that SuperScan performed. Instead of issuing ICMP packets, we configured the program to locate all hosts that answer to connections on TCP ports 25 (SMTP), 80 (HTTP), and 21 (FTP). In this case, only two hosts were located, both apparently running web server software.

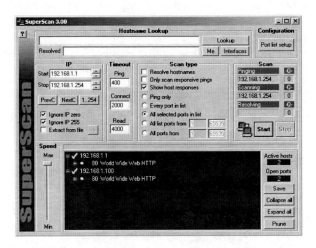

Figure 22.5 SuperScan can locate remotely accessible systems by attempting to connect to commonly used ports.

Traceroute

In addition to scanning, you may also want to use traceroute to discover the path your packets are taking to reach the hosts your scans revealed. The following are some ways to use traceroute (or *tracert* under Windows) to learn about the targeted network:

- Traceroute results will often stop when the trace reaches a firewall. This can be very useful to you as you map out the structure of your network.

- A traceroute to a targeted host reports the networks and systems that the traffic passes through. This information might be useful in determining which paths connect the targeted network to the Internet, and, potentially, what internal devices route packets to publicly accessible systems.

- Sometimes a traceroute returns unexpected IP addresses. For example, you might see an address such as 10.3.1.70, which is most likely an internal network address being "leaked" through a misconfigured or malfunctioning device that performs Network Address Translation (NAT).

At this point of the external assessment, you have gone through several stages of learning about the targeted network. You started off with planning, performed initial reconnaissance, and enumerated systems that were accessible from the Internet. You are now ready to focus on the configuration details of the individual hosts you have uncovered so far.

Service Discovery

Now that you have mapped the targeted network, you are ready to probe individual systems in an attempt to determine which operating system they are running, locate ports that can be accessed remotely, determine the service software running on these ports, and access the services to determine additional host details. This prepares you for the next step, in which you probe discovered systems and services for exploitable vulnerabilities.

Port scanners can probe individual systems and network ranges to locate open ports associated with commonly used services, potential vulnerabilities, or specific exploits. For example, an attacker can run Nmap to find devices that have TCP port 27374 open, which might indicate that they are infected by the SubSeven Trojan.

Nmap

Nmap (http://www.nmap.org/) is one of the most popular and powerful tools for identifying open ports in a system. Nmap can perform different types of scans that help you determine which traffic is allowed to pass through your access control devices. You can use Nmap to perform scans with TCP, UDP, and ICMP packets in an effort to acquire system information. Each Nmap option attempts to connect with the target system in a different way. Nmap is one of the most popular network scanners because of its flexible scanning options and its availability on multiple OS platforms.

The following is an example of a SYN scan directed at a remotely accessible server. It shows the Nmap program performing a SYN scan, as specified by the -sS parameter. The -O option specifies that Nmap should attempt to guess what type of OS the target system is running.

```
# nmap -sS -O 192.168.254.6

Starting nmap 3.75 ( http://www.insecure.org/nmap/ ) at 2004-12-18 09:56 EST
Interesting ports on 192.168.254.6:
(The 1661 ports scanned but not shown below are in state: closed)
PORT    STATE SERVICE
135/tcp open  msrpc
139/tcp open  netbios-ssn
MAC Address: 00:0D:60:F8:FA:62 (IBM)
Device type: general purpose
Running: Microsoft Windows 2003/.NET|NT/2K/XP
OS details: Microsoft Windows Server 2003 or XP SP2
```

> **Tip**
>
> Using Nmap to perform only a SYN scan does not exhaustively determine accessibility of remote systems and services; additional scans, such as FIN, XMAS, and UDP, should be executed as well. This is because different firewalls tend to block different types of discovery activities. By trying more than one scanning method, you can determine how effective your firewall is at blocking these packets.

In this example, Nmap not only determined which ports were open on the host, but also was able to guess its operating system, which might help later when assessing the system for vulnerabilities. Knowing open ports on the remote host enables you to determine versions of the services that are listening on those ports. Often, all you have to do is connect to the ports using a tool as commonplace as the Telnet client. The Telnet client can connect to more than the Telnet service. By providing a port number after the host, you can make the Telnet client connect to any TCP port. For instance, `telnet 192.168.5.12 21`, will make the Telnet client connect to the FTP port on the computer system located at 192.168.5.12.

Telnet and Banner Retrieval

Knowing which versions of applications are in use on the targeted system can help you locate vulnerabilities that might be exploitable over the network. After you know which TCP ports are open on the targeted hosts, you can try connecting to those ports that look particularly interesting. Some of the services that often announce their version when you simply connect to them using the Telnet client are Telnet (TCP port 23), FTP (TCP port 21), and SSH (TCP port 22). For example, you can often obtain the version of the SSH server running on the target by connecting to its TCP port 22, as follows:

```
# telnet 192.168.5.12 22
SSH-1.99-OpenSSH_2.9
```

Some services, such as SMTP (TCP port 25) and HTTP (TCP port 80), require you to issue a request after you connect with Telnet before revealing their version. For example, you can determine the version of the remote web server by connecting to port 80 on the server using the `telnet` command, typing `HEAD / HTTP/1.0`, and pressing Enter twice:

```
# telnet 192.168.5.12 80
HEAD / HTTP/1.0

HTTP/1.1 200 OK
Date: Sat, 02 Mar 2002 00:09:55 GMT
Server: Apache/1.3.19 (Unix) Resin/1.2.2 PHP/4.1.2 mod_ssl/2.8.1 OpenSSL/0.9.6
Last-Modified: Thu, 08 Nov 2004 00:08:32 GMT
ETag: "9cf48-244-3aa6cd80"
Accept-Ranges: bytes
Content-Length: 580
Connection: close
Content-Type: text/html
```

As you can see, this web server seems to be running Apache version 1.3.19 on a UNIX platform, with several modules that might contain vulnerabilities. Port and vulnerability scanners might be able to automatically obtain versions of certain applications. Nmap has had this ability since version 3.4. You activate it using the -sV flag, which stands for *version scan*. Here is an example that shows that Nmap is able to determine versions of the SSH server and web server on the targeted system:

```
# nmap -sV 192.168.254.2

Starting nmap 3.75 ( http://www.insecure.org/nmap ) at 2004-12-18 10:20 Eastern
Standard Time
Interesting ports on 192.168.254.2:
(The 1659 ports scanned but not shown below are in state: closed)
PORT      STATE SERVICE VERSION
22/tcp    open  ssh     OpenSSH 3.5p1 (protocol 1.99)
80/tcp    open  http    Apache httpd 2.0.40 ((Red Hat Linux))
111/tcp   open  rpcbind 2 (rpc #100000)
6000/tcp  open  X11     (access denied)
MAC Address: 00:0C:29:C2:6F:8F (VMware)

Nmap run completed -- 1 IP address (1 host up) scanned in 10.785 seconds
```

You may notice at this point that you are starting to collect a large amount of information about your network. You will need to organize your data collection for it to be any good to you later. One method you may want to use is to build a system matrix that reflects what you know about the targeted systems. Table 22.3 presents an example of one such matrix.

Table 22.3 **A System Matrix Helps Keep Track of Detailed Information Discovered During the Assessment**

System	IP Address	Available Services	Operating System	Version
br2-dc1.abtltd.com	x.x.x.1	25	Cisco 3600	IOS 12.0(5)
smtp.xyz.com 8.11.1	x.x.x.10	22, 25, 53, 110	SunOS 2.6	ESMTP-Sendmail
ftp.xyz.com	x.x.x.15	21, 22, 5631	UNIX (type undetermined)	WU-FTP 2.6.0(1)
www.xyz.com	x.x.x.28	80, 443	Linux	Apache 1.3.22, OpenSSL 0.9.6a
ns1.xyz.com	x.x.x.53	25, 53	SunOS 5.8	BIND 8.2.3

As the amount of information you know about your network grows, the more targeted the next step in the process will be. Network and port scanners bring you closer to the target by locating and analyzing open service ports. A different class of scanners is needed to test these open service ports to detect vulnerabilities. Scanners that are able to obtain detailed information about remotely accessible applications and determine whether they are vulnerable to known exploits are called *vulnerability scanners*. Vulnerability scanners are used to locate exploitable weaknesses in applications and operating systems, as we discuss in the following section.

Vulnerability Discovery

Vulnerability discovery is the assessment step where you start to determine what your findings will be. Sometimes, just the information that your port scanning and banner grabbing gives you is enough to strongly suggest certain vulnerabilities. For instance, if your scanning revealed to you that one of your Windows servers is running Apache 2.0.38, it is likely that the server is susceptible to a directory traversal attack (http://www.securityfocus.com/bid/5434). This can be tricky, though. In the case of this vulnerability, the administrator could have fixed the problem by upgrading the Apache software or by making a change to the Apache configuration file. The first approach would be easily detected because the software upgrade would also cause the banner to change. The second approach, although just as effective at fixing the vulnerability, would not change the banner, leaving us with a false impression of vulnerability. This is the problem that vulnerability scanners are meant to solve. These tools work at the application layer, combining various testing techniques to determine whether a vulnerability exists. Although not perfect, they are a large step beyond what we can accomplish through port scanning alone.

Vulnerability scanners often possess network- and port-scanning capabilities similar to the scanners we have discussed so far, but they can also probe audited systems for vulnerabilities. Unlike port scanners, which typically operate at the transport layer and lower, vulnerability scanners have the ability to locate vulnerabilities at the application layer. By using both port and vulnerability scanners, you can achieve a comprehensive awareness of the state of your network's defenses. We begin by looking at Nessus, an open source vulnerability scanner, which we will then compare to several commercially available alternatives.

> **Note**
>
> Even if you cannot locate any known vulnerabilities in your network, it may still be vulnerable to attack. Unknown vulnerabilities are ones that exist in services you are using but have not been discovered (or revealed) to the computer security community. Because you have no way to know they exist, you will not know to look for them. A proactive approach to this problem is discussed in Chapter 23, "Design Under Fire." However, don't be too concerned. If the computer security community does not know of the vulnerability, the majority of network attackers will not know of it either. It's always better to fix what you can fix first before worrying about harder problems.

Nessus

Nessus (http://www.nessus.org/), a high-quality open source vulnerability scanner, offers the ability to scan for accessible service ports, and it can perform security checks to determine whether known exploits can be applied to discovered systems. Most vulnerability scanners rely on a database of scripted tests they perform to attempt to discover vulnerabilities on scanned computer systems. Nessus refers to these scripts as *plug-ins*. The set of plug-ins available for Nessus is large (currently over 5,800). Plug-ins exist to attempt many classic vulnerability types (for example, remote access) and to assess many types of devices (for example, Cisco, Windows, UNIX). You can also write your own plug-ins either using your favorite scripting language or using the Nessus attack scripting language (NASL), Nessus's internal scripting language.

Tip

All of Nessus's included plug-ins are written in NASL and are available for your review. You can learn a lot about how Nessus operates by examining these scripts. This can be especially useful to learn the limitations of the scripts. If you have a particular finding that continually shows up in your environment, but you have verified that it is unimportant (for example, a false positive), you can look at the script that is reporting the vulnerability to see if it can be improved for your site to produce better results!

While you are performing the vulnerability discovery phase of the assessment, you might decide to audit your systems in stages, according to the function they perform. For example, consider first focusing on your high-profile devices, such as your firewalls. You would then configure Nessus to test for only commonly exploited firewall vulnerabilities. You might then focus special attention on your web servers because of their high visibility and accessibility. Whatever the case, you simply have to select the Nessus plug-in family you require and specify which systems to scan. Nessus plug-ins are grouped into categories, such as backdoors, small services, Microsoft Windows, and CGI abuses.

Tip

Limiting the tests that a vulnerability scanner uses will dramatically speed up the time it takes the scanner to run. This can be very important if you plan to scan frequently or if you have a large network to examine. A good practice is to occasionally run comprehensive scans while running targeted scans much more frequently. Depending on your environment, daily scans may not be too frequent. To make this work, you will need to spend time deciding what tests to include in your frequent scan. A good place to start building your list is the SANS Top 20 Vulnerabilities (www.sans.org/top20/).

After performing a vulnerability scan, Nessus compiles a summary report, illustrated in Figure 22.6, which helps to focus your attention on security weaknesses that require your immediate attention. In this example, Nessus was able to enumerate various user accounts while assessing a Windows file server.

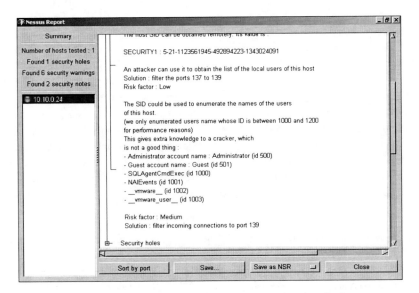

Figure 22.6   A Nessus assessment report summarizes findings
of the vulnerability scan—in this case, of a Windows system.

> **Note**
>
> Although Nessus is an open source tool, Tenable, the company maintaining Nessus, has recently decided to
> start selling the plug-ins it produces. Plug-ins created by the open source community will remain free, and
> Tenable does currently allow free (though delayed) access to its private plug-ins for noncommercial use.

ISS Internet Scanner

ISS Internet Scanner (http://www.iss.net/) is another popular vulnerability assessment
tool, which rivals the thoroughness of Nessus and has the advantages and the disadvantages of being a commercial product. ISS Internet Scanner performs many of the same
functions as Nessus, including port scanning, service verification, and software fingerprinting.

ISS Internet Scanner offers tailored sessions depending on the OS, the role of the system, and the level of thoroughness you desire. For example, if your plan is to assess a
UNIX system that is running Apache, you might select the UNIX web session with the
desired level of thoroughness. The higher level, the more vulnerability checks will be
performed. ISS Internet Scanner also produces high-quality, flexible reports that can be
tailored to executives, management, or technicians.

Figure 22.7 shows a vulnerability detail screen from ISS Internet Scanner. As you
review the vulnerability report, you have a comprehensible description of the vulnerability as well as a path to remedy the problem. In this illustration, you can see that a high-
risk vulnerability in the Microsoft SQL server service has been found. The description of

the "MDAC OpenRowSet buffer overflow vulnerability" shows what impact the vulnerability would have on the system—in this case, allowing an attacker to gain complete control over the SQL server and possibly issue operating system commands. This information will be very useful to you later as you try to prioritize the vulnerabilities in your report. ISS also provides remediation information. In this example, you are directed to Microsoft Security Bulletin MS02-040 to understand how to resolve the vulnerability.

ISS Internet Scanner provides an extensive vulnerability database. In addition, it offers an easy-to-use update feature, guaranteeing that the most current data is available. When a new vulnerability is discovered or when new malicious code becomes publicly available, ISS's X-Force team quickly updates its vulnerability database to allow customers to scan for these items. It is important to note that all the vulnerability-scanning product vendors (including Nessus) claim to provide rapid updates to their database, and, in fact, this is true. It is also true that each tool has some vulnerabilities that it uniquely scans for. For this reason, it is not a bad idea to include more than one vulnerability scanner in your toolbox.

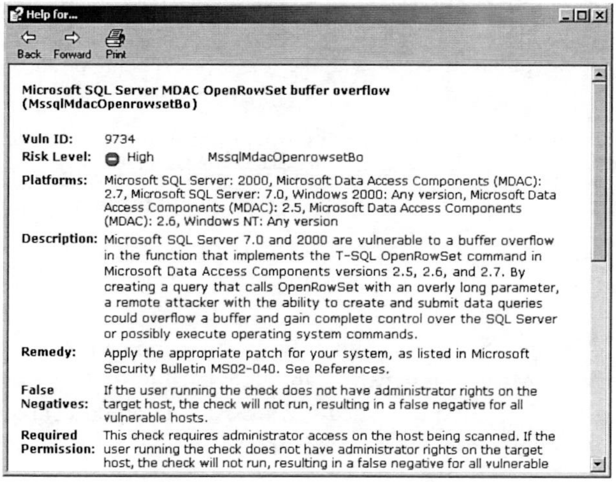

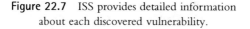

Figure 22.7   ISS provides detailed information
about each discovered vulnerability.

Retina

Retina is a commercial scanner produced by eEye Security (http://www.eeye.com/) that competes with ISS Internet Scanner. Retina provides a clean Windows-based interface, as illustrated in Figure 22.8. Retina offers a single interface that incorporates a vulnerability scanner, an Internet browser, a system miner module (which simulates hacking stimulus), and a tracer utility (which offers traceroute-like functionality). Retina offers a quality solution because of its user friendliness, technical robustness, ability to automatically correct some vulnerabilities, as well as detailed explanations for resolving discovered issues.

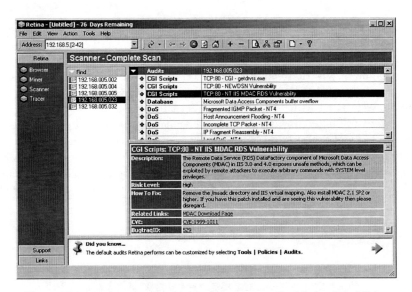

Figure 22.8   In this example, Retina discovers several critical vulnerabilities, including specific problems with the web server running on the system.

Some scanners are better at probing specific operating systems or applications than others. LANguard, for example, is a powerful scanner for probing systems regardless of their OS, but it is particularly effective for obtaining detailed information about Windows hosts.

LANguard

GFI LANguard Network Security Scanner (http://www.gfi.com/lannetscan) provides robust functionality for scanning networks and individual hosts. This tool performs especially well when assessing Windows-based systems. Among other techniques, LANguard can utilize Windows null session connections to execute information-gathering and enumerating processes. LANguard also comes in handy when assessing any device that accepts Simple Network Management Protocol (SNMP) connections. If you are able to guess the target's SNMP community string, which is just like a password, you might be able to access extensive amounts of information regarding this device. In Figure 22.9, LANguard discovers enough information to plan an attack against this Windows XP system.

All four vulnerability scanners we've discussed offer many similar options and functionality. Let's summarize how they relate to each other:

- Nessus is a wonderful open source tool. It has continued to be refined over the years and now competes head-to-head with commercial vulnerability scanners, though its reporting system is not yet as flexible as some of the other choices available. Nessus is also a good choice as a complementary vulnerability scanner.

- ISS Internet Scanner offers mid-size to large corporations a robust vulnerability scanning tool, complete with easy software updates and excellent reporting that can be catered for specific audiences. Many sites already have site licenses for ISS Internet Scanner, especially organizations that already license other ISS software such as the RealSecure IDS.

- Retina is great for scanning mid-size to large corporations. Retina and ISS Internet Scanner are both excellent at locating and providing detailed guidance for vulnerabilities. Retina, however, offers an interface that is somewhat easier to navigate and configure.

- GFI LANguard Network Security Scanner is an excellent comprehensive vulnerability scanner but is particularly good at examining Windows-based systems.

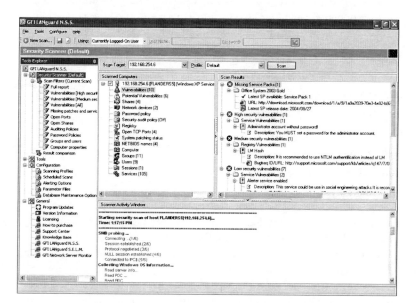

Figure 22.9   In this example, LANguard enumerates sensitive information from a Windows XP system.

You have now completed several steps in your external assessment, starting with planning and continuing to enumerate systems, services, and vulnerabilities. By using a variety of network and vulnerability scanners, you can gain an understanding of the possible weaknesses in your security perimeter. You can learn which service ports can be accessed and exploited from the outside world, and you can discover configuration errors that might result in the network's defenses operating differently from what you originally expected.

You have used these network and vulnerability scanners to gather information about your organization, and your system matrix should be fully populated with an assortment of information about your external devices. The next step of the assessment is to further research what vulnerabilities are likely to affect your systems that are publicly accessible.

Vulnerability Research

One of the problems with automated vulnerability assessment tools is they often report vulnerabilities that do not actually exist. These bogus findings are called *false positives*. You will need to perform some additional research to determine which vulnerabilities are real and which are fake.

As a security analyst, you can research vulnerabilities in effort to determine whether they are real as well as the level of risk associated with them. You will also need to determine the best ways of mitigating each of them. An excellent source of information on vulnerabilities and their resolutions are your software vendors' websites, along with vulnerability announcement mailing lists, such as Bugtraq. You can conduct additional research by checking security-oriented websites such as the following:

- http://www.securityfocus.com/
- http://www.cve.mitre.org/
- http://www.ntbugtraq.com/
- http://packetstorm.widexs.nl/
- http://www.cotse.com/
- http://www.infosyssec.com/
- http://searchsecurity.techtarget.com/
- http://www.secunia.com/

These sites provide much more detail about particular vulnerabilities than is typically provided by a vulnerability-scanning tool. By carefully analyzing the information from the vulnerability announcement, combined with examination of the system the vulnerability was reported on, you may be able to eliminate the vulnerability from consideration. This can be somewhat laborious, but well worth the effort if it allows your administrators to concentrate on what's important instead of wasting time responding to false information.

At this point in the assessment, you have determined what public services you are allowing out to the Internet and whether these services have potentially exploitable vulnerabilities. You still have work to do, though. Your perimeter devices may be allowing more packets to flow through them than required. In addition, other backdoor access to your network may be possible using either modems, wireless devices, or VPN connections. In the next couple steps, you will examine these additional access methods to ensure they are as secure as possible.

Verification of Perimeter Components

In the "Accomodating Change" section of Chapter 19, "Maintaining a Security Perimeter," we described the need to thoroughly test hosts, devices, and applications before deploying them on a production network. Components of the security perimeter should undergo such testing as well, both in the lab environment before deployment and as part of your vulnerability assessments. This part of the assessment focuses on ensuring that access restrictions implemented by your security devices are properly implemented, even if they do not allow access to a vulnerable service on your network. To test whether access controls are properly implemented, you need to be intimately familiar with your security policy so that you can locate deviations from it.

In this section, we concentrate on verifying controls that are implemented by a border firewall to demonstrate what's involved in testing the configuration of a perimeter component; however, the same techniques should be used to verify proper application of the security policy on any other device that restricts the way traffic moves across your network.

As a security analyst who is about to audit the security policy implemented by your firewall, you need to make sure a plan is laid out to systematically validate mechanisms that control components of your infrastructure. You will need to verify that rule sets and ACLs have the intended effect. For each rule in your firewall, whether it allows or blocks traffic, you need to verify that network traffic travels as expected.

Preparing for the Firewall Validation

Your border firewall is primarily responsible for controlling the flow of traffic between the internal network and the Internet. The firewall's assessment should verify that network traffic complies with the intent of the firewall rules. For example, if the firewall rulebase is configured to allow SMTP traffic from the Internet to a mail server that is located in a screened network, you will attempt to connect to the mail server from the Internet to guarantee that traffic passes through the firewall as defined in the rulebase. You must further validate that only SMTP traffic from the Internet is allowed to pass and that all other traffic is rejected by the firewall and logged accordingly. In the event that you are able to connect to the mail server from an unapproved network, you must inspect the firewall configuration to determine the cause of the deviation from your security policy.

Figure 22.10 provides an example of a common network configuration, which we will use to demonstrate how to perform an assessment of the firewall. To test how traffic from the Internet traverses the firewall, we have set up an assessment station outside of the organization's network. We have also configured listener systems to see what packets are able to pass through the firewall. The assessment station is equipped with network and the vulnerability scanners we discussed in the "Network Service Discovery" and "Vulnerability Discovery" sections of this chapter. Listener systems are configured to monitor network traffic in promiscuous mode on internal subnets. The listening systems are configured with packet-sniffing software, such as Tcpdump (http://www. tcpdump.org/). Another graphical alternative is Ethereal (http://www.ethereal.com/), which is available for free and can be used on UNIX and Windows systems.

> **Tip**
>
> Although normally used as an IDS, Snort (http://www.snort.org/) can also be very useful for vulnerability assessment. It can be configured on a "listener" station to watch the network for specific patterns and types of traffic to determine whether your defense lines are filtering against such traffic.

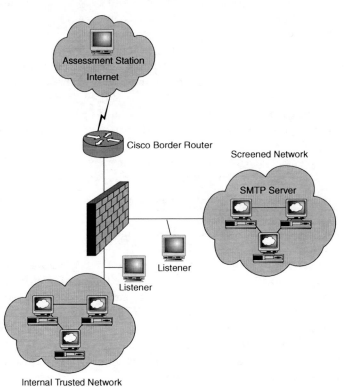

Figure 22.10   Assessment and listener stations are placed at key points of the network to conduct an internal assessment of the border firewall.

Your listener systems monitor packets that pass the firewall and help determine whether access controls succeeded or failed. With logging enabled on the firewall, you can view the log file to determine which packets were accepted or dropped during the audit, but these logs rarely provide as much detail as a listening station that is equipped with a sniffer. To fully audit the border firewall, you must move the assessment station from the Internet to another network segment to validate access controls for each firewall interface.

Verifying Access Controls

To verify that the firewall properly enforces access controls, you can utilize a scanner, such as Nmap or SuperScan, to perform the following tests:

- Verify that the firewall service ports that should be explicitly blocked are indeed blocked and that approved traffic is allowed to pass.
- Verify controls over broadcasts and other types of discovery traffic.
- Verify that authorized firewall management stations are the only devices allowed to establish an interactive session with the firewall.
- Verify that only authorized traffic can cross boundaries of internal subnets.

Your audit of the firewall's configuration begins by attempting to access systems and services that are behind the firewall.

Traffic Restrictions

During the external assessment, you used network scanners, such as Nmap, to determine what devices can be accessed from the Internet. We use the same process, depicted in Figure 22.11, to ensure that unauthorized traffic is blocked by the firewall and that approved traffic is allowed to pass. The arrows represent the inbound discovery requests from the assessment station directed toward the devices located in the screened network.

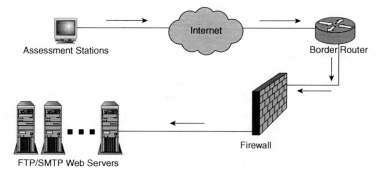

Figure 22.11   The assessment station issues discovery packets in an attempt to reach servers located behind the firewall.

To use Nmap for determining whether the firewall blocks ICMP echo request traffic, you can use the -sP parameter to perform an ICMP scan, like this:

```
# nmap -sP -PE 192.168.1.1-254
```

If your security policy prohibits inbound ICMP traffic, the firewall should block this scan as the assessment station attempts to incrementally scan the 192.168.1.0/24 network. To ensure that the firewall blocked ICMP packets, you can check firewall logs, as well as sniffer logs, on the listener system.

Next, you can attempt to verify that your firewall drops all packets that are not destined for approved network devices. Nmap can perform such scans using the following syntax:

```
UDP: # nmap -sU -p 1-65534 IP_ADDR_OF_MONITOR
SYN: # nmap -sS -p 1-65534 IP_ADDR_OF_MONITOR
```

These two scans will attempt to connect to the monitoring system using every possible TCP and UDP port. You will want to try this with several different monitoring systems located on different interfaces of the firewall. Keep in mind that even if Nmap does not report a success, it is still possible that some of the probe packets made it through the firewall. Your monitoring stations should capture these probes, even if the replies from the probes are blocked by the firewall.

You should also try other Nmap scan types to see if your firewall is effective at blocking all discovery efforts. Here are some of the alternative Nmap scans you should include in this step:

- **ACK scans (-sA)**—These often pass through simple firewalls when SYN scans would be blocked.
- **FIN scans (-sF)**—These scans check to see if the flag used to close a TCP session will pass through the firewall.
- **NULL scan (-sN)**—Sends packets with no flags set. These should not normally appear on a network.
- **Frag option (-f)**—Combines with other scan types to create scans that use many tiny fragment packets. Many firewalls cannot properly handle fragments and may allow them through when they shouldn't.

After you have completed all your scan attempts, you will need to view your monitoring station's packet captures to see what got through. Figure 22.12 shows an example of what this may look like. If you detect traffic making it through your firewall that should have been denied, you will need to research your particular firewall to see how to eliminate the holes. Hopefully, this will be as simple as changing the firewall's configuration. If not, you may need to consult with the firewall vendor.

Firewall Management

You should also ensure that the firewall itself is well protected. An important part of this is control of the management interfaces used to configure and maintain the firewall. You want to verify that an attacker will not be able to connect directly to the firewall. Generally, the firewall should be configured to only allow connections from your administrative hosts. These administrative hosts should reside on a trusted internal management network. To verify that this is the case, attempt to connect to the firewall using its management console from the assessment station that is located on various network segments. You should also verify that the authentication credentials that your administrators use are strong and the credentials themselves are only passed across encrypted communications channels.

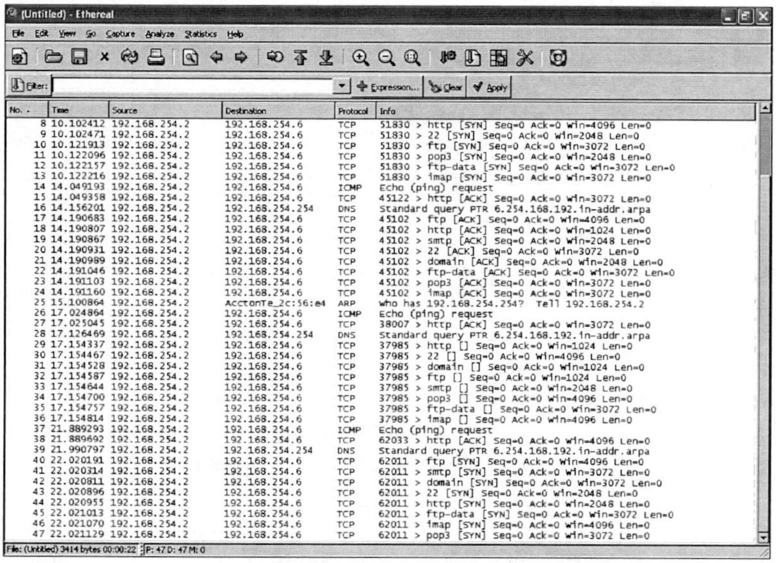

Figure 22.12 An example of some packets that got
through the firewall, captured using Ethereal.

You have analyzed the firewall rulebase and performed an audit to verify that traffic is allowed or denied according to controls that are defined in the security policy. Performing such an internal assessment is critical to locating misconfigurations or vulnerabilities of which an attacker might take advantage. As part of the assessment, you have clearly defined which traffic flows through the firewall. You may also want to apply these tests on other firewalls and routers within your network. Next we will look for other access methods that may expose your network to attack.

Remote Access

If attackers can't come in through the front door, they'll certainly go looking for the back. You will need to ensure that your authorized remote access systems (your backdoors) are well protected. In addition, you'll need to ensure that there are no backdoors you do not know about. In this step, we'll cover wardialing (searching for modems) and wardriving (searching for wireless access points). We'll also talk about VPN and reverse proxy testing.

Wardialing

Wardialing used to be the most popular way for attackers to break into corporate networks. This was before the Internet provided an easier method. Although its popularity has diminished, it is still a widely used technique for breaking past perimeter security controls.

Wardialing is primarily about finding modems within the phone number ranges assigned to your organization. The method is fairly easy. A computer is configured to dial each number and listen for any responding modem or fax tones. When it detects a modem or fax, it records the number and may also attempt to communicate with the responding device to determine what type of system it is. Smarter wardial programs are able to detect many remote access programs and can optionally attempt to log in to any authentication prompts provided by the answering modem.

One popular open source tool you can use for wardialing is THC-Scan from The Hackers Choice (http://www.thc.org). Although not exactly a new tool (the current version was released December 1998), it is still a useful wardialer. It supports the basics of wardialing and can detect modems, faxes, and PBXs, voice mail boxes, and voice (that is, a real person picking up the line).

Another more recent product that you may want to look into is ModemScan, available at http://www.wardial.net. ModemScan runs under Windows and has a user-friendly GUI. Many people find it easier to configure than THC-Scan, though both perform similar functions.

Commercial scanners are also worth examining. The current market leader is PhoneSweep, by SandStorm Enterprises (www.sandstorm.net/products/phonesweep). PhoneSweep supports many advanced features, including the ability to dial out on up to eight modems at one time simultaneously. PhoneSweep also has patented technology to support the identification of devices it detects.

Just as with any other part of your assessment, careful planning pays many dividends when performing your wardial. First, you need to determine which telephone lines belong to your organization. Even more important, you need to identify which numbers within this range are off limits. It is especially critical that you remove any emergency service numbers that may exist at your site. You would not want to block access to police, fire, and rescue numbers during your wardial exercise! All this targeting information needs to be included in your rules-of-engagement document.

You will also want to determine the times you will be wardialing. Getting a complete record of the modems in use in your environment may require conducting multiple wardial exercises during different hours of the day. For instance, users may only turn on their modems after hours to allow themselves access to their workstations from home. You may also want to avoid wardialing during certain periods to prevent business disruption. As with the target information, you will want to record test hours in the rules-of-engagement document.

Next, you will need to assemble your equipment. You will need a computer, modems, telephone lines, and software. It is better if the computer is not connected to your network. This is to prevent the remote possibility of someone dialing in to one of the attachment modems and gaining access to your network. The modems you select should be "real" modems, not Winmodems or any other type of DSP-based modem. Winmodems work by emulating a real modem and may not work as well for wardialing purposes. The telephone lines you use should be plain-old telephone service (POTS) lines. You should also disable any special phone services such as caller ID and call waiting. These can confuse the wardial software. Last, you will need to install and test the software you have selected to use.

Testing is an important part of wardialing. Wardials take a long time to finish. You would not want to conduct several days of wardialing only to find out that your wardialer was malfunctioning. Your test should include steps to verify that every type of connection you expect to encounter is properly identified by the wardialer. Here are some of the devices you may want to identify during your wardial exercise:

- Modems
- Faxes
- People
- Voice mail
- ISDN lines
- Busy lines

You will also need to decide how many rings to allow per number. Many modems will answer after only three rings, but this is configurable. If the modem is set to answer after five rings, and you only wait for four, you will not detect the modem. However, setting the ring count high will drastically slow down your scan. A typical setting is six rings, but you will need to carefully make this decision before proceeding.

Tip

Because many wardialers will default to five rings, you can add security to your site by increasing the ring count for your authorized modems to eight. Although this will make connecting to these modems slower, it may be a small price to pay to avoid detection by modem-based attackers.

Finally, you will perform the wardial. After the wardialer has finished, it should report back to you the telephone numbers with responding devices. Depending on the sophistication of your tool, you may also get other information, including identity and authentication details. For each reported number, you will need to verify whether the number is part of an authorized modem bank or is rogue. All rogue modems should be eliminated from your organization. For the remaining modems, you will want to verify that they effectively limit access to authorized users. This means enforcing the use of good usernames and passwords—or better yet, using a strong authentication system such as RSA's SecureID tokens.

Wardriving

801.11-based wireless LANS are very popular and very inexpensive to implement. In fact, they have become so inexpensive that users have probably started attaching wireless access points they have purchased to your internal network. Most of these have no security turned on, but as we discussed in Chapter 14, "Wireless Network Security," even if they did, attackers may still be able to use them to break into your network. Finding and eliminating these rogue access points is a very important part of securing your perimeter. In addition, you will want to verify that your authorized wireless LANS are properly secured.

Wardriving is the process of moving a wireless LAN receiving station around an area attempting to detect wireless LAN emissions. This can be done walking, driving, or even flying!

Most wardriving is performed using a laptop (or PDA) computer configured with software that sniffs wireless connections. It is also desirable to have a GPS or other type of location device to record exactly where you are when you detect the wireless LAN signals. The information you record in this case is the latitude, longitude, LAN identifier, and signal strength. If you move around and collect enough data, you can create a signal strength footprint that can be overlaid on top of a map. This makes it much easier to physically locate the access point.

> **Tip**
>
> Using an external antenna on the wireless access card you use for wardriving will dramatically increase the amount of access points you will detect. The internal antennas on most cards are toys compared to a good quality external antenna.

Many products exist to perform wardriving. A popular Windows-based program is Netstumbler (http://www.netstumbler.com). It has a well-designed graphical user interface and is reasonably easy to install. Many wardrivers, though, tend not to use it because it has difficulty detecting wireless access points that are not broadcasting their SSIDs.

Kismet is currently the most popular wardriving package. Kismet is available for Linux, and a port for Windows will probably eventually show up. What makes Kismet good for wardriving is that it will capture any wireless conversation that occurs and use this to detect access points, even if the access point is not broadcasting its SSID. In addition, Kismet can output packet captures in Tcpdump format. This makes it easy to analyze packet captures in open source packet-decoding software such as Ethereal. Last, Kismet (and Netstumbler) also supports a GPS interface to grab location data with every packet received. Figure 22.13 shows Kismet running at a recent SANS conference.

The process of performing the wardrive is fairly simple once you have your equipment set up and tested. Simply move your equipment around your facility, recording any signals you receive. If you detect an access point, you should collect enough information to identify it—and hopefully locate it. Later, you will compare the list of access points you found to the list of authorized access points for your site. Any rogue access points should be shut down immediately. This can be significantly complicated if you've got organizations near yours that have wireless LANs set up. In these cases, you may be able to use the location data from your GPS to determine whether the LAN is yours or not.

There are a couple of items to keep in mind if you plan to use a GPS to find access points. First, the GPS signal is line-of-site. If you cannot see the sky, you are probably not receiving any GPS signal. This means no location data inside. In these cases, you will have to manually record your location as you walk through a building. Next, make sure you are using an omni-directional antenna for GPS-based wardrives. Using a directional antenna will skew the signal strength results, depending on the direction the antenna is pointed. Use of directional antennas is still a good idea, though, to detect faint signals that may be coming out of some of your facilities.

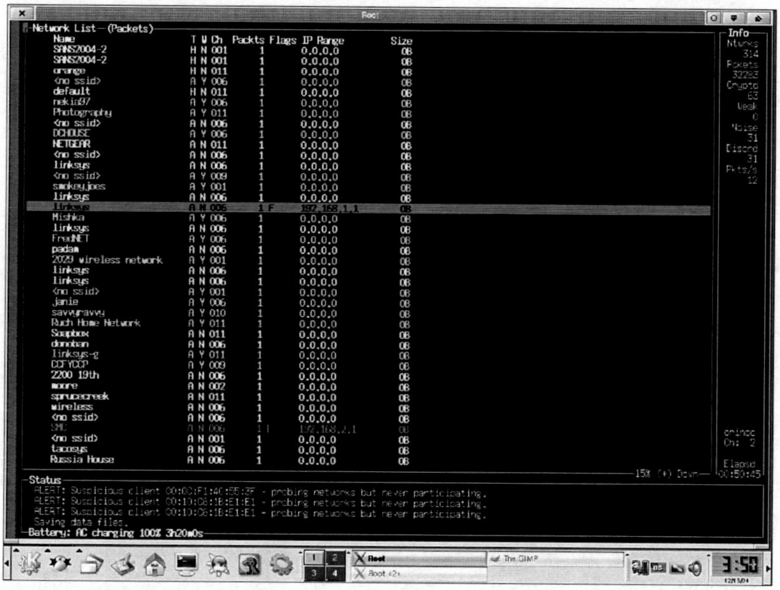

Figure 22.13   Kismet is excellent at detecting wireless access points.

If you are having difficulty tracking down an access point, you may be able to locate it based on the SSID. For instance, if you are near a Starbucks, an access point with an SSID of T-MOBILE is unlikely to be connected to your network! Instead, highly caffeinated customers are probably using it to surf the Internet.

At the end of your wardrive, you should have a good idea of what access points exist in your area. You can use this as a baseline for future scans, which you should conduct regularly. You will also want to verify the security controls for the access points you allow to remain on your network. As with modem-based access, strong authentication is a must. In addition, though, you should make sure that good encryption is used to protect all your wireless LAN conversations.

Note

The RC4-based encryption built in to 802.11 products is *not* considered strong.

VPNs and Reverse Proxies

The last form of remote access we will look at involves VPNs and remote proxies. Because the problems you will encounter are similar between VPNs and remote proxies, for the rest of this section, we will generically refer to both as VPNs. VPNs provide a popular way to allow remote employees to gain access to internal network resources. When well implemented, they can be very secure. However, it is important we verify that several key facets of the VPN are correct. Here are several areas we will need to examine:

- Encryption algorithm and key strength
- Method and strength of authentication
- Access controls
- Client-side restrictions

Encryption

Encryption has proven to be a reliable way of protecting network conversations. However, it is only as good as the algorithm and keys it is built upon. When assessing your VPNs you need to verify that a trusted algorithm is in use and that you cannot connect using weaker algorithms. Many VPN devices will support strong encryption but will agree to use weaker algorithms if requested. Man-in-the-middle attackers may make use of this feature by interrupting the session negotiations that make use of the better algorithms. Some VPNs will then fall back to the weaker systems. To make sure that your VPN does not do this, you should attempt to connect to your VPN using all the algorithms supported by your device and record which ones work. Any successful connections for algorithms or key sizes that are weaker than your policy allows indicates that your VPN may be vulnerable to this type of attack.

Authentication

The next item to examine is authentication. Any type of remote access should be carefully authenticated to prevent attackers from bypassing your perimeter controls. If you are using username/password-type authentication, you will want to make sure that your account policies are effective and that no weak passwords are assigned to your user accounts. Account policies, such as the number of attempts allowed before the account is locked out, can be tested by attempting to get the policy to trigger and noting the effect. If the account should lock out after three attempts, you should verify that this does happen by attempting four incorrect log-in attempts to the same account. Verifying password strength is more difficult.

A variety of password-cracking packages are available for your use. They can be separated into two main categories: online tools and offline tools. Online tools attempt to guess passwords by actually attempting logins. Any protocol that provides a login prompt can be assessed using an online tool. A good example of an online tool is Hydra (http://www.thc.org/releases.php). Hydra can attempt to log in to a target system using many protocols. It supports HTTP Auth, Telnet, FTP, IMAP, POP3, MySQL, and many others. In addition, Hydra is fully parallelized (it can send many simultaneous requests per second). Hydra is also the password cracker that Nessus uses to perform its password cracks.

Offline tools do not attempt to log in. Instead, they work using a copy of your encrypted (actually hashed) passwords. An offline tool works by taking a password guess, encrypting it using the same algorithm as the login process of the system being assessed, and then comparing the resulting value with the stored value. If the values match exactly, that means the guess equaled the password (in other words, the password has been cracked). Offline tools work many times faster than online tools, but you do need to be able to get a copy of the password file from the systems you will be assessing for them to work. You have many offline tools to choose from. On UNIX, many sites choose to use Crack, written by Alec Muffett (http://www.crypticide.com/users/alecm). Crack is primarily used for cracking passwords created using the crypt algorithm. This is the algorithm that most UNIX systems use to create their passwords. However, Crack can be compiled to support many other password algorithms. Crack is a dictionary-based tool that supports sophisticated word permutation. This means that you can feed Crack a list of words, and Crack will take each and perform interesting substitutions and modifications to crack the passwords when users have made small changes to a word to create their passwords. For instance, if the word is *apple*, Crack might try @pple, @pp1e, @pp13, apple1, and so on. This makes it much more likely that Crack will guess a user's password.

Another password cracker you should look into is John the Ripper (http://www.openwall.com/john). John comes preconfigured to crack several password algorithms, including UNIX crypt and Windows LANMAN hashes. It also supports permutation, as well as provides interesting brute force modes where it attempts many combinations of letters, numbers, and symbols to guess the password. With the increasing processing power available to us, brute force methods have become increasingly useful in discovering weak passwords.

The last password-cracking tool we will mention is L0phtCrack (http://www.atstake.com/products/lc). L0phtCrack is a commercial tool that was originally created to attack Windows LANMAN hashes but has recently added UNIX support. It has also added precomputed password tables, which can drastically speed up the process of breaking most English alphanumeric passwords. This is based on the research of Philippe Oechslin and is also implemented in an open source project called RainbowCrack (http://www.antsight.com/zsl/rainbowcrack/). L0phtCrack is an excellent password cracker that is user friendly and supports many useful features. However, it is significantly more expensive than free! If your budget supports it, though, it comes highly recommended.

If you can gain a copy of the password hashes for the system you are testing, use an offline tool. You will get better results faster. If you cannot, use an online tool. Either way, make sure to address this area because it is one of the most common ways that attackers gain access to networks.

In addition to worrying about the strength of the passwords, you need to look at how secure the transfer of the usernames and passwords is. If you allow the use of unencrypted protocols such as Telnet, any eavesdropper in your user environment will be able to capture a user's password. He then has free reign to log in to your network. You can reduce this risk by requiring the use of protocols that encrypt their authentication sessions. For example, if you are using a reverse proxy, you should verify that authentication only occurs after an SSL session has been established. This is only a partial solution, though. What if your users are using a web café to log in to your network? If a keystroke logger is installed on the computer your users choose to use, no amount of encryption will keep the password out of the hands of the attacker. A better, though more expensive solution is requiring strong authentication for all remote access.

Access Controls

A common configuration (some would say *misconfiguration*) of VPNs is to establish a protected connection between two organizations but enforce no restrictions on the traffic that can flow across the VPN. This, in effect, allows both organizations to bypass each other's perimeter security controls. If this actually is what was intended, you do not have any specific tests to perform in this area. However, if you have limited the connections that can be made through the VPN to the set needed by your remote users or remote business partners, while blocking access to more sensitive areas of your network, you will need to verify that these restrictions are being enforced. The methods you will use are identical to the tests you performed during the firewall verification. This time, though, you will be running the tests from a test system that has established a VPN connection into your network. You will want to attempt to scan systems and protocols that you are allowed and not allowed to reach to ensure that the filters are working correctly. You will also want to attempt scans before and after authentication to make sure the VPN device is properly blocking communications prior to VPN establishment.

Client-Side Restrictions

The last item you should examine for your VPNs is the effectiveness of controls on the client. If a user has established a VPN connection to your network, it is possible that an attacker who can compromise the user's computer can route his packets through the user's computer into your network. Some VPN products disable any routing functions while the VPN is established. If your product supports this, you should verify that it is working by attempting to enable the routing function of the user's workstation and sending packets to the workstation destined to your internal network. This will normally require that you establish a static route on your test workstation that sends all traffic destined to your internal IP addresses to the user workstation being examined.

Using antivirus and personal firewall products is also a very good idea for remote users' computers. If you require the use of these types of products, you will want to verify that they are installed, up to date, enabled, and effective. Just as with your public systems, vulnerability scanners can be run against your users' remote systems to check for exposures.

Testing for client-side restrictions is only realistic, though, if you enforce some kind of configuration control on the systems you allow to connect in to your network. If you allow users to connect using their personal systems, or while they are on the road with borrowed or rented equipment, you will have to rely on other controls to protect the access.

Exploitation

As the final active part of your assessment, you may want to consider exploiting some of the vulnerabilities you have uncovered during the exercise. Assessments that include exploitation are normally referred to as *penetration tests*.

The big advantage to including exploits in your assessment is that they demonstrate, in a powerful way, the existence and impact of the vulnerabilities you have discovered. There are no false positives from a successful exploitation. If the exploit worked, you know there was a vulnerability. In addition, there is something much more compelling about having your proprietary data handed to you by a tester than reading a report that states that a vulnerability could potentially expose your organization to information exposures. Simply put, penetration tests can bring home the seriousness of vulnerabilities, in a way that other methods cannot.

The downside to penetration testing is that it is considerably more dangerous than vulnerability scans. It is not uncommon to have an exploit attempt crash its target. This can mean downtime—or worse, lost data. These tests can also take long amounts of time to perform properly, raising the cost of the assessment.

Careful planning precedes any penetration test. Systems that will be targeted should be recently backed up, and the administrators who manage the systems need to be readily accessible to resolve any problems that come up during the exercise. You should also plan to conduct the test during periods of low utilization. Taking down the order-entry system the week before Christmas would not make anyone happy with you!

You will also need to assemble your toolkit of exploitation software. Many sources of exploits are available on the Internet, some of them more reliable (and safe) than others. Good sites to start with are http://www.securityfocus.com/bid and http://packetstorm.widexs.nl. Keep in mind that it is common for Trojan code and other types of malicious software to masquerade as testing software. Be careful where you acquire your exploits. If source code is available, it should be examined, line by line, to ensure the tool only does what you expect it to. In addition, you should test each exploit in a lab setting prior to using it.

If you do not want to go through the trouble of assembling your own exploitation library, you can look into commercial products. One of these is Canvas (http://www.immunitysec.com/products-canvas.shtml). Canvas currently supports a library of over 50 exploits and is relatively inexpensive compared to other tools in this category. Another tool you may want to examine is Core Impact (http://www.coresecurity.com/products/coreimpact/index.php). Core Impact maintains a large library of exploitation methods. It also supports a robust logging system. Every action taken with Core Impact is logged, making it easy to document exactly what you did within the test. An open source alternative to both of these products is Metasploit (http://www.metasploit.com). Although Metasploit is not nearly as comprehensive as any of the commercial products, it's hard to beat the price.

The steps necessary to actually perform a penetration test can be complicated. Penetration testing by its nature is iterative. You will launch exploits that may increase your knowledge of a system or increase your access to a system. In both cases, this may lead to more exploits, which lead to more access and knowledge, and so on. Eventually, you will reach a point where no further exploits are possible or you completely control the systems you are testing. To focus this process, you may want to establish goal states for the test. For instance, you may want to specify that your goal is to reach administrative-level access on your payroll system. In this way, you can definitely determine when the test should end.

At the end of a penetration test, you will examine how far you got into the network and what information and access you were able to gain. In addition, you should go back and see what your server and intrusion detection logs recorded. Were your test efforts noticed? Did administrators take appropriate steps to respond to your intrusion attempts? This information is equally important to your documentation of the vulnerabilities you successfully exploited.

The quality of your documentation is at least as important as the work you have performed. You will need to keep careful records of what you did, when you did it, and what you observed. This is true of penetration tests as well as the overall assessment. In the next section, we will describe how to develop and organize the results of your efforts.

Results Analysis and Documentation

In the last step of your assessment, you will create a final report. You will have collected a large amount of information during your test, and now is the time to analyze it to determine the overall level of security for your network and what changes are necessary to make it completely secure.

Developing your findings can be the hardest part of producing your report. You will need to look at the results of every test you performed to see what they can tell you about the security of your network. Any tests that indicate weakness need to be examined to determine what the true impact of the weakness is to your organization. You will want to use three elements to determine this impact:

- Severity of the vulnerability
- Criticality of the affected system(s)
- Level of threat (how common the exploitation of the vulnerability is)

Once you've developed your individual findings, you will then want to examine the whole set to see if you can locate any common elements to them. You are looking for the root causes of problems, not the individual facts. For instance, if you discovered systems with vulnerabilities that your organization had previously eliminated, it is possible that your process for provisioning new systems on your network is at fault. If you allow systems be installed from the original installation CDs without a process to upgrade the systems to the latest patches before connecting them to your network, you may reintroduce vulnerabilities you have previously fixed. This type of information can be invaluable to identify the important things that need to change to keep your network secure.

When you are ready to write your report, you will want to examine what formats will best convey the information you have developed. There are many report formats you can use, but most will include the following elements:

- **Executive summary**—This section provides a quick overview of what was done, what the major findings were, and what impact these findings may have to the organization.

- **Introduction**—This section includes a description of the tests performed and the scope of the effort.

- **Findings prioritized by risk**—This section will often provide specific remediation advice for each finding.

- **Best practices**—This section documents areas of the network that were particularly strong.

Keep in mind that even though it comes first in the report, the executive summary should be written after the rest of the report is finished. Doing it any other way may cause you to unintentionally skew your results to keep them consistent with the executive summary you created prior to analyzing all the data.

Summary

In this chapter, we examined techniques for assessing the effectiveness of your security perimeter. You are now armed with the tools and techniques used to perform a security assessment of your environment. You can use this knowledge to find security holes in your defense perimeter and to locate vulnerable or misconfigured systems that are accessible from the Internet. You should also be prepared to test your remote access devices to keep these back channels from allowing attackers past your perimeter. We also talked about the value and danger of exploiting your discovered vulnerabilities, and finally we provided guidance on how to assemble your final report.

If you take nothing else away from this chapter, remember that security assessment requires permission! The difference between a hacker and a security professional, between illegal and legal, is authorization. Make sure you have written approval from the proper authorities before starting any type of security assessment. In addition, make sure this authorization spells out exactly what your scope is so that it is clear to everyone involved what you are and are not allowed to do. This will keep you and your organization safe as you verify the effectiveness of your security perimeter.

23

Design Under Fire

THIS CHAPTER DEALS WITH DESIGN UNDER FIRE, which means the practice of looking at our network security designs the same way an attacker would. Analyzing how attackers can compromise our networks helps us find the networks' weaknesses so that we can improve their security. Analysis is a natural follow-up to the testing procedures discussed in Chapter 22, "Assessment Techniques." To implement design under fire, we discuss a process called *adversarial review*, which offers one way to protect our networks, even from vulnerabilities we are unaware of.

Performing an adversarial review might seem redundant because you already included security in your design from the start. However, the testing that occurs in the design stage attempts to determine whether a design functions according to its requirements. Such testing is an essential part of system design, but it tells you little about how secure the design is. It is entirely possible for a network to perform all of its functions exactly right, yet be completely insecure. An entirely different mental process is required to understand how someone else might intentionally break your design, but it is exactly the type of thought process necessary to eliminate the subtle security problems introduced into our networks.

To prepare you to perform an adversarial review, we begin this chapter with a discussion of how an attacker thinks about attacking a network. Then, we ask you to watch over our shoulders while we subject the designs in this chapter to the type of attention they would receive every day if they were implemented and placed on the Internet.

The Hacker Approach to Attacking Networks

Attackers choose the path of least resistance when attacking a network. They start with efforts to discover the architecture of the network and then attempt to exploit any weaknesses they find. Most attackers possess a limited set of attack methods (exploits), which they can use only when particular technologies and configurations (preconditions) exist on their target's network. The discovery process enables them to find out whether the network possesses any of the required prerequisites, so the first line of defense for a network is to prevent as much discovery activity as possible. You can reduce an attacker's ability to learn whether your network is vulnerable by limiting the unnecessary information your network releases using techniques such as filtering ICMP messages, changing application headers, and employing split DNS configurations.

The attacker who gets by your anti-discovery defenses begins to map out the vulnerabilities on your network and match them up against the available exploit techniques. If the attacker finds a match, he can launch the exploit in an attempt to subvert some part of your network. An attacker who does manage to gain some access can use it to leverage more access into the network. The attacker repeats this discovery/exploit process until he runs out of techniques or achieves his attack goals. One of your goals when designing the security for your network should be to frustrate attackers long enough that they go away in search of an easier target. Failing that, slowing them down gives you a chance to detect them.

The designs that we review in this chapter are already good at frustrating attackers. It is our job to see if we can add some additional frustration into their lives by thinking about how they might subvert our networks and using this knowledge to design additional security controls.

Adversarial Review

During an adversarial review, we look for ways an attacker might make use of the devices and the configurations of those devices that you have used to create your network. This process is especially important for those devices you have used to implement your security infrastructure. Remember that the overall security of your network relies on the individual components that make up the network. Security settings on one device can have a dramatic effect on the security of another device. To gain a complete view of the security of the entire network, you must take a careful look at each of the devices that implement your security infrastructure and then analyze how the interaction between devices affects security. Adversarial review provides a useful method for exploring the impact of these interactions.

We are not actually attacking the network during an adversarial review. Instead, we are conducting an analytical thought process that allows us to develop scenarios that someone else might use to attack the network. By creating these scenarios and identifying measures that could be used to prevent them, we can locate flaws in the architecture of the perimeter or potentially weak links that do not follow defense-in-depth principles.

To conduct an adversarial review, you must perform the following activities:

1. Decide what you are trying to prevent. For example, the goal of your adversarial review might be to find a way to deface a website, access an internal database, or perform a denial of service (DoS) attack.

2. Decide where to start the attack. The attack conceived during the adversarial review is frequently launched from the Internet, but it is also useful to start from an internal network segment to see how to defend against the insider threat.

3. From the viewpoint of the attacker, determine the access that remains after all the security device configurations have been taken into account. For example, if your goal is to access a system located behind a firewall, and the firewall only allows TCP port 80 traffic through to this system, your review will have to find a way to either attack the server using TCP port 80 or locate a vulnerability in the firewall to circumvent this restriction. To complete this step, you must review configurations and research vulnerabilities for each device you can communicate with. If you discover vulnerabilities, you must make a judgment about how feasible an attack based on these vulnerabilities is.

4. Determine the impact of taking advantages of any misconfigurations or exploiting any vulnerabilities. Any increases in access gained can then be used to attack additional systems on the network. For example, if you locate a vulnerability that would allow you to take control of an internal server, you can now consider that server under your control and proceed with the review using the system to reach other systems on your network.

5. Repeat steps 3 and 4 as necessary until you have reached the maximum amount of access to the network that you can.

6. Identify additional security controls that would have prevented any of the attacks from succeeding.

One of the most time-consuming parts of the review is step 3. To determine the amount of access an attacker has, you must conduct a detailed analysis of each security device on your network. You will be looking for three key pieces of information:

- What access does the device have to provide to allow normal network usage? For example, a border firewall normally needs to allow TCP port 80 traffic to the public web server.

- What extraneous access is the device providing? Too frequently, the configuration of security devices is overly permissive, allowing access that is not required but is useful to the attacker. For example, a firewall might allow TCP port 80 traffic to the entire De-Militarized Zone (DMZ), not just to the public web server. If a device on the DMZ is running a vulnerable service on port 80, an attacker can exploit it even though access to the device may be unnecessary to the operation of the network.

- Does the device have any vulnerabilities that would allow you to circumvent the security controls? You can use many sources of information on the Internet to research vulnerabilities, including Carnegie Mellon's Computer Emergency Response Team (CERT) at http://www.cert.org and the vulnerability database maintained by SecurityFocus at http://www.securityfocus.com/bid. If you find a vulnerability announcement for your device, you need to carefully review the information to see whether it applies to your environment and, if it does, what you should do to mitigate the problem.

In step 4, you use the access you have discovered to "attack" your network. Thinking like the attacker, you attempt to see whether the access that remains after you have considered each device is sufficient to do significant damage.

Even if you did not find exploitable access in step 3, it is occasionally useful to act as if you had and proceed with the review anyway. New vulnerabilities are discovered in software every day. As an example, consider Microsoft's Internet Explorer web browser. If you were using it in the spring of 2004, you would have had no way of knowing it exposed your network to attack due to an exploitable vulnerability in its drag-and-drop feature (http://www.securityfocus.com/bid/10973). You would have had to wait until the August 2004 for the vulnerability to be made public. This vulnerability had actually been in the software since version 5, which was released in 1999. This means that sites that installed this version or its successors (up to version 6) might have been vulnerable to this attack for over five years. Simulating vulnerabilities during your review allows you to experiment with the impact that an undiscovered vulnerability would have on your network.

Step 5 is an iterative process that requires you to look at where the attacker starts to determine how far he can penetrate the network. If you were analyzing your exposure to an external attack, you would likely start the attack with your public systems. These systems normally come under attack first because they are the most exposed to the Internet. If you have (or simulate that you have) a vulnerability in one of these systems, your next step is to think what attackers could do if they were able to exploit the vulnerability successfully.

Gaining control of one of these systems would allow you to start launching more attacks using the public system as the source. If the access you have discovered during the review allows this public system to attack other computers on your network, and these other systems also have exploitable vulnerabilities, you would be able to control these other systems, moving further into your network. You continue this thought process until you run out of systems that an attacker could access or until you have circumvented the security controls that you care about. At this point, you can look to see how far you, as the attacker, got in the network and what security controls you could implement that would have stopped the attack at each step in the process. Assuming their implementation, you can re-run the analysis to see whether you can figure out any other ways to attack your network. When you have run out of ideas, you are done.

Step 6 ends the adversarial review with the identification of the additional security controls necessary to protect your network. Especially for reviews in which you have included simulated vulnerabilities, the review helps you identify the controls necessary to implement defense in depth. This is the real power of the adversarial review: the identification of the layers of defense needed to help protect you against the unknown.

GIAC GCFW Student Practical Designs

We will draw our examples for this chapter from practical assignments that GIAC students produced as part of the requirements for their GIAC Certified Firewall Analyst (GCFW) certification. The students were asked to create a secure network for a fictitious entity named GIAC Enterprises (GIACE), which is in the business of selling fortune cookie sayings. This is the same source we used for Case Study 4 in Chapter 18, "Sample Designs." In Chapter 18, we explored the major security features for one of the GCFW student's practicals. In this chapter, we will take a different approach when reviewing their designs.

The GCFW students have produced a wide variety of designs for us to choose from. We have chosen to discuss two of them that were awarded honors by the GCFW Advisory Board. During each review, our goal will be to determine if a reasonable scenario exists that would allow an attacker to gain access to the fortune sayings database. As a secondary goal, we will attempt to gain control of as many GIACE systems as possible. Also, both reviews will assume a starting viewpoint of an Internet attacker. A listing of completed practical assignments can be found at http://www.giac.org/GCFW.php.

Practical Design 1

The first design we look at is the security architecture created by Angela Orebaugh. Angela's design is shown in Figure 23.1 and can be downloaded at http://www.giac.org/practical/Angela_Orebaugh_GCFW.zip. It has several interesting features, including the following elements:

- Extensive use of redundancy to produce a high availability network
- Two levels of firewalls from two different vendors to provide defense in depth
- Ingress and egress filtering at the network border
- A screened subnet network to separate publicly accessible servers from internal systems
- A separate management network segment to monitor and administer the network
- The use of VPNs to allow suppliers and partners to gain access to the GIACE network
- IDS systems to monitor the DMZ and internal network segments

As previously mentioned, our goal is to determine if a reasonable scenario exists that would allow an attacker to gain access to the fortune sayings database. Our review will assume that the attack originates from the Internet. Because steps 1 and 2 of the adversarial review process have already been determined, our adversarial review of Angela's design will begin with step 3: determining the access that remains. By examining the security settings of each security device that stands between the Internet and the fortune database, we will determine whether an external attacker can access the fortune database. Looking at Figure 23.1, you can see that this will require us to examine the screening filtering routers at the border of the network, the external firewalls, the internal firewalls, and the database server. After we have finished discussing a device's configuration, we will perform step 4 for that device: determining the impact. After all the devices have been discussed, we will then show how step 5—repeat as necessary—can be used to combine the discovered vulnerabilities to reach our review goal.

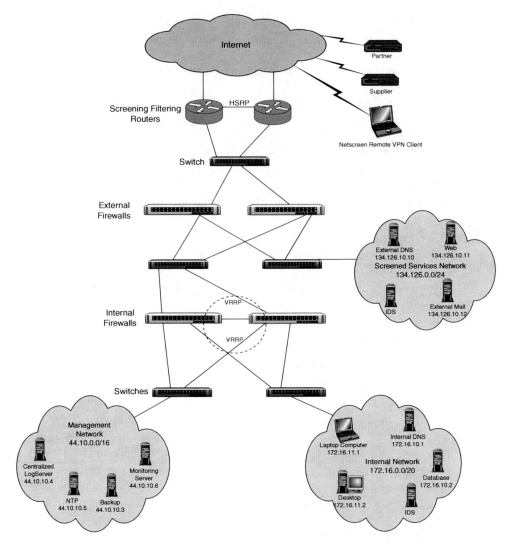

Figure 23.1   Angela Orebaugh's GIACE secure network architecture makes extensive use of redundancy.

Determining the Access That Remains: Screening Filtering Routers

Our discussion begins at the interface between the GIACE network and the Internet. At the border of the network are two Cisco 7200 series routers running IOS 12.x. They connect the GIACE network to the Internet and are configured to use Cisco's proprietary Hot Standby Routing Protocol (HSRP) to enable one of the routers to take over should the other fail. The routers also provide the first opportunity to protect the GIACE network from external attackers by implementing ingress and egress filters. Because the exact filter settings are essential to the implementation of the security architecture, we spend some time going over them.

The Ingress Filter

An ingress filter on the border router of a network can be an effective first step toward securing it. Properly implemented, an ingress filter can block potentially damaging packets before they enter the network. Here is a summarization of the ingress rules for this design, which are applied to the serial interface that is connected on the border routers to the WAN link to the Internet:

- Deny and log packets that have invalid source IP addresses.
- Deny and log incoming packets that are destined to the ports normally associated with FTP, Telnet, Secure Shell (SSH), SunRPC, Network File Service, and Windows Common Internet File Service.
- Allow HTTP and HTTPS packets that are addressed to the web server.
- Allow SMTP packets that are addressed to the mail server.
- Allow IPSec and IKE packets that are addressed to the external firewall.
- Allow "established" TCP packets (with the ACK or RST bits set) that have a destination port greater than 1024. This rule is intended to allow in TCP packets that are part of ongoing TCP conversations initiated from internal hosts.
- Deny and log any other inbound traffic.

The Egress Filter

The egress filter can prevent the site from being used to attack other sites should an attacker manage to gain control of internal systems. The egress filter prevents spoofed packets from leaving the network and is applied on the Ethernet interface that connects the border routers to the interior network:

- Permit traffic to leave if its source address is valid (that is, from 134.126.0.0/16). This is the address that is assigned to the company's internal network.
- Deny and log any other outbound traffic.

As mentioned in Chapter 2, "Packet Filtering," it is a shame that more sites do not implement egress filters. If they did, the opportunity for an attacker to launch attacks on other networks, including distributed denial of service (DoS) attacks, would be sharply limited.

Other Filters

In addition to the ingress and egress filters, the router also has been configured using the following settings to prevent other activities that can cause security problems:

- No Source Routing
- No IP Directed Broadcasts
- No IP Unreachable Messages
- No Cisco Discovery Protocol (CDP) Messages

The first setting, No Source Routing, prevents the router from accepting packets with source routing enabled. If you allow source-routed packets, an attacker can more easily circumvent your ingress filters by spoofing packets with addresses that are allowed by the router. Normally, replies to spoofed packets will not make it back to the attacker. However, with source-routed packets, the attacker can define the return path for the reply. This allows the attacker to set up full TCP connections that appear to originate from a trusted external host. Preventing source-routed packets is a setting that should be used on all border routers.

The second setting, No IP Directed Broadcasts, prevents IP-directed broadcasts. This setting is important for preventing the network from being used in a Smurf attack. Without this setting in place, it is possible that the GIACE network could be used to launch a DoS attack on another network. To prevent this, the routers have been config-ured to drop packets destined to broadcast addresses.

The third setting, No IP Unreachable Messages, helps prevent network discovery activities by telling the router not to generate ICMP unreachable messages. A router generates ICMP unreachable messages on two occasions: when it receives a packet that is destined for itself on a port that it is not listening to, and when it receives a packet that it does not know how to deliver.

Shutting off ICMP unreachable messages makes it harder for an attacker to determine what services are running on the router. It also prevents inverse network scans. If a router generates an ICMP unreachable message when it receives a packet destined for a host that does not exist on a network that the router is directly connected to, an attacker can map the network for live hosts by sending a packet to each address on the network and then watch to see which addresses result in an ICMP unreachable message. A probe that does not return an ICMP packet indicates a live host at that address.

The last setting, No Cisco Discovery Protocol (CDP) Messages, prevents the genera-tion of CDP messages. Cisco routers use CDP to discover information about other neighboring Cisco routers. This information is also useful to attackers, so it has been dis-abled in this design.

Protecting the Routers

Any device that enforces the security policy of a network is a tempting target, and this definitely includes the border routers. Cisco routers have a few popular ways that attack-ers can attempt to gain access. These include logging in to the router using Telnet, downloading or modifying the router's configuration using SNMP, and accessing the router through its HTTP administrative interface. The following steps were taken to prevent these types of accesses:

- Allow login access only from the monitoring server.
- Replace the Telnet protocol with SSH.
- Enable SNMP read access, but restrict it to the monitoring server.
- Enable SNMP read/write access, but restrict it to the monitoring server.
- Disable the HTTP administrative interface.
- Disable other unnecessary services.

Now that we have described the security settings of the routers, let's see if we can figure out a way they might be compromised.

Determining the Impact: Routers

We start step 4 of our adversarial review of the screening filtering routers by looking at the access that remains after all of the routers' filter settings are considered. The major items we note are the settings that allow outside users access to the web, mail, DNS, and VPN servers. This information will be useful to us later when we look at the security of those devices. Meanwhile, some additional items are worth noting about the routers.

The security settings of the border routers are relatively good, and little access remains after the filters and other configuration settings are considered. However, a few areas remain that we should take note of during the review:

- The ingress filter allows anonymous established packets.
- The egress filter allows any internal packet to exit the network as long as its source address is valid.
- SNMP version 1 is enabled.
- Administrative access to the router is only weakly authenticated.

To start with, the ingress filter is allowing established packets through. This allows an attacker to use ACK scanning to discover services on computers behind the routers. In this design, depending on how the external firewalls are configured, this might not be a problem. However, if a firewall was not between the routers and the GIACE network, better filtering settings would be needed at the router. Cisco supports two additional filtering technologies that can help. The first is reflexive access lists (covered in Chapter 2). These allow the router to filter incoming packets based on whether a matching outgoing packet was seen previously. Although this is effective for many types of TCP connections, certain protocols cannot be supported using reflexive lists. For these other protocols, Cisco supports context-based access control (CBAC) filters. CBAC filters can be CPU intensive, so be careful when using them that you do not adversely affect the router's primary purpose—to route packets. More details about CBAC can be found in Chapter 6, "The Role of a Router."

The next area to look at is the egress filter. It allows any internally generated packet to leave the network as long as its source address is valid. This is overly permissive. A number of ICMP packet types should probably be blocked at the egress filter to prevent certain types of discovery activities. For example, ICMP TTL exceeded messages should be dropped to prevent the attacker from using traceroute to discover the structure of the network. In addition, most types of ICMP destination unreachable messages should be dropped to prevent attackers from learning what hosts and services are running on the network.

> **Note**
>
> One type of ICMP destination unreachable message that should not be filtered is code 4 (fragmentation needed and don't fragment are set). RFC 1191–compliant systems use this destination unreachable message to set the optimum maximum transmission unit (MTU). See Chapter 6, "The Role of a Router," and Chapter 17, "Tuning the Design for Performance," for more details.

In addition to filtering ICMP messages, it is worthwhile to block other types of outbound traffic that are unnecessary to the operation of the network. If an attacker were to gain control of an internal system, this would make it harder for him to use the system to attack other systems outside the network. It can also complicate the attacker's ability to download additional exploit tools. In the case of a live attacker, this is probably just an inconvenience. However, if the attacker actually sends a piece of malicious code, such as a worm or virus, egress filtering can prevent the attack from working.

Beyond these issues with the filters, certain problems might allow an attacker to gain control of the actual router. The first of these is the use of SNMP. An attacker who knows the read-only SNMP community name and has access to the SNMP service on the router can learn substantial information about the configuration of the router. An attacker who knows the read-write SNMP community name can change the configuration of the router, including the access control lists (ACLs). To prevent this from happening, the routers have been configured to accept SNMP requests only from the management console. In addition, community names have been chosen that might be hard to guess. Accepting connections that originate from the only monitoring server's address is effective at blocking requests from outside the network. If the attack originates from inside the network, though, the attacker might be able to successively impersonate the monitoring server, allowing him to access the SNMP service if he knows a valid SNMP community name.

Discovery of the community names might be relatively easy. First, the read-only community name was set to "giacpublic." It is realistic to expect that a determined attacker might guess this community name. Second, SNMP version 1 does not encrypt its packets. An attacker who manages to take control of a system that is on the network path between the management server and the router might be able to sniff the community names (including the read-write community name) as they are transmitted to the router. This would allow the attacker to completely compromise the border routers. It is important to mention that the community name weakness has been eliminated in version 3 of the SNMP protocol. Cisco routers fully support this version of SNMP; unfortunately, many SNMP management tools have not been updated to support this enhanced version of the protocol.

The second way that an attacker might be able to gain control of the routers is by logging in to them. Similar to the technique used to protect SNMP, the routers accept login only from the monitoring server, and again, similar to SNMP, an internal attack might be able to bypass this restriction. Additional security has been added by changing the login protocol from Telnet to SSH. Because SSH encrypts the network conversation, an attacker won't be able to sniff a valid password from the network when a login to the routers occurs. However, an attacker could still guess the password. No strong authentication system (such as SecurID) is being used. A simple (weak) username/password combination is all that is needed to access the router. Brute force techniques can be used to guess this password, although the monitoring server would log this activity.

It is also possible that vulnerabilities in the SSH version 1 protocol might be used to gain access to the routers (http://www.cve.mitre.org/cgi-bin/cvename.cgi?name=CVE-2001-0144). In particular, SSH version 1 has a vulnerability that might allow an attacker to recover a session key and allow the session to be decrypted. This could reveal the username and password of the administrator, allowing the attacker to log in to the router.

Tip

The SSH protocol supports public key authentication. However, not all SSH servers implement this feature. This includes the implementation on Cisco routers.

Mention of SSH vulnerabilities is not meant to imply that you should not use SSH to protect your Cisco logins. It is still a useful technique to protect the routers. To make it more effective, consider implementing stronger authentication methods than are used in this design.

Determining the Access That Remains: The External Firewalls

The next layer of defense is a pair of stateful packet filter firewalls being used to implement the external firewall and to terminate the VPNs that allow the business partners and the suppliers to connect to the internal network. The products being used are two NetScreen-100 security appliances. Like the border routers, these appliances are running a high availability protocol to allow one to take over should the other fail.

Note

The NetScreen-100 is no longer produced. Service for this device ends on January 14, 2006. After this date, no additional support, including patches, is available. It is important that you consider end-of-service issues when selecting security products because once the product reaches its end of service, you will no longer be able to keep the device secure. This problem is not specific to NetScreen. Most manufacturers will eventually stop support for their older products.

The NetScreen-100 comes with three network interfaces: untrusted, trusted, and DMZ. In this design, the untrusted interface is connected to the border routers, the trusted interface is connected to the internal network, and the DMZ interface is connected to the screened service network. It uses four different rulebases to control which packets to allow, based on the interface at which the packet arrives. These rulebases are incoming, outgoing, "to DMZ", and "from DMZ". For example, packets that come from the untrusted network and are destined to the internal network are filtered based on the incoming rulebase. Packets that enter the untrusted network and are destined for the DMZ are handled by the "to DMZ" rulebase, and so on. The following sections present the configurations for each rulebase.

Incoming

Table 23.1 shows the rulebase that controls packets heading from the untrusted interface to the trusted interface.

Table 23.1 **Incoming Rulebase for the External Firewalls**

Source	Destination	Service	Action
Border Routers	Log Server	Syslog	Allow
Border Routers	NTP Server	NTP	Allow
Outside Any	External Firewall	IPSec	Allow
Partner and Supplier VPN	Database	IPSec	Allow
Outside Any	Inside Any	Any	Deny

Outgoing

The rulebase in Table 23.2 controls the traffic entering from the trusted interface and destined for the untrusted interface.

Table 23.2 **Outgoing Rulebase for the External Firewalls**

Source	Destination	Service	Action
Monitoring Server	External Firewall	SSH	Allow
Inside Any	External Firewall	Any	Deny
Backup Server	Border Routers	Backup	Allow
Monitoring Server	Border Routers	Ping, SNMP, SSH	Allow
Internal Network	Outside Any	Any	Allow
Inside Any	Outside Any	Any	Deny

To DMZ

The rulebase in Table 23.3 controls the traffic heading for the DMZ network regardless of which interface the traffic entered from (untrusted or trusted).

Table 23.3   **Rulebase for Packets Heading Toward the DMZ**

Source	Destination	Service	Action
Outside Any	Web Server	HTTP, HTTPS	Allow
Outside Any, Internal Network	External Mail Server	Mail	Allow
Internal Network	Web Server	HTTP, HTTPS	Allow
Internal Network	External Mail Server	IMAP	Allow
Monitoring Server	DMZ Any	Ping, SNMP	Allow
Backup Server	DMZ Any	Backup	Allow
Inside Any	DMZ Any	Any	Deny
Outside Any	DMZ Any	Any	Deny

From DMZ

The last rulebase, shown in Table 23.4, defines what traffic is allowed to leave the DMZ network.

Table 23.4   **Rulebase for Packets Leaving the DMZ**

Source	Destination	Service	Action
Web Server	Database	TCP Any	Allow
External DNS	Outside Any	DNS	Allow
External Mail Server	Outside Any	Mail	Allow
DMZ Any	Log Server	Syslog	Allow
DMZ Any	NTP Server	NTP	Allow
DMZ Any	Monitoring Server	SNMP	Allow
DMZ Any	Inside Any	Any	Deny
DMZ Any	Outside Any	Any	Deny

Determining the Impact: The External Firewalls

The cumulative effect of these rulebases is to dramatically limit what type of traffic can flow between the three network zones. It is our job as adversarial reviewers to look for any access that remains after all the rules on the firewalls are put into place and for any vulnerabilities that might exist in the firewalls that an attacker could make use of. A careful review of these settings reveals the following issues:

- Network traffic to the web and mail servers is not tested for invalid requests.
- The web server is allowed unrestricted access to the database server.
- The NetScreen appliance might have a vulnerability that allows the filters to be bypassed.

As stated at the beginning of this chapter, attackers target what they can talk to. In this case, the web server and mail server must be accessible to outside users. If the web server software or the mail server software contains vulnerabilities, this design would not prevent it from being taken over, which is a major concern because services that have had the worst history for security vulnerabilities include web and mail server software. Stateful packet filtering firewalls rely primarily on the contents of the packet header to make their security decision, so they would be unable to detect an attack that uses malformed requests targeted at the web or mail server software. The use of a web proxy and a mail proxy would provide the ability to look at the application data in the packet to determine whether an invalid request is being made. Although this method is not perfect, it would provide better security than relying entirely on the packet header to make the security decision.

The next potential problem is the permissive setting between the web server and the database server. An attacker who managed to gain control of the web server could use it to attack any TCP service running on the database server. This rule should be more restrictive, permitting only the minimum TCP traffic necessary to allow the web server to make the necessary database queries. It is worth noting that the internal firewall does provide this restriction. It only allows the web server to send SQLnet1 (TCP Port 1521) traffic to the database server. You might ask why it is important to restrict the traffic between the web server and the database server at the external firewall when the internal firewall is going to accomplish the same thing. As was stated previously, whenever you can stop a particular problem with multiple defensive techniques, you increase the resiliency of the network to attack.

The last items worth talking about are potential vulnerabilities in the NetScreen devices. Some versions of the NetScreen software are vulnerable to an attack that allows packets into the DMZ that should have been filtered (http://cve.mitre.org/cgi-bin/cvename.cgi?name=CAN-2001-0589). Ensuring that version 2.5r6 or higher is installed on the NetScreen devices will prevent this attack.

Determining the Access That Remains: The Internal Firewalls

The internal firewalls are the last line of network filters for the GIACE network. Their purpose is to provide design redundancy for the NetScreen appliances while protecting the internal and management networks.

The internal firewalls are implemented using a pair of Nokia IP330 firewall appliances running Check Point FireWall-1 version 4.1. Like the NetScreen-100s, the Nokias are stateful inspection firewalls; however, unlike the NetScreen configuration, the Nokias have a single rulebase to control all filtering decisions. Table 23.5 is the configuration of this rulebase.

Table 23.5 **Rulebase for the Internal Firewalls**

No.	Source	Destination	Service	Action
1	Monitoring Server	Internal Firewall	FireWall-1, SSH, ICMP, SNMP	Allow
2	Any	Internal Firewall	Any	Drop
3	Web Server	Database	SQLnet1	Allow
4	Internal Network	Screened Service Network	http, https	Allow
5	Internal Network	NOT (Screened Service Network)	Any	Allow
6	Partner and Supplier VPN	Database	IPSec	Allow
7	Screened Service Network, Internal Network, Border Routers	Log Server	Syslog	Allow
8	Screened Service Network, Internal Network, Border Routers	NTP Server	NTP	Allow
9	Backup Server	Screened Service Network, Internal Network, Border Routers	Backup	Allow
10	Monitoring Server	Screened Service Network, Internal Network, Border Routers	SNMP, ICMP	Allow
11	Monitoring Server	Border Routers, External Firewall	SSH	Allow
12	Any	Any	Any	Deny

Determining the Impact: The Internal Firewall

This filtering layer provides additional protection for the internal network over and above that provided by the external firewalls. Separation of the management network and the internal network is a particularly good idea. As with the external firewalls, though, some access remains after the firewall's security controls are considered. Here are three issues that should be addressed:

- The internal network is granted access to the management network.
- Screened service network hosts can communicate with some internal systems.
- The SSH daemon on the firewall might contain vulnerabilities.

The first issue to address is the protection of the management network. Separating the management network from the rest of the network is a good security precaution. As is the case in this design, management systems frequently have more access rights to the network than other systems, which makes them tempting targets. An attacker who manages to gain control of the monitoring server, for example, would be able to attack most of the security devices on the network. For this reason, the management network needs to be carefully protected; yet this rulebase allows internal systems free access to the management network. Rules 4 and 5 are meant to restrict the internal networks' access to the screened services network while allowing them free access to the Internet, but the rules are more permissive than necessary. Rule 5 says that as long as the destination address is not the screen services network, then the packets—including packets destined for the management network—are allowed.

The next issue to talk about is the control of traffic between the screened services network and the internal network. This rulebase does a good job of limiting screened service systems access to the bare minimum required to allow the network to function; however, any time you allow communication between networks at different trust levels, you need to be extremely careful. To allow logging and time synchronization, the screen services network hosts are allowed to send Syslog entries to the log server and make NTP requests from the NTP server. Both of these systems are located on the management network. If either of the daemons (Ntpd or Syslogd) contains security vulnerabilities, an attacker could gain a foothold on the management network. Because of this, special care should be taken to harden these services.

The rulebase also allows the web server to establish connections with the database server over the SQLnet1 protocol. Again, as with the Ntpd and Syslogd daemons, if the service, which handles the SQLnet1 requests, contains vulnerabilities, it is possible for an attacker to gain control of the database server. In addition, even if the service contains no vulnerabilities, the web server has a normal amount of access to the database service running on the database server. An attacker who controls the web server could cause the database server to perform malicious transactions, such as creating fake supplier invoices. These transactions would be hard to prevent if the web server is normally allowed to request them. Only careful application design that includes substantial validity checks on each transaction could help mitigate this problem.

The last issue to discuss is the reliance on the SSH protocol to administer the firewalls. The Nokia IP330s prior to release 3.4.1 have the same SSH vulnerability we described for the Cisco routers. IP330s running older versions of software that require SSH support should be upgraded.

Repeating as Necessary: Attacking the Whole Network

So far, we have talked about the individual devices that make up the security of the network and how their configurations might open up the network to attack. Let's see what might be possible if we combine all of this information.

Our attack will start by looking for vulnerabilities in the web server, the mail server, and the DNS server. The reason for this is simple; after the routers and firewalls have done their jobs, these are the only systems we can still establish connections to. If any of these systems contain vulnerabilities, we might be able to gain access. For example, if we assume that the web server is running Internet Information Server 5.0, it is possible that the web server is vulnerable to a buffer overflow attack.[1] A successful attack would place us in complete control of the web server.

But wait! Look back at the network diagram in Figure 23.1. Isn't there an IDS located on the screened services network that might detect the attack? The important word here is *might*. Most IDS tools are signature based. If the attack is new or the IDS has not been updated, it is possible that the IDS does not contain a signature for the attack, in which case it would not be able to produce an alert[2]. In addition, in some cases, attacks can be reengineered to specifically avoid detection by IDS tools.[3]

Assuming that we are now in control of the web server, what should we do? This depends on the review goals. If the goal is to embarrass GIACE, we now have enough privileges to deface the website. If we are trying to steal data, we are in a good position to accomplish this as well. The web server needs to be able to query the database server to fulfill its role. We could potentially use this access to query customer account information, steal fortune sayings, or capture any other information that the web server would normally have access to on the database. We could also Trojanize the web server, replacing the scripts that implement the website (CGIs, JSPs, and so on) with versions that record the transactions between the users and the site.

If we want to gain control of more hosts on the GIACE network, the other screened service network systems would be good targets. By using the web server to launch the attacks, we can circumvent the external firewalls and attack any system on the screened service network. What about attacking systems on the internal network?

We still have two layers of firewalls between the internal networks and us. The result of both layers leaves us with limited access from the screened services network. We can send Syslog packets to the log server, NTP packets to the NTP server, and SQLnet1 packets to the database server. As with the web server, we need a vulnerability in the service software if we want to continue the attack. In this case, if GIACE is running Oracle 8i on the database server, it might be possible to proceed. Some versions of Oracle 8i's listener services contain a buffer overflow vulnerability that allows an attacker to gain remote access to the server (http://cve.mitre.org/cgi-bin/cvename.cgi?name=CAN-2001-0499).

Taking over the database server allows us direct access to any of the internal systems, including user workstations. In addition, it allows us to attack any of the systems on the management network. Remember: The internal firewalls do not prevent hosts on the internal network from communicating with the management network. The likely reason for this is that the administrator is using a workstation located on the internal network to log in to management network systems. As was mentioned in Chapter 13, "Separating Resources," using ARP poisoning techniques makes it possible to eavesdrop on the conversations between the internal network and other networks, even though the network is implemented using a switch instead of a hub. If the administrator wants to access management network systems by using Telnet, FTP, or any other protocol that does not encrypt authentication information, we will be able to capture the administrator's username/password combination and use it to log in. This would pretty much be game over because we would then have control of every major system on the network.

You might be asking yourself how realistic this sample attack is. We had to rely on vulnerabilities on the web and database servers to accomplish the attack, and we had to assume that the IDS would not pick up the attack. This is a key point to consider when performing your review. Even when you cannot find a vulnerability for a particular service or system you are running, it can still be useful to assume the existence of a vulnerability to discover the impact it could cause should one be discovered in the future. It is almost beside the point that the products we chose to use to illustrate the example actually contained exploitable vulnerabilities. It is much more important to recognize that even good security architectures can be improved.

These additional steps can be used to improve this design:

- Use proxy firewalls or Deep Packet Inspection firewalls for high-risk services. Web and mail service software does not have a good history for security. If we want to strengthen our border defenses, we need to use firewalls that can look at the content of a message, not just its source and destination.

- Do not allow direct access from publicly accessible systems to back-end systems. Instead, implement middleware systems that enforce reasonable security checks between your public servers and your back-end databases.

- If you must use SNMP, use version 3.0 of the protocol and implement its strong authentication mechanisms. If you cannot use version 3.0, make sure you enable SNMP trap alerts—especially for authentication failures—to enable yourself to detect when someone is attempting to attack the SNMP service.

- Keep all the security devices and public systems up to date with the latest security patches.

Practical Design 2

The second design we will look at is the security architecture created by Sam Campbell. Sam's design is shown in Figure 23.2 and can be downloaded at http://www.giac.org/practical/Sam_Campbell_GCFW.zip. This is an interesting design that has many sophisticated security features:

- The design uses multiple layers of firewalls that are not only from different vendors but are also different firewall types (proxy versus stateful inspection).

- All internal systems use private addresses.

- The public web server is hosted on a server that is running a security-hardened version of HP UNIX.

- Standard daemons for DNS and mail have been replaced with more secure alternatives: djbdns (http://cr.yp.to/djbdns.html) for DNS and Qmail (http://cr.yp.to/qmail.html) for mail.

- A centralized authorization database is maintained using an LDAP server. This server authenticates external customers, suppliers, and partners.
- RSA's SecurID system is being used to strongly authenticate remote users who are then allowed to establish an IPSec VPN with the internal firewall.
- A reverse proxy server implemented using Aventail's extranet product is being used to allow suppliers and partners secure access to the network.

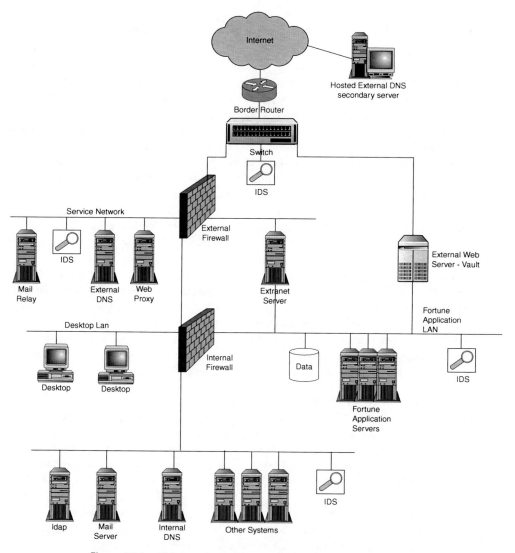

Figure 23.2 This security architecture uses a security-hardened version of UNIX to protect the web server.

Sam's design has five security devices that need to be examined: the border router, the external firewall, the public web server, the internal firewall, and the extranet server. Each of these devices plays a role in determining how much access we can get to the GIACE network. Just as in the previous case study, we provide a discussion of the access that remains for each of these devices and what impact this access would have to the network's security. We wrap up our discussion by showing how all the vulnerabilities can be combined to reach the review goals as well as provide recommendations to improve the security of the design.

Determining the Access That Remains: The External Firewall

As in the previous review, we want to look at each security device to determine what access remains to the attacker after the device is added to the network and find any additional vulnerabilities that might exist in the device. Where appropriate, we assume vulnerabilities so that we can analyze where additional security measures might be warranted.

Because this design's border router is set up similarly to the first design we looked at, we will not spend time discussing it. Beyond the border router, there are two paths into the network: toward the external firewall and toward the public web server. We will begin our discussion by looking at the security implemented by the external firewall.

The design uses a Symantec firewall to provide access control between the Internet and the internal networks. Unlike the stateful firewalls used in the previous design, the Raptor is a proxy firewall. As was covered in Chapter 4, "Proxy Firewalls," this type of firewall acts as a go-between for network connections. This method provides some security benefits, including the ability to hide the structure of the internal network and to make security decisions based on the content as well as the header of the packet.

Proxy firewalls can hide the structure of the network because they act as a middleman for all the network connections. All incoming connections are negotiated at the firewall, which then negotiates a second connection with the system that will actually handle the transaction. This configuration makes it difficult for an attacker to discover details about the host he is attempting to attack. As an example, if an Nmap scan with operating system detection was conducted against a network protected by a Symantec firewall, the result would look like all the public servers were Symantec firewalls.

Discovering a Network Behind a Proxy Firewall

Proxy firewalls are good at hiding the structure of the internal network, but they are not perfect. In a penetration testing assignment I conducted, I ran up against a proxy firewall that allowed external users to FTP into a particular host on the internal network. The firewall's FTP proxy required that you FTP into the firewall and then specify which host on the internal network you wanted to connect to. If you specified the correct host and provided a valid username/password combination, a connection was established. A small programming error in this arrangement allowed me to map the internal network. Here's how it worked: The proxy firewall returned an authorization error if you specify the IP address of a valid host, but did not provide a good username/password. If you specified the address of a nonexistent host, you would get a `connection refused` message. Using this difference, I created a script that attempted to access IP addresses within the typical private ranges (10.0.0.x, 192.168.x.x, and so on). Any address that returned an authorization error meant that I had detected the address of a live host.

The method that proxy firewalls use to protect networks also allows for inherent Network Address Translation (NAT). Because the firewall will act as the public front for all the protected systems, it is the only one that needs to have any public IP addresses. The protected systems can be numbered using any private addressing scheme. This does require that the firewall know which system will handle a particular incoming request. Table 23.6 shows the translation settings used to allow external requests to reach the appropriate internal system.

Table 23.6   **Translation Settings on the External Firewall for the Public Services**

Destination Address	Destination Service	Redirected Address	Description
1.1.1.3	SMTP	Mail Relay	Accept incoming mail.
1.1.1.3	DNS	External DNS	Accept incoming DNS requests.
1.1.2.1	IPSec-ESP	Internal Firewall	Allow remote employees in.
1.1.1.5	HTTPS	Extranet Server	Allow suppliers and partners in.

Because these systems are the only servers that have an external IP address, they are the only systems protected by the firewall that an external attacker will be able to directly communicate with. In our review, we will want to look at the chance that an attacker could use this capability to attack these systems.

Hosts on the inside of the network that will require the ability to initiate external network connections must also have translation rules established on the firewall. Table 23.7 shows the rules for this design.

Table 23.7   **Translation Rules to Allow Outbound Network Connections**

Server	Address to Translate To	Description
Mail Relay	1.1.1.3	Allow outbound mail.
Web Proxy	1.1.1.3	Allow outbound HTTP requests.
Internal Firewall	1.1.2.2	Needed for IPSec UDP key exchange between remote users and the internal firewall.

The implication of this table is that these are the only hosts (besides the public web server, border router, and external IDS) on the GIACE network that will be allowed to initiate connections to the Internet. This means that any attempts to attack the Internet from the service network need to be launched from one of these systems.

Of course, the main purpose for the firewall is to provide access control. Table 23.8 shows the access control settings used in this design.

Table 23.8   **External Firewall Rulebase**

Incoming Interface	Outgoing Interface	Source	Destination	Service	Action
Internet	Service	Any	Ext. DNS	DNS	Allow
Service	Internet	External DNS	Any	DNS	Allow
Internet	Service	Any	Mail Relay	SMTP	Allow
Service	Internet	Mail Relay	Any	SMTP	Allow
Any	Extranet	Any	Extranet Server	HTTPS	Allow
Internet	Corporate	Any	Internal Firewall	IPSec-ESP, IPSec-IKE	Allow
Corporate	Internet	Internal Firewall	Any	IPSec-ESP, IPSec-IKE	Allow
Service	Corporate	Mail Relay	Mail Server	SMTP	Allow
Service	Internet	Web Proxy	Any	HTTP, HTTPS, FTP	Allow
Corporate	Service	Desktop LAN	Web Proxy	HTTP, HTTPS, FTP	Allow
Corporate	Service	Desktop LAN	Any	SSH	Allow, Log
Corporate	Service	Mail Server	Mail Relay	SMTP	Allow
Corporate	Internet	Any	Any	Any	Deny
Internet	Any	Any	Any	NetBIOS over IP	Deny, No Log

> **Note**
>
> The Symantec firewall that was used in this design includes the incoming and outgoing interface in each
> access rule. The names of the interfaces are configured during installation of the firewall. Although the
> interface names are pretty self-evident, it is worth noting that the corporate interface is the one connected
> to the internal firewall.

Determining the Impact: The External Firewall

This external firewall implementation doesn't give us much to complain about. Assuming that the firewall does not contain vulnerabilities that would allow us to circumvent its security rules, the only systems protected by the firewall that an external attacker could initiate a connection with are the mail relay server, the external DNS server, the internal firewall, and the extranet server. For an attack to succeed, one of these servers would have to be vulnerable. However, even if one of the servers is vulnerable to some exploit, the proxy nature of this firewall might prevent the attack from succeeding. As an example, suppose that the Qmail software running on the mail relay server had a buffer overflow vulnerability in its handling of the SMTP HELO command. The firewall's mail proxy limits the format and length of the data that the HELO command supplies. It is unlikely that the data the attacker would need to provide to successfully attack this system would meet these length and format restrictions. This does not mean that this solution is bulletproof. Remember that we should also consider vulnerabilities in the security device. In this case, a quick search on the vulnerability database at http://www.securityfocus.com reveals several problems that could affect its security:

- The firewall's RealAudio proxy contains a potentially exploitable buffer overflow vulnerability (http://www.securityfocus.com/bid/6389). Caused by improper bounds checking within the proxy, under some circumstances, it could lead to complete compromise of the firewall.

- The firewall's HTTP proxy has a few security problems. First, it has an information disclosure vulnerability (http://www.securityfocus.com/bid/5959). This allows an attacker to discover what hosts exist behind the firewall because of an overly revealing error message returned by the proxy. Next, the HTTP proxy has a denial of service vulnerability caused by a problem in the proxy's DNS resolution functionality (http://www.securityfocus.com/bid/5958). Last, it has a bug in its handling of requests that allows an attacker to connect to web servers behind the firewall as long as the web service is on a nonstandard port (http://cve.mitre.org/cgi-bin/cvename.cgi?name=CAN-2001-0483). This vulnerability would not help an attacker browse web materials on this network because no web servers are running on nonstandard ports on the GIACE network. It would enable the attacker to discover what hosts are running on the network, though.

- The firewall may allow attackers to bypass firewall restrictions by piggybacking on on-going connections (http://www.securityfocus.com/bid/5387). This is caused by a weakness in the method the firewall uses to generate its initial sequence numbers.

- The firewall is susceptible to a DoS attack related to UDP packets (http://www.securityfocus.com/bid/3509). The attack is possible because the firewall does not properly handle zero-length UDP packets. This attack would normally be easy to prevent by blocking UDP packets heading toward the firewall at the border router. Unfortunately, this will not work because the firewall must pass UDP packets to allow the remote employees to set up IPSec tunnels with the internal firewall.

- The firewall has a bug in its handling of HTTP proxy requests that allows an attacker to connect to web servers behind the firewall as long as the web service is on a nonstandard port (http://cve.mitre.org/cgi-bin/cvename.cgi?name=CAN-2001-0483). This vulnerability would not help an attacker browse web materials on this network because no web servers are running on nonstandard ports on the GIACE network. It would enable the attacker to discover what hosts are running on the network, though. A hotfix is available to fix this problem.

Neither of these vulnerabilities would help an attacker gain unauthorized access to this network. If no other potential access paths were available for an attacker to use, we might decide to analyze the impact that adding an artificial vulnerability to the network would have. In this case, though, other areas in the network show a greater potential for problems, including the public web server.

Determining the Access That Remains: The Public Web Server

This design uses the highly unorthodox approach of locating the public web server on a host connected directly to the Internet with no firewalls in-between. This host is also acting, for all intents and purposes, as a proxy firewall between the Internet and the Fortune Application LAN. The designer felt comfortable doing this because this is no ordinary web server. The product he has used is an HP Virtual Vault Server. HP Virtual Vault is an HP UNIX–based system that has been heavily modified to increase its security. The biggest change is the absence of an all-powerful root account. Instead, the power of the root user has been separated into 50 distinct privileges. These privileges can be granted or revoked as needed on a per-user, process, or file basis. This provides tremendous power in limiting the impact of service vulnerabilities. Even if an attacker can successfully take over a service on a Virtual Vault, the service might not have enough privileges on the Virtual Vault to allow the attacker to do anything useful. In addition, the Vault comes installed with nothing activated by default. You must manually add interface cards, the web server, and so on, which eliminates the possibility that a vulnerability in a service that is not being used could be used to compromise the Vault. More information on trusted OSs such as the Virtual Vault can be found at http://csrc.nist.gov/secpubs/rainbow/std001.txt.

> **Note**
>
> Multilevel security operating systems, such as HP Virtual Vault Server, have clear security advantages over standard servers and seem easy to recommend from a functionality standpoint. However, before you rush out to implement one, you must carefully consider the additional effort required to install and maintain these systems. These servers can be tricky to configure correctly. The added flexibility in permissions adds complexity in implementation.

The version of Virtual Vault being used for this design comes with an integrated Netscape Enterprise web server. This web server hosts the public website for the GIACE network and is the primary public interface between GIACE and its customers. To perform this role, the web server connects to the Fortune Application Server using its second network interface, which is connected directly to the Fortune Application LAN. This application server implements the back-end processing for the site, including storing and retrieving transaction information in the corporate database and authenticated customers by querying the corporate LDAP server.

Determining the Impact: The Public Web Server

This is an interesting way of implementing the public web server for this site, but it is also somewhat risky. The security of the most critical parts of the GIACE network depends on the strength of a single product: the Virtual Vault. If the Virtual Vault security should fail, an attacker would have access to the "crown jewels" of this network. Placing the public web server behind the external firewall, while increasing the load on the firewall, would provide some additional protection for this critical GIACE resource.

Determining the Access That Remains: The Extranet Server

The extranet server allows partners and suppliers access to the hosts on the Fortune Application LAN. The extranet server is implemented using an Aventail extranet server. The Aventail extranet server is a form of reverse proxy that allows external users, after they have authenticated, to connect to internal systems. To protect the confidentiality of these transactions, including the exchange of authentication data, the Aventail solution encrypts these conversations.

Table 23.9 shows the configuration details for the extranet server.

Table 23.9   **Rulebase for the Extranet Server**

Source	Destination Port	Destination Method	User	Authentication
Any	Application Server	5656	Any	LDAP username/password
Any	Application Server, Shares Server	5656, 80	Any	LDAP username/password and client certification
Any	Shares Server	NetBIOS over IP	Any	LDAP username/password and client certification

As you can see from this information, two classes of access are available. Suppliers are granted access to the application server by providing a valid username/password. After this is performed, the supplier is granted access to port 5656 on the application server, which is where the customer GIACE fortune application is hosted. Partners are granted additional access to the network, but they are required to also provide a client certificate in addition to a valid username/password. All authentication data, including the client certificates, is held on the corporate LDAP server.

The added access granted to the partners includes the ability to connect to a web service located on the application server as well as to connect to the NetBIOS ports on the shares server. This shares server is not shown on the network diagram, but it is located on the Fortune Application LAN. It is used as a place to share files between GIACE and its partners.

Determining the Impact: The Extranet Server

This solution does allow secure access from partners and suppliers, but there are still a few points to be made:

- The use of simple username/password authentication might allow an attacker to guess or brute force a valid password, granting him access to the fortune application. If the fortune application has any exploitable vulnerabilities, the attacker might gain a foothold on the Fortune Application LAN. The use of certificates here would eliminate this risk, but it might not be practical with numerous suppliers. Other strong authentication alternatives, such as SecurID tokens, could also be used; however, if this is not feasible, the only alternative is to make sure the fortune application is carefully designed to prevent misuse.

- The extranet server shares an authentication server (the LDAP server) with the public web server. If the web server is allowed to request new user accounts, it is possible that an attacker could add a web user account and then use it to authenticate to the extranet server. Proper application design would eliminate this possibility, but it is still a good idea to separate the storage of customer and business partner authentication databases.

- The location of the shares server places the GIACE "crown jewels" at unnecessary risk. Authenticated partners are allowed to connect using the NetBIOS protocol to the shares server to share files with GIACE. Depending on the configuration of the shares server, though, this might be sufficient access to allow a motivated attacker to gain control of the server, which in this case would allow him to gain a foothold on the Fortune Application LAN. Although this risk is only a concern if the partner is the attacker or has had his certificate stolen, it is a risk that could easily be mitigated by relocating the shares server.

Determining the Access That Remains: The Internal Firewall

The internal firewall protects the desktop and corporate LANs while allowing remote users to establish IPSec tunnels to the GIACE network. These remote users are authenticated using SecurID tokens. The firewall is implemented using a Nokia IP440 appliance running Check Point FireWall-1 version 4.1. Table 23.10 shows its configuration.

Table 23.10 **Rulebase for the Internal Firewall**

Source	Destination	Service	Action
Desktop LAN	Corporate LAN	DNS, IMAP, LDAP, POP3, SMTP, SSH	Allow
Corporate LAN	Desktop LAN	X, SNMP, Ping	Allow
Mail Relay, Mail Server	Mail Server, Mail Relay	SMTP	Allow
Corporate LAN	External DNS	DNS	Allow
trustedusers@GIACE	Corporate LAN	Any	Client Encrypt
normalusers@GIACE	Corporate LAN	DNS, IMAP, LDAP, POP3, SMTP, SSH	Client Encrypt

Table 23.10   **Continued**

Source	Destination	Service	Action
normalusers@GIACE	Desktop LAN	Any	Client Encrypt
Fortune LAN	Corporate LAN	LDAP	Allow
Fortune LAN	Any	Any	Deny, Log
Desktop LAN	Web Proxy	HTTP, HTTPS	Allow
Any	NTP-Server	NTP	Allow
Any	Any	Any	Deny, Log

Determining the Impact: The Internal Firewall

This is a reasonably secure rule set, especially considering all the other security measures in effect on this network. One point of concern is worth discussing, though.

The use of SSH might allow an internal attacker access to the corporate network. The internal firewall allows the desktop LAN to communicate with the corporate LAN using several protocols, including IMAP and SSH. The use of SSH is probably to allow an administrator, while he is at his desk, to administer corporate LAN systems. At the same time, protocols that allow unencrypted authentication, such as IMAP, are also allowed between the two networks, which might create an opportunity for an internal attacker to gain administrative access to corporate servers.

This access would rely on a couple of configuration details. First, the SSH daemons on the corporate network would need to accept username/password authentication (their default configuration). Second, an administrative user would need to have used the same password for his mail account and his user account on a corporate server. We'll leave it up to you to decide how realistic you think this would be.

To implement the attack, the internal attacker would first use ARP poisoning techniques to convince the local systems that the MAC address of the local interface of the firewall is actually the MAC address of the attacker's system. This method results in all the desktop LAN traffic destined for other networks to be redirected to the attacker's machine. By eavesdropping on all this traffic, the attacker can capture the IMAP authentication session when the administrator goes to retrieve his mail. Using the username/password from this session, the attacker would be able to use SSH to log in to any corporate servers in which the administrator has used the same password.

Prevention of this attack is simple. Make sure all SSH servers are configured to only accept public key authentication and make sure the SSH private keys are well protected. Also, if you must use the nonencrypted mail access protocols (as opposed to IMAP+SSL, for example), create a different set of usernames/passwords just for mail access.

Repeating as Necessary: Attacking the Whole Network

All in all, this is a good security design that would be extremely difficult to attack from the outside. An attack is not impossible, though. Here is a potential scenario that might grant access to the "crown jewels."

As previously mentioned, an inordinate amount of trust has been placed in a single server. If the HP Virtual Vault contained sufficient vulnerability, an attacker would have free access to the Fortune Application LAN. As luck would have it, the version of Virtual Vault that was used contains two key vulnerabilities that might be useful to an attacker.

The first is a buffer overflow in the publisher module of the Virtual Vault's web server. (http://cve.mitre.org/cgi-bin/cvename.cgi?name=CAN-2001-0746). If the web-published module were installed on the Vault, it is possible that an attacker could use this vulnerability to execute arbitrary code at the privilege level of the web server, although this is somewhat unlikely because HP rated the publisher module as "high risk" and did not include it as part of the standard distribution.

The second vulnerability is in Virtual Vault's mkacct command, which creates a new account on the server (http://www.securityfocus.com/bid/1843). This program contains a vulnerability that can allow a local user to add privileges to his account. Using these in combination might allow an attacker to gain control of the web server's account and then elevate his privileges to the point where he is as close to root equivalent as is possible on a Virtual Vault system.

Unfortunately for the attacker, it is unlikely that the web server would have the mkacct privilege, making the second half of this attack impossible. This is the strength of the Virtual Vault system. By limiting permissions to just those required for the job at hand, you drastically reduce the risk of exploitation.

All is not lost for our attacker, though. The web server must have sufficient rights to perform its normal activities. This includes the ability to retrieve customer data, retrieve fortunes, and capture other sensitive data that the web server would normally have access to. In this case, even web server access might meet the goals of the attacker. The lesson here is never to rely too heavily on one solution. Moving the web server behind the external firewall would prevent this attack from succeeding.

Summary

In this chapter, we analyzed the effectiveness of two good security designs. Each provided multiple layers of defense using different security techniques to provide defense in depth, and each would prove difficult for a real-world attacker to break into. However, as good as they were, we were able to identify areas in each that could be improved.

The process we used to accomplish this was adversarial review. Instead of concentrating on what the security architecture prevented, we concentrated on what it might allow. As is often the case, a design might allow far more than you expect. When performing your own adversarial review, keep a few things in mind:

- It is not important what a device is supposed to do. Think about what it could do.
- Pay special attention to the services accessible to the attacker. These are where the attack must start.

- Do not assume that the attacker will always be external. It is a useful exercise to look at each of your network segments to see what an attacker could accomplish if he started his attack from there.

- Pay attention to the ways your design can reduce an attacker's ability to discover your network, but conduct your own review as if the attacker has full knowledge of your design. This might seem unfair, but it is much better to weed out all vulnerabilities, not just the vulnerabilities you think will be easy for an attacker to discover.

It is much better for you to conduct this review than to allow the vast collection of Internet attackers to perform it for you. We hope this chapter has provided you with the incentive to look at your designs in a new light.

References

1 Eeye Advisory AD20010618. "All Versions of Microsoft Internet Information Services Remote Buffer Overflow (SYSTEM Level Access)." http://www.eeye.com/html/Research/Advisories/AD20010618.html. June 2001.

2 M. Handley, C. Kreibich, and V. Paxson. "Network Intrusion Detection: Evasion, Traffic Normalization, and End-to-End Protocol Semantics (HTML)." (Compressed PostScript) (PDF) Proc. USENIX Security Symposium. 2001.

3 Eeye Advisory AD20010705. "%u Encoding IDS Bypass Vulnerability." http://www.eeye.com/html/Research/Advisories/AD20010705.html. September 2001.

24

A Unified Security Perimeter: The Importance of Defense in Depth

WHEN WE WERE YOUNG TEENAGERS, WE WERE fearless. We drove our cars too fast, didn't wear seatbelts; it is amazing we are alive today. Now that we are older, we still drive fast, but we do it in very sophisticated vehicles. We wear seatbelts, our cars have front and side airbags, antilock breaks, and skid management, we pay insurance, and as we age, we eat vitamin A to improve our night vision and we wear special driving glasses. We apply a defense-in-depth approach to driving. What's the difference? Nowadays, with a spouse and kids counting on us, we have something to lose.

Could it be that in our journey as system and network builders a similar thing has happened? Just a dozen years ago, less than half the organizations that employ the readers of this book had a firewall. Today, many of our security operations centers look like NASA control rooms with failover firewalls, VPNs, intelligent IPS switches, antivirus, antispam, IDS (including anomaly IDS to pick up the activity of the worms our IPS switches don't have a signature for), correlation engines, and enough cooling to keep it all running to ice the streets of a really hot city such as Houston, Texas in August. What's changed? We have something to lose. What are we trying so hard to protect? Over the past decade the value of our organizations is measured more and more by the value of our intellectual property (IP). Today, IP accounts for more than half the value of most nonagricultural organizations and is at least 90% of high-tech companies.

Throughout the book, we have touched on defense in depth. We have made an assertion that no single defensive component is enough to protect our information assets. We are at a crossroads as a community, in our desire for ease of use; the most prevalent desktop operating systems simply cannot be secured without resorting to external tools. Do you remember the discussion of rickety operating systems in the preface of this book? If security was as simple as putting a firewall between the Internet and the system needing to be defended, that would be great, but it is not that simple. Even if the system is robust, there is more to do to achieve a reasonable level of risk. The lesson of devastating attacks such as Nimda is that a vulnerable system simply has to browse from a hostile web server and it can be infected. Does this depress you? We hope not. Life is full of risk, damage, and mayhem, yet we not only survive, but we prosper. To prosper, defense in depth is imperative as a design paradigm. Bad things are going to happen. We need to limit the damage to a minimum.

This chapter gives you a lot to think about and helps to tie all the topics of the book together. In the first half of this chapter, we employ the classic castle analogy to help make our perimeter defense points crystal clear as we introduce the problem of the rigid perimeter. At the end of that discussion, we focus on static packet filters and Network Address Translation (NAT) from a defense-in-depth perspective. Then we consider softer perimeter solutions that tie up the attacker's time by absorbing the attacks, much like the crumple zone of your automobile absorbs energy in a crash. We discuss internal defenses, which are the information technology equivalent of the watertight doors built in to ships. Finally, we consider defense in depth for information.

Castles: An Example of Defense-in-Depth Architecture

Castles are often used as an information security analogy; castles typically have a perimeter control that includes one way in and out. Castles also use chokepoints. It is easy to see defense in depth in action; to rescue the princess in the tower, you have to cross the moat and bash down the big door. Then you find yourself in a sally port area, which is similar to an airlock. There are external control doors, an assembly area, an interior set of doors, and only one set of doors opens at a time. So even if you break down one set of doors, you have to cram into the assembly area, where there may be ports through which the insiders can shoot at you. Then you have another set of doors to go through. We can employ many elements from castle architecture in our networks. The border routers and firewalls are used in the same way as moats and sally ports. The castle is not invincible, but the defense-in-depth architecture is one to carefully consider. Castles aren't still in military use today because they had a number of problems that relate to modern perimeter defense. Cannons were a big problem. Backdoors and secret passages did more than a few castles in, and the fact that they were stationary and easy to find was a significant disadvantage. With our networks, we have similar problems. 802.11 wireless access points and modems, especially on auto-answer, are the backdoors and secret passages of our networks. Sites with public address space, like castles, are exposed, stationary, and easy to find and attack.

In the next section of this chapter, we use the analogy of a castle to explore some of the components of defense in depth.

Hard Walls and Harder Cannonballs

Gunpowder and cannons were the primary forces that put castles out of business. Even if you build the walls 60 meters thick—a huge investment of building resources—the attackers can hammer the walls into dust and then breach the perimeter. By using denial of service (DoS) techniques of SYN floods or UDP floods as cannonballs, attackers might not be able to turn your firewall into dust, but they might well be able to shut down your site.

If a firewall—especially an application gateway firewall—is directly connected to the Internet, it probably doesn't have the speed in terms of CPU cycles to withstand a DoS attack. As we covered in Chapter 12, "Fundamentals of Secure Perimeter Design," the border router and firewall deployed together are more robust because the router is faster and can be configured to block many DoS attacks. Thus, a couple layers of defense are more effective than a single layer.

Before the cannon was available, the perimeter breach device of choice for castles and keeps (a keep is the inner sanctuary of a castle) was the battering ram. The actual doorway of the castle tended to be made of metal and wood and was connected to stone, each of which reacts differently to the ram's attack. Wood, for instance, is softer than iron; therefore, the metal fasteners tend to erode the wood as the doorway withstands the shock. The holes in the wood get bigger; the joints weaken, and pretty soon the defense is breached. The functional equivalent for the battering ram is the DoS attack. As discussed in the preface to this book, in our networks, we have the firewall applications on top of operating systems, and attackers might target either the firewall application or the underlying operating system. This was the case with the flaw in Intel Pentium chips, where a single op code command series (F0 0F C7 C8) could halt the processor (http://catless.ncl.ac.uk/Risks/19.45.html#subj5).

We have already discussed using border routers to shield firewalls from attack, but border routers are also susceptible to attack. Many of them do not respond well to ping floods directed against them. In fact, a sufficiently large number of attacking systems directed against the primary backbones might be able to drop portions of the Internet. The solution for an attack against the Internet is outside the scope of this book, but the best answer is related to defense in depth—design the routers and network to be managed by an out-of-band network. A solution to the ping flood against your border router might be to add one more layer. A tool such as Attack Mitigator from Top Layer is an example of a very fast box that can be optimized to stop DoS attacks. Unless these attacks can saturate your entire data pipe, this layer can withstand the attacker's battering ram. Several companies are currently developing similar defenses against distributed DoS attacks, and additional products should be available by the time this book is printed.

Secret Passages

Although it is certainly true that a castle's perimeter can be breached, we should also take a second to think about how well those ancient perimeters worked. Thick stone walls, like firewalls, do work well to help keep the barbarians out. Because they work so well, people invested a lot of effort trying to get around perimeter defenses. A favorite movie trick to circumvent these perimeters is the secret passage. Let's take a minute to examine how easy and likely it is that you might have a tunnel through your firewall that acts as a secret passage, or a leak you are not aware of in your perimeter.

Tunnels Through the Firewall

If the firewall is perceived to be too restrictive, users may find ways to get through it; one of the most common ways is to tunnel through HTTP. There are several ways to do this, including SOAP (Simple Object Access Protocol), non-RFC tunnels, and attacking the web server (putting it under your control and using it to send data via HTTP).

SOAP (Simple Object Access Protocol)

RFC 3288 describes SOAP as a means of implementing web services across the Internet and tunneling through perimeters using HTTP. These tunnels act as third-party servers to forward your message from, say, a system inside your firewall to a server you might not otherwise be able to access.

SOAP can be sent either in a synchronous way (for example, when it contains an RPC call) or in an asynchronous way (for example, when it contains an XML message). The latter is usually the case. SOAP does not care about the content, only about the addressee. You might as well regard it as a simple envelope: It can carry anything. SOAP is not concerned about the content; it just lets the mailman (usually HTTP) deliver the envelope. The first generation of commercial SOAP and XML firewalls is already available from companies such as Xtradyne, Flamenco, and Datapower.

Non-RFC Approaches to HTTP Tunneling

HTTP tunneling does not have to be based on the RFC standards; all you have to do is encode your message properly using HTML and the tunnel will work. On the non-RFC side of the house, dozens of tools, such as the original GNU httptunnel, encapsulate a communication stream in HTTP. For one example, you might want to visit http://www.nocrew.org/software/httptunnel.html. If you look at the data, you will see GET, PUT and POST commands passing through the tunnel. Most even incorporate HTML tags, making these tunnels a bit tough to spot.

If you have an intrusion detection system (IDS), such as Snort, that can perform statistical analysis, or a traffic measurement tool, such as Cisco's NetFlow, you can often detect these HTTP tunnels. If you think about it, when you surf the Web, you specify a URL, wait, and then the page starts to display. In terms of the traffic signature, the client initiates the connection and sends a few bytes to the server, and the server sends a considerable amount of data back to the client. Now to be sure, some web applications enable the client to PUT or POST, so there is a potential for a false positive; however, with a bit of practice, you can detect a number of these tunnels. Of course, technology is not enough. After you detect a tunnel, your organization's policy dictates your next move. Is there a policy against unauthorized connections at your site? Would your organization's policy define a tunnel as an unauthorized connection? If the answer to the preceding two questions is yes, then what actions does the policy permit or require you to take?

Attacking the Web Server

A lot of organizations feel that web server security is not an interesting or important topic. The SANS Institute commissioned a course on Apache security from researcher Ryan Barnett. When it did not sell, we purchased Google AdWords for the Hands On Apache Security class with a number of search words related to web security. Google reported we had such an abysmal "click-through ratio" that it essentially said, "Keep your money," and disabled the search words (http://www.sans.org/onsite/description.php?tid=41).

However, because web servers are Internet facing, they remain under constant attack. If an attacker is able to compromise a web server, he can tunnel information from the server. This is why your IDSs should always alert if your web server initiates a connection to any other system. However, the attacker can still PUT and GET information right in the HTTP stream.

Ryan Barnett conducted an experiment using an open proxy server for a week as a honeypot demonstrates that not only are web servers directly under attack, but they are also being tested to see if they are an open proxy so the attackers can create "proxy chains" (proxy web servers connecting to other proxy web servers) to mask their identity. An article by Barnett and Northcutt describing the experiment can be found at http://www.sans.org/rr/special/http_elephant.php.

PUT Attacks, September 20, 2004

To illustrate that web servers really are under attack, consider an excerpt from the Internet Storm Center's (ISC) Handler's diary dated September 20, 2004:

"Increase in HTTP PUT requests. A report from Ryan stated that he noticed an increase of HTTP PUT attempts to his public web servers over the past few weeks. After looking at the file names attempting to be uploaded, it appeared that this was an attempt to deface his web site."

Some of the file names in his logs included the following:

- `PUT /index.html HTTP/1.0`
- `PUT /at4k3r.htm HTTP/1.0`
- `PUT /ka.htm HTTP/1.0`
- `PUT /kateam HTTP/1.0`
- `PUT /scanned HTTP/1.0`
- `PUT /inf.txt HTTP/1.0`
- `PUT /ownz.htm HTTP/1.0`
- `PUT /hdg.htm HTTP/1.0`

Johannes Ullrich, the ISC's CTO, checked SANS web logs and found similar activity. Fortunately, the attempted defacements were not successful. This highlights the importance of restricting the authorized HTTP request methods on public web servers. This "hack" (the easiest defacement method of them all) can be effectively denied by not allowing the PUT method and also with appropriate `DocumentRoot` directory ownership/permissions. Check your web logs for this type of behavior. A simple Snort rule to `ALERT` on PUT statements for sites that do not expect uploads would also be prudent.

Change in the Perimeter Configuration

Even a performance problem or the perception of a performance problem can lead to the creation of a secret passage—a leak in the perimeter. People just want to get their work done, and if the perimeter is slowing them down, they find ways to get around the perimeter.

Even at highly secured DoD facilities or other high-value assets, security officers might discover that the firewall administrator has changed the web or some other proxy application on the firewall to a simple packet filter. If it happened to you, would you be at a loss as to why the officer would have done such a thing? It does make sense. The primary task of firewall administrators is to create ACLs or rules that open up the firewall. Firewalls might ship with a default rule to deny anything that is not specifically allowed (deny all), but that does not mean the firewall administrator is oriented to deny all. We should never forget the human element. From time to time, this administrator will almost certainly get phone calls or emails from people saying that the firewall is too slow. He knows packet filters are faster than proxy applications, so one day he decides to fix the firewall and switch it from a proxy to a packet filter.

If you are not monitoring your firewall configuration, the first time you realize something is wrong might be when you start seeing attacks from the Internet that are clearly operating-system specific. HTTP, for instance, often gives away operating system information in the protocol headers; therefore, if the attackers run a website, they might know exactly what to target. Of course, this would only be an issue if certain websites on the Internet were malicious. This would be a serious problem for a site that is not interested in using NAT and making all the internal machines private addresses.

An emerging best practice to help protect your site from administrative changes is to continually scan your perimeter from the outside using assessment tools. Managed scan services, such as Qualys (http://www.qualys.com), have subscription offerings so that you can schedule these scans via a web browser interface. They maintain a database of your configuration and provide a variety of canned reports. They also have an interface so that you can build your own reports. This way, if a new port is open or a new IP address becomes active, you can get a report to that effect. From a defense-in-depth perspective, you should seriously consider an active scanning program for any of your systems that can be reached from the Internet. Attackers will certainly scan you, so you had best probe your systems so that you see what the attackers see.

Insider Threats

The insider threat is divided into two major components: people and programs. It never hurts to mention that throughout history, one of the best ways to get into a castle, bank, Secure Compartmented Information Facility (SCIF), or perimeter defense is to pay someone off. An equally effective and potentially cheaper method is the use of spyware and keystroke loggers.

Insider Employees and Contractors

Money is a powerful tool. If a firewall administrator would put a site at risk for free, imagine what a bit of coercion and $100,000 might be able to do. The CERT study on the insider threat, available at http://www.cert.org/archive/pdf/bankfin040820.pdf, shows that 87% of the time, attackers do not use a technically sophisticated approach. Why bother? They can burn a DVD of all your intellectual property, put it in a briefcase, and walk out of the facility.

The defense-in-depth strategy here is to employ good background checks when hiring, do a bit of random monitoring, and keep an eye out for people who come in early, leave late, and work weekends. (Although all my peers work long hours, this is still a classic indicator of problems.) Sudden changes in financial status, signs of alcohol or drug use, and talk of entitlement ("They owe me.") can all be signs of an insider problem.

Insider Programs, Spyware, and Keystroke Loggers

It is a lot of fun to watch the expression on people's faces the first time they run antispyware tools such as Spybot Search and Destroy or Ad-Aware. Here are the links for these tools:

http://www.safer-networking.org/en/download/

http://www.lavasoftusa.com/software/adaware/

Folks that do not run antispyware tools regularly will typically have 60 to 100 spying URLs, a couple of bots, and a keystroke logger or two. We'll probably be plagued with software that spies on where we go and what we do as long as people use browsers that execute software.

Many organizations are not aware of the vulnerabilities browsers have. For instance, see CERT advisory CA 2003-22 (http://www.cert.org/advisories/CA-2003-22.html).

These organizations using vulnerable browsers have probably yielded a lot of information to their unscrupulous competitors that are happy to engage in espionage, one password, one credit card number, one email marked "Proprietary" at a time. In addition to the antispyware tools, part of defense in depth is to eliminate the buildup of information that can be mined. If intellectual property is a significant component of the value of your organization, consider a tool such as CyberScrub (http://www.cyberscrub.com), which deletes temporary Internet files and all the other intelligence information that accumulates on your organization's desktop and mobile systems.

Insider people and programs will always be a significant problem. The classic concepts of the principle of least privilege—letting people and systems have only the access they need to do their jobs, and the separation of duties, especially where money or valuable intellectual property is involved—are two of your best defenses. A third defense is similar to the principle of least privilege: the need to know. The less the insiders know, the less harm they can do. Strictly enforcing the need to know is one way to hide crucial assets in the mist, even from insiders.

Hiding in the Mist

Remember the TV mini series *The Mists of Avalon* from a few years back? The castle dwellers did one smart thing: They used magic to call up mists to hide their castle. The location of castles is one of the big problems in the whole castle concept from the standpoint of military strategy. After the cannon was developed, it became apparent that castles were the perfect targets. They were so big that it was hard to miss them and waste a cannon ball, and you knew just where to find them because they were not mobile and couldn't be hidden. The great news is that we can deploy the functional equivalent of the mists of Avalon on our networks by using NAT. Someone can attack a perimeter in many ways, but if you have private addresses and NAT, the attacks or probes might still work to some extent, but they won't be as useful to the attacker. Suddenly, your internal systems become difficult to find, as if they are hidden in the mists. Imagine listening in on an IRC chat room discussion, and you realize the attackers are experimenting with the latest technique to slip through the perimeter. As you are watching the chat room discussion between Attacker 1 (A1) and Attacker 2 (A2), you see something resembling the following scroll across your screen:

A1: Did it work for you? I've got 10 bots banging.

A2: I got through the firewall and got a box to answer.

A1: Lamers, what OS is it? I bet I can crack it in 10 minutes or less.

A2: Passive fingerprinter indicates it must be a windoze box. It reports its IP is 192.168.1.238.

A1: NAT, better keep scanning.

A2: I don't get it. We found one.

A1: Yeah, but which 192.168.1.238 is it exactly?

Easily 100,000 networks start with 192.168.1, and unless you can nail up a source route or come through a tunnel, you probably can't get to and from one of these networks across the Internet. If you do have public addresses for the internal machines at your site, you should seriously consider transitioning to a NAT and private address structure. It can be the single most valuable tool to prevent successful reconnaissance by those who desire to be your enemy. In the next section, we briefly discuss three classic techniques used every day to penetrate perimeters: setting additional flags with a SYN, fragments, and echo replies. These examples illustrate the point about public and private addresses.

SYN/FIN

Many of the buffer overflows from 1998 through just yesterday often follow reconnaissance using SynScan, which uses a combination of flags found in byte 13 from offset zero in the TCP header, and set both the SYN and FIN flags or bits. For a long time, the SYN and FIN set, in conjunction with an IPID of 39426, has announced the use of the SynScan tool. However, the flag combination can be more than a signature, the idea behind a SYN/FIN attack is to add an additional spurious flag to the SYN to attempt to originate a connection behind a perimeter. Many packet-filtering systems, especially static packet filters, mask on byte 13 of the TCP header checking for the value 2, the value of the SYN flag as the only bit set. The TCP flags are URG, ACK, PSH, RST, SYN, and FIN. FIN is the low-order bit, with a value of 1, if set; SYN is 2, RST is 4, and so on. This is what RFC 793 specifies, so it makes sense that designers of perimeter systems would inspect for a value of 2 in byte 13. SYN/RST, for instance, would not meet the logical test and would be allowed through the packet filter into the internal network, as would SYN/ACK, an ACK only, and so on. The kicker is that both UNIX and Windows systems will respond to a SYN/FIN with a SYN/ACK. SYN/FINs are used to penetrate perimeters and to establish a connection.

This attack is the most dangerous perimeter penetration we are going to discuss; fragments and echo replies are primarily for reconnaissance, as opposed to system compromise attacks.

Reconnaissance with Fragments

In this section, we examine the use of incomplete fragment trains. When this reconnaissance technique is used on a vulnerable site, attackers get a positive answer as to the existence, or lack thereof, of a live host at every address that is checked. Fragmentation occurs when a packet is larger than the maximum transmission unit (MTU) of the next hop in its journey to its destination host.

Only the first fragment has the true header from the original datagram. The other fragments have only the IP header generated by the router that breaks up the original datagram; those fragments do not get their true protocol headers until the destination host reassembles them. This lack of protocol header makes them ideal reconnaissance tools for attackers. Many perimeter devices do not choose to make the blocking decision on anything but the first fragment. An attacker can intentionally send in fragments without the protocol information; these fragments tend to pass through the perimeter to internal systems. If the internal systems have public addresses, a number of things—all bad—could happen. If the system being probed exists, it might receive the fragment. Then, when the other fragments do not arrive, the probed system might respond with an ICMP error messages saying that the reassembly time was exceeded, which tells the attacker that there is a live host at that IP address. If the system being probed does not exist, an internal router might respond with an ICMP host unreachable error message. The attacker then knows an IP address is not active. To defend against this technique, the perimeter must block both outgoing ICMP time exceeded in reassembly messages and ICMP host unreachable messages.

Next, we look at one more way attackers can penetrate perimeter defenses for reconnaissance—using echo replies.

Reconnaissance with Echo Replies

ICMP has two forms: error messages that are never replied to and error messages that take the form of request/reply. ICMP Type 8, Code 0 is an echo request, although it is also known as a *ping*, after the ping program. If an ICMP listener receives an echo request, the listener generally responds with an ICMP Type 0, Code 0 echo reply to tell the original ICMP speaker that the datagram was received.

These request/reply types of ICMP are generally used for network management—for instance, to see if hosts or routers are up. They can also be used for reconnaissance in many cases because echo replies often pass through perimeters; to block them would break outbound ping, and people like to use ping. Therefore, attackers send in echo replies to cause internal routers to respond with ICMP host unreachable error messages. This is known as *inverse mapping*. The only active response from the probed site is for systems that do not exist.

The defense strategy is obvious here. As you learned in Chapter 3, "Stateful Firewalls," stateful firewalls maintain a table and might be able to determine whether or not the echo reply is a response to a ping initiated from within your site. Your design should have a stateful perimeter layer. As an additional layer of protection, you learned about the importance of squelching the outbound ICMP error messages in Chapter 6, "The Role of a Router." If we drop outgoing ICMP unreachable messages, even if our state table fails, we have this second layer of defense. Of course, the best defense would be to employ filtering, thus squelching outbound ICMP and NAT.

Defense on the Inside

Even if you are able to enter a castle though a secret passage, a number of barriers still exist, including those pesky guards with swords, before you can rescue the princess in the tower. Every single person who sees you is likely to either raise an alarm or attack you. Plus there will still be additional locked doors. In the past, this was not so with most of our sites. We did not typically use internal barriers or internal instrumentation. Nowadays, this is beginning to change with network segmentation and even self-defending networks.

The Need for Compartmentalization

I worked for a Navy lab once that was a loose group of multiple Navy bases in different states. They each did different kinds of work and had fairly low interaction, but one day, some "genius" decided that the bases needed a common email system. They selected what I consider the riskiest email client on the face of the earth: Microsoft Outlook. That wasn't the half of it, though; the servicemen wanted a single domain controller for all the users at all the bases. Chapters 12, "Fundamentals of Secure Perimeter Design," and 18, "Sample Designs," talk about single points of failure, but this was the most vulnerable design I have ever seen. If an attacker was able to compromise the single domain controller, every login for every user at every one of those bases would be exposed. If you think about the way they build ships with multiple compartments, each protected by doors, you have a good analogy for building a robust internal network. We need to employ internal barriers, such as appliance firewalls, and place and monitor IDS sensors inside our systems.

If attackers get through the perimeter, we still want to employ layers of defense and instrumentation. Chapter 20, "Network Log Analysis," discusses the kind of information available in log files. The following sections of this chapter review some of the technologies we can employ to really get a clue as to what is going on in our networks as well as how to harden them. These technologies include personal (or host-centric) firewalls, appliance firewalls, physical airgaps, segmenting the network using switches, active network defense, as well as the emerging log fusion products.

Host-Centric Firewalls as Sensors

Personal, or *host-centric*, firewall technology is one of the great breakthroughs in the past few years, and it is clearly a defense-in-depth technology. Firewalls are barriers—one more layer of defense—and that additional layer is valuable in and of itself. Some firewalls do not even allow systems to answer pings.

In addition to being an another layer of defense, host-centric firewalls, described in Chapter 10, "Host Defense Components," are equally as valuable as canaries in a coal mine. In the past century before modern sensors were developed to detect poisonous gas, miners took canaries into coal mines. Canaries are more sensitive to poisonous gas than people, so when the canaries started keeling over, it was time to get out of the mine. Because we have very little instrumentation internally in our sites, a personal firewall can be an early sensor, much like a canary, that alerts us to a serious problem of which we might not otherwise be aware.

If all the writers and editors of this book could be in a very large room with each of you, the readers, we could conduct a poll. If we asked all of you to raise your hands if you use a personal firewall, about 70% of your hands would go up. If we asked you if you run a personal firewall at work behind your corporate firewall, maybe 40% of you would raise your hands. If the members of that last group were asked how many had ever received an alarm on their work personal firewall, almost every hand would stay up. The implications of those alarms are startling. You can chalk up those alerts to one of three things:

- False positives, or errors, by the firewall detection
- Real attacks generated from outside your organization
- Real attacks generated from within your organization

When we instrument an internal network, the results can include finding compromised systems being used to attack other systems and finding employees who are involved in hacking. When choosing a personal firewall solution for your organization, you might want to make the console available with enterprise versions a priority. These are available from Sygate, Symantec, McAfee, and others. In terms of maintaining situational awareness (knowing what is going on inside your network) by having reports coming to a central place, this is a great aid.

Internal Firewalls/Appliances

A number of tools are logwatchers and correlation engines. These are major improvements on the original swatch. Almost all these include a relational SQL database to manage the information. Examples include NetForensics, ArcSight, and Intellitactics' NSM, which are all costly because of the amount of compute power needed to drive the database, the amount of storage they require, and the amount of manual intervention needed to keep them up to date. As these tools mature and integrate with passive OS sniffers such as SourceFire's RNA and Tenable's NeVO, they will enable us to do the same sorts of attack detection and trend analysis, possibly even more than we can do by using a personal firewall console. If we design our networks with multiple internal compartments, possibly using firewall appliances, we have the opportunity for both protection from attacks and detection of attack attempts inside our internal network.

The Case for Airgaps

Nothing beats a genuine, old fashioned, not-connected-to-the-Net airgap. The department of defense has a rule that a classified network has to be airgapped from any unclassified network. That is a sensible rule.

You need an airgap between your networked assets and the servers where you locate your most critical information. What is the information that truly differentiates you from your competition? The SANS Institute is engaged in research into securing systems every day, but its most critical information is either encrypted at rest while on networked computers or stored on airgapped systems if not encrypted. Several of our peers working for startup security companies have told us their software development and lab systems are not connected to a network connected to the Internet. We have discussed the notion of the hard, crunchy perimeter and the soft, chewy interior. The next section of this chapter suggests that we should think a bit about softer, absorbent perimeters. Although that might conjure up thoughts of paper towels, the plan is to discuss honeypots, rate limiting, and failover.

Self-Defending Network (SDN)

If we look at the way attacks come in today, we can clearly see the secret passage analogy is quite accurate: Attacks and attackers don't walk in the front door per se anymore. Our problems come from rogue machines, laptops that have been brought home, put in sleep mode, and connected back up to your network. The problem lies within the machines we don't control, such as those of the contractors and vendors who come on your network to check email and so on.

You might have seen the new advertisements on TV about the Self-Defending Network from Cisco, with the little girl who installs software on her father's computer! A worm immediately tries to infect the machine, but luckily the outbreak is stopped before it can happen, due to the new SDN technology deployed. Let me give you a bit of insight into what is behind the Self-Defending Network.

The Self-Defending Network is a Cisco-led strategy that includes the facility to improve the way a host can attach to your network via the checking of parameters that you set to see if it complies with your security policy, hence enhancing the ability to identify, prevent, and adapt to threats. Obviously, this will not be perfect, but it seems to be a major trend. Similar technology is available from Sygate.

> **Note**
> The authors wish to thank Patrick Ramseier and other Cisco engineers for providing us with the technical content to ensure this section is accurate.

This fundamental element of SDN is called NAC, which is short for Network Admission Control. NAC is an efficient way to leverage the network to intelligently enforce access control based on your endpoint security posture and is currently supported by a number of vendors, including Computer Associates, Symantec, Trend Micro, McAfee, and IBM.

There are a few prerequisites in order for NAC to work:

- Cisco IOS v.12.8(8)T or later
- IOS security image (firewall feature set)
- Cisco Trust Agent (CTA), which must be installed on endpoint devices such as desktops, laptops, and so on
- Support for Extensible Authentication Protocol over UDP (EAPoUDP), a protocol designed to support a number of authentication methods, ranging from MD5 and One Time Password to device-specific solutions such as RSA or Cryptocard
- Cisco Secure Access Control Server (ACS) version 3.3

NAC works by utilizing a software agent called CTA, which will be available as a free download from http://www.cisco.com and potentially embedded in Symantec, McAfee, Trend Micro Virus programs as well as the Cisco Security Agent.

Here are the steps used for the comprehensive compliance validation on a Layer 3 device such as a router:

1. When a new host is attempting to attach to your network, the IP packet triggers an Intercept ACL on your router. The purpose of the Intercept ACL is to initiate the network admissions process; the first step is to query a policy server for a posture. In addition, the NAC program will occasionally query existing hosts to ensure they are the same admitted host they are supposed to be.

2. The default ACL determines the initial or interim network access to be granted to the host.

3. The router then triggers a posture validation by utilizing the CTA. It does that by using Extensible Authentication Protocol over UDP (EAPoUDP). Postures can include antivirus, host-based intrusion prevention, or application-specific postures.

4. The CTA agent gathers the information and sends the posture credentials back to the router via EAPoUDP again.

5. The router then forwards the collected credentials to an access control server (ACS) by using EAP over Radius.

6. ACS can optionally proxy portions of that posture authentication to vendor servers so you can make sure all hosts that enter your network have the right antivirus definition or DAT level for your antivirus policy.

7. ACS validates the posture and then determines the authorization rights, to make sure the host presented is healthy, and whether it needs to be segmented off to be updated or quarantined.

8. ACS then sends the host's authorization policy back to the router.

9. The host IP access is granted, denied, or restricted, depending on the posture assessment.

10. The router periodically reassesses inactive hosts to ensure the posture has not changed. It does this by using a new mechanism called L3 EAP Status Query. This poll makes sure of the following:

- That CTA is still there.
- It is the same validated device.
- The posture hasn't changed.

Active hosts are reassessed as well. If they stop responding to the status queries, a revalidation is triggered.

If a large number of vendors support NAC in the same way the major antivirus players have, you will be able to make sure all your endpoints conform to your security policy before they attach to your network via switch, router, wireless, or any other method. If this is done in conjunction with absorbent perimeters (the next strategy we discuss), you have a very solid security model.

Absorbent Perimeters

For years, the primary advance in perimeter security was the silent drop, where a probe was dropped without a response, such as an ICMP administratively prohibited message. Today, it is possible to construct perimeters that are even harder to probe from an attacker's point of view than these black-hole-style systems. Chapter 10 discusses a number of host-based firewalls, including SunScreen and Psionic PortSentry. One such host-based firewall that remains a bit ahead of its time is NFR's BackOfficer Friendly (http://www.nfr.com/resource/backOfficer.php). This technology incorporates a kind of active defense. If the attacker is scanning for a web server, NFR's BackOfficer Friendly provides a valid HTTP response. It answers to Telnet requests or even Back Orifice pings. The logic is to keep the attacker off base. Raptor firewalls have a similar capability at the perimeter. These devices, possibly in conjunction with the occasional silent drop, make reconnaissance a more challenging proposition for attackers. Other technologies we can employ to create a perimeter that is able to absorb attacks include honeypots, rate-limiting, and failover.

Honeypots

One early example of a honeypot was the deception toolkit (DTK) developed by Fred Cohen and available from his website (http://www.all.net/dtk/dtk.htm). DTK was a state machine written in Perl that made it possible to emulate almost any service. The software came preconfigured to emulate about 20 network services, including a Telnet written in the C language. NFR's BackOfficer Friendly, which we just discussed, can also be considered a state machine. It is a honeypot as well as a personal firewall. Such technology has two major advantages for the organization that deploys it. It tends to tie up the attackers' resources as they are burning their time and effort against the honeypot, and it provides you with information about what the attackers are trying to do.

The Internet Storm Center (ISC) depends on honeypots to capture malicious code, after they determine it is running, by large changes in the destination port number of traffic. In this case, the honeypot is the actual Windows or Linux operating system with a weak security model so that it can be infected. This is an alternative to the state machine approach. The state machine is advantageous because it is unlikely that an attacker can break out of the state machine and use the honeypot to attack someone else. The native operating system is advantageous because it becomes a thousand times more difficult for the attackers to figure out they are dealing with a fake system.

No discussion of honeypots is complete without mentioning the Honeynet project (http://www.honeynet.org/), championed by Lance Spitzner and a number of security researchers. The Honeynet project continues to add to our understanding of attacker techniques and motivation. Today, the Honeynet Alliance is available for organizations interested in fostering research about honeypots. The Honeynet Alliance tends to use actual operating systems for its technology; the original Honeynet was an actual network with firewalls, targets, and an IDS. Today, through the magic on VMware, it is possible to simulate an entire network using only a single computer. This solution is much cheaper and less complex, and it might allow the defensive community to deploy more honeypots. There is also Neils Provost's excellent honeyd, a free software solution that is rapidly becoming the honeypot of choice. More information is available at http://www.honeyd.org/.

Should your organization consider a honeypot? It is an advanced technique. If you already have your perimeter functioning well, an IDS collecting data, and host-based intrusion detection on at least the critical systems, a honeypot might be a next logical step. A honeypot can be deployed on the screened subnet or DMZ as a third DNS server, an FTP server, or any other server. Also, it would draw fire and not be obviously out of place. A honeypot might be the only way to actually capture the full attack if the perimeter is knocking down the traffic. As defenses advance and defenders consider automated response, this technology can be used to help assess threat. Originally, the primary auto-response capabilities were to drop the connection, forge a reset to knock down the attack, and shun the attacker's IP address. Each of these has drawbacks, and a significant potential exists for self-inflicted DoS. Nevertheless, as the attacks we face become ever more sophisticated, auto-response must be considered as a defense-in-depth tool.

In addition to the types of active response we have discussed in this section, another tool to consider is rate limiting.

Rate Limiting

Rate limiting—managing the amount of bandwidth granted to a connection—was developed for Quality of Service (QoS) reasons. Throughout the history of networking, we have had to deal with various degrees of service and capability. Researchers have long proposed various QoS solutions, including buffering, advances in queuing theory, and protocol advances. These are primarily for performance, especially with services that do not react well to changes in throughput, such as streaming audio or video; however, QoS solutions offer fascinating possibilities for creating perimeters that absorb attacks as a defensive methodology. Like any other auto-response, these techniques come with their own problems and dangers, but they are worth considering, especially to buy time to evaluate and respond to an attack. The primary advantage is to avoid tipping our hand to the attacker whose activity we have identified. Rate limiting is similar to the active response and honeypot-style defenses. Also, if we do accidentally target the wrong host with our active defense, we do less damage because we slow the attacks down more than stopping them. The three possible ways to implement rate limiting are in the network switch we control, in effective use of the protocol, and at the application.

Network switches are rapidly becoming more sophisticated, and QoS is available in off-the-shelf products, such as the Entarasys switch. If the IDS detects an attack, it can simply begin to modulate the available bandwidth to the attacker. This might be a security option that managed service providers could deploy. You can't have a conversation with someone in this business for five minutes before you start hearing a story about a customer who made a change without informing him or her, setting off the security alarms and whistles. Not all switches support rate limiting, but there are some fascinating things that we can implement with existing and emerging protocols.

If an attack were UDP based, it would be simple for the perimeter defense mechanisms to issue an ICMP source quench message. This tells the sender to slow down. You can modify the performance of a TCP connection in several ways. If the other side is Explicit Congestion Notification (ECN)–capable, we can send a congestion message and ask the sender to back off. Even if the attacker does not run ECN, we can take a page out of the LaBrea work done by Tom Liston and send an initial response with a small TCP window size and then set it to zero from time to time to keep the attacker from sending data.

These first two approaches—setting a limit using hardware, such as a switch, or ICMP source quench—can easily be set in motion by an IDS as an auto-response, and there have been applications of both. One simple example at the application layer is when a user mistypes his password several times. The response can be to slow down the rate at which the system tells the user that the password is incorrect. We can also consider defense at the application, although this will not be practical until we start using better practices in coding. That said, it is worth noting that the software application might be the best place to detect and respond to certain attacks, such as illegal values and buffer overflows. It would be interesting to see Sendmail and named implementations with a built-in defensive capability. Named, for instance, could trivially identify attempts to use the obsolete query class CHAOSnet. It could send an alert to the defensive systems, respond by delaying the answer, and then possibly transmit a BIND version number that would send attacks down the wrong path, such as 4.9.1, an ancient version of BIND. If such technology does become available, it certainly would help us implement defense in depth.

In this section of the chapter, we have considered several techniques for implementing perimeters that are more flexible than the standard border router firewall–type perimeter. None of these techniques should ever be used in lieu of those technologies, but they can supplement and enhance our perimeter defense. One of the critical issues in a perimeter, of course, is uptime or availability, and one of the most important technologies to help us achieve this is automated failover.

Failover

Failover is the practice of maintaining a hot standby and transferring operations to the standby if the primary fails. When you're considering purchase requirements for firewalls and other perimeter devices, one crucial capability is failover. Many commercial and freeware products and designs seek to balance security and degree of polling, usually through Hot Standby Routing Protocol (HSRP), maintaining NAT tables and connection state, as well as load and performance balancing. If you plan to implement failover, buy all the firewalls at the same time and maintain strict configuration management so that they have the same patch level at all times to avoid problems.

Failover products are dynamic by nature, but it never hurts to ask the manufacturer's technical representatives if it is possible to deploy their products in a failover mode that allows both failover and static routing between the secure or intranet sides of perimeter devices. Static routing helps you avoid the risk that the compromise of a single router could lead to the manipulation of the organization's dynamic routing tables. If an attacker can manipulate the routes, he can cause traffic to pass through an arbitrary IP address he controls. The security mechanism for routing tends to be a password or an MD5 hash, which is not considered fully robust. Passwords can be sniffed, and although MD5 is a strong security mechanism, cryptographic experts have asserted that the implementation for routing was hastily done and is not perfect. Static routes are read from a table; therefore, even if a router is compromised, as long as the remaining routers do not accept ICMP redirects or router discovery messages, they and their routes will remain intact.

Maintaining near 100% uptime is great, but it also means that a failure in our security design, process, or procedure results in our precious information leaking all the faster. Next, we will consider defense in depth with information, covering the problems and some of the solutions we can employ.

Defense in Depth with Information

Defense in depth as a concept goes beyond the protocol to an architecture and orientation of protecting information. One of the goals of this book is a holistic treatment of the perimeter. This includes not just routers, firewalls, and VPNs, but policy, system hardening, intrusion detection, and software architecture. In the final major section of our discussion of defense in depth, we want to revisit the problem of information leakage and also restate the case for encryption.

The Problem of Diffusion

One fascinating security problem is the diffusion of information. An organization might have three levels of information confidentiality: top secret, secret, and confidential. Sooner or later, a classified piece of data ends up on a system or network that is not rated for that level of information.

Today, business can be characterized by intense competition, where a single misstep in information control can be disastrous. We label critical information proprietary, but laptops can be lost and systems can become infected with the Sircam worm and send random files out onto the Internet. AOL versions 6 and 7 both occasionally decide to attach some file that has been recently sent in an email message to someone else. If you're lucky enough to realize this is happening, and you have a slow-enough connection, you can cancel the email; however, if you have a broadband connection and the file is small, it's impossible to stop the email and retrieve the file. It turns out that it is nearly impossible to prevent information diffusion, but we can develop architectures to minimize the problem. Some of the problems we need to design and plan for to minimize diffusion include backdoors, wireless devices, remote controlware, email, and social engineering.

When PCs first started being deployed, modems were controllable problems. They were slow, expensive, and external, so you could find them by walking through your organization. You would think your top firewall and network administrators would know not to leave a modem on a critical system on auto-answer, but administrators can be the worst culprits. After all, it is a lot easier to roll out of bed, dial up the organization, fix whatever is wrong, and go back to sleep than to drive in to fix the problem. Defensive measures include wardialing your own phone numbers with ToneLoc (a free tool) or PhoneSweep from Sandstorm (if you need to use commercial software).

802.11 wireless access points (WAPs) bring a whole new dimension to the problem. At less than $200 each, WAPs will end up all over your organization whether you prohibit them or not. They do not require much skill to set up, and they are simple to eavesdrop on with tools such as AirSnort or any packet sniffer if the data is in the clear. If you are going to run wireless, consider the wireless intrusion detection and prevention tools available from AirDefense and AirMagnet.

> **Tip**
>
> The best advice is to get a wireless card with an external unidirectional antenna, download a copy of Kismet (available from http://www.kismetwireless.net/), and walk your perimeter on a regular basis before someone else does. Kismet runs on Linux, but if you are a Windows user, you can run it from Knoppix, a bootable CD-ROM version of Linux available from www.knoppix.org.

The term *remote controlware* is made up, used to describe the suite of products ranging from Symantec's pcAnywhere (which can be identified by access to port 22, 5631, or 5632) to the HTTP tunneling service available from www.Gotomypc.com. Policy and security awareness training are your primary tools for managing these types of technologies.

If you don't think you have a problem with information leakage via email, try scanning just your email headers for a month. If you want to collect information to demonstrate the problem with diffusion to your management, this can be one of the most powerful ways to do it. Many times, your management will agree to allow you to copy just the subject lines because that is part of the header, the equivalent of the outside of an envelope. You will quickly learn that a lot of sensitive information is sent via email. In addition to policy and awareness training, one old trick is to create a fake acronym and add it to particularly sensitive documents. After all, no one will notice one more acronym. Then you can add this as a string to your IDS so that it alerts if the word you have created crosses your perimeter. Think of it as marker dye for tracking information diffusion.

We have made a case for understanding a bit about how diffusion of information happens in the organization. Although we have offered a number of technical solutions, the best answer is an active and powerful security awareness program. Most security awareness programs consist of a canned brief and a poster or mouse pad with a catchy slogan. We need to do better than this, and we can. The users in our organizations are not stupid; they can set up a modem in auto-answer mode and deploy a wireless access point. The best security awareness program is one that treats the users as peers. Get involved! Perhaps your information security officer is not the most technical person in the organization; if that is the case, help him out. With permission from your manager and security officer, set up a wireless access point and demonstrate AirSnort. In most awareness programs, you see the users nodding off, eyes fixed and brains in a wait state. When you show someone decrypting what people normally think are private communications, the lights go on. After that, users will think twice before using a WAP in the office or at a conference without a VPN. The more your users know, the more capable they will be of making educated decisions. That said, information diffusion happens. There are just too many ways information can become exposed. This final section of the chapter and this book is a reminder of the importance of cryptography in defense in depth.

Cryptography and Defense in Depth

Here's a question for you: What is free for personal use and reasonably priced commercialware, provides defense in depth instantly, is exhaustively reviewed, yet underused? One answer would be Pretty Good Privacy (PGP). PGP is a bit cumbersome to use, and the web of trust needs to be established in advance of need, but for a community of 2 to 200, it's quite serviceable.

Many organizations have implemented Public Key Infrastructure (PKI) by now, but they don't use their solution for encrypting email. As we travel we hear horror stories of users with two-factor authentication, leaving the token component in their USB drive and going home for the evening as a regular practice (that way they don't lose their tokens).

Can PGP and PKI interoperate? Yes, to some extent. PGP can import an X509 certificate as a legacy RSA signature. However, beware: PGP 7 and PGP 8 do not protect the secret key portion of the imported certificate.

> **Note**
>
> To view a set of step-by-step instructions by Ridge Cook for organizations that must have PGP/PKI interoperability, visit http://www.mccune.cc/PGPpage2.htm#X.509.

Microsoft has often been flamed during its history for its cryptography and security practices, yet Windows 2003 Server shipped with Kerberos, IPSec, and encrypting file system support for certificates as part of the operating system. We have the tools we need; we just need to implement them. One government organization in Crystal City, Virginia implemented VPNs from the desk of government officials to the printers. This kept an insider who was not trustworthy from intercepting and reading sensitive data off the network. We should think about this example. Encrypting data at rest and in transit takes a bit of work and a bit of discipline to manage the keys, but it is the most bombproof way to implement defense in depth.

Summary

The threat against our systems and information has never been greater; yet, the primary reason we lose is because we sometimes fail to apply good security design and practice. 2004 was the year of the worm, with over a dozen NetSky versions, reruns of MSBlast, and Sasser. However, almost all the attacks exploited known vulnerabilities for which patches were available. If we take the responsibility to implement sound design and security practice, we can move forward. There is no single silver bullet, no magic product, no vendor that will do it all for us. On the other hand, tools both free and commercial are available that we can use to build an architecture that layers defense in depth.

V

Appendixes

A

Cisco Access List Sample Configurations

THIS APPENDIX COMPRISES TWO ACCESS LISTS that demonstrate possible ways to securely configure a Cisco router as a standalone security device. These sections use best practices as described in Chapter 2, "Packet Filtering," and Chapter 6, "The Role of a Router," listed out so that a complete configuration can be seen in its entirety. The first access list is used to demonstrate a network that has no publicly shared resources, and the second access list illustrates an example of a network with publicly accessible mail, DNS, and web servers.

Complete Access List for a Private-Only Network

The following sample access list is appropriate for a network that has outbound and return traffic only, with no public servers or screened subnets. Most likely, this network is a low-risk/low-budget setup in which security is not first priority. Therefore, a single inexpensive security device is chosen. For an example of an access list that works with public servers, see the next section. Both are designed to work on a Cisco router that runs IOS version 12.0 or later.

```
no ip source-route
no service tcp-small-servers
no service udp-small-servers
no service finger
```

Next are all the commands to be applied directly to the external serial interface, including the `access-group` commands that apply the inbound and outbound filters to it. The `serial 0` interface connects the router to the Internet. We also stop all services that need to be disabled at the interface configuration level.

```
interface serial 0
 ip access-group filterin in
 ip access-group filterout out
 no cdp enable

 no snmp
 no ip direct-broadcast
 no ip redirects
 no ip unreachables
```

The next section is an inbound, reflexive access list called `filterin`, which begins with an ingress filter to prevent spoofing. It is followed by a permit list that only allows in ICMP `packet-too-big` statements. `Filterin` concludes with an `evaluate packets` statement, which checks the reflexive list "packets" to see whether the incoming traffic matches it and will be permitted through. Any traffic that fails the `evaluate packets` check is dropped by an implied `deny all`. However, we append a `deny ip any any log-input` statement so that we can keep track of all denied traffic. If you wanted to open any other services or ports inbound, the `permit` statements would be added here, before the `evaluate packets` line.

```
ip access-list extended filterin
deny ip 190.190.190.0 0.0.0.255 any
deny ip 10.0.0.0 0.255.255.255 any
deny ip 127.0.0.0 0.255.255.255 any
deny ip 172.16.0.0 0.15.255.255 any
deny ip 192.168.0.0 0.0.255.255 any
deny ip 224.0.0.0 15.255.255.255 any
deny ip host 0.0.0.0 any
permit icmp any any packet-too-big
evaluate packets
deny ip any any log-input
```

`Filterout` is next. It is the outbound reflexive access list that was applied to interface `serial 0`. It lists all the traffic types we are allowing out of our network. Through the use of the packet's reflexive access list, the `evaluate packets` statement in the `filterin` access list will determine the return traffic that is allowed back in. You might notice that the last statement under `filterout` is an ICMP `packet-too-big` statement. This statement allows outbound information to other routers that send acceptable return traffic, but with too large of a packet size. This statement is not reflexively inspected; therefore, it doesn't allow for return traffic. ICMP traffic has varying results when it is used in a reflexive access list, so for most applications, it is best to simply apply ICMP in individual inbound and outbound nonreflexive access lists. If your security policy specifies any other outbound traffic (and in turn, return traffic) that isn't already listed here, you can add the `permit` statements to the bottom of the list, following the pattern of the other reflexive statements. To make sure that a statement is treated reflexively, verify that it ends with the keyword `reflect` followed by the identifying list name packets.

```
ip access-list extended filterout
permit tcp any any eq 21 reflect packets
permit tcp any any eq 22 reflect packets
permit tcp any any eq 23 reflect packets
permit tcp any any eq 25 reflect packets
permit tcp any any eq 53 reflect packets
permit tcp any any eq 80 reflect packets
permit tcp any any eq 110 reflect packets
permit tcp any any eq 119 reflect packets
permit tcp any any eq 143 reflect packets
permit tcp any any eq 443 reflect packets
permit udp any any eq 53 reflect packets
permit icmp any any packet-too-big
```

The `ethernet 0` interface is configured and has extended access list number 112 applied inbound as an egress filter, only allowing packets to pass with addresses that match the internal network's address range. This prevents programs that spoof addresses when performing malicious actions from being able to leave your network. This way, you remain a good Internet neighbor. An extended access list format was chosen because it facilitates the use of the `log-input` command. Notice that we add a `deny ip any any log-input` rule to track inappropriate traffic as it attempts to exit the network segment and use `log-input` to enable tracking of MAC addresses.

```
interface ethernet 0
 ip access-group 112 in

access-list 112 permit ip 190.190.190.0 0.0.0.255 any
access-list 112 deny ip any any log-input
```

In the previous examples, the following information is assumed:

- We have two router interfaces: a `serial 0` interface that connects us to the Internet and an `ethernet 0` interface that connects us to our private network.

- This list is a template with suggestions; it shouldn't be considered a full solution for any particular network.

- We want to limit the outbound traffic (and return traffic) to the services that are listed in `filterout`.

- The internal private network number is 190.190.190.0.

- We want to limit our ICMP message interactions to make `packet-too-big` statements the only type we allow out—none is allowed back in. (`Ping` and `traceroute` are disallowed internally.)

- Any use of FTP outbound requires a passive (PASV) FTP client and server support for the same.

- The listing format used for the access list information is for easier reading.

Listing A.1 shows the complete router access list.

Listing A.1   **The Complete Router Access List for a Private-Only Network**

```
no ip source-route
no service tcp-small-servers
no service udp-small-servers
no service finger

interface serial 0
ip access-group filterin in
ip access-group filterout out
no cdp enable

no snmp
no ip direct-broadcast
no ip redirects
no ip unreachables

ip access-list extended filterin
deny ip 190.190.190.0 0.0.0.255 any
deny ip 10.0.0.0 0.255.255.255 any
deny ip 127.0.0.0 0.255.255.255 any
deny ip 172.16.0.0 0.15.255.255 any
deny ip 192.168.0.0 0.0.255.255 any
deny ip 224.0.0.0 15.255.255.255 any
deny ip host 0.0.0.0 any
permit icmp any any packet-too-big
evaluate packets
deny ip any any log-input

ip access-list extended filterout
permit tcp any any eq 21 reflect packets
permit tcp any any eq 22 reflect packets
permit tcp any any eq 23 reflect packets
permit tcp any any eq 25 reflect packets
permit tcp any any eq 53 reflect packets
permit tcp any any eq 80 reflect packets
permit tcp any any eq 110 reflect packets
permit tcp any any eq 119 reflect packets
permit tcp any any eq 143 reflect packets
permit tcp any any eq 443 reflect packets
permit udp any any eq 53 reflect packets
permit icmp any any packet-too-big

interface ethernet 0
ip access-group 112 in

access-list 112 permit ip 190.190.190.0 0.0.0.255 any
access-list 112 deny ip any any log-input
```

Complete Access List for a Screened Subnet Network That Allows Public Server Internet Access

The following is an access list that takes the preceding section's access lists and incorporates inbound access to a screened subnet containing web, mail, and DNS servers. This example would most likely be used for a lower-risk, lower-budget network that needs to use its router as its sole security device. By using an additional interface to serve as a "screened subnet," we allow increased protection while implementing publicly accessible services. All public access servers are assumed to be properly hardened, and because of their volatile nature, any available defense-in-depth measures should be implemented.

In this initial section, we disable unneeded global services. These commands must be configured in global configuration mode:

```
no service finger
no ip source-route
no service tcp-small-servers
no service udp-small-servers
```

Next are all the commands to be applied directly to the external serial interface, including the `access-group` commands that apply the inbound and outbound filters to it. The `serial 0` interface is the one that connects the router to the Internet. We also stop all services to be disabled at the interface configuration level.

```
interface serial 0
 ip access-group filterin in
 ip access-group filterout out

 no snmp
 no ip direct-broadcast
 no ip redirects
 no ip unreachables
 no cdp enable
```

Next is the `filterin` access list, which includes antispoofing commands. This list is followed by ingress lines that allow any web, SMTP, or DNS inbound traffic to the server that handles such a request. It next allows ICMP `packet-too-big` packets, followed by an `evaluate packets` line that reflexively examines any remaining inbound traffic to see if it matches any of the currently temporarily formed reflexive access lists that `filterout created`. This is followed by a statement to log all denied inbound packets.

```
ip access-list extended filterin
deny ip 190.190.190.0 0.0.0.255 any
deny ip 10.0.0.0 0.255.255.255 any
deny ip 127.0.0.0 0.255.255.255 any
deny ip 172.16.0.0 0.15.255.255 any
deny ip 192.168.0.0 0.0.255.255 any
```

```
deny ip 224.0.0.0 15.255.255.255 any
deny ip host 0.0.0.0 any
permit tcp any host 200.200.200.2 eq 80
permit tcp any host 200.200.200.3 eq 25
permit tcp any host 200.200.200.4 eq 53
permit udp any host 200.200.200.4 eq 53
permit icmp any any packet-too-big
evaluate packets
deny ip any any log-input
```

`Filterout` is next, and it starts by allowing response traffic back from the web, mail, and DNS servers. Notice the `est` (established) keyword at the end of these lists. This confirms that only replies are leaving the servers, behaving like an egress list for our screened subnet. Following that is the reflexive access lines that permit outbound traffic and create the reflexive lists that allow inbound traffic. To grant other services outbound access, you would need to add a reflexive access list here. `Filterout` is ended with an ICMP filter allowing `packet-too-big` messages to go through.

```
ip access-list extended filterout
permit tcp host 200.200.200.2 eq 80 any gt 1023 est
permit tcp host 200.200.200.3 eq 25 any gt 1023 est
permit udp host 200.200.200.4 eq 53 any gt 1023
permit tcp any any eq 21 reflect packets
permit tcp any any eq 22 reflect packets
permit tcp any any eq 23 reflect packets
permit tcp any any eq 25 reflect packets
permit tcp any any eq 53 reflect packets
permit tcp any any eq 80 reflect packets
permit tcp any any eq 110 reflect packets
permit tcp any any eq 119 reflect packets
permit tcp any any eq 143 reflect packets
permit tcp any any eq 443 reflect packets
permit udp any any eq 53 reflect packets
permit icmp any any packet-too-big
```

Progressing to interface `ethernet 0`, no outbound list is applied; therefore, any traffic that matches the private network's address range is passed on.

```
interface ethernet 0
 ip access-group filterin1 in
```

`Filterin1` is applied inbound to the `ethernet 0` interface. `Filterin1` contains an egress filter, only allowing traffic that is addressed from the private network's address range to be forwarded to the serial interface. It also contains a `deny` statement, logging all nonstandard egress traffic.

```
ip access-list extended filterin1
permit ip 190.190.190.0 0.0.0.255 any
deny ip any any log-input
```

Ethernet 1 contains `filterout2` and `filterin2`.

`Filterout2` permits network traffic in from the Internet to be forwarded to the web server if it's HTTP traffic, to the mail server if it's SMTP traffic, and to the external DNS server if it's DNS traffic. Notice that these first three lines serve as a basic ingress filter. `Filterout2` also permits ICMP `packet-too-big` messages to pass and supports logging of undesirables through its last statement.

```
interface ethernet 1
ip access-group filterout2 out
ip access-group filterin2 in

ip access-list extended filterout2
permit tcp any gt 1023 host 200.200.200.2 eq 80
permit tcp any gt 1023 host 200.200.200.3 eq 25
permit tcp any host 200.200.200.4 eq 53
permit udp any host 200.200.200.4 eq 53
permit icmp any 200.200.200.0 0.0.0.255 packet-too-big
deny ip any any log-input
```

`Filterin2` allows reply traffic from each of the three public servers out to the serial interface. This serves as a basic egress filter. `Packet-too-big` messages are also forwarded. The `deny any 190.190.190.0` line disables communications between the screened subnet and your private network. This is necessary because the outbound traffic on `ethernet 0` is open to the screened subnet. The next lines allow SMTP and DNS traffic from their particular servers to the Internet. `Serial 1`'s `filterout` then passes this traffic through its reflexive access lists so that it will have the same level of protection as the private network's outbound traffic. If any other outbound traffic is desired from the screened subnet, this is where additional filters are added. These additional filters are added after the `deny` statement that prevents everything except reply traffic from entering the private segment, but before the last statement that logs undesirables. DNS support for the private segment would most likely be handled internally (split DNS) or by an outside party. No DNS zone transfers would take place between the private and screened subnets.

```
ip access-list extended filterin2
permit tcp host 200.200.200.2 eq 80 any gt 1023 est
permit tcp host 200.200.200.3 eq 25 any gt 1023 est
permit udp host 200.200.200.4 eq 53 any gt 1023
permit icmp 200.200.200.0 0.0.0.255 any packet-too-big
deny ip any 190.190.190.0 0.0.0.255
permit tcp host 200.200.200.4 any eq 53
permit udp host 200.200.200.4 any eq 53
permit tcp host 200.200.200.3 any eq 25
deny ip any any log-input
```

In the preceding example, the following information is assumed:

- This list is a template with suggestions; it shouldn't be considered a full solution for any particular network.
- The screened subnet's network number is 200.200.200.0.
- The internal private network number is 190.190.190.0.
- The screened subnet's web server's address is 200.200.200.2.
- The screened subnet's SMTP mail server's address is 200.200.200.3.
- The screened subnet's DNS server's address is 200.200.200.4.
- No other hosts are on the screened subnet.
- We have three router interfaces: a `serial 0` interface that connects us to the Internet, an `ethernet 0` interface that connects us to our private network, and an `ethernet 1` interface that connects us to our screened subnet.
- We want to limit the outbound traffic (and return traffic) to the services that are listed in `filterout`.
- We want to limit our ICMP message interactions to make `packet-too-big` statements the only type we allow out—none is allowed back in. (`Ping` and `traceroute` are disallowed internally.)
- Any use of FTP outbound requires a PASV (or passive) FTP client and server support for the same.
- The listing format used for the access list information is for easier reading.

Listing A.2 shows the complete router access list.

Listing A.2 **The Router Access List for a Screened Subnet Network That Allows Public Server Internet Access**

```
no service finger
no ip source-route
no service tcp-small-servers
no service udp-small-servers

interface serial 0
ip access-group filterin in
ip access-group filterout out

no snmp
no ip direct-broadcast
no ip redirects
no ip unreachables
no cdp enable

ip access-list extended filterin
deny ip 190.190.190.0 0.0.0.255 any
```

Listing A.2 **Continued**

```
deny ip 10.0.0.0 0.255.255.255 any
deny ip 127.0.0.0 0.255.255.255 any
deny ip 172.16.0.0 0.15.255.255 any
deny ip 192.168.0.0 0.0.255.255 any
deny ip 224.0.0.0 15.255.255.255 any
deny ip host 0.0.0.0 any
permit tcp any host 200.200.200.2 eq 80
permit tcp any host 200.200.200.3 eq 25
permit udp any host 200.200.200.4 eq 53
permit icmp any any packet-too-big
evaluate packets
deny ip any any log-input


ip access-list extended filterout
permit tcp host 200.200.200.2 eq 80 any gt 1023 est
permit tcp host 200.200.200.3 eq 25 any gt 1023 est
permit udp host 200.200.200.4 eq 53 any gt 1023
permit tcp any any eq 21 reflect packets
permit tcp any any eq 22 reflect packets
permit tcp any any eq 23 reflect packets
permit tcp any any eq 25 reflect packets
permit tcp any any eq 53 reflect packets
permit tcp any any eq 80 reflect packets
permit tcp any any eq 110 reflect packets
permit tcp any any eq 119 reflect packets
permit tcp any any eq 143 reflect packets
permit tcp any any eq 443 reflect packets
permit udp any any eq 53 reflect packets
permit icmp any any packet-too-big



interface ethernet 0
ip access-group filterin1 in

ip access-list extended filterin1
permit ip 190.190.190.0 0.0.0.255 any
deny ip any any log-input

interface ethernet 1
ip access-group filterout2 out
ip access-group filterin2 in

ip access-list extended filterout2
permit tcp any gt 1023 host 200.200.200.2 eq 80
permit tcp any gt 1023 host 200.200.200.3 eq 25
permit tcp any host 200.200.200.4 eq 53
```

Listing A.2   **Continued**

```
permit udp any host 200.200.200.4 eq 53
permit icmp any 200.200.200.0 0.0.0.255 packet-too-big
deny ip any any log-input

ip access-list extended filterin2
permit tcp host 200.200.200.2 eq 80 any gt 1023 est
permit tcp host 200.200.200.3 eq 25 any gt 1023 est
permit udp host 200.200.200.4 eq 53 any gt 1023
permit icmp 200.200.200.0 0.0.0.255 any packet-too-big
deny ip any 190.190.190.0 0.0.0.255
permit tcp host 200.200.200.4 any eq 53
permit udp host 200.200.200.4 any eq 53
permit tcp host 200.200.200.3 any eq 25
deny ip any any log-input
```

Example of a Router Configuration as Generated by the Cisco Auto Secure Feature

As stated in Chapter 6, the Cisco auto secure command allows for a simplified way to apply best security practices with very little interaction from the administrator. The user would be prompted as to which of the listed access lists auto secure should apply to the Internet-facing interfaces. The default choice would add them all.

Listing A.3 shows a sample router configuration as created by auto secure.

Listing A.3   **An Example of a Configuration as Generated by Cisco Auto Secure**

```
no service finger
no service pad
no service udp-small-servers
no service tcp-small-servers
service password-encryption
service tcp-keepalives-in
service tcp-keepalives-out
no cdp run
no ip bootp server
no ip http server
no ip finger
no ip source-route
no ip gratuitous-arps
no snmp-server
banner k My Banner k
security passwords min-length 6
security authentication failure rate 10 log
enable password 7 XXXXXXXXXXXXX
```

Listing A.3   **Continued**

```
aaa new-model
aaa authentication login local_auth local
line console 0
 login authentication local_auth
 exec-timeout 5 0
 transport output telnet
line aux 0
 login authentication local_auth
 exec-timeout 10 0
 transport output telnet
line vty 0 4
 login authentication local_auth
 transport input telnet
service timestamps debug datetime localtime show-timezone msec
service timestamps log datetime localtime show-timezone msec
logging facility local2
logging trap debugging
service sequence-numbers
logging console critical
logging buffered
int FastEthernet0
 no ip redirects
 no ip proxy-arp
 no ip unreachables
 no ip directed-broadcast
 no ip mask-reply
int Serial0
 no ip redirects
 no ip proxy-arp
 no ip unreachables
 no ip directed-broadcast
 no ip mask-reply
int Ethernet0
 no ip redirects
 no ip proxy-arp
 no ip unreachables
 no ip directed-broadcast
 no ip mask-reply
ip cef
ip access-list extended autosec_iana_reserved_block
 deny ip 1.0.0.0 0.255.255.255 any
 deny ip 2.0.0.0 0.255.255.255 any
 deny ip 5.0.0.0 0.255.255.255 any
 deny ip 7.0.0.0 0.255.255.255 any
 deny ip 23.0.0.0 0.255.255.255 any
 deny ip 27.0.0.0 0.255.255.255 any
```

Listing A.3 **Continued**

```
deny ip 31.0.0.0 0.255.255.255 any
deny ip 36.0.0.0 0.255.255.255 any
deny ip 37.0.0.0 0.255.255.255 any
deny ip 39.0.0.0 0.255.255.255 any
deny ip 41.0.0.0 0.255.255.255 any
deny ip 42.0.0.0 0.255.255.255 any
deny ip 49.0.0.0 0.255.255.255 any
deny ip 50.0.0.0 0.255.255.255 any
deny ip 58.0.0.0 0.255.255.255 any
deny ip 59.0.0.0 0.255.255.255 any
deny ip 60.0.0.0 0.255.255.255 any
deny ip 70.0.0.0 0.255.255.255 any
deny ip 71.0.0.0 0.255.255.255 any
deny ip 72.0.0.0 0.255.255.255 any
deny ip 73.0.0.0 0.255.255.255 any
deny ip 74.0.0.0 0.255.255.255 any
deny ip 75.0.0.0 0.255.255.255 any
deny ip 76.0.0.0 0.255.255.255 any
deny ip 77.0.0.0 0.255.255.255 any
deny ip 78.0.0.0 0.255.255.255 any
deny ip 79.0.0.0 0.255.255.255 any
deny ip 83.0.0.0 0.255.255.255 any
deny ip 84.0.0.0 0.255.255.255 any
deny ip 85.0.0.0 0.255.255.255 any
deny ip 86.0.0.0 0.255.255.255 any
deny ip 87.0.0.0 0.255.255.255 any
deny ip 88.0.0.0 0.255.255.255 any
deny ip 89.0.0.0 0.255.255.255 any
deny ip 90.0.0.0 0.255.255.255 any
deny ip 91.0.0.0 0.255.255.255 any
deny ip 92.0.0.0 0.255.255.255 any
deny ip 93.0.0.0 0.255.255.255 any
deny ip 94.0.0.0 0.255.255.255 any
deny ip 95.0.0.0 0.255.255.255 any
deny ip 96.0.0.0 0.255.255.255 any
deny ip 97.0.0.0 0.255.255.255 any
deny ip 98.0.0.0 0.255.255.255 any
deny ip 99.0.0.0 0.255.255.255 any
deny ip 100.0.0.0 0.255.255.255 any
deny ip 101.0.0.0 0.255.255.255 any
deny ip 102.0.0.0 0.255.255.255 any
deny ip 103.0.0.0 0.255.255.255 any
deny ip 104.0.0.0 0.255.255.255 any
deny ip 105.0.0.0 0.255.255.255 any
deny ip 106.0.0.0 0.255.255.255 any
deny ip 107.0.0.0 0.255.255.255 any
```

Listing A.3   **Continued**

```
deny ip 108.0.0.0 0.255.255.255 any
deny ip 109.0.0.0 0.255.255.255 any
deny ip 110.0.0.0 0.255.255.255 any
deny ip 111.0.0.0 0.255.255.255 any
deny ip 112.0.0.0 0.255.255.255 any
deny ip 113.0.0.0 0.255.255.255 any
deny ip 114.0.0.0 0.255.255.255 any
deny ip 115.0.0.0 0.255.255.255 any
deny ip 116.0.0.0 0.255.255.255 any
deny ip 117.0.0.0 0.255.255.255 any
deny ip 118.0.0.0 0.255.255.255 any
deny ip 119.0.0.0 0.255.255.255 any
deny ip 120.0.0.0 0.255.255.255 any
deny ip 121.0.0.0 0.255.255.255 any
deny ip 122.0.0.0 0.255.255.255 any
deny ip 123.0.0.0 0.255.255.255 any
deny ip 124.0.0.0 0.255.255.255 any
deny ip 125.0.0.0 0.255.255.255 any
deny ip 126.0.0.0 0.255.255.255 any
deny ip 197.0.0.0 0.255.255.255 any
deny ip 201.0.0.0 0.255.255.255 any
permit ip any any
remark This acl might not be up to date. Visit www.iana.org/assignments/ipv4-add
ress-space for update list
exit
ip access-list extended autosec_private_block

deny ip 10.0.0.0 0.255.255.255 any
deny ip 172.16.0.0 0.15.255.255 any
deny ip 192.168.0.0 0.0.255.255 any
permit ip any any
exit
ip access-list extended autosec_complete_bogon
deny ip 1.0.0.0 0.255.255.255 any
deny ip 2.0.0.0 0.255.255.255 any
deny ip 5.0.0.0 0.255.255.255 any
deny ip 7.0.0.0 0.255.255.255 any
deny ip 23.0.0.0 0.255.255.255 any
deny ip 27.0.0.0 0.255.255.255 any
deny ip 31.0.0.0 0.255.255.255 any
deny ip 36.0.0.0 0.255.255.255 any
deny ip 37.0.0.0 0.255.255.255 any
deny ip 39.0.0.0 0.255.255.255 any
deny ip 41.0.0.0 0.255.255.255 any
deny ip 42.0.0.0 0.255.255.255 any
deny ip 49.0.0.0 0.255.255.255 any
```

Listing A.3 **Continued**

```
deny ip 50.0.0.0 0.255.255.255 any
deny ip 58.0.0.0 0.255.255.255 any
deny ip 59.0.0.0 0.255.255.255 any
deny ip 60.0.0.0 0.255.255.255 any
deny ip 70.0.0.0 0.255.255.255 any
deny ip 71.0.0.0 0.255.255.255 any
deny ip 72.0.0.0 0.255.255.255 any
deny ip 73.0.0.0 0.255.255.255 any
deny ip 74.0.0.0 0.255.255.255 any
deny ip 75.0.0.0 0.255.255.255 any
deny ip 76.0.0.0 0.255.255.255 any
deny ip 77.0.0.0 0.255.255.255 any
deny ip 78.0.0.0 0.255.255.255 any
deny ip 79.0.0.0 0.255.255.255 any
deny ip 83.0.0.0 0.255.255.255 any
deny ip 84.0.0.0 0.255.255.255 any
deny ip 85.0.0.0 0.255.255.255 any
deny ip 86.0.0.0 0.255.255.255 any
deny ip 87.0.0.0 0.255.255.255 any
deny ip 88.0.0.0 0.255.255.255 any
deny ip 89.0.0.0 0.255.255.255 any
deny ip 90.0.0.0 0.255.255.255 any
deny ip 91.0.0.0 0.255.255.255 any
deny ip 92.0.0.0 0.255.255.255 any
deny ip 93.0.0.0 0.255.255.255 any
deny ip 94.0.0.0 0.255.255.255 any
deny ip 95.0.0.0 0.255.255.255 any
deny ip 96.0.0.0 0.255.255.255 any
deny ip 97.0.0.0 0.255.255.255 any
deny ip 98.0.0.0 0.255.255.255 any
deny ip 99.0.0.0 0.255.255.255 any
deny ip 100.0.0.0 0.255.255.255 any
deny ip 101.0.0.0 0.255.255.255 any
deny ip 102.0.0.0 0.255.255.255 any
deny ip 103.0.0.0 0.255.255.255 any
deny ip 104.0.0.0 0.255.255.255 any
deny ip 105.0.0.0 0.255.255.255 any
deny ip 106.0.0.0 0.255.255.255 any
deny ip 107.0.0.0 0.255.255.255 any
deny ip 108.0.0.0 0.255.255.255 any
deny ip 109.0.0.0 0.255.255.255 any
deny ip 110.0.0.0 0.255.255.255 any
deny ip 111.0.0.0 0.255.255.255 any
deny ip 112.0.0.0 0.255.255.255 any
deny ip 113.0.0.0 0.255.255.255 any
```

Listing A.3   **Continued**

```
deny ip 114.0.0.0 0.255.255.255 any
deny ip 115.0.0.0 0.255.255.255 any
deny ip 116.0.0.0 0.255.255.255 any
deny ip 117.0.0.0 0.255.255.255 any
deny ip 118.0.0.0 0.255.255.255 any
deny ip 119.0.0.0 0.255.255.255 any
deny ip 120.0.0.0 0.255.255.255 any
deny ip 121.0.0.0 0.255.255.255 any
deny ip 122.0.0.0 0.255.255.255 any
deny ip 123.0.0.0 0.255.255.255 any
deny ip 124.0.0.0 0.255.255.255 any
deny ip 125.0.0.0 0.255.255.255 any
deny ip 126.0.0.0 0.255.255.255 any
deny ip 197.0.0.0 0.255.255.255 any
deny ip 201.0.0.0 0.255.255.255 any

deny ip 10.0.0.0 0.255.255.255 any
deny ip 172.16.0.0 0.15.255.255 any
deny ip 192.168.0.0 0.0.255.255 any

deny ip 224.0.0.0 15.255.255.255 any
deny ip 240.0.0.0 15.255.255.255 any
deny ip 0.0.0.0 0.255.255.255 any
deny ip 169.254.0.0 0.0.255.255 any
deny ip 192.0.2.0 0.0.0.255 any
deny ip 127.0.0.0 0.255.255.255 any
permit ip any any
remark This acl might not be up to date. Visit www.iana.org/assignments/ipv4-add
ress-space for update list
exit
ip access-list extended 100
 permit udp any any eq bootpc
```

B

Crypto 101

*C*RYPTOGRAPHY IS THE PRACTICE AND STUDY OF encryption and decryption. Cryptography is an important part of what makes a Virtual Private Network (VPN) work. This appendix is a primer on how cryptography works. It defines the various terms used for the cryptographic processes so that you can better understand the technologies that are part of the VPN. Cryptography is an immensely complicated and varied field. The purpose of this appendix is to briefly describe the encryption technologies necessary to better understand VPNs and how they work. It is meant to be a supplement for the VPN material that appears throughout the book, primarily in Chapter 7, "Virtual Private Networks," and Chapter 16, "VPN Integration."

> **Note**
>
> Quite a few specific terms are used regularly when speaking of cryptographic technologies. Throughout this appendix, we will define these terms and briefly explain them to facilitate the understanding of the VPN. Don't worry—we only cover those terms you actually need to know!

A discussion of cryptography rarely occurs without the mention of encryption keys. *Keys* are secret values used to encode and decode messages. These values can vary in length, with the length of the key corresponding directly to the security of the encoded message. Encryption keys come in symmetric and asymmetric varieties, which we will discuss in greater detail later in this appendix.

Cleartext and *plain text* are terms that define information before it is placed into an encrypted form. After the same information is encrypted, it is called *ciphertext*.

The formula or method by which information is encrypted is called the *encryption algorithm*, or *cipher* (also spelled *cypher*). An *algorithm* is a mathematical means by which cleartext is transformed into encoded ciphertext.

Encryption Algorithms

Many encryption algorithms are commonly used to protect data. Of these, most can be categorized as symmetric or asymmetric key algorithms—two very different approaches to encryption.

Shared Key: Symmetric

A *shared key*, or *symmetric key*, is an encryption method that uses the same key value for both encryption and decryption. Its use assumes that everyone involved has had time in advance to securely exchange a secret key that no one else knows. This key value is then used to encrypt information that is exchanged. This means of encryption can be fast because the mathematics needed to create ciphertext from a shared secret key does not have to be as complex as the type used with asymmetric algorithms. The main disadvantage to the symmetric algorithm is that it is difficult to remotely exchange keys or start a symmetric exchange with an unknown party and authenticate that person is who he says he is. How can you give a remote party your key if he doesn't already have it? You would need to have a secure channel to pass the key. Because you most likely don't have such a channel (otherwise you wouldn't need to pass the key), you are in the middle of a catch-22. With a symmetric algorithm, we have established confidentiality of data as long as the key remains secret, and we have some basic key-exchange issues.

Many symmetric encryption algorithms are available for use today, including Data Encryption Standard (DES), 3DES, Advanced Encryption Standard (AES), Rijndael, Blowfish, and International Data Encryption Algorithm (IDEA). Of these, DES, 3DES, and AES are the most commonly used encryption algorithms in today's VPNs. DES was an encryption standard set by the National Institute of Standards and Technology (NIST) in 1977. DES, a symmetric algorithm with a 56-bit key, seemed unbreakable with the technology of the time. However, as time has passed and processing power has multiplied, DES has been proven breakable many times.

Does this mean that DES is not a suitable algorithm to use for your VPN? Maybe. You have to weigh the value of your data against the price paid to retrieve it. No one wants his payroll posted on a billboard, but by the same token, it is unlikely that you will install a walk-in vault to protect it from interlopers. (If you would, don't use DES.) Some businesses that are exchanging standard transactions that have no real value to outside parties are effectively using DES as their VPN algorithm because DES is less resource and bandwidth intensive than the stronger alternatives. If you operate a financial institution or you have top-secret information that you are exchanging, don't use DES.

As an interim solution to the vulnerability of DES, 3DES has become popular. Most popularly used with three 56-bit keys for a total of a 168-bit key strength, 3DES provides considerably more protection. Even so, with the breaking of DES, a call went out for a new Advanced Encryption Standard (AES). The winner was Rijndael, an algorithm made by Vincent Rijmen and Joan Daemen, two highly respected Belgian cryptographers. Although AES is considered stronger than 3DES, it has taken considerable time for VPN vendors to add AES support to their products. 3DES is still a fine solution for most secure implementations today, but many organizations are moving to AES as it becomes available in their VPN products.

Symmetric algorithms are important to VPNs because they supply the confidentiality component that the VPN supplies. They work well to protect the heavy burden of the VPN's data flow because of their speed-per-strength advantage over other encryption algorithm types.

Public–Private Key: Asymmetric

Asymmetric key algorithms use a different method of encryption. Two different keys are used: a public key and a private key. The *public key* is used to encrypt the ciphertext, and the *private key* is used to decode it back to cleartext. The interesting thing about this process is the relationship between these two keys. The public key cannot be used to reverse-engineer the private key. Therefore, although ciphertext can be generated by anyone with a copy of the public key, only the person who possesses the private key can decrypt it. For this reason, the mathematics behind asymmetric algorithms are considerably more complex than those used in symmetric algorithms. In turn, asymmetric algorithms are also much slower and more processor intensive.

We still haven't resolved the issue of how to start an encrypted communication session with someone whom you haven't previously been able to exchange keys with. Because the public key cannot compromise the ciphertext, it can be freely distributed. This does not guarantee, however, that the message is coming from the person it claims to be. Despite still lacking guaranteed authentication, integrity, and nonrepudiation, we still have confidentiality of our data and no more key exchange issues.

One popular example of asymmetric key encryption is Pretty Good Privacy (PGP). PGP is a means to exchange information securely with persons whom you might not ever have met face to face. It uses publicly dispersible keys (in coordination with private keys) and even has specific key servers set up for the distribution of these public keys. This way, if the person with whom you are exchanging information has "posted" his public key on a key server, you can search for it by the person's email address or name. Then the communication can begin. Posting public keys to a key server is not a necessary part of the process; keys can just be emailed back and forth.

The two most commonly used asymmetric algorithms are Diffie-Hellman and RSA's public-key algorithm. Diffie-Hellman is used heavily in VPN technology, as a part of the Oakley key exchange protocol. It and Internet Security Association Key Management Protocol (ISAKMP) make up the standard negotiation and key-management option of IPSec, called the Internet Key Exchange (IKE) protocol. Whitfield Diffie and Martin Hellman created Diffie-Hellman in 1976. It was the first of the public key algorithms.[1]

Diffie-Hellman is most commonly used in VPNs as a means to exchange information to set up a symmetric algorithm tunnel using a protocol such as DES or 3DES. The advantages of public-key cryptography are used to allow the creation of an outside connection without previous knowledge. This connection is used to pass the vital symmetric-key information and configuration data that cannot be securely transferred otherwise. Then the symmetric algorithm communication can begin. When using the Diffie-Hellman algorithm in conjunction with a VPN, you have to choose the group type that will be used: group 1 or group 2. The differences between the groups include the size of the prime number that is used (768 bit for group 1 and 1024 bit for group 2) and the length of the prime modulus in 32-bit words (24 for group 1 and 32 for group 2). Group 2 provides more security but takes more processing power to implement.

Although asymmetric algorithms are too slow to be practical as a means to encrypt the main data flow transmitted via the VPN, they are an effective way to exchange key information in the negotiation and key exchange phase of VPN initialization. Because symmetric algorithms have key-exchange woes and faster encryption speeds, asymmetric and symmetric algorithms make an excellent pair. By using asymmetric algorithms to exchange keys to be used for a symmetric connection, you have removed your key exchange issues, while benefiting from the speed advantage of the symmetric algorithm.

Digital Signatures and Hash Algorithms

Digital signatures and hash functions are the missing pieces in our secure communication method. They help provide integrity of data, additional authentication, and nonrepudiation. Digital signatures are meant to prove that a piece of information came from a certain individual or entity. This authentication is accomplished with encryption. If you receive a message that was encrypted with a key that only one other person has, then it is most likely from that person.

However, a symmetric key does not function well in this model because you have all the same key-management issues that occur with standard symmetric key transactions. For this reason, asymmetric encryption has become a popular means to integrate digital signature capability. You can encrypt a document with your private key, and the person to whom you are sending the document can decrypt it with your public key, proving (because you are the only individual with your private key) that the message was from you. Therefore, we have nonrepudiation and integrity checking because any changes in the encrypted text result in jumbled output. However, we lack true confidentiality because anyone with our public key can decrypt the message. The biggest disadvantage of this as a signing method is the sluggishness of asymmetric encryption. A signature should be able to be retrieved in a timely fashion; otherwise, it loses its practicality. Also, anyone with your public key can read the document, so the document loses its confidentiality unless you then encrypt it a second time, adding even more time to the whole process. Wouldn't it be nice to have a means to ensure integrity, authentication, and nonrepudiation and not have the speed disadvantage of asymmetrically encrypting an entire message?

Enter the hash algorithm. Hash algorithms are used to create a "fingerprint" of a piece of information or file. You can use this fingerprint, called a *hash* or *message digest*, to verify that the file has not been changed. If the file changes, so will its hash. This helps guarantee the integrity of the information without having to verify the entire file, bit by bit. With a one-way hash, it is difficult to reverse-engineer the original source information, or find or create information that can produce the same hash. People are confused about how one-way hashes can be verified. If these hashes can't be reversed, how do you know that they correctly represent the original information? The answer is deceptively simple. You take the document for which you are verifying integrity and create a second hash using the same algorithm. You then compare the hashes. If the documents are the same, the hashes will be the same as well. Also, because a one-way hash function is being used, it is unlikely that you just happened upon a document that produced the same hash.

Two of the more popular hash algorithms are Message Digest 5 (MD5) and Secure Hash Algorithm (SHA-1). SHA-1 is the more secure hash algorithm of the two, but it is slower than MD5. In most practical applications, it is okay to use either, unless your security policy dictates the use of the more secure SHA-1. Both algorithms are available and commonly used in VPN setups for integrity checking of information.

Understanding the basics of cryptography is essential for designing, implementing, and maintaining VPN solutions. The use of speedy symmetric encryption algorithms keep data flows confidential, and asymmetric algorithms allow for easy key exchange. Hash algorithms ensure integrity with digital signatures, which provide authentication and ensure nonrepudiation. Combine these technologies and you ensure the three goals of a secure communication channel—confidentiality, integrity, and authentication—can be successfully established.

References

1 W. Diffie and M. Hellman, "New Directions in Cryptography." IEEE Transactions on Information Theory, vIt-22, n.6. November 1976.

Index

E

How can we make this index more useful? Email us at indexes@samspublishing.com

H

J – K – L

N

O

How can we make this index more useful? Email us at indexes@samspublishing.com

Q - R

search engines, 559-560

sensitive information searches, 558

whois searches, 556

recovery phase (incident response), 489

recursive queries, 339

redundancy

firewalls, 313-314

geographic, fault tolerance, 315

intrasite

fault tolerance, 313-314

firewall redundancy, 313-314

switch redundancy, 314

intrasystem, fault tolerance, 312

switches, 314

reflexive ACL (Access Control List), 27, 47

FTP, 49

ICMP, 50

named ACL, 48-49

outbound traffic, 51

PASV FTP, 49

TCP flags, 50

UDP, 50

Regedit utility (Windows), restricting Registry permissions, 233

Regedit32 utility (Windows), restricting Registry permissions, 233

Registration Authorities (RA), digital certificates, 187

Registry (Windows), restricting permissions, 233

remote access phase (network security assessments), 552

VPN/remote proxies

access controls, 584

authentication, 582-584

client restrictions, 584-585

encryption, 582

wardialing, 577-579

wardriving, 579-581

remote access services, deactivating, 228-229

remote authentication, SNMP routers, 147-148

remote commands (UNIX)

deactivating, 228

SSH, 229

Telnet, 228

remote controlware, 636

Remote Desktop service (Windows), deactivating, 228

remote desktop software, 405

risks of, 406

single-session

client integration, 406

perimeter defenses, 407

server integration, 407

uses of, 408

terminal servers

client integration, 408

perimeter defenses, 409

server integration, 408

uses of, 409

VPN case studies, 415-416

remote proxies, network security assessments

access controls, 584

authentication, 582-584

client restrictions, 584-585

encryption, 582

Remote Registry Service (Windows), deactivating, 228

remote system/network monitoring, security of, 483-485

remote users

null sessions, 229-230

r-commands (UNIX), deactivating, 228

How can we make this index more useful? Email us at indexes@samspublishing.com

W

How can we make this index more useful? Email us at indexes@samspublishing.com

X - Y - Z